STUDIES IN
EIGHTEENTH-CENTURY
LITERATURE

STUDIES IN EIGHTEENTH-CENTURY ·LITERATURE

EDITED
by
MIKLÓS J. SZENCZI and LÁSZLÓ FERENCZI

AKADÉMIAI KIADÓ · BUDAPEST 1974

CE VOLUME PRÉPARÉ PAR LES SOINS DE
L'INSTITUT D'ÉTUDES LITTÉRAIRES DE L'ACADÉMIE DES SCIENCES DE HONGRIE
EST OFFERT EN ÉTUDE PRÉPARATOIRE A
L'HISTOIRE COMPARÉE DES LITTÉRATURES DE LANGUES EUROPÉENNES
SOUS LES AUSPICES DE
L'ASSOCIATION INTERNATIONALE DE LITTÉRATURE COMPARÉE

ISBN 963 05 0243 7

CONTENTS

PREFACE

by

ISTVÁN SŐTÉR

"ICLA" has embarked on a large-scale enterprise for the production of a complete history of literatures written in the European languages. The Institute for Comparative Studies at the Sorbonne and the Literary Research Institute of the Hungarian Academy of Sciences have joined forces to produce a history of European literature in the period leading from the Enlightenment towards Romanticism. The emerging outlines of the work now in preparation in the Paris and Budapest workshops suggest that the volume which is to discuss the period between 1770 and 1820 will bring into synthesis the most characteristic features and processes of the European development. That period, the time of the American War of Independence, the French Revolution and the English Industrial Revolution, was indeed a revolutionary epoch which brought about radical changes in the entire European literary scene. New critical and aesthetic ideas emerged, the old literary genres were transformed and, particularly in poetry, the personal note and lyricism became predominant, making the break with the poetic rules of classicism more complete. Nor was the transformation less effective in the field of the novel and the drama; after several tentative attempts the novel was ready to pave the way for the romantic and realistic art of the 19th century.

However, the literary processes and phenomena of this period in Europe were far from uniform, since the countries of Europe represented different stages of economic, political and cultural development. These basic differences allow us to distinguish several cultural zones in the Europe of the late eighteenth century. The differences between certain developed countries of Western Europe and the countries of Eastern, Central, Northern and Southern Europe which developed in different conditions were quite distinct. The radical transformation of European literature began in the mid-18th century in England and France, then from 1770 onwards, it was the literature of Germany which became the torch-bearer of the process. However, both Central and Eastern Europe reacted fast to this transformation. While in the countries of the West great literatures emerged which promoted bourgeois development, in Central and Eastern Europe the aim of bourgeois transformation was combined with the aim of creating autonomous national literatures. Thus the literary trends and movements of the period assumed different functions in Western and in Central and Eastern Europe.

We cannot successfully survey these processes, or comprehend their laws and peculiarities, unless we investigate the European history of this period from the angle of the evolution of a bourgeois and national culture. Similarly, an understanding of the literary phenomena requires a clear view of the emergence of philosophical, social and scientific trends in the various cultural zones of Europe. However, to understand the literary phenomena and processes within the period and to appraise the significance of aesthetical and theoretical literary endeavours, it is important to see certain formations emerging among the themes of literature (they could just as well be called myths) and finally to distinguish the characteristics in the field of poetry, the novel and the drama in the respective zones.

The most important part of the comprehensive work under way in Paris and Budapest must be the analysis of the phenomena and processes of poetry, novel and drama in Europe at the turn of the 18th and 19th centuries.

Hence the projected work should include an ideological and aesthetico-historical survey as well as a thorough analysis in the domain of poetry, drama and the novel.

However, this type of research must be anticipated by a number of preliminary studies. The present volume contains but a few of these studies. We believe that more such studies, or even more volumes, would be needed to discuss the problems of poetry, or the drama and novel in various European literatures or in the specific European cultural zones, respectively.

Our present volume — which eventually can be followed up by several other prepatory volumes before a final synthesis — is but a small contribution to the great work carried on in Paris and Budapest.

THE MIMETIC PRINCIPLE
IN LATER EIGHTEENTH-CENTURY CRITICISM

by

MIKLÓS J. SZENCZI

It has become a commonplace in the history of criticism that the latter half of the eighteenth century witnessed a radical reorientation in literary theory. René Wellek describes the change as the disintegration of the great system of Neoclassical criticism inherited from antiquity and codified in Italy and France during the 16th and 17th centuries, parallel with the crystallization of the new trends into Romantic movements early in the 19th century.[1] M. H. Abrams uses the striking visual metaphors of the mirror and the lamp to bring home the essence of the change: from Plato to the 18th century — he says — the mind was usually compared to a mirror, a reflector of external objects, while the prevailing Romantic conception of the poetic mind is that of a lamp, a radiant projector which makes a contribution to the objects it perceives.[2]

Changing views on the nature and function of poetry and the poet, as of the fine arts in general, are part and parcel of the transition from Classic to Romantic, which was itself a reflection in the medium of art of profound economic, social, and political changes such as the industrial and agricultural revolutions in England, the American War of Independence, and the French Revolution. The social, philosophical, and literary ideals of the Classicist Pope are essentially static: a vast chain of being which binds together the fabric of the universe and of human society; an eternal order, against which sinful pride rebels in vain. In the realm of art the fundamental rule is to follow Nature, conceived of as an invariable standard, as "one clear, unchanged, and universal light". In Pope's eyes Nature is "at once the source, and end, and test of art"; the rules, so dear to the Neoclassical theorist of poetry, "are Nature still, but Nature methodiz'd." The old quarrel between Nature and Art disappears, Nature and Homer prove to be the same, to copy Nature is tantamount to following the ancient, well-established rules discovered by the science of literary criticism.

Such an essentially conservative system of "cosmic Toryism" which stressed the permanent elements in the structure of society, thought, and art, was bound to disintegrate in the social and political upheavals referred to above; the "clear, unchanged, and universal light" of rational deism was lost in the red flames of Orc which swept over revolutionary America in Blake's vision, with a corresponding change from the polished, sophisticated couplets that delighted an aristocratic audience to the long, passionate

---

[1] *A History of Modern Criticism*, Vol. I. The Later Eighteenth Century. Yale Univ. Press, 1965 (1955), p. 1.

[2] *The Mirror and the Lamp*, Romantic Theory and the Critical Tradition. New York, 1958 (OUP, 1953), p. vi.

lines of the seemingly formless Prophetic Books. The gospel of inspiration appears to have triumphed over conscious artistry; Blake advocates an "Art deliver'd from Nature and Imitation" and steeped wholly in Imagination which is the world of Eternity.[3]

The contrast between two poetic creeds, that of the aristocratic Tory poet and the passionate cockney visionary seems absolute. Yet they represent only two extremes in a dialectical process of thought which reaches back to critical theories of Classical antiquity, revealing some inherent contradictions especially during the latter half of the 18th century, only to find a temporary equilibrium in Coleridge's attempt to reconcile the conflicting claims of imagination and truth to Nature.

I

The germ of the antithesis, the fulcrum round which much of subsequent aesthetic speculation revolves, can be traced back to Greek thought. Truth to Nature or the reflection of reality was first recognized as a fundamental principle of fine art by Plato and Aristotle and described by the term *mimesis* or 'imitation'. The value attributed to works of art was connected in their thought with the degree of reality represented in them. In Plato's system, true existence belongs to the realm of Ideas, of which our ordinary world of experience is only a faint imitation (μίμημα), copy (εἰκών), likeness (ὁμοίωμα), or image (εἴδωλον). Since the poet or the painter 'imitates' this shifting world of appearance, he is thrice removed from reality and truth. In the tenth book of the *Republic*, Plato's fullest and best-known discussion of the subject, all poetical imitations are declared to be "ruinous to the understanding of the hearers," on the ground that "the imitator or maker of the images knows nothing of true existence; he knows appearances only . . . The real artist . . . would be interested in realities and not in imitations." Plato has a special complaint against tragic poets who satisfy and delight our "natural hunger after sorrow and weeping" — in fact, against every kind of poetry that "feeds and waters the passions instead of drying them up." He would expel all poetry from his ideal State, except for "hymns to the gods and praises of famous men," and closes his argument with a reference to the "ancient quarrel between philosophy and poetry." The divided mind of the poet-philosopher is, however, revealed in the concluding remarks: we give up poetry much against our will — Plato says — "after the manner of lovers who abstain when they think that their love is not good for them; for we too are inspired by the love of poetry which the education of noble States has implanted in us." Plato challenges the lovers and defenders of poetry to speak on her behalf and to show "not only that she is pleasant but also useful to States and to human life."[4]

Elsewhere he takes up the challenge himself and becomes one of the most eloquent and influential defenders of poetry, regarded not as an art but as pure inspiration. In the *Ion* the poet is described as "a light and winged

[3] *The Laocoon Group* and *A Vision of the Last Judgment*. In *Poetry and Prose of William Blake*, ed. G. Keynes. London, 1956. pp. 580, 639.
[4] *The Republic* X. 595—608, in Jowett's translation.

and holy thing," a man possessed who utters "priceless words in a state of unconsciousness." It is God who is conversing with us through the poets. The *Phaedrus* contains the famous praise of "inspired madness" which transports the soul of the philosopher and the lover from the beauty of the earth to the beauty of the intelligible world. In the *Symposium* the ideas of love, beauty, and the good appear in unison: love is of the everlasting possession of the good, hence of immortality; poets and all artists who deserve the name of inventor are numbered among the creative souls; the beauties of earth may lead up by degrees to the vision of absolute beauty, a blessed possession that will enable one to bring forth, not images of beauty, but realities.[5]

The "dear, gorgeous nonsense" of Plato[6] was echoed by countless critics and poets of the Renaissance, including the Spenser of the *Four Hymns* and Shakespeare's half-serious, half-mocking comments on imagination and the essential kinship of the lunatic, the lover, and the poet. It left its mark even on the sober-minded Aristotle who, in chap. 17 of the *Poetics*, distinguishes two main types of poetic talent: "poetry implies either a happy gift of nature or a strain of madness. In the one case a man can take the mould of any character; in the other, he is lifted out of his proper self."[7]

However, Aristotle's chief claim to a commanding position among literary critics depends on his analysis of the first alternative and the doctrine of 'imitation'. He borrowed the term *mimesis* from Plato and from popular usage, cleared it from all disparaging associations, and made it the cornerstone of his aesthetic thought. In the preamble to the *Poetics* he pronounces practically all the fine arts to be modes of imitation which differ from one another in three respects: the medium, the objects, and the manner of imitation. After a brief discussion of the origin and development of poetry he proceeds to his main task, a detailed examination of tragedy and, to a lesser extent, of the epic.

We must limit our examination of the *Poetics* to a few points only, those which will be hotly debated and variously interpreted in later centuries. One of them is the strictly anthropocentric trend of Aristotle's aesthetic thought: to him the objects of imitation are men in action[8] — even dancing imitates character, emotion, and action.[9] This cuts out the 'imitation' of external nature, descriptive poetry as it came to be written in the 18th century, and even architecture, the glory of Greek art; it secures, on the other hand, a prominent place for music. Butcher calls our attention to the fact that music was held by the Greeks to be the most 'imitative' of the

[5] *Ion* 533—534; *Phaedrus* 245—250; *Symposium* 206—212.

[6] The phrase is S. T. Coleridge's, in *Letters* I, pp. 211—2, ed. E. H. Coleridge.

[7] διὸ εὐφυοῦς ἡ ποιητική ἐστιν ἢ μανικοῦ· τούτων γὰρ οἱ μὲν εὔπλαστοι οἱ δὲ ἐκστατικοί εἰσιν. *Poet.* 17, 1455 a 33—34. The passage is quoted in S. H. Butcher's translation, *Aristotle's Theory of Poetry and Fine Art*, London, 1911[4], pp. 63—64, because this seems closer to the original that I. Bywater's version in *Aristotle on the Art of Poetry*, Oxford, 1909, pp. 48—49. It may be noted that εὐφυής 'of good natural parts, clever' was chosen by John Lyly to designate the hero of his novel, that εὔπλαστος seems to point forward to Keats' 'negative capability' as the distingushing mark of the Shakespearean type of poet, and that the reading ἐκστατικοί, found only in one MS, is required by the sense and confirmed by a 10th century Arabic version.

[8] μιμοῦνται οἱ μιμούμενοι πράττοντας. *Poet.* 2, 1448 a 1.

[9] μιμοῦνται καὶ ἤθη καὶ πάθη καὶ πράξεις. *Ibid.* 1, 1446 a 28. Bywater translates: men's characters, as well as what they do and suffer.

arts, since it is a direct image of character.[10] There are few references to music in the *Poetics*, but Aristotle's position is made clear by passages in Book VIII of the *Politics* where he discusses the training of youth. In his view, musical rhythms and tunes "provide us with images of states of character — images of anger, and of calm; images of fortitude and temperance, and of all forms of their opposites." This is followed by a significant distinction between the method of music and that of the visual arts. "The shapes and colours presented by visual art — says Aristotle — are not *representations* of states of character: they are merely *indications* ... With musical compositions, however, the case is different. They are, in their very nature, representations of states of character."[11] — We shall see that Aristotle's inclusion of music among the 'imitative' arts came to be doubted and severely criticized in the 18th century.

It is clear from the foregoing that imitation, in Aristotle's sense, does not mean passive reflection, photographic reproduction of some material alien to the nature of man; it is, to quote Erich Auerbach's translation of the word *mimesis*, the representation of reality, of human reality, an active ordering of experience. This is shown by Aristotle's remark that the poet, like the painter or any other artist, "must of necessity imitate one of three objects — things as they were or are, things as they are said or thought to be, or things as they ought to be."[12] This opens the doors wide for idealization, on the one hand, and for satire, caricature, and the grotesque on the other. — Another indication is that the rule of necessity or probability is repeatedly stressed as a requirement applicable both to the ordering of incidents and to characterization. A work of art is not a 'slice of life' but an organic whole; the plot of an epic poem, like that of a tragedy, must have for its subject a single action, whole and complete, with a beginning, a middle, and an end. "It will thus resemble a living organism in all its unity and produce the pleasure proper to it."[13]

For Aristotle, as for E. M. Forster, art is an evidence and a creator of order, a function closely connected with its cognitive content. In a famous passage Aristotle proclaims poetry to be "a more philosophical and a higher thing than history: for poetry tends to express the universal, history the particular."[14] He connects the idea of universality with that of probable or necessary sequence, thus foreshadowing not only important aspects of Marxist aesthetics but also contemporary views on poetry as structure. There is an 'objective' orientation, in M. H. Abrams' sense of the term, in

[10] *Op. cit.* pp. 128—9.

[11] *Politics.* VIII v. §§. 18—21, quoted from *The Politics of Aristotle*, translated with notes by Ernest Barker, Oxford, 1948, pp. 404—5. — One is reminded of a similar distinction by Schopenhauer: "Die Musik ist ... keineswegs, gleich den anderen Künsten, das Abbild der Ideen, sondern *Abbild des Willens selbst*, dessen Objektität auch die Ideen sind; deshalb eben ist die Wirkung der Musik so sehr viel mächtiger und eindringlicher, als die der anderen Künste; denn diese reden nur vom Schatten, sie aber vom Wesen." *Die Welt als Wille und Vorstellung*, Drittes Buch, § 52.

[12] ἀνάγκη μιμεῖσθαι τριῶν ὄντων τὸν ἀριθμὸν ἕν τι ἀεί, ἢ γὰρ οἷα ἦν ἢ ἔστιν, ἢ οἷα φασιν καὶ δοκεῖ, ἢ οἷα εἶναι δεῖ. Poet. 25. 1, 1460 b 9—11.

[13] ἵν᾽ ὥσπερ ζῷον ἓν ὅλον ποιῇ τὴν οἰκείαν ἡδονήν. Poet. 23. 1459 a 20—21. — Butcher quotes (p. 189) a close parallel from the *Phaedrus*, a remarkable anticipation of the romantic theory of poetry, with its distinction between mechanic and organic form.

[14] διὸ καὶ φιλοσοφώτερον καὶ σπουδαιότερον ποίησις ἱστορίας ἐστιν· ἡ μὲν γὰρ ποίησις μᾶλλον τὰ καθόλου, ἡ δ᾽ ἱστορία τὰ καθ᾽ ἕκαστον λέγει. Poet. 9. 3. 1451— b 5—7.

Aristotle's distinction of six elements in tragedy and his analysis of the interrelation of structural elements with the emotional impact of drama. The literary critic reveals himself here as a subtle psychologist; his remark on the 'catharsis' or purgation of the tragic emotions of pity and fear has opened a stream of endless discussion,[15] as has the question of 'tragic pleasure', the paradoxical fact that from scenes of pain and suffering the spectator or reader derives aesthetic delight.

It was from the tragic stories enacted on the Greek stage, the heart-rending fate of Oedipus, Antigone, Pentheus, and their peers that the first and most seminal theoretician of poetry drew his main conclusions: that by 'imitating' or representing the actions, emotions, and passions of an individual the poet may create prototypes of humanity, that art can express contents of permanent and universal validity in a sensuous medium, by a judicious selection from the material of everyday experience. It is a great merit of Aristotle's treatise that he does not indulge in abstract theorizing: his method is tentative and pragmatic, his generalizations are based on concrete material, on Homer and the masterpieces of Greek drama. This is a feature which distinguishes him greatly to his advantage from the prescriptive method of most of his Neoclassic successors, with their rigid code of 'rules' which it cost so much pain to overthrow.

The fragmentary nature of the *Poetics* has often been stressed; Humphrey House points out that the theory of catharsis implies a knowledge of the *Nicomachean Ethics* and the *Politics*, while the discussion of the tragic emotions of fear and pity in the *Rhetoric*, Book II, is essential to a full understanding of some central passages in the *Poetics*.[16] S. H. Butcher, in his attempt to reconstruct "Aristotle's theory of poetry and fine art," had recourse to an imposing number of passages culled from a great variety of the philosopher's writings. A more modest task, one more germane to our present inquiry, was undertaken by the Chicago Aristotelian, Richard McKeon, in his study on "Literary Criticism and the Concept of Imitation in Antiquity".[17] He draws an enlightening distinction between the use of Plato, for whom the term 'imitation' "may undergo an infinite series of gradations of meaning, developed in a series of analogies" and Aristotle's more precise and scientific method, for whom "the term is restricted to a single literal meaning" (p. 130). A more critical view of the precision of Aristotelian terminology was taken by Humphrey House who points out inconsistencies even in the use of the crucial term 'imitation' (see pp. 122—3). This is one more reminder that Aristotle's theses must not be treated dogmatically. Many of his works are, in fact, lecture notes for the curriculum at the Lyceum, hence individual remarks must be considered in the context of his extremely stimulating, but not always consistent, edifice of thought.

Contradictions and shifts of meaning become more pronounced in the later history of the term 'imitation', after Aristotle; this process has been

[15] This is partly due to an ambiguity inherent in the text. Butcher points out, and quotes examples to show, that the verb καθαίρειν and the noun κάθαρσις admit of a double construction, with different meanings. *Op. cit.* pp. 253—5.

[16] *Aristotle's Poetics.* London, 1967 (1956), p. 35.

[17] The full text is included in the abridged edition of *Critics and Criticism*, ed. by R. S. Crane. Univ. of Chicago Press, 1957 (1952).

traced in McKeon's article. He points out that a third variant to the meanings of Plato and Aristotle derives from the tradition of writers on rhetoric. Imitation of good models, of other orators and artists is recommended by Isocrates, Cicero, Dionysius of Halicarnassus, Quintilian. McKeon adds the name of Longinus who regards "zealous imitation of the great historians and poets of the past as one of the roads which leads to sublimity."[18]

The next phase is the disappearance of the term 'imitation' from its central place in criticism: literature comes to be judged primarily by its effect on the audience; in Horace's phrase "the poet's aim is either to profit or to please" ("*aut prodesse volunt, aut delectare poetae*"). This is a victory for what Abrams calls the 'pragmatic' theory of poetry, a view of judging art by its psychological impact on the audience. Imitation is relegated to a secondary place: the clever imitator is advised by Horace "to look to life and morals for his real model, and draw thence language true to life" ("*respicere exemplar vitae morumque iubebo/doctum imitatorem et vivas hinc ducere voces*"). In McKeon's summary: "Imitation has been reduced to the imitation of other artists or to reflecting actual conditions or customs."[19]

All these tendencies were to be taken up and developed at some future date, thus the doctrine of "reflecting actual conditions and customs" in a language true to life by 18th century advocates of bourgeois domestic drama.

The temporary eclipse of Aristotle's concept of 'imitation' as the representation of reality led to the emergence of several alternative theories. One of them, as we saw, was tinged with the "affective fallacy", and sought to derive aesthetic value from the psychological effect of a work of art on the spectator or reader. Another tendency, foreshadowing the 'expressive' theories of Romanticism, laid increasing emphasis on the personality of the artist and the psychology of creation. This trend, as C. S. Lewis points out in his admirably concise summary of aesthetic thought from Plato to the Renaissance,[20] arose mainly from prolonged reflection on a single sacred image, the statue of the Olympian Zeus by Pheidias, a work which clearly could not be 'imitated' from an earthly model. The earliest reference to this aspect of Pheidias' statute seems to be by Cicero: "In his mind resided a most splendid concept of beauty, which beholding and keeping his mind fixed on it, he directed his art and hand in harmony with its likeness."[21] The thought reappears a century later in Dio Chrysostom who makes Pheidias say: "What is hardest in making such a work as my Olympian Zeus is that the same image has to be preserved unchanged in the mind of the artist until he has finished the statue, which may be a matter of years."[22] The idea of an internal model is further developed and more pointedly for-

[18] *Op. cit.* p. 139. Allan H. Gilbert translates the Greek title περὶ ὕψους as "On Literary Excellence" and assigns the treatise to about 80 A. D. in his selection of *Literary Criticism: from Plato to Dryden*, Detroit, 1962 (1940).

[19] *Op. cit.*, p. 144.

[20] In *English Literature in the Sixteenth Century*, Oxford, 1954, pp. 318—322.

[21] Ipsius in mente insidebat species pulchritudinis eximia quaedam, quam intuens in eaque defixus ad illius similitudinem artem et manum dirigebat. *Orator*, 2. 9.

[22] Τὸ δὲ πάντων χαλεπώτατον ἀνάγκη παραμένειν τῷ δημιουργῷ τὴν εἰκόνα ἐν τῇ ψυχῇ τὴν αὐτὴν ἀεί, μέχρις ἂν ἐκτελέσῃ τὸ ἔργον, πολλάκις καὶ πολλοῖς ἔτεσι. *Orat.* XII. *De Dei Cognitione*. The model, as Lewis points out, is not a natural object, but an image (εἰκών) in the artist's mind.

mulated by Flavius Philostratus (170 ? — 250 ?) who again cites the works of Pheidias, adding also those of Praxiteles, and for the first time sets the products of imagination against imitations of nature: "Imagination made them, and she is a better artist than imitation. For imitation will fashion what it has seen, but imagination goes on to what it has not seen, supposing it according to the analogy of the real."[23]

The final formulation of the theory was the work of Plotinus in his treatise on Intellectual Beauty. The devout admirer of Plato here corrects and supplements the master's view of art as "the copy of a copy". The central passage runs as follows: "Still the arts are not to be slighted on the ground that they create by imitation of natural objects; for, to begin with, these natural objects are themselves imitations; then, we must recognize that they give no bare reproductions of the thing seen but go back to the Reason-Principles from which Nature itself derives and, furthermore, that much of their work is all their own; they are holders of beauty and add where nature is lacking. Thus Pheidias wrought the Zeus upon no model among things of sense but by apprehending what form Zeus must take if he chose to become manifest to sight."[24] Aristotle's empirical model — the world of human actions, passions, and emotions — has been replaced here by a transcendental ideal as the object of imitation: the realm of Ideas or Reason-Principles ($λόγοι$), from which Nature itself derives.

In Plotinus the wheel has come full circle. Plato's artist or poet was assigned a place below that of the craftsman, since he 'imitates' only objects of sense, earthly copies of models which exist in the intellectual realm of ideas; he is thus the maker of copies of copies, thrice removed from truth. In Plotinus the status of the poet and artist has been raised immeasurably: he has an immediate vision of a supersensuous original, either in his own mind or extrapolated into a transcendental world. The creations of art are 'imitations' of models which exist in the realm of Ideas, have the same ontological status as Nature herself, and often surpass Nature in beauty and order. Between Plato's condemnation and the neo-Platonic exaltation of art stands Aristotle with his emphasis on the universal element in a concrete, sensuous artefact. The three conceptions have this in common that they centre around the relation of art to reality and attribute decisive importance to its cognitive function. The mimetic orientation which forms the subject of our inquiry was soon supplemented by 'pragmatic' theories which have in mind the effect on the audience. Formed under the influence of rhetoric, this latter view was given a classic expression by Horace who enjoined the poet to teach, to please, and to move his reader.

---

[23] "φαντασία", ἔφη, "ταῦτα εἰργάσατο, σοφωτέρα μιμήσεως δημιουργός· μίμησις μὲν γὰρ δημιουργήσει, ὃ εἶδεν, φαντασία δὲ καὶ ὃ μὴ εἶδεν, ὑποθήσεται γὰρ αὐτὸ πρὸς τὴν ἀναφορὰν τοῦ ὄντος." De Vita Apollonii, VI, xix.

[24] Plotinus, The Enneads, trans. by Stephen MacKenna. Third ed. rev. by B. S. Page, London, 1966. "On the Intellectual Beauty." pp. 422—3. The key sentence in the original: (αἱ τέχναι) οὐχ ἁπλῶς τὸ ὁρώμενον μιμοῦνται, ἀλλ᾽ ἀνατρέχουσιν ἐπὶ τοὺς λόγους, ἐξ ὧν ἡ φύσις.

II

In the course of nearly eight centuries, thinkers and critics of antiquity developed some of the main categories of aesthetic thought, centred around the twin concepts of art as a reflection or 'imitation' of reality and as a means of evoking certain responses in the audience. When after a slumber of about a thousand years speculations about the nature of poetry and the arts were resumed, they usually ran in channels marked out by thinkers of Classical antiquity. We cannot undertake to follow the fortunes of the mimetic principle through the centuries of the Renaissance and Neoclassicism. An exception may be made for the modifications by Jacopo Mazzoni in his treatise on Dante.[25] Starting from a division of the imitative arts into two kinds in Plato's *Sophist* (235-6), Mazzoni attributes to Aristotle a division into four species of the genus 'poetic imitation', viz. those of the dramatic-phantastic, the dramatic-icastic, the narrative-phantastic, and the narra-tive-icastic. This is a reminder that loose formulations in the doctrine of *mimesis* began to bring forth a rich crop of subdivisions and conflicting interpretations. Even more noteworthy is the fact that Mazzoni, while admitting that poetry is always an imitative art, stresses the fact that as play it has pleasure as its end, and as play is regulated by the civil faculty. He thus opens the way for multiple definitions of poetry, each of them valid within its own terms of reference, but depending on the angle from which poetry is considered.

While Mazzoni belongs to the later 16th-century Aristotelians, the third earl of Shaftesbury propounded an early 18th-century version of the Neo-Platonic theory. At a time when Locke's empirical philosophy was becoming a mainstay of the Enlightenment, Shaftesbury, through his study of the Cambridge Platonists, reached back to the doctrines of Plotinus and made them the basis of his aesthetic thought. In his *Advice to an Author*, published in 1710, the poet is referred to as a "second Maker," is compared to "universal plastic Nature," since "he forms a whole, coherent and proportioned in itself." "The moral artist — concludes Shaftesbury — can thus imitate the Creator."

M. H. Abrams who quotes the famous passage (p. 280) remarks earlier that although Shaftesbury uses the phrase "universal plastic nature," he "envisions formative nature, on the model of Plato's Demiurge, as creating a fixed and finished universe according to a timeless and changeless pattern." In Abrams' view it was only later that German writers "converted Shaftesbury's completed and static cosmos, whether of nature or art, into an endlessly growing, never finished, process of organic development" (p. 201).

A greater importance to Shaftesbury as an original thinker and aesthetician was attached by Bonamy Dobrée, in a recent volume of *The Oxford History of English Literature*. Dobrée stresses the fact that Shaftesbury rejected Locke's theory of association or his view of the mind as *tabula rasa*, together with the Hobbesian notion of imagination being merely decaying sense. In contrast to such mechanical explanations Shaftesbury insisted

---

[25] *Della difesa della "Commedia" di Dante*, 1587. The references are to the English text in Allan H. Gilbert's anthology, pp. 358—403.

on the creative power of imagination and of the human mind which he regarded as a reflection, even a part, of the plastic General Mind.[26] The dynamic aspect of the imagination becomes even more prominent in Shaftesbury's later work, especially in his *Second Characters* which remained unpublished until 1914. Even so, his doctrine met with a wide European response, especially in Germany, where he exercised a strong influence on Herder, Goethe, Kant, the Schlegels, and Schelling who, in their turn, inspired Coleridge's theory of poetry.

An interesting point is that such anticipations of 'Romantic' theory (really based on Neo-Platonic doctrines) appear in Shaftesbury's writings together with fundamental tenets of Neoclassicism. The main body of his views on art reflects the prevailing rationalism of the times; the sense of order and proportion — he writes — is deeply rooted in the mind; 'Gothic' to Shaftesbury is a synonym of the formless and the false, the models of artistic perfection are to him the writers of Classical antiquity.

III

The conflicting tendencies in Shaftesbury's aesthetic thought are signs of a growing fissure but also of a desire to harmonize the main doctrines of the classical heritage and to adapt them to new developments in European literature. One of the main points at issue was the concept of imitation which, mainly in its Aristotelian form, became the basis of countless varieties of 'rules' and systems of prescriptive aesthetics. The cramping effect of such rules and prescriptions was increasingly felt and critics began to question the validity of the basic premiss, the mimetic principle itself. Some of them tried to reinterpret the concept of *mimesis* either theoretically or by the touchstone of the actual practice of poets and artists, others rejected it outright or limited it only to certain provinces of art.

An attempt to reduce the numerous rules of art to a single principle was made by the French critic Charles Batteux, in a treatise which achieved tremendous popularity, especially in France and Germany.[27] He begins with a playful reference to the big but empty words, such as divine fire, enthusiasm, transport, happy delirium, which critics use to characterize the nature of poetry. Led by the Cartesian desire for a clear and distinct idea he stumbled upon Aristotle's concept of imitation and found in it a key to the nature of all fine art. Batteux is a true son of the mid-eighteenth century in attributing an important role to genius, but he adds that genius cannot go beyond the limits of Nature: its function is not to imagine what cannot be but to find out what is. The genius which digs deepest only discovers what had existed before. An artist of genius is a creator only because he has observed and, conversely, he only observes in order to be able to create.

---

[26] *English Literature in the Early Eighteenth Century, 1700—1740*, Oxford, 1959, pp. 330—1.

[27] *Les Beaux Arts réduits à un même Principe*, Paris, 1746. It was reprinted as Vol. I of Batteux's *Principes de la litterature*, Paris, 1764. All references are to this later edition.

Art must be lifelike — Batteux plays a number of variations on this main theme. Genius, he points out, needs a prop or support for his sustained flight, and this prop is Nature. The artist cannot create or destroy it: he must follow and imitate Nature — all he produces is necessarily imitation.

Batteux defines Nature in generous and comprehensive terms: as a model of the arts, Nature includes all that is, even what may be easily conceived as possible. It is divided into four worlds: the actually existing world, whether physical, moral, or political, of which we form a part; the world of history, filled with great names and famous events; the world of fable, with its imaginary gods and heroes; and finally, the world of the ideal or possible where beings exist only as generalities; imagination draws thence the individuals which it supplies with all the marks of existence and propriety.

In Batteux's eyes, the function of art follows from the above principles: it transfers features from Nature to objects to which they are not natural. Hence the material of the fine arts is not the true but the true-seeming or credible.[28] Poetry, adds the critic, is a perpetual lie or fiction which has all the marks of truth. He also states this central idea in a more general form: what is really artistic in every art consists only of imaginary things, faint shadows, copies and imitations of what really exists.

Batteux's theory is a courageous attempt to reconcile the real and the ideal, the conflicting claims of truth to Nature and imagination, the principles of imitation and artistic illusion. He achieves his aim partly by extending the usual concept of Nature so as to include his 'four worlds', partly by restricting the object of imitation to 'la belle Nature'. This famous phrase is justified by a reference to a passage in chap. 9 of Aristotle's *Poetics*, which Batteux translates or paraphrases rather freely: Aristotle demands, in his version, not a servile copying of Nature, but an "imitation in which we see Nature not as she is in herself, but as she may be or may be conceived by the spirit."[29] Batteux quotes as his examples Zeuxis and Molière's Alceste to give a clear and distinct idea of what he means by 'la belle Nature': "it is not the true which exists, but the true which may be, the true which is also beautiful, which is represented as if it really existed, with all the perfections with which it may be decked."[30]

The relation of genius and imitation is the central subject of Edward Young's *Conjectures on Original Composition*, published in 1759, at the ripe age of 76, after a long career as a satirist and a tragedian, a country parson at Welwyn and, chief of all, the author of *Night Thoughts* (1742—5) which

[28] In the epigrammatic formulation of the original: "ainsi la matière des Beaux Arts n'est point le vrai, mais seulement le vrai-semblable." *Op. cit.*, p. 19. This clearly contradicts Boileau's famous thesis: "Rien n'est beau que le vrai" and its echo in Keats ("Beauty is Truth, Truth Beauty").

[29] "Une imitation, où on voie la Nature, non telle qu'elle est en elle-même, mais telle qu'elle peut être, et qu'on peut la concevoir par l'esprit." *Op. cit.* p. 29. The reference is clearly to the opening sentence in chap. 9 of the *Poetics*: Φανερὸν δὲ ἐκ τῶν εἰρημένων καὶ ὅτι οὐ τὸ τὰ γενόμενα λέγειν, τοῦτο ποιητοῦ ἔργον ἐστίν ἀλλ᾽ οἷα ἂν γένοιτο καὶ τὰ δυνατὰ κατὰ τὸ εἰκὸς ἢ τὸ ἀναγκαῖον. In Butcher's translation: "It is, moreover, evident from what has been said, that it is not the function of the poet to relate what has happened, but what may happen, — what is possible according to the law of probability or necessity."

[30] "Ce n'est pas le vrai qui est; mais le vrai qui peut être, le beau vrai, qui est représenté comme s'il existait réellement, et avec toutes les perfections qu'il peut recevoir." *Op. cit.* p. 32.

brought him European fame. As a satirist Young was overshadowed by Pope, and much of the *Conjectures* is an open or implicit polemic with the doctrines of the dead Neoclassic poet. Early in the course of his argument Young makes a fundamental distinction. "Imitations — he says — are of two kinds: one of nature, one of authors. The first we call originals, and confine the term imitation to the second."[31] This flies in the face of Pope's thesis that "Nature and Homer . . . were the same" (*An Essay on Criticism*, 1711), as of the whole rhetorical tradition which goes back, as we have seen, to antiquity and subsumes the following of good literary models under the term 'imitation'. Young will have nothing of such blurring of outlines: his distinction is sharp and clear, he uses metaphors that again foreshadow the later division into organic and mechanical form, as in the following passage: "An original may be said to be of a vegetable nature; it rises spontaneously from the vital root of genius; it grows, it is not made. Imitations are often a sort of manufacture wrought up by these mechanics, art and labour, out of pre-existent materials not their own."[32] The term 'imitation' has in his use again received a derogatory connotation, though for reasons different from Plato's. Young is well on the way to that uncritical admiration of spontaneity, of untutored genius which pervades so much of later eighteenth-century aesthetic thought. He rejects rules which Pope had regarded as "Nature methodiz'd." In Young's eyes, "rules, like crutches, are a needful aid to the lame, though an impediment to the strong." For him, "all eminence and distinction, lies out of the beaten road; excursion and deviation are necessary to find it; and the more remote your path from the highway, the more reputable."[33]

Such a change in critical standards leads to some important reappraisals. Dryden and Pope, the idols of the Augustan age, are relegated to the lower rank of imitators. Young celebrates the "deathless, divine harmony of three great names," of Milton, Greece, and Rome. But his chief praise among the moderns is reserved for Shakespeare, "a star of the first magnitude." In the quarrel of the ancients and the moderns Young took the side of the former and lamented "the great inferiority" of the latter. Yet he considered the British dramatist the equal of the ancients, because "Shakespeare mingled no water with his wine, lowered his genius by no vapid imitation." In the customary comparison with the learned Ben Jonson, Young gives the preference unhesitatingly to Shakespeare, in accordance with his basic principle. "Jonson, in the serious drama — he says — is as much an imitator as Shakespeare is an original." The reason Young gives for Shakespeare's preeminence is very much like Dr. Johnson's, to be discussed later. Here is the core of a famous passage: "Perhaps he was as learned as his dramatic province required; for whatever other learning he wanted, he was master of two books, unknown to many of the profoundly read . . .; the book of Nature, and that of man. These he had by heart, and has transcribed many admirable pages of them, into his immortal works."[34]

[31] *Conjectures on Original Composition*, quoted from the text as given in *English Critical Essays* (Sixteenth, Seventeenth and Eighteenth Centuries), selected and edited by E. D. Jones. OUP, 1947 (1922), p. 273.
[32] *Ibid.*, p. 274.
[33] *Ibid.*, pp. 277—9.
[34] *Ibid.*, pp. 298—9.

Batteux and Young examined and reinterpreted the term 'imitation' mainly from a theoretical point of view, though they, especially the latter, used it also as a touchstone to determine the value of literary works and to establish a hierarchy of writers. Now we come to critics like Diderot and Lessing who were in the thick of the intellectual and literary struggles of the time and who used critical concepts as weapons to secure victory for their principles in the fight against fossilized literary genres or for the introduction of new ones.

One of the new genres, unknown in France, was the domestic drama which in England could look back to Elizabethan origins and was revived in plays like George Lillo's *The London Merchant* (1731) and Edward Moore's *The Gamester* (1753). It was on the model of such plays that Diderot wrote his *Le fils naturel* (1757) and *Le père de famille* (1758) and produced a French version of Moore's drama (*Le joueur*, 1760). Some of Diderot's best-known critical work consists of dialogues and discourses connected with these plays. But René Wellek points out that these prefaces and postscripts give only a one-sided idea of Diderot's rich and varied critical output. He himself gives a penetrating account of Diderot's changing views, from the rather crude emotionalism, even sensationalism, which characterize the early theories, towards Neoclassical positions tinged with the Plotinian strain, probably inherited from Shaftesbury.[35] We cannot hope to do justice here to the manysidedness of Diderot's volatile genius which is fully revealed in Wellek's succinct, masterly analysis. Our concern is with the concept of imitation, presented from widely different angles at various stages of Diderot's career as a critic.

Most of his aesthetic criticism is concerned with drama and acting. A well-known passage in the early novel *Les Bijoux indiscrets* (1748) implies, as Wellek remarks, wholly naturalistic standards. In Diderot's words, "the perfection of a spectacle consists in such an exact imitation of an action that the spectator, deceived without interruption, imagines that he witnesses the action itself."[36] Diderot confounds here dramatic illusion with deception or the intention to delude, and will be effectively refuted by Dr. Johnson. "It is false — says Johnson in his *Preface to Shakespeare* (1765) — that any representation is mistaken for reality; that any dramatic fable in its materiality was ever credible, or, for a single moment, was ever credited."[37]

Wellek seems right in stressing that the naturalistic devices recommended by Diderot in his earlier theories are meant to produce powerful emotional effect. At this stage "Diderot constantly assumes intense emotional personal engagement as the criterion of poetic greatness" — writes Wellek.[38] But the gospel of emotionalism, even sensationalism, gradually gives place to Neoclassic assumptions. Even Diderot's advocacy of the new genre of domestic drama, Wellek reminds us, is made in terms acceptable to Neo-

---

[35] Wellek reminds us that a translation of Shaftesbury's essay on *Virtue and Merit* was Diderot's first published work in 1745. *Op. cit.*, p. 54.

[36] "La perfection d'un spectacle consiste dans l'imitation si exacte d'une action que le spectateur, trompé sans interruption, s'imagine à l'action même." Quoted by Wellek from the standard edition of Diderot's works, *Œuvres Complètes*, ed. J. Assézat and M. Tourneux, 20 vols. Paris, 1875—79. *Œuvres*, 4, p. 282.

[37] *Dr Johnson on Shakespeare*, ed. W. K. Wimsatt. Penguin Shakespeare Library, 1969 (1960), p. 70.

[38] *Op. cit.*, p. 52.

classical theory. The *drame bourgeois* is thought of as an intermediary between the other dramatic genres. According to Diderot's classification, comedy is about types, tragedy about individuals, domestic drama about *conditions* — a division which Wellek describes as "simply good neoclassical typology."[39] Drama is no longer the purveyor of mere emotion but the imitation of nature, and by 'nature', Wellek is careful to add, Diderot means the typical, the universal, the assumed harmony of nature.[40] The advocacy of a naturalistic technique to produce the maximum of emotional effect is gradually replaced by the Neo-Platonic concept of the internal model which the artist is to follow.

This process, subtly analyzed by Wellek, finds its consummation in the dialogue *Le Paradoxe sur le comédien*. The authenticity of the work, written between 1770—1778 and published only in 1830, has been questioned, yet it is now felt to be in line with the general drift of the critic's development. Diderot's main concern in the *Paradoxe* is the art of acting but the implications of his argument for poetry are far-reaching. Naturalistic expression of feeling is no longer advocated: "if the actor is endowed with extreme sensibility, either he does not act or he acts ridiculously." A great actor must be a close observer of human nature, a man of sharp judgment. Feeling is not a mark of genius; it is always accompanied by weakness of imagination. Diderot now reaches a general conclusion which takes him well beyond the Age of Sensibility, even beyond Romantic ideals, to anti-Romantic, anti-sentimental doctrines of the 20th century. "The great poets, the great actors — he writes in the *Paradoxe* — and probably in general all the great imitators of nature, whatever they are, endowed with a beautiful imagination, with a good judgment, a fine tact, a sure taste, are the least sensitive of all beings ... They are too much occupied with looking, knowing, and imitating to be vividly affected and carried beyond themselves."[41] Close observation, rigorous selection, the creation of an internal model and its translation into a sensuous medium are now considered the characteristic marks of a great artist, the role of imagination and judgment is emphasized — we are well on the way to Coleridge's theory of poetry which attempts to reconcile the claims of truth to nature and the creative imagination. Diderot no longer maintains, as in the passage from *Les Bijoux* quoted above, that the spectator must be deceived into thinking that he sees actions and characters of real life on the stage; he now recognizes that the Cleopatras, Agrippinas, Cinnas of the stage are not historical personages but "imaginary spectres of poetry".[42]

[39] *Ibid*. pp. 53—54.
[40] Wellek quotes from *Œuvres*, 12, p. 81: "L'harmonie du plus beau tableau n'est qu'une bien faible imitation de l'harmonie de la nature."
[41] "Les grands poètes, les grands acteurs, et peut-être en général tous les imitateurs de la nature, quels qu'ils soient, doués d'une belle imagination, d'un grand jugement, d'un tact fin, d'un goût très sûr, sont les êtres les moins sensibles ... Ils sont trop occupés à regarder, à reconnaître, et à imiter, pour être vivement affectés au dedans d'eux-mêmes." *Œuvres*, 8, pp. 419—20. Cf. T. S. Eliot's well-known dictum from "Tradition and the Individual Talent": "Poetry is not a turning loose of emotion, but an escape from emotion; it is not the expression of personality, but an escape from personality." *Selected Essays*, new ed. New York, 1960, p. 10.
[42] "Ce sont les fantômes imaginaires de la poésie." *Œuvres*, 8, p. 372.

Like Diderot, Lessing was also an advocate of the domestic drama which he recreated in his *bourgeois* tragedy, *Miss Sara Sampson* (1755). He analyzed Diderot's theory of drama in no. 48 of his *Hamburgische Dramaturgie* and called him "the best French critic of art." Otherwise, there is little similarity between the mental make-up of these two leading figures of the European Enlightenment. Their historical position was also different. Diderot could look back to the great age of the French baroque and Neoclassicism, the splendour of the court of *le Roi Soleil*; he was editor-in-chief of the *Encyclopédie*, contemporary and often companion-in-arms of such brilliant figures as Voltaire, Rousseau, Condillac, Helvétius, D'Holbach, a leader of the intellectual ferment which culminated in the ideology of the French Revolution. The inheritor of a great national tradition, Diderot broke fresh ground in philosophy and creative writing; in the field of literary theory he reached out in many directions to give a satisfactory account of the mystery of artistic representation. Compared with his wide range and brilliance, his proneness to experiment, Lessing seems more single-minded. His role was primarily that of a pioneer: he created a new type of *bourgeois* drama, pitted himself against the Frenchified Neoclassical theories of Gottsched, found a partial embodiment of his ideals in Shakespeare, rejected the practice and theories of even the greatest French tragedians, Corneille and Racine, and sought support in the teaching of Aristotle.

The traditional strain in Lessing's views on art, especially on poetry and drama, is very strong. This emerges clearly from Wellek's comparison of Lessing with his precursors, especially Johann Elias Schlegel, uncle of the two famous Romantic critics, and Johann Jakob Bodmer. Schlegel devoted several papers to imitation but he stressed the emotional impact of works of art, not their resemblance to reality. He anticipates Dr. Johnson by attacking "the notion of art as deceptive illusion and declares that we are never deceived in the theatre."[43]

Bodmer goes even further in his defence of the non-representational aspect of poetry. In his view, the poet is not an imitator of nature. Rather, "he imitates the powers of nature in transferring the possible into the condition of reality."[44]

Bodmer's view springs from neo-Platonic assumptions and anticipates Coleridge's idea of the true nature of artistic imitation.[45] Lessing will have none of these metaphysical subtleties or transcendental models. His own view of imitation, the basis of his aesthetics, is firmly based on Aristotle and on ordinary human experience. The epigraph of his *Laokoon* comes from Plutarch: the arts differ from each other in the matter and manner of imitation.[46] On the basis of this distinction Lessing rejects the old analogy between poetry and painting, an idea that goes back to Simonides, "the

---

[43] Wellek, *op. cit.*, p. 146. Cf. note 36.

[44] *Critische Abhandlung von dem Wunderbaren in der Poesie*, Zürich, 1740. p. 165. "Die Kräfte der Natur in der Überbringung in den Stand der Wirklichkeit nachzuahmen." Quoted and translated by Wellek, *op. cit.*, pp. 147, 299.

[45] "If the artist copies the mere nature, the *natura naturata*, what idle rivalry! . . you must master the essence, the *natura naturans*, which presupposes a bond between nature in the higher sense and the soul of man." "On Poesy or Art." In *Biographia Literaria*, ed. by J. Shawcross. Vol. II. OUP, 1962 (1907). p. 257.

[46] ὕλη καὶ τρόποις μιμήσεως διαφέρουσι.

Greek Voltaire", and found its best-known expression in Horace's "*ut pictura poesis*". Lessing draws a sharp line between the arts of space and those of time. Painting belongs to the former category, its particular subject consists of bodies with visible characteristics, while actions are the particular subject of poetry. But the difference is not absolute. Since bodies exist not only in space but also in time, painting too can imitate actions but only by indication, by means of bodies. Conversely, actions are necessarily connected with existing beings, hence poetry too imitates bodies, but only indicatively, by means of actions. It follows from these premises that painting, in its simultaneous compositions, can represent only a single moment of an action, while poetry, in the course of its continuous imitation, can make use only of a single quality of bodies. Hence painting must select the most pregnant moment, while poetry must characterize by a single trait, by one picturesque "Homeric" epithet.

"Lessing's main distinction between the arts of space and time — writes Wellek (*op. cit.* p. 163) — is basically sound." But the simple distinction is often overlaid with subtler ramifications. Thus in par. XVII of the *Laokoon* Lessing deals with the objection that the signs of poetry not only succeed each other in time but are also arbitrary; being arbitrary signs (one may argue) they are capable of representing bodies that exist in space. The thought is further developed in a letter to Nicolai (May 26, 1769) which comments on a review of the *Laokoon* by Garve. Here is a passage from the letter quoted and translated by Wellek: "Poetry must try to raise its arbitrary signs to natural signs — writes Lessing —: that is how it differs from prose and becomes poetry. The means by which this is accomplished are the tone of words, the position of words, measure, figures and tropes, similes, etc. . . The highest kind of poetry will be that which transforms the arbitrary signs completely into natural signs. That is dramatic poetry; for in it words cease to be arbitrary signs, and become natural signs of arbitrary objects."[47]

Lessing winds up his argument by referring to the authority of Aristotle who said that "dramatic poetry is the highest, even the only, poetry, and he assigns second place to the epic only insofar as it is for the most part dramatic or can be dramatic."[48]

This highest kind of poetry is the subject of Lessing's main contribution to literary criticism, the 104 numbers of the *Hamburgische Dramaturgie*, a series of papers published twice a week, from May 1, 1767 to April 19, 1768, when Lessing was acting as literary expert and dramatic critic to

---

[7] Wellek, *op. cit.*, pp. 164—5. The original is quoted in Note 77, p. 304: "Die Poesie muss schlechterdings ihre willkürlichen Zeichen zu natürlichen zu erheben suchen; und nur dadurch unterscheidet sie sich von der Prose, und wird Poesie . . . Die höchste Gattung der Poesie ist die, welche die willkürlichen Zeichen gänzlich zu natürlichen macht. Das aber ist die dramatische: denn in dieser hören die Worte auf, willkürliche Zeichen zu sein, und werden natürliche Zeichen willkürlicher Dinge."

[48] *Ibid.*, p. 165. The comparison of dramatic and epic poetry is based on chap. 24 of the *Poetics* which contains one of the major inconsistencies in the use of the term 'imitation'. Whereas at the beginning of chap. 3 Aristotle plainly included narrative among the forms of imitation, he now says that the poet should say as little as possible in his own person, as he is no imitator when doing that: αὐτὸν γὰρ δεῖ τὸν ποιητὴν ἐλάχιστα λέγειν· οὐ γάρ ἐστι κατὰ ταῦτα μιμητής. *Poet.* 1460 a 7—8. On the inconsistency and its source in Plato see H. House, *Aristotle's Poetics*, London, 1967 (1956), pp. 122—3.

the recently organized German-speaking national theatre. The most personal and most pathetic in tone is the last piece condensing nos 101—104. It is the voice of a disappointed man who refuses to be called actor or poet, who disclaims any pretensions to original genius and is content with the modest title of a critic. He speaks with bitter self-mockery about the naive idea of establishing a 'national' theatre when the Germans are not yet a nation. "We are still imitators of everything foreign," — Lessing complains — "especially servile admirers of the French who cannot be admired enough." He asserts his independence by reverting to Aristotle's doctrine of the essence of dramatic poetry, a doctrine based on "innumerable masterpieces of the Greek stage." Lessing expresses his conviction that, especially in tragedy, one cannot depart from the Aristotelian canon without departing from the ideal of perfection.

With this conviction firm in his mind, Lessing undertook a systematic examination of some of the most famous products of the French stage, supposed to follow strictly the Aristotelian rules and proclaimed to be models of perfection. This misconception was — he says — soon dispelled by some English plays which supplied evidence that tragedy was capable of producing quite a different effect from those produced by Corneille and Racine. Lessing advocates a middle course between two dangerous alternatives. He points out that the English plays obviously failed to conform to certain rules so sedulously formulated and proclaimed by the French. Hence it was concluded that the object of tragedy may be attained without following these rules, nay, even in defiance of *all* rules, and that it was mere pedantry to prescribe to genius what he should do or avoid. Lessing rejects both these extremes: he takes his stand on the experience of past ages and thinks it absurd that every poet should rediscover art for himself.[49]

A central portion of the *Hamburgische Dramaturgie* (nos 36—50) is concerned with the restatement of Aristotle's theory of tragedy, starting from an examination of Voltaire's *Merope*. Lessing emphasizes that unity of action was the first law of drama for the ancients, that the unities of time and place merely followed from it. But the French — writes Lessing — never relished true unity of action, having been spoiled by the wild intrigues of Spanish plays before they came to know Greek simplicity; hence they regarded the unities of time and place not as concomitants of the unity of action but as indispensable requirements for the presentation of an action on the stage.[50]

Lessing's views on Spanish drama are most fully stated in the conclusion he draws from a comparison of three plays on the fate of the Earl of Essex, by John Banks, Pierre Corneille, and an anonymous Spanish playwright, respectively (nos 54—68). All genuine Spanish plays — he says — share the characteristics of the latter. Lessing draws an interesting balance of the beauties and blemishes of Spanish drama; the former include an original plot, exciting complications, a sense for the stage, well developed and usually consistent characters, frequent dignity and strength in expression — beauties which are, however, often exaggerated in the direction of the romantic,

---

[49] All references are to L. Magon's edition of the *Hamburgische Dramaturgie*, Berlin, 1952.
[50] No. 46, pp. 174—5.

the adventurous, the unnatural, features that yet compare favourably with the mechanic regularity of most French plays. What really rouses the critic's anger is the figure of Cosme, the clown of the Spanish stage, "this terrible combination of rough horseplay with solemn seriousness, this mixture of the comic and the tragic that has made the Spanish stage notorious."[51] Lessing reveals himself here as a staunch champion of the fourth unity of Neoclassical criticism, the demand for the purity of genre which found a well-known early expression in Sir Philip Sidney's ironic protest against matching "Horn-pypes and Funeralls".[52]

There is a similar Neoclassic rigidity in some of Lessing's views on characterization, especially in nos 33—36 where he discusses Favart's comedy *Soliman II* based on a moral fable by Marmontel. In Lessing's scale of dramatic values, characters are more important than facts; facts are regarded as something accidental and may be common to several persons, while character reveals what is essential and peculiar. Raising the old problem of the relation of poetic to historic truth, Lessing considers it a less serious fault if characters in a drama differ from those as known in history than if characters invented by the poet sin against internal probability or fail to inculcate a moral lesson. Genius may violate the facts of history but we are justified in expecting harmony and purpose (*Übereinstimmung und Absicht*) in all characters created by him. Lessing is very emphatic on this point: there can be no inconsistency in the characters — they must always remain the same, always preserve their identity.[53] The critic here obviously remembers Aristotle's four points to be aimed at in characterization, the last of which is consistency.[54] He even reminds us of Thomas Rymer's extreme formulations of the Neoclassic doctrine of decorum when he goes on to say: "A Turk and a despot must always remain a Turk and a despot, even when he is in love. A Turk who knows only sensual love, must not think of the refinements which the spoilt European imagination connects with this passion." It is one of Lessing's own inconsistencies to combine this ideal of characterizing by rigid types with his admiration of Shakespeare, the great explorer of the contradictions of the human heart, the master of mixed genres.

Lessing admits that inconsistencies are often found in life, in the actual behaviour of real people. But, he adds sternly, such persons cannot be objects of poetic imitation.[55] The reason the critic gives is revealing: inconsistent characters are inadmissible because they fail to give instruction and lack purpose. In Lessing's ethical universe it is purpose that raises man above the lower creation; to compose with a purpose, to imitate with a purpose: this is what distinguishes the genius from inferior artists who only compose in order to compose, who only imitate in order to imitate, who

---

[51] No. 68, p. 262.

[52] *An Apologie for Poetrie*, c. 1583. In *Elizabethan Critical Essays*, ed. by G. G. Smith. Vol. 1. Oxford, 1904. p. 199.

[53] "Nichts muss sich in den Charakteren widersprechen; sie müssen immer einförmig, immer sich selbst ähnlich bleiben." No. 34, p. 130.

[54] τέταρτον δὲ τὸ ὁμαλόν. *Poet*. chap. 15. 1454 a 26.

[55] "Es gibt Menschen genug, die noch kläglichere Widersprüche in sich vereinigen. Aber diese können auch, eben darum, keine Gegenstände der poetischen Nachahmung sein." No. 34, p. 131.

make the means of art their ends. The end is to instruct us what we ought to do or avoid; to acquaint us with the characteristic marks of good and evil, of the proper and the ridiculous.

So far Lessing has hardly gone beyond the limits of the Neoclassical theory; he merely abandoned — as Wellek says — its French version and substituted a "liberalized version of Aristotle which allowed him to satisfy his desire for an ethical realism." Lessing sticks to the basic principle of *mimesis* and the concept of rules.[56]

But there are many aspects in Lessing's critical views which point forward to later theories, even to present trends of thought. Some of them have been examined by the Hungarian scholar Gy. M. Vajda, in a study introducing a Hungarian translation of Lessing's two treatises.[57]

Lessing makes an attempt to reinterpret the mimetic principle in the light of the psychology of attention. In no. 69 of the *Hamburgische Dramaturgie* he quotes a passage from Wieland's *Agathon* where the apparent lack of design in Shakespeare's plays, the mixing of comedy and tragedy is justified by an argument very similar to Dr. Johnson's. "They blame it [this mixing] — writes Wieland — without bearing in mind that his plays are precisely thereby natural pictures of human life."[58]

Lessing, a firm believer in the Neoclassic doctrine of the purity of genres, will have none of this. He has a contempt for the comico-tragic or tragico-comic 'mongrel-play' (Mischspiel) and refuses the appeal to nature. The example of nature — he writes in no. 70 — which is cited to justify the combination of solemn seriousness with merry clowing could equally justify any abortive drama that lacks plan, connection, or human reason. Hence — Lessing concludes — the imitation of nature would either cease to be a fundamental principle of art; or, if it yet remained a basic principle, art itself would cease to be art.[59]

Lessing seeks a way out of the difficulty by drawing a distinction between two senses of nature. It is both true and false — he says — that the mixture of comedy and tragedy, in the drama of 'Gothic' origin, imitates nature faithfully: it imitates only one half, with a total neglect of the other half; it imitates the appearances of nature, without paying the slightest attention to the nature of our feelings and mental powers.[60]

In nature — the philosophic critic points out — everything coheres, everything is in a state of flux and constant transformation. This infinite variety is fit spectacle only for an infinite spirit. If a finite mind wishes to partake in the pleasure of the spectacle, it must acquire a capacity to set limits to what is, in fact, illimitable; it must learn to segregate and to direct its attention to what it thinks essential.

[56] Wellek, *op. cit.*, p. 176.

[57] G. E. Lessing, *Laokoón, Hamburgi dramaturgia*, ed. Gy. M. Vajda. Az irodalomtörténet klasszikusai 1. Budapest, 1963.

[58] "Man tadelt das und denkt nicht daran, dass seine Stücke eben darin natürliche Abbildungen des menschlichen Lebens sind." Quoted in *Hamburgische Dramaturgie*, no. 69, p. 264.

[59] "Die Nachahmung der Natur müsste folglich entweder gar kein Grundsatz der Kunst sein; oder, wenn sie es doch bliebe, würde durch ihn selbst die Kunst, Kunst zu sein aufhören." *Ibid.*, no. 70, p. 266.

[60] " . . . die komische Tragödie, gotischer Erfindung . . . ahmet die Natur der Erscheinungen nach, ohne im geringsten auf die Natur unserer Empfindungen und Seelenkräfte dabei zu achten." *Ibid.* p. 268.

This capacity is exercised by us — Lessing continues — in every moment of our life. It is the function of art to relieve us, in the realm of the beautiful, of the necessity of distinction and segregation and to make the fixing of our attention easier. Whatever we mentally segregate, or wish to segregate, in nature, whether from an object or from the connection of different objects, in respect of time or space, is actually segregated in art and presented to us as clearly and authentically as is permitted by the feelings it wishes to arouse.[61]

Most theorists of artistic imitation, from Aristotle onward, have made it clear that the term, in their use, does not mean mimicry, a photographic reproduction of the details of physical reality, but implies conscious selection by the artist in order to reveal something of more permanent value, such as the universal, an internal or a supersensuous model, the outlines of a 'beautiful nature'. It is Lessing's merit that he tried to reconcile the mimetic, representational aspect of art with the active powers of the human mind, thus paving the way for the synthesis of objective and subjective elements, a synthesis that was to be achieved in the Romantic theory of poetry and fine art.

Even wider vistas of thought, ranging from Aristotle to contemporary Marxist critics, seem to be adumbrated in the discussion which starts with no. 84 of the *Hamburgische Dramaturgie*, occcasioned by the performance of Diderot's *Le père de famille*. The point of departure is Diderot's thesis: comedy deals with kinds, tragedy with individuals.[62] A similar distinction by Richard Hurd is quoted in no. 92: "Comedy makes all its characters *general;* tragedy, *particular.*"[63] Lessing will have no such dichotomy, in respect of characters, between dramatic genres: he wholeheartedly accepts Aristotle's view in chap. 9 of the *Poetics* who pronounced the expression of the general or the universal to be the distinguishing mark of *all* poetry, in contrast to history which tends to express the particular or singular.[64]

It may be remarked here that both these antithetical concepts, regarded as the *differentiae* of poetry and history, respectively, by Aristotle and Lessing, are used by Marxist critics to describe the aesthetic experience, with the addition of a third concept to make up a Hegelian triad. Thus the Hungarian Marxist, György (internationally known as Georg) Lukács sees

---

[61] "Die Bestimmung der Kunst ist, uns in dem Reiche des Schönen dieser Absonderung zu überheben, uns die Fixierung unserer Aufmerksamkeit zu erleichtern. Alles was wir in der Natur von einem Gegenstande, oder einer Verbindung verschiedener Gegenstände, es sei der Zeit oder dem Raume nach, in unsern Gedanken absondern, oder absondern zu können wünschen, sondert sie wirklich ab und gewährt uns diesen Gegenstand, oder diese Verbindung verschiedener Gegenstände, so lauter und bündig, als es nur immer die Empfindung, die sie erregen sollen, verstattet." *Ibid.* p. 268.

[62] In Lessing's translation: "Die komische Gattung . . . hat Arten, und die tragische hat Individua." *Ibid.* nos. 87—88, p. 327.

[63] *Ibid.* no. 92, p. 343.

[64] "Das ist unwidersprechlich, dass Aristoteles schlechterdings keinen Unterschied zwischen den Personen der Tragödie und Komödie, in Ansehung ihrer Allgemeinheit, macht . . . In diesem καθόλου, in dieser Allgemeinheit liegt allein der Grund, warum die Poesie philosophischer und folglich lehrreicher ist als die Geschichte." *Ibid.*, no. 89, p. 334. — The key sentence in the Aristotelian passage is: ἡ μὲν γὰρ ποίησις μᾶλλον τὰ καθόλου, ἡ δ' ἱστορία τὰ καθ' ἕκαστον λέγει. 1451 b 6—7. In Butcher's translation: "for poetry tends to express the universal, history the particular."

the essence of art in presenting a dialectical union of the general, the particular, and the individual; the function of art, in his view, is to represent life in its all-inclusive totality. Lukács draws a significant distinction between the method of science which resolves the process of movement into its abstract elements and tries to grasp in thought the law of interaction between these elements, and the method of art which represents, in a sensuous form, the process of movement in its living unity.[65]

To return to Lessing's more limited application of the terms 'general' and 'particular' to the drawing of character: in no. 95 of the *Hamburgische Dramaturgie* he makes a valiant attempt to prove that Diderot and Hurd, although they require particular characters from tragedy, and general ones only from comedy, yet do not contradict Aristotle who states *all* poetic characters, including those of tragedy, to be of a general or universal nature. Lessing resolves the paradox by pointing out that the word 'general' is used here to mean two entirely different things: in one sense, a 'general character' means what Lessing calls an *overloaded* character (*ein überladener Charakter*), one that unites features collected from a number of individuals; it is — he says — rather the personified idea of a character than a person characterized. In the other sense, a 'general' character means an average of the features observed in a number of individuals; Lessing calls this a *common* or *usual* character (*ein gewöhnlicher Charakter*). — The distinction seems far from clear and Lessing closes his argument on a modest note: he does not propose a system of dramatic theory, nor does he offer a solution of all the problems raised. His only object was to supply food for thought, to spread the *"fermenta cognitionis."*[66]

It lies beyond the scope of this study to follow Lessing's thought in all its ramifications; we must keep to our subject, the changing fate of the mimetic principle. But imitation, or representation, of reality necessarily involves wider issues. What sort of feelings should imitative art arouse? — Lessing asks in no. 79 of the *Hamburgische Dramaturgie*, after witnessing the tragedy of *Richard III;* is it only horror at the crimes of the king, pity with his helpless victims? No — he replies —, events should be viewed in the eternal, endless chain of all things. Here is the rest of the passage in Wellek's translation: "In history all is wisdom and goodness, though it may appear to us that there is blind fate and cruelty in the few links picked out by the poet. Out of these few links the poet ought to make a whole, rounded in itself and complete, fully explained in itself . . . We ought not to be forced to seek a reason outside, in the general plan of things . . . The whole fashioned by this mortal creator [viz. the poet] should be a silhouette of the whole of the eternal Creator. It should accustom us to the thought that as in it all things are resolved for the best, so also will it be on earth."[67]

[65] The reference is to the "Einführung in die ästhetische Schriften von Marx und Engels", written in 1945, as printed in Georg Lukács, *Schriften zur Literatursoziologie*, Soziologische Texte, Band 9. Luchterhand Verlag, Neuwied am Rhein, 1963 (1961), p. 229. Of the three concepts — das Allgemeine, Besondere und Einzelne — the middle one (das Besondere, the particular) has been made the subject of a separate book by Lukács and pronounced to be the central category of aesthetics in his great synthesis, *Die Eigenart des Aesthetischen. Werke*, Band 11—12. Luchterhand Verlag, 1963.

[66] *Op. cit.*, no. 95, pp. 354—5.

[67] Wellek, *op. cit.*, pp. 173—4, with the German original in Note 114, p. 308; in L. Magon's edition, used by us, on p. 300.

The conclusion Wellek draws from this passage is in keeping with prevalent notions about 18th-century thought: "drama — so Wellek sums up Lessing's view — shows us the world rational, transparent to the ethical will . . . His is the 18th-century universe of a benevolent God, a benevolent Nature, and a basically good man." One wonders if this is quite an adequate description of attitudes represented by some of the 'Tory satirists', e.g. by Swift, or Pope in his later years. It is even more open to doubt whether Lessing really failed "to grasp the nature of art," because, together with Diderot and Dr Johnson, he is charged by Wellek to have prepared "the conception of literature underlying the psychological and social realism of the 19th century."[68]

Dr Johnson is one of the ogres in Wellek's great *History of Modern Criticism;* he is described as "one of the first great critics who have almost ceased to understand the nature of art, and who, in central passages, treats art as life."[69] In support of his view, Wellek quotes Johnson saying that literature is "a just representation of things really existing and actions really performed," that novelists should be "just copiers of human manners" (p. 80). Such Johnsonian dicta are, however, merely restatements of the Aristotelian doctrine of imitation; far from treating art as life, Johnson regards it as an imitation, a reflection, a mirror of life. His adherence to Aristotle's mimetic principle is clearly proclaimed in the *Life of Cowley*: "the father of criticism — he says — has rightly denominated poetry τέχνη μιμητική, *an imitative art.*"[70]

The principle of imitation, adherence to the truth of nature is the touchstone in Johnson's critical judgements. He ascribes Shakespeare's preeminence "above all writers, at least above all modern writers" to the fact that he is "the poet of nature, the poet that holds up to his readers a faithful mirror of manners and of life." The thought and the image are repeated in another familiar sentence of Johnson's *Preface* to his 1765 edition of Shakespeare's plays: "This, therefore, is the praise of Shakespeare, that his drama is the mirror of life."[71]

These simple words reveal the true source of Shakespeare's permanent appeal. In the two centuries since the publication of Johnson's Preface the work of the British poet and dramatist has been the subject of countless studies. The Romantic critics concentrated on Shakespeare's poetry but they often employed the analogy of the living organism, too (an analogy first suggested by Plato and Aristotle) when stressing the "homogeneity, proportionateness, and totality of interest" which make each Shakespearean play a distinct poetic universe.[72] The main interest of the 19th century was in Shakespeare's characters, accompanied and followed by a close study of the available texts, the sources of the plays, the theatrical conditions of the

[68] *Op. cit.*, p. 175.
[69] *Op. cit.*, p. 79.
[70] *Lives of the English Poets*, vol. I. Everyman's Library, p. 11.
[71] *Dr Johnson on Shakespeare*, ed. W. K. Wimsatt, Penguin Shakespeare Library, 1969 (1960), pp. 59, 61.
[72] The phrases in inverted commas are from Coleridge's discussion of *Romeo and Juliet;* he also points out "the distinction, or rather the essential difference, betwixt the shaping skill of mechanical talent, and the creative, productive, life-power of inspired genius." From Coleridge's *Lectures*, in *Shakespeare Criticism*, a selection ed. by D. N. Smith. OUP, 1926 (1916), p. 281.

time, the composition of the Elizabethan and Jacobean audience. In the present century the traditional school of literary critics was joined by psychologists of both the Freudian and Jungian brand who examined the plays in the light of the Oedipus complex or of archetypal patterns. The year 1930 has been regarded as a year of sweeping changes: it initiated the close study of Shakespeare's imagery, it also saw the publication of G. Wilson Knight's first important volume which pooh-poohed the usual concentration on the dramatists' 'plots', 'sources', 'characters', 'intentions', and exhorted the reader, instead, to "regard each play as a visionary whole, close-knit in personification, atmospheric suggestion, and direct poetic-symbolism."[73] "We should not look for perfect verisimilitude to life," — the critic tells us — "but rather see each play as an expanded metaphor."[74]

Some of the critical methods introduced in the present century have revealed, no doubt, new aspects of the inexhaustible wealth of Shakespeare's work and have led to a more adequate appreciation. But it is highly significant that Wilson Knight himself, a leading light of Shakespeare's 'new criticism' disclaims much of his revolutionary ardour in the Prefatory Note to the 1947 reissue of *The Wheel of Fire*. "My animadversions as to 'character' analysis — he states — were never intended to limit the living human reality of Shakespeare's people ... It was, and is, my hope — Wilson Knight adds — that my own labours will be eventually regarded as a natural development within the classic tradition of Shakespearian study."[75]

One of the protagonists of modern symbolic interpretation thus admits "the living human reality of Shakespeare's people," a view that coincides with Johnson's. It is comforting to find that in a 1959 symposium of Stratford lectures, after referring to the great variety of contemporary opinions about Shakespeare and the large body of controversy about his work, J. I. M. Stewart singles out "two central works in the history of Shakespeare criticism: Dr Johnson's *Preface* to his edition of the plays, published in 1765, and A. C. Bradley's *Shakespearean Tragedy*, published in 1904."[76]

One should add the remarkable achievement of Marxist critics, especially during the last fifty years. They extended the scope of traditional methods of inquiry beyond the examination of individual characters to the reflection of the life of the whole society, the artistic mirroring of the struggles of social groups, of conflicting social and political forces. The method has proved particularly fruitful in the analysis of Shakespeare's histories and Roman plays; of *Hamlet* viewed as an expression of the crisis in Renaissance thought; of *King Lear* mirroring the clash of two ethical systems and two social formations, the conflict between the medieval vision of the outgoing feudal order and the ruthlessness of nascent capitalism. In its best representatives, Marxist criticism has been able to assimilate the valuable findings of Shakespearean scholarship, including the study of imagery, but has added a new dimension by the stress it lays on the plays as reflecting or 'imitating' forces which are at work in the life of human communities.

[73] *On the Principles of Shakespeare Interpretation*, in *The Wheel of Fire*, London, 1964 (1930), p. 11.
[74] *Ibid.*, p. 15.
[75] *Ibid.*, pp. v—vi.
[76] *Shakespeare's Men and Their Morals*, in *Shakespeare Criticism 1935—1960*, selected by Anne Ridler. OUP, 1963, p. 290.

Johnson's preeminence above Shakespeare's earlier critics, as the dramatist's preeminence above all modern writers, lies in his grasp of essentials, in his ability to distinguish what is central and primary from what is secondary and accidental. He accepts whole-heartedly the Aristotelian doctrine of *mimesis*: Shakespeare "holds up to his readers a faithful mirror of manners and of life"; his drama "exhibits successive imitations of successive actions."[77] But while regarding truth to life an essential requisite of great drama, Johnson never confounds art and life. We have seen him denying that "any representation is mistaken for reality"; he develops the idea in his well-known discussion of the nature of dramatic illusion. Here are some of the key sentences which raise to a new potency arguments used by Johnson's predecessors: "The truth is that the spectators are always in their senses and know, from the first act to the last, that the stage is only a stage, and that the players are only players . . . The delight of tragedy proceeds from fiction." And here is perhaps the most enlightening statement of all: "Imitations produce pain or pleasure," — says Johnson — "not because they are mistaken for realities, but because they bring realities to mind."[78] The true relation of artistic imitation to reality could hardly be put in a terser, more epigrammatic way.

Wellek also notes Johnson's adherence to the concept of 'general nature' and regards it as a survival of Neoclassic theory. He quotes such Johnsonian dicta as "reason and nature are uniform and inflexible" and "human nature is always the same," together with the famous passage from the tenth chapter of *Rasselas*: "The business of the poet — writes Johnson — is to examine, not the individual, but the species; to remark general properties and large appearances: he does not number the streaks of the tulip, or describe the different shades in the verdure of the forest."[79]

The relation of the general and the particular, a major problem of aesthetics, attracted the attention of many 18th-century critics and will be solved only within the dialectical framework of Marxist thought. Johnson accepts the Aristotelian view of poetry as tending to express the universal, together with the conviction that poetry must say something essential about man if it is to have universal appeal. He expands his description of Shakespeare as the poet of nature by adding that "his persons act and speak by the general passions and principles by which all minds are agitated and the whole system of life is continued in motion."[80] Wellek rightly recognizes that what Johnson advocates is "not accurate copying" but rather "the depiction of the general, the universal, the typical," though it seems incorrect to label this method as 'abstractionism'.[81] What Johnson objects to in other dramatists is that they "can only gain attention by hyperbolical or aggravated characters, by fabulous and unexampled excellence or depravity."

[77] *Dr Johnson on Shakespeare*, pp. 59, 71. Cf. Peter Alexander's attempt to combine the views of Aristotle and Arnold ("literature is first and last an imitation or criticism of life"), his emphasis on the connection of fictitious figures with reality ("the creations of the poet's imagination refer us to reality for their interpretation"). *Shakespeare's Life and Art*, New York Univ. Press, 1961 (1939), p. 145.
[78] *Op. cit.*, pp. 70—71.
[79] See Wellek, *op. cit.*, p. 85.
[80] *Dr Johnson on Shakespeare*, p. 59.
[81] Wellek, *loc. cit.*

As against such distortions and exaggerations, it is the praise of Shakespeare that "he has no heroes; his scenes are occupied only by men, who act and speak as the reader thinks that he should himself have spoken or acted on the same occasion." Here we read "human sentiments in human language."[82]

Dr Johnson, the great English eccentric, has often been accused of narrow sympathies in politics and literature. He obviously had very strong likes and dislikes and was always ready to speak his mind. He heartily disapproved of all romantic exaggeration (his hostility to Macpherson and his *Ossian* is notorious) and would certainly have been irritated by the 'hyperbolical or aggravated characters' of Byron's oriental tales. He uses the Aristotelian definition of poetry as an imitative art to launch a violent attack on the 'metaphysical poets' (the label was appended to them by Johnson), since "they cannot be said to have imitated anything; they neither copied nature for life, neither painted the forms of matter, nor represented the operations of intellect."[83]

We cannot enter here into an analysis of Johnson's objections to the "poetry of wit," a task that was to be performed by T. S. Eliot in his essay on the Metaphysical Poets (1921) which contains his famous remarks on the 'dissociation of sensibility' and his placing of Donne and his school "in the direct current of English poetry".[84] A few words must, however, be said about Johnson's *Life of Milton*, a piece of work that roused even the gentle soul of William Cowper to anger.[85] But Johnson does not indulge in groundless vituperation: he is only faithful to his critical principles and has the courage to pass unfavourable judgments on a poet who had become a national institution. He criticizes *Lycidas* because, in his view, "in this poem there is no nature" and because the "inherent improbability" of pastoral poetry "always forces dissatisfaction on the mind." Johnson anticipates much of modern criticism by pointing out that Milton's images and descriptions of nature "do not seem to be always copied from original form, nor to have the freshness, raciness, and energy of immediate observation." He quotes with approval Dryden's remark that Milton saw nature "through the spectacle of books." Even if one admires *Samson Agonistes* as a dramatic *poem*, it is difficult to disagree with Johnson's view that "Milton would not have excelled in dramatic writing." The reason he gives seems just and has been extended by later critics to other realms of Milton's poetry. Milton "knew human nature only in the gross . . . He had read much, and knew what books could teach, but . . . was deficient in the knowledge which experience must confer."[86]

Johnson's conception of art as a "just representation of human nature" precludes any sympathy with the playful or passionate intricacies of the Mannerist or baroque mode, the verbal subtleties of the 'poetry of wit'. He protests against the "combination of dissimilar images", the *discordia concors* which pervade the poetry of the metaphysicals. Neither does he approve of Dryden's "delight . . . in wild and daring sallies of sentiment, in the

[82] *Dr Johnson on Shakespeare*, pp. 60—61.
[83] *Lives of the English Poets*, vol. I, p. 11.
[84] *Selected Essays*, pp. 241—250.
[85] "His treatment of Milton is unmerciful to the last degree" — wrote Cowper in a letter to a friend on October 31, 1779.
[86] *Lives of the English Poets*, vol. I, pp. 96, 105, 111.

irregular and eccentric violence of wit."[87] We have seen Johnson's praise of Shakespeare's characters who express "human sentiments in human language"; he has also praised the dialogues of his plays for their "ease and simplicity" and declared that they seem "to have been gleaned by diligent selection out of common conversation."[88] But Johnson, while admiring the dramatist's excellencies, is not blind to his faults. His love of Shakespeare, like his namesake's, Ben Jonson's, was always "this side idolatry." He sternly rebukes Shakespeare for his "idle conceits" and "contemptible equivocations" and is particularly hard on his puns and quibbles, the symptoms of Shakespeare's linguistic playfulness and verbal curiosity. "A quibble, poor and barren as it is — writes Johnson in a well-known passage — gave him such delight that he was content to purchase it by the sacrifice of reason, propriety, and truth. A quibble was to him the fatal Cleopatra for which he lost the world and was content to lose it."[89]

Thus there seems to be a certain contradiction in Johnson's views on the Shakespearean style though one may argue that his remarks refer to different levels in the dramatist's richly stratified use of language. There is, however, another, more profound contradiction in Johnson's utterances, a conflict between the demand for reality and the demand for morality, duly noted by Wellek who quotes Johnson saying in the *Life of Addison:* "since wickedness often prospers in real life, the poet is certainly at liberty to give it prosperity on the stage. For if poetry is an imitation of reality, how are its laws broken by exhibiting it in its true form?"[90] The demand that poetry, being the mirror of life, should exhibit reality in its true form, is basic to Johnson's aesthetics. In contrast to Lessing's Neoclassic insistence on the purity of dramatic genres, his protest against the mixing of tragic and comic motifs, Johnson praises Shakespeare's practice of uniting "the powers of exciting laughter and sorrow . . . in one composition," since in this way his plays exhibit "the real state of sublunary nature, which partakes of good and evil, joy and sorrow, mingled with endless variety of proportion and innumerable modes of combination." He admits that "this is a practice contrary to the rules of criticism" but adds that "there is always an appeal open from criticism to nature."[91]

Yet the validity of the mimetic principle, the demand that drama should mirror "the real state of sublunary nature" is limited for Johnson by the claims of "moral truth." In listing Shakespeare's defects, Johnson's first and most serious objection is that "he sacrifices virtue to convenience and . . . seems to write without any moral purpose." The most glaring instance of the violation of "moral truth" and of "poetic justice" in his eyes is the fate of Cordelia. "Shakespeare has suffered the virtue of Cordelia to perish in a just cause," — complains Johnson — "contrary to the natural ideas of justice, to the hope of the reader, and, what is yet more strange, to the faith of chronicles." And here is the critic's personal reaction to the terrible fate of Shakespeare's selfless heroine, the embodiment of "pure redeeming

[87] *Ibid.*, pp. 11, 256.
[88] *Dr Johnson on Shakespeare*, p. 60. One is reminded of Wordsworth's doctrine that the language of poetry should be a selection from the language really used by men.
[89] *Ibid.*, p. 68.
[90] Wellek, *op. cit.*, p. 83.
[91] *Dr Johnson on Shakespeare*, p. 62.

ardour'? (the phrase is Bradley's): "I was many years ago so shocked by Cordelia's death — confesses Johnson — that I know not whether I ever endured to read again the last scenes of the play till I undertook to revise them as an editor."[92]

Wellek couples the name of Johnson with those of Tolstoy and Shaw as critics who "complain of Shakespeare's lack of morality" and discovers in Johnson "a slipping of the grasp on the nature of art and an anticipation of standards of realism and moralism which will make art really as superfluous as it seemed to many Englishmen of the 19th century."[93] We have seen that Wilson Knight, a champion of symbolic interpretation, "never intended to limit the living human reality of Shakespeare's people." As for standards of 'moralism' in art, they were introduced long before Johnson or 19th-century Englishmen. Plato was a notorious offender in this respect and so was his disciple and rival, Aristotle. The latter is the grand source and exemplar of the mimetic principle, yet he is not unaware of complexities in the structure or the emotional appeal of a work of art. His psychological bias is obvious in his attribution of the cathartic effect of tragedy to the 'purgation' of pity and fear; this is joined with moral considerations in his analysis of the ideal tragic hero in chap. 13 of the *Poetics*. In Aristotle's view, a perfect tragedy should "imitate actions which excite pity and fear, this being the distinctive mark of tragic imitation. It follows plainly, in the first place, that the change of fortune presented must not be the spectacle of a virtuous man brought from prosperity to adversity: for this moves neither pity nor fear; it merely shocks us."[94] The word μιαρόν used here by Aristotle has clearly a moral connotation.

We cannot enter into the merits of the case so sharply put by Aristotle. Butcher is, no doubt, right when he points out that in the figure of Antigone Greek drama created a guiltless heroine; he calls it a "misplaced ingenuity" which wants to discover in Antigone "any fault or failing which entailed on her suffering as its due penalty."[95] We may add that similar "misplaced ingenuity" has been applied in attempts to assign some "tragic fault" to Cordelia or Desdemona, in order to shift the burden of responsibility to the individual and save the face of the "moral order." The real point at issue is that Aristotle and Johnson, with the other "moralist" critics mentioned above, may be wrong in their interpretation of the function or effect of any particular dramatic character, yet they are right in attaching great importance to the psychological and moral reactions of the audience. The faithful representation of reality, the source and prime requisite of all great art, must be squared with the mental and moral make-up of the recipient. "The poet, described in *ideal* perfection," — writes Coleridge — "brings the whole soul of man into activity."[96]

---

[92] *Ibid.*, pp. 66, 126.
[93] *Op. cit.*, p. 84.
[94] The last sentence of the original, here given in Butcher's version, runs as follows: οὐ γὰρ φοβερὸν ιὐδὲ ἐλεεινὸν τοῦτο ἀλλὰ μιαρόν ἐστιν. *Poet.* 1452 b 35—36. Here is Bywater's translation: "The first situation is not fear-inspiring or piteous, but simply odious to us."
[95] *Op. cit.*, p. 309.
[96] *Biographia Literaria*, ed. J. Shawcross. Vol. II, p. 12.

Intellectual honesty, a readiness always to speak his mind, is an essential characteristic of Johnson the man and the critic. He combines an acute, if limited, artistic sensibility with a fundamental moral seriousness and an endeavour to organize his responses under general aesthetic principles verified by the test of experience. Wellek is right in pointing out that Johnson's criticism "is not defeated by the conflicting theories of realism, moralism, and what is here called abstractionism. The three strands were no doubt reconcilable in his own mind."[97]

'Abstractionism' is the term used by Wellek to denote Johnson's belief in 'general nature', a belief which he shared with Sir Joshua Reynolds, a member of Johnson's club and first president of the Royal Academy. Otherwise, there is little in common between the outspoken, burly eccentric and the fashionable painter of aristocratic society. Walter Jackson Bate who joins their names together in the chapter dealing with "The Premise of General Nature" in his well-known book, calls Reynolds' presidential *Discourses on Art* delivered to students of the Royal Academy (1769—90) "perhaps the most representative single embodiment in English of eighteenth-century aesthetic principles."[98] Several of these discourses or lectures deal with technical problems of painting; here we can discuss only a few points which concern all the arts and, in particular, poetry.

First, there is the stress Reynolds lays on the concept of 'general nature'. He is in the main line of the Neoclassic tradition when he states that "the highest type of criticism . . . refers to the eternal and immutable nature of things."[99] *Discourse III* deals mainly with painting, yet the injunction "to exhibit distinctly, and with precision, the general forms of things" (III, p. 52) is obviously applicable to all art. The classical ideal of excellence, *quod semper et ubique* is stated emphatically in this lecture. The painter "must disregard all local and temporary ornaments, and look only on those general habits which are everywhere and always the same. He addresses his works to the people of every country and every age" (III, p. 49).

The principle established with regard to painting is extended to all branches of creative intellectual activity in the peroration of *Discourse IV*. "The works, whether of poets, painters, moralists, or historians," says Reynolds, "which are built upon general nature, live for ever; while those which depend for their existence on particular customs and habits, a partial view of nature, or the fluctuation of fashion, can only be coeval with that which first raised them from obscurity" (IV, p. 68). The opposition of the general and the particular, widely discussed by theorists of art and literature since Aristotle, is decided here sharply in favour of the former, and immortality is promised only to works that express 'general nature'. Yet Reynolds has to recognize that his formulation is too extreme; earlier in the lecture he admits that "some circumstances of minuteness and particularity frequently tend to give an air of truth to a piece, and to interest the spectator in an extraordinary manner . . . However, — he adds — the usual and most

---

[97] *Op. cit.*, p. 87.
[98] *From Classic to Romantic*. Premises of Taste in Eighteenth Century England, New York, 1961 (1946), p. 79.
[99] Discourse XIII, in *Discourses on Art*, Collier Books, London, 1969 (1966), p. 201. All quotations are taken from this paperback version of the *Discourses on Art* ed. Robert R. Wark, Huntington Library, San Marino, 1959.

dangerous error is on the side of minuteness . . . The general idea constitutes real excellence" (IV, p. 56).

It is on this principle that he establishes a hierarchy among the schools of painting, putting the Roman, the Florentine, and the Bolognese schools first, followed by the best French painters — Poussin, Le Sueur, and Le Brun — whom he regards as a 'colony' from the Roman school. After them come, "but in a very different style of excellence," the Venetian, together with the Flemish and Dutch schools — "all professing to depart from the great purposes of painting," he adds sternly, "and catching at applause by inferior qualities" (IV, p. 60).[100]

One may suspect from the foregoing that the mimetic principle is assigned a rather ambiguous role in Reynolds' aesthetic thought. In the field of painting, 'imitation' means to him "simply the following of other masters, and the advantage to be drawn from the study of their works" (VI, p. 85). It is primarily a way of acquiring an adequate technique, "the true and only method by which an artist makes himself master of his profession" (VI, p. 100).

But the central statements on the mimetic principle and its relation to the imaginative faculty are found in *Discourse XIII*, delivered on December 11, 1786. Reynolds calls it a 'mean conception' of the art of painting which would confine it to 'mere imitation'; he actually goes to the length of declaring that painting "is, and ought to be, in many points of view, and strictly speaking, no imitation at all of external nature" (XIII, pp. 203—4). This startling statement is expounded more fully in Reynolds' penetrating analysis of the nature of poetry. "The very existence of Poetry depends on the licence it assumes of deviating from actual nature." Poetry, Reynolds continues his argument, "sets out with a language in the highest degree artificial, a construction of measured words, such as never is, nor ever was used by man." Once this artificial mode has been established, another principle begins to operate which carries the poem still further from common nature. "That principle — writes Reynolds — is the sense of congruity, coherence, and consistency." With a rare insight into the necessary interrelation between the structural elements of a poetic composition he points out that "having once adopted a style and a measure not found in common discourse, it is required that the sentiments also should be in the same proportion elevated above common nature, from the necessity of there being an agreement of the parts among themselves, that one uniform whole may be produced" (XIII, pp. 205—6).

---

[100] *Discourse IV* was delivered on December 10, 1771. The same principle had been enunciated and a similar hierarchy established by Reynolds twelve years earlier, in a letter published in no. 79 of 'The Idler', on October 20, 1759. "The grand style of painting — he writes here — requires this minute attention to be carefully avoided." He draws a contrast between the Italian painter who "attends only to the invariable, the great and general ideas which are fixed and inherent in universal nature" and the Dutch who attends, "on the contrary, to literal truth and a minute exactness in the detail." In Reynolds' view, the sublimest style is that of Michelangelo, "the Homer of painting"; he expresses his conviction that "in painting, as in poetry, the highest style has the least of common nature." *The Discourses of Sir Joshua Reynolds*, to which are added his letters to 'The Idler.' With an introduction by A. Dobson. Oxford, The World's Classics, 1907, pp. 253—4.

This is a conception of poetry much wider and more generous than Johnson's. Based on the principle of organic unity or of structural consistency, it is comprehensive enough to include the intellectual subtlety of the metaphysicals or the exquisite variety and use of conventions in Milton's *Lycidas*. Reynolds himself employs it to defend the artificialities of the Italian Opera.

The dialectical turn of the critic's mind is shown by the fact that he sees in the arts the working of two different principles: "the one follows nature, the other varies it, and sometimes departs from it. The Theatre", Reynolds continues, "which is said *to hold the mirror up to nature*, comprehends both ideas." He winds up his argument with the important warning, recalling Lessing's, that "no Art can be engrafted with success on another art," the reason being that "each has its own peculiar modes both of imitating nature, and of deviating from it, each for the accomplishment of its own particular purpose" (XIII, pp. 209—210).

But while the manner and degree of imitating actual nature is perhaps the crucial *differentia specifica* that separates and distinguishes the different fine arts from one another, there is, in Reynolds' view, one feature that unites them: all the arts "address themselves only to two faculties of the mind, its imagination and its sensibility." Reynolds emphatically rejects "all theories which attempt to direct or control the Art, upon any principles falsely called rational." He formulates, with some hesitation in his voice, a central doctrine of Romantic aesthetics: "though it may appear bold to say it, the imagination is here [i.e. in the arts] the residence of truth" (XIII, 202). The mimetic principle, the conception of art as a reflection of reality is relegated to a secondary place, the effect of the work of art, the mental state of the recipient moves into the centre of attention. In Reynolds' words, the great end of all the arts is "to make an impression on the imagination and the feeling". The imitation of nature does not always contribute to this end. Hence, the critic concludes, "the true test of all the arts, is not solely whether the production is a true copy of nature, but whether it answers the end of art, which is to produce a pleasing effect upon the mind" (XIII, p. 211).

Seen in the general context of European aesthetic thought Reynolds' statement is not startling for its novelty.[101] But within the framework of conflicting 18th-century theories his achievement has been rightly described as that of having combined and reconciled "classical and broadly romantic values"[102] or having constructed a compromise between two attitudes, viz. 'Classicism', involved with uniformity, reason, and ideal form, and 'Romanticism', concerned with individualism, imagination, and the value of association.[103]

---

[101] In Aristotle's system, Butcher tells us, "the end of the fine arts is to give pleasure (πρὸς ἡδονήν) or rational enjoyment (πρὸς διαγωγήν)." Or, in words recalling more closely those of Reynolds, "the end of fine art, according to Aristotle's doctrine, is a certain pleasurable impression produced upon the mind of the hearer or the spectator." *Op. cit.*, pp. 198—9, 206.

[102] Walter Jackson Bate, *Criticism: The Major Texts*, New York, 1952, p. 254.

[103] Robert R. Wark's Introduction to his edition of the *Discourses on Art*, San Marino, 1959. p. xxx.

IV

Practically all the critics discussed so far agree in the basic 'Classical' assumption that art, at least in its higher reaches, 'imitates' or represents something permanent and immutable, that the object of imitation is some sort of 'general human nature' which has its fixed place in the 'vast chain of being', in an essentially static universe. This conception was gradually undermined, chiefly from two directions: on the one side, by the growing sense of historicism, on the other, by doubts cast on the validity of the mimetic principle itself, and by the stress laid on the creative activity of the artist or the psychological make-up of the recipient.

One of the first English critics to abandon the concept of 'general nature' and to use historical standards in his judgments was Thomas Warton. This is clear not only in his *History of English Poetry* (1774—81) but in an early treatise, *Observations on the Faerie Queene*, published in 1754 when the author was only 26. Warton propounds here the thesis, partly derived from David Hume, that Spenser, no less than Homer, "copied real manners," the difference between the two poets being that "Homer copied true natural manners" while Spenser "was employed in drawing the affectations, and conceits, and fopperies of chivalry." Quoting Hume's words, Warton concludes that Spenser's sophisticated picture of medieval manners was "nothing more than an imitation of real life, as much, at least, as the plain descriptions in Homer, which corresponded to the simplicity of manners then subsisting in Greece."[104]

A similar distinction between 'heroic' and 'Gothic' manners as objects of imitation was drawn eight years later by Richard Hurd in his *Letters on Chivalry and Romance* (1762). Hurd maintains that Spenser's poem must be read and criticized "under the idea not of a classical but Gothic composition," establishes an interesting analogy with architecture ("when an architect examines a Gothic structure by Grecian rules he finds nothing but deformity"), and concludes with the following justification of Spenser's method: "Judge the *Faerie Queene* by the classic models, and you are shocked with its disorder: consider it with an eye to its Gothic original, and you find it regular." This "Gothic original" is found by Hurd in "the established modes and ideas of chivalry."[105]

A radical reorientation in critical theory was inaugurated by the German *Sturm und Drang*. Repudiation of the mimetic principle is one of the characteristic marks of the movement. Their spiritual ancestor, Johann Georg Hamann, whom Goethe regarded the greatest man of the century, expressed his views on poetry in the cryptic utterances of the '*Aesthetica in nuce*', a section of his *Kreuzzüge des Philologen* (1762). He condemns — writes Wellek — "imitation of nature, probability, *la belle nature*, and all the assumptions of neoclassicism . . . His idea of genius is all feeling, imagination, fire, inspiration, originality, creativeness."[106]

---

[104] *Eighteenth-Century Critical Essays*, ed. Scott Elledge, Cornell Univ. Press. Ithaca, N. Y. 1961. Vol. II, p. 772.

[105] *English Critical Essays*, ed. by E. D. Jones. OUP, 1947 (1922), pp. 319—320. An examination of Hurd's *Dissertation of the Idea of Universal Poetry* (1766), discussed by Abrams as an example of the 'pragmatic orientation', lies outside the scope of our inquiry.

[106] Wellek, *op. cit.*, p. 180.

Wellek is careful to point out that all the ideas of the *Sturm und Drang* movement which broke out in the 1770's were "substantially derived from the French sentimentalists and the British primitivists." The same applies to Johann Gottfried Herder who borrowed the bulk of his critical thought from late 18th-century English and Scottish critics. "There is scarcely any idea in Herder," writes Wellek, "which could not be traced back to Blackwell or Harris, Shaftesbury or Brown, Blair or Percy, Warton or Young," although he was also acquainted with the work of his "German predecessors and contemporaries, especially Lessing, Hamann, and Winckelmann."[107] Wellek adds to this impressive list the names of Rousseau, Diderot, and Vico, remarking that the thought of the Italian critic seems to have reached Herder through Cesarotti's notes to Ossian.

But however great Herder's indebtedness to his contemporaries or precursors, his role was essentially that of an innovator and pioneer. When he borrowed from his predecesssors, he borrowed thoughts that point forward to future developments, to dynamic conceptions of poetry. Thus, Wellek reminds us, poetry for Herder is not an imitation of nature, but an "imitation of the creating, naming Godhead" (*"eine Nachahmung der schaffenden, nennenden Gottheit"*). Herder echoes Shaftesbury in comparing the poet to Prometheus and calling him a "second creator, *poietes*, maker."[108]

The results of Herder's rich and varied activity are clearly summed up by Wellek. In him — he writes — "the poetics of neoclassicism is . . . in the process of dissolution. He rejects all its main tenets: the imitation of nature, decorum, the unities, probability, propriety, clarity of style, purity of genre." In place of these discarded ideals, Wellek adds, Herder "began to build a new romantic poetics on the conception of a natural poetry, sensuous, metaphorical, imaginative." Wellek describes Herder as the "great initiator" who "left to others the task of formulating a new, coherent, systematic theory of poetry and literature."[109]

This coherent, systematic theory is identified by Wellek elsewhere as a "formalistic, organistic, symbolistic aesthetics, rooted . . . in the great tradition of German aesthetics from Kant to Hegel, restated and justified in French symbolism, in De Sanctis and Croce."[110] The initial stage in the formulation of this aesthetics, which is obviously nearest to Wellek's own heart, is discussed in the closing chapters of Vol. I of his *History of Modern Criticism*, devoted to the critical views of Goethe, Kant, and Schiller. It lies beyond the limits of our inquiry to examine such new seminal concepts as Goethe's distinction between allegory and symbol, Kant's isolation of the "aesthetic realm from the realm of science, morality, and utility," Schiller's conception of the artist as the "mediator between man and nature" or his distinction between 'naive' and 'sentimental' poetry, to be reformulated by the Schlegels as the opposition of Classical and Romantic literature. These and related ideas may be regarded as antecedents of the Romantic theory of literature, to be discussed elsewhere. Our present concern is with the mimetic principle which continues to play an important role in this period of changing aesthetic concepts. Thus, after his early enthusiasm

[107] *Ibid.*, pp. 176, 181.
[108] *Ibid.*, p. 188.
[109] *Ibid.*, p. 200.
[110] *Concepts of Criticism*, Yale Univ. Press, 1964 (1963), pp. 363—4.

for Herder and the *Sturm und Drang*, Goethe comes to distrust mere subjectivity and recognizes that the roots of poetry are in external reality. Wellek quotes Goethe saying that he wants "to give the real a poetic form" (*"dem Wirklichen eine poetische Gestalt zu geben"*) and even concludes that Goethe's "theory of art has become totally extrovert, turned toward imitation of nature as all classicism was."[111]

Objectivity is, in Schiller's eyes, an essential feature of 'naive' poetry. His treatise *Über naive und sentimentalische Dichtung* (1795—96) is, as Wellek points out, "based on a deceptively simple contrast": 'naive' poetry involves 'imitation of nature', it is fundamentally realistic, objective art, while 'sentimental' poetry is reflective, self-conscious, personal. Typical representatives of 'naive' poetry are Homer and Shakespeare. But 'naive imitation of nature' — Wellek adds — does not mean naturalism for Schiller. "He shares the neoclassical distaste for the 'Dutch' . . . His ideal of 'naive' art is good classicism, an art based on the eternal principles of nature." According to Wellek's final verdict, "Schiller offers a theory of literature which holds firmly to the essential truth of neoclassicism . . . He sums up and salvages the heritage of the 18th century and is yet the wellspring of romantic criticism which spread from Germany . . . throughout Europe."[112]

The building of comprehensive, fairly consistent aesthetic systems was to be mainly the work of German thinkers, yet the bolder scepticism of the British empirical tradition did much to prepare the soil. One of the iconoclasts who dared openly reject the authority of Aristotle was Sir William Jones, a pioneer of Oriental studies, a member of Dr Johnson's literary club, a friend of Burke and Gibbon. As a young man of 26, he published in 1772 a volume of poems, chiefly translations from Asiatic languages; he appended two essays to this collection, one of them bearing the title "On the Arts Commonly Called Imitative." Jones vigorously rejects the Aristotelian thesis, together with its version in Batteux, that all the fine arts rest on the common principle of imitation; this may be true of painting, but he believes that "poetry and music had a nobler origin."[113] He gives an interesting account of the origin of poetry and music, closely resembling that to be given by Shelley half a century later. According to Jones, "poetry was originally no more than a strong and animated expression of the human passions," its principal subjects being praise of the deity and praise of human love. He defines "original and native poetry" as the "language of the violent passions, expressed in exact measure, with strong accents and significant words"; a similar definition is applied to "true music" which is no more than "poetry, delivered in a succession of harmonious sounds, so disposed as to please the ear."

Jones hopes to clinch his argument by an eloquent appeal to the testimony of Biblical poetry. "The lamentation of David," he writes in a well-known passage, "and his sacred odes or psalms, the song of Solomon, the prophecies of Isaiah, Jeremiah, and the other inspired writers, are truly and strictly poetical; but what did David or Solomon imitate in their divine poems?

---

[111] *A History of Modern Criticism*, vol. I, p. 207.
[112] *Ibid,*. pp. 235—9, 254—5.
[113] All quotations are from the reprint in *Eighteenth-century Critical Essays*, ed. Scott Elledge, vol. II. pp. 872—881.

A man who is really joyful or afflicted cannot be said to imitate joy or affliction."

It is obvious that for Jones, as for Thomas Twining after him, 'imitation' involves resemblance; taking the term in a literal and restricted sense, Jones rejects the widespread view that descriptive poetry and descriptive music are 'strict imitations' because — he says — "words and sounds have no kind of resemblance to visible objects".

The problem will be subjected to a more searching analysis by Twining. Jones himself finds the deepest appeal of the fine arts not in imitation but in creative imagination and in sympathy. The artist gains his end, he says, "not by imitating the works of nature, but by assuming her power and causing the same effect upon the imagination which her charms produce to the senses." He draws a significant distinction between the higher reaches of art, "the finest parts of poetry, music, and painting [which] are expressive of the passions and operate on our minds by sympathy" and those inferior parts that are "descriptive of natural objects, and affect us chiefly by substitution," that is, "by raising in our minds affections or sentiments analogous to those which arise in us when the respective objects in nature are presented to our senses".

The interest of the critic is thus shifting from the world represented to the process of expressing passions and to the emotional impact on the audience. The principle of 'imaginative sympathy' will be predominant in the criticism of Hazlitt and his disciple Keats. The Neoclassic orientation of Jones appears clearly in his repeated protests against the "refinements of modern artists," "the numerous fugues, counterfugues, and divisions which rather disgrace than adorn the modern music." The ground of his objection is that "the passions, which were given by nature, never spoke in an unnatural form," an argument closely resembling that used by Johnson in his criticism of the metaphysicals or of Milton.

The animadversions of William Jones against the mimetic principle are those of a brilliant amateur; a systematic examination of the whole problem was undertaken by Thomas Twining, in two dissertations on poetical and musical imitation which he appended to his translation of Aristotle's *Treatise on Poetry* (1789).[114]

In the first of these treatises Twining discusses two questions: in what sense the word 'imitation' may be applied to poetry; and in what sense it was so applied by Aristotle. In Twining's view, every imitation, "strictly and properly so called", must satisfy two essential conditions: the resemblance between the imitative work and the object imitated must be immediate and it must also be obvious. He denies that all poetry is imitation and maintains that "poetry can be justly considered as imitative only by sound, by description, by fiction, or by personation." The first part of the treatise is devoted to a detailed discussion, illustrated by numerous examples, of these four customary senses of the term. Twining's powers of analysis and discrimination are fully displayed here, as is his acquaintance with the work of British theorists of poetic language and music. He states that "the

---

[114] The first of these, "On Poetry Considered as an Imitative Art," is quoted from Elledge, *op. cit.*, vol. II, pp. 984—1004; the second, "On the Different Senses of the Word, Imitative, as applied to Music by the Antients, and by the Moderns," from the first edition of 1789, pp. 44—61.

materials of poetic imitation are words" but adds that words may be considered in two views: "as sounds *merely*, and as sounds *significant*, or arbitrary and conventional signs of ideas." It is only in the first view, i.e. in fairly exceptional cases, when words are considered as sounds merely, when, in Pope's phrase, the sound is an "echo to the sense,"[115] that there can be any resemblance to the things expressed.

In the second sense the word 'imitation' is applied to denote description, "all such circumstantial and distinct representation as conveys to the mind a strong and clear idea of its object, whether sensible or mental." Twining is careful to stress that description, in this sense, is not limited to poetic landscape-painting, what is usually called 'descriptive poetry', but includes description of mental objects, "of the emotions and passions, and other internal movements and operations of the mind." "Poetry, in this view," he says, "is naturally considered as more or less imitative in proportion as it is capable of raising an ideal image or picture more or less resembling the reality of things." It is at this point that Twining's interpretation of the mimetic principle approaches most closely the central category of Marxist aesthetics.

In the third sense of the term, poetical imitation is considered as fiction. Twining employs and develops the Aristotelian distinction between poetry and history: the poet feigns or invents stories, actions, incidents in imitation of real life, of truth, "in *general*, as opposed to that individual reality of things which is the province of the historian." He calls epic and dramatic poems the principal examples of this type of imitation which he distinguishes from the descriptive kind in epigrammatic phrases. "In description," he writes, "imitation is opposed to actual *impression* . . .: in fiction, it is opposed to *fact* . . . Descriptive imitation may be said to produce illusive perception; fictive, illusive belief."[116]

It is because of the absence of the two essential conditions formulated at the outset (the resemblance between the imitative work and the object imitated must be both "immediate and obvious") that Twining considers the application of the word 'imitative' to description and fiction "manifestly extended or improper senses." According to his definition, only one kind of poetry can be considered imitation "in the strict and proper sense of the word": this is dramatic, or, more generally, 'personative' poetry — "that is," he explains, "all poetry in which . . . the poet personates; for here speech is imitated by speech." Fortunately, Twining does not always insist on his rigid definition, shows understanding for "manifestly extended or improper senses" and readily admits that "these different species of imitation often run into, and are mixed with, each other".

In the second part of his first dissertation Twining tries to define the senses in which the word 'imitation' was employed by Aristotle. In his view,

[115] The phrase comes from *An Essay on Criticism* (1. 365), followed by a number of illustrations, including these two:

> Soft is the strain when Zephyr gently blows,
> And the smooth stream in smoother numbers flows;
> But when loud surges lash the sounding shore,
> The hoarse, rough verse should like the torrent roar.

[116] Cf. Coleridge who finds the source of 'poetic faith' in the "willing suspension of disbelief for the moment." *Biogr. Lit.*, chap. XIV.

42

the Aristotelian use is restricted to the latter two meanings discussed above: 'imitative' poetry for the Greek critic is 'fictive' or 'personative'; or as Twining puts it, Aristotle's notion of poetic imitation "seems to have been simply that of the imitation of human actions, manners, passions, events, etc., in feigned history, and that, principally, when conveyed in a dramatic form." Twining repeatedly states that resemblance of sound or description are not included among the Aristotelian senses of imitation — yet in the passage just quoted "the imitation of human actions, manners, passions" hardly differs from the 'imitation' of mental objects, "of the emotions, passions, and other internal movements and operations of the mind" which Twining includes among the objects of 'descriptive' imitation. There appears to be some inconsistency in Twining's rigid delimitation of the different species of imitation; it seems that they "run into, and are mixed with, each other," not only in the actual practice of poets, but in the subtle distinctions drawn by the theorist of poetry.

A similar blurring of outlines may be detected in Twining's discussion of music as an imitative art. The treatise on musical imitation is largely polemical in character, an epitome of the disputes which were raging at the time. The list of authorities quoted and discussed includes the names of Plato and Aristotle, Steele, Hutcheson and Harris, Lord Kames and Dr Burney, Batteux and Rousseau. At one extreme we find the opinion of Dr Beattie who would "strike Music off the list of Imitative Arts"; at the other, the view of the ancients, especially of Aristotle, who saw music in the light of imitations and pointed out its resemblance to human manners.[117] Twining himself steers a middle course between these extremes. He begins his argument by stating that "the whole power of Music may be reduced ... to *three* distinct effects; — upon the *ear*, the *passions*, and the *imagination*: in other words, it may be considered as simply delighting the *sense*, as raising *emotions*, or, as raising *ideas*." In what follows he considers only the last two of these effects, since they constitute the *expressive* power of music — and here Twining comes to his central idea: "Music can be said to imitate, no farther than as it *expresses* something." The rest of the treatise is an elaboration of this thought. He repeats the principle laid down in the first treatise, of resemblance being essential to all imitation, and points out that, when the ancients called music imitative, they thought of its power of raising emotions. But the resemblance, mentioned in the above-quoted Aristotelian passage, cannot be *immediate*, for — as Twining rightly stresses — "between *sounds themselves*, and *mental affections*, there can be no resemblance." Hence, the critic concludes, "the resemblance can only be a resemblance of *effect*."

The gist of Twining's subsequent argument tends to break down the barriers between 'imitation' and 'expression'. He points out that, for the Greeks, poetry and music were practically inseparable — when an ancient

[117] See our earlier discussion of the problem, with references to Butcher's view and the passage in Aristotle's *Politics*, in notes 10—11. Twining sums up Aristotle's distinction between the method of painting and music in this way: the former "can imitate, immediately, only *figures* and *colours;* which are not *resemblances* (ὁμοιώματα) of manners and passions, but only *signs* and *indications* of them (σημεῖα) in the human body: whereas, in Music, the resemblance of manners "*is in the melody itself*" (p. 54). Note that Twining translates the word ἤϑη not by *(states of) character* or *habitual disposition* but by *manners*.

43

writer speaks of music, he usually means *vocal* music, that is, music and poetry united. "This helps greatly — Twining adds — to account for the application of the term *imitative*, by Aristotle, Plato, and other Greek writers, to musical *expression*, which modern writers *oppose* to musical *imitation*." He admits that dramatic music is "often strictly imitative," but the case is different with instrumental music, i.e. of "Music considered in itself, and without words", the expressions of which are "vague, general, and equivocal." There is no doubt, Twining says, that "emotions *are* raised by Music, independently of words," but, he adds, "in the vague and indeterminate assimilations of Music purely instrumental, though the effect is felt and the emotion raised, the idea of *resemblance* is far from being necessarily suggested," hence it can hardly be regarded as imitation. In an interesting footnote Twining returns to his initial statement that music is capable of raising, not only *emotions*, but, through the medium of these emotions, also *ideas*. But he calls this effect very delicate and uncertain — "so dependent on the fancy, the sensibility, the musical experience, and even the temporary disposition, of the *hearer*, that to call it *imitation*, is surely going beyond the bounds of all reasonable analogy. Music, here," — Twining concludes — "is not *imitative*, but if I may hazard the expression, merely *suggestive*."

At the end of his second dissertation, the critic sums up the results of his inquiry. He denies the thesis maintained by Aristotle and Batteux that "Painting, Poetry and Music are all *Arts of Imitation*," while admitting that "they all, in *some* sense of the word, *or other*, imitate" — but the senses of the word are very different when applied to the different arts. In Twining's view, painting, sculpture, and the arts of design in general are "the only arts that are *obviously* and *essentially* imitative"; the sense of the word, when applied to poetry, or music, is entirely different. Hence, Twining concludes, when we include *all* the arts, "without distinction, under the same general denomination of *Imitative Arts*, we seem to defeat the only useful purpose of all classing and arrangement; and, instead of producing order and method in our ideas, produce only embarrassment and confusion."

V

Twining's edition of Aristotle's *Poetics*, with the two treatises on imitation, was published in 1789. Seen from the perspective of the French Revolution, the violent climax of a long period of social, political, and intellectual change, the state of aesthetic theories must have appeared confused enough, the doctrine of imitation "tame and domestic." Representation of reality was overshadowed by a fervent desire to change the structure of reality; the dawn of a new age was enthusiastically welcomed by poets and artists, "the unacknowledged legislators of the world." Their hopes were fixed on the future. The young Wordsworth was full of Messianic expectations, hoping to see a perfect commonwealth established

> Not in Utopia, subterranean fields,
> Or some secreted island, Heaven knows where!
> But in the very world, which is the world
> Of all of us, — the place where in the end
> We find our happiness, or not at all!

To Hazlitt, "the pillars of oppression and tyranny seemed to have been overthrown"; in Blake's ecstatic vision "Empire is no more! and now the Lion and Wolf shall cease."

William Blake, in particular, the fierce Satanist and antinomian of the early Lambeth Books, praised the glories of revolutionary energy, as he "was walking among the fires of hell, delighted with the enjoyment of Genius, which to Angels look like torment and insanity."[118] Much of the old fire was still aflame in his mind when, in the opening years of the 19th century, he wrote his angry annotations to Sir Joshua Reynolds' *Discourses on Art*, edited by Edmond Malone in 1798.[119] The only point in which Blake agrees with the first President of the Royal Academy is to regard the 'imitation' or copying of old masters as the best way of acquiring an adequate technique. He calls Imitation "the meer Language of Art," "Copying Correctly ... the only School to the Language of Art" since, in Blake's view, "Mechanical Excellence is the Only Vehicle of Genius." He is hardest on the Neoclassic concepts of 'general Nature' and 'general knowledge' and takes his stand emphatically on the importance of the particular. Blake's own method and style as a painter and engraver are illustrated by such aphorisms as "All Sublimity is founded on Minute Discrimination," "Grandeur of Ideas is founded on Precision of Ideas." The principle is stated in an extreme form in the well-known sentences: "To Generalize is to be an Idiot. To Particularize is the Alone Distinction of Merit. General Knowledges are those Knowledges that Idiots possess."

Blake firmly believes in what he elsewhere calls "the Holiness of Minute Particulars," yet they are only handmaidens of Art, the essence of which to him is Inspiration and Vision. This central thesis is fully developed in Blake's most sustained critical work, the eloquent interpretation of his own picture, "A Vision of the Last Judgment," built around the contrast between the world of Imagination or Eternity, and the Temporal world of generation.[120]

In the marginalia to Reynolds there are only passing references to the reality of Vision and Revelation, which is connected in Blake's thought with the Platonic doctrine of Innate Ideas. He emphatically rejects the empirical tradition of British philosophy, Locke's view of the mind as *tabula rasa*. For Blake, "Man is Born Like a Garden ready Planted and Sown. This World is too poor to produce one Seed." "I always thought — Blake adds — that the Human Mind was the most Prolific of All Things and Inexhaustible."

For the later Blake, the poet of *Milton* and *Jerusalem*, the fundamental fact is the divinity of Man, while for his Romantic contemporaries, the chief problem was the relation of Man and Nature. Blake sought to derive art from the Intellectual Principle. "All Forms are Perfect in the Poet's Mind," he wrote in the annotations to Reynolds, "but these are not Abstracted nor Compounded from Nature, but are from Imagination." In *The Ghost of Abel*, etched in 1822 and dedicated "To Lord Byron in the Wilderness," Blake reaffirmed his belief in the transcendantal supremacy

[118] *The Marriage of Heaven and Hell*, Poetry and Prose of William Blake, ed. G. Keynes. London, 1956. p. 183.

[119] Our references are to the text of the Annotations as given by Keynes, pp. 770—812.

[120] *Ibid.*, pp. 637—652.

of the dynamic, imaginative principle. "Nature has no Outline — he wrote —, but Imagination has. Nature has no Tune, but Imagination has. Nature has no Supernatural and dissolves; Imagination is Eternity."[121]

Blake's doctrine of art assumes an increasingly religious colouring, the boundaries between religion and art disappear. To the engraver of the Laocoon Group, "Jesus and his Apostles and Disciples were all Artists," Biblical events are interpreted as symbols of changes in artistic representation: "Israel deliver'd from Egypt — writes Blake —, is Art deliver'd from Nature and Imitation."[122] In 1826, a year before his death, Blake's glosses on Wordsworth's poems praising the influence of nature on poetic imagination express a vigorous dissent. "Natural Objects always did and now do weaken, deaden and obliterate Imagination in Me" — states Blake. He sees in Wordsworth "the Natural Man rising up against the Spiritual Man Continually, and then — Blake adds — he is No Poet but a Heathen Philosopher at Enmity against all true Poetry or Inspiration." All this criticism of Wordsworth, the "Poet of Nature", as Shelley called him, is perfectly in keeping with Blake's central idea, repeated on the margin of Wordsworth's *Poems:* "One Power alone makes a Poet:Imagination, The Divine Vision."[123]

Blake's eyes are fixed on the upward path that leads to the great consummation when all Human Forms awake "in the Life of Immortality."[124] Seen from such an angle, Nature, and, together with it, the imitation or representation of Nature, are regarded as impediments and are summarily rejected. But the main current of romantic feeling and theory took a different course; poets and thinkers strove to break down the barriers between man and nature, to overcome the sharp Cartesian dualism of matter and spirit. The young Coleridge eagerly responded to

> the one Life within us and abroad,
> Which meets all motion and becomes its soul.

He developed one of the numerous romantic myths which tried to bring home to the reader the unity of all living beings.

> And what if all of animated nature
> Be but organic Harps diversely fram'd,
> That tremble into thought, as o'er them sweeps
> Plastic and vast, one intellectual breeze,
> At once the Soul of each, and God of all?[125]

The range of reality thus described was extended by Wordsworth so as to include "a presence",

> a sense sublime
> Of something far more deeply interfused
> Whose dwelling is the light of setting suns,
> And the round ocean and the living air,

[121] *Ibid.*, p. 584.
[122] *Ibid.*, pp. 580—2.
[123] *Ibid.*, p. 821.
[124] *Jerusalem IV;* in Keynes, p. 567.
[125] *The Eolian Harp*, written in 1795, quoted from Coleridge's *Poetical Works*, ed. E. H. Coleridge. OUP 1969 (1912), pp. 101—2.

And the blue sky, and in the mind of man;
A motion and a spirit, that impels
All thinking things, all objects of all thought,
And rolls through all things.

The famous passage from *Tintern Abbey* was subjected to a merciless criticism by William Empson who calls the thought "muddled," full of "philosophical ambiguities," an attempt, "rather shuffling, ... to put across as much pantheism as would not shock his readers."[126] Empson's objections may be partly right — the passage certainly cannot claim the clarity of a mathematical deduction, yet the critic has to admit that he enjoys the lines very much, obviously not only for the sound and images but for the thought and feeling expressed in them: the sense of the unity of all things, a sense reinforced by the poet's further statement that he is "pleased to recognize / In nature and the language of the sense" the anchor of his purest thoughts, the soul of all his moral being.

The unitive tendency of Wordsworth's vision is unmistakable; it is a heroic attempt to reintegrate all levels of experience, to reconcile matter and spirit, Man and Nature, the human and the divine. In between the two passages quoted comes the reference to "all that we behold / From this green earth," to

all the mighty world
Of eye, and ear — both what they half create,
And what perceive.

In a footnote Wordsworth mentions the close resemblance of the line to an "admirable line of Young's," the exact expression of which, however, he does not recollect.[127] But there is a more significant resemblance to the views of Immanuel Kant, with his emphasis on the active, constitutive function of the human mind, both in sensation and thought. In his Introduction to the *Critique of Pure Reason* (1781) Kant admits that "all our knowledge begins *with* experience," yet he denies that "it all originates *from* experience." There is also the possibility that "experience is itself made up of two elements, one received through impressions of sense, and the other supplied from itself by our faculty of knowledge on occasion of those impressions."[128] The "Copernican revolution" hinted at in these words and developed in the system of Kant's critical philosophy had a tremendous influence on all subsequent thought; A. K. Thorlby, in a recently published book, couples Kant's name with that of Rousseau as of two master minds who "established the fundamental polarity of nature and subjectivity between which the wide arc of Romantic inspiration was so often to play."[129] An examination of Kant's impact on the Romantic theory of poetry cannot be attempted

[126] *Seven Types of Ambiguity*, Meridian Books, New York, 1961 (1930), pp. 172—4.
[127] Wordsworth, *Poetical Works*, ed. T. Hutchinson; a new edition, rev. by E. de Selincourt, OUP 1969 (1904, 1936), pp. 163—5.
[128] Quoted by A. K. Rogers in *A Student's History of Philosophy*, New York, 1964³ (1901, 1907, 1932), p. 380.
[129] *The Romantic Movement*. In the series: Problems and Perspectives in History. London, 1966, p. 102.

here; for our purposes it is sufficient to note that Coleridge's doctrine of the imagination is largely based on Kantian pronouncements in the *Critique of Pure Reason*,[130] and that the important distinction between the regulative and constitutive function of ideas, a cornerstone of Coleridge's thought, is found in the *Vorrede* to Kant's *Critique of Judgment* (1790).

Intellectually, the age of Romanticism was a syncretic age; poets and thinkers borrowed freely from each other and from their predecessors. Coleridge's 'plagiarisms' from Schelling and A. W. Schlegel are notorious; his indebtedness to Platonic philosophy is even more pervasive. Chapter XII of *Biographia Literaria*, proclaiming that "all knowledge rests on the coincidence of an object with a subject"[131] is largely based on Schelling and Plotinus. — We may remark in passing that one of Goethe's *Zahme Xenien*, on the unity of object and subject, the kinship of the human percipient with the physical world and the divine principle, can also be traced back to Neo-Platonic thought.[132]

We have seen that the imitative and expressive interpretations of art were drawing closer to each other in the theories of some later 18th-century critics, especially of Thomas Twining. The Kantian view of the constitutive, nomothetic function of the mind, the doctrine of the essential unity of object and subject was to put the final seal on the union of two seemingly distinct conceptions, one of them describing art as an 'imitation' or representation of reality, the other as the expression of subjective emotions or of the creative working of the imagination. Thus in the 1802 *Preface to Lyrical Ballads* Wordsworth characterizes all good poetry both as "the spontaneous overflow of powerful feelings" and as "the image of man and nature".[133] Fifteen years later, Coleridge recalls his conversations with Wordsworth, soon after their first meeting, "on the two cardinal points of poetry, the power of exciting the sympathy of the reader by a faithful adherence to the truth of nature, and the power of giving the interest of novelty by the modifying colours of imagination."[134]

The quest for unity, especially the doctrine of the harmony of man and nature, which pervades so much of early Romantic poetry, soon came to be regarded as an illusion. The hero of *Childe Harold's Pilgrimage* could enthuse in the Wordsworthian manner amidst the scenic grandeur of Switzerland:

[130] " . . . imagination is a necessary ingredient of perception itself. . . . Since the imagination is itself a faculty of *a priori* synthesis, we assign to it the title, productive imagination . . . Experience itself . . .(is) . . only possible by means of this transcendental function of imagination." Quoted in *Romantic Criticism: 1800—1850*, ed. R. A. Foakes. London, 1968, pp. 214—5.

[131] Vol. I, p. 174 in Shawcross's edition.

[132]
> Wär' nicht das Auge sonnenhaft,
> Die Sonne könnt' es nie erblicken;
> Läg' nicht in uns des Gottes eigne Kraft,
> Wie könnt' uns Göttliches entzücken?

Goethe's *Sämtliche Werke*. Jubiläums-Ausgabe, Band 4: p. 59. Cf. Plotinus, *Ennead* I. 6, in MacKenna's translation: "To any vision must be brought an eye adapted to what is to be seen, and having some likeness to it. Never did eye secc the sun unless it had first become sunlike, and never can the Soul have vision of the First Beauty unless itself be beautiful." *Op. cit.* p. 64.

[133] *Literary Criticism of William Wordsworth*, ed. P. M. Zall. Regents Critics Series. Univ. of Nebraska Press, 1966, pp. 42, 50.

[134] *Biographia Literaria*, vol. II, chap. XIV. p. 5.

48

> I live not in myself, but I become
> Portion of that around me; and to me
> High mountains are a feeling

Rapturous emotion is, however, followed by bitter reflection:

> but the hum
> Of human cities torture.

The gulf between the two worlds has become unbridgeable:

> Our life is a false nature; 'tis not in
> The harmony of things.

The same contrast is often voiced by Shelley:

> I love snow, and all the forms
> Of the radiant frost;
> I love waves, and winds, and storms,
> Everything almost
> Which is Nature's, and may be
> Untainted by man's misery.

The high hopes raised by the French Revolution soon died down; the contrast between sanguine expectations and sober, grim reality gave rise to "romantic irony," the sense of "*Zerrissenheit.*" The world of external nature, "untainted by man's misery," seemed a last refuge — but even this hope was shattered when the view of Nature as the realm of idyllic peace, "the soul of man's moral being" was being ousted by Tennyson's vision of "Nature red in tooth and claw/With ravine," a fearful anticipation of the Darwinian world.

Poetry, like the arts in general, is subject to the historical process, to changing modes of thought and feeling expressed in a succession of styles, depending in the last instance on changes in the life of human communities. The same applies, *mutatis mutandis*, to the succession of critical theories, though with an important difference. Embedded in the historical process, they necessarily possess many features of an ephemeral, temporary interest; but as avenues to knowledge, they contain elements of objective truth, of truth to be approximated by a continual process of experience and reasoning. The real nature of art, like that of the physical universe, being inexhaustible in wealth and variety, can only be known by constant approximation; yet there are certain coordinates, set up in accordance with the nature of the subject examined, that may render the approach easier. The four coordinates defined and used by Abrams to classify critical theories seem as good as any. According to his scheme, "attempts to explain the nature and worth of a work of art" may be divided into four broad classes. "Three will explain the work of art principally by relating it to another thing: the universe, the audience or the artist. The fourth will explain the work by considering it in isolation, as an autonomous whole."[135]

It is in accordance with these four coordinates of work, universe, audience, and artist that Abrams distinguishes four main orientations in art criticism,

[135] *The Mirror and the Lamp*, pp. 6—7.

giving rise to what he calls objective, mimetic, pragmatic, and expressive theories, respectively. He admits that "any reasonably adequate theory takes some account of all four elements," yet, he adds, "almost all theories . . exhibit a discernible orientation towards one only." We have seen at the outset of our inquiry that Abrams uses the metaphors of the mirror and the lamp to illustrate the shift from mimetic to expressive theories during the period under review.

One cannot resist the impression that Abrams considers the change an advance, in the same way as Wellek considers the "formalistic, organistic, symbolistic aesthetics, rooted . . . in the great tradition of German aesthetics," obviously superior to the theories of Diderot, Lessing, and Dr Johnson who, in his view, illustrate "the failure of the age to grasp the nature of art" and prepare "the conception of literature underlying the psychological and social realism of the 19th century."[136]

Abrams actually calls "the mimetic orientation . . . probably the most primitive aesthetic theory"[137] where the word 'primitive' may admit of different interpretations; the meanings given in the Concise Oxford Dictionary include not only 'early, ancient', but 'old-fashioned, rude'. We have seen that the word *mimesis*, used as an aesthetic term, had acquired widely different senses in antiquity. The range of meanings became even more extended in the usage of its modern equivalents, probably reaching its widest extension in Batteux, with his description of the four 'worlds' of Nature, the beautiful aspects of which fine art imitates.

It seems that the term 'imitation', in its most legitimate use, denotes the representational aspect of art. Mimesis, as an aesthetic term, means the representation of reality. There are, of course, different meanings attached to the word 'reality', in accordance with the intellectual background or philosophical outlook of the artist and his audience, the temper of the age, and many other factors. Abrams distinguishes the empirical and transcendental ideals as objects of imitation; we have seen that Aristotle, Lessing, Johnson consider human actions, passions, and emotions the proper sphere of art, while the interaction of the individual and society has been moving into the centre of attention since the rise of the realistic novel. If interpreted in this sense, the range of reality 'imitated' or represented in a literary, verbal masterpiece is comprehensive enough to include Dante's vision of the Divine Rose, the tormented soul of Shakespeare's Scottish thane, the vast, Homeric panorama of *War and Peace* and *Quiet flows the Don*, the oppressive phantasmagoria of Kafka's world. Far from being a 'primitive' aesthetic theory, the mimetic principle has universal validity; it asserts that the subject matter of all fine art is human experience, that art is a special way of "assimilating, or taking possession of, the world,"[138] that it turns towards 'nature' or the 'universe', a term which, in Abrams' use, includes "people and actions, ideas and feelings, material things and events, or supersensible essences."[139] With the objects of imitation characterized in such generous terms, it seems unnecessary to mark a sharp temporal caesura between the mimetic and the expressive orientations, especially as we have

[136] *Concepts of Criticism*, pp. 363—4; *A History of Modern Criticism*, I, p. 175.
[137] *Op. cit.*, p. 8.
[138] "Освоение мира" is the expressive Russian phrase.
[139] *Op. cit.*, p. 6.

50

seen that the unity of object and subject is of cardinal importance both in the practice and the theory of several outstanding early Romantics. We should also bear in mind the special case of music, an art which may equally be described in terms of imitation and of expression.

The concept of mimesis is particularly useful in delimiting the realms of science and the fine arts. Speculations on this point begin with Aristotle, with his distinction between the methods employed by the historian and the poet: "one relates what has happened, the other what may happen." It is on this ground that Aristotle calls poetry "a more philosophical and a higher thing than history: for poetry tends to express the universal, history the particular."[140] The distinction is echoed, in some form or other, throughout the history of criticism; in the 18th century it was transformed into an antinomy of the methods of poetry and science. Preference was accorded unequivocally to the poet by Wordsworth in an eloquent passage of the 1802 *Preface to Lyrical Ballads*; his praise is closely bound up with the cognitive function of poetry. For Wordsworth, "Poetry is the breath and finer spirit of all knowledge; it is the impassioned expression which is in the countenance of all Science." The statement must be read in the light of another statement quoted above, about poetry being "the image of man and nature". In Wordsworth's eyes, as in Aristotle's, the mimetic and cognitive aspects of poetry and art are inseparable.[141]

We cannot enter here into a discussion of Shelley's aesthetic views, whose *Defence of Poetry* (1821) was, as is well known, a serious, passionate reply to Thomas Love Peacock's witty, mocking article on *The Four Ages of Poetry*, published in the previous year. The gist of Peacock's argument is that "barbaric manners and supernatural interventions are essential to poetry" which, having passed through the ages of iron, gold, and silver, has now reached the age of brass and is rapidly moving towards extinction. "A poet in our times — wrote Peacock — is a semi-barbarian in a civilized community." He contrasts "the highest inspirations of poetry . . .: the rant of unregulated passion, the whining of exaggerated feeling, and the cant of factitious sentiment" with those qualities that make a philosopher, a statesman or "in any class of life a useful or rational man" and pronounces this sentence on poetry: "as the sciences of morals and of mind advance towards perfection, as they become more enlarged and comprehensive in their views, as reason gains in ascendancy in them over imagination and feeling, poetry can no longer accompany them in their progress, but drops into the background, and leaves them to advance alone."[142]

We cannot hope to do justice here to Shelley's magnificent riposte to "reasoners and mechanists." He glorifies imagination as "the great instrument of moral good," but what concerns us here is his linking of the mimetic and cognitive aspects of art, a conviction the poet shares with Aristotle and Wordsworth. "A poem is the very image of life expressed in its eternal truth" — writes Shelley. For him, "poetry is at once the centre and circumference of knowledge" — a thought closely paralleled in Wordsworth's

---

[140] *Poetics* 9. 2—3. 1451 b 4—7. See note 14.

[141] See note 133 and *Literary Criticism of W. Wordsworth*, ed. by P. M. Zall, pp. 50, 52.

[142] Quoted from *Peacock's Four Ages of Poetry, Shelley's Defence of Poetry, Browning's Essay on Shelley*. Ed. H. F. B. Brett-Smith. The Percy Reprints, no. 3. Oxford, 1921.

panegyric: "Poetry is the first and last of all knowledge — it is as immortal as the heart of man."

A century and a half has elapsed since the debate of Peacock and Shelley, a period of almost incredible triumphs for science — yet poetry shows no signs of moving towards extinction or losing its hold on the minds of people. Peacock's diagnosis has proved false, and the relation of art and science has been subjected to renewed scrutiny. We conclude this survey with an examination of some of the views expressed by two eminent critics who start from very different ideological premises yet show a wide area of agreement in essentials.

One of them is an American, John Crowe Ransom, who devoted a study to the mimetic principle in a collection of essays first published in 1938.[143] Ransom points out that "the doctrine of mimesis was the foundation of the Greek aesthetic" and adds: "it is probably the best foundation for any aesthetic." The contrast between the methods of science and art is stated in simple terms. In Ransom's view, "there are two ways of transcribing nature ... One is by graphs or formulas that record the universal relations ... in nature." These instruments of cognition constitute all that we include under science. "The other transcript — he says — is the one which makes imitations or full representations of nature, and these are the works of art." Mimesis, understood in this sense, "aims at a kind of cognition which is unknown to pure science ... It wants to recover its individuals, abandoned in science, in business, and in affairs."

Ransom is usually classed among the "Southern critics" and there is, no doubt, a deep-seated suspicion of industrialization and scientific advance implicit in the contrast formulated by him. He sees "the dualism between science and art" continually widening "by reason of the aggressions of science" and pins his hopes for the future on art. "As science more and more completely reduces the world to its types and forms — he says —, art, replying, must invest it again with body."

The contrast formulated in a rather extreme way in *The World's Body* was developed more fully and convincingly three years later in a book which added a new term to the critical vocabulary.[144] Ransom discusses the views and tendencies represented by four 'new critics', viz. I. A. Richards, William Empson, T. S. Eliot, and Yvor Winters. In the course of the discussion he touches incidentally on some of his favourite ideas[145] but the crucial argument is reserved for the last chapter. Ransom's central contention here is that "the differentia of poetry as discourse is an ontological one. It treats an order of existence, a grade of objectivity, which cannot be treated in scientific discourse." The latter offers "reduced, emasculated, and docile versions" of the actual world, while "poetry intends to recover the denser and more refractory original world which we know loosely through our perceptions and memories."[146]

[143] *The World's Body*, Louisiana State Univ. Press, Baton Rouge, 1968 (1938), pp. 193—211.
[144] John Crowe Ransom, *The New Criticism*. New Directions, Norfolk, Conn. 1941.
[145] Thus e. g. he maintains that the actual world is unlike its scientific transcripts; science pictures a "docile and virtuous world" while poetry, which pays due attention to the "concrete and insubordinate" material components, provides a more "realistic" kind of cognition. See pp. 42—43.
[146] *Ibid.*, p. 281.

Ransom seeks to support his theory by referring to the views of Charles W. Morris, the semanticist, whom he calls "the nearest approach of a philosopher, or aesthetician, with an ontological account of poetry." The chief difference between the scientific and aesthetic ways of knowledge is that the signs employed in scientific discourse are mere signs or "symbols," which have no other character but that of referring to their semantical objects. Aesthetic signs, on the other hand, are "icons" or images: as signs they refer to semantical objects, but as iconic signs they also resemble or imitate these objects.[147] In Ransom's view, "the iconic character of aesthetic signs . . . amounts to a late restoration of the old commonsense doctrine of art as 'imitation', to which Plato and Aristotle adhered."

While in scientific discourse the reference of a single symbol is uniform and limited, in aesthetic discourse symbols are replaced by icons, and "the peculiarity of an icon is that it refers to the whole or concrete object and cannot be limited." Ransom's example of an icon is our image of Prince Hamlet, which is a particular, and never twice the same. "A particular has too many properties, and too many values" — he explains.

"The world of art is the actual world which does not bear restriction" — concludes the critic. The world of actual objects is marked by a "qualitative density, or value-density," unknown to the scientific understanding. "The discourse which tries systematically to record this world is art."[148]

Ransom stresses repeatedly the cognitive aspect of art; for him, "aesthetic discourse is objective knowledge." His earlier hostility to science seems to have died down; he now thinks that "the scientific and aesthetic ways of knowledge should illuminate each other; perhaps they are alternative knowledges — he adds in a more liberal mood —, and a preference for one knowledge over the other might indicate an elemental or primary bias in temperament."[149]

Another outstanding contemporary critic who has found a firm basis for his aesthetic theory in the concept of mimesis is the Hungarian György Lukács. We have mentioned, in our discussion of Lessing, Lukács's thesis that art represents life in its totality, together with his distinction between the methods followed by science and art.[150] The ideas briefly outlined in an article written a quarter of a century ago have been developed in full in the two volumes of Lukács's great work on aesthetics.[151] True to the fundamental principles of Marxist philosophy, Lukács regards fine art as a special kind of the reflection of objective reality, different in kind from the way in which reality is reflected or mirrored in the sciences. "The scientific mirroring of

---

[147] *Ibid.*, pp. 283—5. Cf. Lessing's distinction between arbitrary and natural signs and the discussion in Plato's *Cratylus* where the question is raised whether names are significant "by nature," having some intrinsic appropriateness to the thing signified, or only significant "by convention," i.e. by arbitrary imposition. On this point see A. E. Taylor, *Plato: The Man and his Work*. London, 1963[7] (1926), pp. 77—84.

[148] *Op. cit.*, pp. 290—3.

[149] *Ibid.*, p. 294. We may add here that A. K. Thorlby notes the recent trend in American academic thought "to concentrate interest on what might be called the epistemological aspects of literature, literature as a form of knowledge." *Op. cit.* p. 27.

[150] See p. 28 and note 65.

[151] *Die Eigenart des Aesthetischen, Werke*, Band 11—12. Luchterhand Verlag, 1963. A Hungarian version, *Az esztétikum sajátossága*, in two vols, was published by Akadémiai Kiadó, Budapest, in 1965. Our references are to the latter version.

reality — writes Lukács — wants to get rid of all sensuous and intellectual determination, wants to represent objects and their relations as they exist in themselves, independent of consciousness. The aesthetic mirroring, on the other hand, starts from, and is directed towards, the human world."[152] It is not fanciful to see here a fundamental kinship with the views shared by critics like Aristotle, Lessing, and Johnson who stress the anthropocentric direction of all great art; nor is it surprising that Lukács employs the traditional term *mimesis* to denote the special kind of mirroring or reflection that characterizes the fine arts. The first three chapters of his book examine the reflection of reality in everyday life and in the sciences, together with the process by which art becomes separated from everyday life; Chapter 4 is devoted to a discussion of the abstract forms of the aesthetic reflection of reality, while the subsequent six chapters, within the compass of 470 pages, discuss "Problems of mimesis," ranging from the origin of aesthetic mirroring to the characteristics of the relation between subject and object in aesthetics.

Lukács's great work, a modern vindication of the mimetic principle, cannot be analyzed here; but there is one point in the Introduction which reveals the originality of his conception and method, compared with that of his idealistic predecessors. He protests against all views that would regard the aesthetic realm as something "eternal" or "non-temporal." Objective reality, mirrored in a variety of ways — he points out — is not only subject to constant change: the change shows very different directions, lines of progress. Hence, Lukács concludes, reality itself, considered objectively, is historical in character. We have seen that Lukács stresses the objective nature of scientific cognition; science is 'disanthropomorphic' in its reflection of reality, "it represents objects and their relations as they exist in themselves, independent of consciousness." The case is quite different with the aesthetic reflection of reality: "there has never been an important work of art that did not bring to life, by specific artistic means, the historical *hic et nunc* existing at the time represented. Content and form of artistic masterpieces — Lukács continues — cannot be separated from the soil from which they sprang." It is precisely in works of art that the historical character of objective reality is manifested, through the union of subjective and objective elements.[153]

The mimetic principle, the view of art as an imitation of life, a representation of nature, or the mirroring of reality is a magisterial line in the history of aesthetic thought, from Plato and Aristotle to Ransom and Lukács. During the space of nearly twenty-four centuries the concepts thus joined together have often been examined, variously interpreted, the validity of the principle itself questioned, its range of reference limited by considering other aspects of art. The clash of conflicting opinions was especially sharp during the latter half of the eighteenth century. It is a historical merit of the critics of the time that they subjected the concept of mimesis, the theory of aesthetic imitation to a close scrutiny, gave it a more precise formulation, and prepared the way for the synthesis achieved first in Romantic criticism and, on a higher plane, in Marxist aesthetics.

[152] *Az esztétikum sajátossága*, I, p. 21.
[153] *Ibid.*, pp. 19—22.

VOLTAIRE. LES PROBLÈMES DE LA POÉTIQUE ET DE L'HISTORIOGRAPHIE

par

LÁSZLÓ FERENCZI

I

« Dieu seul est grand, mes frères » — c'est ainsi que Masillon commença l'oraison funèbre de Louis XIV, nommé grand déjà lors de son vivant. La mort du roi (1715) amèna au jour les passions et les haines cachées, «les provinces, au désespoir de leur ruine et de leur anéantissement, respirèrent et tressaillirent de joie», dit Saint-Simon, homme de confiance du Régent, l'un des représentants éminents de la contre-révolution aristocratique. Saint-Simon avait la nostalgie de l'heureuse époque précédant la centralisation. Il est le dernier grand représentant de la littérature autobiographique, apologétique, semi-clandestine, d'esprit d'opposition qui naquit après la Fronde, c'est-à-dire après le triomphe de l'absolutisme, en même temps que son opposé, le classicisme. Les écrivains de cette tendance pouvaient relater en prose des événements personnellement vécus. Il s'agit de Madame de Sévigné et de La Rochefoucauld, de Retz et de Saint-Évremond.[1] Pour des raisons idéologiques on peut, également, leur rapprocher Fénelon. L'auteur de *Télémaque* déploya une vive activité politique — semi-légale — durant les deux dernières décennies du règne de Louis XIV. Il détesta les ministres d'origine roturière, blâma le gallicanisme, condamna la politique extérieure et surtout l'acceptation de le succession espagnole. Il attaqua aussi le commerce et tout ce que le mot «luxe» contenait.[2]

Après la révolution de 1688, la fortune de Louis XIV changea: l'Angleterre de Guillaume d'Orange, puis celle de la reine Anne, en raison de la consolidation du pouvoir économique à l'époque de la restauration des Stuart, arrêta l'expansion française, fit échouer la politique extérieure, ce qui provoqua et justifia l'absolutisme. Si après le Traité de Westphalie, puis particulièrement après les Traités des Pyrénées, il semblait que la lutte menée durant un siècle et demi entre la France et les puissances Habsbourg pour l'hégémonie européenne se décida en faveur de la première, tout changea en 1715. Le rôle de juge-arbitre joué par l'Angleterre, surtout après la mort de Joseph Ier, devint un fait indiscutable. L'Ambassadeur anglais qui arriva à Paris en 1714 fut surpris par le vif intérêt que l'on portait à son pays. Les alliés traditionnels de la France, la Suède et la Turquie étaient en déclin tandis que la Russie tendait à devenir, à une vitesse vertigineuse, une grande puissance si bien que les grands écrivains français du XVIIIe siècle prêtaient une attention particulière au miracle russe, non seulement Montesquieu, Voltaire ou Diderot, mais également le duc de Saint-Simon. L'électeur de Brandenbourg devint roi en Prusse, et

---

[1] Cf. F. Combès, *Madame de Sévigné Historien*, Paris 1885, pp. 2—4.
[2] Cf. Roland Mousnier, *Les idées politiques de Fénelon. La plume, la faucille et le marteau*, Paris 1970, pp. 77—92.

Louis XIV ne reconnut le nouveau roi qu'après une longue résistance. Le souverain français comprit que la rivalité des Bourbons et des Habsbourg devenait un anachronisme.

Le duc d'Orléans devint le Régent d'une France encore puissante, mais sans suprématie dans une Europe complètement changée. Son premier acte fut d'annuler le testament de Louis XIV — avec le concours du parlement jusqu'alors condamné au silence — puis il libéra les jansénistes emprisonnés et rappela les libertins. Dans sa politique extérieure, le Régent s'allia à l'Angleterre, pour des causes dynastiques, contre le roi d'Espagne, Philippe V, arrière-petit-fils de Louis XIV, prétendant au trône français. Voltaire qui, en général, ne jugeait pas la politique extérieure de la France, blâma l'attitude du Régent contre Philippe V et Alberoni: «C'était en effet une guerre civile, que le jeune roi de France fit sans le savoir» (*Siècle de Louis XV*, chap. I.).

En 1715, lorsque commence l'abolition d'un régime avec une vitesse encore jamais vue, le classicisme français (qui, selon l'opinion générale doit, au moins en partie, son triomphe à Louis XIV et qui est marqué par les noms de Boileau, Racine, Molière et La Fontaine) est épuisé depuis longtemps. Le classicisme est l'un des grands «ismes» de la littérature française, qui aspire à la suprématie. Le classicisme d'exigence universelle, impersonnel, pratiquant surtout le vers, fait appel — face aux influences italiennes et espagnoles ou à la poésie française antérieure — aux classiques antiques dont il se dit unique et légitime héritier. Ce classicisme identifie Paris et la Cour à l'Europe, son idéal de valeur à la valeur elle-même. Il apporta une nouveauté fondamentale à laquelle il doit aussi son triomphe. Il a, certes, trouvé une doctrine toute achevée, mais la doctrine, fut-elle le mieux élaborée, est une chose, sa mise en application en est une autre. Le grand paradoxe du classicisme est qu'il voile sa nouveauté en se rappelant aux autorités. La plupart des drames présentés au cours des années 1670 étaient irréguliers, ce sont tout de même les classiques qui gagnèrent par leur innovation, par leur force artistique et enfin par le soutien que le roi leur apporta: les écrivains qui réussissaient ne s'étaient pas ou à peine compromis à l'époque de la Fronde ou en d'autres occasions d'opposition.

Racine, Boileau et Bossuet sont également courtisans de roi, la carrière des écrivains et celle de l'évêque dépendent de la bienveillance du roi. La poésie de Boileau, les pièces de Racine, le *Discours sur l'Histoire Universelle* et la *Politique tirée de l'Écriture Sainte* sont les apologies du pouvoir royal, du moins dans un des sens de leur explication. Les écrivains classiques et l'évêque de Méaux sont les grands 'restrictifs', ils repoussent à l'arrière-plan les différentes espèces de l'individualisme, de l'imagination, de la fantaisie et de la liberté individuelle. Les écrivains citent Aristote dans le domaine de l'esthétique lorsque selon la juste remarque de Saint-Évremond: «Descartes et Gassendi découvrent des vérités qu'Aristote ne connaissait point.»[3] Bossuet qui soutient le roi, même contre le pape, se défend contre les 'subversifs': Gassendi, Grotius, Spinoza et même contre Hobbes. Un fait qui caractérise l'époque: les *Essais* de Montaigne ne sont pas publiés entre 1669 et 1724. L'univers des classiques et de Bossuet est un univers méditer-

[3] Saint-Évremond, *De la tragédie ancienne et moderne. Critique littéraire*. Introduction et notes de M. Wilmotte, Paris 1921, p. 106. Saint-Évremond écrit également: «Corneille a trouvé des beautés pour le théâtre qui ne lui (Aristote) étaient pas connues», *ibid*.

rannéen et celui de la Contre-Réforme, tandis que Paris, siège de la nouvelle monarchie triomphante française, est le centre de l'Europe. Bossuet considère Lous XIV comme celui qui accomplit l'œuvre de Constantin le Grand, et Boileau déclare du roi:

> «. . . à l'exemple des dieux
> soutiens tout par toi-même et vois tout
> par tes yeux.»

Racine lui aussi, en dit autant.

Que nous le considérions à travers les œuvres ou à travers les générations, la grande vague du classicisme est terminée en 1715. Et, lorsque les attaques se multiplient contre le régime de Louis XIV, que cela ne soit que par l'activité du Régent, par la conception de Fénelon ou par celle de Saint-Simon, on attaque, et théoriquement et pratiquement, les bases esthétiques du classicisme. Ce sont les rimes, les vers en général, les trois unités qui sont jugés. Les genres représentatifs du troisième quart du XVIIe siècle sont le drame et la poésie. Le premier tiers du XVIIIe siècle est caractérisé par la voie triomphale du roman, autrefois dit irrégulier et méprisé par les classiques, du roman, qui, à l'époque, à part la lettre de Huet, n'avait pas de théorie.

II

C'est dans les œuvres de deux écrivains — jeunes en 1715 — que retentit avec le plus de nuances la question «comment continuer?»: ce sont Montesquieu et Voltaire qui posent cette question. Pour la postérité et surtout pour les étrangers, ils semblent être des alliés, cependant ils se portaient l'un à l'autre un intérêt plein de méfiance. Leur trait commun — pour ainsi dire à l'instant de leur prise de conscience — fut de reconnaître la transformation de la situation de l'Europe et de constater sans équivoque que la situation privilégiée de la France avait cessé, que le parallélisme de l'expansion et de l'isolation qui caractérisait la politique de Louis XIV, aussi bien que la philosophie et la conception historique de Bossuet ou l'esthétique de Boileau étaient insoutenables, que l'orientation étrangère et l'échange culturel étaient absolument nécessaires. Ils sont tous les deux ennemis de l'anarchie, mais ils trouvent que le meilleur remède à l'anarchie réside dans la tolérance religieuse. Ils nient l'exigence de l'unité religieuse de Bossuet. Selon Montesquieu et Voltaire l'anarchie est évitable par plusieurs autres moyens, mais toujours basés sur la tolérance. Montesquieu et Voltaire énumèrent les variantes de gouvernement de valeur plus ou moins égale. Ils nient la religion unique aussi bien que le monopole de l'unique forme de gouvernement, celui de l'unique politique et de l'unique philosophie, de l'unique goût et de l'unique esthétique. L'un pose la question de la légitimité d'une théorie constitutionnelle qui se restreint à un État unique, l'autre nie l'historiographie ne concernant qu'un seul État. Ils sont les instaurateurs de la théorie politique et de l'historiographie comparatistes et universelles et les précurseurs de la littérature comparée.[4] Cela, ils le font

---

[4] C'est surtout Étiemble qui accentue le rôle de Montesquieu et de Voltaire: *La poésie au XVIIIe siècle*, in *Histoire des littératures* 3, sous la direction de Raymond Queneau, Paris 1958, p. 819, et *Comparaison n'est pas raison*, Paris 1963, p. 83.

tous les deux de manière différente, face au providentialisme, aux «causes finales» de Bossuet, et les paroles de Trygne R. Tholfsen sont valables pour tous deux: «The historians of the Enlightenment moved beyond more narrative and took first steps in the direction of a systematic understanding of history as a process embracing the whole of human activity, in all its diversity and mutability.»[5] Mais tandis que Montesquieu «a pour but de rendre l'histoire intelligible» et «veut passer du donné incohérent à un ordre intelligible», comme le dit Raymond Aron,[6] Voltaire donne, justement, et cela au contraire de Montesquieu, un rôle décisif au hasard. Pourtant, c'est finalement un contraste politico-social plus profond qui cause leur différence. Au début du XVIIIᵉ siècle, les controverses sur les origines de la monarchie française s'accentuent. Selon Montesquieu c'est le renforcement du pouvoir royal qui cause la perte de la liberté française: «la mort de Charles VII fut le dernier jour de la liberté française».[7] Par contre, Voltaire attend la liberté justement par le renforcement du pouvoir royal, il est parfois royaliste malgré le roi,[8] et il n'aurait pas accepté l'affirmation de Saint-Simon selon laquelle Louis XIV croyait seulement diriger.(Mais il ne faut pas oublier que Voltaire, royaliste et disciple de Newton, n'accepte pas la théorie du droit divin.[9]) Louis XIV avait défendu Boileau, Racine et Molière contre leurs adversaires de grand pouvoir, il ne resta pendant et après le régime du Régent que la Bastille et les bâtons pour Voltaire, bien qu'il soit déjà un écrivain célèbre au temps de l'affaire Rohan. La liberté saluée par Saint-Simon signifie pour Voltaire le manque de liberté.

Althusser cite Vaughan: «. . . tous les théoriciens politiques des XVIIᵉ et XVIIIᵉ siècles sont *à l'exception de Vico et de Montesquieu*, des théoriciens du *contrat social*.»[10] Voltaire n'est pas non plus partisan du contrat social et si nous n'y prêtions pas une attention particulière, nombreuses parties de *Candide* nous resteraient incompréhensibles. Lorsque par exemple Candide dit au Baron dans le Quinzième Chapitre: «Maître Pangloss m'a toujours dit que les hommes sont égaux, et assurément je l'épouserai» (Cunigonde), il s'appuie sur les théories de Leibniz et de Wolff. Montesquieu est l'adversaire du contrat social parce qu'il est aristocrate. Voltaire, bien qu'il haïsse les privilèges féodaux, n'a jamais été démocrate. Dans *Candide* il raille à la fois l'orgueil des feudataires allemands et le contrat social.

Les opinions de Montesquieu et de Voltaire diffèrent aussi dans leur jugement sur le commerce. Et c'est là encore une question fondamentalement politique et sociale. Tous les deux insistent sur l'importance du commerce pour l'État moderne, tous les deux s'occupent du rapport, d'une part,

[5] Trygne R. Tholfsen, *Historical thinking*, New York—Evanston—London 1967, p. 93.

[6] Raymond Aron, *Montesquieu. Les étapes de la pensée sociologique*, Paris 1967, p. 28.

[7] Montesquieu, *Œuvres Complètes* I. Texte présenté et annoté par Roger Callois, Paris 1949, p. 1099.

[8] «When Voltaire came to Paris after Madame du Châtelet's death, Louis XV was embroiled with the clergy in a major struggle for power; here was a fine opportunity to express his political opinions to a large public. But it seemed that Voltaire would have to be a royalist without, and perhaps even despite, his king . . .», Peter Gay, *Voltaire. The Party of Humanity*, New York 1964, p. 30.

[9] «The chief theoretical attack on the Divine Right and on the Religion came from the Scientific Revolution of the seventeenth century.» J. L. White, *The Origins of Modern Europe*, London 1964, p. 25.

[10] Louis Althusser, *Montesquieu. La Politique et l'Histoire*, Paris 1959, p. 15.

entre le commerce et la liberté bourgeoise et d'autre part, entre le commerce et l'art, mais ils traitent de ce rapport de manière et avec une intensité différentes. Ce qui pour Montesquieu, l'aristocrate, n'est qu'une constatation des faits, est pour Voltaire, le bourgeois, un programme politique, et aussi une justification de son attitude. «C'est l'esprit du commerce qui domine aujourd'hui» dit l'un avec indignation[11] tandis que selon l'autre la grande faute de la noblesse française est justement celle de ne pas faire de commerce. Les expériences de Voltaire en Hollande puis en Angleterre lui font conclure que l'évolution de la liberté individuelle, celle du commerce, de la science et de l'art sont toutes en fonction l'une de l'autre. L'enthousiasme de Voltaire pour le commerce se trouve particulièrement éclairé par ce que dit l'éminent historien Henri Sée: «N'est-ce pas un fait significatif que dans la bourgeoisie de la plupart des villes la première place soit occupée par les hommes de loi, avocats ou procureurs, ou encore par les gens de finance, employés de la ferme générale, ou receveurs des impositions royales? C'est seulement dans les grands ports que les négociants jouent un rôle de premier plan.»[12] Voltaire se rend compte que le grand empire anglais a été fondé du moins partiellement — contrairement à celui des espagnols et des français — par des personnes privées et par des sociétés privées et que ce sont également celles-ci qui en profitent et qui en font profiter l'État; tandis qu'en Espagne l'argent abonde des colonies, enrichit le trésor royal, alors que le pays s'appauvrit. La doctrine de Mandeville sur l'intérêt privé et sur le bien commun arrive à temps. Madame du Châtelet traduit en français la *Fable of the Bees*; le penseur anglais sépare la doctrine économique de la morale, renforce la confiance et la foi de Voltaire dans le rôle et l'importance de l'individu. La liberté du commerçant anglais et celle de Pierre le Grand prouvent les possibilités de l'individu qui triomphe du sort et de la tradition, qui surmonte les institutions et qui soumet l'État à ses propres intérêts — tout en assurant l'évolution de l'État, car le commerçant anglais et Pierre le Grand développent tous les deux la civilisation et la culture lorsqu'ils favorisent l'évolution de l'industrie, du commerce, de la communication et de la science. En Angleterre les affaires commerciales mettent fin aux conflits religieux et en Russie, Pierre le Grand brise l'opposition de l'Église: ils résolvent les problèmes qu'il est impossible de résoudre ailleurs, explique Voltaire en faisant allusion à la France.

Lous Althusser cite aussi les paroles de Voltaire: «Montesquieu n'avait aucune connaissance des principes politiques relatifs à la richesse, aux manufactures, aux finances, au commerce. Ces principes n'étant point encore découverts...»[13] Raymond Aron renforce au fond l'opinion de Voltaire: «l'économie, telle qu'il la voit, est essentiellement agriculture et commerce... L'originalité des sociétés modernes qui est liée à l'industrie, n'apparaissait pas à la philosophie politique classique, et, à cet égard Montesquieu appartient à cette tradition. En ce sens, on peut même dire qu'il est antérieur aux encyclopédistes.»[14] Voltaire, bourgeois, poète et commerçant est en ce sens proche des Encyclopédistes. On comprend ainsi que les formes de gouvernement ne l'intéressent pas: «Le meilleur gouvernement

[11] Cité par Dédieu, *Montesquieu. Sa vie, son œuvre*, Paris 1942, p. 101.
[12] Henri Sée, *La France économique et sociale au XVIIIe siècle*, Paris 1925, p. 4.
[13] Althusser, *op. cit.*, p. 57.
[14] Aron, *op. cit.*, p. 45.

n'est ny le républicain ny le monarchique mais celuy qui est le mieux administré».[15] Montesquieu et Voltaire sont les défenseurs de la liberté de l'individu. Mais ils désirent l'assurer de manière différente; Montesquieu sur une base judiciaire politique, tandis que Voltaire — sous l'influence de Petty ou indépendamment de lui — sur une base économique.

Montesquieu et Voltaire découvrent chacun Montaigne, et chacun a étudié les grands philosophes anglais des XVIIe—XVIIIe siècles. La constitution et la philosophie anglaises mènent Montesquieu au système de *l'Esprit des Lois*. Par contre, Voltaire apprend des Anglais le respect des faits, l'empirisme renforce son opposition au système.

Il y a encore une différence fondamentale entre eux, qui détermine aussi les différences mentionnées ci-dessus. Voltaire est artiste,[16] Montesquieu est savant. Voltaire est poète qui proclame la priorité de la poésie, mais qui, tout en déclarant que si le vers est une vieille chose par rapport à la prose, n'en conclut pas que la poésie représente le passé comme beaucoup de ses contemporains le firent. La langue maternelle de Voltaire est le vers, il déclare: «Écrit en prose qui veut, mais en vers qui peut.»

Montesquieu ne nie pas non plus l'importance de la littérature dans la vie privée ni dans celle de l'État, mais Voltaire l'aggrandit de façon presque provocante. Sa situation personnelle dépend de la situation sociale de la poésie. Sa déclaration: «Sommes-nous tous princes ou tous poètes?», faite avant l'affaire de Rohan, exprime à la fois sa confiance en soi et ses exigences sociales.

Malherbe, ce triste courtisan déçu et solitaire, cruel diagnostiqueur ne trouve la poésie importante que pour lui-même et dans son orgueil — s'il ne confronte pas l'intérêt de l'État et l'intérêt de la poésie, du moins les sépare-t-il l'un de l'autre. Racine espère tout au plus que le souvenir du poète durera autant que celui d'un général. Dans le système de valeur de Voltaire, par contre, l'importance de la poésie est unique. Un pays, un siècle et un homme sont définis en fonction de leur rapport avec la poésie. Les quatre époques que Voltaire relève de l'histoire de l'humanité sont appréciées et valorisées parce que les arts florissaient alors, et que le commerce était le plus développé. La poésie est une nouvelle religion laïque. Voltaire écrit dans l'esprit de Baudelaire à l'occasion de la mort de l'actrice française, Mademoiselle Lecouvreur que l'Église ne permit pas d'enterrer.

«Non, ces bords désormais ne seront plus profanes;
Ils contiennent ta cendre; et ce triste tombeau,
Honoré par nos chants, consacré par tes mânes,
Est pour nous un temple nouveau!»

[15] *Voltaire's Notebooks*, ed. Theodore Besterman, Genève 1952, p. 465.
[16] André Suarès écrit: «Voltaire est l'action même, il n'est pas artiste, il n'écrit pas pour faire une œuvre belle mais vaincre dans la guerre des idées ... Toutefois, un chef-d'œuvre est toujours une forme de l'art. Voltaire, qui n'est pas artiste, l'a été dans *Candide*.» *Sur Candide*, *Présences*, Paris 1926, p. 254. Je n'accepte pas la déclaration de Suarès, qui d'ailleurs exprime l'avis de la plupart des érudits et des critiques. Quant à moi, je suis absolument d'accord avec Jean Roudaut: «On a accoutumé de juger le XVIIIe siècle comme un siècle sans poésie. Qu'est-ce à dire? ... N'est-ce pas plutôt l'idée que nous nous faisons de la poésie qui se révèle insuffisante, puisqu'elle est incapable de rendre compte de ce qui s'écrivit au cours de ce siècle? Il serait bon de revenir à une notion plus large de la poésie ...» *Poètes et grammairiens au XVIIIe siècle. Anthologie*, Paris 1971, p. 9.

Le *Discours en vers sur l'homme* explique de façon indiscutable les raisons pour lesquelles Voltaire considère la poésie en tant que pouvoir: elle donne le bonheur à l'individu, elle influence notre entourage le plus proche comme le plus large, parce qu'elle crée une valeur. Et c'est alors que naît la théorie du génie au sens moderne du mot. La qualification «moderne» est importante, car, comme Bray le prouva, le XVIIᵉ siècle français, y compris Chapelain, ne nia jamais la théorie du génie.[17] Le XVIIᵉ siècle honorait sous le mot de génie l'auteur des chefs-d'œuvre, l'artiste le plus parfait, comprenait par cette notion la capacité indéfinissable qui distingue le grand artiste du moyen. Le génie est la notion immanente de l'art ou du chef-d'œuvre. La théorie du génie au sens moderne du mot commence à se développer lorsque l'effet de l'artiste génial dépasse les limites de l'art, lorsque l'artiste exige — comme Voltaire — que l'art soit le créateur des plus importantes valeurs sociales, lorsqu'il doit produire de nouvelles valeurs face aux valeurs traditionnelles, lorsque l'importance de la littérature se dépasse elle-même, lorsque la littérature cesse d'être la servante d'autres valeurs (de la religion, de la philosophie, de la raison d'État), lorsqu'elle se revendique le rôle de formation sociale. Le bon citoyen, enseigne Voltaire, n'est ni le noble, ni le prêtre, ni le soldat, mais l'artiste et le commerçant, les créateurs de valeur qui *prouvent* leur possibilité individuelle. La tâche du roi est de soutenir le commerce et l'art, c'est pour cela qu'il estime Louis XIV, bien qu'il n'ait pas été d'accord avec nombre de ses mesures, ainsi celle de la révocation de l'Édit de Nantes (Saint-Simon non plus, d'ailleurs). «Le luxe ne perd pas les grands états, il les enrichit et les polit»,[18] écrit Voltaire contre toutes les espèces de puritains dans la défense du commerce et aussi dans celle de la poésie.

Il y a une autre différence entre l'artiste et le savant. Étiemble a beau considérer — bien qu'à juste titre — Montesquieu et Voltaire comme les fondateurs du comparatisme, leur attitude est fondamentalement différente. Il n'est pas question de vouloir nier l'importance des écrits esthétiques de Montesquieu — et c'est Ehrard qui a accentué jadis l'importance de son voyage en Italie,[19] mais ceux-ci découlent logiquement de son esprit comparatif, ce sont, pour ainsi dire, les déductions théoriques de la confrontation des lois, des coutûmes, des constitutions et des religions. Pour Voltaire cependant, le comparatisme ne signifie pas la généralisation des expériences politiques, historiques, mais — avant tout — une exigence concrète, pratique. Il écrit la *Henriade*, qui ressemble et diffère des grandes épopées antérieures, il lui faut donc défendre et expliquer son œuvre. Son drame est différent de celui de Racine, il lui faut motiver cet écart. Il travaille non seulement pour le public français, mais aussi pour celui d'Angleterre et en général pour le public européen, il doit prêter attention aux différentes réactions du public. C'est à cause de ses tâches concrètes, que les commentaires théoriques, esthétiques et autres, expressément techniques, stylistiques se suivent accompagnés de remarques sociologico-littéraires. Dans son *Essai sur la poésie épique* il répète justement en conséquence des comparaisons faites que le génie crée les règles au lieu de se soumettre à elles et en

[17] Cf. Bray, *La formation de la doctrine classique en France*, Paris 1951², p. 87.
[18] *Voltaire's Notebooks*, ed. Besterman, Les Délices, Genève 1968², p. 585.
[19] Jean Ehrard, *Montesquieu critique d'art*, Paris 1965.

mentionnant quelques tragédies, il prononce l'un des principes fondamentaux — bien que discuté — de la poétique du XXe siècle: «On aura besoin en quelque sorte d'une définition pour chacune d'elles.» D'une façon empirique, en faisant avec hâte l'éloge de la littérature classique et celle de certaines autres, modernes, il arrive à la découverte du fait de la «Weltliteratur» (il n'en connaît pas la notion elle-même); la «Weltliteratur» signifie pour lui l'influence réciproque et l'égalisation. Il écrit dans les *Lettres Philosophiques*: «Les Anglais ont beaucoup profité des ouvrages de notre langue; nous devrions à notre tour emprunter d'eux, après leur avoir prêté» et, avec encore plus de généralisation dans l'*Essai sur la poésie épique*: «Si les nations de l'Europe, au lieu de se mépriser injustement les unes les autres, voulaient faire une attention moins superficielle aux ouvrages et aux manières de leurs voisins, non pas pour en rire, mais pour en profiter, peut-être de ce commerce mutuel d'observations naîtrait ce goût général qu'on cherche si inutilement.» L'œuvre importante est une valeur de littérature mondiale pour Voltaire, et son exigence à développer le goût général vient de l'intention et du projet de conserver les valeurs et non pas de les jouer les unes contre les autres. C'est la comparaison qui sert au jugement de la valeur et de goût. «Il ne suffit pas pour connaître l'épopée d'avoir lu Virgile et Homère; comme ce n'est point assez, en fait de tragédie, d'avoir lu Sophocle et Euripide.» Lorsqu'il désire transmettre la littérature anglaise au public français, il se trouve devant un problème auquel ni Boileau, ni Montesquieu n'avaient à faire face: celui de la théorie de traduction des vers et par conséquent celui de la nouvelle sorte de définition de la poésie. «... rien de pis que de traduire un poète mot pour mot ... une énergie qui fait le poète ... la pièce est une espèce de musique ...» remarque-t-il dans les *Lettres Philosophiques*.

III

Depuis Corneille, Voltaire est le premier grand écrivain français qui fut élève des jésuites. Il est disciple du Collège Louis-le-Grand qui crée l'élite, d'où sortent aussi les futurs ministres de Louis XV, amis de Voltaire et où étudiera aussi plus tard Robespierre. (Montesquieu est étudiant au Collège de Juilles de teinte janséniste.) C'est des jésuites qu'il apprend l'importance du théâtre dans l'éducation,[20] qu'il tient l'intérêt pour l'histoire[21] et le penchant vers le compromis. Les jésuites missionnaires rassemblèrent une énorme matière sur la Chine, ils font même une concession à la doctrine de Confucius pour la «provocation» de Pascal et de la Sorbonne. Le grand discours satirique d'accusation *Les Lettres Provinciales* prouvent l'intérêt, pour ainsi dire, exclusif des jésuites pour la vie moderne; c'est d'eux que Voltaire apprend sans doute les possibilités de différents modèles et projets, la souplesse d'esprit, le penchant pour l'empirisme et ce n'est pas dû au hasard, si — à son retour d'Angleterre —, il attendait — même s'il devait

---

[20] Ronald S. Ridgway, *La propagande philosophique dans les tragédies de Voltaire*, Studies on Voltaire and the eighteenth century, vol. XV, Genève 1961, p. 45.
[21] Cf. Jean Ehrard et Jacques Roger, *Deux périodiques français de 18e siècle*, in *Livre et société dans la France du XVIIIe siècle*, Paris—La Haye 1965, p. 42.

être déçu — d'être soutenu dans l'expansion des idées de Newton contre le cartésianisme.[22] Sa confiance inébranlable dans la volonté et dans le pouvoir individuel est avant tout le résultat de l'éducation jésuite. C'est sa confiance absolue en lui-même qui distingue Voltaire des grands écrivains de la seconde moitié du XVIIe siècle. Et bien qu'il lui arrive plus d'une fois de flatter avec servitude, bien qu'il nie souvent — à cause des persécutions constantes — être l'auteur de ses œuvres, il ne peut vraiment pas dire de lui-même, comme Boileau le fait: «rarement un esprit ose être ce qu'il est».

Bien que lorsqu'il commença ses études dans le Collège Louis-le-Grand, le pouvoir de la Société eut atteint son sommet, en France, l'éducation jésuite n'aurait naturellement pas été suffisante à créer cette confiance de soi, son courage, sa vocation et le rôle qu'il joua. Il faudra aussi pour Voltaire que les formes rigides qui existaient sous Louis XIV, fléchissent à l'époque de la Régence, il lui faudra l'autorité de la littérature française acquise justement au cours du grand siècle et reconnue en France comme à l'étranger, il lui faudra le public français et celui des différents pays étrangers qui entretenaient leurs écrivains, et les différents protecteurs de haut rang dont les divergences de vue lui assuraient une liberté d'action, et l'incertitude qui caractérisait l'Europe du XVIIIe siècle, et le manque de tradition des nouvelles grandes puissances du continent; et il lui faudra enfin la fortune qui lui assurait son indépendance individuelle. Après son évasion de Potsdam, il écrit franchement dans ses *Mémoires:* «la pauvreté énerve le courage».

Les jésuites le formèrent sous le signe du classicisme, avec Boileau. Ce sont les jésuites qui lui donnèrent la répugnance du roman, si bien qu'il approuve en silence son ancien professeur, le père Porée lorsqu'il commence en 1738 sa campagne contre le roman, et de plus, même après avoir écrit *Candide*, Voltaire nommera «frivole» le genre du roman, c'est, il est vrai, en discutant alors avec Jean-Jacques Rousseau. L'un des grands paradoxes de Voltaire, est de dédaigner jusqu'au bout le roman d'abord à cause du goût classique puis à cause de la philosophie, alors que selon le jugement de la postérité, c'est dans ce genre qu'il créa la valeur la plus durable. L'opinion de la postérité est juste, si elle ne conduit pas — selon la pratique générale — à négliger ses drames et ses poèmes. Cependant il faut encore faire honneur au sens des réalités de Voltaire, qui, malgré son antipathie, perçoit la nouvelle vague du XVIIIe siècle, et développe son propre genre caractéristique en utilisant les résultats de *Mille et une Nuits* traduit par Gallard, ceux de Le Sage, de Prévost, de Montesquieu et des Anglais.[23]

Les rapports de Voltaire et du XVIIe siècle sont compliqués. Il est le défenseur du règne de Louis XIV contre Montesquieu et les conceptions ou les courants les plus différents (aristocratie, parlement, encyclopédistes). Il interrompt ainsi pour un temps le *Siècle de Louis XIV* à cause de la méfiance de Fleury. En effet le cardinal pressent que l'œuvre qui traite de l'époque du Roi Soleil est un programme, un appel à continuer l'ancienne politique. C'est par cette analogie que l'on identifie à celle de Boileau — en général — la position de l'esprit de Voltaire pour la poésie. On la considère même comme son imitation rigide, étroite. Selon les paroles de Philippe van Thieghem, Voltaire «représente, sans aucun doute, la tradition, et fut le frein

[22] René Pomeau, *La religion de Voltaire*, Paris 1956, p. 234.
[23] Jacques van den Heuvel, *Voltaire dans ses contes*, Paris 1967, pp. 20—30.

le plus puissant aux tentatives de révolution littéraire».[24] Mais la tradition et le «frein» ne se présupposent pas nécessairement et nous pensons que ce n'est pas le cas pour Voltaire.

Sans nous engager dans les détails, nous pouvons dire que la politique française de l'époque moderne est caractérisée depuis François Ier par le perpétuel recommencement et le manque de traditions (guerre de religion, Henri IV, Régence, Richelieu, Mazarin et la Fronde, le gouvernement personnel de Louis XIV, la Régence).

Le perpétuel recommencement marque encore davantage la littérature: Clément Marot qui, de toute la poésie française du Moyen-Age, ne fit grâce qu'à Villon, fut lui-même rejeté par la Pléiade, celle-ci par Malherbe (ce dernier est, pour ainsi dire, l'unique écrivain de la littérature universelle qui n'inventa pas d'ancêtres pour lui). Théophile de Viau se tourne contre Malherbe, et l'enseignement de la fin du XIXe siècle, selon lequel un chemin droit mène de Malherbe à Boileau est réfuté depuis longtemps. Seuls les étrangers mettent un trait d'union entre les noms de Corneille et de Racine. Saint-Évremond précise l'abîme qui se trouve entre les poètes de *Cid* et de *Bérénice* et lui aussi, tout comme Madame de Sévigné est du parti de Corneille. Le classicisme qui triomphe après 1661, s'épanouit jusqu'au tournant du siècle, La Motte, Fénelon et les autres attaquent ses principes les plus importants, et le roman commence aussi sa voie triomphale. Il est vrai que Malherbe, Corneille, Chapelain, Boileau, Molière et Racine sont tous les poètes de la France unie, il est donc possible de tracer une sorte de tradition au XVIIe siècle, mais les écrivains de la contre-révolution aristocratique (par exemple Saint-Simon et Fénelon) discutent justement cette unité qui prend corps en la personne du roi. Lorsque Voltaire commence sa carrière, le point d'interrogation est posé aussi bien au sujet de la France unie de Louis XIV qu'au sujet de la littérature du grand siècle.

Voltaire est le premier grand écrivain et philosophe qui insiste sur la continuité de la culture française (même s'il ne remonte que rarement avant l'époque de Malherbe), il est le seul qui ne s'efforce pas de recommencer, mais de continuer, d'innover, d'élargir dans le cours du processus de continuité. Boileau pensait seulement au public de Paris, Voltaire à celui de toute l'Europe, Boileau identifiait la littérature à quelques écrivains du XVIIe siècle et à leurs ancêtres «fabriqués», aux classiques antiques, Voltaire réfléchissait dans une conception de Weltliteratur. Boileau se tourne vers les antiques contre les Espagnols, les Italiens, les écrivains du XVIe siècle et à quelques exceptions près, contre ceux de la France du XVIIe siècle. Voltaire ramène les Italiens et les Espagnols (que Madame de Sévigné et La Fontaine avaient toujours gardés et découvre aussi les Anglais sur lesquels Saint-Évremond attira le premier l'attention) sans renier l'antiquité, ni le XVIIe siècle de Boileau. Voltaire est le premier grand représentant de l'unité de la tradition et de la nouveauté de la littérature française. Il est traditionnaliste, mais pas conservateur, c'est un innovateur, mais il ne brûle pas les ponts derrière lui. Ses rapports avec Shakespeare et avec Pascal en sont les meilleures preuves. Dès 1718, il voit de toute évidence que le drame classique français est épuisé. Il découvre Shakespeare, et il se défend par lui contre l'esthétique de Racine et de Boileau. Dans la deuxième partie de sa vie, lorsque l'in-

---

[24] *Petite histoire des grandes doctrines littéraires en France*, Paris 1950, p. 67.

fluence de Shakespeare et de toute la littérature anglaise commencèrent à menacer sa propre position et celle du drame classique, il se tourna contre l'auteur de *Hamlet* en se référant à Racine et à Boileau. Selon les documents de Besterman, les contemporains apprécièrent le discours de Voltaire à l'Académie contre Shakespeare, comme une revanche des défaites subies en mer.[25] Dans les deux cas, en découvrant Shakespeare et en protestant contre le culte naissant de Shakespeare, Voltaire lutte contre le despotisme du modèle littéraire unique. Il défend d'abord ses innovations, puis ce qu'il observe de la tradition française. Dans aucun des cas il n'est apologétique: il formule des réserves contre Shakespeare dès les premiers débuts, et même à la fin de sa vie, il ne cessera de critiquer Racine et Boileau.[26]

C'est Mario Sina qui a relevé dernièrement, sur les traces de Lanson, que la critique de Pascal faite par Voltaire est une partie de son attaque contre le XVIIe siècle. Le savant italien commente ainsi la 25ème lettre des *Lettres Philosophiques*: «Demolire Pascal significava allora per Voltaire demolire il cattolicesimo, per proclamare la validità della religione naturale.» Sina fait sentir d'une façon convaincante l'unité fondée sur les contrastes entre cette lettre et les autres qui présentent Newton, Locke et les religions d'Angleterre.[27] Un des faits intéressants de la culture et de la politique françaises du XVIIe siècle — prouvant l'impossibilité d'une catégorisation rigide, sans pouvoir nous apesantir ici sur les détails —: c'est que le Port Royal qui, une fois, soutenu par le cardinal de Retz et avec lequel depuis la Fronde le roi voulait toujours en finir, influençait la littérature de l'opposition tout comme la littérature officielle. Pascal eut son influence tout autant sur La Rochefoucauld et sur Madame de Sévigné que sur Boileau et sur Racine ou sur Bossuet. Pascal qui, comme savant, était extrêmement individualiste, et qui selon les belles paroles de Sainte-Beuve était caractérisé par les mots «trouver pour son compte»[28], cherchait dans le domaine du moral les principes absolus d'autorité. Il est impossible de savoir si c'est sa maladie, son effroi des tendances antihumanistes de la science, sa déception envers la philosophie moderne — c'est lui qui parle le premier des «romans» de Descartes — ou le renforcement du pouvoir royal qui le rapprochent du jansénisme. Voltaire retourne la critique de Pascal sur Montaigne, c'est-à-dire qu'il fait gloire à l'auteur des *Essais* d'avoir osé se peindre soi-même, d'avoir su douter. Si en se fondant sur des œuvres précoces, il était possible de noter les différences qui existaient entre Voltaire et Pascal par le contraste de l'optimisme et du pessimisme, cette suggestion est annulée par *Candide* et les autres œuvres tardives. Leurs différences fondamentales ne se relèvent pas dans la 25ème lettre des *Lettres Philosophiques*, mais dans *Candide*, dans cette encyclopédie jusqu'alors inconnue des «misères de l'Homme». Pascal qui écrit l'apologie du christianisme considère les misères comme un état naturel ou du moins les accepte-t-il comme telles, trouve la délivrance en Dieu. Voltaire croit lui aussi en Dieu, mais il rend l'histoire et le destin de l'homme indépendants de Dieu, il se «réfugie» dans le travail.

---

[25] Besterman, *Voltaire*, London and Harlow 1969, p. 130.
[26] Voir le texte de l'édition de Kehl du *Temple du Goût*, in Voltaire, *Le Temple du Goût*, Édition critique par E. Carcassonne, Paris 1938.
[27] Mario Sina, L' «*Anti-Pascal*» *di Voltaire*, Milano 1970, p. 13.
[28] *Causeries de Lundi*, Paris s. d., V. p. 523.

La base du système des valeurs chez Voltaire est le travail, ses *Notebooks* nous en donnent, entre autres, des arguments suffisants: «Posuit eum in paradizo voluptatis ut operatetur, donc l'homme est né pour le travail» (p. 311) ou «L'homme est né pour le travail, comme l'oiseau pour voler dit Job; donc le travail n'est pas un châtiment» (p. 383). Le travail donne une occupation «personnelle» et comme le travail est une valeur en soi, il crée des valeurs nouvelles. C'est là la base philosophique, morale et économique de la conception historique opposée aux actes des rois. Le travail, «la difficulté vaincue» joue déjà un rôle important dans l'esthétique de Boileau, mais Voltaire donne une validité générale à une exigence esthétique. Dans *Le monde comme il va* Babouc conseille justement sous l'effet du travail, à l'ange Iturel de ne pas démolir Persépolis. Chez Voltaire, le travail est une affaire commune et privée tandis que la religion, le rapport avec Dieu est une affaire personnelle. Mais de là aussi naît une autre différence essentielle qui existe entre Pascal, les grands écrivains de la seconde moitié du XVIIᵉ siècle et Voltaire: l'appréciation du rôle de l'individu. Selon Janet, Pascal ne supposait même pas qu'il puisse avoir une influence sur la politique, et cette remarque est d'autant plus importante qu'il n'y a pas longtemps que l'on a découvert que Pascal connaissait très bien Hobbes. Voltaire et ses héros cherchent, jusqu'à l'extrême; Candide, devenu actif à la fin de ses aventures, donne symboliquement l'exemple de l'individu qui se révolte contre ses contraintes.[29] La volonté devient à nouveau créatrice et invulnérable, mais l'héroïsme cornélien de l'honneur se transforme en héroïsme du travail et de la recherche, tandis que chez Pascal et chez les grands écrivains de la seconde moitié du XVIIᵉ siècle, la volonté est secondaire et faible. Les héros de *Bérénice* se soumettent au destin, c'est-à-dire à l'intérêt de l'État, les héros de Voltaire se révoltent contre l'asservissement. Voltaire qui, comme Hobbes et Bossuet, tient l'anarchie pour le plus grand mal et qui s'efforce de renforcer le pouvoir royal, serait incapable de vivre dans l'état «laïque» de l'un ou dans l'état «ecclésiastique» de l'autre, il cherche sur les traces de Spinoza et surtout d'après ses expériences en Angleterre et ses propres impressions individuelles, un État capable de défendre ses citoyens malgré soi-même. Mais il n'en trouve pas: «mais quelle patrie choisirait un homme sage, libre, un homme de fortune médiocre, et sans préjugés?» — demande-t-il dans le *Dictionnaire Philosophique* sous les mots *État, gouvernements*, vers 1757. Il ne donne naturellement pas de réponse à la question mais ne crée pas d'utopie et ne se réfugie pas non plus dans la religion: la dualité de l'activité et du doute le défend et l'oppose à Pascal.

Le contraste et la critique n'empêchent pas Voltaire d'apprécier Pascal: «... le premier livre de génie qu'on vit en prose fut le recueil des *Lettres Provinciales*, en 1656. Toutes les sortes d'éloquence y sont renfermées. Il n'y a pas un seul mot qui, depuis cent ans, se soit ressenti du changement qui altère souvent les langues vivantes. Il faut rapporter à cet ouvrage l'époque de la fixation du langage» — écrit-il dans le *Siècle de Louis XIV*. Ainsi dans la première édition en 1734 du *Temple du Goût* écrit presque en même temps que la 25ème des *Lettres Philosophiques*, il parle favorablement de l'artiste Pascal. Le rôle de Voltaire dans l'histoire de la

<hr />

[29] Christopher Thacker, *Introduction critique*, in Voltaire, *Candide ou l'Optimisme*, Édition critique par Christopher Thacker, Genève 1968, p. 25.

critique française est décisif. Il s'intéressa vivement aux nouveaux genres du XVIIᵉ siècle, il souligne que La Rouchefoucauld[30] et Pascal étaient parmi les plus grands créateurs de la littérature française. Par sa critique, il rehaussa justement l'importance exceptionnelle de Pascal.[31]

Voltaire n'aime pas Boileau en tant qu'individu, en tant que critique il l'accuse quelquefois de ne pas juger selon son goût, mais selon ses préjugés personnels. Il blâme sa campagne satirique contre Chapelain, la trouve indigne d'un homme de lettres et il défend Quinault et Fontenelle contre lui. De son œuvre, il admire avant tout l'*Art Poétique* (comme Montesquieu), mais trouve une partie des odes et des satires superflues et dépassées (la postérité n'est pas entièrement de cet avis depuis Sainte-Beuve). Cependant, leurs points de vue sont identiques dans les questions esthétiques essentielles. Bien que Voltaire n'accepte pas la conception de Pascal: «l'homme sans foi ne peut connaître ni le vrai bien, ni la justice», il accepte d'autant plus une des thèses fondamentales de Boileau, l'unité du vrai et du beau — déjà découverte dans l'antiquité — qui en provient. Et il approuve de toute façon la conscience, le souci minutieux et l'exigence de la raison de Boileau. Il prend aussi parti, avec ferveur, pour les trois unités; que nous pouvons considérer d'après les preuves du roman, du drame et du film du XXᵉ siècle, comme l'une des possibilités très importantes de la condensation artistique. Le *Boileau ou mon testament* est loin d'être le résumé dogmatique des règles de Boileau, c'est plutôt le portrait du maître de sa jeunesse peint avec des éléments biographiques par le vieil écrivain toujours plus solitaire en 1769 à cause des nouvelles tendances littéraires. Voltaire ne défend pas une technique, mais un principe: celui de la raison et de la conscience, du contrôle critique de moins en moins à la mode, et une attitude, fondée sur sa culture, pourtant il ne prêche en aucune manière des règles, des modèles à suivre. C'est dans ce poème qu'il résume le plus expressivement son opinion du XVIIᵉ siècle:

«Siècle de grands talents bien plus que de lumière.»

L'un de ces grands talents, de ces grands hommes est certainement Bossuet. «Son *Discours sur l'Histoire Universelle* ... n'a eu ni modèle, ni imitateurs. Si le système qu'il adopte, pour concilier la chronologie des Juifs avec celle des autres nations, a trouvé des contradicteurs chez les savants, son style n'a trouvé que des admirateurs.» (*Siècle de Louis XIV*. Chap. XXXII.) Bossuet est un écrivain et un adversaire honoré, Voltaire a des objections essentielles contre sa conception historique basée sur la Providence qui enchaîne justement l'individu. Il nie que l'histoire soit l'histoire de l'Église, il nie que le processus historique soit unique, il est lui-même partisan de l'histoire cyclique qui est à cette époque le démenti énergique de l'histoire basée sur la Révolution (bien que chez Vico, la la Providence soit un leit-motif). Il nie que l'humanité ait pour origine un seul ancêtre et il regrette que le monde de Bossuet soit étroit, qu'il ne s'étende pas aux histoires arabes, chinoises et à celles de l'Orient en général.

[30] Claude Mauriac, *La Rochefoucauld — Maximes, De la Littérature à l'alittérature*, Paris 1969, p. 83.
[31] Cf. J. S. Spink, *French Free-Thought from Gassendi to Voltaire*, London 1960, p. 312.

IV

Après 1715, la France a été obligée de reconnaître que l'hégémonie fait place à l'équilibre des puissances, l'isolation à l'orientation. Entre Érasme et Marx, Voltaire, contemporain de Montesquieu, est un écrivain qui réfléchit dans la totalité de l'Europe. Sa découverte est fondamentale: aucune histoire, celle de la France pas plus que les autres, ne peut être écrite en soi. L'idée elle-même n'est pas neuve. Hérodote que Voltaire critiqua aigrement pour ses fables, et Thucydide qu'il estime par contre beaucoup, y font déjà allusions, puis Polybe, «plus ancien que Tite-Live et plus homme d'État»[32], qui, sous l'influence d'un texte d'Aristote, est le premier théoricien de la conception cyclique de l'histoire, déclare, après les expériences de la IIe guerre punique, que l'histoire d'aucun pays ne peut être écrite, isolément de celle des autres pays. Cependant après que Rome fût devenue la seule puissance méditerranéenne, cette doctrine perdit peu à peu de son importance. Cela pour deux causes: d'une part, l'évolution autonome privilégiée de l'Empire; d'autre part le manque de la liberté dont les historiens romains se plaignirent tant. L'historiographie perdit le sens de l'histoire universelle, même si au Moyen-Age beaucoup de livres étaient écrits intitulés 'Histoire universelle'. L'historiographie s'occupa non sans exemples contraires de questions psychologiques et morales au lieu d'analyser les causes politiques, sociales ou économiques. Machiavel remet encore les problèmes politiques au premier plan, mais seul Guicciardini reconnaît que l'histoire de l'Italie ne peut être écrite sans mentionner l'histoire des conquérants du pays. Et c'est Voltaire qui, en partant de ses propres expériences concrètes et soutenu aussi par les aspirations sociologiques de Montesquieu, place l'histoire de la France dans un contexte historique universel et ne prête pas attention à l'Europe seule, mais aussi au monde extérieur à l'Europe. Comme Kosminsky le dit, c'est lui qui élimine l'idée selon laquelle l'Europe est le centre.[33] Et c'est parallèlement — sans que la priorité vaille la peine d'être cherchée, car le processus est réciproque — que Voltaire aperçoit que les valeurs d'une seule littérature sont incompréhensibles en soi et que l'une des conditions du rafraîchissement de la littérature est l'interpénétration.

Nous ne pouvons parler d'histoire littéraire au sens moderne du mot avant Voltaire, et nous ne pouvons même pas trouver un travail ainsi conçu dans l'énorme étendue de son œuvre, mais les faits de la littérature (la vie, les œuvres des écrivains, la réaction du public) sont des faits historiques, les parties importantes, très appréciables de l'histoire d'une époque. L'*Essai sur les mœurs* et le *Siècle de Louis XIV* ont des chapitres importants relatifs à la vie littéraire. Si les faits et les événements de l'art et de la littérature sont des événements appréciables et considérables de l'histoire, il s'en suit que l'évolution de l'histoire en histoire mondiale implique aussi la transformation de la littérature en littérature universelle, mais dans ce cas les causes et les conséquences sont interchangeables. Ce sont les circonstances de

---

[32] Voltaire, *Essai sur les mœurs*, Introduction, bibliographie ... par René Pomeau, Paris 1963, I, p. 188.

[33] « В своих главных трудах отказывается от обычного европоцентризма и стремится охватить историю всех народов мира. » Е. А. Косминский, *Вольтер, как историк, Вольтер, стати и материали*, под ред. В. П. Волгина, Москва-Ленинград 1948, p. 160.

l'époque qui font que Voltaire voit tout de même des limites plus larges pour l'histoire que pour la littérature, car les politiques de Charles XII, de Pierre le Grand ou de Frédéric le Grand agissent et réagissent sur la politique française tandis que les littératures suédoise, russe ou allemande n'eurent guère d'influence sur la littérature française. Mais Voltaire réagit vivement à la culture allemande, il apprécie surtout Leibniz, qu'il accueille même dans le *Temple du Goût* (peut-être sous l'influence de Fontenelle), et qu'il honore dans le *Siècle de Louis XIV* du titre de «peut-être le savant le plus universel de l'Europe», ce qui est le plus grand éloge possible chez lui. Leibniz aperçut sans doute le premier la tournure que prit la politique mondiale à la fin du XVIIe siècle, il écrivit dans un fragment latin intitulé: *État de l'Europe au début du nouveau siècle*: «finis seculi novam rerum faciem aperuit».[34]

Voltaire prête la plus grande attention à la culture contemporaine de l'Angleterre en raison de son statut toujours croissant de grande puissance et à cause de la floraison de la philosophie, des sciences et de la littérature anglaises de l'époque. Il estime non seulement les maîtres de sa jeunesse: Swift, Pope, Newton ou Locke (il gardera la fierté d'avoir lui-même popularisé les deux derniers en Europe), mais il suit aussi les «nouveaux»: il écrit alors qu'il est déjà un historien connu, que Hume écrit la meilleure œuvre historique, alors qu'un quart de siècle auparavant il avait déclaré que les Anglais n'avaient pas vraiment de bons historiens; il estime Sterne qu'il considère d'ailleurs comme un descendant de Scarron.

Brumfitt fait remarquer que lorsque Voltaire attaque la conception méditerranéenne de Bossuet, il ne peut alors condamner que les disciples de XVIIIe siècle de l'évêque de Meaux, car à l'époque où il écrivait le *Discours sur l'Histoire Universelle* il existait incomparablement beaucoup moins de sources sur la Chine, qu'à l'époque des années de la réalisation de l'*Essai sur les mœurs*.[35] Voltaire ne crée pas un système philosophique — car il se caractéries lui-même en disant de Bayle qu'il était «assez sage, assez grand pour être sans système» —, mais un système pratique empirique. Sous l'influence des faits et par la force des choses il élargit son univers. Dierjavine suggère par exemple que les affaires de Calas et de Sirvène sont en liaison avec l'attention croissante de Voltaire pour la Chine.[36] Voltaire intègre les nouvelles connaissances dans les anciennes, il rattache les faits philosophiques, physiques, historiques, littéraires et politiques les uns aux autres. Ses récits sont imposés par les nouvelles connaissances qui transforment les genres du XVIIe siècle.[37] Ses œuvres répondent à La Bruyère qui écrit: «Tout est dit, et l'on vient trop tard, depuis plus de sept mille ans qu'il y a des hommes, et qui pensent.»

La guerre de succession espagnole est le grand échec de la diplomatie française. Si elle réussit un quart de siècle plus tôt, à l'époque de la guerre

[34] Cité par Denis de Rougemont, *Vingt-huit siècles d'Europe*, Paris 1961, p. 121.
[35] J. H. Brumfitt, *Introduction*, in Voltaire, *La Philosophie de l'Histoire*, Critical ed. with an Introduction and Commentaires, *Studies on Voltaire and the eighteenth century*, vol. XXVIII, Genève 1963, p. 32.
[36] К. Н. Девжавин, *Китай в философской мысли Вольтера, Вольтер, стати и материали*, под ред. М. П. Алексеева, Ленинград 1947, p. 91.
[37] I. O. Wade, *Voltaire and Candide. A study in the fusion of the history, art and philosophy*, Princeton 1959, p. 67.

de Hollande à utiliser son allié suédois, la France ne peut arriver cette fois à conclure la paix entre la Suède et la Russie, c'est-à-dire à délivrer l'armée suédoise. La Turquie, elle reste neutre. C'est Voltaire qui fait la chronique de ce nouveau monde transformé, c'est lui qui écrit, comme le rend conscient Pomeau, l'histoire contemporaine de l'Europe.[38] La grande partie de son œuvre — sans égard aux genres — est la démonstration des variantes de la société et de la culture du XVIIIe siècle. Le public contemporain apprécia l'*Œdipe* comme le reflet des conflits entre les jansénistes et les jésuites. Besterman doute de la justesse de cette interprétation.[39] Ceci probablement à bon droit, mais après la rigidité de la religion existant au cours des dernières années de Louis XIV les spectateurs contemporains de la pièce reconnurent peut-être leurs propres pensées, cachées dans quelques passages, contraires aux points de vue de l'Église. Malgré cela, il serait faux de déduire l'anticléricalisme militant des années 1750—1770 de Voltaire à partir du texte du drame présenté en 1718. La tradition d'injurier les prêtres dans la littérature française remonte au Moyen-Age. Dans *Œdipe*, l'attaque de l'Église est juste ce que le fidèle élève des jésuites peut se permettre rien que pour le plaisir de suivre le ton de la société. La valeur de cette œuvre ne réside pas dans la critique, mais dans la présentation d'une atmosphère, d'un sentiment de la vie, que laisse deviner l'un des premiers vers: «Et la mort dévorante habite parmi nous.» Depuis la fin de la guerre de succession espagnole il n'y a guère qu'une demi-dizaine d'années ...

Dans l'*Henriade* Voltaire exprime sa fidélité envers les Bourbons lorsqu'on attaque le pouvoir royal du point de vue judiciaire et politique. L'épopée est la justification du pouvoir royal contre l'anarchie de la noblesse qui provoque l'affaiblissement de la civilisation et la décadence de la culture. L'auteur se prononce pour une France sans partis et prend des distances avec Genève aussi bien qu'avec Rome. Dans l'*Henriade* Voltaire s'enthousiasme pour l'Angleterre et cela concorde avec la conception de la politique extérieure du Régent. Les *Lettres Philosophiques* sont un recueil de reportages sociologiques sur la vie religieuse, politique, commerciale et artistique de l'Angleterre. D'ailleurs en Angleterre tout n'avait pas plu à Voltaire. Selon ses *Notebooks* parus récemment, la liberté de presse, qui lui était justement si importante, était bien imparfaite. Mais ces œuvres destinées ouvertement ou semi-ouvertement au grand public gardaient bien ce secret ...

La première étude historique, la chronique intitulée *Histoire de Charles XII* raconte les victoires et l'échec du récent souverain sudéois signalant déjà la sensibilité de Voltaire pour les rapports de la politique européenne. Quelques lignes de l'*Histoire de Charles XII* font comprendre pourquoi, un quart de siècle plus tard, les aventures de Candide se termineront en Turquie: «... la rapacité et la tyrannie du grand-seigneur ne s'étendent presque jamais que sur les officiers de l'empire, qui, quels qu'ils soient, sont esclaves domestiques du sultan; mais le reste des musulmans vit dans une sécurité profonde, sans crainte ni pour leurs vies, ni pour leurs fortunes, ni pour leur liberté» (Livre cinquième). C'est pour cela que le «bon vieillard» put répondre à Pangloss sans risque de se tromper: «... jamais je ne m'in-

---

[38] René Pomeau, *Politique de Voltaire*, Paris 1963, p. 21.
[39] Besterman, *op. cit.*, pp. 75—76.

forme de ce qu'on fait à Constantinople; je me contente d'y envoyer vendre les fruits du jardin que je cultive» (Chapitre trentième).

Des alternances de ce genre sont très caractéristiques: chacun des nouveaux genres correspond à la découverte d'un nouvel aspect de la réalité contemporaine[40]. Le *Temple du Goût*, essai sociologique et esthétique, critique et pamphlet, écrit en vers et en prose — qui provoqua en son temps une vive opposition en raison de ses critiques sur Boileau et sur Racine — est déjà l'esquisse du *Siècle de Louis XIV*, tout comme l'*Henriade*. Carcassonne qui fit l'édition critique de cette œuvre en 1938, dit que le passage dans lequel Voltaire «veut rehausser la valeur sociale de l'intelligence . . . est un chapitre des *Lettres Anglaises* égaré dans le *Temple du Goût*».[41] Bien que Voltaire considère toujours le rapport entre la société et l'art dans son contexte, c'est justement par là qu'il dépasse les commentaires et les remarques purement techniques. En lisant les *Commentaires sur Corneille* nous nous intéressons moins au fait que tel mot de Corneille est désapprouvé par Voltaire ou non, mais plutôt à la manière dont l'auteur lie la domination du drame espagnol au temps du Cid à la prépondérance politique de l'Espagne. D'ailleurs il explique l'intérêt toujours croissant du continent pour la langue et littérature anglaises par le pouvoir indiscutable que l'Angleterre a sur la mer. Le *Temple du Goût* est également intéressant par son point de vue d'histoire de l'esthétique, ceci à cause de l'accent mis sur *les rapports entre les arts*.

Le *Siècle de Louis XIV* est un énorme tableau, qui commence par l'exposition rapide de la situation européenne. L'œuvre qui traite des questions politiques, sociales, économiques, familiales, religieuses, morales et esthétiques est à la fois une œuvre de la *science pure* et de la *propagande*.

Le catalogue qu'il y joint de la plupart des écrivains français, se termine en caractérisant nettement le point de vue de Voltaire pour les arts: «Il sera difficile désormais qu'il s'élève des génies nouveaux, à moins que d'autres mœurs, une autre sorte de gouvernement ne donnent un tour nouveau aux esprits.»

En 1737 Voltaire pensait encore (comme Bayle et Bolingbroke) que l'histoire ancienne n'était intéressante qu'en tant que curiosité, que l'histoire vraiment importante et vraiment instructive était l'histoire moderne, qui commença à la fin du XVᵉ siècle. Son opinion changea assez vite, l'*Essai sur les mœurs* est sa première grande expérience pour comprendre le présent par le passé. Cet essai fut suivi par la *Philosophie de l'Histoire*, qui traite des époques plus anciennes encore, qui rivalise déjà ouvertement avec Bossuet. Sa dernière grande œuvre historique, les *Fragments historiques sur l'Inde* traitent de la colonisation et du «partage du monde». Entretemps parurent *Candide* que Wade nomme «fictional *Essai sur les mœurs*» et le *Dictionnaire Philosophique*. Ce dernier est à la fois poème en prose, récit, dialogue, histoire et philosophie.

---

[40] «In the *Histoire de Charles XII* (1731) the idea implicit in the *Henriade* that one man can account for a great part of a nation's success or failure is presented explicitly and forcefully.» M. L. Perkins, *Voltaire on the source of national power*, *Studies on Voltaire and the eighteenth century*, vol. XX, Genève 1961, p. 149.

[41] Carcassone, *op. cit.*, p. 14.

Lorsque Voltaire, qui avait déjà fait de sérieuses recherches pour la *Henriade*, écrivit l'*Histoire de Charles XII*, il était déjà considéré comme l'écrivain le plus célèbre de la France. Il n'est donc pas surprenant qu'il s'occupe de l'histoire, il ne fait que poursuivre une grande tradition, qui avait commencé avec Dante et Petrarque. Le classicisme et sa propre expérience artistique influencent son historiographie. Mais l'effet est double: son historiographie, elle aussi, influence ses récits et ses pièces.

Avant d'aller en Angleterre, il devait bien se rendre compte de l'épuisement du drame classique français. Qu'il en fut conscient ou non, son rapide et spectaculaire succès était dû au manque de rivaux contemporains importants. Malgré l'*intermezzo puritain* Voltaire trouve en Angleterre une vie théâtrale florissante et un drame d'effet choquant, très différant du théâtre français. Il y trouve ce dont Houdar de la Motte reprochait l'absence en France: l'action. Voltaire discute à *Bérénice* «le nom de Tragédie, pour lui substituer celui de l'Élégie en Dialogue» (*Temple du Goût*, texte de Rouen). Il critique Shakespeare, mais «la plupart des idées bizarres et gigantesques de cet auteur ont acquis au bout de deux cents ans le droit de passer pour sublîmes» (*Lettres Philosophiques*, Dix-huitième lettre).

Il est enthousiasmé par la force, la productivité et l'élan de Shakespeare et, même par son irrégularité, surtout parce qu'il a du succès. Boileau n'a-t-il pas écrit:

«N'offrez rien au lecteur que ce qui peut lui plaire.»

Le succès retentissant de Shakespeare bien que les meilleurs écrivains anglais le considèrent avec quelques critiques aurait dû donner à réfléchir à Voltaire, justement à cause du conseil ci-dessus, et d'autant plus qu'il voulait gagner aussi le public anglais, d'une part par ambition naturelle d'auteur, d'autre part pour renforcer sa position contre Paris, mais aussi à Paris. Voltaire, épigone prétendu du drame de Racine, fit des innovations fondamentales dans la technique du théâtre et du drame. Il est vrai que Nisard les prit soigneusement en compte[42], Émile Deschanel les répéta de nouveau[43], mais Nisard n'avait pas de crédit car il ne comprenait pas ses contemporains romantiques, Deschanel non plus, parce qu'il infléchissait trop les innovations vers le drame romantique justement lorsque celui-ci était en train de s'épuiser. Ainsi la critique de Lessing exerce-t-elle presque sans obstacle son influence jusqu'à nos jours, alors que ses arguments soient quelquefois directement amusants, lorsqu'il prouve par exemple la médiocrité de Voltaire par l'applaudissement de son public jusqu'à son apparition sur la scène.

On peut résumer ainsi les innovations dramaturgiques de Voltaire: il apporte plus d'actions dans le drame et l'accélère (il le fait pencher vers l'histoire, il en accentue l'événement, l'acte et le fait au lieu d'accentuer la psychologie), il réduit les harangues (il les omet dans ses œuvres historiques malgré la tradition antique et humaniste). Il chasse l'aristocratie de la scène. Aurait-il osé de mettre ce fait en parallèle avec le rôle historique fortement modéré qu'il destine à l'aristocratie? Il travaille sur une scène aggran-

---

[42] Paul Nisard, *Histoire de la Littérature Française*, Paris 1863³, Vol. IV., Chap. V.
[43] Émile Deschanel, *Le théâtre de Voltaire*, Paris 1888, p. 414.

die, l'importance des décors augmente: n'est-ce pas là un symbole de l'élargissement de son monde par rapport à celui de Racine?

La scène de Voltaire change aussi thématiquement. Il puise, certes, chez les antiques, mais, malgré la mise en garde de Racine, il choisit aussi des thèmes français. Il adapte également des histoires chinoises et américaines. Il dépasse le domaine méditerranéen non seulement en tant qu'historien, mais aussi en tant qu'auteur de drames et de récits. C'est l'historiographie qui *sanctifie* pour le poète les thèmes exotiques, *non canoniques*.

Enfin il transforme progressivement le théâtre en une chaire politique. Ce n'est pas que le drame classique n'ait été politique, Jasinski voit la justification des différents actes de Louis XIV dans les pièces de Racine.[44] Les tragédies de celui-ci sont des apologies au moins d'un certain point de vue, tandis que celles de Voltaire sont des défis. Racine approuve, Voltaire attaque. Selon Pomeau, Voltaire écrit à la fois *Sémiramis* et la parodie de *Sémiramis*. C'est une excellente remarque, un flagrant délit de Voltaire lorsqu'il franchit les limites des genres et des points de vue, mais je ne puis être d'accord avec la conclusion de Pomeau, selon laquelle cette pièce est une œuvre mal réussie justement à cause de ce caractère.[45]

Voltaire exécute ses innovations fondamentales dans les cadres «officiels» du drame classique, il garde les trois unités et la rime. Cela ne fait qu'accroître la tension de ses meilleurs drames: la dialectique tradition—nouveauté, conservation—transformation-de-la-forme aiguisent le conflit. C'est l'*Oreste* qui prouve le mieux la force dramatique de Voltaire. Le thème est antique, la forme est racinienne, mais la motivation est toute neuve. La solution mythique classique (ne prêtons point attention ici aux grandes différences qui règnent entre Éschyle, Sophocle et Euripide) se change en une solution historico-politique. La victoire d'Oreste est expliquée ou motivée selon la théorie des sciences politiques des XVIIe et XVIIIe siècles et selon les expériences des grands événements historiques.

Voltaire veut également faire valoir les principes esthétiques classiques dans l'historiographie. C'est en 1740 qu'il écrit à Argental: «Il faut dans une histoire, comme dans une pièce de théâtre, exposition, nœud, et dénouement.» En étudiant l'*Histoire de la Russie*, il écrit à Souvalov: «J'ai toujours pensé que l'histoire demande le même art que la tragédie, une exposition, un nœud, un dénouement, et qu'il est nécessaire de présenter tellement toutes les figures du tableau, qu'elles fassent voir le principal personnage, sans affecter jamais l'envie de le faire valoir.»

Mais l'exigence de la structure dramatique ne se réalise complètement que dans l'*Histoire de Charles XII*, elle ne se fit valoir ni dans le *Siècle de Louis XIV*, ni dans l'*Essai sur les mœurs*, ni dans la *Philosophie de l'Histoire* — et ni dans *Candide*. L'énumération des causes probables peut se rapprocher de la compréhension de la conception historique et esthétique de Voltaire.

Dans les drames et dans la chronique *(Histoire de Charles XII)* c'est le le destin du *principal personnage*, qui détermine l'œuvre. Tous les autres personnages lui sont subordonnés, donc l'histoire porte en soi la structure de l'œuvre, l'ordre des épisodes, l'accélération ou le ralentissement de l'action. Le nombre des personnages secondaires est limité, bien que, par la

[44] Jasinski, *Vers le vrai Racine*, Paris 1954, II., p. 558.
[45] R. Pomeau, *Voltaire par lui-même*, Paris 1955, p. 60.

nature du sujet, il y ait beaucoup plus de rôles dans l'*Histoire de Charles XII* que dans *Œdipe* ou dans *Sémiramis*. Par contre, le *Siècle de Louis XIV* n'est plus la chronique d'un roi: «Ce n'est pas seulement la vie de Louis XIV qu'on prétend écrire; on se propose un plus grand objet. On veut essayer de rendre à la postérité, non les actions d'un seul homme, mais l'esprit des hommes dans le siècle le plus éclairé qui fut jamais» (Chapitre Premier). L'exigence de l'exposition—nœud—dénouement d'Aristote est assuré par les actes d'une seule personne, ceux du *principal personnage* dans le drame et la chronique. Et bien que Voltaire n'ait jamais renoncé au culte des grands hommes, à partir du *Siècle de Lous XIV* ce sont les mœurs, les institutions, les coutumes, les problèmes politiques, culturels et sociaux qui l'intéressaient davantage que les actes de la personnalité, fut-elle la plus éminente. Voltaire qui déclare plusieurs fois — assez sincèrement — que les actes des rois l'ennuient déjà, écrit en 1740: «On n'a fait que l'histoire des rois, mais on n'a point fait celle de la nation. Il me semble que pendant quatorze cents ans, il n'y ait eu dans les Gaules que des rois, des ministres et des généraux, mais nos mœurs, nos lois, nos coutumes, notre esprit ne sont-ils donc rien?» Il résume très expressivement son opinion dans le *Dictionnaire Philosophique*: «On exige des historiens modernes plus de détails, des faits plus constatés, des dates précisés, des autorités, plus d'attention aux usages, aux lois, aux mœurs, au commerce, à la finance, à l'agriculture, à la population.» Entre parenthèse, il faut cependant noter: la scission dans l'historiographie française entre les érudits et les humanistes durait jusqu'à la Restauration.[46]

Le sujet de l'historiographie n'est donc plus seulement l'acte d'un seul homme. Les nouveaux types de faits historiques et les relations compliquées entre les hommes, les institutions, les coutumes et les lois *forcent les cadres de la structure dramatique et rendent impossible la réalisation de l'idéal* que nous venons de citer.

Pour terminer, il est encore une cause qui a contrarié la mise en pratique de la technique des pièces de théâtre dans l'historiographie. Les tragédies de Racine et celles de Voltaire, et l'*Histoire de Charles XII* racontent des histoires achevées. L'écrivain en connaît la fin, il n'a qu'à motiver sa matière pour atteindre les effets artistiques et dramatiques nécessaires. Les grands tableaux historiques de Voltaire sont essentiellement inachevés Le *Siècle de Louis XIV*, par exemple, ne se termine pas à la mort du roi d'une part, parce qu'une partie des problèmes surgis alors n'ont pas encore été résolus, d'autre part, parce que l'écrivain lui-même aimerait qu'il continue, qu'il ne soit pas une période close de l'histoire de la France, mais qu'il serve de mesure à Louis XV. L'inachèvement est encore plus sensible dans *Candide*, œuvre de fiction.

V

Grimm a écrit: «Il ne faut pas juger cette production avec sévérité: elle ne soutiendrait pas une critique sérieuse. Il n'y a dans *Candide* ni ordonnance, ni plan, ni sagesse, ni de ces coups de pinceaux heureux, qu'on rencontre dans

---

[46] Voir Louis Halphen, *Introduction à l'Histoire*, Paris 1946, pp. 73—76.

quelques romans anglais de même genre; vous y trouverez en revanche beaucoup de choses de mauvais goût, d'autres de mauvais ton, des polissonneries et des ordures qui n'ont point de voile de gaze qui les rende supportables; cependant la gaieté, la facilité, qui n'abandonnent jamais Voltaire . . . rendent la lecture de *Candide* fort amusante.»[47]

Candide a vraiment étonné Grimm, habitué à l'esthétique aristotélienne. La série d'aventures est apparemment arbitraire, on peut la continuer même après la conclusion de «cultiver notre jardin».[48] Et l'apparition de *Candide* au début du roman est, elle aussi, incertaine ou fortuite. Il n'y a pas de véritable exposition et de véritable dénouement à l'exemple d'Aristote. Et cependant, depuis Flaubert, nous pensons que *Candide* est le chef-d'œuvre de Voltaire.

C'est l'*Histoire éthiopique* d'Héliodore qui est le récit protohistorique des amoureux qui se poursuivent à travers le monde. Ce livre était très populaire aux XVIIᵉ et XVIIIᵉ siècles et il connut beaucoup d'imitations. Voltaire transmet la variante moderne du roman grec à l'époque de la guerre de Sept Ans, en Europe et en Amérique de Sud. L'histoire elle-même est très simple: Candide cherche Cunigonde. L'action est extrêmement rapide, elle se déroule en deux ans, le lieu est varié, mais unifié, et ces qualités rappellent de loin le drame classique français. On peut sentir tout au cours de *Candide* que c'est un maître absolu du théâtre qui l'écrivit, quelqu'un qui donna de l'importance non seulement à la parole, mais à la mise en scène, aux décors et jusqu'aux gestes des acteurs. Nous y distinguons trois sortes de dialogues, l'auteur en signale le lieu et le décor pour chacun des cas. Pour le premier dialogue, seul le *fait* de la conversation est important, non pas le texte lui-même, l'auteur (le metteur en scène) indique seulement que ses héros (les acteurs) parlent de quelque chose. C'est là, le *dialogue muet*. Dans le second cas, l'écrivain (le narrateur) raconte ce dont les héros (les acteurs) discutent, c'est le *dialogue cité*. Dans le troisième cas, l'écrivain communique mot à mot la conversation elle-même, c'est le *dialogue*. Ce dernier a lieu lorsqu'un changement effectif arrive au héros, lorsque, par exemple, Candide devient soldat.

Le monde de Candide est plus restreint que fut celui de Scarmentado dix ans plus tôt. Dans ce dernier, le héros qui s'exprime à la première personne du singulier s'en va jusqu'en Perse, en Chine et en Turquie. Il résume ainsi ses pénibles aventures: «J'avais vu tout ce qu'il y a de beau, de bon, et d'admirable sur la terre: je résolus de ne plus voir que mes pénates. Je me mariai chez moi: je fus cocu; et je vis que c'était l'état le plus doux de la vie.» Ce récit écrit en 1747 s'oppose aux hypothèses qui attribuent la fin de l'optimisme de Voltaire au tremblement de terre de Lisbonne en 1756. Selon le témoignage de *Dichtung und Wahrheit* c'est dans la vie de Goethe que ce tremblement de terre eut une importance décisive. Tout de même nous ne

[47] Cité par J.-G. Prod'Homme, *Vingt chefs-d'œuvre (du Cid à Madame Bovary) jugés par leurs contemporains*, Préface d'Albert Thibaudet, Paris 1930, p. 105.

[48] Gilbert Highet écrit: «The story of Candide has no pattern—except the elementary pattern of constant change and violent contrast, which can scarcely be called a pattern at all. Indeed, it would be perfectly easy for us, if a new manuscrit of the book were discovered containing half a dozen fresh chapters on the adventures of Candide in Africa or in China, to accept them as genuine.» *The Anatomy of Satire*, Princeton 1962, p. 10. Au début de mes recherches j'ai cru la même chose. Mais les éléments historicosociologiques de *Candide* ont fait changer ma conception.

voulons pas nier que le tremblement de terre de Lisbonne — la première catastrophe naturelle connue tout de suite par le grand public — n'ait influencé Voltaire. Ceci lui signale que la nature pouvait aussi bien intervenir dans la vie de l'homme que la politique, la religion, la guerre, l'évolution scientifique ou autre. Il augmente le nombre des faits à considérer et fournit des matériaux à son œuvre.

Le moment de la création de *Candide* est un moment exceptionnel. C'est une époque de transition entre le monde fermé de la féodalité et celui du capitalisme, une transition entre le spectaculaire représentatif (le Versailles de Louis XIV) et la maison bourgeoise. En simplifiant vraiment le problème: si nous demandions de quoi dépend la sûreté des hommes, Racine répondrait: de Louis XIV, Balzac: du succès des affaires, Diderot et surtout Beaumarchais interviendrait peut-être: elle dépend de la protection (de la défense) de la famille. Voltaire ne donne aucune réponse aussi définitive et aussi simple. Sa vie est une suite perpétuelle de perte de sûreté, il est, par conséquent, contraint à découvrir des choses toujours nouvelles. A l'époque de Racine et à celle aussi de Balzac, c'est la politique intérieure qui s'avère la plus importante; au cours de la vie de Voltaire c'est la politique extérieure qui prime.[49] (Le sort de Voltaire lui-même dépend de la politique internationale.) Le XVIIe siècle est l'époque de six grandes révolutions en Europe bien qu'elle ne manque pas de guerres. Au XVIIIe siècle il n'y a pas de révolution en Europe jusqu'en 1789, mais ce siècle est l'époque des guerres mondiales qui s'étendent sur trois, quelquefois sur quatre continents.

Le monde du roman *Candide* est un monde plus ou moins uni. Cette unité est créée par les différentes institutions internationales ou des types de personnes supranationales. La papauté est une institution du Moyen-Age, la Compagnie des jésuites est une institution moderne, elles sont toutes les deux supranationales. Des jésuites allemands, polonais et italiens fonctionnent au Paraguay et si les jésuites ibériques y sont moins aimés à cause des guerres contre l'Espagne, les jésuites sont d'abord les représentants d'un ordre supérieur aux nations et seulement après, les membres d'un État. (C'est d'ailleurs l'une des causes pour lesquelles le gallicanisme *lutta toujours contre la Société*.) Ce sont les commerçants parcourant le monde qui représentent le nouveau type de l'internationalisme.

Le troisième signe de l'internationalisme, typique du XVIIIe siècle, se trouve dans le fait que le Candide allemand discute en compagnie de Martin, hollandais, avec le grand seigneur italien Procurante, à propos de la littérature anglaise. Il n'est pas important de ce point de vue que Procurante exprime plus ou moins les aversions qu'avait alors Voltaire contre la littérature anglaise. C'est le sujet de la conversation qui est essentiel si nous tenons compte du statut social des partenaires. Ce genre de conversation n'aurait eu lieu autrefois qu'en latin et entre savants humanistes sur des sujets classiques ou bibliques.

Le quatrième signe de l'internationalisme est traditionnel mais prend un ton nouveau à l'époque moderne: c'est la présence partout des juifs, qui, selon Voltaire, jouent un rôle important dans l'économie monétaire internationale.

---

[49] Merle L. Perkins dit: «For Voltaire, foreign policy as much as domestic planning builds or weakens the nation.» *Voltaire's concept of international order, Studies on Voltaire and the eighteenth century*, vol. XXXVI, Genève 1965, p. 18.

Ce sont ces forces de soutien qui rendent authentiques les aventures de Candide et qui unifient les différents pays et les différentes contrées. Sous la forme du roman il généralise ce qu'il dit de l'unité du monde chrétien en tant qu'historien. Voilà pourquoi nous comprenons que Voltaire ne mène pas ses héros en Chine ou au Japon, bien qu'il y ait dans l'œuvre une allusion à ce dernier. Ses héros n'ont rien à faire dans une autre civilisation, dans une autre structure de pouvoir. En ce temps (1758) la Chine ou le Japon ne seraient qu'une sorte d'utopie. Cette circonstance est caractéristique à l'époque où *Candide* fut écrit. Car même s'il y a une allusion à la colonisation (après l'épisode de l'Eldorado), l'Asie ne faisait point encore partie — du moins le semblait-il — de la sphère d'intérêt des pouvoirs colonisateurs européens. Cela changea quelques années plus tard, le Traité de Paris donna les mains libres aux Anglais en l'Inde et je crois savoir que Voltaire fut l'un des premiers à employer le terme de «partage du monde» au sens moderne.

Voltaire respecte obstinément les faits. C'est toujours le dernier événement, celui du moment même, qu'il fixe et qu'il tente d'insérer dans le système toujours souple de ses connaissances, avec une réceptivité qui le rend capable de percevoir le tout-nouveau. Voltaire n'a qu'un seul système, si on peut appeler système la conception, selon laquelle au XVIIIe siècle il faut réfléchir à la base de la politique universelle, et c'est ce système qu'il nourrit des faits concrets sous l'influence de l'empirisme anglais. Nous savons qu'il n'y a, pour ainsi dire, point d'épisode dans *Candide*, dont Voltaire n'ait déjà fait allusion ailleurs, en tant qu'historien, publiciste ou correspondant. La Vieille parle de «cet honnête Eunuque», qui «avait été envoyé chez le Roi de Maroc par une Puissance Chrétienne», pour conclure «avec ce Monarque un traité...». Dans le *Siècle de Louis XIV* et aussi dans l'*Essai sur les mœurs* Voltaire parle de cette négociation. Dans le roman, Voltaire mentionne cet événement du point de vue du sort d'un homme privé (celui de la Vieille). Dans les œuvres historiques il le met dans le contexte de la rivalité des grandes puissances.[50]

A cause de la densité héritée du drame classique et à cause du tempo du roman nous ne nous rendons souvent pas compte que Voltaire condense la confrontation des mondes en quelques mots, alors que nous croyons seulement découvrir une nouvelle chiquenaude donnée à Leibniz. Candide, refugié d'Allemagne en Hollande, «demande l'aumône à plusieurs graves personnages qui lui répondirent tous que, s'il continuait à faire ce métier, on l'enfermerait dans une maison de correction pour lui apprendre à vivre». Voltaire confronte en une seule phrase l'éthique catholique et *die protestantische Ethik*.[51] Il est naturel que Candide, originaire de Westphalie, demande l'aumône et également naturel qu'il soit menacé. A partir du début du XVIIIe siècle «l'on abandonne définitivement la conception de la charité chrétienne: on considère la pauvreté comme une tare, comme 'le produit de la paresse et du vice'; c'est alors également que l'on applique 'de nouveaux remèdes contre la misère' en réprimant sans pitié la mendicité et le vagabondage. C'est l'époque où paraissent le *Giving als no charity*, de Defoe (1704), et la *Political arithmetic* de Petty», comme écrit Henri Sée en citant

[50] J'ai emprunté l'exemple à l'édition critique de C. Thacker, *op. cit.*, pp. 271—272.
[51] L'expression doit, naturellement, à Max Weber.

les paroles de Tawney.[52] On refuse l'aumône à Candide en Hollande, et pourtant Candide lui-même la donne à Venise malgré le conseil du Martin. Le destin de Paquette et de Giroflé justifie plus tard que cette action fut nuisible. Il est possible que — vu dans le contexte de l'œuvre entière — la scène ait une intention pédagogique dans le sens du 'Giving als no charity'. La mendicité est un vice, nous affirme même Voltaire en écrivant sur Mélon.

En revenant au monde du roman *Candide*, il est étrange que Voltaire ne mène pas le jeune homme allemand en Russie. Il ne le fit pas parce que la Russie était alliée à la France à l'époque de la Guerre de Sept Ans ou parce qu'il respectait vraiment très sincèrement les réformes de Pierre le Grand. Mais il ne conduit pas non plus son héros dans les pays scandinaves protestants, ni même en Angleterre. C'est à cause d'un événement politico-militaire que Candide renonce à mettre pied en terre anglaise, et ainsi Candide (et Voltaire) ne critique pas la *société* anglaise. Il est vrai que Procurante dit à Venise: «Je serais content de la liberté qui inspire les génies anglais, si la passion et l'esprit de parti ne corrompaient pas tout ce que cette précieuse liberté a d'estimable.» Mais c'est là aussi une question plus politique que sociale. D'ailleurs les luttes des partis anglais préoccupaient et gênaient toujours les Français, Montesquieu en attendait même l'écroulement de l'Angleterre, durant un certain temps.[53] En ce qui concerne la Hollande, lorsque Candide commence à travailler, il se trouve bien. Il n'a pas besoin de s'en réfugier. C'est le tremblement de terre qui — durant un *voyage d'affaires* — met fin à ses relations hollandaises. Mais, il est vrai aussi, qu'un commerçant hollandais trompe Candide qui se trouve vengé par un bateau espagnol. (L'Espagne est l'alliée de la France à cette période.) Dans *Candide*, Voltaire se moque des adversaires politiques de la France, et des siens dans le domaine personnel, social et artistique. Je voudrais relever que Candide ne confronte pas l'Eldorado à l'Europe entière, et surtout pas à la Hollande ou à l'Angleterre, mais avant tout à la Westphalie et secondairement à l'Église catholique. Ce n'est pas seulement en Eldorado qu'il n'y a pas de prêtres, mais essentiellement en Prusse, comme nous pouvons le lire dans ses *Mémoires* de même date.

Comment faut-il expliquer l'Eldorado? Est-ce une utopie ou le modèle d'un pays à réaliser ou la parodie de l'un et de l'autre? Voltaire écrit dans ses *Notebooks:* «On se moque de la république de Platon, mais celle de Sparte existait, et plus sévère; celle de Crète aussi.» (p. 359) Aujourd'hui, c'est un lieu commun de l'histoire de la philosophie de dire que Platon emprunta à Sparte certaines idées. Voltaire a peur de cet Eldorado, même si, comme le démontre Bottiglia, il y a certaines ressemblances entre l'Eldorado et le dernier jardin de Candide.[54] Il en a peur, et pour le moins, ce pays ne lui plaît pas. Il n'y a pas de théâtre dans Eldorado, les arts n'y florissent pas. Il n'y a pas de place pour l'initiative individuelle, et il semble qu'il n'y ait pas là-bas de propriété privée. Et pourtant Voltaire haïssait les ennemis de la propriété privée.

[52] Henri Sée, *Dans quelle mesure puritains et juifs ont-ils contribué au progrès du capitalisme? Science et philosophie de l'histoire*, Paris 1928, p. 310.

[53] Schwarcz Gyula, *Montesquieu elmélete* (Théorie de Montesquieu), Budapest 1889, p. 34.

[54] Bottiglia, *The Eldorado episode in Candide, Publications of the Modern Language Association of America*, Menashe, Wisconsin, 73, 1958, pp. 341—342.

L'Eldorado qui n'est pas moins absurde, ni moins réel que n'importe quelle autre scène du roman, est un tournant dans la vie du principal personnage. C'est là qu'il arrive à avoir de l'argent et à partir de là, son comportement change. Jusqu'alors il est serviteur et à partir de ce temps il devient seigneur et même s'il continue à être à la merci des aventures, il a au moins un but, et l'argent lui donne, de toute façon, le pouvoir et la sécurité. (Le niveau et le caractère de sa dégradation changent.)

Le monde dans lequel se meuvent les héros de *Candide* est un monde de hasards et de catastrophes. La guerre et la faim sont considérées depuis longtemps comme des désastres naturels dans la littérature, Voltaire en ajoute un autre: la «banqueroute». L'échec du système de Law peut être qualifiée de première crise économique au sens moderne du mot. C'est en confrontant la nouveauté du monde de *Candide* au *Télémaque* qu'elle se révèle le mieux. Télémaque est également à la merci du destin, mais à la fin la Providence récompense la vertu. Dans *Candide* il n'y a pas de Providence, ni décompensation. Il n'y a pas non plus de vertu absolue, objective ni d'idéal subjectif de vertu, créé par l'individu. Ce sera un des dons du romantisme. La souffrance du fils d'Ulysse est souvent un châtiment parce qu'il n'écoute pas son Mentor. Candide a deux mentors, dans les personnes de Pangloss et de Martin. Mais ces mentors ne le préservent pas. Ils expliquent, ils argumentent et le temps passe ainsi. Ils donnent quelque consolation, car le fait de parler apaise, les héros du roman connaissent le plaisir de la parole pour la parole. Voltaire est un excellent psychologue, mais nous nous en apercevons rarement, parce que le tempo des nœuds est infiniment rapide. C'est-à-dire que Voltaire consacre une demie-phrase, une allusion à ce que d'autres auteurs traiteront durant des pages. (C'est pour cette raison que l'on nie d'ailleurs souvent que *Candide* soit un roman.) D'autre part les héros de *Candide* — en général — ne s'analysent pas. La Vieille, par exemple, ne raconte pas sa vie pour justifier l'unité prétendue ou véritable de sa personnalité, mais pour divertir ses compagnons de voyage. Pourtant l'auto-analyse est souvent identifiée à la psychologie.

Martin et Pangloss sont le reflet, l'un de l'autre. Ils ne s'étonnent de rien et acceptent tout, l'un sur la base de l'harmonie préétablie, l'autre à cause de la nature humaine. Même malgré le titre précis du roman: *Candide ou l'optimisme*, il semble que c'est jouer avec les mots que de parler d'optimisme ou de pessimisme. Martin affirme à Candide: «Votre pendu se moquait du monde». Et dans le dernier chapitre Pangloss avouait «qu'il avait toujours horriblement souffert; mais ayant soutenu une fois que tout allait à merveille, il le soutenait toujours, et n'en croyait rien».

La source originelle de Pangloss est Leibniz, «the great compromiser of the age».[55] Pangloss «qui était aussi curieux que raisonneur» (Chap. Trentième), identifie la raison à la réalité. Il explique la cause de tout et ne demande la justesse de rien. Il accepte et approuve le 'status quo' au nom de l'harmonie préétablie. Il est le philosophe de l'immobilité. Le «meilleur des mondes possibles» ne signifie pas que le monde soit bon, mais qu'il ne peut pas être meilleur. Pangloss et Martin n'emploient que des termes différents: l'un emploie le bon, l'autre le mal. Ils discutent sur les mots, et

[55] Peter Gay, *The Enlightenment, An Interpretation. The Rise of Modern Paganisme*, London 1967, p. 203.

non sur les choses. Tous les deux sont possédés d'une idée fixe, et ils ne veulent pas, n'osent pas ou ne peuvent pas y changer quelque chose. C'est la Vieille et Cacambo qui sont différents. Ces derniers — et Candide avec eux — mettent par leur simple activité un point d'interrogation aux faits mêmes. L'œuvre n'est pas une confrontation de l'optimisme et du pessimisme, mais celle de l'immobilité et de la mobilité. Peter Gay écrit: «Voltaire transforms Candide, sprung from the genre of picaresque tales, into a Bildungsroman, the story of an education» et y ajoute «(Candide) it was part of Voltaire's own evolution into an aggressive social reformer».[56] *Candide* est doublement un Bildungsroman. D'abord en tant que genre, ensuite parce qu'il exprime des expériences et des méditations de Voltaire. Il fait prendre conscience de la situation donnée, démontre une conclusion possible et ne l'accepte pas. Son comportement psychologique est analogue à celui de Goethe. Werther se suicide, Goethe continue à vivre. Candide ferme (ou essaie de fermer) la porte de son jardin, et Voltaire de Délices, élargit son domaine.

Candide contient beaucoup de phrases sur les guerres et sur les combats. Cependant, d'une part de la description des institutions, des coutumes et des mœurs, d'autre part la matière accumulée de ses connaissances, prouvent que Voltaire n'identifie pas l'histoire à celle des guerres des dynasties. Nous apprenons par l'édition critique de Christopher Thacker que Voltaire concentra dans son roman des connaissances énormes qui égalent celles de Thomas Mann. On ne peut percevoir une importante partie de ces connaissances qu'à l'aide de notes, tellement elles s'insèrent dans le texte de base. Le roman picaresque est une encyclopédie. Voltaire écrit dans l'introduction de l'*Essai sur les mœurs :* «Je voudrais découvrir quelle était alors la société des hommes, comment on vivait dans l'intérieur des familles, quels arts étaient cultivés . . .» Dans Candide il s'agit:

a) de la production — celle de la veille de la révolution industrielle, et naturellement du caractère agricole;
b) du commerce, de l'économie;
c) de l'armée;
d) de la religion, de l'Église;
e) de la politique internationale;
f) des questions intérieures et dynastiques;
g) de l'art et de la science comme faits sociaux et comme faits individuels.

Il n'est pas question de la famille bourgeoise, dont la découverte et la mode commençait en ce temps-là. Voltaire traite des problèmes de la science et de l'art aussi bien dans *Candide* que dans le *Siècle de Louis XIV*. La science et la littérature peuvent être des éléments importants, organiquement insérés dans la structure des œuvres romanesques et des œuvres historiques.

*

«Ordures . . .» — dit Grimm. Voltaire, historien de Louis XV, exécute l'un des plus importants tournants de la littérature moderne. On connaît la distinction d'Aristote: la comédie «veut représenter les hommes inférieurs»,

---

[56] *ibid.*, pp. 199—200.

la tragédie « veut les représenter supérieurs aux hommes de la réalité ».[57] « La comédie est l'imitation d'hommes de qualité morale inférieur . . . »,[58] « la tragédie est l'imitation d'une action de caractère élevé et complet ».[59] Cette distinction fait déjà place à une autre — mais bien prudemment — dans les *Lettres philosophiques*. « Œdipe, Électre appartient aux Espagnols, aux Anglais, et à nous comme aux Grecs. Mais la bonne comédie est la peinture parlante des ridicules d'une nation, et si vous ne connaissez pas la nation à fond, vous ne pouvez guère juger de la peinture. » (Dix-neuvième lettre)

Pourtant même Vauvenarges, en établissant une comparaison entre Racine et Molière, donne en raison de « la supériorité du genre sublime » la priorité à l'auteur de la tragédie, « bien que l'un et l'autre aient parfaitement connu le cœur de l'homme ». Il reproche même à Molière ses « sujets trop bas ». La distinction d'Aristote dure jusqu'au moment où le grand homme ou le caractère noble ne peut sortir que d'une seule classe sociale, et jusqu'au moment où la littérature est le porte-parole de la réalité hiérarchisée par un point de vue éthique. Le travail, par exemple, passe presque pour ignoble depuis Platon. Voltaire emploie plus d'une fois les notions du bien et du mal, et même en 1778, il écrit : « Pour l'histoire, ce n'est après tout, qu'une gazette ; la plus vraie est remplie de faussetés et elle ne peut avoir de mérite, que celui du style. » Tout de même, Voltaire est aux temps modernes l'un des premiers de ceux qui donnent une plus grande importance à la découverte de la réalité (qu'il considère un principe éthique fondamental) qu'à l'attachement aux normes éthiques actuelles et esthétiques. Le roman fait entrer dans la littérature toute une lignée de héros ignobles et de sujets trop bas, que ce soit pour des fins morales comme par exemple chez Prévost, ou contrairement, comme chez Scarron, de deux générations plus tôt. Le grand changement, cependant, intervient avec Voltaire. Non seulement parce qu'il arrive du côté du drame classique et de la chronique, classique elle-aussi, et qu'il accentue par là le caractère dramatique du changement, mais aussi parce qu'il crée un nouveau système de valeurs — en louant le travail, en rehaussant les commerçants, les industriels, les artistes et les savants, en rejetant les prêtres et les soldats à l'arrière-plan, en échangeant pour ainsi dire les personnages de catégories nobles ou viles, et parce qu'il réalise cela dans le cadre d'une œuvre ayant un genre spécifique. De nombreux liens rattachent *Candide* au roman picaresque — bien qu'il en soit différent par l'absence de forme autobiographique —, nous pouvons dire que c'est ainsi la synthèse du picaresque, de l'historiographie et de la philosophie. C'est de la connaissance elle-même que Voltaire fait une question éthique pour *Candide*, plus expressivement que pour ses œuvres historiques. Il continue par là, la voie déjà amorcée par Machiavel et par Mandeville, vers la science « pure » et vers la littérature réaliste du XIXe siècle. C'est justement en conséquence de l'évolution commencée ou accélérée par *Candide* que nous n'apercevons pas d'ordures là, où Grimm en voit, et c'est ainsi que la critique de Vauvenarges sur Molière perd son sens.

Enfin, il nous faut relever encore une question : bien qu'Aristote ait déjà séparé l'une de l'autre, l'historiographie et la poésie, Plutarque, Suetone

[57] Aristote, *Poétique*, Texte établi et traduit par J. Hardy, Paris 1932, p. 31.
[58] *ibid.*, p. 35.
[59] *ibid.*, p. 36.

mais aussi Tacite et Salluste ont rapproché la première de la seconde. Il est caractéristique que Tacite lui-même ait été trop politique pour Saint-Évremond, et c'est pourquoi il vota pour Salluste. À l'époque de la contre-réforme, l'influence de Plutarque est particulièrement forte; la biographie qui fait le récit de la vie d'un homme d'État, en se basant surtout sur les questions morales et psychologiques, créa une école. Les tragédies historiques des XVIe et XVIIe siècles (et presque toutes les tragédies sont historiques — même *Hamlet*) ont puisé chez Sénèque et Tite-Live, chez Plutarque et Suétone (et ailleurs encore, naturellement), mais jamais chez Thucydide, que Hobbes caractérise comme le «most Politic Historiographe that ever write»,[60] ni chez Polybe,[61] apprécié d'ailleurs par Balzac et Bossuet. La source des tragédies était donc l'historiographie morale-politique, et non pas l'historiographie socio-politique. Lorsque Voltaire parle des institutions, des coutumes, des mœurs, des sciences, du droit, et non seulement des actes d'une personne particulière, il détache radicalement — malgré toute son exigence classique — l'histoire des formes alors traditionnelles de la littérature, pour rapprocher de nouveau les deux par son roman *Candide*.

Le *Candide* offre la synthèse de deux exprériences différentes: celle de l'histoire et celle de la poétique. Si nous examinons cette œuvre sous l'angle d'une négation philosophique, elle pourra parfois nous sembler n'avoir ni ordre, ni plan. Mais si nous analysons le roman en partant de la structure politico-mondiale et sociale du XVIIIe siècle, nous comprenons qu' il est, au contraire, très strictement ordonné, les éventualités étant toujours bien motivées. Si nous regardons ses héros comme nous le ferions pour les héros du roman du XIXe siècle, nous ne leur trouvons ni personnalité, ni psychologie. Mais si nous pensons à la tragédie classique, nous rejetons cette conception. Nous ne connaissons pas moins les héros de *Candide* que ceux de Balzac ou de Stendhal. Mais Voltaire nous les présente non pas de manière épique, mais dramatique.

---

[60] Cité par Rex Warner, *Introduction*, in Thucydides, *History of the Peleponnesian War*, translated with an introduction by Rex Warner, Baltimore—Maryland 1954, p. 5.

[61] Selon Ervin Zaitschek, *Corneille-tanulmányok* (Études sur Corneille), Budapest 1931, pp. 50—51. Corneille emprunta une description de Sophonisbe à Polybe.

THE CRISIS OF ENGLISH COMEDY
IN THE EARLY EIGHTEENTH CENTURY

by

KÁLMÁN G. RUTTKAY

Although the past decades have witnessed some reawakening of interest in eighteenth-century English plays both on the stage and in learned papers, the bulk of critical writings dealing with them is still relatively small, their tone far from enthusiastic, and, to say the least, the century is not regarded as a glorious period in the history of English drama. It would seem logical that the quality of the plays produced during that age is responsible for the largely negative critical appreciation, and that the so-called and oft-mentioned neglect of eighteenth-century drama is not purely the result of a conspiracy of later generations of perverse critics and literary historians.

Even those who are obviously sympathetic cannot deny the fact that the general standard of English drama is lower in the eighteenth century than in the preceding Restoration era, and even more so than in the Elizabethan age. Registering these differences in value, one of the sympathetic critics, W. D. Taylor, goes so far as to conclude that one reason "why the quality of drama depreciated was that the eighteenth century enjoyed a rich dramatic heritage. It did not need to produce great new plays for its Garricks and Macklins. It had Shakespeare, Jonson, Fletcher, Wycherley, Dryden, and Congreve, in their original strength or watered down to please prudes and pedants . . . Of the thirteen parts Garrick chose to appear in during his farewell performances at the beginning of 1776, ten are from plays written before 1730."[1]

Less absurdly naive, but ultimately not much more convincing is the reasoning of A. Nicoll who, while he admits that it is difficult to find an explanation for the "absolute neglect of eighteenth-century comedy," believes to have discovered "an answer to the problem . . . in the theatre of the Victorian era. The drama of the nineteenth century was fundamentally unliterary, and the contempt shown for it by the more dignified critics was extended to the earlier era. Romantic criticism extolled the Elizabethans; everything from 1660 onwards was evil. In addition to this, we must note both the love of novelty displayed by nineteenth-century audiences and the growth of the 'long run'. In days when all theatres had their constantly changing repertories, many old plays could be revived and several scores were regular 'stock-plays' which reappeared season after season. The cry for novelty, however, urged the managers to produce new pieces, and the disappearance of the repertory system limited the number of individual dramas that could be performed in any one season. The eighteenth-century plays which had held the boards till about 1830 or 1840 gradually vanished;

---

[1] W. D. Taylor, Introduction to his edition of *Eighteenth Century Comedy*, London [1st publ. 1929], repr. 1961, World's Classics 292, pp. X—XI.

a few are still remembered by their names only, most of them have been entirely forgotten."[2] Writing as he does, in this case, of "lesser English comedies of the eighteenth century," he does not have to confront the major plays of the century with those of other periods, consequently he can do without a full-scale historical survey or valuation of the whole dramatic output of the century, and can restrict his attention to certain favourable aspects, such as the "essentially theatrical" quality of these plays. "Genuine *flair* for the theatre atones for much; literary quality has, after all, to bow in the playhouse to acting quality."[3]

All the same, he is fully aware of the problem of values, as is clearly seen in *A History of English Drama 1660—1900*, where this question cannot be avoided, and where he accepts the fact of "decay," at least as a point of departure. "A period of decay and disintegration it was in many ways," he admits, including in the "period" not only the eighteenth century, but practically the whole of the seventeenth as well. "In no wise can it be denied that, as we watch the drama progressing from 1610 to the end of the eighteenth century, we see in general only a retrograde movement, arrested at moments, in the early years by men such as Ford and Shirley, in the later by others such as Dryden and Otway and Congreve and Steele, but moving nevertheless relentlessly along the one inevitable path."[4] If Nicoll does not deny the fact of decline he discovers in it elements which prevent him from drawing absolutely negative conclusions. "The more we come to analyse this period of the drama, . . . the more we come to realise that the retrograde movement so apparent on the surface was countered by a series of forward developments, never carried to artistic fulfilment in those years, but of boundless significance when we carry our gaze onwards to our own times."[5] This historically sound view is sometimes blurred in the analytical chapters, both by certain inconsistencies and naivity, and also by the sheer bulk of the impressive material which, occasionally, proves hardly tractable; on the whole, however, Nicoll manages to present the process of "decay and disintegration" as one of fermentation rather, with manifold products and by-products ranging "from *Cato* and *The Conscious Lovers* to the flimsiest of pantomimes and the silliest of Italian operas,"[6] and he relates the process to the changes in the social stratification of the audience and in the intellectual, moral, and political climate of the theatre and the history of other literary forms.

The decline of English drama in the early eighteenth century (which is the period covered by this paper) is certainly not to be understood to have been a decline in numbers, whether of plays or playwrights; on the contrary, it would seem that there were far too many of both, and it is easier to list the writers who did not write for the stage than those who did. Of the major authors of the period Defoe, Swift, and later Samuel Richardson are the

[2] A. Nicoll, General Introduction to his edition of *Lesser English Comedies of the Eighteenth Century*, London (1927), repr. London, 1931, World's Classics 321, pp. VII—VIII.

[3] *Ibid.*, p. XV.

[4] A. Nicoll, *A History of English Drama 1660—1900*, Vol. II., *Early Eighteenth Century Drama*, Cambridge (1925) 1952³, pp. 1—2.

[5] *Ibid.*, pp. 1—2.

[6] *Ibid.*, p. 1.

most notable exceptions. Pope tried his hand at writing drama, burning his finger badly over *Three Hours After Marriage* (1717) in which he collaborated with his friendrs Gay and Arbuthnot. Such eminent figures as Thomson and Young, whose names are kept alive by their poetic achievement, were authors of a number of dramas. Fielding's activity as playwright, before he turned novelist, is well known, and another future major novelist, Tobias Smollett, had the privilege, as a young author coming to London in 1739, to have his tragedy *The Regicide*, an only play, rejected by Garrick. The latter was, however, partial enough to put on ten years later another only play, *Irene*, a short-lived tragedy by his friend Samuel Johnson who had earned some reputation and was to earn much more in other fields of literature, outside the drama.

Unsuccessful or deservedly forgotten plays by otherwise important writers are only a negligible fraction of the whole dramatic output of the period; the vast majority came from the pens of people who would be overrated by being classed even as "minor dramatists of the age." What is to be specially noted is a statistically significant percentage of anonymous plays and one-play writers.[7] Most of these nondescript authors were in a rather awkward position, being neither gentlemen writers nor successfully established professionals; and while they were penning their fulsome dedications, they could not help feeling that the "people of quality" addressed were losing control of the stage, and playwrights were facing an audience whose tastes and demands were less predictable and, consequently, less easy to satisfy than not long before.

The Prologue to Charles Hopkins's tragedy *Friendship Improv'd: or, The Female Warriour* (1700) is a characteristic piece giving evidence of an author's sorry plight.

> Long has our Author beat his addled Brains
> To purchase Fame, but can't find Ways and Means.
> They talk of Fame, but 'tis the thought of many,
> They ne'er regarded that, nor writ for any,
> But wholly plodded how to turn the Penny.
> That is the Plot, which every Poet lays;
> Thither drives all their aim and now a-days,
> Faith, 'tis the only Plot you'd find in Plays.
> Yet when poor Author is in greatest need,
> Seldom, ah! seldom does his Plot succeed.

And the Prologue ends on the same note:

> No Money left, — but Lines exceeding number.[8]

If all this had been no more than a poet's "complaint to his empty purse," intended to work on a patron's heart and money-bag, it would have been

---

[7] See *ibid.*, p. 8.
[8] Charles Hopkins, *Friendship Improv'd: or, The Female Warriour. A Tragedy*, London, 1700, Prologue, Sig. A$_3$v, ll. 1—10. and 38.

relatively easy to remedy the evil, and the lines could be dismissed as an umpteenth variation on an age-old theme. Read in context, however, they show that this was not the case, and the "poor Author" was faced with a new kind of dilemma which personal patronage could no longer solve.

> His [the author's] way would be in this unlucky Age,
> Not to write for, but write against the Stage.
> The moneyed men would then his Cause defend:
> City Security's a special Friend.
> — — — — — — — — — — — —
>
> But Poets with the love of Courts are curst,
> Which leave them Poets, as they found them first:
> Thought wholly for the smallest trust unfit,
> And reckon'd useless, for their very Wit:
> Whose only Wages is their homely board,
> What Shares, the Back-Stair Pages can afford,
> Or, when Fate smiles, a dinner with a Lord.[9]

The line "Not to write for, but write against the Stage" is to be read not only in the textual context of the Prologue but in the historical context of the great controversy formally beginning with Jeremy Collier's wholesale attack in *A Short View of the Immorality and Profaneness of the English Stage* (1698) after a series of sporadic, preparatory explosions of anti-stage feeling over a rather long incubation period and carried on with intermittent vehemence for about thirty years. It appears to have been a warfare between unequal forces since even the most dedicated supporters of the stage could not well say that there was absolutely no ground for the charges brought forth by Collier, Arthur Bedford, William Law, and a shoal of minor but equally militant figures against the English stage, with what it inherited from the last four decades of the seventeenth century. "Even Voltaire, . . . looking back upon English drama, was shocked at its license" — says Edmund Gosse.[10]

In 1693 it was still possible for John Dennis, then engaged in a controversy with Thomas Rymer, author of an earlier and different *Short View*, to put the following statement into the mouth of Freeman, one of the speakers in the dialogue of *The Impartial Critick:* "Our Theatre may be said to be the School of Vertue, upon two accounts. First, because it removes the greatest Obstructions to Vertue, by reducing the Passions to a just mediocrity, from their violence and inequality. And Secondly, because it teaches some Moral Doctrine by the Fable, which must always be allegorical and universal."[11] The questions involved in the debate were theoretical, and the ideas of "Vertue" and "Moral Doctrine" could be conceived in dramaturgical, aesthetic and psychological terms, without reference to actual moral

---

[9] *Ibid.,* ll. 11—14., 24—30.
[10] E. Gosse, *Life of W. Congreve,* London, 1888, p. 99.
[11] J. Dennis, *The Impartial Critick,* London, 1693. In *The Critical Works of John Dennis,* ed. E. N. Hooker. Baltimore, 1939, 1943, [to be referred to as Hooker], Vol. I., p. 35.

practice, whether individual or collective, private or public. But even while he was penning these lines, the great controversy was in the offing.

In 1694, proposals were published for a national reformation of manners, and the fourth "Consideration" was *"To supplicate their Majesties* [William III and Mary], *That the publick Play-Houses may be suppressed"*. This is followed by three pages of vituperation against the theatres which "have a direct tendency . . . to corrupt and vitiate the minds of the generality of all sorts, more or less, though more immediately of *all who frequent them,"* especially the youth, alluring them "into the love of, and delight in *Idleness,* excessive *Vanity, Revellings, Luxury, Wantonness, Lasciviousness, Whore-doms,* and such *Debauches."* The theatres are *"Nurseries* and *Seminaries* of *Vice"* and: "It is more than a little suspected, that it hath been and still is one grand design of those *Priests* and *Jesuits,* who adhere unto the *French Interest,* to introduce and keep up these Publick *Play-Houses* on purpose.

1. *To obdurate the Conscience of Professors* . . .

2. To *Mollifie and Effeminate the English Valour,* that we may be broken in pieces when our Martial Neig[h]bour Nation shall Invade us".[12]

In somewhat milder language, the Religious Societies recommended "to every Person concerned in this *Society,* to consider the many Inconveniencies, (and many times Sins) which attend *Ale-House-Games,* and wholly to decline them. And to shun all unnecessary resort to such Houses and Taverns, and wholly to avoid lewd *Play-Houses."*[13]

At a session of the SPCK on Jan 6th 1704, it was "order'd that 200 Copies of Mr. Colliers Letter or Disswasive from Play-houses be bought, and brought to the next meeting."[14] Also, the Society's own letter against the theatres, drafted by Dr Bray, was discussed and, a week later, further steps were taken in order to make their participation in the systematic campaign against the stage more organized and effective.

When Vanbrugh was to become manager of the new theatre he had built in the Haymarket, "several Members of the Society for Reformation of Manners" asked Thomas Tenison, Archbishop of Canterbury, to intervene and prevent this "great Mischief to *Religion,"* richly larding their petition with quotations from Vanbrugh's plays to prove how immoral he was, how he had ridiculed the clergy, and so on.[15]

The Grand Jury, meeting in Bristol on december 6th, 1704, expressed their apprehensions about "the late Permission given to the *Publick Stage,* within the Liberties of this City, from whence some have conceiv'd Hopes, it shall be tolerated always; and Countenance, or at least Connivance givn' to *Acting* of Plays and *Interludes* within this City and County, which (if it should be) will exceedingly eclipse the good Order and Government of the City, corrupt and debauch our *Youth,* and utterly ruin many *Apprentices* and *Servants,* already so *Unruly* and *Licentious,* that they are with great Difficulty kept under any reasonable Order or Government by their Masters.

[12] *Proposals for a National Reformation of Manners, etc.,* Published by the Society for Reformation, London, 1694, pp. 14—16.

[13] J. Woodward, *An Account of the Rise and Progress of the Religious Societies,* London, 1698², pp. 124—125.

[14] E. McClare (ed.), *A Chapter in English Church History,* London, 1888, p. 257.

[15] *A Letter from several Members of the Society for Reformation to . . . Thomas . . . Archbishop of Canterbury,* London, Dec. 10, 1704, p. 4.

. . . in all Ages, *Acting* of *Plays* and *Interludes* hath been attended with all Manner of *Profaneness*, *Lewdness*, *Murthers*, *Debauching* and *Ruining Youth* of *both Sexes*, infusing *Principles* of *Idleness* and *Extravagancy* into all People that resort to them. We hope your Worships seriously will consider of Effectual Methods to prevent them, and with the greatest Zeal and Fervency will put the same in Execution, when it is apparent that all the Methods to correct and keep them within modest Bounds (where they are tolerated) have proved ineffectual: And all Wise Men are convinced that there is no Methods [sic] of hindering or preventing their Mischiefs, but by totally suppressing them. Your Worships Task is not so difficult, Preventing Remedies being more natural and easy than Punishing. And we humbly conceive you have Reason more cogent to stir you up to this Work, than offer themselves to Cities and Places where they have been tolerated, abounding with *Gentry* and *Nobility*, whose *Estates* and *Leisure* render such Extravagancies more tolerable. But if in such Places their direful and calamitous Effects have been so sensibly felt, how much more in a City not to be upheld but by Trade and Industry, will they be insupportable? We therefore do not doubt but all the due Care will be taken by your Worships to redress and prevent these Grievances, that a Stop may be put to the further Progress of *Immorality* and *Profaneness*, and the Work of *Reformation* carried on, so earnestly press'd by Her Majesty's Proclamation, whose Pious Endeavours *God* has so signally owned in the great Victories with which he hath blessed Her Arms, whose Glorious Example we doubt not but you will follow, to your lasting Honour and Renown, and the Encouragement and Comfort of all good Citizens."[16]

In spite of this protest the theatre in Bristol was established, but the Grand Jury did not give up their struggle against it. In 1706 they renewed their petition: "we would humbly recommend to Your Worships utmost Care and unanimous Zeal, to search out and pursue the most effectual and lawful Methods for crushing the newly erected *Play-House*, that *School of Debauchery* and *Nursery of Profaneness*, where *Vice* and *Lewdness* appear Bare-faced, and Impudent, *Swearing* notoriously Practised and Recommended: The Danger and Growth of which, we have been seasonably warned against by our Right Reverend *Divines* from the *Pulpit*."[17]

It is evident from what has been quoted that the most militant enemies of the stage launched their attacks not only against its immorality but its existence. Arthur Bedford who spared no effort to prove "the *Stage* to be a *Sink of Sin*, a *Cage of Uncleanness*, and the Original Cause of all our Profaneness; directly tending to root out all *Religion*, contemn the Laws of *God* and *Man*, and affront such as pay a Regard to either"[18] was, indeed, very moderate when he offered the alternative of "an intire Reformation or a total Suppression of the *Stage*" to "stop the Mouths both of *Atheists* and *Papists*," if regard was to be taken to "the Glory of *God*, the Welfare

[16] *Tha* [sic] *Presentment of the Grand Jury, met at the General Quarter-Sessions of the Peace, the Sixth Day of December, 1704, in A. Bedford, The Evil and Danger of Stage-Plays*, London, 1706, pp. 223—226.

[17] *Part of the Presentment of the Grand Jury, met at the General Assize of Gaol Delivery, the 15th Day of August, 1706. Ibid.*, p. 227.

[18] *Ibid.*, p. 25.

of *Religion*, the Securing it from *Contempt*, the Promoting of it at home, or the Propagating of it abroad."[19]

An alternative like this must have been welcome to the other party, indicating as it did the line of defence for them to take. Acknowledging that the stage was actually corrupted, they argued that, potentially at least, it could be the "School of Vertue." Dennis brought out his prompt answer to Collier's *Short View*, in 1698, under the very significant title: *The Usefulness of the Stage, to the Happiness of Mankind, to Government, and to Religion*, and he was shrewd enough to make it clear from the very first that his business was "a Vindication of the Stage, and not of the Corruptions or the Abuses of it."[20] He did not try to deny that "the Abuses are so great, that there is a Necessity for the reforming of them"; adding, however, "not that I think, that, with all its Corruptions, the Stage has debauch'd the People,"[21] and he went to some length to prove that "the Corruption of Manners, is not to be attributed to the Licentiousness of the Drama."[22] He pointed out that the "Corruption of Manners upon the Restoration, appear'd with all the Fury of Libertinism, even before the Play-House was re-establish'd, and long before it could have any Influence on Manners; so that another Cause of that Corruption is to be inquir'd after, than the Re-establishment of the Drama; and that can be nothing but that beastly Reformation, which, in the Time of the Civil Wars, was begun at the Tail, instead of the Head and the Heart; and which opprest and persecuted Mens Inclinations, instead of correcting and converting them, which afterwards broke out with the same Violence, that a raging Fire does upon its first getting Vent. And that which gave it so licentious a Vent was, not only the Permission, but the Example of the Court, which, for the most part, was just arriv'd from Abroad with the King, where it had endeavour'd, by Foreign Corruption, to sweeten, or, at least, to soften Adversity and having sojourn'd for a considerable Time, both at *Paris*, and in the *Low-Countries*, united the Spirit of the *French* Whoring, to the Fury of the *Dutch* Drinking. So that the Poets who writ immediately after the Restoration, were obliged to humour the deprav'd Tastes of their Audiences."[23]

Whether " 'tis evident, that the Corruption of the Nation is so far from proceeding from the Play-House, that it partly proceeds from having no Plays at all,"[24] and whether Dennis's historical analysis, anticipating in a nutshell the Freudian theory of repression and sublimation, is absolutely correct in representing the wave of Restoration libertinism as a backlash of the moral rigidity of the Puritan interlude, are questions not very much to the point. What matters more, for the purpose of the present paper, is that Dennis, with all his formidable skill in reasoning and an arsenal of sound arguments, was inevitably under a heavy handicap in comparison with the enemies of the stage who could act more efficiently by using the power, authority, even the administrative machinery, of organizations and institutions. The clergy, however divided over questions of dogma and

[19] A. Bedford, *The Great Abuse of Musick*, London, 1711, pp. 107—108.
[20] Hooker, Vol I., p. 147.
[21] *Ibid.*, p. 146.
[22] *Ibid.*, p. 155.
[23] *Ibid.*, p. 154.
[24] *Ibid.*, pp. 154—155.

ecclesiastic policies, was, naturally enough, unanimous in the condemnation of plays which did not spare the cloth; consequently, the pulpits of the Church of England were at the disposal of the anti-stage propaganda hall-marked with the name of Jeremy Collier, a non-juror.[25] As has been shown, the various religious and semi-religious bodies which united a considerable number of laymen and clergymen of different persuasions to reform morals and promote Christian knowledge gave full moral and administrative support to the campaign.

The anti-stage movement was so strong and organized that its exponents were in the position to urge legislation and administrative measures to suppress or at least regulate the theatres, even if these demands of theirs were never fully met. Moreover, they could see that the Court, no longer the stronghold of libertinism it had been in Charles II's time, was well disposed to them, and King William III who rebuked courtiers for swearing in his presence, or Queen Anne who insisted on having the latest number of *The Spectator* with her tea, were their allies. An early example of royal sympathy was the favour shown to Jeremy Collier himself, whose "book was upon the whole thought so laudable a work, that King William, soon after it was publish'd, granted him a *nolo prosequi*, when he stood answerable to the law for his having absolved two criminals, just before they were executed, for high treason."[26]

It would be too simplistic to call either William or Anne a middle-class monarch or even to believe that the "moneyed men" with their "City Securities" ironically mentioned in the lines quoted from the Prologue to Hopkins's *Friendship Improv'd* had brought about a social, moral and intellectual revolution which changed the climate of the Court as much as that of the play-house. This is not to deny that there were many changes, and that these were connected with the increased importance of the "moneyed men"; but these were the result of a long and slow process of transformation following the Glorious Revolution, a revolution in name only. Certain trends in the process had become marked by about the turn of the century and produced unmistakable symptoms, such as the Collier controversy. The fact, however, that in spite of the vehemence of the first attacks, it was drawn out over a period of three decades, amply proves that the contrary trends were by no means too weak. The "immoral" and "profane" plays continued to be revived, pruned, here and there, of the most outrageous indecencies of the dialogue, occasionally with a scene omitted or

[25] That the stage was thought to be a menace to religion as such can be illustrated, among others, by a passage from No. 8. for Dec. 1717, of *The Entertainer*, a paper with High Church and Tory affiliations: "That vile Composition [i.e. Colley Cibber's *The Non-Juror*] (let his Pretences be otherwise) is not a *Satyr* upon a particular Set of Persons, but is levelled directly at the Christian Priesthood. ... The World is arrived to a fine Pass, when the Membership of the *Catholick Church*, Disputes upon the *Nature of Schism*, and the *Divine Right of Episcopacy*, are to be debated scoffingly by the Devil's Agents in his own Academy. For the *Play-house* to give Rules to the *Pulpit*, looks as if *Antichrist* was upon Earth already. Such Practices are to tincture the Minds of the *Gallery-Mob* with Infidelity and Atheism; for 'tis not to tell them that the *Nonjurors* are in the *wrong*, but that *No Religion* is in the *Right*." In vol. form, London, n. d., pp. 46—49.

[26] C. Cibber, *Apology*, (1740), repr. London, 1938, Everyman 668, p. 143.

rewritten. What is more, even the new plays produced after the publication of Collier's *Short View*, e.g. those by Susannah Centlivre, did not all fully conform to the demands of the reformers. But changing the whole repertoire overnight or abandoning completely the old tradition of writing was impossible, not only for technical reasons but also because the audience was not a homogeneous body of moral reformers. The anonymous compiler of *The English Theophrastus*, possibly Abel Boyer, included in this work a passage elucidating the point in question: "To please the *Pit* and *Galleries* he [the dramatist] must take care to lard the Dialogue with store of luscious stuff, which the righteous call Baudy; to please the new Reformers he must have none, otherwise gruff *Jeremy* will lash him in a third *View*."[27]

It was far from easy to "please the new Reformers" who seem to have demanded always more and more. Collier's catalogue of the vices of playwrights appears short and simple in comparison with the one abstracted by Arthur Bedford from *An Act at Oxford* (1704) by Thomas Baker who "is guilty of *Swearing, Cursing, Exposing the Universities, and Societies for Reformation, the Aldermen and Officers, Marriage and Religion* it self, and pleads for *Pimping* and *Whoring*."[28] Most interesting in this list is the reference to aldermen and officers who, with the rise in social importance of the citizens they represented, were to enjoy the same freedom from ridicule as the clergy. Again, this did not necessarily mean that the traditionally ridiculous representation of the "Citt" (or the clergyman for that matter) was immediately abandoned, but it certainly indicated that the reforming critics were aware of the unquestionable fact that the social scale was shifting, and warned playwrights to revise their ideas of social respectability.

Nor was it easy for the contemporaries, whether participants or merely observers, to judge the achievements and prospects of the intermittent controversy, and it is perhaps no wonder that the majority of the enemies of the stage should have been dissatisfied with the state of affairs. Optimistic statements registering progress were few and cautiously worded, like this: "Some faint Dawnings of Reformation seem to appear, and things begin to recover a better Aspect than formerly. Mr. *Collier* (to whom the Age can never be sufficiently grateful) has given the Stage such a Blow, as in time I'm perswaded will Ruin or Reform it. The very Answers to his Writings do but add to his Triumphs, and loudly confess what feeble Arguments Vice is supported with."[29] Statements in general, even those made decades after the publication of the *Short View*, sound as if nothing had improved since then. In *The Great Abuse of Musick* (1711), Arthur Bedford attacked the play-houses, the "Synagogues of *Satan*,"[30] as vehemently as in *The*

---

[27] [A. Boyer?], *The English Theophrastus: or, the Manners of the Age*, London, 1702, p. 16. Excerpts repr. in facs., ARS, Ser. 1., No. 3., Ann Arbor, Mich., 1947.

[28] A. Bedford, *The Evil and Danger of Stage-Plays*, London, 1706, p. 11.

[29] Preface to *Divine Hymns and Poems on Several Occasions*, By the E. of Roscommon, Mr. Dryden, Mr. Dennis, Mr. Norris, Mrs. Kath. Phillips, Philomela and others, London, 1709, Sig. A_6r. It is interesting to note the absurdity of the tribute paid to Collier in a preface to a volume which contains poems by such eminent anti-Collier writers as Dryden and Dennis.

[30] A. Bedford, *The Great Abuse of Musick*, London, 1711, p. 62.

Evil and Danger of Stage-Plays (1706). William Law took the trouble to bring out a bigoted pamphlet called *The Absolute Unlawfulness of the Stage-Entertainments Fully Demonstrated* as late as 1726, provoking Dennis to write *The Stage Defended* (1726), his last contribution to the stage controversy, in which he pointed out not only that Law was wrong but that he was ignorant of the subject he had taken up. Nevertheless, it was Law's pamphlet that was reprinted several times during the following decades, whereas Dennis's answer made no stir. In a public letter printed in 1728, "Philanthropos" wrote to Law: "I do with a great deal of Pleasure, subscribe to your Praise, where my own Sense and Reason, as well as the common Cause of Mankind, do not interfere. Particularly, in your just and reasonable Accusation of the *Stage*, which I can't but think (at least as it is now manag'd) an Entertainment altogether unbecoming a *Religion*, much more a *Christian* Society."[31]

In 1732 we find another pseudonymous writer, "Ruth Collins," author of *The Friendly Writer, and Register of Truth*, a Quaker monthly, quoting Law "who was a Man of sound Knowledge," in a paper which opens with an invective against the theatres: "My Friends, I think I cannot, in any wise, better begin the Work which I have undertaken for this Month, than by an Exhortation to ye all against the Abomination of PLAY-HOUSES, which are rising up as so many Temples of *Satan*, in every Corner of the Town."[32] Two months later, reporting on an epidemic in London, the pious "Ruth" declared its cause to be "the great Wickedness of this perverse and stiff-necked Generation, which is yet more froward and rebellious than their Forefathers; this is plainly to be noted, with Grief do I declare it, by the rising up in every Corner of the Town of so many new Abominations call'd PLAY-HOUSES, those *Temples* of *Satan*, against which I witnessed in my Monthly Labour for the Ninth Month call'd *November;* but little Heed was given to my Rebukes. For observe, my Friends, this Sickness spreads and rages in every Part of this great Town, so do the PLAY-HOUSES; this Sickness kills abundance of Souls, so do the PLAY-HOUSES, yea verily, more than the Sickness; wherefore I say unto ye, those *Temples* of *Satan* are a heavier Visitation than this Sickness."[33]

Symptomatic as it might be in many other ways, the invective of "Ruth Collins" can be discounted as Quaker propaganda; it is both too exaggerated and too general to pass for criticism, especially after more than thirty years of the stage controversy which had produced arguments also, not only high-flown rhetoric. Real criticism, however, must be considered, particularly criticism coming from people who did not use the stage as a whipping-post, who, in fact, were sympathetic and anxious to do it a good turn, and, more particularly, if it was made at a time when the heat of the great controversy had actually cooled off and passions were no longer high. Good examples of this kind of criticism can be found, from as late as the mid-forties, in *The Female Spectator* of Elizabeth Haywood. A practising dramatist herself, she was convinced that "a good Play is an elegant Entertainment for those

[31] Philanthropos [pseudonym], *A Letter to Mr. Law; Occasion'd by reading his Treatise on Christian Perfection with a Copy of Verses Address'd to the same Author*, By a Lover of Mankind, London, 1728, p. 5.
[32] Ruth Collins [pseudonym], *The Friendly Writer, and Register of Truth*, Book the Third, Nov., 1732, p. 3.
[33] *Ibid.*, Book the Fifth, Jan., 1732, p. 10.

of the highest and most elevated Capacities, and cannot but afford some Improvement to the dullest and least inform'd," and "that there is no Kind of Diversion whatever, in which three Hours may so agreeably and profitably be spent." That is why she thought that "among the many Misfortunes of the present Age . . . the visible Decay of the Stage may be well accounted not the least, since nothing can be a greater Proof how much the general Taste is vitiated, than to neglect an Entertainment in which Pleasure and Instruction are blended, for others, which the best that can be said of them is, that they afford some Amusement to the Senses."[34] Two years later the paper resumed the subject: "The Stage, which was designed the School of Morality, and by mingling Pleasure with Improvement, to harmonize the Mind, and inspire Amity among Men, has, in some Theatrical Representations, been most shamefully prostituted to Ends, the very reverse, and not only Gentlemen who happen to live out of *London*, but the most eminent Citizens who live within the Sound of *Bow* Bell, made a public Ridicule: A Country 'Squire and an Alderman of *London* are sure to be the Characters to excite Laughter: — Our modern Writers are more polite than *Shakespeare, Johnson,* and their Contemporaries, who always made the Fools in their Plays Court-Parasites, or at least Jesters, but the City and Country are now the only Places from which a Buffoon is to be picked. The Sarcasms vented here and elsewhere have often a Poignancy in them, which cannot but be resented by those who have Understanding enough to perceive when they are affronted, and sometimes occasion Heart-burnings against those who encourage, and seem to be pleased with the Ridicule; which are no way agreeable to that Cordiality and Good-will which ought to subsist between every Community of a Nation, in order to render the Whole a truly happy People."[35]

It is difficult to believe, and, on theoretical assumptions, it is not really possible, that more than forty years after the publication of Collier's *Short View* the evils of the stage should have been virulent enough to justify the amount of hostile or benevolently anxious criticism that was currently produced. That all the campaigning against the stage had not been wholly ineffective was testified by a most authentic witness, indeed more than a witness, Colley Cibber who, in the multiple capacity of actor, playwright and manager, had a practitioner's first-hand experience of the issues of the great controversy which, he knew well, could not be ignored, and, willynilly, he himself came to be an important contributor to the transformation of English drama during the decades of the controversy. Looking back on Collier's activity, he could be objective enough to say: "it must be . . . granted that his calling our dramatic writers to this strict account, had a very wholesome effect upon those who writ after this time. They were a great deal more upon their guard; indecencies were no longer writ; and by degrees the fair sex came again to fill the boxes on the first day of a new comedy, without fear or censure."[36] Indeed, he spoke of "that remarkable

[34] *The Female Spectator*, Book V., 1744. In vol. form: Vol. I., London, 1745, pp 320 – 321.
[35] *Ibid.*, Book XXI, 1746. In vol. form: Vol. IV., London, 1746, p. 136.
[36] Cibber, *op. cit., loc. cit.*

period," meaning approximately the years 1710—1730, "when the stage, during my time upon it, was the least reproachable."[37]

Nevertheless, long after Cibber's *Apology* appeared, the traditional critical opinions continued to be voiced, sometimes in rather unlikely places, such as an essay on the novel, "the New Species founded by Mr. Fielding," published anonymously in 1751 by Francis Coventry, who found it necessary to make an excursion into the field of criticising the drama and include a reference to "those barren Writers of Comedy, who have no other Way of pleasing, but a scandalous Coincidence with the deprav'd Taste of a vicious Audience."[38] In the same year an instalment of a discourse attributed to Thomas Cooke appeared, which lashed the contemporary English stage at length, in the manner familiar from a long line of preceding anti-stage pamphlets. "The Success which many dramatic and other Pieces have met with through many Years passed in this Kingdom presents a melancholly Prospect to those who are zealous in forming the Manners of each rising Generation. The *English* Stage, which should be the School of Virtue and Wisdom, is too often the Representation of what ought to be concealed from Persons of all Denominations: and, instead of Wit and Humour, most of our Comedies abound with what the judicious must call Ribaldry and Impertinence; and the greatest, far greatest, Part of our Tragedies are void of the Sentiments which enrich the Mind, and of that Language which adorns Virtue, and which makes those Impressions in the Heart which prove of general Utility: from such muddy Springs, with which may be ranked many Books and Pamphlets not dramatic, flow various Tides of Immorality. Many who go from a Play which furnishes them with Nothing but deformed and noxious Ideas become hurtful to themselves and to Society: and such the Effect of other Writings equally bad: I shall not give any of the Titles of the Pieces, or the Names of the Authors, which are public Nu[i]sances, that I may not disgrace these Pages with them, and because I would not feed the Curiosity of those who are too apt to warp towards Depravity." The main point of the discourse was that "the Regulation of the Stage is worthy the Care of Legislature," in view of "the Deluge of Filth which may overflow the Land" and the "Offences [which] will spread in private Families," and the theatres themselves "would be greater Gainers by the Performance of commendable Pieces than of such as merit Reprehension; for Parents then, and all Heads of Families, would be earnest in promoting a School of Virtue and Politeness."[39]

It is surprising that this should have come from Cooke, who had expressed more lenient views in his *Considerations on the Stage, and on the Advantages which arise to a Nation From the Encouragement of Arts* published twenty years earlier, in opposition to "several grave Divines" who "have thought fit to write and preach against dramatic Performances," and endeavouring "to point out the Benefits arising from them when under proper Regulations, and to shew how much they conduce to the Advancement of

---

[37] *Ibid.*, p. 241.

[38] [F. Coventry], *An Essay on the New Species founded by Mr. Fielding: With a Word or Two upon the modern State of Criticism*, London, 1751, p. 42.

[39] [T. Cooke], *A ... Discourse ... [prefixed to] An Ode on the Powers of Poetry*, London, 1751, pp. 3—4.

Virtue, and consequently to the Destruction of Vice."[40] He vindicated the stage not only on a theoretical level, and in general terms, but supported his statements by illustrative names and titles. Having examined *King Lear* as altered by Tate, Shadwell's *The Squire of Alsatia* and Addison's *Rosamond*, he said: "I could add many more, which would bear as strict a moral Examination, from the same Authors, from *Beaumont* and *Fletcher*, *Dryden*, *Lee*, *Otway*, *Steel* [sic], *Phillips*, *Cibber*, and some few other dramatic Poets, who may be properly sayed, in many of their Plays, to have adorned Morality."[41] He stressed the moral usefulness of comedy in which "the Objects of Pleasure are made Lures of Instruction,"[42] and asked: "If some few Objections may be made to the present Management of our Theatres, is it reasonable that dramatic Performances should be entirely prohibited?"[43] Years later he still proved himself to be for the stage, saying in a Prologue that "The Curse of Fools was mighty Dryden's Lot," and he spoke with derision of "A Collier, Blackmore, and a Herd of Foes."[44]

The contrast between these opinions taken from Cooke's signed, earlier writings and those quoted from the unsigned discourse of 1751 attributed to him are so great that one is tempted to believe that the later work has been wrongly ascribed to him. More important, however, than the possible inconsistencies in Cooke's successive attitudes, or even the question of authorship, is the fact that a discourse should have demanded legislation against the theatres in 1751, when the Licensing Act had been in force since 1737, and that the demand should have been penned in the style of pamphlets published thirty, forty, even more than fifty years earlier.

By the mid-century there could have been no unspent arguments or passions left against the English stage, and the phrases, so familiar from the great controversy, were kept alive not by the heat in which they had been originally coined but very largely by the persistence of *clichés*. Also, at least in part, by a new wave of dissatisfaction provoked no longer by the "immoral" and "profane" plays but, ironically enough, by those which came to replace them. There were, of course, critical utterances which were concerned with the new evil phenomena only, such as *A Satirical Epistle to Mr. Pope*, published anonymously by one Lorleach in 1740 who did not feel it necessary to resort to the traditional vocabulary and reasoning of the Collier controversy when he catalogued the symptoms of the decline of the stage.

[40] Affixed to T. Cooke, *The Triumphs of Love and Honour, a Play*, London, 1731, pp. 47—48.
[41] *Ibid.*, p. 68.
[42] *Ibid.*, p. 62.
[43] *Ibid.*, p. 69.
[44] T. Cooke, *Prologue the Sixth. Spoke by Mr. Milward to the Country Wife*. Mr. Cooke's Original Poems, ... London, 1742, p. 167. For the Collier controversy see chiefly, Sister Rose Anthony, *The Jeremy Collier Stage Controversy*, Milwaukee, 1937, and J. W. Krutch, *Comedy and Conscience after the Restoration*, New York, 1924. Also, I have to mention, with gratitude, an excellent diploma work in manuscript, by Miss E. Zombory, now one of my colleagues at the English Department in the University of Budapest, Hungary. An important chapter on the social implications of the stage controversy can be read in J. Loftis, *Comedy and Society from Congreve to Fielding*, Stanford, 1959, pp. 20—42. Loftis's statements concerning "two major forces" in contemporary dramatic criticism, "a moralistic one leading from Collier and an aesthetic one leading to Pope," (p. 41) are of particular interest.

Now view the Town, and search all o'er to find,
But one improv'd, in Habit, or in Mind:
Lo ! *Tragedy* sinks, Now's her fatal Time,
She drops — and in her stead see *Pantomime*.
Now *Harlequin* in triumph spreads his reign,
From *Sadlers-Wells*, to noted *Drury-Lane*.
Orpheus and *Eurydice* at length appears,
The mangl'd Produce, of sixteen long Years.
Peers, Lawyers, Cits, they all in Thousands run,
T'admire the active Feats of nimble *Lun:*
The Comic Vein, no longer now can please,
Now nought goes down, but *Metamorphoses* !
Who can now bear the sad, the doleful Stage,
When *Pistoll* apes, *Othello's* manlike Rage?
Away to Oratorio's now they throng,
Discourse and Action vanish in a Song.[45]

In very many cases, however, the well-worn stock phrases of the Collier controversy, the "decline of the stage," the "depravity of taste," the "corruptions of the age" or of "the vicious audience," and so forth, were extended to include, or transferred to cover, evils different from those which had been the original target of the first attacks. E.g. the passages from *The Female Spectator*, already quoted[46] as a late variety of traditional moral criticism, indicate simultaneously a new orientation of critical thinking. However "shamefully prostituted" the stage might be "in some Theatrical Representations," it was "designed the School of Morality"; and "a good Play" was "an elegant Entertainment for those of the brightest and most elevated Capacities," and what really showed "the visible Decay of the Stage" and the vitiation of "general Taste" was not only that "the most eminent Citizens" were ridiculed but that the play, at its potential best "an Entertainment in which Pleasure and Instruction are blended," came to be neglected "for others, which the best that can be said about them is, that they afford some Amusement to the Senses."

There are two reasons why old and new critical objections mingled easily. One is that the dissatisfaction with entertainments which afforded "some Amusement to the Senses" only was not so new after all. Even if pantomimes, harlequinades (not to mention masquerades and other spectacles and turns which could hardly be called theatrical) became a rage from as late as the mid-twenties of the century, largely owing to the "active Feats of nimble *Lun*," i.e. John Rich, and, to some extent, to the tireless managerial experimenting of that dauntless charlatan, Heidegger, dancing on the stage and the appeal of scenic attractions had been gaining ground for a long time before. Similarly, the craze for Italian opera, whether dating from the first night of *Arsinoe* (1705) or the real break-through of the genre, Handel's *Rinaldo* (1711), had been anticipated by the growing fashion of singing in plays, or between acts, the more and more frequent appearance of Italian singers and instrumentalists on the stage and the "consort" platform, and,

[45] *A Satirical Epistle to Mr. Pope*, London, 1740, p. 7.
[46] See Notes 34, 35.

last but not least, by the "English" or "dramatic" operas performed well back in the seventeenth century. Adverse critical remarks were duly provoked and, as early as 1682, the Duke of Buckingham declared that

> ... Dances, Flutes, *Italian* Songs, and Rhime
> May keep up *sinking* Nonsense for a time.
> But that may fail, which now so much o'er-rules,
> And *Sence* no longer will *submit* to Fools.[47]

Collier himself, though "granting the *Play-House Musick* not vicious in the Composition," was suspicious of it, as "the design of it is to refresh the *Idea's* of the *Action*, ... For this Reason among others the *Tunes* are generally Airy and Gaillardizing: They are contriv'd on purpose to excite a sportive Humour, and spread a Gaiety upon the Spirits. ... This sort of Musick warms the Passions, and unlocks the Fancy, and makes it open to Pleasure like a Flower to the Sun. ... A Lewd *Play* with good Musick is like a Loadstone *Arm'd*, it draws much stronger than before ... Musick is almost as dangerous as Gunpowder; And it may be requires looking after no less than the *Press*, or the *Mint*. 'Tis possible a Publick Regulation might not be amiss."[48]

If the objections to the sensuous appeal of the stage were, in a rudimentary form, included in the early writings which elaborated more specifically the charges of immorality and profaneness, and, consequently, these objections were not chronologically new in the strict sense of the word, nor were the principles behind them essentially different from the ones which manifested themselves in the main questions of Collier's *Short View* and the pamphlets written against it or in its defence. This is the second reason why the opinions on the stage changed less than the stage itself throughout the period here surveyed. With its targets and emphases shifting, criticism continued to be essentially moral. The tide of alleged immorality and profaneness was checked and made to withdraw, however slowly; but was the flood of "sight and sound" more welcome? The dilemma critics found themselves faced with was most clearly demonstrated by the critical reception of Italian opera.

A musical play with a decent libretto, moreover, one performed in a language which the majority of the audience did not understand, could certainly not corrupt the mind, but it could not improve it either. Pleasure without instruction was aesthetically abominable because morally unwholesome: it afforded "some Amusement to the Senses" while it simply starved the mind. The better an opera was, the more strongly it appealed to the senses; its specific artistic value was, then, in an inverse ratio to its moral usefulness, whereas a straight play spoken in the mother tongue had at least the chance of combining a maximum of delight with a maximum of instruction. The "deluge of Filth" exerting its corrupting effect directly and immediately was, after all, an evil which it was easy to recognize and

[47] J. Sheffield, Duke of Buckingham and Normanby, *An Essay on Poetry* [1st ed.: *An Essay upon Poetry*, 1682], 2nd ed., London, 1691, p. 27.
[48] J. Collier, *A Short View of the Immorality and Profaneness of the English Stage.* [1st publ. 1698], 3rd ed., London, 1698, repr. in facs., München, 1967, pp. 278—279,

possible to remedy; in the long run, it was probably less damaging than "sweet stupidity" and "Italian nonsense" which threatened to replace "British sense", or "enervate" and "effeminate strains" which were a real menace to "British valour." Critics who tended to go to extremes argued that opera, a "foreign luxury," jeopardized British liberty and independence and was encouraged by the political enemies of the country abroad and at home, who intended to put the Stuart Pretender on the throne and bring Great Britain under French yoke. Also, as it was "Italian Popery," it could be instrumental in shaking the foundations of the Church of England.

That such absurd views were current enough is evident from an anonymous satire, *The Devil to Pay at St. James's* (1727), which ridiculed them *à propos* of the quarrels of the two famous Italian prima donnas, Cuzzoni and Faustina Bordoni. "God forbid I should judge amiss, yet I cannot but think there is more in this Matter than People are aware of; who knows but they are sent here to raise Dissentions among true Protestants! There are too many shrewd Causes of Suspicion.

1. They come from *Rome;*
2. The Pope lives at *Rome;*
3. So does the Pretender.
4. The Pope is a notorious Papist;
5. So is the Pretender,
6. So is Madam *Faustina,*
7. And so is Madam *Cuzzoni.*
8. King *George* (God bless him) is a Protestant;
9. The Papists hate the Protestants;
10. The Pope hates King *George;*
11. The Pretender can't abide him.
12. But Madam *Cuzzoni* and *Madam Faustina,* love the Pope, and in all Probability the Pretender.

"From whence I infer, that it is not safe to have Popish Singers tolerated here, in *England;* but on the contrary, it would be a great Security to the Protestant Interest to have a Clause added to some Act of Parliament, obliging all Foreign Singers, Dancers and Tumblers, to abjure the Devil, the Pope, and the Pretender, before they appear in Publick."[49]

Incidentally, with all its satirical exaggeration, this sounds hardly more absurd than the absolutely serious reference, already quoted from the *Proposals for a National Reformation of Manners* (1694), to "one grand design of those *Priests* and *Jesuits,* who adhere to the *French Interest,* to introduce and keep up these Publick *Play-Houses* on purpose," among others to "*Mollifie and Effeminate the English Valour,* that we may be broken in pieces when our Martial Neig[h]bour Nation shall Invade us."[50]

Criticism of Italian opera, even at its most vitriolic or extreme, lacked the genuine polemic heat characteristic of many writings produced in the Collier controversy, because the anti-opera campaign was carried on practi-

[49] *The Devil to Pay at St. James's . . .*, London, 1727, 99. 4—5.
[50] See Note 12.

98

cally with no one to oppose it and turn it into a real controversy. The "operatic party" gave the genre financial and administrative support, mainly
through the Royal Academy of Music organized for the purpose, but the
charges against Italian opera were left very largely unanswered. Written
expressions of sympathy came in the form of occasional remarks made
privately, in letters exchanged between ladies or gentlemen of quality,
amateurs who complained of the vicious taste of the town which would not
tolerate such a polite entertainment; but public writers did not set their
hearts on vindicating Italian opera. While opinions were very much divided
over the charges of immorality and profaneness, critics of Italian opera
were a solid body united by their hostility towards the genre, and the
principles which they shared and put into practice with relatively few individual differences.

The Tatler and The Spectator which contributed little to the Collier controversy (Steele's sallies against Etherege and Ravenscroft being the most
notable instances) rarely missed an opportunity to attack or ridicule the
absurdities of Italian opera, a genre as incompatible with common sense
as with the British genius and very much inferior to spoken drama.[51]
What these periodicals were doing in their casual and urbane fashion had
been done by Dennis, more systematically and more violently, in An Essay
on the Opera's After the Italian Manner, which are about to be Establish'd on
the English Stage: With some Reflections on the Damage which they may bring
to the Publick (1706) some arguments of which were to reappear in his An
Essay upon Publick Spirit (1711).

If it may appear strange to see Steele and Addison joining forces, even
though not in a formal alliance, with Dennis whose relationship with both
was far from amicable, it is not less strange to see Dennis in agreement,
concerning the dangers of music, with Collier, Bedford, and Law whom he
opposed so fiercely over the alleged immorality and profaneness of the
stage. But, divided as they were over the issues of that controversy, it
has to be emphasized again, what Dennis and other supporters of the drama
never failed to emphasize, that they were vindicating the stage as a potential
school of virtue, and not the undeniable abuses of it; and though they came
to different conclusions they were convinced as much as the opposite party
that the stage, as indeed art in general, was to unite entertainment with
instruction, and that entertainment without instruction was morally unwholesome. The reason why this fundamental principle was more evident
in the anti-opera campaign was that it was generally accepted not only on
the highest, theoretical level, but it was interpreted and applied much the
same way on the lower, practical levels as well. Critics, as a rule, demanded
from an opera the kind of "reasonable" delight which only a play could
have given, and, not getting it, blamed the genre for their own error.

[51] It should be noted that Addison himself had made an unlucky effort with Rosa-
mond (1707), to defeat Italian opera by anglicizing it. For more details on the critical
reception of Italian opera in England, and the importance of The Tatler and The
Spectator in this respect, see chiefly, F. Montgomery, "Early Criticism of Italian
Opera in England," Musical Quarterly, 15 (1929), pp. 415—425, A. E. Betz, "The
Operatic Criticism of the Tatler and Spectator," Musical Quarterly, 31 (1945), pp.
318—330, K. G. Ruttkay, "The English Critical Reception of Italian Opera in the
Early Eighteenth Century," Studies in English and American Philology, Vol. I.,
ed. by L. Kéry and N. J. Szenczi, Budapest, 1971, pp. 93—169.

Even those who had had their brief spells of flirtation with Italian opera in the early phase of the fashion turned against it sooner or later. Aaron Hill who had had an important share in the production of Handel's epoch-making *Rinaldo* in 1711 came to hold a contemptuous opinion of the genre.

> Near opera's fribling fugues, what muse can stay?
> Where wordless warblings winnow *thought*, away!
> Music, when *purpose* points her not the road,
> Charms, to betray, and softens, to *corrode*.
> Empty of sense, the soul-reducing art
> Thrills a slow poison to the sick'ning heart.
> Soft sinks *idea*, dissolute in ease,
> And all life's feeble lesson is, to *please*.[52]

And it was Hill who urged Handel to free the British people from their "Italian bondage"[53] by setting dramatically sound English librettos, thus creating a new kind of English dramatic opera, which Handel formally never did, though he more than met the demand in his English oratorios which gave full scope to his dramatic genius.

Incidentally there had been repeated efforts to create an English variety of Italian opera. John Hughes who was exceptionally lenient towards Italian opera and did not share "the Opinion of those who impute" the encouragement "given to *Italian* Musick, to an Affectation of every thing that is Foreign," wrote the words of *Calypso and Telemachus* (1712) as "an Essay for the Improvement of Theatrical Musick in the *English* Language, after the model of the Italians"; but even he protested that it "cou'd never have been the Intention of those, who first promoted the *Italian Opera*, that it shou'd take the intire Possession of our Stage, to the Exclusion of every thing of the like kind, which might be produc'd here." He did not subscribe to the "late Opinion . . ., that *English* Words are not proper for Musick." Admitting that "the *English* Language is not so soft and full of Vowels as the *Italian*," he asked "whether too great a Delicacy in this Particular may not run into Effeminacy?" — making a point, in the form of a tentative question, which was often made by hostile critics in the form of a definite charge. Admitting that "the Success of Entertainments of this kind depends chiefly on the Musick, and that it is not natural to expect any thing exact in the writing," he nevertheless insisted that these "Dramatical Entertainments . . . shou'd be perform'd in a Language understood by the Audience,"[54] which shows that even a most sympathetic and understanding person like Hughes could not entirely free himself from certain habits of thinking derived from traditional criticism which recognized the spoken drama as the legitimate form of stage entertainment.

In social terms, the marked division into friends and foes of Italian opera showed a distinct though not simple class pattern: it was in taste, not

---

[52] A. Hill, "The Tears of the Muses". *The Works of the late Aaron Hill*, London, 1753, Vol. IV., pp. 175—176.
[53] In a letter written to Handel, on Dec. 5th, 1732, *op. cit.*, Vol. I., pp. 115—116.
[54] John Hughes, Preface to *Calypso and Telemachus. An Opera* (1712). John Hughes, *Poems on Several Occasions*, London, 1745, Vol. II., pp. 11—15.

necessarily in birth as well, that the former could be called aristocratic and the latter middle-class. The division and its social implications were strongly felt by contemporaries of the Italian fashion. When, in December 1707, it was arranged that "the House in the *Hay-Market* should be taken up wholly for *Opera's*, and that in *Drury-Lane* for Plays," John Oldmixon's periodical, *The Muses Mercury*, commented: "Perhaps the Distance of the House in the *Hay-Market* from the Scene of Business in the City was to its Disadvantages: For 'tis very certain, that a very good part of the Audience for *Plays* came from that Part of the Town, where Mr. Collier's Arguments prevail'd most. As for *Opera's*, the Expence of that Diversion is a little too great for such as declare for exact Oeconomy; and as the *Great* chiefly encourage them, they are now nearer than ever to their Protectors."[55]

Time seems to have brought no considerable change: Italian opera continued to exert the same limited appeal, as is testified by a passage from another periodical, Ambrose Philips's *The Free-Thinker*, written more than ten years after the one just quoted. "*Operas* are a very elegant Diversion; but more confined in *England*, by reason of the Expence required to support them; and, because the People are not, so universally, prepared to understand the Language of Musick, as they are to apprehend Expressions of Wit and Sense: Therefore, amongst us, Operas cannot, yet, be so properly accounted Publick Shews, as Entertainments for a Select Audience."[56]

No doubt, opera was an expensive entertainment, but this alone was not sufficient to make it an exclusive diversion of "the Great"; after all, the "moneyed men" could have afforded to support it if they had found its delights worth their money. Nor is it likely that money, or rather the lack of money, was solely responsible for the decline in the quality of straight plays, as was suggested, again in *The Muses Mercury:* "If Plays were bad, 'twas chiefly because there was but a bad Price paid for them, and the Poets cou'd not be at the Expence of much Thought, at the Rate their Poems went off at. Half the Encouragement given to them, which has been given to such as are concern'd in the Performance of Opera's, wou'd have produc'd Plays that shou'd always have pleas'd. For we have no Reason to doubt, but there are Genius's now living who are qualify'd to succeed as well as their Predecessors: And by *Succeed*, we do not mean to *Take*, but to *Deserve*."[57] Half a year later, however, the same column of the same periodical sounded less hopeful: "As for *Comedies*, there's no great Expectation of any thing of that kind, since Mr. *Farquhar*'s Death. The two Gentlemen who would probably always succeed in the Comick Vein, Mr. *Congreve* and Capt. *Steel* [sic], having Affairs of much greater Importance to take up their Time and Thoughts. And unless the *Players* write themselves, the Town must wait for Comedy till another *Genius* appears."[58]

Linking Congreve's name with Steele's was correct in so far only as neither the one nor the other was active at the time as a comic dramatist; but even

[55] *The Muses Mercury*, Vol. I. No. 12., Dec., 1707, pp. 287—288. Cf. Loftis, *op. cit.*, pp. 11—14.
[56] *The Free-Thinker*, No. 68., Nov. 14, 1718. In vol. form: Vol. I., London, 1722, p. 89.
[57] *The Muses Mercury*, Vol. I., No. 3., March, 1707, p. 76.
[58] *Ibid.*, Vol. I., No. 9., Sep., 1707, p. 218. In Vol. I., No. 5., May, 1707, p. 124., the obituary tribute paid to Farquhar in the same column ended: "And such as love to laugh at the *Theater* [sic], will probably miss him more than they now imagine."

this was a merely formal coincidence of negative factors, and otherwise there was nothing in their respective careers to justify any parallel between the two writers. They could easily pass for the representatives of two generations, even of two centuries, which they were not by dates, since Steele, born in 1672, was only two years younger than Congreve, and both died in the same year, 1729. But while Steele made his name after 1700 with *The Christian Hero* (1701) and three comedies written in rapid succession, *The Funeral* (1701), *The Lying Lover* (1703), and *The Tender Husband* (1705), and he abandoned the stage to return to it with *The Conscious Lovers* (1722) after an interval of seventeen years during which he was far from inactive, busying himself with "Affairs of much greater Importance" indeed, and emerging as a major public writer of the early eighteenth century, Congreve had produced all his important works by the turn of the century, after which time he withdrew more and more both from the stage and all forms of public activity, literary or otherwise, and lived at ease as a gentleman, turning out, every now and then, bits of elegant verse, but the reputation he enjoyed in the world of letters until his death was a reputation earned with the works he had written by 1700.

Not that the two were enemies, the one entering full tilt the field of literature and the other finding it advisable to retreat before him in order to avoid a confrontation. On the contrary, Steele and Congreve were nearest to each other when the former was about to take up writing as a career and the latter was about to exchange it for a gentleman's life. About this time the atmosphere of Will's coffee-house, the haunt of Dryden, was not less congenial to Steele than to Congreve; and when a number of wits belonging to that circle joined, under Tom Brown's leadership, to revenge themselves on Sir Richard Blackmore, the "city bard" who had dared to publish *A Satyr Against Wit* (1700), Steele participated in the action, while, strangely enough, Congreve did not.[59] And the production of *The Way of the World* (1700), Congreve's last and best comedy, which was rather coolly received at first, was an occasion for Steele to pay his tribute to the "great author" who, at a time "When pleasure's falling to the low delight,/ In the vain joys of the uncertain sight," and when "rude spectators" knew no "sense of wit . . . But in distorted gesture, farce and show," dared "to write only to the few refined." And:

> Yet tho' that nice Ambition you pursue,
> 'Tis not in *Congreve*'s Power to please but few.
> Implicitly devoted to his Fame,
> Well-dres'd barbarians know his awful Name
> Tho' senseless they're of Mirth, but when they laugh,
> As they feel Wine, but when, 'till drunk, they quaff.[60]

[59] Blackmore's satire appeared as printed in 1700, but it came out, most probably, late in 1699. The wits replied with *Commendatory Verses, on the Author of the Two Arthurs, and the Satyr against Wit* (1700). Another writer whose participation was at least as strange as Steele's is Dennis. Both he and Steele came to hold, shortly after this episode, views which were not alien to Blackmore, and the two were becoming more respectful of his person, if not necessarily admirers of his poetry.

[60] R. Steele, "To Mr. Congreve, Occasion'd by his Comedy called »The Way of the World«." The Occasional Verse of Richard Steele, ed. R. Blanchard, Oxford, 1952, p. 12.

In his judgment of the audience, Steele voiced an opinion similar to Congreve's who printed the play with a dedication to the Earl of Montague, in which he worked off his resentment for the near-failure of *The Way of the World* in a subtly ironic way. "That it succeeded on the stage, was almost beyond my expectation; for but little of it was prepared for that general taste which seems now to be predominant in the palates of our audience." He detached himself not only from the audience for whom the play was evidently too good but from the majority of writers as well. "It is only by the countenance of your Lordship, and the *few* so qualified, that such who write with care and pains can hope to be distinguished: for the prostituted name of *poet* promiscuously levels all that bear it."[61]

Was Congreve's fastidiousness (shared, as we have seen, by Steele also) a display of aristocratism? Was the audience not fit to appreciate his play, because it was becoming increasingly middle-class, or, at least, markedly heterogeneous? Were the "rude spectators" and "well-dressed barbarians" mentioned by Steele, tradesmen with low tastes? It would be tempting to believe that the case was as simple as e.g. W. D. Taylor makes it out to have been, saying: "Farce, ballad-plays, pantomime, dancers, performing animals of all kinds, became immensely popular even in the regular theatres — perhaps because of the new audience, the honest citizens and their wives, who now thronged them." But the authority he quotes in his own support, happens to give evidence to the contrary. "Colley Cibber says of the patentee of Drury Lane in 1707: 'His point was to please the majority, who could more easily comprehend any thing they saw, than the daintiest things that could be said to them.' "[62] It is significant that Cibber spoke of "a majority" without even hinting that this was made up of "the honest citizens and their wives," as, indeed, it was not. Nicoll seems to be on safe ground when he says: "It must not be presumed, of course, that the audience, suddenly and in a few years, changed entirely its character, or that even in the last portion of this period [i.e. 1700—1750] the atmosphere of the theatres was middle class rather than aristocratic. If anything, the air of eighteenth-century London was more "fashionable" than it had been before; and only too many of the richer middle class aped the manners and the vices of the People of Quality. All that can be said is that the body of spectators was larger than it had been, that the middle classes were growing in importance and power, and that the close connection between Court and theatre was for ever shattered."[63] And again: "The theatre was midway between two extremes. It was not universal as in Shakespeare's time, and it was not aristocratic as in the time of the Restoration; it was merely fashionable."[64]

If this was the case throughout the period surveyed, it would be illogical to conclude from Congreve's and Steele's remarks, *à propos* of the reception of the play, that it was a puritanic, middle-class audience that failed to respond sympathetically on the first night of *The Way of the World*, in 1700. Indeed, the increasing demand for spectacle, referred to by Steele, could not be blamed on people who came "from that Part of the Town, where Mr.

[61] W. Congreve, *The Way of the World*, [1700]. In G. H. Nettleton—A. E. Case (eds.)، *British Dramatists from Dryden to Sheridan*, Boston, 1939, p. 309.
[62] Taylor, *op. cit.*, p. IX.
[63] Nicoll, *A History of English Drama 1660—1900*, vol. II., p. 8.
[64] *Ibid.*, p. 11.

103

Collier's Arguments prevail'd most.''[65] On the contrary, the more consistently middle-class these spectators were in their manners, morals, tastes and demands, the more they rejected the merely sensuous pleasures which the rapidly developing "show business" of the early eighteenth century afforded, as we have seen. And even if there were spectators at the theatre who were "honest citizens" by their social status, some or perhaps many of these were *nouveaux riches* in their habits and aped, as Nicoll has suggested, "the manners and vices of the People of Quality," merely following, not setting, the fashion. An ironic comment in Aaron Hill's periodical, *The Plain Dealer*, can be quoted to show where contemporaries looked for the social root of this particular evil: "Who does not observe, That *Dancing of Jigs, Masquerades, and Sarabands*, are Improvements in Learning, which the happy Genius of our *Nobility*, and the vast Encouragement they give to *Wit*, have brought, already, to their full Perfection?''[66]

The Way of the World very nearly failed, because it was too subtle not only for the minority of the audience who went to see a play expressly to draw a positive moral from it, but for the majority as well, the habitual play-goers who had been used to, and demanded, the "immorality and profaneness" of the traditional comedies of manners, including Congreve's own earlier plays. That the difference between *The Way of the World* on the one hand, and *The Old Bachelor* (1693), *The Double-Dealer* (1694), and *Love for Love* (1695) on the other, was considerable, the author himself knew and admitted; he even prided himself on it, though not, perhaps, without some misgivings. In the dedication to the Earl of Montague, already quoted, he referred to "Terence, the most correct writer in the world" who had "great advantages to encourage his undertakings; for he built most on the foundations of Menander: ... and Menander had no less light in the formation of his characters from the observations of Theophrastus, of whom he was a disciple; and Theophrastus, it is known, was not only a disciple, but the immediate successor of Aristotle, the first and greatest judge of poetry. These were great models to design by; and the further advantage which Terence possessed, towards giving his plays the due ornaments of purity of style, and justness of manners, was not less considerable from the freedom of conversation, which he was permitted him with Laelius and Scipio, two of the greatest and most polite men of his age. And indeed, the privilege of such a conversation is the only certain means of attaining to the perfection of dialogue." The real point, without which this theoretical and historical digression would have been somewhat out of place in a dedication, was made in the sequel, where Congreve drew a parallel: "If it has happened in any part of this comedy, that I have gained a turn of style, or expression more correct, or at least more corrigible, than in those which I have formerly written, I must, with equal pride and gratitude, ascribe it to the honour of your Lordship's admitting me into your conversation, and that of a society where everybody else was well worthy of you, in your retirement last summer from the town; for it was immediately after that this comedy was written. If I have failed in my performance, it is only to be regretted, where there

[65] See Note 55.
[66] *The Plain Dealer*, No. 59, Oct. 12, 1724. In vol. form: London, 1730, vol. II., p. 16.

were so many, not inferior either to a Scipio or a Laelius, that there should be one wanting equal to the capacity of a Terence."[67]

The differences between *The Way of the World* and the author's earlier comedies were not merely stylistic. Congreve himself may have been aware that while he was advocating an ideal of correctness which he derived from antiquity, namely Terence's practice and, ultimately, Aristotle's theory of the drama, he kept an eye on his formidable contemporary, Jeremy Collier also, whom it was, indeed, difficult to ignore at the critical stage the comedy of manners had reached by the turn of the century. The comic dramatist of the period could do two things: he could either take the line of least resistance and revert to farce, or to turn genteel. The ironic Prologue to *The Way of the World* shows that Congreve declined to do the first and was only half willing to do the second.

> Some plot we think he [i.e. the author] has, and some new
>   thought;
> Some humour too, no farce; but that's a fault.
> Satire, he thinks, you ought not to expect;
> For so reformed a town who dares correct?
> To please, this time, has been his sole pretence,
> He'll not instruct, lest it should give offence.[68]

The Way of the World seems to have been the maximum of concession Congreve was willing or able to make; at least this can be logically concluded from the fact that this was his last full-length original comedy, and although he did not break all connections with the stage, his career as a dramatist ended when he was only thirty. Steele, on the other hand, whose first comedy, *The Funeral*, was produced a year after *The Way of the World*, took off from the point where Congreve had stopped. Looking back on *The Funeral*, John Hughes found "many lively Strokes of Wit and Humour" in it, but he confessed that he was "more pleas'd with the Touches of Humanity in it, than with any other Part of the Entertainment," and borrowing "*Plautus*'s own Remark," he said that "by the Representation of such Plays even *good Men may be made better*."[69] His chief concern, however, was not with the play itself but with the concept of comedy which the play exemplified, and that is why his criticism is of special theoretical interest. Admitting that if "ever Mirth can lay claim to a full Scope and Indulgence, it is in the Business of Comedy," he maintained "that a Comick Poet who shou'd only propose to himself the raising of Laughter, whatever might be his Success in that, wou'd be a wretched Writer. It is this that has given occasion to distinguish such low Performances by the name of *Farce*." The fact that he rejected farce as "low", did not imply that he approved of the comedy of manners as "high": in fact, he seems to have been so much opposed to any kind of laughing comedy that he did not care to distinguish between the two. When he disclaimed "the lively Jest, the smart Repartee, or the

---

[67] Nettleton—Case, *op. cit.*, pp. 309—310.
[68] *Ibid.*, p. 295.
[69] *The Lay-Monk.* No. 9., Dec. 4, 1713. In vol. form: *The Lay-Monastery*, 2nd ed., London, 1714, p. 57.

witty Conceit" to be essentials of comic drama, he rejected qualities which were more characteristic of the comedy of manners than of farce, and he stated that it is not these "but the natural Views of Life, the moral Painting, the Manners, the Passions, the Follies, the Singularities, and Humours; in a Word, it is the Human Heart in all its odd Variety, pleasantly represented, that makes up the elegant Entertainment of Comedy. In this the Author presents Mankind to his Audience; in the other Way of Writing he only exhibits *Himself*." What follows is of particular interest: "I was never better pleas'd than with an uncommon Observation made by a celebrated modern Writer, concerning the *Heautontimorumenos* of Terence; namely, that *in that excellent Comedy there are Passages which wou'd draw Tears from a Man of Sense, but not one that will provoke his Laughter*. I believe the Reader will not be dissatisfy'd to see this Remark further exemplify'd by Two very fine Instances, the last of which that ingenious Writer would never have mention'd. The first is an Ancient Comedy by *Plautus*, the other is a Scene in the *Funeral*, or *Grief Alamode*, by Mr. *Steele*."[70]

That celebrated modern writer was evidently Steele, anticipating in the form of a casual remark what he was to develop in more detail later in the Preface to *The Conscious Lovers*, his last and most mature play (produced in 1722 and printed the year after), a classic of comic drama turned respectably middle-class, designed "to be an innocent performance."[71] Writing in 1713, Hughes may have judged *The Funeral* in the light of Steele's later works, in fact, all his major writings, with the one notable exception of *The Conscious Lovers* which is of a later date. But he had the rest of his comedies to form his views by, *The Lying Lover* and *The Tender Husband*, organic links between the first and the last of the author's comedies, and he could, of course, bear in mind Steele's more recent contributions to *The Tatler* and *The Spectator* which answered, but for their form, Hughes's description of "the elegant Entertainment of Comedy" quoted above.

A year after Hughes's *Lay-Monk* paper, Steele also looked back on an early play of his, not *The Funeral* but *The Lying Lover*, and as he did so in an *Apology for Himself* where he obviously wanted to make a point, and at a time when the moralistic trend in literature had become dominant, he probably found it difficult not to overstate his case. To show how far he had carried the "Inclination to the Advancement of Virtue," pursuing it "even in things the most indifferent, and which, perhaps, have been thought foreign to it," he referred to *The Lying Lover*, quoting passages from its Preface in which he had declared, as early as 1703, his belief that "it would be an honest Ambition to attempt a Comedy, which might be no improper Entertainment in a Christian Common-wealth." From the same Preface he quoted another important statement concerning the anguish and sorrow expressed in one of the episodes of the play, which "are perhaps an Injury to the Rules of Comedy, but I am sure they are a Justice to those of Morality." Moreover, he did something in his *Apology* that he had not done in the Preface: he paid his tribute to Collier in person. "Mr. *Collier* had, about the Time wherein this [i.e. *The Lying Lover*] was published, written against the Immorality of the Stage. I was (as far as I durst for fear

[70] *Ibid.*, pp. 53—54.
[71] R. Steele, *The Conscious Lovers*, (1723). The Preface. In Nettleton—Case, *op. cit.*, p. 439.

of witty Men, upon whom he had been too severe) a great Admirer of his Work, and took it into my Head to write a Comedy in the Severity he required." And he went so far in his own defence as to say: "I can't tell . . . what they would have me do to prove me a Churchman; but I think I have appeared one even in so trifling a Thing as a Comedy: And considering me as a Comick Poet, I have been a Martyr and Confessor for the Church; for this Play was damn'd for its Piety."[72]

The rapid development of a waggish and rakish young wit of Will's into a martyr for the church and morality must be highly interesting for a biographer of Steele: it is, however, no less interesting as an illustration in a particular phase in the history of English drama. Indeed, taking the path Steele actually did take appears to have been inevitable, but less so for reasons of his own than for the pressure of historical coincidences brought to bear on comedy. Similarly illustrative is the activity of Colley Cibber who started acting and writing for the stage before the publication of Collier's *Short View*, at a time when the Restoration tradition of the comedy of manners was still strong, but there were signs to warn a man of Cibber's practical sense that this tradition could not be carried on long with impunity. In 1696, two years before the publication of Collier's first anti-stage pamphlet, he "amazed audiences . . . with *Love's Last Shift*, a comedy in which the rakish hero is strikingly reclaimed by his faithful wife,"[73] and continuing to work in this vein, he contributed substantially to the establishment and development of the genre which is variously called the comedy of sensibility, sentimental, genteel, domestic, or, sociologically speaking, bourgeois comedy.

Farquhar, another dramatist who started under strong Restoration influences, even after Collier had launched his attack, also proceeded towards greater decency and gentility, getting farthest in his last play, *The Beaux' Stratagem* (1707), where he exploited certain stock situations of the comedy of manners in a way which was by no means traditional, causing, for instance, his unscrupulous hero to have a guilty conscience and turn honest at the critical moment, foreshadowing, as it were, the attitude of Fielding's Tom Jones;[74] or allowing an ill-treated wife to escape from her matrimonial distress into divorce, not adultery as had been the rule with Restoration dramatists.

"Sympathy, not with the characters on the stage, but as exemplified in their own actions; the relating of art to life; the return to a highly artificial love of natural scenery and rural landscape; and the deliberate enunciation of a moral or social problem — these appear the commonest features of the sentimental comedy in the early years," says Nicoll, adding: "Sentimentality of this type is a distinctly English development," and though

---

[72] *Mr. Steele's Apology for Himself and his Writings; Occasioned by his Expulsion from the House of Commons*, (1714). In R. Steele, *Tracts and Pamphlets*, ed. Rae Blanchard, Baltimore. 1944. pp. 311—312.

[73] P. A. W. Collins, "Restoration Comedy." In B. Ford (ed.), *The Pelican Guide to English Literature*, vol. 4., *From Dryden to Johnson*, repr., Hammondsworth, 1968, p. 160. — Congreve said, "it has a great many things in it that are like wit, that in reality are not wit." Quoted in the notes to *The Complete Works of William Congreve* ed. M. Summers, (1924), repr. New York, 1964, Vol. I., p. 78.

[74] See Taylor, *op. cit.*, p. XVIII.

he discovers traces of it in the early seventeenth century and finds it present even in the late Restoration period, he emphasizes the importance of "the dramatists of the reign of Anne" who brought this type of sentimentalism "several steps forward". Originally an English speciality, sentimental comedy did not remain limited to England. "French playwrights, seeking for novelty, seized upon Steele and Cibber, and, from imitations of English sentimental dramas, came to elaborate a still more philosophic, tearful, pathetic comedy — the *comédie larmoyante* — which in its turn crossed the Channel to influence deeply the dramatic writers of the later eighteenth century."[75]

It was not without any opposition, though, that sentimental comedy came into its own. What Steele said in his *Apology* with reference to some of the emotions presented in *The Lying Lover*, namely that they were "perhaps an Injury to the Rules of Comedy, but . . . a Justice to those of Morality," was not only a rhetoric device; it was generally true of sentimental comedy which really did offend against the established rules of comedy. The question was whether the moral profit offered was acceptable as a compensation. Ironically enough, it was John Dennis again who was loudest in deprecating the new dramatic fashion. Not that anything could have been more welcome to him, as a moralist, than a play which advertised virtue; but while he was an ardent propagandist of the view that moral instruction was indispensable in a work of art, he was as staunch an upholder of the rules which were to be observed in the composition of that particular work of art. Being temperamentally militant, a born controversialist, he was in his element when he had someone or something to disagree with, and he was ready to put up a fight over partial differences of opinion with people whose other views he essentially shared. His vindication of the stage against Collier is a case in point, and so is his opposition to the comedy of sensibility.

In one of his diatribes against Colley Cibber, Dennis called him "a certain vile Scribbler for the House in *Drury-Lane*, who is an errant Mountebank; not only for railing at the Rules, but for Metamorphosing Tragedy into Comedy, and Comedy into Tragedy." The sequel is, of course, ironical, with the reference to Cibber's tragedies "the Language of which is peculiarly adapted to excite Laughter" and his comedies which "perform the Effect of Tragedy: He never offers at a Jest, but the very offer at it moves a Terror; and 'tis no sooner out, but it moves a Compassion."[76] Even in the ironical context, the charge that Cibber was metamorphosing tragedy into comedy and *vice versa*, sounds genuine. In some ways this was precisely what the comedy of sensibility had achieved; and to one who venerated the rules as Dennis did, mixing the "kinds" was a sin. However, he venerated the rules not because they were hallowed by the authority of critics ancient and modern, but because he was convinced that the rules worked, and that the writer who violated them weakened the effect of his work and, by doing so, defeated his own end, the end of all art, which was to join a maximum of instruction with a maximum of delight. With reference to *The Conscious Lovers* he said that "the Force of any kind of Writing consists chiefly in

[75] Nicoll, *A History of English Drama 1660—1900*, vol. II., pp. 179—180.
[76] Dennis, *The Characters and Conduct of Sir John Edgar, . . .* , (1720), Hooker, vol. II, p. 199.

that which distinguishes it from all other Kinds. Now the Ridicule being that which distinguishes Comedy from every other kind of Poetry, the *Comick Force* must consist in that."[77] He had no use for comedy without real comic characters (which sentimental comedy at its best necessarily was), feeling that much of the potential moral profit was lost. In his *Letters on Milton and Wycherley* he explicity stated that "as 'tis the Business of a Comick Poet to correct those Irregularities and Extravagancies of Men's Tempers which make them uneasie to themselves, and troublesome and vexatious to one another, for that very Reason, your witty Fools are very just Subjects of Comedy, because they are more troublesome and shocking in Conversation to Men of Sense, than any other sort of Fools whatsoever."[78]

By Dennis's standards the comedy of sensibility was, then, no comedy. In a particularly revealing passage he defined his own concept of comedy in contrast to the practice of the writers of sentimental comedies, Steele in especial. "How little do they know of the Nature of true Comedy, who believe that its proper Business is to set us Patterns for Imitation: For all such Patterns are serious Things, and Laughter is the Life, and the very Soul of Comedy. 'Tis its proper Business to expose Persons to our View, whose Views [probably: Vices] we may shun, and whose Follies we may despise; and by shewing us what is done upon the Comick Stage, to shew us what ought never to be done upon the Stage of the World."[79] But even though he was a great admirer of antiquity, it was not in the classical comedy of ancient Greece or Rome that he found his idea embodied. He found the type of comedy which answered his description of the genre nearer in time and nearer home. He maintained that "as 'tis the Business of a Comick poet to cure his Spectators of Vice and Folly, by the Apprehension of being laugh'd at; 'tis plain that his Business must be with the reigning Follies and Vices. The violent Passions, which are the Subjects of Tragedy, are the same in every Age, and appear with the same Face; but those Vices and Follies, which are the Subjects of Comedy, are seen to vary continually: Some of those that belonged to our Ancestors, have no Relation to us; ... What Vices and Follies may infect those who are to come after us, we know not; 'tis the present, the reigning Vices, and Follies, that must be the Subjects of our present Comedy: The Comick Poet therefore must take Characters from such Persons as are his Contemporaries, and are infected with the foresaid Follies and Vices."[80] The type of comedy which met these demands was, of course, the comedy of manners.

Dennis's insistence on the contemporary nature of comedy meant that its subject matter and characters were changing with time, the "reigning Follies and Vices" of one generation being different from those of another. He could have been expected to say that this was the playwright's concern only, and that the critic's standards to judge a comedy by were unchanged, because so were the rules which the dramatist was to observe in making up the topical raw material into a finished play. Contrary to expectations, however, Dennis seems to have come to the conclusion that the concept of

[77] Dennis, *Remarks on The Conscious Lovers*, (1723), Hooker, vol. II, p. 261.
[78] Dennis, *Letters on Milton and Wycherley* (1721—1722), Hooker, vol. II, p. 233.
[79] Dennis, *Defence of Sir Fopling Flutter*, (1722), Hooker, vol. II. p. 245.
[80] *Ibid.*, p. 248.

comedy also was subject to change, and critics would do well to take it into consideration. This is not to say that Dennis had an elaborate theory of historical criticism which he applied consistently. Consistency was, after all, not one of his virtues, as indeed it could not well be since he was engaged in controversy all his life, compelled to act on the spur of the moment in order to score a hit. On occasion, and for practical, tactical purposes, however, he could be as modern and flexible as he could be rigidly dogmatic and old-fashioned. Whatever his motives might be, he certainly gave a fine instance of how the historical point of view should be applied, when he gave a blow to the idea of 'genteel comedy', defending Etherege and rebuking Steele at the same time. Talking of *The Man of Mode, or, Sir Fopling Flutter*, Etherege's play, which Steele never ceased to disparage, he said: "either Sir *George Etheridge* [sic] did design to make this a genteel Comedy, or he did not. If he did not design it, what is it to the Purpose, whether 'tis a genteel Comedy, or not? Provided that 'tis a good one: For I hope, a Comedy may be a good one, and yet not a genteel one. The *Alchimist* is an admirable Comedy, and yet it is not a genteel one. We may say the same of *The Fox*, and *The silent Woman*, and of a great many more. But if Sir *George* did design to make it a genteel one, he was oblig'd to adapt it to that Notion of Gentility, which he knew very well, that the World at that Time had, and we see he succeeded accordingly. For it has pass'd for a very genteel Comedy, for fifty Years together. Could it be expected that the admirable Author, should accommodate himself, to the wrong headed Notions of a would be Critick, who was to appear fifty Years after the first Acting of his Play: A Critick, who writes Criticism, as Men commit Treason or Murder, by the Instigation of the Devil himself, whenever the old Gentleman owes the Knight a Shame?"[81]

Ironically enough, no sooner had Dennis charged Steele with using the critical standards of one period for a product of another, than he himself committed the same blunder, except that he committed it the other way round. Looking forward, with malicious eagerness, to the production of *The Conscious Lovers*, and knowing well what he might and might not expect from it, he declared: "Whenever *The Fine Gentleman* [the provisional title of Steele's play] . . . comes upon the Stage, I shall be glad to see that it has all the shining Qualities which recommend Sir *Fopling*." He pretended to hope to see that Steele's "Characters are always drawn in Nature, . . . that they are the just Images of our Contemporaries, and of what we every day see in the World."[82] Characters, he said in another paragraph of the same essay, "not only ought to be drawn truly in Nature, but to be the resembling Pictures of our Contemporaries, both in Court and Town."[83] Dennis should have taken for granted the fact that Steele's contemporaries were necessarily different from Etherege's, and he should have concerned himself with what was the gist of his statement, that is to say, whether Steele's stage characters were as close replicas of his contemporaries in the reigns of Anne and George I as Etherege's had been of his own in Charles II's time. But again, as so often, Dennis was inconsistent, and instead of concentrating on this, the

[81] *Ibid.*, p. 244.
[82] *Ibid.*, p. 250.
[83] *Ibid.*, p. 245.

110

essential question, he made a point of showing that, contrary to Steele's opinion, Dorimant, in Etherege's comedy, was a fine gentleman. Even if Etherege did not design him for one, "the Character is ne'er the less excellent on that Account, because *Dorimont* [sic] is an admirable Picture of a Courtier in the Court of King *Charles* the Second. But if *Dorimont* was design'd for a fine Gentleman by the Author, he was oblig'd to accommodate himself to that Notion of a fine Gentleman, which the Court and the Town both had of a fine Gentleman at the Time of the writing of this Comedy. 'Tis reasonable to believe, that he did so, and we see that he succeeded accordingly. For *Dorimont* not only pass'd for a fine Gentleman with the Court of King *Charles* the Second, but he has pass'd for such with all the World, for Fifty Years together."[84]

What was, then, Dorimant? A "resembling Picture" of a courtier of the Restoration era, or a projection of the "Notion of a fine Gentleman" current at the time, or an embodiment of the timeless, evergreen ideal of the same? Anyway, the vindication of the character as a fine gentleman would have been pointless even if there had been no flaw in Dennis's reasoning. After all, the most memorable character of the play, the real "hero" is not Dorimont but Sir Fopling Flutter, a fact which must have been welcome to Dennis, since it was perfectly in keeping with the most important thesis of his theory of comedy. He restated this thesis in the closing paragraph of his *Defence of Sir Fopling Flutter*, saying that he would have been glad to see, among others, "that instead of setting us Patterns for our Imitation, which is not the proper Business of *Comedy*, he [i.e. Steele] makes those Follies and Vices ridiculous, which we ought to shun and despise."[85]

It might be suggested, however, that in producing their "witty fools," Restoration dramatists were not, or not only, showing their skill at contemporary portraiture, hitting off "just Images" and "resembling Pictures" of models whom they could daily meet "in Court and Town," but were observing the current "Notion" of the "witty fool." That is to say, they, too, were setting patterns, except that these were negative patterns, ideals in reverse.

It is difficult to tell how far the idea that moral improvement could and should be achieved by means of presenting examples to the contrary, was a real motive behind the comedy of manners or just a handy excuse for its immorality and profaneness, worked into a theoretical thesis by people like Dennis. He, for one, seems to have been sincerely convinced of the truth of this thesis which he reiterated times without number both in defence of the comedy of manners and as an argument against the comedy of sensibility. In principle Steele and Dennis agreed that comedy, as all art, should instruct and delight at the same time; otherwise they were wide apart. The indirect method of instruction was unacceptable to Steele not so much in Dennis's theoretical presentation as in Etherege's actual practice of it. In one of his *Spectator* papers Steele said: "It cannot be denied, but that the Negligence of every thing, which engages the Attention of the sober and valuable Part of Mankind, appears very well drawn in this Piece," but he did not see Etherege's excellence in presenting vice as a

[84] *Ibid.*, pp. 244—245.
[85] *Ibid.*, p. 250.

subtle and effective means to a moral end. On the contrary, he damned this "whole celebrated Piece" as "a perfect Contradiction to good Manners, good Sense, and common Honesty," and found "nothing in it but what is built upon the Ruin of Virtue and Innocence."[86]

In less than a month's time Dennis's *Defence of Sir Fopling Flutter*, which was as much an attack on Steele as a vindication of Etherege, was answered by Benjamin Victor, a friend of Steele's who published *An Epistle to Sir Richard Steele, on His Play, Call'd, The Conscious Lovers*. In this Victor expressed his view which was Steele's also, putting the rhetorical question: "Is it possible . . . that *De—s* can be so void of Shame to attempt to prove, that vicious Characters is the only Business of Comedy, and that their corrupt Examples have the same design'd Effect upon the Audience as a virtuous honourable Character."[87]

But this was, essentially, not a rhetorical question, nor was it as simple as Victor would have it. A play which chose to ridicule fools and scoundrels baffled in their silly hopes or vicious designs, and another which guided nice people, possibly through agonies and dignified suffering, to a well-deserved happy ending (a feature meant to make the play a comedy) instructed *and* pleased differently. Provided, of course, that they did, which depended less on the motives professed by or attributed, more or less legitimately, to the authors, than on the dispositions of critics and audiences to respond in one way or another. Dennis's and Steele's controversy over the concept of comedy hinged not only on their respective views concerning the relative moral utility of the techniques of direct and indirect instruction, but as much, if not more, on their variance on the point of "delight," the aesthetic, dramaturgical and psychological effects and all other features coming under the heading, which were, of course, not separable from the possible edifying value of the plays. Their differences were, primarily, not temperamental; the whole affair was not a personal combat between two idiosyncratic writers but a clash of an older and a younger man of letters who stood for two generations, two schools of taste.

Not content with the attack he had made on *The Conscious Lovers* in advance, Dennis followed up the production of the play with his *Remarks* on it, a longer and more elaborate pamphlet than its predecessor had been. Among others, he took issue with two of Steele's propositions which were of particular importance to the comedy of sensibility. "When Sir *Richard* says, that anything that has its Foundation in Happiness and Success must be the Subject of Comedy, he confounds Comedy with that Species of Tragedy which has a happy Catastrophe. When he says, that 'tis an Improvement of Comedy to introduce a Joy too exquisite for Laughter, he takes all Care that he can to shew, that he knows nothing of the Nature of Comedy." Steele, Dennis said, "seems not to know that Joy, generally taken, is common like Anger, Indignation, Love, to all Sorts of Poetry, to the Epick, the Dramatick, the Lyrick: but that that kind of Joy which is attended with Laughter, is the Characteristick of Comedy; as Terror or Compassion, according as one or the other is predominant, makes the Characteristick of Tragedy, as Admiration does of Epick Poetry." Dennis

[86] *The Spectator*, No. 65, May 15, 1711.
[87] Quoted in Hooker, Vol. II., p. 498.

naturally agreed that "weeping upon the Sight of a deplorable Object is not a Subject for Laughter, but that 'tis agreeable to good Sense and Humanity," adding, however, that by saying so Steele "says nothing b ut what all the sensible Part of the World has already granted; but then all that sensible Part of the World have always deny'd, that a deplorable Object is fit to be shewn in Comedy." But Indiana's case he found "deplorable, and the Catastrophe downright tragical."[88]

To raise laughter was certainly not Steele's aim. As early as 1703, he had declared in the Prologue to *The Lying Lover* that "to detain th' attentive knowing Ear,/Pleasure must still have something that's severe." At the same time, he said that "He [the author] offers no gross Vices to your Sight,/Those too much Horror raise for just Delight."[89] More than ten years later, when he was patentee of Drury Lane and argued that the representation of virtuous, or at least, innocent things on the stage "will bring a new Audience to the House," he said, "This will naturally have the desired Effect, and Folly will be ridiculous without being, at the same Time, so mixed with Vice, as to make it also Terrible."[90] The absence of the terrible was not enough to make Steele's plays pass for comedies with Dennis, not only because instead of laughter they raised compassion, which was another "Characteristick of Tragedy," but also because Steele dismissed from his stage the representation of vice which was, to Dennis's mind, as indispensable in a comedy as that of folly. Insisting that comedy should instruct by negative examples, he very nearly demanded a kind of terror or horror himself, when he advertised "witty Fools," as we have seen, "because they are more troublesome and shocking to Men of Sense, than any other sort of Fools whatsoever."[91] Too much laughter might, however, absorb the shock, and as a result, folly and vice might appear simply amusing, or even attractive as Collier and other reformers suggested; or folly and vice might fail to provoke laughter and the moral shock might be submerged and lost in the far greater one given to the aesthetic sense, which was what Steele's above statements implied.

Instead of shocking people into a state of mind in which virtuous behaviour was the reasonable and, as Dennis believed, the only alternative to what was ridiculed on the stage, Steele intended to make his audiences, even through the agency of tears, emotionally malleable and susceptible to the moral beauty of the instances presented on the stage. This again was not a difference in methods only. Dennis supported the indirect technique of the comedy of manners as one which suited "Men of Sense." Steele, on the other hand, though he too spoke of "reason and good sense," used these terms in a context which modified their meaning very considerably. With reference to some incidents in his play which "are esteemed by some people no subjects of comedy," he expressed his views, already quoted, on the object of comedy, and in particular, on the "joy too exquisite for laughter," and

[88] J. Dennis, *Remarks on a Play, Call'd, The Conscious Lovers*, (1723), Hooker, Vol. II., pp. 259—260. (Slightly misquoted.)
[89] In *The Occasional Verse of Richard Steele*, ed. R. Blanchard, Oxford, 1952. p. 41.
[90] R. Steele, *Town-Talk. In a Letter to a Lady in the Country*, No. 6, Jan. 20, 1715—16. In *Richard Steele's Periodical Journalism* 1714—16, ed. R. Blanchard, Oxford, 1959. p. 232.
[91] See Note 78.

went on to say, "I must, therefore, contend that the tears which were shed on that occasion flowed from reason and good sense, and that men ought not to be laughed at for weeping till we are come to a more clear notion of what is to be imputed to the hardness of the head and the softness of the heart; and I think it was very politely said of Mr. Wilks, [the actor who played Myrtle in the first production of *The Conscious Lovers*] to one who told him there was a general [Charles Churchill] weeping for Indiana, 'I'll warrant he'll fight ne'er the worse for that. To be apt to give way to the impressions of humanity is the excellence of a right disposition and the natural working of a well-turned spirit."[92]

The general's tears and the praise he received for shedding them indicated far-reaching changes in habits and tastes and the underlying system of values. With moral sensibility becoming a fashion, the "fine gentleman" of the 1720's differed conspicuously from that of the 1670's or 80's, and the Man of Sense was giving way to another ideal, the Man of Feeling. It is difficult to tell to what extent, if any, all this was due to a direct or indirect influence of Shaftesbury's essentially un-Christian thesis that man was virtuous by nature; indeed it seems more likely that sentimental comedy and Shaftesbury's moral philosophy were parallel and simultaneous manifestations of one and the same trend. The sentimentalization of comedy was becoming pronounced about the turn of the century which was also the time when Shaftesbury started publishing his writings, and also when the controversy about the immorality of the stage began in earnest. Amusing as it would be to show the righteous Christian Collier and the deist Shaftesbury holding each a hand of the comic muse and leading her, in perfect unison though with different motives, on the path of virtue, it would be a grossly simplified presentation of facts the interrelationships of which are far too intricate to be reduced to that of cause and effect. If, nevertheless, chronological priority has to be and can be established, the demand for greater sensibility had been expressed in terms of aesthetics before Shaftesbury put a line on paper, or Collier's *Short View* appeared. And again it is Dennis who can supply a good instance.

It is true, as has been shown, that he was to defend the comedy of manners against both Collier and Steele, on aesthetic grounds and also because it appealed to "Men of Sense"; nevertheless, he had postulated some time before these controversies that passion was a criterion of poetry, a view which he was to hold throughout his life. Anticipating some of Shaftesbury's ideas in his criticism,[93] he advocated the claims of the heart, though not in comedy. As early as 1696, he had declared, that "a Poet ought always to speak to the Heart. And the greatest Wit in the World, when he ceases to do that, is a Rhimer and not a Poet. For a Poet, that he may be sure to instruct, is oblig'd to give all the Delight that he can, ... Now nothing that is not pathetick in Poetry, can very much delight: For he who is very much pleas'd, is at the same time very much mov'd; and Poetical Genius, ... is it self a Passion. A Poet then is oblig'd always to speak to the Heart. And it is for this reason, that Point and Conceit, and all that they call Wit, is to be for ever banish'd from true Poetry; because he who

[92] R. Steele, *The Conscious Lovers*. Preface. In Nettleton—Case. *op. cit.*, p. 439.
[93] See Hooker's *Introduction* in Hooker, Vol. II., pp. LXXV—LXXVI.

uses it, speaks to the Head alone. For nothing but what is simple and natural, can go to the Heart: and Nature (humanly speaking) can be touch'd by it self alone."[94] The contradiction between Dennis's insistence on passion and his utter negation of the comedy of sensibility is perhaps not so great as it appears to be. He included comedy in the category of "the less Poetry" which "is an Art by which a Poet incites less Passion," that is to say, less than in "the greater Poetry," an Art "by which a Poet justly and reasonably excites great Passion, that he may please and instruct."[95]

Dennis's criticism of the comedy of sensibility was not necessarily wrong because it remained ineffective, and the fact that the genre flourished practically unchallenged until the 1770's when Sheridan and Goldsmith restored laughter to its rights, was a sign not so much of the vitality of the genre as of the protracted crisis English comic drama, or rather English drama in general, was undergoing. Occasionally there was a comic play of a non-sentimental type which had a long run, e.g. *The Beggar's Opera*, or *Tom Thumb*. But even Gay's brilliant play, a masterpiece in its own right, which had enough vitality to score a tremendous success for itself and start a fashion for its kind, failed to revivify comic drama as a whole. Though not comparable to the concentrated attack launched on the comedy of manners thirty years earlier, the sporadic objections to its alleged destructive effect should not be ignored. They showed that the crisis of English comedy, which was a crisis of English criticism also, was not over.

The confusion of moral and aesthetic principles in criticism revealed how conflicting the demands of a heterogeneous audience were. No doubt, moralization met one of the genuine demands, but when it became excessive and exclusive, it disgusted many people who otherwise were quite willing to accept it in smaller doses and in an enjoyable mixture. A play which raised laughter by presenting virtue, without making virtue itself ridiculous, would have appealed to the moral and aesthetic sensibility of more people than one which forced a positive moral through direct instruction. This is, however, what the comic dramatists of the period could not or would not produce. Simultaneously with the long crisis of English comedy, there were achievements in non-dramatic genres which proved that this was not impossible. Sir Roger de Coverley, or later, Parson Adams, or much later, Dr Primrose, to name but three well-known varieties of the same type, who provoked smiles perhaps rather than boisterous laughter, were as unlike any of Etherege's fine gentlemen as Steele's Bevil Junior, and, incidentally, were not only more amusing but more instructive than the latter. It would be wrong to suggest that this was the only type of hero in the prose genres. Sir Charles Grandison, for instance, could have been very much at home in a comedy of sensibility. On the whole, however, the fictional kind of the moral essay, and later the novel in particular, presented the solution which could have ended the crisis of English comedy.[96] And indeed, it is significant that the laughing comedies of Sheridan and Goldsmith (the latter a novelist and playwright) were written for, and favourably received by, a novel-reading public.

[94] J. Dennis, *Remarks on a Book Entituled, Prince Arthur, an Heroick Poem* . . . (1696), Hooker, Vol. I., p. 127.
[95] Dennis, *The Grounds of Criticism in Poetry*, (1704), Hooker, Vol. I., p. 338.
[96] Cf. Loftis, *op. cit.*, p. 137.

ENGLISH POETRY IN THE AGE OF SENSIBILITY. A TYPOLOGICAL APPROACH

by

M. SZEGEDY-MASZÁK

0. PROGRAMME

The following essay is part of a "work in progress." Most of the stylistic formulae used in it have been worked out in preliminary studies published either in periodicals or in collections of essays.[1] In its final form the text will be presented as a dissertation consisting of three chapters devoted to the philosophic, aesthetic, and stylistic features of late 18th-century English poetry. This essay is a short preliminary version: the literary corpus examined is almost reduced to the material included in *The Oxford Book of Eighteenth Century Verse* (Chosen by D. N. Smith, 1926). (In the dissertation we shall deal with the poetry of Thomson, Shenstone, Johnson, Akenside, Collins, the three Wartons, Gray, Churchill, Smart, Goldsmith, Percy, Langhorne, Chatterton, Cowper, Macpherson, Crabbe, Blake, and Burns in separate sections.) Throughout all phases of the work a stylistically oriented t y p o l o g i c a l method is used.

0.1 THE ENLIGHTENMENT IN ENGLAND (1660—ca 1800)

The Enlightenment has two faces; it is the combination of two philosophical tendencies: Rationalism and Empiricism. Within the long period of the English Enlightenment three phases can be distinguished.

0.1.1 *The Restoration Age (1660—1700)*

In the forty years between (a) the opening of the theatres and (b) the death of Dryden, the failure of Congreve's last comedy, and the publication of Jeremy Collier's attack on the theatre, Empiricism and Rationalism existed side by side, neither was predominant. Some writers of the Baroque were still active (Milton, Marvell, Bunyan), what is more, Milton was writing his greatest works at this time. Yet the literature characteristic

---

[1] Csokonai: A magánossághoz (Csokonai: Ode to Solitude), *Irodalomtörténeti Közlemények*, 1969, pp. 281—90; A XVIII. századi angol irodalom a kutatás tükrében (18th-Century English Literature, A Guide to Research), *Irodalomtörténeti Közlemények* 1969, pp. 315—30; A strukturális vizsgálat alkalmazásának lehetősége az összehasonlító irodalomtudományban (Structural Approach and Comparative Literature), *Helikon*, 1970, pp. 238—50; Az angolszász és francia stilisztikai kutatások főbb irányai (Trends in Anglo-American and French Stylistics), *Helikon*, 1970, pp. 420—48; Szintakszis, metafora és zeneiség Kassák A ló meghal a madarak kirepülnek című költeményében (Syntax, Metaphor, and Music in Kassák's Autobiographic Poem) in *Formateremtő elvek a költői alkotásban* (The Dominant Elements of Poetic Form), Budapest, 1971; Az átlényegített dal (The Transformation of the Lied) in *Az el nem ért bizonyosság* (A Collection of Studies on Arany's Early Lyric), Budapest, 1972.

of the late 17th century showed a steady development towards creating a Neoclassical style, through a transition from the Baroque (Cowley, the early Dryden), making use of certain stylistic devices developed by late Renaissance (Jonson, Herrick) and Baroque (Marvell) authors. In this first phase a decidedly aristocratic literature was produced, with satire (Rochester, Dryden) and comedy (Etherege, Wycherley, Shadwell, Congreve, Vanbrugh, Farquhar) as its main genres, and Rochester, Dryden, and Congreve its best writers.

0.1.2 *The Age of Neoclassicism (1700—1740)*

In the first decades of the 18th century Rationalism seemed to gain in significance. English literature got as close to Neoclassicism as ever. That is to say, by no means so close as the French. This fact might have been an advantage for later development, but it also meant a "narrowness of mind" which even Dr Johnson admitted and even about the greatest English Neoclassicists: Swift and Pope.[2] There were many signs, the associationist theory and the activity of Shaftesbury among them, showing the way towards the next phase, the Age of Sensibility, of which the first important poem was published as early as the mid 20's, but until about the appearance of *Pamela* and the death of Pope, the typical works had been written in agreement with Neoclassical aesthetics. After 1740 this was no longer so, in spite of the fact that Dr Johnson, the most important critic, and Gray, one of the best poets of the second half of the century, tried to stick to a Neoclassical interpretation of style; Fielding, the most important Neoclassical novelist of England wrote most of his works in the middle of the century, and Smollett broke loose from the norms set by this predecessor only in his last work, *Humphry Clinker* (1771).

Neoclassicism can be taken for the culmination of a development which started in the Renaissance. In medieval literature signs used in literature were purely symbolic, i.e. they were meant *not* to be similar to the things symbolized by them, so the law of exclusive disjunction served as basis for the semiotic system; while in Neoclassicism signs were halfway between symbol and icon, i.e. they were meant to resemble their signified, so the law of non-disjunction became the basic principle of the semiotic system.

In poetry two Horatian genres: urban satire (Swift, Pope, Prior, Arbuthnot, Gay) and rural meditation (Lady Winchilsea, Pope); in prose the picaresque (Defoe, Fielding's *Jonathan Wild*, all the narrative fiction of Smollett, except his last work), and the periodical essay (Addison, Steele) were the forms of expression most characteristic, and Swift, Pope, Addison, Defoe, and Fielding the greatest writers of English Neoclassicism.

0.1.3 *The Age of Sensibility (1740—1800)*

After about 1740 a new kind of style emerged which essentially was neither post-Classical nor pre-Romantic, but had a relative independence of its own. Naturally, one cannot speak of any break in the continuity of English literature. Still, the most characteristic and greatest writers of the

[2] Johnson, *Lives of the English Poets*, (The World's Classics ed.) I, p. 301.

second half of the century (e. g. Sterne, Smart, or Blake) cannot be explained in terms of either the previous or the next period.

Neoclassical artists were Aristotelian in aesthetics, looking upon the work of art as a closed object. Of the three possible interpretations of style they insisted on its grammatico-rhetorical aspect; style for them was ornate form, the technique of exposition, a kind of dress. The writers of the Age of Sensibility, on the other hand, were followers of Pseudo-Longinus, developing the conception of style as "mentis character," a conception which implied a strong emphasis on the work of art as an act, a process, on art as productivity, and thus on the psychology of creation. The idea dawned upon these writers that there was a single voice in the works by the same author, and with it a strong reaction came against Neoclassical distinctions between genres. If for Pope, influenced by Bolingbroke's deism in *Essay on Man*, every kind of creation seemed to exist only in its result, as a finished product and an autonomous whole, Blake, who dismissed Rationalism, even if he could not make more than tentative advances towards the only way out of it: dialectical thought, viewed creation both in a theological and in an artistic sense as a process still going on at the moment when we observe it. The structure of the works most typical of the Age of Sensibility (e. g. *Tristram Shandy* or *A Song to David* or *Jubilate Agno*) was modelled on the operative character of consciousness, and this idea was one of the distinguishing qualities of such critics of the age as, for instance, Lord Kames or Hugh Blair. Furthermore, this central aesthetic concept is the basis of works whose genre traditionally appears to be outside the domain of belles lettres, such as Gibbon's *Decline and Fall* and *Autobiography* or Boswell's *Life of Johnson*.

The appearance of this new type of semiotic system was simultaneous with the transformation of science at the end of the 18th century, when scientists turned towards the analysis of practice, as, for instance, economists went beyond examining the exchange of money and focused on the dynamics of productivity.

The Romantics, in a way, returned to an Aristotelian phenomenologist view of the work of art, invalidating, or at least taking the edge off, the antiformalism implicit in the literature of the later 18th century, though they developed an entirely new idea of artistic form. One cannot help coming to the conclusion that the Age of Sensibility was much fuller of contradictions and daring experiments than either the preceding or the next period. It was an age which saw many tentative advances and recoils. Some of its writers (Young, Gray, even Thomson) produced works so diverse that it is not easy to believe that they were written by the same person. One can assume that all this seeming disorder was connected with changes in English society more vehement than either before the middle of the 18th or after the beginning of the 19th century: the Age of Sensibility corresponded to the beginning of the Industrial Revolution, the Agrarian Reforms, the disappearance of a highly characteristic countryside, and the emergence of a middle-brow reading public.

As to the favourite genres, satire began to lose its dominance and was cultivated mostly by those who had a certain nostalgia for the literary model set up by Pope (Young, Johnson, Gray, Churchill, Goldsmith). Descriptive-meditative poetry, on the other hand, became even more significant than before; the major work of all the typical poets of the age (Thomson, Gray, Collins, Shenstone, Goldsmith, Cowper) was written in that genre. Other genres which previously had not seemed to be more than by-products of the main development became integral parts of the most characteristic literature produced in the second half of the 18th century. The oriental tale (Johnson, Beckford) and the artistic letter (Gray, Walpole) seem to be cases in point. Furthermore, new genres appeared, such as the epistolary novel (Richardson, Goldsmith, Smollett), the Gothic romance (Walpole, Mrs Radcliffe, Cl. Reeve, Monk Lewis, C. B. Byron), the song (Blake, Burns), or the prose-poem (Macpheson). In verse Johnson, Smart, and Blake, in prose Richardson, Smollett, Strerne, A usten, Gibbon and Boswell brought a contribution to literary evolution on a European scale.

The end of the Age of Sensibility is marked by a sudden stylistic change in the work of Wordsworth and Coleridge, the result of which was the first edition of their *Lyrical Ballads* (1798), but there are overlaps with the next period: the vogue of the Gothic romance did not cease after 1800, and Blake, Crabbe, and Austen produced some of their most characteristic work in the first two decades of the 19th century. From this one must conclude that the Age of Sensibility, in the same way as Neoclassicism and Romanticism, means first of all *a type of literature* which was dominant in a period (1740—1800) but appeared earlier and continued to exist later.

Although the Age of Sensibility brought a dramatic model of its own, the so-called *drame bourgeois* (Lillo, Edward Moore) has much less aesthetic value than the late variants (Goldsmith, Sheridan) of a model developed during the Restoration. That is why (before a concrete typological analysis of the poetry) we shall briefly sum up stylistic and structural changes only in the aesthetically relevant prose and verse genres.

0.1.3.1 Diction as the main stylistic feature characterizing poetry written in the Age of Sensibility

The experiments which the Age of Sensibility brought in the field of diction were sometimes so daring that they foreshadowed evolution in the second half of the 19th century (Whitman, Rimbaud, Hopkins). Experimentation was backed by the *stylistic influence* of

(a) the Bible (Macpherson, Smart, Blake),
(b) Milton (Thomson, Shenstone, Beattie, Blake)
(d) the ballads (Chatterton, Burns), and
(e) alliterative verse (Collins).

It is not easy to arrive at generalizations about the tentative advances and recoils that characterize the poetry of the Age of Sensibility. Still, one can distinguish *conservatives* inclined to keep an eye on Neoclassical models from *innovators* aiming at more or less daring experimentation. Although there were writers who represented the first tendency from one and the second from another point of view, the central figures of the two groups, Johnson on the one hand and Blake and Sterne on the other, seem to represent the two extremes quite definitely. Needless to say, these two terms do not at all imply value judgments: Johnson and Goldsmith were finer poets than most of the experimenters. The aim of the conservatives was to limit (Johnson, Goldsmith), while that of the innovators was to enlarge *vocabulary* (Macpherson, Blake).

On the level of *syntax*, the first group kept close to, while the second departed from, the syntax of Pope and Swift, which had been decidedly objective, that is, it had made use of as many logical formulae as possible and stayed pretty close to the syntax of discursive prose. Some of the experimenters aimed at a partial deformation of logical syntax, manipulating euphonico-associative effects (Collins, Macpherson), others went as far as to create a kind of pseudo-syntax (Blake, Sterne).

In Johnson's poetry and prose *metaphors* are relatively few, but most of them are verbs, i.e. words having a metaphoric influence on relatively many words. The works of Thomson, Collins, Macpherson, or Blake, on the other hand, are full of weak metaphors, mostly adjectives with no far-reaching effect. Johnson or his friend Goldsmith tried to purify diction, making dead metaphors alive, Blake and the less daring experimenters employed a mixed, impure diction, creating many new metaphors, enlarging the territory of meaning. Vocatives (apostrophes) and personifications, the two most characteristic Neoclassical types of metaphor predominant even with Young, Thomson, Gray, or Collins, disappeared in the mature work of Cowper and Blake, Johnson's circle still took similarity for the basis of metaphor, whereas others unconsciously re-interpreted it, making its basis an identity in which the poet's mind is involved.

As a consequence of all these developments in syntax (of which metaphor is, after all, a constituent) the *epigrammatic formula* still very frequent with Thomson or Gray disappeared with Blake, *rhetoric devices* still favoured by Churchill, Gray, or Gibbon were dismissed by Cowper, Crabbe, or Austen, and in verse *end-stopped* couplets were replaced by either many *enjambements* (Cowper, Crabbe) or *metric irregularities* (Blake).

0.1.3.2 Other structural and stylistic changes

The purpose of this essay is to concentrate on one aspect of stylistic change, to examine how far the poetic diction of the second half of the 18th century is different from that of the earlier and later periods. Yet we wish to indicate that in other stylistic and structural domains similar changes can be observed from the middle of the century. *The addressee of a poem* written by Young or Thomson is, in most cases, a definite person or a personified abstraction, whereas by the end of the century either there is no definite addressee (Blake), or occasionally, it is the fictive self of the poem (Cowper). On the *semantic level* the more conservative writers emphasized the denotative meaning of a word (it is by no accident that Johnson compiled a dictionary), remaining in the territory of meaning conquered by their predecessors. Blake or Smart, on the other hand, developed new connotations, enlarged the territory of meaning; and so their poetry is full of ambiguities. Johnson (like Pope or Fielding) aimed at giving parallel impulses to the reader, whereas *Tristram Shandy* can be annoying for a hostile reader especially because the impulses supplied by it are extremely heterogeneous. In other words, semantic units in Neoclassical literature are related to one another as parts to wholes, whereas the *global structure* of an epistolary novel as well as that of Blake's quasi-mythological system is based on conjunction/disjunction relationships. One-sided contrasts characteristic of Neoclassicism *(The Dunciad, Tom Jones)* are replaced by dialectical oppositions *(Clarissa, Tristram Shandy*, Blake, Austen), bridge- or arch-forms comprising an uneven number of parts (3 in the case of *Tom Jones*) by more open forms implying a use of semantic pauses/contrast-forms. The examples of *Jubilate Agno* and *Tristram Shandy* illustrate well how late-18th-century writers sought non-linear, intertextual modes of organization, making use of a more complex temporal and motivic structure, and of a functional use of quotation.

0.1.3.3 The Age of Sensibility in other literatures

The Age of Sensibility was a phase in literary evolution which all European literatures underwent. English literature was the first to arrive at this stage; that is why English influence was foremost in the second half of the 18th century. Therefore, a comparative approach to the period (whose idea can be merely suggested here) first ought to deal with

(a) *direct influences.* To mention but a few examples: The example of Thomson's *The Seasons* (1726—30) played an important rôle in the formation of French descriptive-reflexive poetry as represented by Saint-Lambert's *Les Saisons* (1769), l'abbé Delille's *Les Géorgiques* (1770), and *Les Jardins* (1782), Roucher's *Les Mois* (1779), or Lemierre's *Les Fastes* (1779). In a similar way, the motivic structure of *Tristram Shandy* (1760-7) served as model for the renovation of German prose fiction started by Wieland, in *Der goldene Spiegel* (1772) and *Die Geschichte des weisen Danischmend* (1775), or Richardson's technique was a major direct or indirect influence on practically all epistolary novelists, from Jean-Jacques Rousseau to Laclos, from Goethe to the Hungarian Kármán. Yet

(b) *analogies independent of influence* are even more revealing proofs of the unity of the Age of Sensibility in European literature. Writers who in all probability did not know about each other developed a very similar model of the same genre. This is the case, for instance, with the Pindaric ode as cultivated by such poets as Gray and Collins, Jean-Baptiste Rousseau, Écouchard Lebrun and André Chénier, Csokonai and Berzsenyi. On several levels of diction: in the use of rhetoric (Jean-Baptiste Rousseau, Écouchard Lebrun), vocatives and personifications (Panard, Dayka, Csokonai), epigrammatic formulae (Panard, Dayka), or in the connotative interpretation of such key-words as solitude (Jean-Jacques Rousseau, Léonard, Goethe, Dayka, Csokonai, Berzsenyi). Continental poets show close analogies with their English contemporaries.

0.1.3.4 The Age of Sensibility in the other arts

We wish to end the introductory part of this essay with a few tentative suggestions about the possibilities of extending the term "Age of Sensibility" to the other arts. After 1768 there is a kind of experimental period in music which bears analogies with the *Sturm und Drang*, which we regard as a local variant of the Age of Sensibility, in the same way as Metaphysical poetry must be considered a national variant of the Baroque. In such works as Haydn's *Symphonies* Nos 26 (in d minor, *"Lamentazione,"* ca. 1768), 39 (in g minor, ca. 1768), 44 (in f minor, *"Abschied,"* 1772), 49 (in f minor, "La Passione," 1768), and 52 (in c minor, 1771—3), several of his string quartets and piano sonatas; Mozart's *Miserere* (in a minor, K. V. 85), *Kyrie* (in d minor, K. V. 90), *Psalm: De Profundis* (in c minor, K. V. 93), *Ouverture* to his oratorio *Betulia Liberata* (in d minor, K. V. 118, 1771), *Mass* (in C minor-major, K. V. 139), d minor *String Quartet* (K. V. 173, 1773), little g minor *Symphony* (K. V. 183, 1773), F major piano *Sonata* (K. V. 280, 1774), or, among later works, the e minor violin and piano (K. V. 304, 1778) and the a minor piano (K. V. 310, 1778) *Sonata*, the d and c minor *Piano Concertos* (K. V. 466 and 491, both from 1785), the beginning of the C major *Piano Concerto* (K. V. 503); Boccherini's symphony *La Casa del Diavolo*, Brunetti's b minor *Symphony* (1779), Simon le Duc's c minor Adagio in his e flat major *Symphony* (1776—7); or in several contemporary works written by Vanhal, Gassmann, Dittersdorf, Ordonnec, or Franz Beck, we find a heavy stress on the minor mode, driving, syncopated rhythms, melodic motives built on wide leaps, harmonies full of tension, pointed dissonances, discordant suspensions, diminished chord sequences, extended modulation, greater breadths of dynamics (abrupt fortissimi) and accentuation, and a fascination with contrapuntal devices. All these stylistic changes prepared the way for Beethoven, who was as much *the* composer of the Age of Sensibility, as Goethe its greatest literary artist.

In the visual arts the situation of Goya is comparable to that of the two great Germans: he is not yet a Romantic, but is no more a Classicist, and sums up the best of all the tentative experiments made by such lesser artists as Füssli (Fuseli), Flaxman, Blake, Prud'hon, Mortimer, Falconet, or Piranesi.

1. THE PSYCHO-PHILOSOPHIC DIMENSION:
THE POETIC SELF AND THE OUTSIDE WORLD

1.0 THE CONSERVATIVE VISION:
THE WORLD AS A SYSTEM OF POWERS KEPT IN BALANCE

Where am I? I am part of a Great Chain of Being. Behind the most ambitious works of English Neoclassicism: *Gulliver's Travels* (1726), *Essay on Man* (1732), *Tom Jones* (1749), and *The Lives of the Poets* (1781), there is the general formula that
"All creatures are necessarily imperfect, and at an infinite distance from the perfection of the Deity."[3] The world picture of English Neoclassicism is essentially Conservative, its main document being William King's theodicy *De origine mali* (1702), a work written under the influence of Leibniz. On this scale of life

> There must be, somewhere, such a rank as Man; ...
> Why has not Man a microscopic eye?
> For this plain reason, Man is not a Fly.

[3] *An Essay on the Origin of Evil* by Dr William King, trans. from the Latin with Notes and a Dissertation concerning the Principle and Criterion of Virtue and of the Passions; by Edmund Law, London, 1732[2], p. XIX.

123

This is the best of all *possible* worlds, which (and this shows how grossly Voltaire misunderstood and misrepresented Leibniz) does not imply that this world is good, but only that any better world would be metaphysically impossible. It is only in that sense that

" . . . 'Whatever IS, is RIGHT.' "

" . . . On superior powers
Were we to press, inferior might as ours:
Or in the full creation leave a void,
Where, one step broke, the great scale's destroyed: . . .
From Nature's chain whatever link you strike,
Tenth or ten thousandth, break the chain alike."[4]

The backbone of this world picture is the principle of plenitude. *"Midas se trouva moins riche, quand il n'eut que de l'or."*[5] Cultural history consists of a series of interconnected systems. In the value theory implied in the principle of plenitude one can see the germ of the cult of diversity which finally replaced the abstract norms of Neoclassicism.

Early 18th-century social analysis in England was based on the notion of the Great Chain of Being. The world of that most self-consciously Neoclassical novelist, Henry Fielding, is a telling proof of this. In his picture of a highly stratified, hierarchic social organization each man has his bounded sphere assigned to him, within which he has a special function to fulfil. Society as an integrated whole has no mercy for anyone who has strayed outside his proper sphere, the one appointed to him.

In the 18th century Whig and Tory were no mere party labels: they represented two equally important trends in thought. Neoclassicism was created chiefly by a Tory circle of writers including Oxford, Bolingbroke, Ormond, Prior, Arbuthnot, and Gay, besides Swift and Pope. The last important document of the Tory sense of decadence was John Brown's *Estimate of the Manners and Principles of the Times*, which appeared in the very year when Pitt became prime minister and brought the victory of Liberal belief in progress, the perfectibility and essential goodness of man. The Tory vision of the world, the ideological basis of English Neoclassicism, was essentially pessimistic. Influenced by La Rochefoucauld, the Tory satirists held that evil is not in human institutions but in man. The authors belonging to that tradition, from Swift to Johnson, had an exceptional moral honesty in not dissociating themselves from evil, not pushing it away, or locating it in some other man or place. For them evil was not *there* and *at that time* but *here* and *now*. Through a painful and humiliating self-examination they tried to trace the defects of society back to the defects of human nature.

Towards the middle of the century the tough-minded suffered a heavy blow, a great loss of credit. Those retaining something of Swift's or Pope's tragic sense were forced to move into opposition, and the influence of the French Enlightenment met with a breezy insouciance and complacency that had been anticipated by Addison. Being a Christian humanist, Swift

---

[4] Pope, *An Essay on Man*, I, ll. 48, 193—4, 294, 241—6.
[5] Leibniz, *Essais de Théodicée*, in *Œuvres philosophiques*, Paris, 1900, II, p. 163.

124

wrote in opposition to the Enlightenment, (Cartesian) rationalism, experimental and theoretical science, the new conception of man, the new and sudden wealth of England and of the upstart middle class (probing into the origin of that wealth), and centralization, chiefly because he thought that the Enlightenment was built on false premises and indulged in Utopian hopes which he detested and thought as cheap as cynicism. His measuring rod, Lemuel Gulliver, was an ordinary man exempt from such extremes:

> Placed on this isthmus of a middle state,
> A being darkly wise, and rudely great:
> With too much knowledge for the Sceptic side,
> With too much weakness for the Stoic's pride,
> He hangs between; in doubt to act, or rest;
> In doubt to deem himself a God, or Beast;
> In doubt his Mind or Body to prefer;
> Born but to die, and reas'ning but to err;
> Alike in ignorance, his reason such,
> Whether he thinks too little, or too much:
> Chaos of Thought and Passion, all confus'd;
> Still by himself abused, or disabused;
> Created half to rise, and half to fall;
> Great lord of all things, yet a prey to all;
> Sole judge of Truth, in endless error hurl'd:
> The glory, jest, and riddle of the world ![6]

As for Pope chance meant the absence of art,[7] so the source of pessimism for Swift was a constant fear of disorder menacing the balance of the Great Scale of Existence. The end of *Gulliver*, showing how the hero is driven mad, is a striking proof of how much aware he was of that danger.

The key-word for Swift and Pope and Johnson was moderation. And here it should be at least mentioned that their position was not so far from that of Voltaire, who was, essentially, also a man of compromise (see his *Discours sur la modération* or *Charme des fables*). They distrusted science and were anti-intellectual because they pitted themselves against all sorts of excess. Thackeray saw them in a negative perspective because their positions were poles apart: the Tory satirists prophetically foresaw the corruption of Liberalism at the beginning of an evolution which attained its highest phase only in the middle of the 19th century. The critical practice of Johnson is an epitome of this world view. A good writer must have genius, industry and taste, learning, wit, imagination, and judgement, must have a doctrine to state; he must be original but simple, both "analytick" and general, elegant, yet sublime. He is expected to write for a "common reader" and in a "middle style," knowing the proper limits, having never too much of any quality, running to no extreme.

This ideal balance, the state in which the inside is at harmony with the outside, the self with the surrounding universe, is the essence of the

---

[6] Pope, *An Essay on Man*, II, ll. 3–18.
[7] Pope, *An Essay on Criticism*, l. 362.

world view behind European Neoclassicism. Locke was the first to formulate it, Voltaire identified the centre with God and its circumference with his creation:

> Dans le centre éclatant de ces orbes immenses
> Qui n'ont pu nous cacher leur marche et leurs distances,
> Luit cet astre du jour par Dieu même allumé;

Turgot interpreted the relation between the present and the non-present in a similar way: *"Le moment présent est un centre où aboutissent une foule d'idées enchaînées les unes aux autres"*; Buffon, Rivarol, and Vauvenargues defined the situation of man in the universe in like terms: *"un centre où tout se rapporte, un point où l'Univers entier se réfléchit," "Le moi dans les animaux et dans l'homme est la plénitude du sentiment; il est produit par la convergence des facultés vers un point unique," "Un esprit étendu considère les êtres dans leurs rapports mutuels; il saisit d'un coup d'œil tous les rameaux des choses; il les réunit à leur source et dans un centre commun; il les met sous un même point de vue; enfin il répand la lumière sur de grands objets et sous une vaste surface."* Dryden tried to prove the necessity of this balance with his dramas; Addison thought the work of art must reflect this organization of the world, having a "center that collects and gathers into it the Line of the whole Circumference," and in this idea he was followed by Bodmer, Goethe, and Humboldt. Pope and Montesquieu summed up all these analogous relations with a single image:

> The spider's touch, how exquisitely fine!
> Feels at each thread, and lives along the line.

"L'âme est dans notre corps, comme une araignée dans sa toile."[8]

1.1 WORLD WITHOUT CENTRE AND WITHOUT MEANING

For the poets of the second half of the century the bottom of the world had fallen off: they were disoriented, they did not find the ruling principle of the universe and, consequently, did not find their position in the world either. The aesthetic consequences are well-known: the work of even the best poets of the age is extremely unequal, their most ambitious works (from *The Seasons* to *The Task*) are read in parts and not in whole, and there is a kind of "dissociation of sensibility" in them; Johnson was indeed right to observe that each poet had too much of one and too little of another of the qualities necessary in great literature. To give but one example:

[8] Voltaire, *La Henriade*, chant 7, passage quoted in *l'Encyclopédie*, in the article "Soleil"; Turgot, *Œuvres*, Paris, II, p. 626; Buffon, *Histoire naturelle*, Imprimerie Royale, III, p. 8; Rivarol, *Discours préliminaire du Nouveau Dictionnaire*, Hambourg, 1797, p. 146; Vauvenargues, *Introduction à la connaissance de l'esprit humain*, Œuvres, éd. Gilbert, I, 13; Dryden, *Preface to Troilus and Cressida, A Parallel of Poetry and Painting*, Essays, ed. W. P. Ker, OUP, I, p. 208, II, p. 143; Addison, *The Spectator*, no. 415, June 26, 1712; Pope, *An Essay on Man*, I, ll. 217—8; Montesquieu, *Essai sur les causes qui peuvent affecter les esprits et les caractères*. Cf. Georges Poulet, *Les métamorphoses du cercle*, chap. iv, "Le dix-huitième siècle", pp. 73—101.

Collins lacked principle, whereas Gray had more than enough of it. The antecedents of this change can be traced back to the earlier period, when isolated poets began to lose their sense of a centre. The Quietist Mme Guyon, for instance, admired and translated by Cowper, wrote of an

> Être d'une immuable essence:
> Cercle sans principe et sans bout,
> Qui n'a point de circonférence,
> Son centre se trouvant partout.[9]

Marvell in *Upon Appleton House* showed his awareness of a topsy-turvy universe, and the picaresque story as written by Defoe presented a chaotic world. Prior, the least Augustan of the Tory satirists, in a single poem rather surprisingly suggested that he was not so much sure of, as in search for, a ruling principle in the universe:

> In vain We measure this amazing Sphere,
> And find and fix its Centre here or there;
> Whilst its Circumference, scorning to be brought
> Ev'n into fancied Space, eludes our vanquish'd Thought.[10]

Shaftesbury, the most important theoretical anticipator of the Age of Sensibility, laid the basis of that bad cosmic consciousness which characterizes the second half of the century:
"Oh glorious nature! ... Thy being is boundless, unsearchable, impenetrable. In thy immensity all thought is lost, fancy gives over its flight, and wearied imagination spends itself in vain, finding no coast nor limit of this ocean, nor, in the widest tract through which it soars, one point yet nearer the circumference than the first centre whence it parted."[11]

Unlike the Neoclassical period, the Age of Sensibility was relativistic; it saw a world whose boundaries were unknown, in which everything was related to everything, and any point could become a centre, *"tous les êtres circulent les uns dans les autres,"* as Diderot, one of its leading theoreticians wrote.[12] Kant was the only philosopher of the century who could create an entirely unified system, which proves not only that he was the greatest thinker of the age, but also that he took so big a stride forward to the next age that he can be neglected as not characteristic from our point of view.

The loss of any sense of a centre went so deep that it penetrated into the organization of literary life. The Augustan Neoclassicists were both urban and urbane to the greatest possible extent. They insisted on living spiritually in the centre of culture. After 1740 Johnson was the only serious artist who kept to that tradition — that is why between Pope and the best Romantics he was the only English poet who cannot be called provincial. Shenstone and Cowper, Langhorne and Lloyd, Austen and Crabbe, and even Gold-

---

[9] Mme Guyon, *Poésies et cantiques spirituels*, Paris, 1790, III, p. 3.
[10] Matthew Prior, *Poems on several occasions*, ed. A. R. Waller. Cambridge, 1905, p. 278.
[11] Shaftesbury, *Characteristics*, London, 1900, II, p. 98.
[12] Diderot, *Le Rêve de d'Alembert*, éd. J. Lough. Cambridge UP, p. 113.

smith, became alienated from London and dismissed the great Augustan idea as irrelevant. Even such a self-consciously civilized poet as Gray saw a catastrophic clash between the values of town and village life, and in his famous *Elegy* tended to side with the latter. The destruction of one of the greatest talents, that of Churchill, proves that there was more than an element of truth in Cowper's or Lloyd's moral contempt for contemporary urbanity:

> "In cities vice is hidden with most ease,
> Or seen with least reproach; and virtue, taught
> By frequent lapse, can hope no triumph there
> Beyond th' achievement of successful flight."

> "The harlot muse, so passing gay,
> Bewitches only to betray."[13]

The fact of the matter is that the great social event of the period, the Industrial Revolution, was recorded only in its negative consequences. Both poets cited above, as well as Goldsmith and Crabbe, thought that the profit was less considerable than the loss: they saw in the rural communities destroyed by industrialization a tradition which had been the backbone of national culture:

> . . . a bold peasantry, their country's pride,
> When once destroy'd, can never be supplied.[14]

The conclusion is probably not too far-fetched that what happened in England in the late 18th century was comparable to urbanization in East Europe in the middle of the 20th century.

Urbanity vs. provincialism is the most frequent variant of the most characteristic thematic contrast that the reader can find in post-Augustan poetry: that of appearance vs. reality. Its other relatively frequent variant is of related interest: a contrast between the past and the present (as in Shenstone's *Song* starting with the line "How pleas'd within my native bowers" or in Goldsmith's *The Deserted Village*), resulting in a pessimism best exemplified by Beattie's verses on *Solitude*, in the sense of national decadence running through the 4th book of *The Task*. From Shenstone (*Elegy, He complains how soon the pleasing novelty of life is over*) to Helen Maria Williams (*To Hope*) all the poets are tortured by a loss of belief and an alienation from their surroundings. In this respect Cowper, whose main themes are continual disappointment (*On the Receipt of my Mother's Picture out of Norfolk*) and resignation (*The Statesman in Retirement*), is probably the most characteristic case. The political consequences of this attitude were obvious: Cowper (*On the Loss of the Royal George*) as much as John Scott of Amwell (*The Drum*) felt nothing but disgust at hearing about military glory. The English poets dismissed violence as an unsatisfactory means to put an end to a confusion from which they saw no way out: George Canning's verses published in 1797 in *The Anti-Jacobin* illustrate how

[13] Cowper, *The Task* I, l. 689—92; Lloyd, *The Temple of Favour*, The Poetical Works. London, 1774, II.
[14] Goldsmith, *The Deserted Village*, pp. 55—6.

great a contempt the English poet had for such radicals as Paine, who hoped for a simple solution of social troubles.

Dissatisfied with the culture of their own time and having realized that the culture which they could fall back upon provided no longer a metaphysically objective morality, these post-Augustan poets had to choose between two roads: either they could accept a totally relativistic ethos — the fact that they could never produce a long poem which was more than a series of momentary illuminations proves how serious that temptation was — or they could look to some past culture for authority as an ethical model. The first path (later trodden by the Browning of the dramatic monologues) they were afraid to take. As they had to admit that rural/peasant culture was not to survive industrialization, they desperately turned to the historical past, thus trying to give orientation to their painfully meaningless world. There is no doubt that traces of that nostalgia can be felt as early as Pope's four *Pastorals* or in the Theocritan and Spenserian undertones of Gay's *Shepherd's Week*, but it became predominant only in Dodsley's *Collection of Poems* (1748—58), which included Shenstone, Lyttelton, Akenside, Mason, Gray, Collins, and the elder Wartons. A sign of how deeply they were sunk in nostalgia was that they gave the highest praise to the epic, a genre which none of them tried to write. Johnson summed up the bad conscience characteristic of the whole generation: "Our grandfathers knew the picture from life; we judge of the life by contemplating the picture."[15]

Gray and Blake can be regarded as two dissimilar extreme cases of this nostalgia: the entire work of both is, in a way, imitation on a large scale. The relatively small œuvre of the first had been written by a university scholar who one after another turned to various cultural inheritances for inspiration. The bulk of the latter poet's work was produced by an eclectic mind prone to "yoke violently together" the most disparate mythological tradition. One thing was common to both: neither created an original system. The first volume of the painter-poet, *Poetical Sketches* (1769—78) was a conglomeration of half-digested cultural material ranging from Spenser (*To the Evening Star, To Morning, An Imitation of Spenser*) and Shakespeare (*King Edward the Third*) to Milton (*Prologue*) and Percy (*Fair Elenor, Mad Song*), sometimes blending several styles in a rather crude way: the King James Bible with Ossian (*The Couch of Death, Contemplation, Samson*), or the *Song of Solomon*, Milton, and Thomson (*To Spring, To Summer, To Autumn, To Winter*). If one compares the more mature *Tiriel* (ca. 1789) and the even later *Milton* (1804—8), which combine thematic material drawn from *Oedipus at Colonus* and *King Lear*, and Platonic with Biblical symbolism, respectively, with Pope's *Eloisa*, inspired by an Ovidian and a medieval model, one cannot help observing that with Pope the two lines of allusion strengthen, whereas with Blake they rather obscure each other. The conclusion is inescapable that imitation in the later 18th century is a sign of enervation rather than of energy.

It should be admitted, however, that imitation at that time had a meaning quite different from what was meant by it in the 19th century. When judging 18th-century poets, we should forget about the 19th-century con-

[15] Johnson, *Lives* I, p. 145.

notation of the word and should rather think of that sort of free re-creation, admitting even a strong burlesque deformation of the model, which we can meet in the work of Ezra Pound.

As for the poets imitated, in the first half of the century numerous poems had been written in Pope's manner or Young's more Neoclassical style (for both Browne's *A Pipe of Tobacco* is an example). Cowper's early couplet satires were probably the last poems in which there was a faint reminiscence of the vein of the *Epistle to Augustus* and the *Epistle to Dr. Arbuthnot*. In the middle of the century even Classical models lost their dominance. After Gray no significant Pindaric ode was written until the Romantics; and Collins's four *Persian Eclogues*, Chatterton's three stanzaic pseudo-medieval *Eclogues*, Churchill's anti-Scot pastoral dialogue, *The Prophecy of Famine*, and the anti-pastoral poems written by Goldsmith and Crabbe, *The Deserted Village* (1770) and *The Village* (1783) marked the various phases of the deformation of the pastoral. Besides Cowper's eight satires already mentioned Collins's *Ode to Evening* was the last important poem with Horatian undertones. Of all the poets of sensibility the earliest, Thomson, was the most Latinite. And even this was partly due to his being a Scotsman; in Scotland the tradition of Latin scholarship had been much stronger than in England. Scots learned to speak Latin and used it when staying abroad. Yet even among his works *The Seasons*, the earliest, was the only one full of Virgilian connotations. After Thomson's death only the *Georgics* kept their influence, and quite understandably, for they asserted the strength of human control over the non-human world, a control which the late 18th century was so uncertain of. That was why both Cowper (in *The Task*) and Blake (in the description of the vermin of the wine press in *The Four Zoas* and in *Milton*) drew upon them.

After 1750 the poets turned towards cultural models which the Augustans entirely neglected. Gray adapted Norse *(The Fatal Sisters, The Descent of Odin)* and Welsh *(The Bard, The Descent of Owen)* material, Chatterton wrote his pseudo-Middle English Rowley poems, Blake in his *Tiriel* took to the Icelandic *Edda*, as translated in 1770 by Percy from Mallet's *Northern Antiquities*. It must be emphasized that all these works were very free and highly stylized adaptations of works which themselves had been written not much before. The "ancient Germanic" culture represented in Blake's *The Four Zoas*, for instance, had Gray's *The Fatal Sisters* and *The Descent of Odin* and Macpherson's *Fingal* for its sources. The later 18th century knew incomparably less about folk or medieval art than the Augustans knew about the Rome of Augustus, and, what is more, it did not want to know more about either. Macpherson's "ancient times" were as subjective as William Morris's Middle Ages.

Although a few poets had their own special sources of inspiration: Sir William Jones "translated" Hafiz (*Poems*, 1772), Thomas Russell and other fifth-rate versifiers returned to Petrarch, who as a major literary model had fallen out of favour in England with the appearance of the Metaphysical poets (*Sonnets and Miscellaneous Poems*, 1789), Burns continued the tradition of the great Scottish poets of the late Middle Ages, yet the major models of post-Augustan imitation were confined to the work of three poets neglected by Neoclassicism: Spenser, Shakespeare, and Milton. Of the three Shakespeare in fact had not too much influence on poetic practice:

his art served rather as a slogan against Neoclassicism (as in Collins's *Ode on the Popular Superstitions of the Highlands of Scotland*, ca. 1749, Joseph Warton's *The Enthusiast*, 1744, or Churchill's *The Rosciad*, 1761), the enigmatic inconstancy of Hamlet might have given suggestions to Sterne to create his amoeba-like character Yorick, but even in Blake's *The Book of Thel* (1789) the allusions to his fifteenth *Sonnet* are insignificant beside the overwhelming reminiscences of the mutability cantos (esp. Book III, Canto VI) of *The Faerie Queene*. And the recreations of Spenserian stanza are numerous, Shenstone's *The School-Mistress* (1742), Thomson's *The Castle of Indolence* (1748), Beattie's *The Minstrel* (1771—4), and Burns's *The Cotter's Saturday Night* are only the most famous among them. The debts of William Mason's *A Monody to the Memory of Mr Pope* and Collins's finest poem, the *Ode to Evening*, to Milton's *Lycidas* are conspicuous, the 17th-century poet's blank verse is recreated with more or less success in Thomson's *The Seasons*, Young's *Night Thoughts*, Mallet's *Amyntor and Theodora*, and Shenstone's *Love and Honour*. On one level at least, *The Task* is a Miltonic parody, *The Book of Urizen* a burlesque anti-*Paradise Lost*, Satan's famous journey from Hell, as described in *Paradise Lost* (Book II) is the basis of Urizen's journey in *Vala* (Night VI). Such syntactic devices as, for instance, inversion for the sake of alliteration:

Of beasts — the beaver plods his task;[16]

show that even Smart, the least imitative British poet of the age, could not resist his stylistic influence.

In this preference for Spenser and Milton as models for imitation we can see a further proof of enervation. The later 18th century turned not to Shakespeare or the Metaphysical poets, the great representatives of a national verbal style, but to Spenser and Milton, poets who wrote in a highly idiosyncratic, Latinite nominal style. They tried to mingle disparate conceptual material, at the risk of obscurity. Blake, the greatest English poet of the second half of the 18th century, embodied the strength and weakness of the Age of Sensibility on a grand scale: he made an attempt to combine the heritage of his two great predecessors and created a poetry which in power is comparable to theirs but has similar pitfalls, too. *Lyrical Ballads* was a landmark in the history of English poetry precisely because it dispensed with Spenserian-Miltonic clichés.

1.2 STOICISM

How to escape from their sense of meaninglessness: that was the most serious question to be answered. Different (and sometimes even the same) poets took to different paths. One temporary, and, in the long run, not too efficient solution was Stoicism. An appeal to the Stoa had been implied sporadically in the Neoclassical attacks against excess, in John Pomfret's *The Choice* (1700) and in some of the poems written by Prior *(For My own Monument, Jinny the Just)*, but the world view of the major Augustans

---

[16] Smart, *A Song to David*, st. 25, 1. 1.

had been unified and balanced enough; and so they still could regard Stoicism as essentially irrelevant. Swift showed his contempt for it in the presentation of the Houyhnms, and remarked that

"The Stoical Scheme of supplying our Wants, by lopping off our Desires, is like cutting off our Feet when we want Shoes."[17]

The Stoic interpretation of the relation of the ego and the outside world did not gain ground until the appearance of the second generation of the Age of Sensibility and doubts had been cast on its validity by the time Blake began to publish. For those who held this view of the world, the self was driven along the circumference of a circle whose centre was unknown to him.

> What idle progeny succeed
> To chase the rolling circle's speed,
> Or urge the flying ball?

In Gray's opinion man should not give himself up to lamentation. Wisdom consists in learning to suffer our fate in silence, for "man is not born to happiness" as Johnson wrote.[18] All creatures are at the mercy of some great power:

> Alas, regardless of their doom,
> The little victims play!
> No sense have they of ills to come,
> Nor care beyond today:
> Yet see how all around 'em wait
> The Ministers of human fate.[19]

In Johnson's works or in Akenside's *Ode to the Evening Star* this power might be identified with a God whose residence is unknown. Gray is much vaguer about this unknown driving force, the only thing which he seems to be certain about is that its existence necessitates a peaceful resignation on man's part, which became the ruling modality of the tone of many characteristic poems written between Gray and Blake: William Whitehead's ode, *The Enthusiast* (1754), Mrs Greville's *A Prayer for Indifference* (1759), Sir John Henry Moore's tale *The Duke of Benevento* (1778), and Crabbe's early *Life* (1779) were among them. The tradition of 18th-century English poetical Stoicism ended with Cowper, in whose work resignation had entirely lost its heroic character.

1.3 DIALECTICAL THOUGHT

The poets who preceded Blake tried to revive an old tradition which had seen its first great revival in England during the Renaissance. Blake instinctively arrived at a much more radical conclusion which, later, turned out to be the only relevant antidote to Rationalism. The outlines of a dia-

[17] Swift, *Thoughts on Various Subjects.*
[18] Gray, *Ode on a Distant Prospect of Eton College*, ll. 27—30; Johnson: *Lives* II, p. 381.
[19] Gray, *Ode on a Distant Prospect of Eton College*, ll. 50—6.

lectical contrast can be seen in the Baroque, especially in a great late-Baroque political poem, Marvell's *An Horatian Ode*. As Blake, Marvell, too, wanted to reconcile opposite qualities, but the direction of his approach was the contrary: the late Metaphysical poet set himself the task of demonstrating multiplicity, whereas for the later poet multiplicity meant semblance beyond which, on the level of reality, total unity can be revealed. The novelist who came closest to Blake in his conception of the inseparability of contrasting qualities was Sterne. Yet neither could go along the whole length of the path leading to the idea of dialectics. It was Goethe who, after having suggested the dialectical relation of subjectivity and objectivity as early as in his *Werther* (1774):

"Wie die Natur sich zum Herbste neigt, wird es Herbst in mir und um mich her. Meine Blätter werden gelb, und schon sind die Blätter der benachbarten Bäume abgefallen"[20]

arrived at a completely dialectic mode of organization in the conceptual framework of *Faust*. He made the decisive step towards the total rejection of the Cartesian dualism of body and mind and the fusion of the inner and the outer world, which, through Schelling:

"Die Natur soll der sichtbare Geist, der Geist die unsichtbare Natur sein"
August Wilhelm:

"Das griechische Ideal der Menschheit war vollkommene Eintracht und Ebenmaß aller Kräfte, natürliche Harmonie. Die Neueren hingegen sind zum Bewußtsein der inneren Entzweiung gekommen, welche ein solches Ideal unmöglich macht; daher ist das Streben ihrer Poesie, diese beiden Welten, zwischen denen wir uns geteilt fühlen, die geistige und die sinnliche, miteinander auszusöhnen und unauflöslich verschmelzen."

"Die antike Kunst und Poesie geht auf strenge Sonderung des Ungleichartigen, die romantische gefällt sich in unauflöslichen Mischungen; alle Entgegengesetzten: Natur und Kunst, Poesie und Prosa, Ernst und Scherz, Erinnerung und Ahndung, Geistigkeit und Sinnlichkeit, das Irdische und Göttliche, Leben und Tod verschmelzt sie auf das innigste miteinander."

and Friedrich Schlegel:

"nicht bloß alle getrennte Gattungen der Poesie wieder zu vereinigen, und die Poesie mit der Philosophie und Rhetorik in Berührung zu bringen. Sie will, und soll auch Poesie und Prosa, Generalität und Kritik, Kunstpoesie und Naturpoesie bald mischen, bald verschmelzen, die Poesie lebendig und gesellig, und das Leben und die Gesellschaft poetisch machen."

and Coleridge and Wordsworth, who interpreted Schelling's *In-Eins-Bildung* as imagination which reconciles the subjective with the objective, by which "the many, becomes one" and

"elements of the most different nature and distant origin are blended together into one harmonious and homogeneous whole,"[21]

became the basis of Romantic aesthetics.

[20] Goethe, *Die Leiden des jungen Werther*, Werke, Salzburg, 1949, II, p. 439.
[21] Schelling, *Werke*. 1797, II, p. 55; A. W. Schlegel, *Über dramatische Kunst und Literatur*. Heidelberg, 1817, I, pp. 24—5, II, p. 55; Friedrich Schlegel, *Kritische Schriften*, München, 1956, p. 37; Coleridge, *Biographia Literaria*, Oxford, 1907, II. pp. 220—1; Wordsworth, *Conversations and Reminiscences Recorded by the (Now) Bishop of Lincoln*, *Wordsworth's Prose Works*, ed. Grosart, III, p. 465.

How far had Blake gone along this line of development? If taken out of their context, some of his statements seem to be those of a dialectical thinker:

"God is in the lowest effects as well as in the highest causes."

"I tell you, no virtue can exist without breaking these ten commandments."

"God is within and without: he is even in the depths of Hell."[22]

In the opposition of Oothoon and Leutha in *Milton*, and in that of Jerusalem and Vala, who stand to each other as soul to body, there is the implication that they had been as one before the Fall, and so they would be in Eternity. The debate between the Neoplatonic and the alchemical philosophies ends on unanswered questions in *The Book of Thel* (1789) and *The Tyger*, but in his *Visions of the Daughters of Albion* an answer is accepted:

"Does not the eagle scorn the earth and despise the treasures beneath?
"But the mole knoweth what is there, and the worm shall tell it thee.
"Does not the worm erect a pillar in the mouldering church yard
"And a palace of eternity in the jaws of the hungry grave?"[23]

which is that of the alchemists, who used the dialectic method:

> Heaven Above, Heaven Beneath,
> Starres Above, Starres Beneath,
> All that is Above, is also Beneath;
> Understand this, and bee Happy.[24]

All this would point to the conclusion that Blake was moving towards a dialectical interpretation of the world. It is true that this tendency, which had been entirely absent from the early *Songs* and *Tiriel*, became stronger later, still *The Marriage* (ca. 1790—3) and the *Visions*, works of his middle phase, are by-products of his career. In his late and by far most important phase he reverted, though not without vacillation, to a Neoplatonic view of matter and spirit, regarding the latter as substance and the former as shadow.

1.4 LIBERAL EVOLUTIONISM

At the beginning of this chapter we mentioned a progressivist sense of existence, the entire opposite of the Tory view of man. The roots of this optimistic consciousness of reality go back to a minor variant of Neoclassicism, represented chiefly by Addison. His complacency:
"Though I am always serious, I do not know what it is to be melancholy."[25]
led to an entirely didactic view of literature: the sole aim of literature is to make man better and enlighten his understanding. Towards the middle of the century this smugness became characteristic of many works produced

---

[22] Blake, *Annotations to Lavater's Aphorisms on Man* 630, *The Marriage of Heaven and Hell* plates ll. 22—4,: *Jerusalem* plate 12, 1. 15.
[23] Blake, *Visions of the Daughters of Albion*, plate 5 1. 39— pl. 6 1. 1.
[24] Thomas Vaughan; *Magia Adamica* (1650), Works. London, 1919, p. 183.
[25] Addison, *The Spectator*, no. 26.

by the generation following that of Pope: among the novelists it was Fielding, of the poets the first generation of the Age of Sensibility, that of Thomson and Young, who had most of it. This feeling of existence produced some of the worst poetry of the century, the sheer didacticism of Thomson's *Rule Britannia*, and it spoiled both his *Autumn* and most of *Night Thoughts*. Neither of these poets had any sense of evil, for both "philosophic melancholy" was a necessary but only a first stage, they were absolutely certain that the only possible change was from darkness to light. In "Night Nine" Young, by far the lesser poet of the two, amended Pope's

> Go, wondr'ous creature! Mount where Science guides,
> Go, measure earth, weigh air, and state the tides;
> Instruct the planets in what orbs to run,
> Correct old Time, and regulate the Sun, . . .
> Go, teach Eternal wisdom now to rule —
> Then drop into thyself, and be a fool![26]

to "be a God."

In the second half of the century the optimistic, nationalistic interpretation of history expressed by Thomson in *Britannia* (1727) and *Liberty* (1735) became so much the official view that all the better poets were forced to move into opposition, only second-rate talents were occupied with supporting what was in no need of any support: Garrick, who echoed Thomson's *Rule Britannia* in his praise of the strength of Britain's native oak *(Heart of Oak)*, John Cunningham, who maintained, in striking contrast to Goldsmith or Crabbe, that the poor peasants were the happy ones *(The Miller)*, or an anonymous poet, singing hosannas of military glory *(The British Grenadiers)* at a time when Cowper rejected it as a theme unfit for serious poetry, whose main concern was with human values. There was only one exception: that of Burns. True, his patriotism was that of a minority, a subdued nation, its tendentiousness aimed at the popularising of an opposition, and so went against the general current *(Scots wha hae)*, yet it obliged him to write some of his worst poetry *(The Cotter's Saturday Night)*. He, too, was complacent about conditions in the countryside which troubled so much his best contemporaries.

It must be admitted that optimistic evolutionism had left its mark even on Johnson's evaluation of the past. In his notoriously unsystematic mind there was at least a temptation to dismiss works and periods as no longer relevant, for the world had grown wiser since that. Thus, *Chevy Chase* "is chill and lifeless imbecility," one of *The Canterbury Tales* "seems hardly worth revival," and the same prejudice violates his appreciation of Milton or leads him to speak of "the licentious festivity of the Restoration," when "a total disregard of every moral" prevailed.[27] Yet it is a long way from the half-nostalgic half-sceptic Johnson, who held reservations about all human activities, to the writers at the turn of the century, who all started with a Liberal outlook. Some remained Liberals all during their lifetime (Wordsworth), others went on to a Democratic (Jefferson), Radical (Byron), or

[26] Pope, *An Essay on Man* II, ll. 19—22, 29—30.
[27] Johnson, *Lives* II, p. 69, I, pp. 447, 322, 98, 149.

even Socialist phase (Godwin, Paine). The early English Socialists laid stress on the one-way movement from the self to the the outside world, and had a condescending attitude toward even the most splendid achievements of the past. Paradoxical as it may seem, by the end of the 18th century the Socialist Godwin and Paine, and they alone, were entirely optimistic about the human predicament, besides the official view held by the Liberal government. No other serious and morally honest writer was completely sure that "Man is perfectible,"[28] and that his prospective conquest of the universe is not only possible but also solves all his problems.

1.5 TO BREAK THROUGH LIMITS: PANTHEISM

Moll Flanders was probably the first literary work of art where a complete externalization was suggested. But there it had been no more than a secondary implication, in the form of an unrealized aim. Gray, in the middle of the century, asked the question "How far can man fulfil himself" in sharp terms in his *Elegy*. But the answer had not come before Romanticism. It was probably Fichte who first observed that a development in time always implied a similar change in space. Romanticism brought a great interest in the human will which had been entirely absent in the Age of Sensibility. Will meant action, which, in turn, led to the expansion of the self in the outside world. For Pico man's aim was to assimilate the world; Fichte made his task to impose himself on it. It was this recognition which put an end to the Age of Sensibility. August Wilhelm Schlegel, Coleridge, and Novalis were those who formulated the new poetic aim:

"eine symbolische Darstellung des Unendlichen."

" . . . the universe itself! What an immense heap of *little* things! I can contemplate nothing but *parts*, and parts are all little. My mind feels as if it ached to behold and know something great, something one and indivisible."

"Wir suchen überall das Unbedingte, und finden immer nur Dinge."[29]

and Byron and Hugo those who most completely realized it. Neither of them is ever alone with himself, in himself. Both seek self-realization in the outside, in an expansion to embrace reality. But their attitude to this expansion is different from that of Godwin: they do not hail it, to them it does not appear as a conscious aim, but as a temptation which they are unable to resist. Senancour, Lamartine, Vigny, and Nerval show different phases of the recognition that the expansion of the self in the universe leads not so much to self-realization as to self-annihilation of any durable self.

[28] Godwin, *Enquiry Concerning Political Justice*, U. of Toronto P, 1946, I, p. 86.
[29] A. W. Schlegel, *Vorlesungen über schöne Kunst und Literatur*, 1884, p. 90; Coleridge, *Letter to Thelwall*, 16 Oct. 1797; Novalis, *Blütenstaub* Werke, Heidelberg, 1953, I, p. 307.

1.6 THE VAPORIZATION OF THE SELF

Charles Baudelaire, the poet who had most courage, even more than Nerval who looked into the abyss of self-annihilation and shrank from it, marks the end of this line of development and the starting point of a new one. In his poetry everything is in perpetual oscillation, the barriers between inside and outside, here and everywhere, now and at any time are broken down. He has given an aswer to all the questions of poetic ontology that tormented poets in the Age of Sensibility; and brought to its end an evolution that had been started as a departure from Neoclassicism.

1.7 BEYOND THE CIRCLE: TRANSCENDENTALISM

Not all poets followed, however, this main direction. Smart and Blake, for instance, took a by-path. Their starting-point was summed up by the former with great clarity:
"For in my nature I quested for beauty, but God, God hath sent me to sea for pearls."
In the terminology of both poets selfhood is a Satanic manifestation and as such must be rejected. Feeling impelled to search for God, they turned to nature. But, unlike the Pantheists, they found that their spiritual adventure had not been finished yet, for
"Nature is (also) the work of the Devil. The Devil is in us, as far as we are in Nature."[30]
If the descriptive poets of the Age of Sensibility, from Thomson to Cowper, derived meaning from observation, Smart and Blake reversed the process: with them meaning pre-existed. Of the two poets Blake has been taken for a Romantic, but without justification. Unlike the Romantics, he rejects the circumference of the outside world in the manner of Orthodox Neoplatonic Christianity:
"I assert for My Self that I do not behold the outward Creation and that to me it is hindrance and not Action; . . . I look thro' it and not with it."
For him the outside world has existence only in the mind, as maya:
"Mental Things are alone Real; what is call'd Corporeal, Nobody knows of its Dwelling Place."[31]
In innocence, the only state in which ontological truth is accessible for us, the circumference is semblance and the beyond is reality.

> To see a World in a Grain of Sand
> And a Heaven in a Wild Flower,
> Hold Infinity in the palm of your hand
> And Eternity in an hour.

[30] Smart, *Jubilate Agno* B MS 1, 30; Edith J. Morley (ed.); *Blake, Coleridge, Wordsworth, Lamb, etc. Being Selections from the Remains of Henry Crabb Robinson*, Manchester, 1922, p. 10.
[31] Blake, end of *A Vision of the Last Judgement*, The Complete Writings. Oxford University Press, 1966, p. 617.

The opposite state of experience, the one associated with Romanticism, is that of fallen man, in which the love of the body destroys that of the soul, and even the material world is destroyed because externalized:

"Art thou a visionary of Jesus, the soft delusion of Eternity?
"Lo I am God, the terrible destroyer, and not the Saviour.
"Why should the Divine Vision compel the sons of Eden
"To forego each his own delight, to war against his spectre?
"The Spectre is the Man. The rest is only delusion and fancy."[32]

This world for Blake is an underworld, a death in life into which the soul descends through the gate of birth from an infinite and eternal life-in-death. The alienation from eternity is compared either to death (as in *Tiriel*) or to a dream (as in *The Little Girl Lost* and *Found* or in *Vala*). Yet Blake's finest painting, the so-called Arlington Court tempera, showing Odysseus as he sheds his natural garments, most clearly shows that Blake regarded this downward attraction of spiritual man as only a temporary decline. His perception of existence was cyclic: in *The Mental Traveller* he presented innocence as both an initial and a terminal state. Fundamentally he was an optimist, because he thought, like Rousseau who might have influenced him with his theory of education through Mary Wollstonecraft, that the soul was incorruptible, incapable of defilement; in his definition sin was extraneous to the soul. This explains his interpretation of *Paradise Lost* and his denunciation of the God of the *Old Testament*. How could he make outcasts of the devils when evil can be only transitory? Blake asks. And that question brings him close to Milton's half- or unconscious preference for Satan, to Milton's great admirer, Richardson, who by supernatural rewards made a happy ending for Clarissa, and even to Godwin, who came to the same conclusion from an opposite direction.

The main source of Blake's optimism was the Hermetic tradition: "Neither can anything perish, or be destroyed in the World, the World being contained and embraced by Eternity."[33]

The decline from spirituality to materiality is followed by a necessary renewal. The world is transient in the soul, and art must not be concerned with this world. That is why Blake dismissed Wordsworth's poetry, and no doubt he was right to point out that their aims were diametrically opposed: "I see in Wordsworth the Natural Man rising up against the Spiritual Man Continually, and then he is No Poet but a Heathen Philosopher at Enmity against all the true Poetry of Inspiration."[34]

Blake's poetry was not the ouverture of Romanticism in England, but the culmination of an earlier period to which Romanticism brought a reaction.

[32] Blake, *Auguries of Innocence* ll. 1—4; *Vala or The Four Zoas* I, ll. 337—41.
[33] *The Divine Pymander of Hermes Mercurius Trismegistus*, transl. from the Arabie by Dr (John) Everard (1650), London, 1884, p. 61.
[34] Blake, *Annotations to "Poems" by William Wordsworth*, p. 1.

Blake and Rousseau were men whose eyes met once, they agreed in their critique of the notion of guilt, in their disbelief in the finality of evil, but otherwise they were turned in opposite directions: Blake tried to forget the self and get beyond even its circumference, whereas Rousseau was in search of the self. Although for different reasons, a tragic sense of life was inconceivable for both. Crime in their system of ideas does not lead to punishment but to remorse. In *The Four Zoas* both Los and Urizen repent. At this point they came close to Hegel's excusively ethical view of tragedy. The German thinker, too, was so much oriented toward the future that he also shot wide of the mark: interpreting history as the unfolding of the Absolute and art as ontodicy, he looked upon tragedy as eternal justice working itself out.

Rousseau's sense of existence, however, is more contradictory than that of Blake or Hegel. In his thought much as the soul is tempted by a progressive conquest of the world, a re-creation of the landscape, it is also afraid that expansion leads to multiplication and, in the long run, to disappearance:

"N'allez pas vous figurer qu'en étendant vos facultés vous étendez vos forces; vous les diminuez, au contraire, si votre orgueil s'étend plus qu'elles."

Recognizing a sort of antipathy, a gap which he cannot bridge between the self and the circumference:

"Ils ont creusé entre eux et moi un abîme immense que rien ne peut plus combler ni franchir, et je suis aussi séparé d'eux pour le reste de ma vie que les morts le sont des vivants."

he arrives at the conclusion that one must stay in the centre and renounce all expansion not to lose one's identity:

"Commençons par redevenir nous, par nous concentrer en nous, par circonscrire notre âme des mêmes bornes que la nature a données à notre être;"

"Le monde réel a ses bornes, le monde imaginaire est infini: ne pouvant élargir l'un, rétrécissons l'autre; car c'est de leur seule différence que naissent toutes les peines qui nous rendent vraiment malheureux."

"Ô homme! resserre ton existence au-dedans de toi, et tu ne seras plus misérable."

"Je sens mieux, de jour en jour, qu'on en peut être heureux sur terre qu'à proportion qu'on s'éloigne des choses et qu'on se rapproche de soi."[35]

Rousseau abhorred the gardens of Versailles, because they were dominated by straight lines leading the eye too far, and preferred the English gardens for their serpentines which did not give frightfully large perspectives. A serpentine lets the soul return to itself: this idea had been pointed out first by Hogarth in *The Analysis of Beauty* (1753), was expanded by Burke in *A Philosophical Inquiry into the Sublime and the Beautiful* (1756), and became the ruling principle of the global structure of *Tristram Shandy* (1760—7) and *The Task* (1785). The last of these is a most complete poetic realization of Rousseau's feeling of identity: Cowper is afraid of the dangers implied in the outward movement of fancy and finds pleasure in the inward movement of aesthetic pleasure.

[35] J.-J. Rousseau, *Émile*, éd. Garnier, p. 60, *Ébauche des Rêveries*, fragm. 19, éd. Pléiade, p. 1170, *Émile* p. 60, *Lettres morales*, lettre 6, *Correspondance* II, p. 369; *Émile* pp. 59, 63; *Lettre à Henriette*, 4 nov. 1764, *Correspondance* XII p. 29.

The origin of this withdrawal of the poetic self, as that of most types of *Weltanschauung* characteristic in the Age of Sensibility, goes back to the Baroque, to Herrick's and Marvell's interest in the tiny. Theoretically it was a possible implication in John Dennis's explanation of "enthusiasm" put forward in *The Advancement and Reformation of Modern Poetry* (1701). Yet in the first half of the century there were only two works which suggested the backward motion of the self: *Clarissa*, where objective events had been replaced by subjective reactions and *The Castle of Indolence*, the first European poem which presented a state of mind on a grand scale without appealing to an epic strain, ascribing (whether consciously or not is beside the point) an entirely positive value to passivity. The consequences of the sense of existence characterizing this poem (exceptional not only in contemporary literature but also in Thomson's work) were later pointed out by Cowper, in *The Task*. For both poets subjectivity was not a conscious program but the inescapable consequence of the void which the Enlightenment left after having destroyed earlier moral values. There was only one writer who drew the most radical consequences from the fact that the Enlightenment could not supply the world with a new ethical system: the marquis de Sade, whose *La philosophie dans le boudoir* (1795) marks the end of a process started by La Mettrie, in his *L'homme machine* (1745). All the others tried to evade the crux of the problem. Thomson and Cowper turned to immediate imaginative experience which in earlier poetic approach to the world had always been preceded by analytic reflection. Thus they came to an intuitive apprehension of the basis of the *Erlebnisdichtung* to be formulated by Fichte:

"*Merke auf dich selbst: kehre deinen Blick von allem, was dich umgibt ab, und in dein Inneres; ist die erste Forderung, welche die Philosophie an ihren Lehrling tut. Es ist von nichts, was außer dir ist, die Rede, sondern lediglich von dir selbst.*"[36]

Thomson defined the gap of non-identity between the self and the universe, Cowper went further: for him the outside world appeared as hostile:

> . . . though seeming sweet
> Be still a pleasing object in my view;
> My visit still, but never my abode.

Of all the English poets of the 18th century Thomson and Cowper came closest to the sense of life which is a characteristic feature of German Romanticism:

"*So viel hab' ich, ohne noch für die Presse darüber nachgedacht zu haben, heraus, dass in unserer Idee von der Totalität eines jeden Menschen ein Hauptzug, ein Brennpunkt, ein Punctum Saliens vorglänze, um welches sich die Nebenpartien abstufend bilden . . .*"

"*Die höchste Aufgabe der Bildung ist, sich seines transzendentalen Selbst zu bemächtigen, das Ich seines Ichs zugleich zu sein.*"

[36] Fichte; *Wissenschaftslehre*, Vorwort.

"*Wir träumen von Reisen durch das Weltall: ist denn das Weltall nicht in uns? ... In uns, oder nirgends ist die Ewigkeit mit ihren Welten, die Vergangenheit und Zukunft.*"[37]

For Descartes the foremost task had been to know the world, for the Romantic it was to know yourself, he projected himself into the universe only to know himself in it.

"In looking at objects of Nature while I am thinking . . . I seem rather to be seeking, as it were asking for, a symbolical language for something within me that already and forever exists, than observing anything new."

"I describe what I imagine."[38]

The starting point of this development was *The Castle of Indolence,*where Thomson departed from the tradition of 18th-century descriptive verse and valued insight so much more than sight that the painted landscape became not only the substance but also the setting of a dream, the poetic self dreamt for himself an appropriate land to dream in. If Cowper was much aware of one of the dangers latent in Romanticism: the annihilation of the self, Thomson anticipated that evolution which resulted in an identification of poetry with creative dreaming:

$$\text{"}\textit{Die Welt wird Traum, der Traum wird Welt.}\text{"}^{39}$$

and in an extreme subjectivism inherent in the work of Novalis, Poe, Guérin, Amiel, and Schopenhauer.

2. THE AESTHETIC DIMENSION

2.1 RATIONALISM VS. PRIMITIVISM

In the final analysis the basic change in 18th-century aesthetics can be reduced to a simple formula:

$$\text{Art} = \text{Idea} > \text{Nature} \rightarrow \text{Art} = \text{Nature} > \text{Idea}$$

This is, however, a gross simplification. The different phases and aspects of that development show a far more complex picture. An acceptance of the tenets held by Descartes and Hobbes implied a belief in the possibility of a rational comprehension of the world. In England only third-rate poets endorsed Rationalism without any reservation: Mary Lee (Lady Chudleigh), for instance, who in *The Resolve* (1703) defined reason as a superior faculty which "all inferior Faculties obey," or Charles Mordaunt (Earl of Peterborough), who in his verses addressed to *Chloe* (1723) identified the wonderful with the rational. Without going to such extremes, the essence of a rational aesthetic was accepted even by the Janus-faced Pope, at least in the didactic (and probably less valuable) part of his output. Thus, in *An Essay on Man* his aesthetic position was as closely attached to Rationalism as that of Boileau: in Nature he saw a reflection of Art. This doctrine

---

[37] Cowper, *The Task* I ll. 249—51; Jean-Paul Richter, *Der Jubelsenior, Sämmtliche Werke*. Berlin, 1841, X p. 204; Novalis, *Blütenstaub* 30, *Werke* I pp. 315, 310—1.
[38] Coleridge, *Anima Poetae*, Boston, 1895, p. 115; Keats, *Letter to George Keats*. 18 Sept. 1819, Letters, OUP 1934, p. 343.
[39] Novalis, *Heinrich von Ofterdingen*, pt II, opening poem.

held sway for a long time, as can be illustrated with the poetic practice of even those poets of the Age of Sensibility who were full of Augustan nostalgia. A characteristic example is Langhorne's *The Evening Primrose* (1771). Like his predecessors, Langhorne starts with an idea of which the following description is an illustration.

Rationalism implied an interpretation of literature as "an universal language"[40] of which the rules can be formulated. Of Horace's *dulce et utile* the second was emphasized: the primary aim of all Neoclassicists, from Dryden to Johnson, was to mend, "to point a moral."[41] How much influence this doctrine had can be seen if one compares Gray's Pindaric, *The Progress of Poesy* (1754) with Keats's *Ode on a Grecian Urn* (1819). Any sort of didactic, educative aim of poetry is rejected by the Romantic poet, whereas the poet of the Age of Sensibility, who, in Gray's case, had a half-resentful admiration for the Augustans, still hopes to civilize people's passions and manners.

What were the means of rationalistic-minded Neoclassical writers to that end? Wit, learning, and eloquence, as Pomfret defined them in *The Choice* (1700). And by eloquence he meant the same use of an entirely fixed system of rhetorical devices which characterized the poetry of his contemporary, Jean-Baptiste Rousseau. Wit was something more complex, more difficult to attain, even because of the great tradition behind it. There is no doubt that Dryden curtailed the complexity of wit, and Addison and Pope even further narrowed its territory, the first in *The Spectator*, the second in his correspondence with Wycherley and what originally had been its by-product, *An Essay on Criticism*, discarding much of a great late-Renaissance and Baroque heritage. Still, the difference remained fundamental between eloquence and wit: eloquence even second-rate talents could give; wit was possessed only by the great.

> "In Men, we various Ruling passions find,
> In Women, two almost divide the kind;
> Those, only fix'd, they first or last obey,
> The Love of Pleasure, and the Love of Sway.
>   That, Nature gives, and where the lesson taught
> Is but to please, can Pleasure seem a fault?
> Experience, this; by Man's oppression curst,
> They seek the second not to lose the first."

> "A Fool quite angry is quite innocent;
> Alas! 'this ten times worse when they *repent*."[42]

Constant changes from the predictable to the unpredictable and backwards characterize all poetic languages. The quotations show that wit = rhetorical device + double meaning. A characteristic species of the latter was the constant oscillation between literal and metaphorical language: the title of Pope's *The Rape of the Lock* can be cited as a well-known example. After

---

[40] Johnson, *Lives*, I, p. 305.
[41] Johnson, *The Vanity of Human Wishes*, l. 222.
[42] Pope, *Moral Essays* II (1732—4) ll. 207—14; *An Epistle from Mr Pope To Dr Arbuthnot* (1731—4) ll. 107—8.

Pope's death the field of this kind of wit became limited to those poems which were written after the most characteristically Augustan poetic model of satire. Walpole's *To Lady Anne Fitzpatrick when about Five Years old, with a Present of Shells* (1772), Gray's *Ode On the Death of a Favourite Cat* (1747), and Goldsmith's *Retaliation* (1774) are cases in point. In each the constant shifts from one level to the other serve to underline the contrast between appearance and reality: Walpole, like Prior in his verses *To a Child of Quality Five Years Old*, written almost seven decades before (1704), addresses a child *as if* she were an adult; Gray *seems* to be uncertain whether his subject is an animal or a woman:

> What female heart can gold despise?
> What Cat's averse to fish? . . .
> (Malignant Fate sat by, and smil'd) . . .
> A Favourite has no friend! . . .
> Know, one false step is ne'er retriev'd,

and Goldsmith on the literal level *pretends* to draw a friendly portrait of Burke, whereas on the metaphorical level his lines are full of scathing irony:

> . . . 'twas his fate, unemploy'd, or in play, Sir,
> To eat mutton cold, and cut blocks with a razor.[43]

Why could the English not produce a literature of so purely a Neoclassical type as the French? One of the reasons for this might be that before Rationalism, the philosophical basis of Neoclassical aesthetics could have its full development, a reaction was started against it. The Puritans were essentially pragmatic-minded rationalists. They omitted all subjects from the curricula which they considered not reasonable (i.e. profitable). Inasmuch as Hobbes's philosophy was taken for an extension of Cartesianism, the Restoration became prejudiced against both. And if one does not mean to simplify the case, one must grant that the Restoration was not merely being reactionary in its violent reaction against Rationalism. Hobbes not only took God from man, but also wished to eliminate those aspects of life which had necessitated religion. As a result of a discontent with this system, an opposition to science developed. The members of the Royal Society came to the conclusion that it was not advisable to formulate laws too early, so they set out to accumulate data in the hope that there would come the time for generalizations. Theologians made a painful effort to prove that the world was vaster than Hobbes' system. It was at this point that the Cambridge Platonists became significant. Henry More with his *Antidote Against Atheism* (1652) started a campaign whose aim was to call attention to spiritual aspects of life neglected by Rationalism. In their distrust of reason, the major Neoclassicals, from Swift, whose *Gulliver* is, among other things, a satire directed against Rationalism and science, to Johnson, who in his *Prologue spoken by Mr. Garrick* (1747) contrasted philosophy with nature, were surely indebted to this circle of Protestant thinkers, as much as the scientists themselves, who went literally spirit-hunting. Glanvill published

[43] Gray, *On the Death of a Favourite Cat*, ll. 23—4, 28, 36, 38; Goldsmith, *Retaliation* ll. 41—2.

143

A full and plain Evidence Concerning Witches and Apparitions as early as 1668, and Boyle declared that humble ignorant people knew more about nature than men of learning. It was with this same argument that Addison praised *Chevy Chase* in *The Spectator*, and that the writers of the Age of Sensibility produced their wish-fulfilments: Gothic novels, "ancient barbaric" poems (Collins, Gray, Percy, Macpherson, Chatterton, Blake), or Scottish "folk-songs" (Burns). Perhaps we do not exaggerate if we say that the Cambridge Platonists who, trying to prove the existence of spirituality, referred to the function of the supernatural in folk-tales, unconsciously started a development whose final result was the discovery of folk-art:

"*Die Gelehrten indessen versaßen sich über einer eigenen vornehmen Sprache, die auf lange Zeit alles Hohe und Herrliche vom Volke trennte, die sie endlich doch entweder wieder vernichten oder allgemein machen müssen, wenn sie einsehen, da ihr Treiben aller echten Bildung entgegen, die Sprache als etwas Bestehendes für sich auszubilden.*"[44]

In England it was with Blake that the anti-Rationalist reaction culminated. On the Continent Rousseau with his *Discours sur les sciences et les arts* (1750) and *Discours sur l'inégalité* (1754), in England Sterne had prepared the way for him. In Blake's terms man had fallen from an innocence which did not know any kind of uniformity to a visionless, loveless experience (*The Echoing Green, Holy Thursday*). The second of these two modes of being was identified with conceptual or discursive reason, with Newton's science, and the philosophy of Descartes, Locke, and the Enlightenment; in the formulation of the first he was indebted to Berkeley, who, like Blake himself, drew upon the Neoplatonic and Hermetic tradition. Blake elaborated this contrast of incompatible visions of existence in both prose (in the now lost *Annotations to Locke*, the *Annotations to Sir Joshua Reynolds's "Discourses,"* ca. 1808, and the *Annotations to Berkeley's "Siris,"* ca. 1820) and verse, first in the form of a debate (as in the *Visions of the Daughters of Albion*, 1793), later through a re-interpretation of the Fall (in *The First Book of Urizen*, 1794, *Vala, or the Four Zoas*, 1795—1804, and in *Milton*, 1804—8). As the Cambridge Neoplatonists or the Tory satirists, Blake, too, emphasized that reason was limited (οὐρίζειν: "to bound/limit"), what lay outside its boundaries was essential to humanity. Urizen (who in *Jerusalem* is called the Spectre) had cast out his counterpart, Ahania, but unsuccessfully, for life could not exist without non-rationalistic values. Thus Blake's was fundamentally the same position as the one that had been maintained by Henry More, more than a century earlier. The poet's originality was in his attack on the rationalistic interpretation of time and space. Originally, so Blake said in the Introduction to *The Songs of Experience* and *The Four Zoas*, Los (Time) and Enitharmon (Space), the complementary agents of perception, had an imaginative flexibility, the faculty of expansion and contraction, but with the Fall they became frozen, that is, fixed, rigid, even dead, and, at the same time, their original harmony was destroyed, so that time could not be projected into space, could not be spatialized any more. At this point the possibility was open for Blake to re-establish the balance between the self and the universe,

[44] Arnim, *Von Volksliedern*, Deutsche Literatur in Entwicklungsreihen, Romantik X, pp. 117—8.

the inside and the outside, between subjectivity and objectivity, which balance made the work of Pope and Swift so much superior to that of all their successors with the exception of Sterne. But Blake could not quite make up his mind whether he sided with a Neoplatonic or a dialectical interpretation of the world, and, consequently, fell short of realizing Pope's integrated sense of existence on the higher level of organic form. But the greatest poet of the Age of Sensibility, Goethe, was his only contemporary who could achieve this, and Blake could develop a more consistent sense of existence and create a more integrated poetry than any English poet since Pope.

In one respect, however, Blake, who brought so many factors of 18th-century Primitivism to a head, went against the general current: in his interpretation of Nature. Being a Neoplatonist, it was inevitable for him to regard Nature as semblance; and so he broke away from one of the main ideological tendencies of his age which gave a highly positive value to Nature and took her for an essential source of Primitivism.

Some of the sources of 18th-century Naturalism were certainly literary: late Renaissance writers like Montaigne (especially through his idea of the noble savage referred to as early as the first epistle of Pope's *An Essay on Man*) and Shakespeare (several works, as, for instance, Walpole's verses addressed to *Anne Greville, Countess Temple, appointed Poet Laureate to the King of the Fairies,* 1763, prove that from this point of view *A Midsummer Night's Dream* was the most influential among his plays, although one may also think of Perdita's plea for nature against art in Act IV of *The Winter's Tale*), and some Baroque nature poets like Marvell (witness the plea for the wilderness against the formal garden, for landscape as a retreat from the social place in *The Mower against Gardens*, or echoes of *To His Coy Mistress* in the scientist-poet Erasmus Darwin's *The Loves of the Plants,* 1789). The 18th century put all these works into a new context, thereby modifying their meaning. In a few cases one can even say that the later reading was definitely a misunderstanding of the original work. Rousseau's version of *Robinson Crusoe* in *Émile* is an extreme case. Having found one of his favourite themes, that of the dignity of labour in Defoe's work, the Swiss author read the "back to nature" theme into it, which in his own mind became associated with the first theme, not recognizing that Defoe's aim was fundamentally anti-primitivistic: he thought of the urbanization of Nature as the only solution of the conflict between the values of urban and rural life.

By Nature the Neoclassicists meant chiefly "human nature." Johnson was the last who used it in this sense in *The Lives of the Poets* (1779—81), at least in England, for among the great civilized Western Continental countries it was in France where the Neoclassical use of the term survived longest, until as late as Hugo's Preface to *Cromwell* (1827). The change was probably started by Addison, who meant, first of all, non-human nature by it:

"If we consider the works of Nature and art, as they are qualified to entertain the imagination, we shall find the last very defective, in comparison of the former; for though they may sometimes appear as beautiful or strange, they can have nothing in them of the vastness and immensity which afford so great an entertainment to the mind of the beholder."

As a theoretician he anticipated the attitude of the first generation of the Age of Sensibility: that of Dyer, who in *Grongar Hill* (1726) reversed the arch-Neoclassical formula and put description first and its meaning second, or the theory and practice of Thomson:

> . . . who can paint
> Like Nature? Can imagination boast,
> Amid its gay creation, hues like hers?[45]

Description ceased to be illustrative but could not be creative yet: there was still a long way from allegory to symbol, and it was only in the Romanticism of the most radical type (Novalis, Keats, Nerval) that description could be entirely simultaneous with meaning. The disorientation and divided conscience of the later 18th century can be observed in the use of description, too. The poets of the Age of Sensibility still separated meaning from description, but they were ashamed of their didacticism. Hence their belief that non-didactic Nature was always superior to Art which, they thought, must be inevitably didactic. It was in this sense that they contrasted corrupt taste and frigid art with "Nature's simple charms" (Joseph Warton: *The Enthusiast*, written in 1740, and *Ode to Fancy*, 1746), "sober truth" with Nature (Collins: *Ode on the Popular Superstitions of the Highlands of Scotland*, ca. 1749), "Learning" with "inherent Genius" (Gilbert West: *The Second Olympick Ode*, 1749); praised the complexity of natural beauty (Beattie: *The Minstrel*, 1771), or attacked books over which "the mind inactive lies" (Hannah More: *The Bas Bleu*, 1784).

Unlike the Neoclassicists or the Romantics, the typical poets of the Age of Sensibility, with the exception of the transcendentalist Smart and Blake (who, in this respect, meant a departure from the main aesthetic current) believed in Nature's aesthetic superiority to art:

> . . . nature works as if to mock at art,
> And in defiance of her rival pow'rs;
> By these fortuituous and random strokes
> Performing such inimitable feats
> As she with all her rules can never reach.[46]

They anticipated Romanticism, so far as they recognized an intrinsic significance in nature — in *The Task*, for instance, evening and a vale are associated with composure and harmony, both of which are to be taken as essential co-ordinates of a wisdom that is opposed to knowledge —, but were unable to carry their anti-Classicist reaction to its logical end and arrive at the dea of an organic form which could bring Art to a level with Nature, and thus bridge the gap between description and meaning.

Tlhe main driving force behind this recognition of an intrinsic aesthetic vaue in Nature was undoubtedly Pantheism, first populari zed by the second generation of the Age of Sensibility. For Joseph Warton, Akenside, later ifor Smart, William Whitehead, or John Cunningham, even later for the

[45] Addison, *The Spectator* no. 441, 25 June 1712; Thomson, *The Seasons*, "Spring", ll. 468—70.
[46] Cowper, *The Task*, V ll. 122—6.

early Southey, Nature represented a created harmony as contrasted with original Chaos. Listening to "Nature's universal song" was identical with an awareness of God. This awareness, which they called "enthusiasm," was meant to be a pre-reflexive state of mind. The later poets of the Age of Sensibility would have liked to free themselves from the conventions of Augustan reflexive verse and get at an *Erlebnisdichtung*, a poetry of experience which precedes ideas — the subtitle of Cowper's *The Shrubbery* ("Written in a Time of Affliction", 1773) is a manifestation of that desparate attempt. Their desire to strip the poetic treatment of Nature of all connotations accumulated in the past urged the sonnetteers of the generation immediately preceding that of Wordsworth: Charlotte Smith (in her *Sonnet Written at the Close of Spring*, 1782) and Bowles (in his *Sonnet At Ostend*, 1787) to praise the child's clear eyes for a totally non-intellectual vision of Nature, and the young Wordsworth and William Gifford praised for the same reason the Swiss peasant's "eye sublime" (*Descriptive Sketches*, 1793) and "folktale" (*The Baviad*, 1794).

By this time, however, England lagged behind in anti-rationalistic theory; Germans took the lead in a movement which had been started in England more than a hundred years before. The above-mentioned were but timid tentatives in the same direction where Herder made aesthetically definitive discoveries in his *Über den Ursprung der Sprache* (1770): in the formulation of a hypothesis concerning the existence of a half-dead, pre-rational primitive language. Herder's ideas in themselves did not become important in Western Europe (in East-European countries his transitional ideas were taken for ends and their erroneous influence resulted in a characteristic but fundamentally retrograde and provincial literature which became a blind alley and hindered these literatures in their later development), they were significant

(a) as the logical conclusion of the Primitivism of post-Augustan poets who aimed at an anti-Classicist poetics but could not achieve it, so they made painstaking efforts to discover it in the distant past which they tried to re-create;

(b) as far as it gave a great impetus to Romanticism to move from allegory to symbol, and thus actually realize the possibility implicit in 18th-century Primitivism and create a new poetics. In England Blake was the only poet who could anticipate the Romantic symbolist representation of Nature, and even he succeeded in doing this only in a single lyric: *The Tyger*, otherwise his fundamentally non-Romantic vision of existence and poetics obliged him to remain an allegorist.

2.2 THE VOCABULARY OF SENSIBILITY

2.2.1 *Mental Capacities*

2.2.1.0 The Deformation of the Meaning of Wit

Through its history of two hundred years the concept of wit had undergone significant modifications: for the late Renaissance and Baroque poet it had been a means to create a sense of multiplicity and complexity of forms in the reader; the Neoclassicist made it a device with which he could suggest that the organization of the world observed a limited number of rules. In the Age of Sensibility it lost its dominance but neither got an entirely new meaning nor disappeared until the beginning of Romanticism. The significant change had started with Pope in his later period, who in the second *Moral Essay* (1732—4) spoke of a balance of fixed principles and fancy, and no longer thought of wit as the only basis of literature, in contrast to his own earlier *An Essay on Criticism* (1711). A sense of the loss of objective values can be detected in Johnson's *Lives of the Poets* (1779—81), when the author speaks of wits instead of wit (as in *The Life of Cowley*) or of the balance of wit and genius (as in *The Life of Savage*). The more conservative, as Burns, in his *Epistle to James Smith* (1786), or William Gifford, in *The Baviad* (1794), would stick to this harmony between wit and fancy, sense and genius, a characteristic tenet of the modified, liberalized later Classicism of the later Pope or of Johnson.

2.2.1.1 Genius: Originality

The poets of the Age of Sensibility fought for an anti-Classicist idea of style on three levels, going deeper and deeper into the core of the work of art. The first term they tried to replace wit with was genius. It had been a fairly conventional term, widely used by Pope in his later works:

> . . . were there One whose fires
> True Genius kindles, . . .
> . . . they left me GAY,
> Left me to see neglected Genius bloom,
> Neglected die !⁴⁷

Because of its very familiarity, the term remained too loose to be of much use. One could speak of Scotland's genius when referring to the poetry of Thomson or Burns, vaguely alluding to a kind of distinction which set these poets apart from all the English poets of their century; one could even speak of Europe's genius, as Young actually did in *The Foreign Address* (1734). Later poets could not give more concrete meaning to it either:

> ". . . GRAY:
> Whose lofty Genius bears along
> The conscious dignity of Song;"
> "Genius is of no country, her pure ray
> Spreads all abroad, as gen'ral as the day;"
> ". . . GENIUS, rising from a dark despair,
> His long-extinguished fires relume."⁴⁸

The history of this term provides indeed a good illustration of the painstaking efforts of late-18th-century writers to break away from a Neoclassicism which they greatly admired and work out new critical concepts. Johnson,

[47] Pope, *Epistle To Dr Arbuthnot* ll. 193—4, 256—8.
[48] Mason, *Ode to a Friend* (1746) ll. 54—6; Churchill, *The Rosciad* (1761), *The Oxford Book of Eighteenth Century Verse*, p. 415; John Wolcot, *An Apologetic Postscript to Ode upon Ode* (1787), ll. 67—8.

for example, used the word either when another term would have served much better (as instead of "talent" in "his genius was not dramatick"), or put it into a phrase which contains no information, because it is either entirely impressionistic ("the lustre of genius") or supplies us with a useless definition ("that particular designation of mind, and propensity for some certain science or employment, which is commonly called Genius").[49] Johnson's case, who was, we should remember, the greatest and most conservative critic of his time and the best and most Neoclassical poet between Pope and Blake, shows how far confusion violated even the best minds of the later 18th century in England. If in the field of poetic ontology disorientation was the touchstone of the Age of Sensibility, in aesthetics it was no less so. No other critic comparable in stature lacked so badly a system as Johnson.

Although genius was one of his basic terms in the *Lives*, onty twice made he an attempt at anything like a definition. One of these suggests more than denotes:

" . . . genius, that power which constitutes a poet; that quality without which judgement is cold and knowledge is inert; that energy which collects, combines, amplifies, and animates;"

It is only in the second case that he enumerates what qualities constitute genius in his opinion: invention, imagination, and judgement. Of these, as he asserts in another passage,

"The highest praise of genius is original invention."[50]

In the whole of the *Lives* genius meant an originalily that is incompatible with imitation. In this Johnson did not go farther than Addison, who, in his essay on the pleasures of the imagination, opposed genius, "nobly wild and extravagant" to "Bel Esprit," "refined by convention, reflection, and the reading of the most polite authors."[51] Both Addison and Johnson thought of genius and imitation as two incompatible capacities, the first of which was probably to be preferred, but they censured the excesses of genius. There were only some poets, like Young in his *Conjectures on Original Composition* (1759), Lloyd in his epistle written to Garrick on *Shakespeare* (1760), Churchill in *The Rosciad* (1761), or the last associationist poet-critic, Thomas Brown, who tried to make genius the basic term of an anti-Classicist poetics. Their failure was due to the vulgarity and artificiality of the opposition originality vs. imitation, which they wished to solve with "either/or", not realizing the dialectics of their relationship.

2.2.1.2 Fancy

Others tried to go to a deeper level, substituting the concept of fancy for that of wit. In the case of some poets the term did not seem to denote more than a personified psychic quality, a specific characteristic feature of poets: Benjamin Stillingfleet in his sonnet on *True Ambition* (1746), Thomas Warton in his sonnet sequence (1777), or Burns in *Mary Morison* used it in this rather vague sense. Yet even in the work of such a second-rate poet as

[49] Johnson, *Lives* I p. 259, II p. 131, I p. 2.
[50] Johnson, *Lives* II pp. 308, 325—6, I p. 133.
[51] Addison, *The Spectator* no. 160.

Mason there appeared a quality referring to the psychology of creation, of a kind that had been absent from any interpretation of either wit or genius: he tried to remind the reader that fancy, unlike wit or genius, was also a curse for its possessor,

"For Fancy is the friend of Woe."[52]

Thus, Mason anticipated an important idea behind the emotionalist tendency of Romanticism, an idea which was formulated explicitly in Shelley's *Defence of Poetry* (1821), Musset's *Nuit de mai* (1835), and Petőfi's *Adorján Boldizsárhoz* (1848); and was consciously rejected by the representatives of the Stoical strain of Romanticism: by the mature Byron, by Vigny (especially in *La mort du loup* 1838) and Arany (*A rab gólya*, 1847). The first of these Romantic tendencies, expressing "the spontaneous overflow of powerful feelings" clearly owes much to 18th-century emotionalism, whereas the second, controlling "emotion recollected in tranquility"[53] in a Stoic manner, implies a rejection of the cult of sensibility.

2.2.1.3 Imagination

Two of Mason's contemporaries, Thomson and Collins, both far better poets than him, measured the consequences of his recognition of the dangers of fancy, in *The Castle of Indolence* (1748) and the *Odes* (1747). Both used the term fancy but they associated it with an intermediate territory between everyday and poetic reality. For Thomson it meant a means to an end, a faculty which could help us to produce and understand the psychological state of sentiment. Collins, after having spoken of fancy in the *Ode Written in the beginning of the Year 1746* and the *Ode to Evening,* in the *Ode, On the Popular Superstitions of the Highlands of Scotland* moved to what he regarded as the higher sphere of the imagination, somewhat anticipating Coleridge. Both Thomson and Collins found themselves on the horns of fundamentally the same dilemma: having discovered a new kind of poetic experience, they had to justify its lawfulness. But their specific point of view was different: Thomson sought for a psychological justification, Collins tried to lay the basis of a new poetics. Having replaced wit with fancy, later with imagination, the younger poet had to find an idea of discipline attached to it, comparable to the concept of judgement in rationalistic, Neoclassical poetics. He failed to find, however, the new kind of organic form, which was not worked out before the Romantics. As a result, there remained a sense of duality of mind: he either recoiled from a total commitment to the values of the imagination (as in his ars poetica, the *Ode on the Poetical Character* or in the first and last stanza of the *Ode, On the Popular Superstitions of the Highlands of Scotland*), or produced chaotic verse (as in his ode on *The Passions*), justly censured by Johnson.

It is not difficult to see why imagination was suited more to replace wit than either genius or fancy; its denotation had been much more concrete from the very beginning. Through the root of the word ("image") it could take its origin from Locke's description of perception, elaborated in *An Essay*

---

[52] Mason, *Ode to a Friend* (1746) l. 20.
[53] Wordsworth, Preface (1800) to the *Lyrical Ballads*, Karl Beckson ed. *Great Theories in Literary Criticism*, New York, 1963, p. 260.

Concerning Human Understanding (1690). 18th-century English poetry developed side by side with the successive post-Lockean interpretations of imagination, started by Addison. The more conservative poets, the Thomson of *The Seasons*, or Gray, created a poetry along the lines of the more conservative theoretical formulations expounded by Scottish rhetoricians like Robert Andrews (*A Hint to British Poets* 1757) or Hugh Blair (*Lectures on Rhetoric and Belles Lettres* 1759—83) who by imagination meant a descriptive use of images. More experimental works, *Night Thoughts*, *The Castle of Indolence*, or the work of Collins, urged Johnson to write, if somewhat reprovingly, of the "flights of imagination," of that function of the imagination which implies the suggestion of the vastness of the universe:

"... the imagination can with great facility range the wide field of Nature, contemplate an infinite variety of objects, and, by observing the similitude and disagreement of their several qualities, single out and abstract, and then suit and unite those ideas which will best serve its purpose."[54]

Richard Hurd, author of a *Discourse Concerning Poetical Imitation* (1751) and *Letters on Chivalry and Romance* (1762), went so far as to characterize the world created by the imagination as immanent, Robert Lowth (*De sacra poesi Hebraeorum*, 1753) and William Duff (*An Essay on Original Genius*, 1767) defined this immanent world as consisting of images produced by great passion. And here again it is time to emphasize the fundamental difference between the Age of Sensibility and Romanticism: for the writers of the earlier period images take their interest from their source, whereas for Romanticism they are interesting because of their effect on the reader: the shift of emphasis is from the psychology of creation to that of effect. That is why Wordsworth rejected post-Augustan poetry and that is the fundamental difference between the confusion of Collins's *The Passions* and the integrity of *Kubla Khan*.

Most poets and theoreticians of the Age of Sensibility gave a narrower meaning to imagination than the Romantics. There was a similar rupture between what Blake and the Romantics meant by the term, but for the opposite reason: Blake made the signifié Imagination cover far too wide a semantic territory. As all contemporary theoreticians, he also took a Shakespearean passage as starting point:

> The Poets eye in a fine frenzy rolling
> Doth glance from heaven to earth, from earth to heaven,
> And as imagination bodies forth
> The forms of things unknowne, the poets pen
> Turnes them to shapes, and gives to aire nothing
> A locall habitation, and a name.
> Such tricks hath strong imagination.

But, as befitted a Transcendentalist, he censured Shakespeare for calling "aire nothing" what in fact was the only true reality.

"This world of Imagination is the world of Eternity ... This World of Imagination is Infinite and Eternal, whereas the world of Generation, or Vegetation, is Finite and Temporal. There Exist in that Eternal World the

[54] Johnson, *Lives* II, pp. 381, 43.

151

Permanent Realities of Every Thing which we see reflected in this Vegetable Glass of Nature. All Things are comprehended in their Eternal Forms in the divine body of the Saviour, the True Vine of Eternity, The Human Imagination, . . ."

"Imagination" (for which he sometimes uses inspiration as a synonym) is the faculty which helps us to understand the real nature of existence.

"Abstract Philosophy warring in enmity against Imagination
(Which is the Divine Body of the Lord Jesus, blessed for ever)."[55]

Since Jesus had most of this faculty, he could see most clearly the limitations of the rational mind, as we are told in *The Ever-Lasting Gospel*. The Last Judgement, so goes the main argument of *The Vision of the Last Judgement*, brings a triumph of the Imagination over Reason. After Jesus it is the inspired man (the poet) for whom Imagination is accessible to a considerable degree, but in each man there must be a trace of it, according to *The Laocoön*. The conclusion is inescapable that by imagination Blake meant all sorts of spiritual activity, that is, any manifestation of what he called reality as opposed to semblance. Within the poet's own frame of reference it might have had a concrete meaning, but outside it (and the Romantics rejected Blake's sense of existence and the resulting system of poetic ontology as irrelevant) it was vaguer and less useful that the above-mentioned non-Transcendentalist interpretation of imagination.

2.2.2 *States of Consciousness*

2.2.2.0 Sentiment — Feeling — Emotion

Thomson can be read as the first poet of the Age of Sensibility chiefly because he was the first to feel a temptation to see the essence of art as self-expression. In the first canto of *The Castle of Indolence* he tried to write poetry with the aim of expressing authentic and intensive emotions. Being as much aware of the formlessness implicit in such a poetry, as Collins was of the similar dangers of the imagination, he added a second canto to the first in which he tried to reject this kind of poetry and the world view behind it. But the antidote turned to be much less successful, so his work became a starting point for later development, somewhat in spite of his intention. From him to the end of this line of development there was still a long way: in Thomson the emotional patterns had been present in the form of an underlying structure, feeling had always been a connotation subsequently added to a discursive-logical unit of meaning; for Cowper the starting point and the basis of meaning became feeling itself. It is important to emphasize that this development, which is generally and rightly called Sentimentalism, is only one facet of the far more complex Age of Sensibility. There is not a shade of doubt that the fact that the contemporary reading

---

[55] Shakespeare, *A Midsummer Night's Dream* V. i, ll. 12—8; Alexander Gilchrist, *Life of William Blake*, London and Cambridge, 1863, I p. 364; Blake, *The Vision of the Last Judgement* pp. 69—70, *Jerusalem* plate 5, ll. 58—9.

public, that of Richardson, Mackenzie, and Austen, was largely female, was an important factor in this process. The influence of Sentimentalism was, as it is well-known, far-reaching all over Europe. Even the Conservative Johnson had to admit that "originality of sentiment" was at least one component which could make literature interesting; Herder, the most representative theoretician of the age, regarded the perfect expression of an emotion as the only task of poetry,[56] and most of the minor French poets of the time (Moncrif could provide a most characteristic example) tried to realize that aim. There was only one English poet who rejected outright the cult of self-expression: Blake. For him true art expressed the essence of universal humanity, i.e. the self-less world that had preceded and would follow earthly life. Self-expression, by its very nature, meant pretence, for it tried to make semblance appear as reality, so it was bad art of a very dangerous sort. And this sheds much light on his unique historical position. While many trends of the Age of Sensibility had come to a head in his œuvre (sometimes even in an extremely intense form), because of his largely inherited Neoplatonic system of ideas (which no significant contemporary of his shared), he was also a lonely figure, an end in historical development. The Romantics fundamentally rejected his world view and poetics, Pre-Raphaelitism and Art Nouveau distorted them, Surrealism was probably the only later current which could make his art *appear* as a beginning, but even their interpretation was rather a conscious misreading than a true rendering.

Romanticism started as a rejection of the cult of self-expression, too, but for an entirely different reason. Wordsworth's 1800 Preface to the *Lyrical Ballads* shows the decisive change: from a conception of art as a (special kind of) result of emotion to a conception of art as the origin of (a special kind of) emotion. And the latter doctrine implied the total rejection of the 18th-century cult of emotion, and anticipated the *ars poetica* of High Romanticism, proclaiming the superiority of art to any non-aesthetic passion (cf. Keats: *Ode on a Grecian Urn*).

2.2.2.1 Melancholy and Spleen

What were the predominant states of consciousness whose connotative emotions the poets of the later 18th century were mostly interested in? The cult of "heavenly melancholy," the emotional colouring of both the descriptive poetry of "this melancholy Vale," and the verse tales of "mirth turn'd to melancholy,"[57] owed much to Hamlet's character newly re-discovered and to other Renaissance versions of the medieval humour: in Montaigne, in *As You Like It*, and in Burton's *The Anatomy of Melancholy* (1621).

It is not difficult to understand why these poets were so preoccupied with melancholy: they saw a form of psychological alienation in it, a state which the dispossessed, rootless self, having lost its stability, may fall into. The pitfalls of the related state: spleen Sir Richard Blackmore was already

---

[56] Johnson, *Lives* I, p. 382; Herder, *Terpsichore*, II, Werke, Herausg. v. Suphan, XXVII. Berlin, 1881, p. 171.
[57] Smart, *A Song to David* l. 65; Burns, *The Cotter's Saturnay Night*, l. 69; Charles Dibdin, *Poor Tom, or the Sailor's Epitaph* l. 15.

aware of; being a physician, he wrote of it as of an insidious disease degrading the body. The later Pope, in the second of his *Moral Essays* (1735), and David Lewis in *When none shall rail* (1732), tried to find its cure in irony. For them, however, it had been not more than a danger threatening a well-built system of ideas. This was no longer so for Matthew Green and Thomson, who in *The Spleen* (1737) and *The Castle of Indolence* set themselves a similar task, but could not supply the reader with any convincing antidote, they were too successful in the presentation of illness, but not at all in their efforts to reverse the argument and establish a distance from what had been represented. Spleen was one of those things Johnson felt nervous about,[58] and that state of mind which the narrator of *Tristram Shandy* would have liked to escape from by relating a story, but in vain. This struggle is at its most desperate in Cowper's *Olney Hymns* (1771—2), *Yardley Oak* (1791), and *The Castaway* (1799), poems which make their author (together with *The Task*) one of the finest poets of his time. In them he tried to depersonalize himself and speak through a mask. His lack of success in this pretension reveals an existential failure, a total disintegration of the self, but leads to an artistic success, to a dramatization of the conflict between appearance and reality.

2.2.2.2 Solitude

One of the chief difficulties in a description of 18th-century psycho-aesthetic vocabulary is that although a limited number of key-words were used all during the century, the meanings attached to them were widely different, sometimes even contradictory. The stature and seriousness of a writer depended very often on how complex and intensive meanings he could assign to the familiar frame of reference. On close view it becomes clear that Neoclassicism involved a concern with the social and moral, the Age of Sensibility with the personal and spiritual aspects of existence.

As in several other cases, in the attitude towards solitude, too, the later 18th century could draw upon Renaissance and Baroque antecedents, on Montaigne's teaching about Stoic contemplation, later developed by Théophile de Viau, St-Amant, Marvell, and Cowley. The idea was modified in its essence by the gregarious Neoclassicists, for whom seclusion was identical with a retreat from the bigger society to their own set, to a company of intimate friends:

> Near some fair Town, I'd have a private Seat,
> Built Uniform, not Little, nor too Great: . . .
> In my Retreat . . .
> I'd Chuse two Friends, whose Company wou'd be
> A great Advance to my Felicity:
> Well Born, of Humours suited to my own,
>
> Give me, O indulgent Fate !
> Give me, yet, before I Dye,
> A sweet, but absolute Retreat, . . .

[58] Johnson, *Lives*, I, p. 352, II, p. 42.

> Give me there (since Heaven has shown
> It was not Good to be alone)
> *A Partner* suited to my Mind,

And even this intimacy had to be only temporary, just for a change for civilized man who
". . . wisely went only so far from the bustle of life as that he might easily find his way back, when solitude should grow tedious."

Real solitude would have upset the balance of the inside and the outside, which, for them, meant the basic principle of existence. He who retires from the world will find himself deserted as fast, if not faster, by the world.

> Each bliss unshar'd is unenjoy'd,
> Each power is weak unless employ'd
> Some social good to gain. . . .
> . . . man was made for man.[59]

It is no wonder that those post-Augustan poets who pined for the old scale of values, as Gray (in *The Bard*) or Goldsmith (in *The Deserted Village*), looked upon solitude as a form of destitution.

The typical attitude to solitude in the next period is the exact opposite of this: a totally positive evaluation of seclusion. The tacit acknowledgement according to which poetry was identical with self-expression obviously led to the conclusion that, as William Julius Mickle made it clear in his ballad-imitation *Cumnor Hall* (1784), in solitude man is not alone.

> Man is never less alone,
> Than when alone; . . .

> In crowded courts I feel myself alone,[60]

The "careless," "flowery" solitude of Thomson's *Hymn on Solitude* (1729), *The Seasons*, and *The Castle of Indolence*, Green's seclusion in which man can "enjoy a calm thro' life" *(The Spleen)*, Isaac Hawkins Browne's "contemplative solitude" (*The Fire Side: A Pastoral Soliloquy*, 1735), Akenside's "my happy solitude" *(Inscription)*, Collins' (*Ode to Evening*, 1747) and Langhorne's "pensive pleasures" (*The Fables of Flora*, 1771), Beattie's ambitionless retreat (*Retirement*, 1760) and echoing, "lone valley" (*The Minstrel* 1771) as well as, outside England, the similarly modified pastoral world of Rousseau's *Le verger des Charmettes*, Gessner's, Léonard's, Berquin's idylls, Csokonai's ode *A magánossághoz* (1800) were all variations on this theme. The exteriorization of the psychic world which became characteristic of that tendency in Romanticism that culminated with Hugo took its origin from the 18th-century populating solitude with natural objects, as can be seen in the early Byron, who took up the familiar 18th-century idea and

---

[59] Pomfret, *The Choice* ll. 5—6, 69, 76—8; Anne Finch, Countess of Winchilsea, *The Petition for an Absolute Retreat* ll. 1—3, 48—50; Johnson, *Lives*, I, p. 11, II, p. 433; William Whitehead, *The Enthusiast*, ll. 70—2, 96.
[60] Anonymous, *The Retirement* (1730) ll. 4—5; Lady Mary Wortley Montagu, *In Answer to a Lady who advised Retirement* (1750) l. 3.

developed it at a rate and in a direction that would have been unimaginable
in the earlier period:

> To sit on rocks, to muse o'er flood and fell,
> To slowly trace the forest's shady scene,
> Where things that own not man's dominion dwell,
> And mortal foot hath ne'er or rarely been;
> To climb the trackless mountain all unseen,
> With the wild flock that never needs a fold;
> Alone o'er steeps and foaming falls to lean;
> This is not solitude; 'tis but to hold
> Converse with Nature's charms, and view her stores unroll'd.
>
> But midst the crowd, the hum, the shock of men,
> To hear, to see, to feel, and to possess,
> And roam along, the world's tired denizen,
> With none who bless us, none whom we can bless;
> Minions of splendour shrinking from distress!
> None that, with kindred consciousness endued,
> If we were not, would seem to smile the less,
> Of all that flatter'd, follow'd, sought, and sued;
> This is to be alone; this, this is solitude![61]

This positive attitude to seclusion is, then, a link that connects the two
ages: the Age of Sensibility started a revaluation later to be developed in
a new direction by Romanticism. Some 18th-century writers, however, held
a more ambivalent view of solitude, which distinguishes them sharply from
the Romantics as much as from the Neoclassicals. The origin of their view
might be traced back to the work of Defoe who, both in the first essay
"On Solitude" of his *Serious Reflections* and in *Robinson Crusoe*, pointed
out that solitude, isolation might be a result of a leaning towards the
uncanny, of individualism and the pursuit of self-interest, that is, it may be
a form of alienation and have a degrading influence on human values.
(It should be noted that at this point the greatest of the Tories, Swift and
Pope, who had none of the easy complacency of their lesser contemporaries,
would have agreed with him, so Defoe's opinion can be taken as an interesting variant of the Tory view.) It was in this deeper sense that Burke called
solitude one of the "general privations" which, by its very nature, together
with "Vacuity, Darkness, and Silence," had something of the sublime in it.[62]

Still more interesting is Cowper's attitude, for whom solitude appears as
an experience which cannot claim to be pleasant but which is inevitable
(see, for example, *The Shrubbery* 1773). He sees only too well the logic
behind the argument shared by the majority of poets from Lady Montagu
to Byron, but reverses their value judgement: solitude can be dangerous,
precisely because it is not loneliness:

> Absence of occupation is not rest,
> A mind quite vacant is a mind distressed.[63]

---

[61] Byron *Childe Harold's Pilgrimage* II, xxv—vi.

[62] Burke, *A Philosophical Inquiry into the Sublime and the Beautiful* (1756) pt. II,
section vii.

[63] Cowper, *Retirement* ll. 623—4.

In Romanticism, except in the work of exceptionally Neoclassical-oriented poets, personified abstractions disappeared, and solitude, together with melancholy, spleen, etc. lost its concrete, fixed, allegorical denotation and became a vaguely connotative word used mostly in the plural (as early as in Wordsworth's *The Prelude* 1799—1805), in a rather everyday sense. It was only with Baudelaire that it regained a complexity of meaning but only as a subordinate trait of symbols of contemplative life (*Les chats* 1851).

2.2.3 *Spheres of Association*

2.2.3.1 The Sublime

The Age of Sensibility brought a great change in the meaning of aesthetic concepts. Neoclassical beauty had been intimately connected with symmetry and usefulness; waste or desolate places were excluded from what had been accepted by a general consent to be objects of aesthetic pleasure. The Age of Sensibility put all these under the heading of the sublime, which it regarded as superior to the beautiful. The aesthetic revolution of the later 18th century consisted in the demolishing of the identification of the aesthetically valuable with the agreeable. The change of taste had begun with Thomas Burnet, who in his *Telluris Theoria Sacra* (1684) pointed to a possible interest one might take in contemplating such natural deformities as, for instance, the Alps. The idea was developed by Addison, who distinguished between three sources of imaginative pleasure: the Great, the Uncommon, and the Beautiful, and as specimens of the first mentioned "an open champaign country, a vast uncultivated desert, huge heaps of mountains, high rocks and precipices, or a wide expanse of waters".[64] Akenside

> ("Diff'rent minds
> Incline to different objects: one pursues
> The vast alone, the wonderful, the wild;
> Another sighs for harmony and grace,
> And gentlest beauty.")

and Burke (in his *Inquiry*) still spoke of the sublime and the beautiful as alternatives of equal value, but the accumulation of poetry (started by Young with his *Night Thoughts* and Gray with his later and more experimental poems such as *The Progress of Poesy*, 1754, *The Bard*, 1754—7, etc.) made even Johnson reformulate the distinction as one between the sublime and the elegant, the former representing the top level of aesthetic value.[65]

2.2.3.2 The Gothic

Towards the middle of the century the intensification of the influence of the sublime was due partly to the supporting influence of the Gothic. The definition of the meaning of this latter term meets serious difficulties

[64] Addison, *The Spectator* no. 412.
[65] Akenside, *The Pleasures of Imagination* III 456—550; Johnson, *Lives* pp. I 122, 14, 370, 231, 203.

because of its various and rather loose uses. Johnson, for instance, might have referred to the Middle Ages when speaking of "the Gothic ages." But earlier Addison had expounded a non-historical denotation of the word: taking Gothic architecture as a model, he called all art Gothic which lacked simplicity and hunted after artificial ornaments.[66] In the middle of the century Horace Walpole started a revival of Gothic architecture, and as a result of this, all poetic qualities associated with it were sought after by the poets. With a few exceptions, all the Romantics rejected Neoclassicism, hailing Gothic art as much more superior. The vacillation that characterized the Age of Sensibility had also a very positive side to it: implying an objective historical perspective that had been unknown to the Neoclassicists and was denounced later by the Romantics. A characteristic example of this objectivity was Thomas Warton's *Verses on Sir Joshua Reynolds's Painted Window at New College, Oxford* (1782), making allowances for the rival aesthetic claims of the British portraitist and the Gothic.

In the descriptive presentation of Nature there existed no clear-cut division between the sublime and the Gothic. Poems like Joseph Warton's *The Enthusiast* (1744) or Beattie's *The Minstrel* (1771) prove that the two indeed overlapped. On the basis of such indirectly descriptive poems as Robert Blair's *The Grave* (1743), John Armstrong's *The Art of Preserving Health* (1744), Thomas Warton's *The Pleasures of Melancholy* (1747), or Collins's *Ode, On the Popular Superstitions of the Highlands of Scotland* (ca. 1749) one can maintain that the Gothic appears to be a specific department within the sublime, characterized mainly by a very limited but characteristic vocabulary:

> "Till now, I never heard a Sound so *dreary:* . . .
> In *grim* Array the *grizly Spectres* rise,
> *Grin horrible*, and obstinately *sullen*
> Pass and repass, . . .
> . . . *horrid Apparition*, tall and *gastly*,"

> "What *solemn twilight!* . . .
> . . . th' impending trees
> Stretch their *extravagant* arms athwart the *gloom*."

"dreary dreams"; "gliding ghosts"; "glimm'ring mazes"; "lurking"; "sullen eyes"

> "To some *dim* hill that seems uprising,
> To his *faint* eye the *grim and grisly shape*,
> . . . at *midnight's solemn* hour, . . .
> . . . on their *twilight tombs aerial* council hold."

> "Beneath yon' *ruin'd Abbey's moss-grown* piles
> . . . thro' the *gloomy void*
> That far extends beneath their ample arch
> As on I pace, religious *horror* wraps

[66] Johnson, *Lives* I pp. 195—6; Addison, *The Spectator* nos 62, 70.

My soul in *dread* repose.
. . . while *airy voices* talk
Along the *glimm'ring* walls, or *ghostly shape*,
. . . at distance seen, invites with beck'ning hand"

"aweful solitude"; "mystic visions"; "bewild'ring Fancy."

This "Gothic vocabulary" was, in fact, the result of an inexorable process during which the image of an apocalyptic garden was turned into that of a demonic garden, the pastoral world was totally deformed. It served as a means of expressing a sense of gloom in such otherwise widely different poems as *The Castle of Indolence*, Mason's *Ode to a Friend* (1746) and *The English Garden* (1772), Beattie's *The Retirement* (1760), the works of Macpherson, or Wordsworth's *Lines written near Richmond* (1789). This gloom had two aspects: on the one hand, it implied a dissatisfaction with social conditions (see especially *The Deserted Village* or *The Village*); on the other, it was yet another form of the psychological alienation of the poetic self most explicitly formulated by Henry Gifford, in *The Baviad* (1794):

' . . . forth I rush, from vale to mountain run,
'And with my *mind's thick gloom* obscure the sun.[67]

In two respects the Gothic sphere of associations prepared the way for at least certain Romantic trends:

(a) through the discovery of the supernatural. By the 1790's, when Burns wrote his *Tam O'Shanter* (1791), Matthew Gregory Lewis *The Monk* (1795), and Coleridge his early verse (1796), words denoting the supernatural had become parts of the common code of both prose and verse. Yet here again the important difference between the two ages should be emphasized. As far as the story level is concerned, Lewis' *Alonzo the Brave and Fair Imogine* (included in *The Monk*) and Keats's *The Eve of St Agnes* (1819) are very much alike, but Lewis was interested only in horror as the emotional basis of the story, whereas Keats re-created the story in the same way as he "re-created" the Grecian urn, and to the same purpose: viewing it as a symbolic embodiment of the autonomous world of art which is more lasting than any kind of emotion.

(b) by laying stress on the Northern origin of the English. By no means is it true that the English became conscious of their nationality in the Age of Sensibility. Certainly, much patriotic verse was written at the time — most of it on a very low level. But different models of national consciousness had replaced one another since at least the Renaissance. The significance is, for us, in the rupture between the national awarenesses of the age of Neo-classicism and that of Sensibility. For Pope's generation the English were a nation closely related to the Romans of Augustus' time and the French under the reign of Louis XIV. For Blake this concept of the nation as a special kind of civilization was quite alien. The formative influences on him, the *Eddas* (echoed in the passage relating the fettering of Orc, in *The Book of Urizen* and *The Four Zoas*), northern Gothic art, Young, Gray, Blair

[67] *The Oxford Book of Eighteenth Century Verse*, p. 694.

(all the three illustrated by him), Macpherson (whose imagery of evanescent light, mist, and solitude he tried to raise from a descriptive to an allegoric level, whose vocabulary influenced that of *The Book of Thel*, whose names occur in many of his works, from *Tiriel*, ca. 1789 to *Milton*, 1804—8), Chatterton, Percy, and Swedenborg, inspired him in developing a Northern-Germanic myth, with the purpose of finding in it an equivalent of Graeco-Roman mythology. In Blake's poetry the cult of the Gothic culminated: it became the only possible form of the sublime. Reversing the moral of *King Lear*, the author of *Tiriel* endorsed the values of an imagined Northern past which was even more savage and barbaric than the world of Wagner's *Ring*:

"As valour was the only virtue among the northern nations, cowardice was the only vice. The first intitled them to the joys of the Valhalla; the latter subjected them to an uncomfortable eternity in the regions of Hela . . . The coward who suffered himself to be taken off by disease, or to be extinguished by age, brought disgrace on his friend as well as misery upon himself. The relations of the aged often prevented the reflections, which otherwise might have fallen upon themselves, by putting them to a violent death. Children have been known to precipitate their parents from rocks, whilst the devoted persons exhibited every demonstration of gladness and joy."

This scale of values the Romantics did not accept and the Augustans would have shrunk from. Later Blake drew even more drastic conclusions from it, and discarded Greek culture which at one time he had loved.[68]

3. THE POETIC DIMENSION: GENRES

"Truth indeed is always truth, and reason is always reason; they have an intrinsick and unalterable value," wrote the Neoclassical critic. Genres for him constituted a system, in the sense of the *Summa* of Thomas Aquinas, of divisions and subdivisions. Each genre involved a certain height of diction: some were suited to the sublime, others to the elegant, etc.[69] The importance of this for aesthetics and literary theory should not be neglected: in the theory of genres the achievement of Neoclassicism is lasting. In the Age of Sensibility a dissolution of genres began, the concept of form as a logico-rhetorical construction was replaced with that of form as an organism. The organic theory suggested that either there were as many genres as poems or all poems belonged to a single genre. This single genre they identified with the lyric, the genre whose neglecting had been the major flaw of Neoclassicism. The Age of Sensibility thus developed a new theory of form best embodied in the pure lyric — a theory and a norm that had been predominant ever since.

[68] Macpherson, *An Introduction to the History of Great Britain and Ireland*, 2nd enlarged ed. 1772, p. 305; Blake, *Letter to Dr Trusler*, Aug. 16, 1799, The Complete Writings p. 792, Preface to *Milton* (1804—8).
[69] Johnson, *Lives* I pp. 48, 22.

What had been the chief Neoclassical genres that lost their relevance in the second half of the 18th century?

3.1.1 *Satire*

Which in the first half permeated poetry on all levels, from major (*The Dunciad*), through minor (Prior: *An English Padlock* 1705, *For My own Monument*, ?) to second-rate anonymous popular poetry (*In good King Charles's golden days*, 1734). But though it started later, Neoclassicism (which made satire a norm in non-fictional poetry) came to an end earlier in England than in France. Young's *Love of Fame* (1725) was the first work to point towards the decline of the chief genre of the age: a series of satires in intention, it was, actually, an early example of the *Mischgedicht*: the strong sublime element in the diction spoiled the satiric effect. And so satire lost its predominance in England earlier than in France, where it was still favoured in the middle of the century (see, for instance, Gresset's anti-church satires). There can be no doubt, nevertheless, that the earlier decline of Neoclassical genres in England was partly due to the fact that Neoclassicism itself was weaker, more provincial in Britain than in France: in two characteristically Classicist genres: tragedy and fable, it could not produce works of lasting value.

3.1.2 *Epigram*

A further sign of the weakness of English Neoclassicism was that behind the masterpieces of the two towering geniuses there was no solid body of minor verse. The gap between the few major poets and the countless third-rate talents was too large. The fact that lesser versifiers like Samuel Wesley, Abel Evans, John Byrom, or Sir Charles Hanbury Williams, cultivated mainly the epigram, which had been regarded by both the great French and the great English Classicists as a minor genre and enjoyed an immense vogue in the second and declining phase of French Neoclassicism (Fontenelle, Baraton, Jean-Baptiste Rousseau, Piron, Panard, Ecouchard-Lebrun, Guichard, Rulhière), was a natural consequence of this. Yet although no significant poem had been written in the genre, the epigrammatic was one of the main stylistic qualities of Augustan verse, especially in those poems which were written in the genre of the

3.1.3 *Epistle*

As Boileau before and Voltaire after them, the Augustans were intent to raise the epistle from the level of merely occasional didacticism. Throughout the century poets went further and further in the deformation of the Classical model: Christopher Anstey went so far as to compose a letter as written by and to a fictitious person, bringing the genre as close to the epistolary novel as the Hungarian prose writer Mikes, half a century before. The temptation to renovate the epistle lasted as long as the century: it is a telling evidence that even Burns and Blake made serious attempts at it.

The Age of Sensibility brought no more than the deformation of inherited genres, it was only with the Romantics that the old hierarchy of genres entirely disappeared. So, it was only these latter who entirely put aside the tradition that lay behind the epistolary form.

The backbone of that tradition was the speech situation raised to the poetic level, implying a strong sense of the audience, closely associated with the concept of the communal function of poetry. Pope, in his *Epistle to Dr Arbuthnot* (1735), was speaking as a member of a small civilized society to another member of the same community. In the Age of Sensibility, as, for instance, in Goldsmith's poetry, this community became even more intimate, and in Cowper's work, which stands at the end of this tradition, either the audience became reduced to a single person in so close an intimacy with the speaker that she (for, in most cases, the addressed person was an imaginative "encodage" of Mrs Unwin or Lady Austin) could be taken for his double, or the psychological state expressed verged on privacy. Yet — such is the gift of the great — of all 18th-century poets it was Pope who, in *Eloisa to Abelard* (1717), went furthest towards anticipating Romantic and post-Romantic developments, in deforming the Ovidian model of the heroic epistle in such a manner as to open a path for the dramatic monologue.

3.1.4 *Pastoral*

Pastoral was the only genre with a tradition unbroken since the Renaissance that had been kept alive by the Neoclassicists. True, after Tonson's *Miscellanies* (1709), which began with Ambrose Philips's *Pastorals* and ended with those of Pope, it fell into the hands of such second-rate talents as Byrom (*A Pastoral* 1714) or Browne (*The Fire Side* 1735). In the Age of Sensibility this minor non-didactic strain of Augustan verse survived only in Scotland (John Cunningham: *A Day* 1761, William Julius Mickle: *There's nae Luck about the House* 1769), while in England the major poets deformed the genre so much that, as we have seen, a kind of anti-pastoral tradition evolved.

3.2 NEOCLASSICAL GENRES MODIFIED

3.2.1 *Meditative-Descriptive Verse*

The essential difference between Augustan descriptive verse such as Pope's *Pastorals* or *Windsor-Forest* (1713) and the reflective-descriptive poems of the Age of Sensibility was due to a successively stronger emphasis on the emotional bearings of Nature on man and a shift of emphasis from the general to the particular qualities of landscape. These two factors werethe driving forces behind the development started with *The Seasons*. John Scott of Amwell summed up the second principle in his appraisal of Thomson's work:

"Some Criticks have supposed, that poetry can only deal in generals, or in other words, that it cannot subsist with any very minute specification of particulars. To such, this passage [the description of birds building their nests, from "Spring"] might well be produced as a proof, that their opinion is erroneous."[70]

The aesthetic implications drawn from Newton's *Opticks* were the rationale of the first important poets of the new model of descriptive verse: Young and Thomson. It was Locke who, quoting a letter written to him by the great scientist, first suggested that since excessive light might cause blindness, light was ambivalent.[71] One of the reasons of the superiority of *The Seasons* over *Night Thoughts* is that while the contrast between darkness and light in Young is, in the final analysis, one-sided and melodramatic, the conceptual meaning of Thomson's work is far more complex: he distinguishes between the "beauty" of familiar and quiet light and excessive light which is "sublime," majestic, but also terrifying, almost like the darkness at the end of *The Dunciad*.[72]

3.2.2 *Elegico-Ode*

The traditions of the ode and the elegy had met in Dryden's *To the Pious Memory of the Accomplisht Lady Mrs Anne Killigrew* (1693). Still, the elegico-ode was a combination specifically characteristic of the Age of Sensibility. Neoclassical elegico-odes, such as Dryden's or Pope's, were imaginative representations of human achievement. The second generation of the Age of Sensibility, coming after Young and Thomson, brought the elegico-ode closer to meditative-descriptive verse. Their model of the elegico-ode can be, in fact, regarded as a second phase in the development of reflexive landscape poetry.

Three elements had gone into its formation:

(a) The structure of the odes of Collins, Akenside, Lord Melcombe (George Bubb Dodington), William Whitehead, Smollett, or Cowper prove that the Horatian ode, which had had its earlier masters in Thomas Randolph and Marvell, meant the greatest influence on this mixed genre. Landor's odes, Coleridge's *Dejection* (1802), and Wordsworth's *Ode to Duty* (1805), the last of which stands quite alone in its author's mature output and is a survival of his earliest style, are the last poems in this line and the last odes of the Age of Sensibility.

(b) The modality of the diction used in all these odes is elegiac, which is a natural consequence of the non-tragic yet disoriented sense of existence that prevailed. With Shenstone and Goldsmith (and, of course, in Gray's *Elegy*) this elegiac element was so strong that it became more important than the first: they wrote odic elegies rather than elegico-odes.

(c) Non-didactic Pindaric ode was an ideal which a single poet of the Age of Sensibility, Gray, influenced by Gilbert West's translation of Pindar (1749), tried to assimilate in such not too successful poems as *The Progress*

[70] John Scott of Amwell, *Critical Essays on Some of the Poems of Several English Poets*. London, 1785, p. 315.
[71] M. H. Nicolson, Aesthetic Implications of Newton's *Opticks*, in J. L. Clifford (ed.), *Eighteenth Century English Literature. Modern Essays in Criticism*. New York, 1959, p. 200.
[72] Thomson, *Summer* ll. 437—9, 884—8.

of Poesy or *The Bard*. Gray's experiment was a partial failure: his achievement was more considerable than Cowley's but less so than Dryden's — and
even Dryden's was by no means a brilliant success. A trace of the Pindaric
tone can be felt in most 18th-century odes, but the Pindaric lay fundamentally outside the scope of the Age of Sensibility. With the emergence of
Romanticism the Horatian ode fell into disgrace and the Pindaric became
one of the genres most suited to the poets, witness the line of great Pindaric
odes starting with Wordsworth's *Intimations of Immortality* (1807). All the
major Romantics and even Tennyson and Swinburne wrote important odes;
their purely lyrical tradition is in plain contrast with the didactic aims of
the preceding age.

The most characteristic structural feature of the odes written in the later
18th century is in their beginning. Most of these poems start with a personification (Gray: *Ode on the Pleasure arising from Vicissitude*, ca. 1754—5)
which is almost always connected with an apostrophe (Collins: *Ode on
Simplicity, Ode to Evening* 1747; Gray: *Ode on a Distant Prospect of Eton
College* 1742, *The Progress of Poesy* 1754; Smollett: *Ode to Independence*
1773). This general formula was slightly modified sometimes, by adding
a simple replacement metaphor to it (Michael Bruce: *Ode to the Cuckoo* 1770)
or an apposition (James Grainger: *Solitude* 1755), or the first line might
serve as an apposition to the title, and the apostrophic personification could
be delayed (Elizabeth Carter: *Ode to Wisdom* 1747).

3.2.3 *Verse Tale*

It is easy to see why it took more time for poets to revise the Augustan
model of the verse tale. The epic-oriented Neoclassicists, Prior (*Jinny the
Just*, ?), Addison (*The Campaign*, 1705), Pope, and Gay (*Fables*, 1727)
elaborated specific variants of it, the most important of which was the
mock-heroic. Later poets, too, had an aversion to the epic mode and did
not feel themselves certain enough about their aims to touch types of poetry
which their predecessors excelled in. That is why the deformation of the
Augustan model of the verse tale was not attempted until about the last
third of the century. The experiments pointed in two directions:

(a) towards a subjectivization of the narration (Burns: *Tam O'Shanter*,
1791, John Wolcot: *Apple Dumplings and a King*, 1787), as a result of
which the narrator's metalanguage came into the foreground, and so the
story became, at least on one level, that of the narration (Cowper: *The
Diverting History of John Gilpin*, 1782), anticipating the Byronic epico-
lyrical narrative situation (Sir John Henry Moore: *The Duke of Benevento*
1778).

(b) towards an objectivization of the narration. George Crabbe, the
finest epic poet of the Age of Sensibility, represented this trend. Reducing
the narrator's commentary to the minimum, in the best letter of *The Borough*
(1810), in *Peter Grimes*, and in the numerous brilliant sections of the *Tales*
(1812), *Procrastination, The Patron, The Widow's Tale, The Mother, Arabella,
The Lover's Journey, Edward Shore*, and *The Brothers*, he concentrated
on the direct presentation of the situation as much as, and came close to
the high level of, Jane Austen.

3.3.1 *Ballad*

Other poets tried to reach the same goal as Crabbe: the liberation of the tale from the instrumentality of a (self-)conscious speaker within the ballad tradition. From John Cunningham's Miller who
" . . . sings the last ballad he bought at the fair:"[73]
as well as from other sources we know that the ballad was one of the most popular genres of the age. It goes without saying that all 18th-century ballads were specifically 18th-century recreations of a late medieval genre. It must be taken for granted, too, that long before Percy's *Reliques* (1765) there had been more (David Mallett: *William and Margaret*, 1724) or less (William Hamilton, of Bangour: *The Braes of Yarrow*, 1724) free imitations of these ballads. Such a poem as *The Friars of Orders Gray* shows that Percy drew upon the ballad in the same way as others drew upon Spenser, Shakespeare, or Milton, and recreated as much his material as Gray in his pseudo-Norse poems: the last stanzas, for example, bring a characteristically 18th-century happy ending. The ballad revival represented by Percy, Chatterton, and such lesser poets as William Julius Mickle (*Cumnor Hall*, 1784) or John Logan (*The Braes of Yarrow*, 1784) must be seen as a further wisha fulfilment, manifestation of the desire of a disoriented age to obtain - balanced sense of existence through the re-interpretation of past values

3.3.2 *Lyrical Ballad*

Owing to its peculiar position among the genres, its connexion with the epic, lyrical, and dramatic mode, the ballad could be a most suitable starting point for development in the direction of the dissolution of genres. Under the term ballad contemporary usage also included popular narrative songs (Henry Carey: *The Ballad of Sally in our Alley*, 1729), highly civilized, meditative epistles (Lady Mary Wortley Montagu: *The Lover*, 1747), or stylized, pastoral meditations (Shenstone: *Pastoral Ballad*, 1743). All these poems had one common trait: they were monologues involving a situation, lyrics with a dramatic setting, and pointed towards such lyricized ballads as Chatterton's *Mynstrelles Songe* (1777) or *Auld Robin Gray* (1776), written by Lady Anne Lindsay.

As the verse tale, the ballad also developed in two opposite directions. Here, too, the subjectivizing tendency pointed towards Romanticism, which meant by no means that it produced the better works. *Lyrical Ballads* can be taken as the culmination of this development. Such a poem as Coleridge's *Songs of the Pixies* (1796) summed up the results of the evolution of the short epico-lyric in the Age of Sensibility: the shift from an appeal to an external standard of judgement to an emphasis on deriving meaning from the poetic context, from a view of the dramatic situation as a rhetorical device or allegory to its metaphor-like interpretation. From this point of view one can say that the Age of Sensibility raised a problem which it could not solve. Qualitative changes had to come in other spheres of poetic art before a solution was found.

[73] John Cunningham, *The Miller* (1760) l. 12.

3.3.3 *Hymn*

Besides destroying the old divisions between the genres, the poets of the later 18th century made steps towards accepting the lyric as the norm of all poetry. This was a very slow, though inexorable process. Hymn-writers certainly made an advance, but their connections with Neoclassical theories were as strong as those of the odists: most of the hymns start with an apostrophe (Charles Wesley: *A Morning Hymn*, 1740, *O Thou who camest from above* . . . , 1762), to which in many cases a personification was added (Gray: *Hymn to Adversity*, 1742, John Wesley: *Thou hidden love of God*, 1738), and even John Newton and Cowper used many characteristically Neoclassical, explicit metaphors such as appositions in their *Olney Hymns* (1779).

Hymn-writing was backed by Methodism, which was comparable to German Pietism in its contribution to the cult of emotion. The two finest hymn-writers: Smart and Cowper clearly represent two phases of a development: the shift of emphasis from the external world to psychological insight.

3.3.4 *Song*

Smart and Cowper, while almost arriving at the pure lyric, did not throw Augustan rhetoric to the winds. Two younger poets, Blake and Burns, *seemed* to go further: their songs were the only pure lyric written in the period. Of the two only Blake was an innovator. But even he turned away later from the song and developed in quite a different direction. Burns in his songs was not only very repetitious (cf. for example *The Banks o' Doon* and *Ye Flowery Banks*) but wrote some of the worst poetry of his age, full of deep-seated vulgarisms below the level of a Béranger, quite close to that of cheap pop-songs:

> That sacred hour can I forget,
>   Can I forget the hallow'd grove,
> Where by the winding Ayr we met,
>   To live one day of parting love?
> Eternity will not efface
>   Those records dear of transports past;
> Thy image at our last embrace —
>   Ah! little thought we 'twas our last![74]

His historical situation was extremely advantageous: the English, ignorant of the Scottish context, mistook him for a reformer. Actually, his whole output was within a strong national tradition. His best poems, such as *Holy Willie's Prayer*, a satirical dramatic lyric, represent an interesting by-path but are not in the main line of development.

His historical significance is limited to his being a songwriter. In this field he did better what his predecessors, Mrs Cockburn or Jane Alliott had done in their poems published in Herd's *Scottish Songs* (1776). In his

---

[74] Burns, *Thou lingering star* (1799) ll. 9—16.

refurbishing of old songs and writing new songs to old airs he was as far from folklore as Percy and Macpherson: his songs are full of echoes of his reading which was similar to that of his contemporaries, it included Shakespeare, Milton, Thomson, Shenstone, Sterne, Mackenzie, and Robert Fergusson. Like Percy, Macpherson, or Chatterton, he was a minor talent, had less originality than Smart, Goldsmith, Cowper, or Crabbe.

4. THE STYLISTIC DIMENSION: DICTION

What are the common features of, and the differences between, the style of Neoclassicism and the Age of Sensibility? In this last chapter we shall try to find a tentative answer to that question, concentrating on how the function of the same stylistic devices had changed over the years and how later poets explored formulae that had been neglected by their predecessors.

4.1 SYNTAX

4.1.1 *Repetition*

Such a simple syntactic formula as repetition is indispensable in all kinds of poetry. Still, the change in its function was decisive: in Neoclassicism it had been a means of rhetorical emphasis, as in Lady Winchilsea's *A Nocturnal Reverie*, where the same line opens the long description and the didactic closure, thus emphasizing that the two are representations of the same reality on two different planes *(a B a c)*, or in Pope:

> She speaks, behaves, and acts just as she ought;
> But never, never, reach'd one gen'rous Thought.

while in poems composed in the Age of Sensibility it either acted out the rôle of an elegiac modifier of diction:

> "Ah me, my friend! it will not, will not last!
> This fairy-scene, that cheats our youthful eyes!"

> " . . . trembling, shrinking from the spoiler's hand,
> Far, far away thy children leave the land. . . .
> I still had hopes, my latest hours to crown,
> Amidst these humble bowers to lay me down; . . .
> I still had hopes, for pride attends us still,
> Amidst the swains to shew my book-learned skill, . . .
> I still had hopes, my long vexations past,
> Here to return — and die at home at last."

> "I saw the hearse that bore thee slow away,
> And, turning from my nurs'ry window, drew
> A long, long sigh, and wept a last adieu!"

" 'Such, such were the joys
When we all, girls and boys,
In our youth time were seen
On the Ecchoing Green' "[75]

or was the sign of the poet's (emphatically anti-Classicist) aspiration for song-like effects. Of this innumerable examples could be cited not only from the work of Burns, but also from the Scottish ballad- and song-imitations:

"O say not soe, thou holy friar;
I pray thee, say not soe:"

"They're dowf and dowie at the best,
Dowf and dowie, dowf and dowie,
Dowf and dowie at the best,
Wi' a' their variorum;
They're dowf and dowie at the best, . . .

May dool and sorrow be his chance,
Dool and sorrow, dool and sorrow,
Dool and sorrow be his chance,
And nae say, wae's me for him!
May dool and sorrow be his chance,"[76]

The fact that the refrain, hardly used by the Augustans, became so popular in the second half of the century (*Rule Britannia*, Chatterton's *Mynstrelles Songe*, Blake's *The Echoing Green* provide examples of very different types) was a natural consequence of this poetic tendency, and the same principle underlies even the repetition of the first stanza with a slight change (Burns: *Thou lingering star*, Blake: *The Tyger*).

4.1.2 *Parallelism*

Parallelism, as a special kind of repetition, is also a general characteristic of poetic language. Still, one can see a shift in emphasis between the usage of the two periods in question. The earlier poets did not often use sentences of identical structure, they preferred phrase parallelisms within longer units of widely different rhetorical construction:

"Nor Wish'd, nor Car'd, nor Laugh'd, nor Cry'd:
And so They liv'd; and so They dy'd."

"Not the Beauty she has, nor the Wit she borrows,
Gives the Eye any Joys, or the Heart any Sorrows. . . .

"Thou wonderful Creature! A Woman of Reason!
Never grave out of Pride, never gay out of Season!"

[75] Pope, *Moral Essays* II (1735) ll. 161—2; Shenstone: *Elegy, He complains how soon the pleasing novelty of life is over* (ca. 1748), ll. 1—2; Goldsmith, *The Deserted Village* ll. 49—50, 85—6, 89—90, 95—6; Cowper, *On the Receipt of my Mother's Picture out of Norfolk.* ll. 29—31; Blake, *The Echoing Green* (1789) ll. 17—20.
[76] Percy: *The Friars of Orders Gray*, (1765) ll. 53—4; John Skinner, *Tullochgorum*, (1776) ll. 29—33, 65—9.

"How happy is the blameless Vestal's lot!
The world forgetting, by the world forgot.
Eternal sun-shine of the spotless mind!
Each pray'r accepted, and each wish resign'd;
Labour and rest, that equal periods keep;
'Obedient slumbers that can wake and weep';
Desires compos'd, affection ever ev'n,
Tears that delight, and signs that waft to heav'n."

"O ruddier than the Cherry,
O sweeter than the Berry,
O Nymph more bright
Than Moonshine Night,"

"The Flow'r most sweet, the Nymph most fair;"

On many occasions the Neoclassicist poet combined the uses of phrase parallelism and elision:

"Give me, O indulgent Fate!
Give me, yet, before I Dye,
A sweet, but absolute Retreat,
'Mongst Paths so lost, and Trees so high,"

" 'What St. John's skill in state affairs,
'What Ormond's valour, Oxford's cares,
'To save their sinking country lent,
'Was all destroy'd by one event.'"[77]

Sometimes one can find sentences of the same structure in their verse, as in Parnell's *A Hymn to Contentment* (1714), Gay's *Blouzelinda's Funeral* (1714), David Lewis's *When none shall rail* (1732), or James Miller's *The Life of a Beau* (1737), and, conversely, phrase parallelisms in late 18th-century poems like Wordsworth's *Lines, written near Richmond* (1789) Southey's *The Widow* (1797), or in Mrs Chapone's *To Stella*, written in the middle of the century (1755), although this latter shows a deviation from the exact symmetry of Augustan parallel phrases:

Suspicion pale, and Disappointment sad,
Vain Hopes and frantic Fears his heart damn.[78]

Still, the sentence constructions in the poetry of the first decades of the century had been generally more complex, conforming to all the principles of traditional logic; the simplification of syntactic patterns by the extensive use of sentence parallelisms began only with the generation following that of Pope. Countless examples could be quoted, let it suffice to refer to a few

[77] Prior, *An Epitaph* (1718) ll. 61—2; Charles Mordaunt, Earl of Peterborough, *Chloe* ll. 8—9, 21—2; Pope, *Eloisa to Abelard* (1717) ll. 207—14; Gray, *Song (Acis and Galathea* II, 1732), ll. 1—4; William Broome, *The Rose-Bud* (1727) l. 16; Anne Finch, Countess of Winchilsea, *The Petition for an Absolute Retreat* ll. 1—4; Swift, *Verses on the Death of Dr. Swift* (1739) ll. 373—6.
[78] Hester Mulso, Mrs Chapone, *To Stella* (1755) ll. 59—60.

poems in which they play an important rôle: Mallet's *William and Margaret,* (1726), Sir Charles Hanbury Williams's *An Epigram of Martial, imitated* (1755), *The Vanity of Human Wishes, The Pleasures of Imagination, The Deserted Village,* Sheridan's *Song* (*Here's to the maiden of bashful fifteen,* 1777), Blake's *Night* (1789), or Burns's *The Silver Tassie* (1790). Sentence parallelism was often combined with metaphor: the similarity between two sentences was emphasized by making them vehicles of the same tenor:

" 'Tis all a cloud, 'tis all a dream;"

or the second sentence functioned as the tenor, the first as the vehicle, and vice versa:

"(The web is wove. The work is done.)"[79]

Both Augustan and late-18th-century verse aimed at cumulative effects, but in different ways: the first, the expression of a balanced sense of existence, fundamentally metonymical and based on the principle of contiguity, by periphrasis; the second, the manifestation of a disoriented *Weltanschauung*, essentially metaphorical and governed by the principle of contrast, by a series of parallel sentences leading up to a conclusion (Collins: *Ode to Evening*, Churchill: *The Rosciad*). There was only a single poem which could combine both principles in a higher synthesis: *The Tyger*, in which Blake superposed an *a b a* pattern on a series of rhetorical questions, and so produced an implicit conclusion and got close to the organic form propounded and realized by the Romantics.

4.1.3 *List*

List had been a favourite stylistic device with the Augustans: in prose Swift was a great master of it, in verse Pope (*To Mrs M. B. on her Birth-Day*, 1724), Philips (*To Signora Cuzzoni*, 1724), and Gay (*To a Lady on her Passion for Old China*, 1725) used it most frequently. Later poets, Collins (*The Passions*), Joseph Warton (*The Enthusiast*), Smollett (*Ode to Leven-Water*, 1771), Goldsmith (*The Deserted Village*), Christopher Anstey (*Letter containing a Panegyric on Bath*, 1766), and Cowper (*The Task*) followed the example of their predecessors; the function of the list did not undergo any important change in their hands. There was, nevertheless, one poet: Smart who, like Sterne in prose, put it to new uses. In *Jubilate Agno* he formed two lists, each governed by wordplay as an organizing principle, and subordinated them to a basic antiphonal structure:

"*Let* God's creatures worship him; *For* His existence is demonstrated
by the following example."

In *A Song to David* he went even further in experimentation, anticipating such poets as the later Mallarmé or Butor. Three introductory stanzas are followed by an adjective list, of which each member is successively developed. After a stanza of transition a noun list comes with brackets, a list within the list: *a (z) b (y) c (x)*, etc. The next noun list is preceded by transitional

[79] Sir William Jones, *A Persian Song of Hafiz* (1772) l. 28; Gray, *The Bard* (1754—5) l. 100.

stanzas and followed by 2 stanzas containing an apostrophe interrupted by 10 stanzas relating incidents. One stanza of praise prepares 21 stanzas repeating ADORATION. The last 15 stanzas produce a powerful cumulative effect, based on an adjective list, each member of which is, in turn, raised from the positive to the comparative and superlative degrees. A verb list in the last line brings the poem to its end with an exceptional control over a tremendous tension.

It cannot be our task here to analyze this extraordinary poem. From our point of view it suffices to say that in it the poet made use of repetition, parallelism, and list which was far more complex than, and a great development on, the comparable technique of the two greatest Augustans. The Age of Sensibility produced only one other poem, *The Tyger*, which was on the level of *A Song to David* as an artistic achievement. Of the two works priority must be granted to Smart's poem because of its much greater length: it is one of the very few longer poems that have a close-knit formal organization. *A Song to David*, as both the Romantics and Yeats knew, is one of the greatest English poems ever written.

4.1.4 *Dislocation*

Relatively simple dislocations of syntax are numerous in Augustan and even in those later poets who had no talent enough to break away from the Augustan idiom:

"Never since I was born, did I hear so much wit;"

"Blest, who can unconcern'dly find
  Hours, days, and years slide soft away,"

"But such terrific charms as these,
I ask not yet:"

In most cases it is endowed with the function of the emotional colouring of exclamations:

"How blest, how happy should I be,
Were that fond glance bestow'd on me !"

  "Oh, had I the Wings of an Eagle, I'd fly,
Along with bright Phoebus all over the Sky."

"Hark ! from yon Covert, where those tow'ring Oaks
Above the humble Copse aspiring rise,
What glorious Triumphs burst in ev'ry Gale
Upon our ravish'd Ears !"

" . . . Of joys departed
Not to return, how painful the Remembrance !"[80]

---

[80] Swift, *A Soldier and a Scholar* (1732) l. 159; Pope, *Ode on Solitude* (ca. 1700) l. 9—10; William Mason: *Ode to a Friend* (1746) ll. 49—50; Gay, *To a Lady, On her Passion for Old China* (1725) ll. 3—4; John Dyer, *The Enquiry* (1726) ll. 17—8; William Somervile, *The Chace* II: "Harehunting", The Oxford Book of Eighteenth Century Verse, p. 280; Blair, *The Grave*: "Friendship," The Oxford Book of Eighteenth Century Verse. p. 306.

From the second quarter of the century poets tended to put away this use of syntactic dislocation; from Dyer's *Grongar Hill* (1726) bracketing became the most favoured type of dislocation. Besides Smart, Churchill (*The Rosciad*, 1761, *The Prophecy of Famine*, 1763) mastered the art of long interpolations.

4.1.5 *Elaboration*

Periphrasis and tirade had been among the distinctive qualities of Augustan verse, and the beginning of Collins's *Ode to Evening* and Smart's works prove that even the later poets made occasional use of them. Lady Winchilsea's *A Nocturnal Reverie* (1713), a one-sentence poem, illustrates that the Augustans could go to extremes with their fondness of elaboration. In this paper we cannot give a systematic treatment of all its organizing principles, but here are some basic types:

(a) syllogism-like formula:

> stanza 1 (statement)
> 2 If
> 3 If
> 4—5 If
> 6 Then   (Lady Chudleigh: *The Resolve*, 1703)

(b) delayed predicate:

> "In the worst inn's worst room, with mat half-hung,
> The floors of plaister, and the walls of dung,
> On once a flock-bed, but repair'd with straw,
> With tape-ty'd curtains, never meant to draw,
> The George and Garter dangling from the bed
> Where tawdry yellow strove with dirty red,
> Great Villers lies — alas! how chang'd from him,
> That life of pleasure, and that soul of whim!"[81]

(c) gradation (Young: *Night Thoughts* I)
(d) circular patterns: So pass my Days ...
> Thus do I live ...

> (John Philips: *The Splendid Shilling*, 1701)

Later poets departed from these norms, first by jumbling several traditional patterns together, as Collins at the beginning of his *Ode to Simplicity*, incorporating a bracket and a dislocation into an elaboration, then by deforming the very patterns, as Bowles in his *Sonnet July 18, 1787*. The aesthetic rationale behind these poets was the same as the one behind Sterne, creator of Walter Shandy, born and professional rhetorician. Having set up a conflict between the rhetorical prescriptions for delivery and the emotion of the speaker, they arrived at the creation of a non-argumentative and non-logical syntax.

A subtle change can be observed in the development of antithesis. Antithesis is the most common form of elaboration, the organizing principle of

[81] Pope, *Moral Essays*, III (1733) ll. 299—306.

172

poems as different as William Walsh's *The Despairing Lover* (1704), Prior's *Answer to Chloe Jealous* (1718), or Richard Savage's *To a Young Lady* (1733). Pope's *Eloisa to Abelard* is built on a series of homologous antitheses:

nature	vs.	calmness
Eloisa	vs.	Abelard
life	vs.	death

and variants of the antithesis between the natural and the artificial underlies the work of Gay. The nearest parallel of a similar global structure in fiction is, of course, *Tom Jones*.

The last poetic works with this sort of antithetical composition were *The Seasons* and *Night Thoughts*. On close view it becomes clear that the conceptual meaning of the latter can be reduced to a single antithesis (light vs. Darkness) + a melodramatic ending. *The Seasons* is a much more sophisticated poem: although it lags behind the formal perfection of *Eloisa*, still its organization is of the same type:

light	vs.	darkness
motion	vs.	stasis
sound	vs.	silence
fertility	vs.	sterility
potential	vs.	actual vision
boundless	vs.	limited

Notwithstanding its far-reaching influence — its echo can be heard as late as the first book of *The Task* and the antithetical pair of genitive metaphors that form the conclusion of Crabbe's early *Life* (1779) —, this sort of antithetical construction is not typical of the Age of Sensibility. An irreconcilable conflict replaced it, first in *The Castle of Indolence*. It is true that Thomson originally planned to reconcile emotion and conscience, but he was unable to devalue the "castle of indolence" built up in the first canto. In spite of his conscious intention, he became the first in a line of poets who painfully lacked a centre in the world and saw existence in terms of irreconcilable alternatives: those of innocence and experience (the earlier Gray: *Ode on Spring, Ode on a Distant Prospect of Eton College, Sonnet on the Death of Mr. West*), the good and the great (the later Gray: *Elegy written in a Country Churchyard, The Progress of Poesy*), the natural and the cultivated (Smart: *A Song to David*), the conventional and the personal, the expected and the actual, faith and perception (Cowper: *Olney Hymns*).

4.1.6 *Epigrammatism*

The epigrammatic was a mode of expression in vogue with the Neoclassicists. Pope raised it to the highest artistic level in the didactic half of his work:

> In Faith and Hope the world will disagree,
> But all Mankind's concern is Charity:
> All must be false that thwart this One great End;
> And all of God, that bless Mankind, or mend.[82]

---

[82] Pope, *An Essay on Man* III ll. 307—10.

Later poets appealed to it especially in conscious imitations of Augustan satire: Gray in the *Ode on the Death of a Favourite Cat*, Cowper in his early satires. As a consequence of the considerable influence of Augustan models on his poetry, it frequently occurs in the work of Burns, outside the songs.

Epigrammatism had an important structural function in 18th-century verse: the text was built around an epigrammatic germ (as in Swift's *On Poetry: A Rhapsody*, 1733), or, more often, an epigrammatic line ended the stanza:

> "Renown is not the Child of indolent Repose."
> "Care of itself too fast advances."[83]

In the majority of cases the epigram served as the culmination of the whole poem: this was the closure most widely used by the Augustans, *vide* Congreve's *Nil Admirari* (1729), Prior's *To a Child of Quality* (1704), Steele's song *Me Cupid made a Happy Slave* (1707), Pope's *Ode on Solitude* (ca. 1700), Gay's *To a Lady On her Passion for Old China* (1725), or Abel Evans's *On Blenheim House* (1714). The poets of the Age of Sensibility used it much less frequently — Thomson's *To the Reverend Mr Murdoch* (1750) and Blake's *Song* (*My silks and fine array . . .* , 1783) are examples taken from the work of the first and last generations of its poets.

The main function of epigrammatism was closely connected with the didactic interpretation of poetry. In most cases pointing a moral meant an allusion to some stock theme: mutability (one of the basic subjects in Voltaire's shorter poems; William Julius Mickle's *Cumnor Hall*, 1784 and Mrs Hunter's *My Mother bids me bind my Hair*, 1794 are characteristic English examples), the circle of Fate (Gray's *Elegy*), a variant of the proverb "East and west, home is best" (Goldsmith: *The Traveller*, 1764, Burns: *Epistle to Dr Blacklock*), or the contrast made between happiness and learning (Burns: *Epistle to Davie* 1786). The poets of the later 18th century made tentative departures from the didactic model of poetry, trying to get rid of maxims, replacing it with didactic direct speech (Churchill: *The Rosciad*), playing on the ambiguity of literal and/or metaphorical meaning:

> "Full many a flower is born to blush unseen,"

or turning the moral into a rhetorical question:

> "Who would not cherish dreams so sweet,
> Though grief and pain may come to-morrow."[84]

4.1.7 *Paradox*

Sudden change from the literal to the metaphorical level:

> "A shameless woman is the worst of *Men*."
> "I wake: How happy they who wake no more."
> " . . . where ignorance is bliss,
> 'Tis folly to be wise."[85]

---

[83] Thomson, *The Castle of Indolence* II, l. 450; Sir John Henry Moore, *Song* (1783) l. 28.
[84] Gray, *Elegy Written in a Country Churchyard*, (1750) l. 55; Wordsworth, *Lines Written near Richmond, upon the Thames, at Evening* (1789) ll. 15—6.
[85] Young, *Love of Fame* V (1725), "The Manly Lady" l. 20; *Night Thoughts* I (1742), The Oxford Book of Eighteenth Century Verse, p. 216; Gray, *Ode on a Distant Prospect of Eton College* (1747) ll. 99—100.

was only one form of the deviation from the Augustan norm of closure. In Augustan poetry maxims and epigrammatic closures characterized the main tradition, but there was also a minor strain of paradox-like formulae and endings:

> "For oh ! Eternity's too short
> To utter all thy Praise."

> "The sober Follies of the Wise and Great;"

> "The whilst poor mortals startle at the sound
> Of unseen footsteps on the haunted ground."

> "I am a poor Workman as rich as a Jew,"

> "My Day or Night myself I make, . . .
> A loss I ne'er can know."[86]

Rejecting the didacticism of epigrammatism, the poets of the later 18th century explored the possibilities implicit in this minor strain, making a rule of what had been rather unusual:

> "They hear a voice in every wind,
> And snatch a fearful joy."

> "And weep the more because I weep in vain."

> "But such terrific charms as these,
> I ask not yet . . . "

> " . . . all the dread magnificence of heaven, . . .
> What dreadful pleasure ! . . . "

> " . . . hope to pierce the sacred gloom."[87]

Besides the shifts from the literal to the metaphorical plane and the juxtaposition of usually contradictory adjectives and nouns, paradox-like antitheses are characteristic features of the style predominant in the Age of Sensibility:

> "I aim at Thee, yet from Thee stray."

> " 'Thou thynkest I shall dye to-daie;
> 'I have beene dede 'till nowe,"[88]

[86] Addison, *Hymn* ("When all thy Mercies, O my God . . ." 1712) ll. 51—2; Pope, *To Robert Earl of Oxford and Earl Mortimer* (1722) l. 10; Thomas Tickell, *Kensington Garden* (1722), "Fairies" ll. 31—2, *The Oxford Book of Eighteenth Century Verse* p. 182; John Byrom, *Contentment, or The Happy Workman's Song,* (ca. 1750) l. 1; Colley Cibber, *The Blind Boy,* (1734) ll. 9, 12.
[87] Gray, *Ode on a Distant Prospect of Eton College,* ll. 39—40; idem, *Sonnet on the Death of Richard West* (1742) l. 14; William Mason, *Ode to a Friend* (1746) ll. 49—50; James Beattie, *The Minstrel* (1771) "Nature's Charms", *The Oxford Book of Eighteenth Century Verse,* pp. 495—6; Sir William Jones: *A Persian Song of Hafiz,* l. 30.
[88] John Wesley, *Hymn* ("Thou hidden love of God . . . " 1738) l. 12; Chatterton. *Bristowe Tragedie* (1772) ll. 321—2.

4.1.8 *Alliteration*

If viewed in historical perspective, 18th-century poets but started a cult
of the paradox to culminate in Byron's Romantic irony. In the use of alliteration, another means of deforming the logical syntax of the Neoclassicists,
the Age of Sensibility experimented in a far more radical way than the
Romantics. Between the Baroque (Crashaw) and what might be called a
British variant of Surrealism (Dylan Thomas), the later 18th century was
the period when certain poets went furthest in creating a consistently
auditory and anti-visual poetry. For the Augustans to appeal to the reader's
ear was a minor affair in poetry. Alliteration with Pope is scarce:

> " . . .sensible soft Melancholy."

Among the Neoclassicists Savage, a minor talent and an exceptional figure,
was the only poet who seemed to be interested in it:

> " . . . launch'd me into Life without an Oar. . . .
> A Lawful Lamp of Life by Force your own !"[89]

In the Age of Sensibility, on the other hand, all poets made an extensive
use of alliteration, from the first to the last generation:

> " . . . the Stock-dove breathes,
> A melancholy Murmur thro' the whole."

> "While Solitude, and perfect Silence reign'd: . . .
> Plac'd far amid the melancholy Main,"

> "There is a kindly Mood of Melancholy,"

> "Your hardy labors: let the sounding loom
> Mix with the melody of ev'ry vale."

> "Fair fancy found, and bore the smiling babe
> To a close tavern: . . ."

> "Down on the vale of death, with dismal cries,
> The fated victims shuddering cast their eyes"

> "Lasting life, and long enjoyment
> Are not here, and are not yet."

> "Or with languid silence stand
> Midway in the marshy pool."

> "Deem not, devoid of elegance, the sage,
> By Fancy's genuine feelings unbeguil'd,
> Of painful Pedantry the poring child,"

---

[89] Pope, *On a Certain Lady at Court* (1732) l. 8; Richard Savage: *The Bastard* (1728),
"The Bastard's Lot", *The Oxford Book of Eighteenth Century Verse*, p. 210.

"Beneath the precipice o'erhung with pine;
While waters, woods, and winds, in concert join,"

"Whose song, sublimely sweet, serenely gay,"

"Moping awhile, in sullen mood
    Droops the sweet mourner — but, ere long,
Prunes its light wings, and pecks its food,
    And meditates the song:
Serenely sorrowing, breathes its piteous case,
And with its plaintive warblings saddens all the place."

"Danger and death attend delays."

"Softest on sorrow's wounds, and slowly thence,
   (Lulling to sad repose of weary sense)"

"The mournful magic of their mingling chime"

"With sweet May dews my wings were wet,"

"Rough is the road, your wheel is out of order —
Bleak blows the blast; — your hat has got a hole in't,"[90]

The quotations are from widely different genres. The cult of alliteration is indeed a distinctive feature of late-18th-century style; in the Romantic era we can find nothing comparable to the daring and complex experiments of Collins or Gray.

4.1.9 *Objective → Subjective → Pseudo-Syntax*

And now to sum up. According to the theory which backed Augustan diction, vocabulary was foremost, syntax only of secondary importance. Johnson, when criticizing poets because of their harsh, coarse, impure diction, always meant an unsatisfactory selection of words.[91] Yet diction also included matters closely connected with syntax: the juxtaposition of generic names and properties that are adequate to determine less generic terms, simile, personification, apostrophe, exclamation, or periphrasis. The strict limits and systematizing principles of Augustan diction were the result of a long evolution started by Spenser and continued by his imitators and

---

[90] Thomson, *Spring* (1728) ll. 612—3, *The Castle of Indolence* (1748) I, ll. 260, 263; John Dyer: *The Ruins of Rome* (1740) and *The Fleece* (1757) III, *The Oxford Book of Eighteenth Century Verse*, pp. 276—7; Joseph Warton, *The Enthusiast* (1744), *The Oxford Book of Eighteenth Century Verse*, p. 361; William Falconer, *The Shipwreck* (1762), III, *The Oxford Book of Eighteenth Century Verse*, l. 429; Smart, *The Psalms of David* (1765) XIII, ll. 35—6; John Cunningham, *Day* (1761) ll. 55—6; Thomas Warton, *Sonnet Written in a blank leaf of Dugdale's Monasticon* (1777) ll. 1—3; Beattie, The Minstrel (1771), "Nature's Charms" and "Nature and the Poets", *The Oxford Book of Eighteenth Century Verse*, pp. 496—9; Cuthbert Shaw, *Monody to the Memory of a Young Lady* (1768), "Time's Balm", *The Oxford Book of Eighteenth Century Verse*, p. 505; Sir John Henry Moore, *The Duke of Benevento* (1778) l. 141; Bowles, *Sonnet July 18, 1787*, ll. 2—3, *Sonnet at Ostend* (1787) l. 11; Blake, *Song* ("How sweet I roam'd . . ." 1783) l. 9; George Canning, *Sapphics* (1797) ll. 2—3.
[91] Johnson, *Lives* I, pp. 112, 48, 275.

"the tribe of Ben," and depended on the fixed hierarchy of genres. Neoclassical syntax was, likewise, objective, determined by the already fixed system of logic. The consequence of this was a high degree of syntactic expectation, which, in turn, necessitated what Johnson called "the art of concluding . . . (the) sense in couplets."[92] The subdued couplet tended to subdue those forms of syntactic complication which would have worked against logical rules. When Pope translated the second and the fourth of Donne's satires (1713?) into Neoclassical idiom, he had to introduce endstops. The abolition of logical syntax in the later decades brought inevitably the decline of the heroic couplet; for the poets of the end of the century (Cowper, Crabbe) enjambement became indispensable.

The use of logical syntax implies a belief in an ordered universe; objective syntactic patterns correspond to the rules of law in a civilized community. The dislocation of syntax in the second and last third of the century was intimately connected with the unbalanced *Weltanschauung* that prevailed. The Augustans held that conceptual thinking outstripped thinking in images; the representative poets of the Age of Sensibility thought that the truth was the other way round. Interpreting association in a subjectivist manner, they lost their awareness of denotation. In the middle of the century Collins deformed objective syntax and created a highly idiosyncratic style, substituting euphonic for logical connections, making wild inversions, using a markedly nominal style in order to place emphasis on states of being and appearance rather than on process and activity:

> "I view that Oak, the fancied Glades among,
>   By which as Milton lay, His Ev'ning Ear,
> From many a Cloud that drop'd Ethereal Dew,
>   Nigh spher'd in Heav'n its native Strains could hear:"[93]

Smart and Blake were even more radical in their reaction:

> "Where o'er the mead the mountain stoops,
>   The kids exult and brouse."

> "Hear the voice of the Bard!
> Who Present, Past, and Future sees,
> Whose ears have heard
> The Holy Word
> That walk'd among the ancient trees,

> Calling the lapsed Soul,
> And weeping in the evening dew;
> That might controll
> The starry pole,
> And fallen, fallen light renew!"[94]

Are the children on the mountain or on the mead? Is it the Bard or the Holy Word who is "Calling the lapsed Soul"? Is it the Bard, the Holy Word,

[92] Johnson, *Lives*, I, p. 61.
[93] Collins, *Ode on the Poetical Character* (1747) ll. 63—6.
[94] Smart, *A Song to David* (1763) ll. 155—6; Blake, *Introduction to the Songs of Experience* ll. 1—10.

or the lapsed Soul who "might controll/The starry pole"? No single answer can be given to these questions. These two poets occasionally made syntax perfectly ambiguous, questioning its very function, thus anticipating 20th-century poetry.

4.2 METAPHOR

Neoclassical diction demanded an extreme economy in the use of metaphor. This economy, from another point of view, can be regarded as a kind of poverty. The Augustan poet was sure of his audience, he knew that he lived in an intellectual centre and could fall back on a long tradition. The circle of intellectuals which he was member of and which he addressed had a common language, and in his poetry he set himself the task of perfecting that language. Towards the middle of the 18th century the structure of English society changed, the reading public became larger but also more heterogeneous. The poets could not have the same confidence in their audience, they did not know exactly for whom they were writing. They could not "imitate," for they lost their awareness of tradition, of a common denominator, the general principles of literary communication, and had to depend much more on personal idiosyncrasy in the creation of their personal style.

Still, Augustan diction had not quite lost its hold over poets until the second generation of the Romantics. (In France the same was true: Hugo was, as it is well known, still indebted to Neoclassical diction.) The Age of Sensibility tried to make original imagery determine the structure of poetry, but this tendency remained a reaction against the Augustan poverty of metaphor, its aim was not fully realized before the French Symbolists. The modernity of the last forty years of the 18th century consisted in the new notion of the poet as a solitary human being facing non-human nature, which replaced the Augustan picture of the poet as a member of an urban society adressing its other members. Instead of an urban maker, the poet of the Age of Sensibility was a seer of sublime visions who remained an improviser until the new poetics was completed by Symbolism. That is why all sustained efforts remained fragmentary until *Les Fleurs du Mal* (1857).

4.2.1 *Metaphors explicit in their nature*

4.2.1.1 Personification and Apostrophe

4.2.1.1.1 Personification

18th-century poetry inclined heavily towards the animating principle in poetry. When examining the rôle of personification, we are watching a fundamental principle of Neoclassical literature at work. Of all types of metaphor, this was used most frequently by practically all 18th-century poets, what is more, there is no other period when personification would occur so often in poetic texts. In the second half of the century their number became somewhat diminished, but this numerical change is not considerable enough to draw any decisive conclusion from it. We may note in passing that allegorical personification was the Neoclassical device which survived longest, it hindered the development of the Romantic lyric and was dismissed only by the Symbolists.

We may observe, however, a slight change in the object of personification, towards the middle of the century. In Augustan literature almost exclusively abstractions had been personified; later poets more often addressed Nature (Erasmus Darwin: *The Economy of Vegetation*, 1792, IV), the image-like concept of a season (Cowper: *The Task*, 1785, IV), or parts of a landscape, such as a river (Thomas Warton: *Sonnet to the River London*, 1777), a valley (Blake: *To Spring*, 1783), or a rose (Darwin: *The Loves of the Plants*, 1789, I). Analogous to this, a structural modification can be noted: in plain contrast to the exceptionally conservative Johnson, who reduced the number of personifications and immensely elaborated them with the help of intense verb metaphors (esp. in *The Vanity of Human Wishes*, 1749, one of the best poems of the century), poets more prone to experiment tried to weaken the syntactic influence of personified abstractions, by putting aside verbs and using a genitive + an adjective (Burns: *Thou lingering star*, 1790), a genitive (Cowper, in the closure of *On the Receipt of my Mother's Picture out of Norfolk*, 1798), or, in most cases, an adjective (Gray: *Ode on a Distant Prospect of Eton College*, 1742, Mrs Chapone: *To Stella*, 1755, Burns: *Ae fond kiss*, 1792) as the means of personification, sometimes turning even the genitive or adjective into a metaphor, and so creating a metaphoric group of a complexity quite alien to the concise clarity of Augustan diction (Burns: *Highland Mary*, 1799). A sign of this growing impatience with personified abstraction was that even Gray, so fond of the device, played it down in his best poem, the *Elegy written in a Country Church-Yard* (1750), by making it ironical. Another phase of the struggle with this trait of Neoclassical style can be represented by Blake and the Romantics. The older poet could use personification no more in the brilliant Popean or Johnsonian manner, for his vocabulary was extremely poor in transitive verbs. Yet until the very end of his career, he could not produce any other means of grafting metaphor grammatically into the organism of the poem. Wordsworth, Shelley, and sometimes even Keats tacked an "s" on the end of abstractions, thereby making them neither abstract nor concrete enough, evading a problem which only the Symbolists could solve.

4.2.1.1.2 Apostrophe

What we have said of personification is also true of apostrophe: this is the other most distinctive quality of Augustan style. The difference is that apostrophe had served also as the main structural principle in the opening of poems of odic modality, and continued to hold the same function in the Age of Sensibility, from William Oldys's *The Fly* (1732), though Mason's *Ode to a Friend* (1746), Collins's *Ode to Simplicity* (1747), Smart's *A Song to David* (1763), Bowles's *Sonnet July 18, 1787*, Blake's *The Lamb* (1789), to Cowper's *On the Receipt of my Mother's Picture out of Norfolk* (1790).

As in the field of personification, here, too, a slight shift of emphasis can be felt towards the end of the century, as regards the addressee of the poem. In the Neoclassical era the poem was, as a rule, addressed to a non-fictive person. Such apostrophes are scarce in later verse, except for the most conservative poets (Burns: *Mary Morison*, ?), they are replaced

(a) sometimes by the whole of mankind (Charlotte Smith: *Sonnet written at the Close of Spring*, 1782; such exaggerations had been unfamiliar for the Augustan mind which thought in terms of intimacy), an animal (Burns: *To a Mouse*, 1785), or flowers (Erasmus Darwin: *The Loves of the Plants*, 1789), and mostly by inanimate constituents of nature: the stars (E. Darwin: *The Economy of Vegetation*, 1792, IV), a river (Wordsworth: *Lines Written near Richmond, upon the Thames, at Evening*, 1789), or a dell (Coleridge: *Reflections on having left a Place of Retirement*, 1796);

(b) by an indefinite person, a "stranger" who is also a "Traveller" (Charles Wesley: *Wrestling Jacob*, 1742). In Blake's system his equivalent is a "mental traveller," man hastening to the end of his journey, passing through different states (*For the Sexes: The Gates of Paradise*, 1793, rev. 1818; *The Mental Traveller*, 1803?, *Milton*, 1804—8). The Romantics, first Southey in his *Poems* of 1797, put the wanderer into the far larger and more general context of the mythos of romance, drawing heavily on the long archetypal tradition of constant attempts at the creation of an idealized summer world that had started with *The Odyssey* and had the traveller's journey, the wanderer's quest in its centre. There can be not a shade of doubt that this archetypal character, re-discovered by a few poets of the Age of Sensibility, in a new context became the main driving force of Romanticism.

4.2.1.1.3 Apostrophe + Personification

These two technical devices became so intimately connected in Neo-classicism, the one strengthening the other, that no great change can be detected in its use throughout the century. The continuity was almost impeccable: like the Augustans (Addison: *A Letter from Italy*, 1701, Prior: *Solomon*, 1718, II), later poets (Green: *The Spleen*, 1737, Young: *Night Thoughts*, 1742, Akenside: *The Pleasures of Imagination*, 1744, Thomson: *The Castle of Indolence*, 1748, II, William Mason: *The English Garden*, 1772, I, Burns: *Epistle to James Smith*, 1786, Coleridge: *Songs of the Pixies*, 1796) hardly used it in intermediary position, save in longer poems; in lyrics it assumed the rôle of an effective *Auftakt* (Lady Winchilsea: *The Petition for an Absolute Retreat*, 1713, Thomas Parnell: *A Hymn to Contentment*, 1714, Thomas Tickell: *An Ode inscribed to the Earl of Sunderland at Windsor*, 1720; — Thomson: *Hymn on Solitude*, 1729, *Ode*, 1750, Smollett: *The Tears of Scotland*, 1749, Shenstone: *Written at the Inn at Henley*, 1751, Akenside: *An Ode to the Country Gentlemen of England*, 1758, Smart: *On a Bed of Guernsey Lilies*, 1764, Blake: *To Spring*, 1783, Thomas Osbert Mordaunt: *Verses written during the War*, 1791).

Two modifications are worthy of notice:

(a) instead of abstract concepts, a visually imaginable season, part of the day (Cowper: *The Task*, 1785, IV), or elements of landscape, a town (Thomas Russell: *Sonnet to Oxford*, 1789), "banks and braes and streams" (Burns: *Highland Mary*) were personified and addressed to;

(b) except for one or two cases (Gray: *Ode on a Distant Prospect of Eton College*, 1742, Helen Maria Williams: *To Hope*, 1790), the poets of the Age of Sensibility did not embody it in other elements, figures and tropes of Augustan rhetorical paraphernalia.

4.2.1.2 Metaphorical Economy/Poverty

As to the territory of meaning covered by metaphors, the later decades of the century brought a fairly radical reaction. The Augustan poets perhaps never created a new metaphor, they always relied on the stock of clichés which even provincial readers were familiar with:

> "Thy bounteous Hand with worldly Bliss
>   Has made my Cup run o'er,"

> "Most souls, 'tis true, but peep out once an age,
>   Dull sullen pris'ners in the body's cage:"

To take but the second and far more successful fragment, we can trace it back to Dryden's

> " . . . imprison'd in so sweet a cage
>   A soul might well be pleas'd to pass an age"

— which, in turn, are but a variation on Donne's

> "She, whose faire body no such prison was
>   But that a soule might well be pleas'd to passe
>   An age in her."[95]

Pope counted on the reader's having read the two earlier poems, and expected of him to compare the three passages as variants of the same familiar image.

Not taking interest in the creation of original metaphors, such a great Neoclassicist as Pope had to find other means of expression which could have a function analogous to the metaphorical: in his verse capital names, allusion, pun, juxtaposition, and dialogue took on a metaphorical colouring, and the mock-heroic served as a metaphor of tone. Later poets could do without these highly ingenious surrogates, for they not only broke down the strict boundaries of metaphorical possibilities — after the first generation of the poets of the new period (Thomson) only second-rate (Beattie) or very conservative (Burns) poets did not try their hands at creating new metaphors —, but also diminished the number of explicit metaphors, i.e. those forms of imagery which contain both the metaphorical (vehicle) and the literal (tenor) term stated.

4.2.1.3 Simile

Besides reducing the number of mythological comparisons which the verse of Pope or Gay had been so full of, they further developed one and rejected another kind of simile used by the Neoclassicals. For the Augustans in a simile the emphasis could be placed on either exemplification/illustration/decoration:

> "Are not Ambition's hopes as weak?
>   They swell like bubbles, shine and break."

[95] Addison, *Hymn*, (1712) ll. 33—4; Pope, *Elegy on the Death of an Unfortunate Lady*; (ca. 1717) ll. 17—8; Dryden, *To the Duchess of Ormond* ll. 118—9; Donne, *The Second Anniversary*, (1612) ll. 221—3.

or the creation of a rather complex impression of likeness and tension:

"Soft as the slumbers of a saint forgiv'n,"

Trying to get rid of didacticism, the later poets preferred this latter type:

"It seems that like a Column left alone,
    The tottering remnant of some splendid Fane,
        Scape'd from the fury of the barbarous Gaul,
    And wasting Time, which has the rest o'erthrown;
        Amidst our House's ruin I remain
        Single, unpropp'd, and nodding to my fall."

"Dost thou hear the voice of the king? It is like the bursting of a stream, in the desert, when it comes, between its echoing rocks, to the blasted field of the sun!"

"The moon, like a flower,
In heaven's high tower,
With silent delight
Sits and smiles on the night."[96]

Still, the best poets of the later 18th century recognized that the decorative element could not be dispelled unless the simile were in organic relation with the context. The Augustans knew only of two related kinds of elaborating the simile: they either combined it with a rhetorical device like inversion:

"We harden like trees and like rivers grow cold."[97]

or built it into a larger rhetorical pattern:

$$a \text{ (statement} - s\text{(imile)}_1 - b \text{ (question)} - s_2 - c\text{(conclusion)}$$

(Swift: *Stella's Birth-Day*, 1728)

The more original poets of the later age reacted against such a rhetorical solution, but from the works of Macpherson they could see how damaging an influence the creation of isolated similes could have on the poem as a whole. That is why they made up their mind to employ less similes but elaborate them on a larger scale, devoting several lines to each of the term of the comparison, thus anticipating a characteristically Romantic technique. Goldsmith's, Cowper's, and Blake's similes about "some lone miser" (at the beginning of *The Traveller*, 1764), "a gallant bark from Albion's coast" (near the end of *On Receipt of my Mother's Picture out of Norfolk*, 1790), and a cloud (*The Little Black Boy*, 1789) are characteristic examples.

[6] Gay, *To a Lady, On her Passion for Old China*, (1725) ll. 57—8; Pope, *Eloisa to Abelard* (ca. 1716) l. 255; Thomas Edwards, *Sonnet on a a Family Picture* (1748) ll. 9—14; Macpherson, *Temora* (1763) III, *The Poems of Ossian III*, Vienna, 1801, pp, 63—4; Blake, *Night* (1789), ll. 5—8.
[97] Lady Mary Montagu, *The Lover* (1747) l. 48.

4.2.1.4 Apposition

From Swift to Coleridge, poets used appositions invariably, without much development. Only two changes were of any consequence:

(a) The Augustans were chary of attaching more than one metaphor to a literal term. Having lost their sense of a world in which everything had its distinctive value, the poets of the Age of Sensibility revealed their relativistic mental make-up by connecting a series of appositions with the same word (Walpole: *Anne Grenville, Countess Temple*, 1763).

(b) For the Neoclassicists apposition was a means of animating the inanimate world. Their less anthropocentric successors reversed the formula (Burns: *Thou lingering star*, 1790).

4.2.1.5 Copula Formula

The history of the use of the copula formula is analogous to that of apposition: the later modifications were neither more considerable nor more various. In Augustan usage the rôle of this type of metaphor had been to embody elements of stock wit in an epigrammatic manner. The poets of the Age of Sensibility deprived it of this function and

(a) either combined it with other forms of metaphoric expression, such as personification:

> "Procrastination is the Thief of Time"

> "For Fancy is the friend of Woe."

or with a means of deforming logical syntax, such as dislocation:

> "The hungry worm my sister is;"

(b) or they weakened its categorical, logical character by putting the copula into the conditional:

> "The brightest jewel in my crown
> Wad be my queen, wad be my queen."[98]

4.2.2 *More Implicit Metaphors*

4.2.2.1 Verb vs. Genitive/Adjective

The Age of Sensibility reduced to a minimum the number o f verb metaphors, the only type in which Augustan verse, considering its general metaphorical poverty, had been rich enough, and relied heavily on genitives and adjectives. Chapman, the translator, and Pope, imitator of Virgil, started a tendency which the poets of the mid- and late 18th century made

---

[98] Young, *Night Thoughts* I (1742), *The Oxford Book of Eighteenth Century Verse* p. 217; William Mason, *Ode to a Friend* (1746) l. 20; David Mallet, *William and Margaret* (1724) l. 49; Burns: *O, wert thou in the cauld blast* (1796) ll. 15—6.

very much of, and which, in short, can be called the adjective style. From Thomson onward many of the leading poets tended to tack the "-y" suffix to substantives and prefer participial adjectives to active verbs. In the work of Thomson, Akenside, and Gray the relative proportion of adjectives rose to a higher level than in that of any earlier poet, and with Collins the trend reached its highest imaginable point. Because supplying the reader with far too numerous qualifying terms, value judgements, means of differentiating, his poetry creates an impression of giddiness and obscurity; the intensity of the information has been lost in the qualifying process. His is an extreme case but nevertheless illustrates a central weakness of later-18th-century English poetry.

4.2.2.2 Replacement

Going upwards on the ladder of metaphorical types, from the explicit to the implicit, we find replacement. The highest form of metaphorical mimesis, symbol, is a species in this category. The Augustans had hardly if ever used replacements, whereas in the work of their successors they occurred more and more frequently. Yet these latter could not depart in a drastic way from the norm of intelligibility, one of the governing principles of Neoclassical poetics. They produced metaphors which appeared to be implicit but of which the literal term

(a) had been stated

   (1) either in the title:

     "Stern rugged Nurse !"   (Adversity)

     "In yonder Grave a Druid lies"   (Thomson)

     "O Nymph, compar'd with whose young bloom

     Hebe's herself an ancient fright;"   (a young lady)

   (2) or earlier in the text:

     "Flowers of the sky ! ye too to age must yield;"   (stars)

(b) could be guessed

   (3) from the whole context of the poem:

     "Come, O Thou Traveller unknown,
     Whom still I hold, but cannot see,"   (God)

     "Dear charming nymph, neglected and decried,
     My shame in crowds, my solitary pride;"   (poetry)[99]

   (4) or, in the case of a (half-)dead metaphor, on the basis of traditional usage (cf. the little bark/slow barge in Lord Melcombe's *Ode*, 1761 and in Book I of Erasmus Darwin's *The Economy of Vegetation*, 1792).

[99] Gray, *Hymn to Adversity* (1742) l. 13; Collins, *Ode on the Death of Thomson* (1749) l. 1; Walpole, *To Anne Fitzpatrick, when about Five Years old, with a Present of Shells* (1772) ll. 1—2; Erasmus Darwin, *The Economy of Vegetation* (1792), *The Oxford Book of Eighteenth Century Verse*, p. 683; Charles Wesley, *Wrestling Jacob* (1742) ll. 1—2; Goldsmith: *The Deserted Village* (1770) ll. 411—2.

4.2.3 *Explicit/Allegorical vs. Implicit/Symbolical*

Of the two aspects of the literary work of art, corresponding to Horace's *dulce et utile*, Neoclassicism laid stress on the latter. When starting a reaction against this didactic conception of art, the Age of Sensibility gave the first impetus to a development that has been going on ever since. There is no doubt that the Augustans could rely on the allegorical tendencies of previous ages, but Pope's generation went to an extreme: the image of the book of Fate in the first Epistle of *Essay on Man* (1733), to mention but one example, is the most clearcut allegory one can imagine; if compared to it, the gambling analogy in Congreve's *The Way of the World* (1700) had still something of the complexity of Baroque imagery. Among later writers first novelists set out to right the balance — Richardson's Lovelace can be taken as the first step towards the deformation of allegory. In poetry the process was much slower: even mid-century poets like Gray conceived their metaphors mechanically and could not integrate them into the context:

> "And melancholy, silent maid
> With leaden eye, that loves the ground,"[100]

Until the time of Blake and the very late Cowper only isolated passages bear witness to the poets' intention to move further away towards a less outspoken form of expression, by leaving the reader uncertain whether the words should be taken in a metaphorical or a literal sense:

> "I make (may heav'n propitious send
> Such wind and weather to the end)
> Neither becalm'd, nor over-blown,
> Life's voyage to the world unknown."[101]

or pointing out, at the end of a poem, the close resemblance of the allegorical figure and the fictive self (Thomas Russell: *The Maniac*, 1789). This latter path was chosen later by Cowper, too, who in his last poem *The Castaway* (1799) went as far in the personalizing of allegory as any poet can go without becoming a Symbolist. (It is a telling fact that Arany, that Hungarian contemporary of Baudelaire's who also stopped on the verge of Symbolism did the same in his epico-lyric *A rab gólya*, 1847).

The Castaway shows how much the ideas of a lyric-centered poetics and of Symbolism were bound together. And this close connection explains why Blake, after having failed to become a Symbolist, was obliged to leave the territory of the lyric. In his poetry there are many replacement metaphors but they all have a relatively fixed meaning in Blake's system of ideas: the antithesis of the Tyger and the Lamb, the child and the aged blind man, Urthona and Los, Orc and Luvah, etc. represent hell and heaven, eternity and our temporal world; red, blue, and golden-white signify, respectively, love, wisdom, and the celestial state that is above both; Enitharmon is the moon, mother of souls, Persephone the earth, mother of bodies,

---

[100] Gray, *Hymn to Adversity*, ll. 27—8.
[101] Green, *The Spleen* (1737), *The Oxford Book of Eighteenth Century Verse*, p. 288.

the tree and the looms are allegories of generation, the butterfly is Psyche, the valley and the cloud stand for the body, the southern gate leads to eternity, the northern to the temporal death-in-life, and so forth.

Blake's attitude to allegory was contradictory:

"Fable or Allegory are a totally distinct and inferior kind of Poetry. Vision or Imagination is a Representation of what Eternally Exists, Really and Unchangeably. Fable or Allegory is Form'd by the daughters of Memory. Imagination is surrounded by the daughters of Inspiration,"

"Allegory address'd to the Intellectual powers, while it is altogether hidden from the Corporeal Understanding, is My Definition of the Most Sublime Poetry;"[102]

He dismissed naturalistic art as inferior, but for an aesthetically wrong reason: because in Nature he saw the work of the Devil. Instead of creating his own world of images, he relied on the ready-made stock of the public and didactic system of emblems developed by Neoplatonism. He believed that everything in the world was symbolic in its very nature, a sensible representative of a spiritual essence, accepting Swedenborg's idea that the whole material world corresponded to a spiritual universe. The result was an incomplete realization of the metaphoric principle. His pseudo-symbols are arbitrary, they do not embody their designata but point to them. As the tenor is not lost in the vehicle, the reader is forced to look for explanation in the poet's system of ideas as separate from the poetry. Occasionally he could transcend this inherited ideological pattern in short lyrics; his most brilliant success: *The Tyger* is much greater, because far more ambiguous that the intention behind it.

Blake illustrates both the originality and the weakness of the poetry written in the Age of Sensibility: he broke fresh ground by expressing his dissatisfaction with a utilitarian, didactic conception of poetry, but failed in the full realization of his aim. The fact that only Symbolism could find a satisfactory solution for his problem proves the significance of the questions posed by the age of which he was the most important English poet.[103]

---

[102] Blake, *A Vision of The Last Judgement* (1810), *The Complete Writings*, p. 604, *Letter to Thomas Butts* 6 July 1803, *ibid.* p. 825.

[103] I am considerably indebted to *Eighteenth Century English Literature. Modern Essays in Criticism*, ed. by James L. Clifford (New York, 1959); to *Purity of Diction in English Verse*, by Donald Davie (London, 1952); to *Les métamorphoses du cercle*, by Georges Poulet (Paris, 1961); to *Blake and Tradition*, by Kathleen Raine (Princeton, N. J., 1968); to *The Poetry of Vision. Five Eighteenth-Century Poets*, by P. M. Spacks (Cambridge, Mass., 1967); and to *Romanticism in Perspective*, by L. R. Furst (London, 1969).

LE SETTECENTO ET LE ROMANTISME ITALIEN

par

PÉTER SÁRKÖZY

I

Le XVIIIe siècle italien est l'un des siècles les moins connus par le grand public. Il est vrai que les noms de Vivaldi, Métastase, Goldoni, Alfieri, Longhi et Piranesi sont connus, mais la croyance qui considère le settecento uniquement comme une époque de décadence, d'étouffantes cours princières, de mondains et de Casanova, se maintient toujours. Dans les milieux professionnels, par contre, les recherches les plus approfondies sont consacrées précisément aux problèmes du Settecento. C'est le positivisme qui commença l'étude d'ambition scientifique du Settecento en étendant l'époque du Risorgimento à l'époque précédente au XVIIIe siècle, également. L'analyse autonome du Settecento se rapporte aux noms de Benedetto Croce et d'Adolfo Omodeo[1] et c'est à la suite des travaux d'Antonio Gramsci, Luigi Salvatorelli, Franco Venturi, Giorgio Candeloro, Franco Valsecchi et Furio Diaz[2] que se cristallisait l'aspect historique selon lequel c'est l'époque italienne des Lumières qui prépara la péninsule italienne au grand mouvement politique et spirituel du siècle suivant: le Risorgimento.[3]

La mise au jour d'exigence scientifique de la culture et de la littérature de l'époque italienne des Lumières ne devient possible que sur la base d'une analyse économique, sociale et politique du XVIIIe siècle avec une perspective européenne.[4] Des échanges de vues de niveau international,[5] des travaux

---

[1] B. Croce, *Storia del Regno di Napoli*, Bari 1925; *Storia d'Italia dal 1871 al 1915*, Bari 1928. — Adolfo Omodeo, *L'età del Risorgimento italiano*, Messina 1931; *Difesa del Risorgimento*, Torino 1951.

[2] A. Gramsci, *Il Risorgimento*, Torino 1952. — L. Salvatorelli, *Il pensiero politico italiano dal 1700 al 1870*, Torino 1935; *Pensiero e azione del Risorgimento*, Torino 1943. — F. Venturi, *La circolazione delle idee*, Rassegna storica del Risorgimento, XLI, 2—3, 1954; *Saggi sull' Europa illuminista*, Torino 1954; *L'illuminismo nel Settecento europeo*, Histoire moderne, 4, Göteborg 1960. — G. Candeloro, *Storia dell'Italia moderna, Le origini del Risorgimento*, Milano 1956. — F. Valsecchi, *Storia illustrata d'Italia* Editore Vallardi, Settecento, Milano 1959.

[3] C'est Saverio Bettinelli qui emploie le premier l'expression de Risorgimento, au sens moderne du mot, dans *Risorgimento d'Italia dopo Il Mille*. Plus amplement v. Walter Maturi, *Risorgimento Enciclopedia Italiana* XIX, 1936; *Interpretazioni del Risorgimento*, Torino 1962.

[4] R. Moscati, *Gli stati italiani nell'equilibrio politico europeo nella prima metà del secolo XVIII*, Roma 1967. — Br. Caizzi, *Storia dell'industria italiana dal XVIII secolo ai giorni nostri*, Roma 1967. — F. Venturi, *Socialista e socialismo nell'Italia del Settecento*, Rivista storica italiana, LXXV, 1. 1963. — R. Rosario, *Risorgimento in Sicilia*, Bari 1950; *Risorgimento e il capitalismo*, Bari 1950. — A. Bobbio Accame, *Poesia e scienza nella letteratura del Settecento*, Roma 1968.

[5] E. Cassirer, *La filosofia dell'Illuminismo*, 1935. — P. Hazard, *La crise de la conscience européenne*, 1935. — Horkheimer–Adorno, *La dialettica dell'Illuminismo*, 1965. — F. Diaz, *Filosofia e politica nel Settecento francese*, Torino 1962.

de synthèse historique et idéologique qui s'y relient,[6] suivent l'exploration toujours plus complète de la vie culturelle du XVIIIᵉ siècle. Dans le domaine des publications de caractère scientifique des textes du XVIIIᵉ siècle, une nouvelle édition critique vit le jour qui a embrassé l'œuvre de tous les écrivains importants. L'étude d'ensemble de la littérature du Settecento dans les anthologies de genres à conception différente, prouve l'accroissement de l'intérêt théorique.[7] Les éditions critiques des périodiques de l'époque, sont également importantes.[8] Le grand nombre des traitements critiques des textes du XVIIIᵉ siècle, parus après la dernière guerre, influença sensiblement la nouvelle appréciation de la littérature du Settecento.[9] L'un des plus grands soucis de l'histoire de la littérature italienne se trouve dans la synthèse, dans la récapitulation historique complexe de valeur générale de la littérature de l'Italie divisée en morceaux, aussi dans sa mentalité. Il y a ainsi un décalage, dans les recherches relatives au Settecento, entre les monographies partielles exigentes et les traitements théoriques. Après Benedetto Croce ces dernières s'évaluèrent en deux directions. L'une des conceptions — dont le représentant principal est Mario Fubini[10] — démontre, suivant l'enseignement de Croce, que le classicisme reposait sur une poétique humanistique, tandis que l'autre polémise, par des preuves exactes, des interprétations confondant les siècles. Les partisans de cette conception sont Binni et Diaz.

Les chercheurs du Settecento restent dans les cadres de deux groupes de problèmes: celui de la différence entre l'Arcadie et «l'illuminisme», et celui du néo-classicisme particulier à la deuxième partie du XVIIIᵉ siècle qui s'y relie étroitement. Mario Fubini et ses successeurs font remonter la littérature du Settecento à l'Arcadie et ils analysent la façon dont prend naissance la nouvelle pensée poétique et se développe un combat inspiré par l'Arcadie dans les différents milieux du goût littéraire et du renouvellement culturel. La conception de Fubini était largement modifiée et souvent discutée,[11] Walter Binni fut le seul à élaborer un travail de synthèse appro-

---

[6] A. Vallone, *Dal Caffé al Conciliatore. Storia delle idee*, Lucca 1953. — A. Plebe, *Che cosa è l'Illuminismo*, Roma 1967.

[7] *UTET I Classici italiani*, Torino 1956. — B. Maier, *Lirici del Settecento*, Milano 1959. — E. Bigi, *Dal Muratori al Cesarotti — Critici e storici della poesia e delle arti del Settecento*, L—IV, Milano—Napoli 1960. — Bonora–Fubini, *Antologia della critica letteraria*, I—IV, Torino 1962. — A. Rosa—M. Vitale—C. Salinari—G. Petronio, *Il Settecento e l'Ottocento*, Milano 1967.

[8] G. Gozzi, *L'Osservatore*, 1900. — Baretti, *Frusta letteraria*, 1932. — P. Verri, *Il Caffé* 1945. — G. Gozzi, *Gazeta Veneta*, 1955.

[9] C. Carista, *P. Giannone «giureconsulto» e «politico»*, Milano 1947. — E. Codignola, *Illuministi, giacobini e giansenisti nell'Italia del Settecento*, Firenze 1947.–G. Dorfles, *Estetica del mito*, Milano 1967. — W. Binni, *Arcadia e Metastasio*, 1963; *Goldoni*, 1958. — A. Momigliano, *Studi goldoniani*, Venezia-Roma 1959. — N. Sapegno, *Poetica e poesia del Parini*, Roma 1960. — A. Piromalli, *G. Parini*, Firenze 1966. — V. Branca, *Alfieri e la ricerca dello stile*, Firenze 1948. — A. Vecchi, *L'opera religiosa del Muratori*, Modena 1955. — S. Bertelli, *Erudizione e storia in L. A. Muratori*, Napoli 1960. — F. Tessitore, *Lo storicismo giuridico-politico di V. Cuoco*, Torino 1962.

[10] M. Fubini, *Pietro Metastasio*, Firenze 1939; *Stile e umanità di G. B. Vico*, Firenze 1946; *Arcadia e illuminismo — Questioni e correnti*, Milano 1949; *V. Alfieri*, Firenze 1953; *Dal Muratori al Baretti*, Firenze 1968⁴; *Romanticismo italiano*, Firenze 1953; *Ugo Foscolo*, Firenze 1962.

[11] C. Calcaterra, *Parnaso in rivolta*, Bologna 1951; *Il Barocco in Arcadia*, Bologna 1950; *La melica italiana dalla seconda metà del Cinquecento al Rolli e al Metastasio*,

190

fondi.[12] Binni constate des périodes et des changements nettement différenciés dans l'art du Settecento; l'Arcadie ne peut ainsi couvrir le siècle entier, elle ne représente que l'art du rationalisme italien, son activité s'insérant comme un filtre entre le baroque et le néo-classicisme. Le néo-classicisme constitue l'autre problème central des recherches du Settecento. Ce problème surgit dans l'interprétation du néo-classicisme préromantique, sensualiste de la fin du XVIIIe siècle, et non pas dans la différence entre le néo-classique fondé sur l'idéal de beauté de Winckelmann et le classicisme de l'avant-siècle. L'histoire de la littérature italienne utilise depuis un siècle le terme « préromantique »,[13] mais l'explication qu'elle en donne n'est pas sans équivoque. Selon M. Fubini, le préromantisme ne représenterait pas seulement l'art de la fin du siècle, mais une tendance secondaire qui empreigne toute la littérature italienne du XVIIIe siècle. Walter Binni, par contre, explique la naissance du préromantisme italien par la crise du rationalisme italien et de l'optimisme des Lumières. Selon lui, le préromantisme est l'atmosphère d'une époque qu'on peut définir ainsi: «Il nome del preromanticismo designa un periodo che ha la sua tipica atmosfera, ma sopratutto vive come avvio ad una civiltà letteraria più organica, come svolgimento e abbandono di una poetica nella sua piena maturità. Periodo in cui provvisorie sintesi si realizzano su residui di una cultura consumata e su spunti di una nuova sensibilità su fermenti ancora torbidi, ma capaci di incidere sul linguaggio tradizionale, di scommuoverlo entro i suoi chiari limiti aulici.''[14]

Plusieurs chercheurs — dont Mario Puppo aussi[15] — affirment que le romantisme italien n'a pas d'aspirations idéalistiques comme le romantisme allemand, bien que le goût classique de Foscolo, de Monti et de Leopardi s'accorde avec le goût néo-classique keatsien et hölderlinien de l'avant-siècle, de sorte que dans le cas de la littérature italienne on peut parler d'un néo-classicisme s'étendant des Lumières au romantisme, comme dans les littératures de l'Europe centrale. L'héritage du Settecento ne se manifeste donc pas seulement dans les rapports sociaux et politiques; c'est la littérature et la culture du XVIIIe siècle qui prépare le libre développement de l'art de l'époque du Risorgimento; les romantiques italiens reçoivent en héritage du précédent siècle l'idée de la nation, de l'unité nationale, de la solidarité, l'aspiration à une langue nationale et à une culture unie, à l'élaboration d'un nouveau style fondé sur la liberté de la pensée et sur la nouvelle sensibilité.

Bologna 1951; *Arcadia e antiarcadia*, Bologna 1964. — G. Toffanin, *Eredità del Risorgimento in Arcadia*, Bologna 1923; *L'Arcadia*, Bologna 1958. — G. Petronio, *Parini e l'illuminismo lombardo*, Milano 1961.

[12] W. Binni, *Arcadia e Metastasio*, Firenze 1963; *Classicismo e neoclassicismo, nella letteratura del Settecento*, Firenze 1963; *Preromanticismo italiano*, Firenze 1962. — Binni–Diaz, *Il Settecento Garzanti*, 1968.

[13] E. Bertana, *Arcadia lugubre e preromanticismo*, 1908.

[14] Binni, *Preromanticismo italiano*, Firenze 1962, p. 8.

[15] *Discussioni linguistiche del Settecento*, Momenti e problemi della storia dell'Estetica, III., 1957.

II

La péninsule italienne est démembrée, divisée depuis la chute de l'Empire romain jusqu'en 1870, durant mille cinq cents ans, et la pensée de l'unité sociale et politique ne se prononce concrètement qu'après l'activité des grands prédécesseurs tels que Dante et Petrarque, à la suite de la Révolution française et des guerres de Napoléon. La prospérité des royaumes des villes, la richesse de la Renaissance italienne montrèrent déjà certains signes annonciateurs de l'unité italienne, mais les illusions des Cola di Rienzo et de Machiavel furent définitivement dissipées par les campagnes conquérantes en Italie de Charles VIII, par les guerres sévissant durant des siècles sur la péninsule italienne et par la dépendance espagnole d'un siècle et demi.

Cependant l'équilibre européen des dynasties hispano-franco-Habsbourgiennes changea vers les années 1700. La conséquence pour l'Italie en fut un nouveau morcellement de territoire, sacré par le traité d'Utrecht en 1713 et celui d'Aachen en 1748. Le démembrement territorial, la dépendance politique de l'étranger semblent les plus stables et c'est alors que la vie économique se trouve à son niveau le plus bas. Pourtant ce sentiment de stabilité, la relative tranquillité de la politique intérieure et de l'indépendance donnent la possibilité d'un début du réformisme italien. Les petits États italiens (la Lombardie, la Toscana, le royaume de Naples) qui ne peuvent pas être considérés comme indépendants dans leurs affaires étrangères, commencent à se détacher de plus en plus de la capitale et à développer leur propre direction politique de caractère italien. Les projets de réforme des gouvernements éclairés (Du Tillot) mobilisent les idées italiennes, de nouvelles forces se révèlent, la péninsule italienne commence lentement à prendre conscience. L'Italie, isolée jusqu'alors, a tendance à s'ouvrir aux acquisitions étrangères du siècle des Lumières, c'est ce que prouve la diffusion et la popularité en Italie des œuvres littéraires et scientifiques françaises et anglaises, le grand nombre de traductions et la publication prompte de l'édition révisée de l'Encyclopédie (1752, Lucca).

C'est dans des circonstances spécifiquement italiennes que font leur apparition les tendances informatives caractéristiques aux Lumières italiennes: la littérature juridique, politico-économique, économico-sociale, sociologique. La culture de la deuxième moitié du XVIIIe siècle doit beaucoup aux influences anglaises, françaises et allemandes, mais là ce n'est pas un emprunt passif, car elle dispose d'un fort caractère individuel qui nuance et colore considérablement le tableau des Lumières européennes. Cesare Beccaria, les frères Verri, Algarotti, Giannone, Galiani, Genovesi étaient connus partout en Europe.

Nous pouvons constater donc que l'Italie, même divisée, même connaissant son niveau économique le plus bas, malgré sa dépendance et son état arriéré n'est plus l'ancienne Italie immobile de l'époque de la contre-réformation. C'est ce que prouve aussi le fait que la pensée de la solidarité, de l'unité nationale italienne, du futur État national italien commence à se prononcer à partir des années 1760, à un moment où la division semble justement être définitive.

Dans les œuvres des écrivains de l'époque italienne des Lumières il est de plus en plus question de la nation et de la nécessité de l'unité et ce que les membres de l'Arcadie ne déclaraient qu'en défense des traditions culturelles au début du siècle, devient une nécessité économico-politique chez Galiani et Genovesi et un programme politique chez Gianrinaldo Carli et Vincenzo Cuoco.

L'exigence de l'unité politique et économique ne vit le jour qu'à l'époque républicaine, mais la conscience de l'unité culturelle qui l'avait précédée date de bien plus loin. L'idée d'une unique appartenance culturelle existait déjà à partir de 1200 en Italie, Dante, Petrarque, Lorenzo il Magnifico et Machiavel la traduisirent déjà, mais la base sociale de la conscience de l'unité intellectuelle manquait durant des siècles. L'Arcadie, l'école des poètes fondée en 1690 à Rome par la reine Christine qui avait pour un de ses buts de rallier les artistes de la péninsule italienne, joua un rôle important dans la détermination de l'aspect culturel du XVIIIe siècle. C'est dans le cadre de l'Académie de l'Arcadie que se réalisa, pour la première fois dans la vie culturelle de l'Italie, l'idée de l'égalité et de la démocratie. Les poètes de pastorales se déclaraient égaux sans distinction de rang ou de lieu de naissance, ils ne se distinguaient que selon certaines contrées d'Arcadie et selon les types de vers utilisés. Ce fait distingue en grande mesure l'Arcadie du rang des salons et des académies de l'époque, car c'est là le premier signe de libération dans la vie culturelle italienne, la voie de développement de la pensée d'unité, et nous comprendrons que même à la fin du siècle, lorsque la pratique de la poésie pastorale devient une fiction vide, les grands personnages de l'époque voient dans l'Arcadie le symbole des traditions littéraires nationales et ils se sentent honorés de prendre place parmi les membres de l'Arcadie (comme Alfieri).

Nous observons aussi le renforcement de la pensée nationale dans les manuscrits où les écrivains de l'époque s'engagent pour la défense de la culture nationale en polémisant avec des auteurs français et anglais qui critiquent la situation de la littérature en Italie. Le premier exemple en est la polémique Bouhours—Orsi,[16] dans laquelle les notabilités culturelles italiennes défendent les valeurs de la culture et de la langue italienne, tels Manfredi, Salvini, Zeno, Francesco Montani et L. A. Muratori. Ce dernier, dans ses travaux philologiques (*Della perfetta poesia italiana*, 1706, *Riflessioni sopra il buon gusto intorno le scienze e le arti*, 1708) tâche de démontrer, contre l'opinion défavorable de Bouhours sur la langue italienne, que celle-ci ne s'est pas altérée durant les siècles, qu'elle n'est pas mourante, et qu'au contraire, elle s'amplifie et évolue. C'est ainsi que la *Questione della lingua* devient le mobile le plus important des idées nationales italiennes.

Ce fut Dante qui commença la discussion sur la langue nationale italienne dans *De Vulgari Eloquentia*; l'époque de l'humanisme en fait une question centrale.[17] Le Cinquecento (Pietro Bembo et Leonardo Salviati) élabore

[16] G. G. Orsi, *Sette dialoghi in difesa del classicismo contro l'anticlassicismo francese*, 1905.

[17] La première discussion sur la *Questione della lingua* — la question de la langue italienne — eut lieu en 1435 dans l'antichambre de l'appartement du pape Eugène IV entre F. Biondo, L. Bruni et d'autres humanistes, puis y prirent part au cours des siècles suivants des personnalités telles que: L. B. Alberti, Lorenzo il Magnifico, G. G. Trissino, N. Machiavel, P. Bembo, L. Salviati et la discussion se poursuivit à travers le XVIIIe siècle jusqu'à Alessandro Manzoni et I. G. Ascoli. Faute d'une littérature italienne unie, c'est la *Questione della lingua* qui représentait pour ainsi dire la tradition de l'histoire de la littérature italienne, aussi ses problèmes ne peuvent-ils pas être considérés uniquement comme linguistiques. Littérature: B. Migliorini,

les canons au-dessus de toute critique du Trecento de Florence de la langue littéraire italienne, qui seront sacrés par l'Académie et le *Grand Dictionnaire Crusca* (1606). Ainsi, il y a deux langues qui vivent l'une près de l'autre aux XVII—XVIIIe siècles: la langue littéraire nationale, instrument des érudits, tout à fait restreinte et stérile et la langue commune, de caractère peu cultivé, fragmentée en différents dialectes. Au XVIIIe siècle, sous l'effet des influences spirituelles étrangères, la discussion linguistique tourne autour de la fonction de la langue. Les philosophes italiens ont besoin d'une langue «utile» et non «savante», ils exigent la simplification du style, de nouveaux mots, qui conviennent aux nouvelles idées et, contrairement à la structure artificielle des phrases du Cinquecento et de Boccaccio, ils aspirent à une langue en prose, de structure directe, selon le modèle français. Ainsi, le problème du renouvellement de la langue fait porter l'intérêt des anciens sujets rhétoriques aux questions culturelles, politiques et sociales italiennes. Les polémistes commencent à voir de plus en plus clairement l'étroit rapport entre la langue commune et la nation et ils cherchent la raison des imperfections de la langue italienne et l'absence d'une langue nationale dans des facteurs historiques et sociaux. Saverio Bettinelli affirme: «Je pense cependant que si l'Italie avait un vrai centre, un lieu unificateur, elle serait beaucoup plus riche en art, aussi en littérature, mais peut-être même en sciences que n'importe quelle autre nation.»[18] Et Giuseppe Baretti, qui fut peut-être l'un des participants les plus importants et les plus intransigeants des discussions linguistiques fonde, dans sa préface aux œuvres complètes de Machiavel, son parti pris contre la langue de Trecento de Florence, sur une opinion qui rallie la langue, la politique et l'histoire: «Les années de Florence étaient un temps très différent: c'était l'époque de la liberté républicaine, celle des discussions publiques devant le peuple, d'une vie politique partagée par toute la ville; et, par conséquent, la langue aussi, était différente: forte, claire et vivante ... Mais aujourd'hui Florence est un Lilliput, comment veut-elle que sa langue soit répandue pour toute l'Italie.»[19] Les innovateurs les plus hardis, Caffé et Melchiore Cesarotti veulent parvenir à l'amélioration de la situation de la langue et de la culture par l'amélioration de la situation de l'État. Ils proclament: «Lorsqu'un écrivain écrit des choses intelligentes et intéressantes en une langue que tous les Italiens comprennent, et lorsqu'il les écrit avec goût, sans ennuyer les lecteurs, il faut dire de cet écrivain que c'est un bon écrivain et qu'il est un écrivain italien ... Chaque mot que tous les habitants d'Italie comprennent est d'après nous un mot italien ... Nous déclarons que nous écrirons sur ces pages dans une langue que les gens cultivés comprendront de Reggio Calabria jusqu'aux Alpes.»[20] «Plus une langue montre de changements, plus c'est là, le signe sûr du

---

Storia della lingua italiana, Firenze 1960. — Vitale, *La Questione della lingua*, Palermo 1960. — Devoto, *Profilo di Storia della lingua italiana*, Firenze 1953. — A. Schiaffini, *Momenti di Storia lingua*, Firenze 1953. — M. Puppo, *Discussioni linguistiche del Settecento*, Torino 1957. — L. Rosiello, *Linguistica illuministica*, Bologna 1965. — S. Battaglia, *Il problema della lingua dal Baretti al Manzoni*, Napoli 1965. — C. Calcaterra, *L'ideologia negli studi linguistici del Settecento*, Bologna 1946. — Gy. Herczeg, *Az illuminizmus stílusvítáinak társadalmi háttere* (L'arrière-plan social des discussions de style de l'illuminisme). Filológiai Közlöny, Budapest 1961/1—2.
[18] Cité par M. Puppo, *Discussioni linguistiche del Settecento*, Torino 1966, p. 290.
[19] *Op. cit.*, p. 239.
[20] *Il Caffé*, 1945, pp. 20—21.

changement révolutionnaire des idées de la nation qui parle cette langue, et c'est du genre des changements de la langue que l'on peut présumer du domaine de changement des idées.»[21] «La vie de la langue correspond à la vie de la nation et dépend du sort du peuple auquel elle appartient.»[22] L'essence de la langue ne peut être autre chose qu'un génie formé de tous les composants de la nation, et représentant la totalité des caractères nationaux[23] — en d'autres termes: l'exigence d'une langue italienne moderne et nationale commence à se former de plus en plus nettement, et elle est naturellement contenue aussi dans l'idée de l'unité nationale. D'autre part, il est très intéressant de voir que la conception d'une langue nationale ne se développe pas seulement dans les milieux des innovateurs: les pédants, les académiciens, les puristes luttent pour la défense de la langue nationale contre les innovations.[24] Parmi ces derniers se distingue l'œuvre du piémontais Gianfranco Galeani Napione qui, malgré sa conception traditionnelle de la langue, contient déjà des pensées nettement nationalistes: «La langue est un des liens les plus importants qui attachent à la patrie.» «Disposer d'une propre langue, la soigner, l'aimer, l'estimer et l'utiliser aux occasions les plus intimes et les plus solennelles est l'un des facteurs les plus importants qui puissent attacher les hommes à la terre qu'ils habitent.» (*Dell'uso dei pregi della lingua italiana*, 1791)[25]

La *Questione della lingua* marque une des époques les plus importantes de l'histoire de la langue italienne, celle du dernier tiers du XVIIIe siècle, où la question de la langue devient essentiellement une question culturelle, littéraire et politique. Ce n'est pas le hasard qui fait que jamais autant de personnes ne s'occupent des questions linguistiques et stylistiques qu'à l'époque des Lumières et que les participants aux discussions sont moins des écrivains et des savants que des critiques, des rédacteurs de journaux, des hommes de loi, des philosophes, des économistes et des hommes politiques — ce qui témoigne de la présence des problèmes sociaux et politiques dans la question de la langue. Même les participants à la controverse sont conscients de la fonction sociale et politique que peut remplir le moyen d'action linguistique, ils savent bien que la modernisation de la langue littéraire traditionnelle qui entrave l'évolution culturelle et sociale, la création d'une langue nationale unique contribuent largement au développement d'une nouvelle Italie démocratique et unifiée.[26] Ce n'est pas un hasard si la première revue des romantiques italiens, le *Conciliatore* (1818—1819) considère

[21] Beccaria, *Frammento sullo stile*, Il Caffé, 1945, p. 131.

[22] Cesarotti, *Corso preliminare al Corso ragionato di letteratura greca. Opere Scelte*, Firenze 1945, p. 203.

[23] M. Puppo, *Discussioni linguistiche del Settecento*, Torino 1966, p. 408.

[24] G. Gozzi, *Giudizio degli antichi poeti sopra la moderna censura di Dante attribuita ingiustamente a Virgilio*, 1762. — C. Gozzi, *Marfisa Bizzarra*, 1768; Chiaccheria de C. Gozzi intorno alla lingua litterale italiana e alcune ricerche sopra il libro intitolato «Saggio sopra la lingua italiana» . . . 1796; *Ragionamenti sopra una causa perduta*, 1798. — S. Bettinelli, *Discorso sopra la poesia italiana*, 1781; *Saggio sull'eloquenza*, 1782. — M. Borsa, *Del carattere nazionale italiano e di un certo gusto dominante in letteratura straniera*, 1786. — G. B. De Velo, *Sulla preminenza di alcune lingue e sull'autorità degli scrittori approvati dai grammatici*, 1789.

[25] M. Puppo, *Discussioni . . .*, p. 495.

[26] G. Petronio, *Illuminismo, preromanticismo, romanticismo e Lessing*, Società, 1957. — Gy. Herczeg, *Az illuminizmus stílusvitáinak társadalmi háttere*, Filológiai Közl. 1961/1—2.

le *Caffé*, la revue des Lumières italiennes et Cesarotti, le grand rénovateur de langue comme ses prédecesseurs et que c'est dans l'esprit de ces prédecesseurs qu'il rédige la conception historique en perspective nationale, l'importance du soin des traditions nationales, celle de la fonction sociale de la littérature et l'exigence de la langue nationale. Car l'unité de langue n'est pas un but abstrait, mais un moyen et une voie de consolidation et de conservation de la communauté nationale, de la création d'un équilibre entre les couches sociales, comme l'écrit A. Manzoni: «Après l'unité du gouvernement, des armes et des lois, c'est la langue nationale unie qui rend étroite, vivante et florissante l'unité d'une nation.»[27]

Cependant, les écrivains éclairés du *Caffé* (hommes de loi, économistes et hommes d'État) n'avaient pas seulement transmis le mythe de la langue nationale à l'époque suivante, mais aussi le sentiment national lui-même. C'est leur patriotisme éclairé (ou cosmopolite) qui en est la première manifestation.[28] En Italie — et toute l'histoire du *Caffé* le prouve — c'est l'expansion de l'esprit cosmopolite qui avait stimulé le développement des idées nationalistes, c'est-à-dire le sentiment d'unité et un patriotisme franchissant les frontières qui séparaient les petits États se répandant dans toute l'Italie. Les intellectuels italiens éclairés reconnaissent dans le sentiment d'unité culturelle européenne la solidarité culturelle italienne millénaire et c'est sur elle qu'ils fondent leurs ambitions italiennes. Les Lombards, les Toscans, les Napolitains, etc. commencent à se sentir non seulement Lombards, Toscans et Napolitains, mais aussi Européens, et en même temps à se dire et à se sentir Italiens, de façon cosmopolite. Gianrinaldo Carli écrit dans un numéro du *Caffé* de l'année 1765 un manifeste ardent sur «Le pays des Italiens» où celui qui arrive d'une ville étrangère doit refuser le nom d'étranger, car «un Italien n'est pas étranger en Italie comme un Français ne passe pas pour un étranger en France . . .», il termine ses paroles par l'exclamation: «Soyons donc de nouveau Italiens, pour ne pas cesser d'être des hommes!» Filippo Buonarroti, le chef des républicains italiens interprète ainsi les pensées de Rousseau: il n'y plus de Napolitains, de Florentins, de Milanais, de Turinois, seulement des Italiens, car «tous les Italiens sont frères l'un de l'autre».[29] L'idée caractéristique de patriotisme avancée par le milieu du *Caffé* trouve donc vite une formulation concrète après la Révolution française parmi les jeunes intellectuels affluant à Milan des différentes villes d'Italie (F. Buonarroti, V. Cuoco, P. Pagano, F. Galiani).[30] Les espoirs italiens trop hardis seront déçus par Napoléon, et l'unité italienne créée par les armes françaises tombe de nouveau en péril après la chute de Napoléon. Mais le Royaume Uni, œuvre de Napoléon, ouvre déjà un nouveau chapitre dans l'histoire de l'Italie, la possibilité de l'unification politique devient plus réelle. Si l'époque de la restauration rétablit la division territoriale et la dépendance politique, elle ne peut effacer dans les Italiens les souvenirs de l'époque des réformes, des Lumières et de la révolution.

[27] *Pagine manzoniane sulla Questione della lingua*, Milano 1960, p. 83.

[28] M. Cesarotti utilise lui-même l'expression du patriotisme éclairé dans sa brochure *Patriottismo illuminato*, 1797.

[29] D. Cantimori, *Giacobini italiani*, Bari 1924, p. 157.

[30] A. Salza, *L'idea della patria nella letteratura del Settecento avanti la Rivoluzione*, Campobasso 1918.

Et l'anéantissement des illusions des réformateurs — ce que reflètent fidèlement l'œuvre de Foscolo, le roman national d'Ippolito Nievo — prouva que le dévouement des grands personnages ne suffit pas à la création de la nation italienne, et comme Vincenzo Cuoco résume en 1801 dans les conclusions du Settecento: « . . . on ne peut mener à victoire une révolution sans la participation du peuple, et le peuple ne bouge pas pour des mots, mais seulement pour l'amélioration de son propre sort ».[31]

III

L'héritage du Settecento s'exprime dans le romantisme italien, entre autres, dans la pensée nationale. Mais les esthétiques et les *ars poetica* du XVIIIe siècle sont également intéressants et significatifs, car ils préparent dans une grande mesure les Italiens à la réception du nouvel idéal poétique romantique.

Il est naturel que l'héritage poétique de la Renaissance joua un rôle très important même au cours du Settecento. Et si l'époque du baroque modifia déjà cet absolutisme poétique, ce n'est que le XVIIIe siècle qui apporte le vrai renouveau esthétique. L'Arcadie, déjà, fait un retour — du moins théorique — à la conception pragmatique de l'art, fondée sur Horace. Selon Crescimbeni: «le bon poète est celui qui sait la juste mesure de l'utile et de l'agréable, pour enseigner en amusant et amuser en enseignant»,[32] mais la plupart des poètes de l'Arcadie essaient encore de trouver cela dans l'imitation. C'est ainsi que seront renouvelés les trésors que constituent les sonnets de Petrarque, les vers classiques (les odes de Pindare, les chants d'Anacréon, les melodrames). Après le baroque, le retour aux mètres classiques, l'exigence de la formulation lyrique claire sont les premiers pas vers la création d'une langue poétique italienne moderne. Le mépris de l'Arcadie par le romantisme ne provient d'ailleurs pas de là, mais du fait que la plupart des poètes arcadiens, comme Frugoni, ne furent point capables de réaliser le programme «utile-dolce», et ainsi la réforme de goût du classicisme de l'Arcadie restait formelle. L'«erreur humaniste» (Toffanin)[33] commise par la culture italienne postérieure est imputée à l'Arcadie; car celle-ci affirme en effet que les poètes italiens — contrairement à la pratique des autres littératures européennes qui développent progressivement leur propre poésie autonome, différente des modèles antiques — ne consentent pas à renoncer à la force des traditions culturelles nationales, force qui peut unir l'Italie, et ne renoncent pas non plus aux traditions antiques. C'est ce qui explique l'énergie avec laquelle ils combattent le pédantisme académique, ennemi de l'esprit innovateur, et, en même temps, l'opposition inconsciente aux influences étrangères plus radicales, et ceci justement pour défendre les traditions italiennes afin que la culture italienne garde son caractère italien au moment de la division et de la dépendance politique, c'est-à-dire: afin que la culture du Settecento italien fasse siennes les nouvelles idées européennes d'une part et s'appuie d'autre part sur les résultats de plusieurs siècles de la culture italienne.

[31] V. Cuoco, *Saggio storico sulla rivoluzione napoletana del 1799. Scritti vari*, Bari 1924, p. 157.

[32] Crescimbeni, *Dialoghi della volgar poesia*, Roma 1700, p. 83.

[33] G. Toffanin, *L'Arcadia*, Bologna 1958.

Ludovico Antonio Muratori est peut-être l'un des personnages les plus importants et les plus innovateurs dans le rafraîchissement des idées italiennes du XVIIIᵉ siècle, c'est lui qui commence l'étude scientifique et la nouvelle publicaon de l'héritage culturel italien. La Crusca, à son tour, essaie de mobiliser les intellectuels italiens en s'opposant au pédantisme, et introduisant en Italie les pensées européennes. Il est le premier propagateur italien du carésianisme, mais dans son livre intitulé *Riflessioni sopra il buon gusto internole scienze e le arti* (1708) il prête à la poésie une bien plus grande importance que la conception mathématique n'en fait. Il la définit comme une activité créatrice et prépare ainsi la thèse fondamentale de la liberté créatrice et de l'imagination, qui sera l'objet des débats sur le style dans les années soixante. Selon Piccolomini la vraie réalisation de la poésie sera le «verosimile».

C'est en 1725 à Naples, dix ans avant Baumgarten, que paraît le *Scienza Nuova* de Giambattista Vico, dont les livres (*Della sapienza poetica* et *Della discoperta del Vero Omero*) marquent, selon Benedetto Croce, le début de la théorie moderne européenne. Si nous pouvons observer chez Muratori une tentative de concilier le rationalisme et les traditions culturelles italiennes, nous retrouvons la même intention chez Vico qui veut mettre en harmonie la philosophie et la philologie. Vico, tout comme Muratori, ne peut se faire au sec intellectualisme rationnel, selon lui, l'auteur de la poésie n'est pas la raison, mais l'imagination, qui est une question de don, par conséquent, la poésie ne peut se fonder sur l'imitation. L'éblouissement, l'imagination du baroque, deviendra dans la théorie de Vico un concept réunissant sensation et sentiment qui donnent naissance à l'œuvre artistique inspirée par des impressions sensitives. Chez Vico, la fantaisie est le moyen qui reflète le contenu, une saisie de la réalité qui précède le raisonnement. Selon Vico, ce ne sont pas les poètes de bon goût (Horace, Petrarque) qui se tiennent au plus haut sommet des valeurs lyriques, mais les poètes primitifs, les artistes ayant une imagination vive, ceux qui interprètent les passions, les vrais sentiments humains, qui ne respectent d'autres règles que l'instinct de leur propre génie, comme Homère et Dante. C'est en se référant aux grands mythes que Vico affirme que les métaphores et les images de la langue poétique sont les enfants de l'imagination exaltée. C'est encore Vico qui met en route le mythe de la poésie spontanée, et fait découvrir un Homère nouveau. Ses pensées trouveront un public compréhensif dans le romantisme, tout comme Herder et Hamann. Ainsi, même si Vico n'avait pas d'influence directe sur le romantisme allemand,[34] il favorise l'expansion en Italie des théories de Herder et de Hamann arrivés aux mêmes conclusions, et de ce fait il facilite le développement du romantisme italien.[35]

[34] Benedetto Croce tenta de démontrer l'influence de Vico dans les œuvres de Herder et de Hamann. B. Croce, *Hamann e Vico–Saggi sul Hegel*, Bari 1913. Voir aussi: Gemmingen, *Vico, Hamann und Herder*, Munich 1918. — E. Auerbach, *Vico und Herder*, Deutsche Vierteljahrschrift für Literatur, Wissenschaft und Geistesgeschichte, 10, 1932.

[35] On peut voir survivre les doctrines de Vico dans les œuvres suivantes: F. A. Astore, *La filosofia dell'eloquenza della ragione*, 1783. — G. Gentile, *Saggio filosofico sull'eloquenza*, 1795. — T. Natale di Monterosato, *La filosofia Leibniziana esposta in versi toscani*, 1756. — V. Gaglio, *Riflessioni sopra l'arte di ben criticare*, 1759. — A. Pepi, *Saggio sopra l'uso della critica*, 1772.

L'esthétique de Vico n'a pas eu d'effets proportionnels à son importance théorique sur son époque. C'est le *Ragion poetica* de Gian Vincenzo Gravina (1708) qui devient le canon du classicisme italien du XVIIIᵉ siècle. Gravina se contente de l'explication de l'art par l'imitation, mais il rejette l'idée d'une poésie des jeux formels. Le programme, «cose non parole», qui deviendra la devise du cercle du *Caffé* est lancé également par Gravina. Pour lui, la poésie est «l'utile e diletto insieme». Giuseppe Parini réalisera plus tard dans sa poésie l'art poétique de Gravina. C'est l'esthétique de Gravina qui fit le plus grand effet sur son époque, son écho à l'étranger est également importante. Cela est dû en partie aux traductions de ses œuvres (1748, Roquier, en français; 1806, Mathias, en anglais), en partie à l'activité d'Antonio Conti qui développa sa théorie sur l'inspiration poétique, l'imagination et l'imitation à partir de ses instructions.[36]

Les esthéticiens italiens de la première partie du XVIIIᵉ siècle sont importants même à l'échelle européenne, non parce qu'ils précèdent Addison, Burke, Hume, Du Bos et Batteaux — d'ailleurs ce sont ces derniers qui déterminèrent la pensée esthétique du siècle, et non pas les Italiens — mais surtout parce qu'ils défendirent en Italie, l'idée de l'activité créatrice poétique et la liberté de l'imagination tout en élaborant en même temps les thèses esthétiques du rationalisme et du sensualisme. En 1764 Bernardo Tanucci attaque publiquement Voltaire dans ses discours prononcés à Pise; il l'accuse de vouloir tuer le beau dans la poésie et de condamner ainsi à mort la poésie elle-même. L'insolite dans la réalisation poétique, la défense de l'autonomie de l'art prennent leur naissance en Italie. On découvre d'influences anglaises chez Conti, et d'influences françaises chez Martello. En territoire allemand, c'est M. Pagano qui est plus connu, mais l'influence en Europe de l'esthétique classiciste italienne se fait remarquer également dans la correspondance de trente années entre le comte Pietro Calepio et Bodmer et dans les éditions des œuvres de Calepio à Zurich.

Le succès du sensualisme en Italie, l'aboutissement au sensualisme sont la conséquence logique de l'aversion éprouvée par la culture italienne pour le rationalisme. C'est le sensualisme qui aida à résoudre le conflit entre le rationalisme et la tradition poétique italienne. Selon les représentants italiens du sensualisme, la vraie valeur de l'œuvre artistique réside dans l'effet esthétique qu'elle exerce sur le lecteur, dans le «piacere». Grâce à Condillac et à Du Bos, de nouveaux concepts entrent dans la poétique italienne, comme: raison — sentiment — sensibilité — illusion.[37] Condillac qui vécut à Milan entre 1764 et 1767 et qui était en relation avec les milieux du *Caffé* et de l'Accademia dei Transformati, joua un rôle direct dans la formation des théories sensualistes italiennes.[38] Évidemment, ce n'était pas

[36] A. Conti, *Prose e poesie*, 1756, selon Croce c'est une œuvre équivalente à l'esthétique de Baumgarten.

[37] Plusieurs études naquirent en Italie sous l'influence des sensualistes. F. Algarotti, *Lettere sulla pittura e sull'architettura*, 1753. — S. Bettinelli, *Dell'entusiasmo nelle belle arti*, 1769. — C. Beccaria, *Ricerche sulla natura dello stile*, 1770. — P. Verri, *Discorso sull'indole e del piacere e del dolore*, 1773. — F. Soave, *Note sul bello*, 1775. — M. Pagano, *Discorso sull'origine della natura della poesia*, 1783. — M. Pagano, *Del gusto delle belle arti*, 1785.

[38] B. Pergoli, *Condillac in Italia*, Faenza 1908. — H. Bedarida, *Condillac à Parme*, Annales de l'Université de Grenoble, 1924. — R. Spongano, *Il sensismo e la poesia di G. Parini*, 1933. — L. Rosiello, *Linguistica illuministica*, Bologna 1965.

dû au seul Condillac si au cours des années soixante les esthéticiens italiens s'intéressèrent particulièrement à l'interprétation sensualiste du « bello ideale ». C'est alors que commence à s'affirmer, en Italie, la croyance en les différentes formes du beau, qui sont valables même si elles ne peuvent pas être ramenées aux genres et aux règles antiques. C'est ce qu'affirme aussi Baretti dans son livre dirigé contre Voltaire. C'est alors que naît la pensée de la relativité des goûts, et que Melchiorre Cesarotti déclare que le véritable critique « est le concitoyen de tous, il est membre de tous les peuples et comprend toutes les langues du beau ».

A part du sensualisme, l'influence de Winckelmann est très forte sur le développement de l'idéal du beau du XVIIIe siècle, son *Geschichte der Kunst des Altertums* paraît en 1779 à Milan. Si Winckelmann ne put changer fondamentalement la conception italienne de l'art, il fournit des bases à une théorie selon laquelle la tâche de l'artiste consiste à créer des formes parfaites, à rassembler harmonieusement les plus beaux côtés de la réalité. Et pourtant, malgré l'influence de Winckelmann, le culte de l'art grec ne l'emporta pas celui du romain — pas tellement par les vestiges d'Hercule que par la force des pensées nationales.

En Italie, l'imitation de la nature, le règne du principe d'imitation continue d'exister sous les différentes influences (tradition culturelle, rationalisme, sensualisme néo-classique selon Winckelmann), même s'il ne s'agit plus de décrire la nature de manière arcadienne, mais d'offrir une optique tout à fait idéalisée dont les éléments perdent petit à petit tout lien avec la vraie nature. Ce processus s'observe bien au cours du dernier tiers du XVIIIe siècle, dans l'intérêt porté au monde de la mythologie, l'inclination vers les paysages d'Homère et d'Ossian dans les ruines des jardins anglais, où on croyait avoir trouvé le monde sensible et affiné des formes parfaites.

Nous pouvons toutefois constater que le classicisme italien du XVIIIe siècle n'est point concevable comme une unité monolithe,[39] il y a une diffé-

---

[39] Les opinions relatives au néo-classicisme commencent à prendre forme d'après les théories de L. Settembrini et de G. Carducci, puis, après B. Croce, les recherches italiennes sur le néo-classicisme et ses variantes prennent un élan sous l'effet de l'œuvre de Mario Praz (*Gusto neoclassico*, Napoli 1939), un article écrit sur le néo-classicisme dans le dictionnaire littéraire Bompiani. Praz examine les changements de goût dans les beaux-arts, surtout, des affinités de Milton—Poussin—Tasso, de Winckelmann jusqu'aux auteurs de l'Empire. Un autre livre de Praz, *Panopticum romano*, Milano—Napoli 1967, présente une conception analogue. Praz publia des études spéciales sur Foscolo et sur le néo-classicisme, sur le style mêlant Ossian et l'antiquisation et sur le style napoléonien; il prépare aussi la réhabilitation de Canova. A. Momigliano (*Gusto neoclassico e poesia neoclassica* — *Cinque saggi*, 1945), V. Borghini (*Dal Barocco al neoclassicismo*, 1946), W. Binni (*Poetica neoclassica*, in *Classicismo e neoclassicismo*, 1963), F. Ulivi (*Settecento neoclassico*, 1957) continuent cet examen complexe fait dans l'intérêt d'une histoire commune de la littérature, de la critique et des beaux-arts. Dans son introduction à la *Discussioni linguistiche del Settecento*, M. Puppo souligne la convergence des orientations culturelles et stylistiques dans les discussions linguistiques allant de Muratori à Cesarotti, tandis que dans son essai écrit pour le volume III du *Momenti e problemi di storia dell'estetica*, il qualifie le classicisme de trait dominant le culture littéraire italienne, il proclame la continuité sans rupture avec le passé, le lien entre le classicisme du début du XIXe siècle et l'humanisme de l'Arcadie du XVIIIe siècle. A. Momigliano sépare de façon convaincante le classicisme d'Horace enseigné aux écoles du néo-classicisme dont il esquisse trois articulations: l'arcadienne (celle-ci se caractérise par le goût alexandrien, hellénistique, telle que la

200

rence sensible entre le rationalisme arcadien du début du siècle, le classicisme humaniste, le néo-classicisme mêlé d'influences sensualistes des années soixante — qu'on peut ramener à Winckelmann —, et le néo-classicisme préromantique de la fin du siècle qui assure le passage vers le romantisme. C'est ce que semble prouver aussi le fait que les romantiques italiens assimileront sans aucune difficulté la doctrine du double type de beauté de Mme de Staël-Schlegel, en conséquence de la thèse relative aux genres d'idéal de beauté simultanés, thèse déjà acceptée au Settecento.

IV

C'est chez Muratori et chez Gravina qu'apparaît, en Italie pour la première fois, l'exigence d'une littérature «cose non parole», qu'approfondira le cercle rationaliste du *Caffé*. Mais la définition de la «littérature des choses» est loin d'être sans équivoque, les différents *ars poetica* s'en occupent au XVIIIe siècle italien depuis Algarotti jusqu'à Alfieri.

Le personnage de clé des Lumières italiennes, Francesco Algarotti, dans son jugement porté sur les œuvres littéraires attribue une importance décisive à la profondeur du sujet et à son utilité sociale. Et en même temps, quant à la question de l'imitation, c'est lui qui proclame le premier la liberté de l'imagination créatrice dans l'Italie du XVIIIe siècle. Selon Algarotti, la poésie et les beaux-arts dépendent directement de l'imagination, ils sont les créations libres de celle-ci, dont les éléments peuvent cependant être ramenés aux sentiments et à la pratique. Ce dernier phénomène, Algarotti le nomme imitation. L'ami d'Algarotti, Saverio Bettinelli développe ses idées sur la poésie italienne dans ses lettres d'Angleterre et dans son *Del Risorgimento d'Italia*. Par rapport à la culture anglaise et européenne, il trouve décadente la culture italienne du XVIIIe siècle, et c'est en opposition avec celle-ci qu'il formule sa propre esthétique dans l'*Entusiasmo delle belle arti* (1768). Dans son œuvre, il réclame la légitimité de l'art basé sur l'imagination: «l'entusiasmo è una elevazione dell' anima» ou selon une autre formule: «la passion et l'exaltation artistique ne sont rien d'autre que l'élévation de l'âme dans un état où l'approche et la vue extraordinaire et inhabituelle des choses transmettent la passion aux autres». Bien que le travail de Bettinelli ne puisse égaler la conception de l'art de Shaftesbury, Lessing et Diderot,[40] il prépare la définition romantique de l'individualité

---

poésie de Savioli); la napoléonienne (le grand culte de l'antiquité, la poésie scénique, allégorique de Monti, le désir monumental, l'amalgame de l'ossianique et de l'antique en baroque) et l'idéalistique (alexandrien, Foscolo). Il ramène toujours les caractéristiques du néoclassicisme à Winckelmann. Les œuvres de W. Binni rehaussent la nouvelle sensibilité, qui est à la base du néo-classicisme, mais aussi sa phase soumise, mais contraire aux tendances romantiques à un certain moment. La divorce entre les deux poésies — celle du néo-classicisme et du romantisme est la plus apparente dans la doctrine du majestueux (celui d'Apollon, d'Ossian). Un classicisme particulier se développe dans la période des Lumières de Savioli à Parini. Binni trace l'évolution depuis Winckelmann, en passant par le chemin du plutarchisme, de la vertu bourgeoise jusqu'à Monti, contemporain de David et jusqu'à Foscolo, chez qui, selon lui, le néo-classicisme est un modèle de perfection (Foscolo est déjà le précurseur de Hölderlin et de Keats).

[40] B. Croce s'occupe de l'importance esthétique de l'œuvre dans son *Estetica*, Bari 1928, p. 267.

et de la création poétiques en donnant la description empirique de la psychologie du processus créateur poétique et la conception de l'«entusiasmo
poetico». Sa conception du génie est également originale (chapitre «Genji ed
ingegni»). En réunissant le génie («ingegno, ma grande») et l'enthousiasme
(«fantasia, ma forte», «cuore, ma risentito») il arrive, si l'on peut dire, presqu'à
la formulation romantique de la création poétique, mais ensuite il revient
à la proclamation éclairée d'un art fondé sur le «buon gusto», qui a une fonction éducative, qui corrige la société, parce que «la poesia è un arte amabile
et divertente».[41] A la fin de sa vie, Saverio Bettinelli est devenu l'opposant
principal des traductions préromantiques.

C'est le cercle du *Caffé* qui représente le plus assidûment les conclusions
du rationalisme appliquèes à l'art, entre 1764 et 1766 à Milan. Leur activité
comporte une nette opposition à toute érudition formelle, à l'explication à
la lettre du «cose non parole», une certaine opposition à l'art-même, et la
sérieuse décision de mettre la poésie et la philologie au profit de fins sociales
afin que «les œuvres littéraires ne soient pas gratuites, mais qu'elles aient
une utilité». Mais ils ne firent qu'employer machinalement les principes
du rationalisme cartésien dans la solution des problèmes littéraires, linguistiques et stylistiques; Guiseppe Baretti avait raison d'attaquer ces
excès d'une pratique et ce manque de style dans ses articles écrits sur un
ton acerbe (*Frusta letteraria* Nos XIII, XIX, XXII, 1764). Les représentants
du cercle du *Caffé* écrivirent, eux aussi, de travaux esthétiques; ainsi, le
véritable système esthétique de Pietro Verri est exposé dans son étude intitulée *Discorso sull'indole del piacere e del dolore*. Benedetto Croce en pense
retrouver la psychologie profonde dans l'anthropologie pragmatique de
Kant, et, selon lui, le pessimisme irrationnel de Verri réapparaît non seulement chez Leopardi mais même chez Schopenhauer. D'après Carmela,
tandis que la branche optimiste du sensualisme italien (Genovesi) reste
idéalistique, classiciste comme les exemples français et allemands, la branche
pessimiste représentée par P. Verri correspondrait à une tendance préromantique et éclairée du sensualisme qui annonce le *Conciliatore*.

L'un des premiers représentants du sensualisme italien, issu également du
cercle du *Caffé*, Cesare Beccaria utilise les éléments psychologiques d'Alembert et de Condillac dans son étude intitulée *Ricerche sulla natura dello
stile* (1770), il les insère dans sa propre théorie des associations. Il place le
secret de l'effet esthétique de l'œuvre littéraire, la source de l'enthousiasme
dans l'harmonie du contenu et du style. Chez Beccaria, le style, la technique
dépendent de l'équilibre entre l'idéal principal, l'idéal secondaire et l'idéal ex-
pressif. C'est Beccaria, qui, en Italie, ouvre la voie vers les recherches sur
la base d'une profonde psychologie, de la stylistique moderne. Ce n'est pas
par hasard que les romantiques citent l'étude stylistique de Beccaria au
même titre que le travail psychologique de Vico. De son époque, cette
œuvre ne connaît pas de loin le succès de son livre de philosophie du droit,
cela d'une part parce qu'elle reste inachevée, d'autre part parce que Beccaria
n'emprunt pas ses exemples stylistiques à la littérature de sa propre époque,
mais aux œuvres des classiques de l'Antiquité.

Ce sont Carlo Goldoni et le grand poète de l'époque Giuseppe Parini qui
offrent un modèle littéraire proche de l'idéal du *Caffé*. L'ars poetica de

[41] Puppo, *Discussioni* . . . p. 410.

Parini se rattache d'une part aux traditions arcadiennes, à l'Accademia dei Transformati, d'autre part au cercle du *Caffé*. Comme Fubini et Binni démontrèrent, la poésie de Parini va de l'Arcadie à travers la *Poesie di Ripiano Eupilino* jusqu' au classicisme éclairé-utilitariste («Va per negletta via / ognor l'util cercando / la calda fantasia / che sol felice quando / l'util puó al vanto / di lusinghevol canto»). Les titres des odes font également allusion au caractère didactique de la poésie utile (*L'innesto del vaiuolo, Salubrità dell' aria, La magistratura, L'impostura*), dont les thèmes accusent une forte ressemblance avec ses articles écrits pour le *Caffé* et le *Parini Gazzetta di Milano*. Dans son travail inachevé: *De' principi generali e formatosi delle belle lettere applicati alle belle arti* (1775), il met en rapport, sous l'influence du sensualisme, la réalisation artistique et le désir naturel de l'âme de s'exprimer. Après la lecture de l'*Entusiasmo* de Bettinelli il déclare, lui aussi, que «la verità dell'arte è nella spontanea e retta natura delle passioni di cui è generata», mais sa propre poésie n'est pas encore inspirée par la passion spontanée — il est retenu par la tempérance arcadienne, l'exigence de l'équilibre lyrique, la moralité religieuse, la sobriété linguistique et le bon goût, car «il fine delle arti si è cagionar piacere».

Si Saverio Bettinelli définit la poésie comme une distraction aimable, chez Parini, la poésie «est l'art de l'imitation et de la coloration en vers, de manière à ce que ceux qui l'entendent s'enflamment avec des sentiments semblables à ceux du poète». Vittorio Alfieri sera le premier poète italien à exclure la conception «dilettare» de son propre ars poetica, il va déclarer en effet que la poésie est «una impedita volontà di vivere», dont la base est le «forte sentir» et l'«impulso naturale», et que le poète ne doit pas être un éducateur, mais un «autoritas poeta», «voce della libertà». Le *Del principe e delle lettere* (1785—1786) montre, malgré toutes ses contradictions théoriques, le fait de la rupture avec la poésie éclairée. Selon Alfieri, la poésie est l'enfant de la liberté et de l'inspiration: «On ne peut formuler et exprimer vigoureusement ce que le poète ne sent pas.» Le poète doit d'abord «apprendre à reconnaître en soi l'impulsion sublime, puis à la diriger quand il l'aura reconnue ... Lorsque le poète éprouve cette émotion naturelle, il doit écrire et non pas imiter.» Il ne renie pas la beauté de l'art fondé sur l'imitation, «non è tuttavia negato il bello del tutto, ma è sempre un bello d'imitazione, in cui originalità nessuna li tradisce pur mai», mais il donne sa préférence absolue aux œuvres nées d'une véritable inspiration poétique, de l'«entusiasmo». Contrairement à la conception classiciste du génie, Alfieri le place au-dessus des autres hommes; selon lui, le vrai poète ne l'est pas par son art de décorer, par la précision de ses vers, mais par sa passion originaire et individuelle. Il est vrai que les drames en forme parfaite d'Alfieri signifient le sommet du classicisme et non pas le romantisme, mais la personnalité du poète, son comportement individuel sont déjà tout à fait nouveaux, il succède au type de l'intellectuel réformiste éclairé de la fin du siècle et représente déjà par sa vocation le type d'artiste de l'époque du Risorgimento. Et un autre trait caractéristique qui est le sien consiste à accepter avec fierté d'être Italien. De Foscolo à De Sanctis, le XIXe siècle italien n'honore pas seulement le prédécesseur en Alfieri, mais aussi le poète national, le compagnon de Dante au XVIIIe siècle, il vénère en lui le proclamateur de la liberté, de l'indépendance, de la démocratie humaniste, celui qui hait éternellement la tyrannie. Comme l'écrit De Sanctis: «Chaque

fois que l'Italie est réssuscitée pour la liberté, c'est avec un grand enthousiasme qu'elle salue Alfieri, et qu'elle se reconnaît en lui. »[42]

Les précurseurs d'Alfieri sont: Baretti, en ce qui concerne la passion vé-
hémente et la franchise implacable, et Cesarotti qui élabore la théorie du
génie qui va s'incarner en Alfieri.

On ne pourrait dire de Giuseppe Baretti qu'il ait été des plus populaires
des hommes de lettres de son époque, même son successeur, Ugo Foscolo, ne
le désigne que comme «le singe de Johnson» pourtant ce critique qui se
montrait quelquefois excessif dans ses jugements, était une des personnalités
les plus intéressantes de son époque, et il contribua par ses attaques impla-
cables aux troubles de l'eau tranquille de la culture italienne, au refoulement
des positions éclairées exagérées s'opposant à la littérature. C'est en tant
que directeur du théâtre italien à Londres que Baretti subit l'influence de
Samuel Johnson. Durant son activité en Angleterre, il considère que faire
connaître et défendre la littérature et la langue italiennes sont de ses devoirs essentiels. Mais après s'être établi à Venise, il commence sa campagne
dans les rubriques de la *Frusta Letteraria* (1763—1765) contre les conditions
culturelles arriérées d'Italie, contre le pédantisme de Crusca, c'est-à-dire
contre les *caféistes*, adeptes de Voltaire, adversaires proclamés de la littérature. Baretti se débat donc en plusieurs directions à la fois: contre l'aca-
démisme, le pédantisme, le traditionalisme, dans la défense de la liberté de
la poésie, de la spontanéité, mais il attaque aussi les innovations, parce
qu'il n'y voit que des imperfections, l'état arriéré des écrivains italiens par
rapport au niveau européen: «Nos auteurs ne sont pas encore aussi bons que
les Anglais, ou les Français, pour que leurs œuvres plaisent autant aux
personnes cultivées qu'aux personnes non-cultivées. »[43] Son opinion sur le
style de Beccaria, de P. Verri et de Goldoni est peu favorable. «Oh glorieuse
Italie, quels beaux Molières tu produis» dit-il de Goldoni, et sur l'œuvre de
renommée mondiale de Beccaria, il déclare: «Una cosaccia scritta bastardamente.» La répugnance pour le ton critique de Baretti est naturelle de la
part du cercle du *Caffé*, des académiciens et plus tard, des romantiques.[44]
Selon Tommaseo, Baretti emprunta beaucoup de choses aux critiques
anglais, à l'exception de la pondération et la tempérance, pourtant Baretti
voulut, avec raison, introduire en Italie — même si avec quelque excès —
l'esprit critique que représentaient en Angleterre Swift, et Johnson.

L'esthétique de Baretti s'avère assez contradictoire dans les rubriques
de la *Frusta*. Par contre, une explication s'en montre dans son *Discours sur
Shakespeare et monsieur Voltaire* qui date de 1777 et qui est destiné à être
l'œuvre principale de sa vie; il y déclare que Voltaire par son peu de savoir
anglais, ne peut donner un jugement valable sur Shakespeare et qu'il ne
peut surtout pas accuser le grand écrivain dramatique de barbarisme et de
manque de style à partir de la position du drame classique français, car le
goût étant relatif, les écrivains doivent développer différemment leur sujet
chez les différents peuples, aux différentes époques, dans des circonstances
historiques et sociales différentes. Cet engagement de Baretti en faveur de
la poésie spontanée — que son publicisme violente de la *Frusta* ne gêne pas

---

[42] Cité par G. Sallay: *Az olasz felvilágosodás kérdései* (Les problèmes des Lumières
italiennes), Irodalomtörténeti Közlemények, 1961/3.
[43] *Scelta delle lettere familiari*, Bari 1912, p. 337.
[44] Voir: P. Verri, *Opere*, 1947, vol. I. pp. 69—81.

cette fois —, ce respect du génie poétique coïncident avec le mouvement du Sturm-und-Drang. Du point de vue du goût, selon Baretti, les facteurs déterminants sont l'originalité, la liberté et l'imagination. Son autre optique de la conception du goût est l'exigence de l'objectivité, le «gusto del concreto», mais cette objectivité est autre que le pragmatisme des *cafféistes*, Baretti insiste en particulier sur le problème des traductions: la simple interprétation du sujet n'a pas le génie original de l'œuvre. Il réclame également l'originalité de la langue et du style des écrivains. Il propage le curriculum vitae de Benvenuto Cellini, découvert en 1728, en opposition à la prose affectée, traditionnelle de Boccaccio. «Le passionné Benvenuto décrit sa vie sans penser au sujet et à la manière dont il écrit ... Et pourtant, le tableau qu'il peint de soi plaît aux connaisseurs de la littérature, parce qu'il est clair et net, on voit que ce n'est pas l'application, mais la fantaisie rapide et flamboyante qui lui donna le jour.»[45] Selon Baretti, les grands écrivains depuis Dante jusqu'à Shakespeare «ne suivirent que, tous, les inspirations de la nature.»[46] Dans sa campagne contre la structure de phrase de Boccaccio, Baretti ne professe donc pas la structure directe de la phrase, menée au triomphe par les philosophes linguistiques français, mais la liberté de l'écrivain, l'instinctivité et le naturel de l'expression poétique.

Nous pouvons donc trouver grand nombre de découvertes vraiment intéressantes dans les œuvres de Baretti, mais nous devons insister sur le fait que ses constatations et ses découvertes ne constituent un système ou une théorie que vaguement. Les historiens de la littérature italienne (Binni), ont relevé que la révolution esthétique de Baretti s'est arrêtée à la simple « piace — non piace». Son maître, le docteur Johnson dit de lui: «Il avait peu d'idées personnelles, mais il savait se battre pour elles de tout cœur.» Cette constatation est aussi, et en même temps, un jugement positif, car bien que Baretti n'ait pas dépassé le niveau de son époque en tant que philosophe ou philologue, il fait, en tant que critique, le précurseur d'Alfieri et des critiques du *Conciliatore* qui le rejetèrent. C'est avec lui que commence en Italie la critique littéraire du contenu, celle conçue sur la «verista».

V

Chez Algarotti, Bettinelli et Baretti l'attirance pour un goût différent du classique traditionnel est nettement perceptible. Mais Algarotti est retenu par la forme de vie «cortegiano», par le respect du rationalisme; Bettinelli finit par s'habituer au goût néo-classique, et Baretti n'avait pas assez d'esprit systématique et d'indépendance pour exprimer ses pensées. Le sensualisme laissa ses empreintes profondes sur les œuvres du grand poète de l'époque, Guiseppe Parini, mais sa culture arcadienne ne permit pas à ses sentiments de prendre le dessus dans son art lyrique. Ainsi, la première œuvre sentimentale — ou œuvre préromantique comme dit Binni — est une traduction: l'*Ossian* de Melchiorre Cesarotti.

Dans la littérature et dans le goût italien, l'œuvre de Melchiorre Cesarotti constitue la transition du rationalisme au sensualisme vers la fin de ce siècle sentimentaliste néo-classiciste. Déjà la carrière de Cesarotti est caractéristique pour l'époque qui précède le romantisme. Ayant terminé le sémi-

---

[45] *Contro la prosa boccaccesca*, in Puppo, *Discussioni* ... p. 215.
[46] *Frusta letteraria*, 13. nov. 1763.

naire de Padoue, Cesarotti devient le professeur de rhétorique du séminaire, il s'occupe de la traduction d'œuvres antiques et classiques, et sera l'un des plus excellents philologues classiques de son époque. Il écrit et traduit des poèmes, mais ne devient vraiment célèbre qu'en 1763 par sa traduction d'*Ossian*, qui fut la première dans son genre en Europe. Il est, à côté de Condillac, l'un des savants très estimés de la cour de Parme, il y est professeur des littératures grecque et hébraïque. Le sommet de sa pensée scientifique est constitué par ses deux essais sur la philosophie des langues. Napoléon l'estime beaucoup pour sa traduction d'*Ossian*, il l'invite d'abord à remplir des fonctions d'ambassadeur, puis lui assure une pension. Cesarotti passe ses dernières années à Selvazzano. Il met sous presse toutes ses œuvres, qui paraissent en quarante volumes à partir de 1800 et qui contribuent considérablement à la formation du goût romantique italien. C'est le cercle du *Conciliatore* et Manzoni qui adoptent les thèses linguistiques de Cesarotti. De Sanctis se base sur ses thèses esthétiques lorsqu'il élabore son histoire de la littérature. Selon Benedetto Croce, dans la culture italienne, le rôle de Herder revient à Cesarotti, non seulement pour sa profondeur philosophique, mais aussi en raison de son attirance pour les sentiments tels que ceux d'Ossian, pour les poésies populaires italienne et espagnole. D'autre part, Melchiorre Cesarotti joue un rôle déterminant dans la vie de son pays: Padoue et Vénétie, c'est lui qui est l'initiateur de l'école esthétique de Padoue, du *patavinitas*, dont on perçoit les traces dans l'art de I. Nievo, A. Fogazzaro, et même jusqu'à P. P. Pasolini.

Dans l'œuvre de Cesarotti, on peut distinguer trois périodes plus importantes. La première s'étend jusqu'à la traduction d'*Ossian*, elle est fondamentalement classiciste, arcadienne. A cette époque, il s'enthousiasme encore pour la structure et pour la langue des tragédies de Voltaire, il les traduit même en italien. Chose curieuse: Alfieri qui écrira des drames strictement classicistes, mais qui, affectivement, se nourrit déjà de l'Ossian, trouve ses traductions de Voltaire: «des écrits de goût de jeunesse». Cesarotti écrit ses poèmes dans le style de Marino et de Conti (*Sonetti amorosi, Cinto di Venere*), il fait preuve de son attirance pour la mythologie dans ses imitations de contes allégoriques (*Telegono, Callista e Filetore, Megillo e Ibindo, Amore giardiniere*). La culture arcadienne-éclairée, classique équilibrée de sa première période de création détermine l'œuvre entier de Cesarotti et cela reste sensible, même quand il révalorise, à la suite d'Ossian, son goût classique de jeunesse.

C'est C. Sackville, qui séjournant à Venise en 1762, apprend à Cesarotti la nouvelle des poèmes d'Ossian parus pour la première fois à Londres en 1758. Plus tard, il lira le volume de Macpherson intitulé *Fragments of Ancient Poetry* collected in the Highlands of Scotland, publié en 1760, qui fit un tel effet sur lui qu'il les traduit en six mois, simultanément avec l'étude de Blair, le premier traducteur d'Ossian, crû alors second. Macpherson et Cesarotti travaillent pour ainsi dire en même temps sur Ossian, c'est justement à cette époque que commence en Angleterre la discussion sur Ossian, ce qui pousse Macpherson à produire de nouvelles traductions et à faire de nouvelles manœuvres, et ce n'est qu'en 1765 que paraîtront tous les vingt-deux poèmes d'Ossian. La discussion sur l'originalité n'intéresse pas Cesarotti, il est ébloui par le nouveau goût découvert dans les poèmes: «Votre Ossian m'a tout à fait enthousiasmé, Morven est devenu mon Parnasse . . .»,[47] écrit-il à Macpherson. Celui-ci répond à Cesarotti en mai 1763, par John Udney, consul de Venise. Il tâche de prouver l'authenticité de l'œuvre dans sa lettre, bien que Cesarotti n'ait pas demandé d'information sur l'origine, et il envoie d'autres chants encore. Encouragé par son succès en Italie et en Europe, Cesarotti continue la traduction, et il publie l'Ossian entier complété d'un indice de vocabulaire d'Ossian, en 1772; il a un succès retentissant. Selon Zanella, son contemporain, ce sont les merveilleuses traductions d'Ossian qui ont délivré le public italien empêtré dans le style emphatique de Frugoni; Carrer trouve l'Ossian «mirabile traduzione»; selon Alfieri, Cesarotti «vibratamente verseggia nell'Ossian». Nous pouvons comprendre ce culte d'Ossian en analysant les traductions et les explications de texte de Cesarotti. Il nous faut voir l'une des causes de cette fièvre pour Ossian — outre la nouveauté des épopées primitives et du caractère de barde — dans l'imposture de Macpherson. Il orna et compléta les chants gaéliques aux sentiments primitifs, selon le goût de son époque, par des motifs et des images de Milton, de la Bible et d'Homère, par les éléments de la poésie de Young et de Gray, par la nouvelle sensibilité, le culte des tombeaux (des vingt-deux chants traduits, onze seulement ont leur variante originale). Par ce semblant de primitivité, d'originalité, il fournit justement la poésie lyrique à laquelle le public aspirait après Gray et Young. Ce sont également ces sentiments et passions qui saisissent Cesarotti, son tempérament de poète l'explique, l'atmosphère de la décadence l'intéressait même avant l'Ossian. L'intérêt qu'il avait porté antérieurement à Démosthène en est la preuve, ainsi que ses une ou deux fables, comme celle, par exemple, du *Momo giornalista*; et sa correspondance aussi, révèle son grand intérêt porté depuis longtemps à la littérature des nations du Nord, aux éléments de poésie populaire d'atmosphère mystérieuse, aux œuvres de Haller, Gessner et de Klopstock.

Dans les annotations et les préfaces de Cesarotti à l'Ossian, nous trouvons un grand nombre de citations qui permettent de placer la nouveauté affective de la poésie lyrique d'Ossian au centre du culte d'Ossian: «Je vois la valeur et la beauté principales de l'Ossian dans ses amours qui surviennent avec tant de délicatesse et de minutie»;[48] «Ce dessin si exact est très rare chez Homère»; «Il faut écouter Homère, et sentir Ossian»;[49] «Chez Ossian . . . es amours sont fondées sur le s entiment, aussi sont-elles délicates.»[50] «Ossian lest un poète sensible, qui veut réaliser l'idéal de sa propre âme, il s'efforce d'abord d'atteindre le beau et non pas le croyable»; «Ossian est le génie de la Nature sauvage, ses poèmes ressemblent à ses propres héros celtiques, et aux forêts celtiques, ils nous terrifient, mais on y sent vivre les dieux»; «Ossian est présent dans l'action et il en vit tous les détails. Il fond les vibrations de son propre cœur dans son pathos»; «. . . il poema è interamente lirico», «Ossian presenta due specie di poesie, una in parole per gli orecchi, e l'altra in cenni per l'anima.»[51]

En Ossian, Cesarotti rend hommage au génie de la nature sauvage. Il écrit: «Celui qui aspire à la gloire du poète universel, doit saisir les grandes

[47] *Opere scelte*, vol. III, 1946.
[48] *Epistolario*, I; *Note all' Ossian. Opere scelte*, II, Pisa 1801, p. 120.
[49] *Op. cit.*, p. 23.
[50] *Op. cit.*, p. 205.
[51] *Op. cit.*, pp. 123—131.

beautés universelles de la Nature.» Le culte de la nature remonte sans
doute à Vico, et cela prouverait déjà le goût romantique du traducteur,
mais les citations ci-dessus sont contradictoires. Cesarotti fut tout d'abord
saisi par les passions, les sentiments des chants de Macpherson; le vrai
naturel — celui de Homère — semble encore rude au poète élevé dans la
contemplation arcadienne-géorgique de la nature. Lorsque Cesarotti écrit
à Macpherson que l'Ossian ne prouve pas seulement la supériorité de la
poésie antique sur l'actuelle, mais montre aussi les défauts de la poésie homérique, nous constatons que Cesarotti est resté l'homme du classicisme.
Cesarotti étudie l'Ossian en le croyant original, en tant que philologue classique, mais son enthousiasme est éveillé par le modernisme, le sentimentalisme des chants de Macpherson, par rapport à Homère. Mais Ossian, jugé
meilleur que Homère, rend la langue et le goût poétiques italiens plus
ouverts pour la découverte, justement, de Homère. Il est intéressant de
suivre Cesarotti dans ses notes et dans ses essais, pour voir la manière dont
il compare Homère et Ossian. «Tandis que les héros grecs sont brutes et
indignes, les héros d'Ossian sont de vrais chevaliers, idéals et parfaits,
et Ossian lui-même est un poète sensible . . .»[52]

La traduction de Cesarotti a une grande importance dans l'évolution de
la langue poétique italienne du XVIIIᵉ siècle, car la langue d'Ossian était
tout à fait nouvelle par rapport à la pratique poétique traditionnaliste,
classiciste, arcadienne, et ausssi à la pratique «illuministe». Il est vrai que
Parini atteint le sommet de la langue poétique néo-classique italienne dans
son *Mattino*, mais la poésie élégante et musicale de Parini n'était point
capable d'assurer un renouvellement du lyrisme. Cesarotti, par contre, dans
sa traduction d'Ossian, rend la langue lyrique italienne propre à l'expression
des sentiments originaux. Cette œuvre représente le commencement du
style sentimental italien. Le traducteur lui-même est conscient de l'importance de son travail, il essaie de «tentare una strada in gran parte nuova».
Dans la préface à l'édition de 1763, Cesarotti proclame clairement: «J'ai
tenté d'offrir un poète original à l'Italie. Et de plus, sans exemple, ni prédécesseur qui aurait pu m'aider dans mon travail, et dans une langue qui
est riche, il est vrai, mais tout à fait stérilisée par le règne absolu des grammairiens, — ainsi j'ai offert l'aspect d'un duelliste moyen engagé contre un
géant . . . Je sais très bien que plus d'une expression de ma traduction ne
seraient admises dans un poème italien, mais je me flatte d'avoir réussi à
les planter dans la langue italienne afin qu'elles donnent une couleur à
notre langue lyrique, peu heureuse en nombreux aspects, et qu'elles servent
aussi à quelques idées de style.»[53] Cesarotti pressent dans son Ossian le
nouveau goût et style sentimentaux, et il a trouvé le moyen de l'introduire
dans la pratique poétique italienne, si bien que ses traductions ne trouvent
pas d'adversaires, mais des disciples. Il y parvient grâce au principe «io
consulto con la ragione e spiego con sentimento». Comme Macpherson, il
mêle de nouveaux éléments au texte anglais, d'ailleurs en traduction non
stylisée. Dans ses traductions, il y a au fond une fusion entre le goût et la
langue arcadiens-néo-classicistes et la manière d'expression d'Ossian. Ses

---

[52] *Opere scelte*, I, p. 235.
[53] *Ossian*, I, Pisa 1801, pp. 5—6.

traductions sont caractérisées à la fois par l'innovation et une prudente fidélité aux traditions italiennes. Tandis que les traducteurs italiens de Young et de Gray subtilisent la poésie anglaise en une poésie de l'Arcadie, Cesarotti ne rend pas arcadienne, mais conserve le style original des poèmes d'Ossian, bien qu'il ne rompe pas pour autant avec la langue poétique arcadienne. Il ne rend pas Ossian arcadien, mais «ossianise» plutôt l'Arcadie. Les annotations ajoutées à son Ossian prouvent bien son intention de faire accepter les innovations, et dans son «Indice poétique d'Ossian» (Indice poetico di Ossian, ossia catalogo classificato delle principali bellezze che si trovano nelle poesie di lui), il explique cas pour cas le pourquoi de la beauté des poèmes d'Ossian, et le secret de l'effet émotif produit par les nouvelles images poétiques. Pour que la poésie lyrique d'Ossian ne semble pas trop insolite et incompréhensible au lecteur italien encore non initié au goût nouveau, Cesarotti ajoute au texte de Macpherson, il complète les associations sentimentales, les explique pour ainsi dire, et donne ses raisons dans les notes par lesquelles il a complété le texte anglais; Cesarotti qui dispose d'une grande culture classique, découvre instinctivement les passages dont Macpherson compléta les textes gaéliques par des motifs empruntés aux poètes antiques, et lui aussi, il rend plus clairs les poèmes d'Ossian en utilisant des comparaisons homériques et pindariques déjà acceptées par la poésie italienne. «Dans le vers "tu pel ciel deserto — solo ti mori", j'ai pris "ciel deserto" de Pindare. C'est ainsi que j'ai uni les expressions des deux génies, qui furent, pour ainsi dire, écrites l'une pour l'autre» Binni démontre que le texte italien de Cesarotti contient même des réminiscences de Métastase.

En résumé nous constatons que Cesarotti essaie de se délivrer, dans sa traduction, des préciosités de la poésie lyrique classique «illuministe»-rationaliste, fort étrangères à la langue d'Ossian fondée sur des associations sentimentales, cependant il prend garde à la compréhensibilité de ses associations, à la conservation des traditions de la pratique poétique italienne. C'est ainsi que l'Ossian italien garde le «sublime» connu de la poésie de Parini, mais sera «terribilmente sublime»; il revît le «magnifico» arcadien, mais sera «terribilmente magnifico».

Cette découverte d'Ossian par Cesarotti représente donc vraiment un tournant décisif dans le goût lyrique du XVIIIe siècle: le commencement d'une poésie type nouveau, qui n'est pas encore romantique, mais qui contient plus d'un élément de la future langue romantique italienne et la possibilité pour le poète de donner expression à ses propres sentiments dans les tableaux lyriques. Cesarotti en était conscient et considérait lui-même son œuvre comme une production artistique et esthétique et se disait «traduttore originale». Walter Binni est du même avis, il parle d'intermédiaire, d'entremise au lieu de traduction, il appelle l'Ossian italien «mediazione». Croce approuve: «Binni a raison d'écrire qu'il faut regarder la traduction d'Ossian par Cesarotti avec la mesure de la vraie poésie, car son trésor poétique, les ondes de ses sentiments représentent une valeur, une découverte, selon leur propre aspect, d'un nouveau monde, d'une nouvelle poésie, qui était en même temps une poésie italienne.»[54]

[54] Le compte rendu sur l'étude de W. Binni (*M. Cesarotti e il preromanticismo*, Critica, 6, 1941 et 1, 1942) par Croce apparut dans le numéro du 20 mai 1942 de la *Critica*.

La traduction italienne de l'Ossian connut un succès unanime en Italie et en Europe. Cependant, les tenants du point de vue traditionnel voient des signes du dépérissement de la langue et de la poésie italiennes dans l'introduction de la nouvelle langue lyrique, dans les traductions préromantiques de plus en plus nombreuses. Dans son œuvre intitulée *Del carattere nazionale del gusto italiano e di un certo gusto dominante in letteratura straniera* (1784), M. Borsa accuse Cesarotti de faire dégénérer la langue italienne. Melchiorre Cesarotti — qui était avant tout un philologue — se donna pour tâche de justifier par des études théoriques le droit et l'importance de la réforme du style et de la langue.

C'est en 1785 qu'il publie son essai philosophique et linguistique, écrit dans le style de Condillac et de De Brosses, le *Saggio sopra la filosofia della lingua*. Malgré son titre, l'ouvrage est plutôt pratique que théorique. La philosophie n'y est nécessaire que pour proclamer l'usage libre de la langue lyrique en se référant aux résultats des théories sensualistes et à celles de Vico, pour faire accepter l'exigence de la raison et du bon goût dans l'appréciation des œuvres poétiques, et jeter les bases d'une réforme de la langue qui ne change pas le génie de la langue italienne et qui assure la plus grande richesse et la plus grande applicabilité des expressions poétiques.[55]

Il commence son livre par les constatations de la Crusca selon lesquelles il existe des états linguistiques idéaux qui sont aptes à exprimer les sujets nouveaux, les objectifs spirituels des époques à venir. L'auteur veut infirmer cette thèse par les preuves de la philosophie linguistique et par l'histoire de la langue, et prouver le contraire. Dans la première partie de son traité il établit ses propres thèses linguistiques. Aucune des langues ne peut originellement être dite supérieure à telle autre, car elles sont nées toutes de la même manière. Aucune des langues n'évolue selon un projet prémédité. Aucune des langues ne se forme selon le désir des autorités. Aucune des langues ne peut se prétendre complète, parfaite car les langues évoluent continuellement. Aucune des langues ne peut être assez riche pour ne pas avoir besoin de nouvelles richesses. Aucune des langues n'est stable, car les langues changent continuellement selon la pratique qu'en font les écrivains et le peuple. Dans la deuxième partie de son traité, Cesarotti s'occupe des questions de la langue nationale en se penchant séparément sur les problèmes de la langue parlée et sur ceux de la langue écrite. Il constate que l'usage général de la langue doit constituer la base d'une langue nationale. Ensuite il s'occupe du côté rhétorique de la langue, du changement à fonction stylistique des paroles et des éléments linguistiques à valeur de parole, des modes de création du mot. Il prouve l'absurdité de figer l'état linguistique d'époques antécédentes dans une norme par le changement de signification des mots à plusieurs sens et il prouve aussi par là la nécessité de rafraîchir la langue «si nous voulons que l'expression littéraire rencontre le sentiment, car cette rencontre est à la base de toute beauté et de toute vivacité du style.»[56] Il consacre des chapitres particuliers aux questions de l'étude des phrases et des mots, aux avantages de la structure directe des

---

[55] Puppo, *Discussioni* . . . p. 417.
[56] *Op. cit.*, p. 381.

phrases («Condillac et Batteaux, les grands Français, désirent rendre plus logique la structure de phrase»),[57] pour la nécessité de créer de nouveaux mots («un nouveau mot est utilisable s'il convient à l'harmonie intérieure de la langue»),[58] il cite comme exemple les œuvres néologistes de Buttner et Michaelis, l'emprunt des mots est surtout justifié par les dialectes. La quatrième partie donne un aperçu historique sur les quatre siècles de la *Questione della lingua*. Son travail se termine par le projet d'évolution de la langue italienne, par la proclamation de l'exigence d'établir un comité linguistique italien, de préparer des dictionnaires étymologiques.

Le traité de Cesarotti paraît à Padoue en 1785. Les discussions qu'il provoque[59] contribuent en grande partie à la formation de la théorie linguistique du romantisme, conçue par Manzoni. Naturellement, on ne tarde pas non plus à l'attaquer. Ce n'est qu'un disciple de Cesarotti qui répond à G. B. de Velo,[60] mais lorsque l'opinion de De Velo sera partagée par des personnalités telles que S. Bettinelli, C. Gozzi[61] et le piémontais Gianfranco Galeani Napione qui publie en 1791 son travail linguistique de teinte nationaliste intitulé *Dei pregi della lingua italiana*, Cesarotti complète l'édition de 1800 de son livre par le *Rischiamenti apologetici* et par sa lettre adressée à Napione. Il y fait hommage aux sentiments patriotiques de Napione, mais souligne aussi que sa proposition de renouvellement du style et de la langue ne signifient pas le dépérissement de la langue italienne, bien au contraire, c'est en l'acceptant que la langue italienne deviendra importante et cultivée. La réforme de la langue est nécessaire parce que les langues évoluent et les écrivains n'ont pas seulement le droit, mais aussi le devoir de faire évoluer et de compléter la langue. «Les grands écrivains se sont toujours gardé le droit et la liberté de leur propre exemple.»[62] «Le grand écrivain, qui exprime avec originalité l'esprit de son époque, n'a pas l'intention de changer de force le génie encore brut de la nation, il le réveille, le presse et contribue à son renforcement et à son évolution.»[63] Cesarotti réclame, tout comme Napione, l'étroite liaison entre la patrie et la langue, et il ne voit pas le véritable amour pour la patrie et pour la langue dans l'immobilité, mais justement dans l'ouverture vers le nouvel esprit, vers les nouvelles conceptions, «d'où la langue et la nation s'enrichissent également». Par la proclamation de l'emprunt motivé des mots étrangers, il ne veut pas affaiblir le caractère nationale de la langue italienne, il veut au contraire le renforcer par là. «Vous ne serez plus prisonniers des

[57] *Op. cit.*, p. 358.
[58] *Op. cit.*, p. 381.
[59] Appréciations: A. Juan, *Dell'origine de'progressi e dello stato attuale d'ogni letteratura*, Parma 1799. — C. Sibillato, *Sopra lo spirito filosofico delle lettere*, 1786. — C. B. Cornician, *Dei piaceri dello spirito* ... 1790. — G. Barbieri, *Intorno allo stile poetico*, 1791. — A. Zendrini, *Riflessioni sul sistema della mitologia allegorica*, 1791. — I. Martignoni, *Del gusto in ogni maniera di amene lettere e arti*, 1793. — L. Cerretti, *Delle vicende del buon gusto in Italia*, 1805. Attaques: A. Anelli, *Cronache di Pindo* (poèmes), des études de M. Borsa, G. B. De Velo, Gozzi et Napione.
[60] G. B. De Velo, *Sulla preminenza di alcune lingue e sull'autorità degli scritti approvati dai grammatici*, 1789. — Réponse de Zendrini, *Ristampa di un articolo del giornale d'Aletopoli*, 1789.
[61] C. Gozzi, *Chiaccheria di Carlo Gozzi intorno alla lingua litterale italiana e alcune ricerche sopra il libro intitolato Saggio sopra la lingua italiana dell'abate Melchiorre Cesarotti ... Il tutto è diretto ai lettori della Marfisa Bizzarra ...*, 1796.
[62] Puppo, *Discussioni* ... p. 415.
[63] *Op. cit.*, p. 410.

dictionnaires, ni des Cruscistes, ni de grammairiens, ni des antiques, ni des néologues, ni des singeurs de français, ni des affectés — mais vous serez Italiens et modernes, qui se serviront de la langue italienne avec un grand naturel et une grande liberté, selon vos propres sentiments.»[64]

Nous pouvons dire que l'une des parties les plus intéressantes de l'étude, le noyau idéologique de l'œuvre, se trouve dans la question du *génie de la langue*. L'idée en parvient aux philosophes sensualistes par la théorie rationaliste du Port-Royal. Le génie de la langue signifiait un aspect linguistique qu'on ne pouvait pas traduire dans la grammaire universellement valable pour toutes les langues, il signifiait la capacité invective qui ne se laisse déduire d'aucune règle. Au XVIIIe siècle, le génie perdit le sens traditionnel du mot, il commence à signifier la partie de la capacité créative qui représente le caractère individuel dans la création.[65] Chez Condillac, le génie de la langue comprend la relation logique, théorique des connaissances entre la langue et les idéaux composant le.génie de la nation. Dans la théorie de Condillac et de Vico, ce sont les circonstances de la nature, le climat et les traits historiques et sociaux fondés sur ces dernières qui déterminent le caractère des peuples. C'est sur cette base que Condillac affirme l'invariabilité du génie linguistique. L'explication de Condillac sur le génie linguistique eut un retentissement dans la conscience linguistique et philosophique italienne déjà avant Cesarotti. Algarotti en parle dans ses essais intitulés *Saggio sopra la necessità di scrivere alla propria lingua* et la *Sopra la lingua francese* (1750), Saverio Bettinelli s'occupe de cette question dans la deuxième partie de *Del Risorgimento d'Italia* (Genii ed ingegni). Chez Bettinelli le génie est la concrétisation de l'enthousiasme de l'écrivain («ingegno, ma grande», «fantasia, ma forte», «cuore, ma risentito»). On trouve une définition du génie proche de cette dernière dans le *Discours* de Baretti, et dans l'étude de P. Verri intitulée *Pensieri sullo spirito della letteratura italiana*, mais Cesarotti est le seul à approcher la question d'une façon vraiment philosophique.

Cesarotti fait sienne la conception de Condillac sur le génie linguistique, mais il suit les traces de Vico,[66] quant à l'origine de la langue, au développement du génie linguistique et surtout dans la question de l'imagination poétique. Il divise le génie linguistique en génie grammatique et en génie rhétorique. Chez Cesarotti, le génie linguistique n'est pas une forme déterminée des spécificités nationales, mais une aptitude d'organisation entre les caractères nationaux entremêlés. Selon Cesarotti, ce n'est pas le génie grammatique constant (la structure), mais le génie rhétorique (l'usage de la langue et du style) qui donne du dynamisme à la langue, et ce génie rhétorique est avant tout déterminé par la pratique de l'écrivain. Selon Cesarotti, «la vie de la langue correspond à la vie de la nation et dépend du sort du peuple auquel elle appartient»,[67] donc le changement du génie de la nation ne détermine pas les changements du génie grammatique, mais ceux du génie rhétorique, tandis que le génie grammatique reste inchangé. «Le

[64] Lettera al conte Giafranco Galeani Napione, *Opere scelte*, II, p. 195.
[65] Ce changement de sens du terme du génie se manifeste dans la discussion entre Napione et Cesarotti: faut-il comprendre «uomo di spirito», «uomo di genio», «uomo d'ingegno» ou «uomo di seno»?
[66] Voir: *Bibliografia Vichiana* I, Napoli 1947.
[67] *Opere scelte*, II, p. 303. a

génie grammatique est le vrai défenseur de la langue, mais il n'enlève pas la liberté de perfection au génie rhétorique.»[68] Le génie rhétorique n'est autre chose que le système linguistique des sentiments et des idées qui prédominent dans les diverses nations et qui opèrent par l'activité des écrivains. («Sistema generale dell'idea e dei sentimenti che predomina nelle diverse nazioni e che per opera degli scrittori improntò la lingua delle sue tracci.») Le génie rhétorique de toutes les langues change et évolue donc nécessairement. Ce processus peut éventuellement être retardé, mais ne peut être empêché ou arrêté définitivement.

Pour fournir la justification du nouveau goût littéraire, Cesarotti publie, en même temps que son travail linguistique, un essai esthétique, le *Saggio sulla filosofia del gusto*, qui par son importance et sa profondeur ne vaut pas sa philosophie linguistique, mais qui est tout de même, malgré sa tempérance arcadienne, une vraie apologie des traductions de l'Ossian. Il forme ses principes esthétiques sur la base des *Réflexions critiques sur la poésie, la peinture et la musique* (1719) de Du Bos, mais il est fort influencé aussi par Gravina et Beccelli.

Dans son livre, Cesarotti fait également une différence entre les conceptions de génie et de bon goût, et il prouve cette distinction par deux poètes. Le génie est représenté par Dante, relégué plutôt en arrière-plan par le XVIIIᵉ siècle, et le bon goût par Petrarque. Dans le cadre du goût, il distingue le «gusto fattizio» affecté et le «gusto della natura». Cesarotti fonde encore le beau esthétique entièrement sur le bon goût et c'est ce fait qui prouve que son point de vue n'est pas encore romantique. D'autre part, lorsqu'il poursuit son raisonnement dans *Ragionamento sopra l'origine e i progressi dell'arte poetica* de 1762, il distingue deux sortes de plaisir vécu, «l'un provient de la nature, l'autre des préjugés dirigés par la civilisation et par les coutumes».[69] On ne voit plus ici la sympathie pour la poésie primitive qu'on trouve chez Vico. Le sensualisme et le sentimentalisme font tous deux appel à l'imitation de la Nature. Selon Cesarotti, cependant, l'art poétique — si proche qu'il soit des sciences naturelles — ne peut se limiter au reflet extérieur, fortuit de la Nature, il doit être un reflet passionné, spirituel, intérieur. «Celui qui examine sa propre âme et son propre cœur, y découvre toutes les règles de la poésie.»[70] Le vrai poète, comme Homère, prend les règles de son propre art «dans l'analyse a priori de la Nature, dans la relation à peine changeante des objets et de l'homme.»[71] L'inspiration poétique naît de l'instant, de l'instinct, du sentiment et l'art poétique, de l'éveil philosophique conscient de soi, et c'est ce dernier qui change sous l'effet de la critique et du goût public.

Pour le principe de la liberté du poète, Cesarotti puise dans Bacon, Du Bos, Fontenelle, Voltaire et Batteaux. Selon lui, le principe de la liberté du poète ne supporte pas l'existence a priori de règles artistiques, le poète est libre de règles extérieures, il ne lui faut suivre que les règles qu'il a en lui-même. Cesarotti s'appuie sur les vues de Vico sur l'art — il deviendra ainsi le précurseur des découvertes romantiques de Vico — mais à la diffé-

[68] Puppo, *Discussione* . . . p. 473.
[69] *Nota all' Ossian*, I, p. 205.
[70] *Opere scelte*, II, p. 244.
[71] *Nota all' Ossian*, I, p. 205.

rence de celui-ci, il trouve que l'imagination primitive est un chaos merveilleux, où s'allument, il est vrai, de véritables flammes («un caos da cui scappava qualche scintilla di luce»), mais que le développement de la vraie poésie ne peut résulter que de l'évolution de la culture et de la société («i singoli geni poetici, consapevoli della loro umanità e arte come Orfeo, i quali ammansarono la mente selvatica e ferina dei primitivi e promossero la civiltà artistica, fino alla formazione di un codice poetico»). C'est là une révalorisation néo-classiciste du «poeti teologi» de Vico. Il tient pour inaccessible le «fantastico universale» de Vico, car la variation infinie de la Nature exclut la possibilité que la poésie puisse jamais atteindre un niveau de reflet aussi profond que celui de la philosophie. Ainsi, la perfection artistique est relative, elle aussi, car elle dépend du génie national («dal genio particolare della nazione che la coltiva») et c'est pour cela qu'il donne beaucoup d'importance au rôle public des artistes: il «porta il poeta al massimo sua funzione civile, a una gloria di educatore e di profeta, pari a quelli degli eroi, ma implica arbitrio del gusto dominante, della moda». La conception déjà presque romantique du rôle prophétique du poète se mêle ici d'une façon intéressante à l'exigence néo-classiciste de l'obligation du poète de suivre le bon goût, car la beauté absolue (piacere assoluto) est propre à la Nature («dell'assoluto universale immutabile»), mais il y a aussi une autre beauté, «piacere relativo», «piacere nazionale» qui est créée par la culture et la civilisation. Cette dernière varie selon les peuples et les époques, c'est sur celle que doit se fonder la création poétique, dite «meraviglioso poetico». C'est cette confusion de vues esthétiques que Binni nomme attitude préromantique; Cesarotti en atteint le sommet quand il identifie le génie artistique au concept du bon goût, et fait de ce génie une catégorie majeure des beaux arts: «il genio che presiede alle arti del bello, ella dirige ugualmente il conoscitore che giudica e l'inspirato che dette.»[72] Ce sont les mêmes pensées du *Saggio sul gusto* qui sont développées davantage dans le *Saggio sul Bello*[73] conservé en fragments seulement, où nous trouvons aussi des aveux concernant sa traduction d'Ossian: «Un bois bien arrangé peut être beau en lui-même aussi, mais s'il est composé de cypres de cimetière, il éveille mieux le doux sentiment de la mélancolie, les idées de la faillibilité humaine et de la mortalité . . .» C'est ce qui avait conduit Cesarotti vers Ossian, car Ossian «è un cuore profondamente sensibile», où «vit la mélancolie qui est le vrai signe du génie, une âme, qui dissoud ses propres sentiments dans les objets de son entourage». C'est à partir d'Ossian que Cesarotti arrive à la définition du nouveau type de poète idéal: «sopratutto abbia vigoria di pensamento e quel sublime dell'anima senza di cui la sublimità della parola non è che fumo e rimbombo.» «Tu veux être poète? Examine-toi pour savoir si tu disposes des conditions de la mission d'Appollon, examine-toi bien et ne confonds pas la flamme rapidement éteinte de la fantaisie enfantine avec le saint et éternel flamboiement du génie.» Pour Melchiorre Cesarotti la «poesia del sublime» est déjà «un più dell'estetico», plus que de l'art, c'est-à-dire qu'il approche la poésie et la personne du génie poétique du point de vue du romantisme.

[72] *Opere scelte*, II, pp. 219—224.
[73] *Opere scelte*, I, pp. 340—365.

214

VII

Le succès de l'Ossian fut particulièrement grand en Europe Centrale, troublée par les questions nationales. La connaissance d'Ossian s'étend par les publications et les traductions toujours nouvelles qui se succèdent à l'époque du tournant du siècle: celles de Cesarotti, en italien 1763, 1772; celle de Denis, en allemand, 1775; de Petersen, en allemand, 1782; de Le Tourneur, en français, 1777; de Batsányi, en hongrois, 1795; de Rhode, en allemand, 1800; de Stolberg, en allemand, 1806; de Ahlwardt, en allemand, mesure gaélique, 1811; de Kazinczy, en hongrois, 1816. Sous l'effet des traductions se développe une vraie fièvre d'Ossian, l'utilisation fréquente des noms des personnages d'Ossian comme prénom en est une preuve (Malvine, Oscar). Des dictionnaires et des ouvrages linguistiques paraissent pour la langue d'Ossian, en Allemagne avant tout (Tales of Ossian for Use and Entertainment, 1784 Nürnberg. — Ein Lesebuch für Anfänger im Englischen), où Ossian est vénéré comme un héros germanique antique; on rêve, à travers ses chants, d'une culture antique du Nord qu'on peut confronter au classicisme gréco-latine. L'influence d'Ossian enrichit, avec Perdy, le genre des imitations allemandes des ballades traditionnelles. Chateaubriand emporte à ses promenades romantiques Homère dans une de ses poches et Ossian dans l'autre, et il puise dans Ossian pour son épopée chrétienne. Madame de Staël nomme Ossian directement l'«Homère du Nord», et Mihály Vörösmarty a recours surtout à Ossian pour créer le style romantique de *Zalán futása*.

La transposition et l'explication préromantiques-classiques d'Ossian par Cesarotti a incontestablement un grand rôle dans l'engagement de l'Europe à cette fièvre d'Ossian. Ils influencèrent le sort et le style de toutes les traductions européennes par l'intermédiaire de l'Autrichien M. Denis. Herder remarque d'ailleurs la tempérance néo-classique de la traduction d'Ossian par Cesarotti–Denis: «Trotz alles Fleisses und Geschmacks und Schwunges und Stärke der deutschen Übersetzung bin ich gewiss, dass unser Ossian nicht der wahre Ossian mehr sei.»[74] La participation italienne à l'ossianisme européen demande encore des recherches, mais on constate toutefois que le travail de Melchiorre Cesarotti a un effet décisif sur le développement du nouveau style de la fin du XVIIIe siècle italien, dit style préromantique. Les traductions d'Ossian par Cesarotti sont suivies par d'autres: celle de Leoni en 1813, puis par celle de Monti. A propos de ce dernier, Torti di Bevagna constate en 1824 que les motifs de la poésie d'Ossian s'insèrent complètement dans le romantisme italien.[75] Des anthologies, contenant les morceaux les plus lyriques d'Ossian paraissent en même temps que les nouvelles éditions: elles ont une influence évidente sur l'art de Foscolo et de Leopardi aussi.

En Italie, l'ossianisme se mêle de l'influence de Young et de Gray que Cesarotti traduisit également. L'ossianisme et le youngisme expriment parfaitement la nouvelle sensibilité. Selon le contemporain L. Cerretti, Young et Ossian sont les principaux responsables de la «destruction du goût» en Italie.

---

[74] Herder, *Fragmente aus Briefwechsel über Ossian und Lieder alter Völker.*
[75] *Bellezze poetiche di Ossian imitate del cav. Monti.*

L'influence des littératures européennes eut un effet décisif sur le développement du goût préromantique italien. Il y en avait certaines marques déjà au début du siècle, mais la vraie période des traductions anglaises, allemandes et françaises ne commence qu'à partir de 1760:

1763 — Cesarotti: *Ossian*;
1768 — A. Loschi: *Le Notti di Young*, *Les Nuits de Young*, d'après la traduction française de Le Tourneur;
1771 — A. Alberti traduit Young, de l'original, en prose;
1771—1775 — G. Bottoni: traduction de Young, en vers (elle connaît deux éditions);
1778 — C. B. da Fermo traduit la *Meditazione sopra i sepolcri* de Hervey, dans la même année Cesarotti traduit aussi l'*Elegia sopra un cimitero campestro* de Gray;
1779 — Pagani-Ceva: traduction de Gessner avec une étude de Bertola (*Saggio delle poesie pastorali del Sig. Gessnero*);
1781 — E. C. Turra: traduction de Gessner;
1796 — Salom: traduction de *Werther*.

En dehors de ceux-là, Baretti et G. Gozzi traduisent et diffusent J. Thomson dans leurs revues; le premier succès de Swift en Italie est attaché au nom de Gaspare Gozzi. Shakespeare est traduit par Conti, Rolli et Baretti. Fénelon, Marmontel, Lessing, Klopstock, Haller, Diderot, Prévost, Marivaux, Destouches et Beaumarchais sont connus et exercent un effet important sur le goût littéraire italien de la fin du siècle.

Mais la plupart de ces traductions n'atteint pas le niveau lyrique de l'*Ossian* de Cesarotti. A. Loschi rend compte ainsi de sa propre pratique de traducteur: «Comme les couleurs dans lesquelles Young trempe son pinceau sont tellement sombres qu'elles provoqueraient de l'ennui chez le lecteur habitué à des couleurs plus gaies, j'ai trouvé qu'il valait mieux rafraîchir les parties à effet monotone par d'autres, plus gaies.»[76] Botta joint à sa traduction de Young, la lettre qui lui adresse Métastase déjà en âge avancé. Le grand maître arcadien y avoue qu'il a beau admirer la poésie de Young, il ne peut s'y accoutumer, car: «ostinato costume di mostrarci sempre gli oggetti dal lato lor più funesto».[77] C'est justement pour cela que la traducteur change le ton pessimiste du texte original. Ce tableau de couleurs assez variées et le niveau inégal des traductions sont fort attaqués par les critiques au goût néo-classique de l'époque: Bettinelli, Parini, Foscolo et Alfieri aussi. Baretti écrit dans la *Frusta letteraria*, que le Settecento italien n'a rien produit de plus «que des histoires et des romans galants, 'bastardamente' traduits».

La véritable cause des insuffisances des traductions italiennes de la fin du XVIIIe siècle consiste dans le fait que les traducteurs étaient privés de la liberté d'écrivain — surtout dans le domaine de la prose — dont disposaient les auteurs français, anglais et allemands des œuvres originales. Les traducteurs devaient se conformer au style littéraire italien et ainsi ils raccourcirent et déformèrent les œuvres. Voilà l'erreur de style qui est surmontée dans l'*Ossian* de Melchiorre Cesarotti, voilà la nouvelle manière de traduire

[76] Cité par Binni, *Preromanticismo italiano*, 129.
[77] *Op. cit.*, p. 150.

et le style qu'il justifie dans ses études théoriques et c'est grâce à cela que le cercle du *Conciliatore* peut être considéré comme le précurseur des traductions romantiques.

Dans sa monographie d'importance fondamentale, Walter Binni remarque que dans l'analyse des traductions ce ne sont pas les déviations du texte original qu'il faut souligner, mais leur contribution considérable, malgré la qualité médiocre, à la création d'une atmosphère préromantique italienne à la fin du siècle («il dovere è di precisare l'effetto preromantico delle tradizioni, il suo grado di novità sulla via del romanticismo»).[78]

L'intérêt pour la culture antique commence déjà dans les milieux de l'Arcadie, l'effet des vestiges de Winckelmann et de Herculanum ne fera que l'augmenter. Dans le dernier tiers du siècle, la peinture des ruines connaît une grande floraison en Italie également (Piranesi, Parini, Guardi, Galliari). Les ruines jouent un rôle important dans les décors du théâtre et le culte italien des jardins de ruine anglais se répand aussi. Ce culte des ruines apparaît en même temps que le culte de la Bible et celui de la mort (V. Landi. L. Cerretti, A. Cesati), commence la mode romantique qui mène des châteaux du Moyen-Age jusqu'à Berchet (Rezzonico, D. Saluzzo). L'intérêt porté à l'Orient se renforce, Domenico Sestini publie en 1784 ses lettres de voyage en Turquie, beaucoup d'écrits paraissent sur la Roumanie et sur la Pologne. Alberto Fortis dans sa description de voyage intitulée *Viaggio in Dalmazia* (1774), reproduit une ballade populaire sur la mort de l'Aga Hassan, que Gœthe traduit en allemand.

L'influence des traductions apparaît tout d'abord dans les œuvres des traducteurs, Gozzi écrit les *Fiabe* d'après Klopstock et Pope, cette œuvre sera la lecture favorite des romantiques allemands. Les œuvres italiennes originales seront avant tout influencées par Young, Gray, Hervey et Ossian. On trouve des traces d'Ossian aussi bien chez Pindemonte (Arminio), que dans l'*Inno al Sole* de Foscolo, ou dans l'*Il Bardo* de Monti. La poésie funéraire italienne, dont le sommet sera l'*I Sepolcri*, commence par *Le visioni* (1766) hautement estimé aussi par Varano, Leopardi et par Monti. Le plus grand personnage de la poésie funéraire est Alessandro Verri, ses principales œuvres sont: *Le avventure di Saffo* (1782) (à ce propos Foscolo donna à Sappho le nom de «Werther en jupe»); la traduction en prose de l'*Iliade* (1789); *Notti romane al sepolcro degli Scipioni* (1792); *Vita di Erostratta* (1793). A la poésie des nocturnes et du sépulcre appartiennent également la *Notte* de Parini dans une certaine mesure, poème que Foscolo cite comme l'exemple italien de la «poésie romantique», ainsi que les œuvres intitulées *Cimiteri* et *Poesie campestri* de Pindemonte et les œuvres de nombreux poètes moins importants de la fin du siècle. Les *Confessions* de Rousseau auront une influence décisive sur les romans d'analyse de la fin du siècle et de la première partie du siècle suivant. Les poètes allemands traduits par Bertola, Denina et Corniani exerceront leur influence en même temps que les essais de Bertola. Le récit de voyage en Allemagne par Bertola, le *Viaggio sul Reno e ne'suoi contorni* (1787) est, à côté de l'Ossian de Cesarotti, une des œuvres les plus évoluées parmi celles qui sont nées du goût préromantique. Carducci nomme Bertola «le premier touriste italien romantique».

[78] *Op. cit.*, p. 163.

C'est ainsi que se développe, à la suite de la traduction d'Ossian, l'atmosphère littéraire italienne de la fin du siècle, que Binni est tenté d'appeler une nouvelle Arcadie préromantique où s'enracine la conception esthétique disant que la vraie poésie et le vrai art ne peuvent se contenter ni de l'imitation de la nature, ni de celle des poètes modèles, mais uniquement de l'ambition d'exprimer les passions du cœur. Chez Alfieri, le raisonnement mélodramatique didactique de Parini est déjà disparu. Ce sont le grand élan, la flamme brûlante des sentiments qui seront les vraies valeurs de ces œuvres écrites en forme classique. La noble conscience d'être prédestiné au sort de poète trouvera ses prolongements chez Foscolo.

Mais il fallait une préparation culturelle et sentimentale conformes au développement du génie d'Alfieri. Et c'est là le mérite de Melchiorre Cesarotti et des traducteurs. L'héritage légué par le Settecento à la poésie romantique de l'Ottocento est la possibilité de créer une langue littéraire libre, réaliste, cultivée et une voie délivrée des pédants et des cruscistes. La synthèse du style affectif et poétique de l'Ossian aide l'éclosion du romantisme italien, qui la dépasse naturellement. C'est pour cela que Foscolo pourra écrire dans *La chioma di Berenice* (1803): «Come può l'uomo nato fra i popoli di gran tempo usciti dallo stato eroico e sotto il beato cielo d'Italia, imitare la magnifica barbarie di Ossian e cercare di transportare nelle sue solitudini? Beh io, volando con l'immaginazione e quei tempi, guidò fra le sue montagne quel ricco poeta e siedo devoto sulla tomba, ma io grido ad un tempo agli Italiani: lasciate quest'albero nel suo terreno, poichè trapiantate tralignerà.» Cette exclamation de Foscolo pourrait bien marquer une borne, dans le temps, c'est à ce moment que se terminent définitivement le Settecento et l'époque du préromantisme et commence l'art nouveau, l'époque moderne, le romantisme, l'époque du Risorgimento.

RÉFLEXIONS SUR LE STYLE LYRIQUE FRANÇAIS AU SIÈCLE DES LUMIÈRES

par

LÁSZLÓ GÁLDI

1. Il est temps de découvrir quelques aspects positifs sinon du génie, mais au moins de la sensibilité et de la technique des poètes français du XVIIIe siècle. La méthode que nous proposons de suivre diffère essentiellement des synthèses antérieures:[1] au lieu de créer un s y s t è m e, un petit traité de stylistique et de poétique sur la base des textes étudiés, nous préférons céder aux suggestions de H. Morier,[2] de Yves le Hir[3] et d'autres stylistes: en essayant de respecter, dans la mesure du possible, la s t r u c t u r e d'un certain nombre de textes, nous espérons pouvoir mieux saisir la v a l e u r d'un s t y l è m e[4] dans un contexte donné. Nous allons tâcher de grouper les textes choisis selon les g e n r e s qu'ils représentent: n partant de *l'ode,* c'est-à-dire du s t y l e s u b l i m e,[5] nous descendrons peu à peu vers la *chanson* qui, sans représenter nécessairement le s t y e e b a s, reflète plutôt les diverses sphères du s t y l e m o y e n. A propos ld chaque genre nous devons citer aussi bien des textes plus ou moins tradie tionnels que des textes plus modernes; il est presque superflu de dire quce qui, d'une manière générale, caractérise le style poétique du XVIIIe siècle, c'est une tendance d'éloignement souvent à peine perceptible du tyle[e] poétique du siècle antérieur. Dans le domaine du vocabulaire ce «glissemsent» vers quelque chose de nouveau est particulièrement net; c'est pourquoi, au cours de nos analyses textuelles, nous renverrons souvent, à défaut d'un vocabulaire spécial de la langue du XVIIIe siècle, aux données fournies par les dépouillements de Littré et de Robert; inutile d'ajouter que si 'on possédait un dictionnaire spécial de la langue du XVIIIe siècle, nos indlications, communiquées cette fois sous bénéfice d'inventaire, pourraient être beaucoup plus précises.[6] Au point de vue de la filiation des stylèmes lexicaux, nous devons tenir compte surtout des attestations a n t é r i e u r e s;

[1] V. les synthèses bien connues de A. François, F. Brunot, Ch. Bruneau, etc. sur l'état de la langue du XVIIIe siècle.
[2] *Psychologie des styles,* Genève s. d. [1959].
[3] *Analyses stylistiques,* Paris 1968.
[4] Nous entendons par là tous les éléments de l'énoncé qui sont susceptibles d'avoir une certaine valeur stylistique. La mise en valeur des stylèmes virtuels dépend toujours d'une interférence complexe du contenu et de la forme.
[5] En parlant du XVIIIe siècle, on doit toujours tenir compte de la théorie classique des t r o i s s t y l e s, même si les limites de ceux-ci commencent à s'effacer. Sur la théorie des trois styles v. l'étude de E. R. Curtius, *Die Lehre von den drei Stilen in Altertum und Mittelalter.* Romanische Forschungen, 1952, pp. 57—69. Sur le prestige de cette théorie en France v. aussi Y. Le Hir, *Esthétique et Stylistique de la Pléiade au Parnasse,* Paris 1960, p. 138 et suiv.
[6] V. surtout les notes de nos analyses; il eût été inutile d'encombrer le texte même d'un grand nombre de références lexicographiques.

néanmoins, dans les cas les plus frappants, nous allons signaler aussi la reprise des trouvailles des poètes du XVIIIᵉ siècle par la génération posté-rieure, plus exactement par les grandes figures du romantisme français.[7]

2. Conformément au caractère général de ce recueil d'études, la plupart de nos textes remontent à la deuxième moitié du XVIIIᵉ siècle ce qui, évi-demment, nous permet de mieux saisir les tendances d'innovation. On peut dire que nous allons passer en revue l'évolution du style lyrique de Jean-Bap-tiste Rousseau à André Chénier; en guise de conclusion, après avoir précisé les particularités stylistiques d'une série de genres, nous tenterons de jeter un coup d'œil sur le texte de la *Marseillaise*: on y trouvera, comme nous allons le voir, une très singulière synthèse du classicisme mise au service du progrès social et de la Révolution.

3. Avant d'aborder l'analyse de nos textes, il faut s'inscrire en faux contre la thèse que toute la poésie du Siècle des Lumières est née sous le signe de la raison. Pour infirmer cette conception traditionnelle, il suffit de citer dans un ordre rigoureusement chronologique les déclarations alléguées par Ph. Van Tieghem comme autant de preuves en faveur du «rationalisme poé-tique».[8]

La première citation date du début du XVIIIᵉ siècle; elle émane de la plume de La Motte, c'est-à-dire d'un auteur plutôt théoricien que poète:

> . . . Marchons sur de plus sûrs vestiges
> Malgré l'éclat de ses prestiges,
> L'Erreur n'est jamais de saison
> Dans le *bon sens* soyons plus fermes
> Et n'employons jamais de termes
> Qu'avec l'aveu de la Raison . . .[9]

Quatre ans plus tard La Motte, ce nouveau Malherbe — dépassant en pédante sévérité même son illustre prédécesseur — s'attaque déjà à l'En-thousiasme (ce qui veut dire que, dès le début, cette poétique du «bon sens» avait des adversaires!); il attribue à sa Muse — qui, «n'est ni une Pythie, ni une Ménade» — les propos suivants:

> . . . Tes chants ne pourront me plaire
> Qu'autant que la Raison sévère
> En concerteras les accords.[10]
> . . . pourquoi de *hardi* Pindare
> S'imposer l'exemple *bizarre*?[11]

---

[7] Tous ces rapprochements se heurtent à une difficulté presque insurmontable: beaucoup de poètes du XVIIIᵉ siècle ne figurent guère parmi les sources de Littré, sans parler de la documentation — assez lacuneuse pour les XVIIᵉ et XVIIIᵉ siècles — de Robert.

[8] Cf. *les grandes doctrines littéraires en France. De la Pléiade au surréalisme*, Paris 1963, pp. 141—142. Il est curieux de noter que pour des raisons qui nous échappent, Ph. van Thieghem n'a point respecté l'ordre chronologique de ses citations.

[9] *Ode: Les Poètes ampoulés*, 1707.

[10] Le travail du poète est donc à comparer à celui du compositeur; même dans l'art de celui-ci La Motte apprécie plutôt: la maîtrise que l'inspiration en tant que disposi-tion beaucoup moins soumise au contrôle de la raison . . .

[11] *L'Enthousiasme*, 1711.

Opposons une cinquantaine d'années plus tard l'opinion de D'Alembert; il est facile d'en conclure à un conflit presque inévitable des règles classiques et de l'inspiration spontanée. «On y veut», écrit D'Alembert de l'ode, «de l'inspiration de commande qui est bien froide; on y veut de l'élévation, et l'enflure est à côté du sublime; on y veut de l'enthousiasme et en même temps de la raison; c'est-à-dire, non pas tout à fait, mais à peu près les deux contraires».[12]

D'Alembert conseillait de ne pas exagérer l'importance des règles;[13] il faudra attendre encore dix ans pour que Diderot essaie d'établir, malgré l'incompatibilité «enthousiasme — raison», le rôle propre à chaque facteur dans le processus de création.[14]

C'étaient donc les encyclopédistes qui, ayant une connaissance plus fine de la psychologie de la création poétique, entraient en lice contre la prépondérance du rationalisme en matière de poésie; il est évident que sans leur intervention, la poésie lyrique du XVIIIe siècle n'eût pu atteindre un certain affranchissement des lois et des règles d'une esthétique périmée. Inutile de dire que l'influence de J. J. Rousseau, créateur d'une nouvelle variété de la prose rythmée,[15] a également fourni un précieux appui à ce processus de renouveau poétique.

4. Pour illustrer l'*ode*, un des genres les plus discutés de l'époque, nous n'allons examiner qu'un seul texte tardif: la célèbre Ode de Philippe-Denis Ecouchard-Lebrun (1729—1807) sur le vaisseau «*Le Vengeur*». Evidemment, c'est un poème de circonstance, mais l'événement historique qu'il a perpétué semble être tout à fait exceptionnel dans l'histoire de la poésie française. Comme il est notoire, il ne s'agit point d'une victoire navale, mais d'un vaisseau de guerre dont l'équipage révolutionnaire, préféra couler le 1er juin 1794 pour éviter ainsi la capitulation devant la flotte anglaise. C'est de ce vaisseau sacrifié que Lebrun créa, aux dernières années du XVIIIe siècle, une sorte du «bateau ivre» rimbaldien: le poème entier est fondé sur un paradoxe où, comme on va voir, il est facile de discerner même un symbolisme fort subjectif.[16]

On néglige bien des fois[17] de reproduire les 5 premières strophes de ce beau poème; néanmoins c'est précisément dans ce préambule souvent omis qu'on découvre non seulement les ornements mythologiques propres au goût postclassique, mais aussi une strophe ayant la valeur d'une profession

[12] *Réflexions sur la poésie et sur l'ode en particulier*, 1760.
[13] «Aussi ne nous occupons-nous pas des règles d'un genre où tout vient des dons du poètes. » (ibid.)
[14] *Réflexions sur l'ode*, 1770.
[15] Yves Le Hir a bien raison de renvoyer à la déclaration suivante de J. J. Rousseau au sujet du style de ses *Confessions:* «Il faudrait pour ce que j'ai à dire, inventer un langage aussi nouveau que mon sujet.» (*Rhétorique et Stylistique de la Pléiade au Parnasse*, Paris 1960, p. 155.) Le professeur Le Hir ajoute à bon droit: «Cela porte au-delà du lexique.» (ibid.)
[16] On a fort peu parlé des poètes du XVIIIe siècle comme précurseurs des symbolistes; il n'en est pas moins vrai que dès l'époque que nous allons étudier les images ternes de l'allégorie conventionnelle tendent à céder la place à des symboles tantôt explicites, c'est-à-dire commentés par le poète lui-même, tantôt à des symboles implicites. Sur ces notions stylistiques v. L. Gáldi, *Précis de stylistique française*, Budapest 1967, pp. 86—89.
[17] Cf. par exemple l'anthologie de A. Lagarde et L. Michard, *XVIIIe siècle. Les grands auteurs français du programme*, IV. Paris s. d. [1960], pp. 362—363.

de foi théorique. A ceux qui se détournaient «du *hardi* Pindare» (v. plus haut un aveu de la Motte) le vieux Lebrun, (âgé à cette époque de 65 ans), riposte par la strophe II de son texte:

> Plein d'une *audace pindarique*,
> Il faut que des hauteurs du sublime Hélicon,
> Le premier trait que lance un poète lyrique
> Soit une flèche d'Apollon.

Ne soyons pas dupes de ce qu'il y a de vétuste dans ce langage plein d'allusions mythologiques et de noms antiques, mis en relief aussi par la rime![18] Outre ces éléments conventionnels, il faut signaler avant tout la nouveauté de plusieurs syntagmes attributifs: pour *audace pindarique, le sublime Hélicon* (en tant que symbole du style s u b l i m e) et *flèche d'Apollon* les dictionnaires ne nous fournissent aucun point de repère antérieur.[19] Ce qui caractérise le style de cette espèce d'ode moderne, c'est un mélange constant des ornements d'allure gréco-latine et des motifs originaux, suggérés par un certain moment historique.

Les strophes III—IV sont fondées sur une comparaison inattendue: même la «froide colère» d'un volcan comme l'Etna est passée par les *fleuves brûlants* de ce singulier incendie:

> L'Etna, géant *incendiaire*,[20]
> Qui, d'un front embrasé, fend la voûte des airs,
> Dédaigne ces volcans dont la *froide colère*
> S'épuise en *stériles*[21] éclairs.

> A peine sa fureur commence,
> C'est un vaste incendie et des *fleuves brûlants*.[22]
> Qu'il est *beau de courroux*,[23] lorsque sa bouche immense
> Vomit leurs flots étincelants!

[18] Cf. plus haut (Iére strophe) *Rhodope/Calliope* et plus bas (strophe VI) *j'adore/Bosphore*, etc. Les rimes de ce genre pullulent chez bien des poètes de l'époque comme par exemple J.-B. Rousseau, on les retrouvera chez maints parnassiens comme J. M. de Hérédia.

[19] A propos de l'expression *audace pindarique* il est à rappeler que le poète mineur Ch. H. Millevoye ne tardera pas à s'inspirer précisément de cette strophe de Lebrun, cf. «Embrasé de feu *lyrique,* / J'osais jusque dans les cieux, / Suivre l'aigle *audacieux* / En son essor *pindarique*» (L., au mot *pindarique*). — Selon R., *sublime* (s. v.) peut bien être l'épithète des mots *cime* ou *sommet*; malheureusement aucun exemple littéraire n'illustre ces constructions. — Les *flèches d'Apollon* sont à rapprocher de celles de l'amour (qui servaient de modèles aux premières), cf. Choderlos de Laclos: «Les *flèches de l'amour*, comme la lance d'Achille, portent avec elles le remède des blessures qu'elles font» (R., au mot *flèche*).

[20] L'emploi de ce latinisme adjectivé est rare au XVIIIe siècle. Aucune trace d'autres «géants *incendiaires*» comme qualificatifs de volcans; rappelons pourtant une phrase moins abstraite, mais fort pittoresque de Chateaubriand: «C'est en vain que Néron prospère; Tacite est déjà né dans l'Empire ... bientôt il ne fera voir dans le tyran ... que l'histrion *incendiaire*» (R., s. v.).

[21] Mot rare aux XVIIe—XVIIIe siècles; cf. pourtant une phrase tirée du style dramatique de Voltaire: «Qu'importent vos serments, vos *stériles* tendresses?» (L.)

[22] Aucun exemple antérieure, mais l'image pénétrera bientôt dans le style romantique européen, cf. all. *Feuermeer, Flammenmeer, Glutmeer*, hongrois *lángfolyam, tűzfolyam*, etc.

[23] Dans ce contexte même un terme aussi conventionnel que *flot* peut être suivi d'un qualificatif insolite. Cf. la note 22.

La strophe IV est aussitôt interprétée, dans l'esprit de la Révolution, par les vers suivants:

Tel éclate un *libre génie*,[24]
Quand il lance aux tyrans *les foudres de sa voix*.[25]
Telle[26] à flots indomptés sa *brûlante harmonie*[27]
Entraîne les sceptres des rois.[28]

Cette strophe nous impressionne aussi bien par ses innovations lexicales et phraséologiques que par la densité des idées qu'elle révèle. En lisant les vers de ce genre, on pense généralement à Victor Hugo,[29] et d'ailleurs, qui ne reconnaîtrait pas dans les exclamations de cette espèce un prélude aux Iambes d'Auguste Barbier?

Les antécédents que nous venons d'examiner font mieux comprendre la strophe VI: le poète y rejette son masque pour se présenter comme un chantre de la Liberté. L'accord final de son credo est déjà formulé à la 1ère personne:

Toi, que je chante et que *j'adore*,
Dirige, ô *Liberté*:[30] mon vaisseau dans son cours,
Moins de vents orageux tourmentent le Bosphore
Que la mer terrible où je cours.

«Passa la nave mia . . .» disait jadis Pétrarque; en 1794, Lebrun reprend la même image d'origine antique (cf. Horace, etc.) pour peindre non pas un

[24] Dans la langue classique proprement dite *génie* était plutôt un synonyme d'*"esprit"*, cf. Racine (*Britannicus*): «*Mon génie* étonné tremble devant le ciel» (L., v. aussi un exemple analogue chez Voltaire: «*Ton génie* alarmé te parle par ma bouche.» Ibid.). Inutile d'ajouter que l'expression *libre génie* est une allusion directe non seulement au culte de la liberté, mais aussi à celui de l'individualité. En all. *Genius* a, dès la «Goethe-Zeit», un sens correspondant; cf. chez le poète hongrois F. Kölcsey (1790—1838): *Az én geniusom* (Mon génie).

[25] Il convient de noter que le 'feu', la 'foudre' et d'autres phénomènes analogues jouent un rôle essentiel dans les images et les métaphores de ce texte; les motifs de ce genre semblent inséparable du ton pindarique. En même temps *les foudres de la voix* trahissent aussi l'influence de certaines réminiscences bibliques.

[26] Même si la phrase se termine à la fin du vers 2, la répétition anaphorique des vers 1 et 3 sert à créer un lien très solide entre les deux unités syntaxiques ou quatrain.

[27] Cf. la note 24. Nous n'avons relevé aucune analogie lexicale et phraséologique. Une *brûlante harmonie* eût été inadmissible selon les lois de la «Klassische Dämpfung» (L. Spitzer). Le XVIIIe siècle n'avait plus pour but d'étouffer la révélation poétique des sentiments. Cf. aussi l'expression *à flots indomptés* (v. 3.).

[28] En 1794 cette phrase où il est facile de découvrir des effets de synesthésie, ne fait que résumer les résultats de la Révolution; en même temps c'est une menace à l'adresse des «léopards» mentionnés plus bas. V. la note 34.

[29] Cf. par exemple Lagarde-Michard, *op. cit.* p. 362. Ce renvoi au langage épique de Hugo ne met point en relief l'élan révolutionnaire de l'ode de Lebrun.

[30] Impossible de ne pas remarquer l'affinité de cette attitude avec celle de Petőfi; outre les analogies historiques, Béranger constituera un important chaînon de cette filiation. Auparavant cette personnification allégorique eût été impossible; les modèles de cette tournure sont à chercher chez les prosateurs; rappelons aussi un passage de Voltaire: «Crois-moi, *la liberté*, que tout mortel *adore*, /Donne à l'homme un courage, inspire une grandeur/ Qu'il n'eût jamais trouvé dans le fond de son cœur» (L., au mot *liberté*). Les aveux de ce genre révèlent aussi ce qu'il faut entendre, à cette époque, par *libre génie* ('esprit affranchi de ses préjugés').

moment de calme, mais la *mer terrible*[31] de l'histoire. D'une manière générale, c'est l'immensité de la mer qui sert de cadre à l'apothéose d'une catastrophe et d'un génie qui aspire à l'immortalité.

Les strophes VIII—IX développent encore mieux le motif «passa la nave mia . . .»; au vers 2 de la strophe IX paraît aussi le nom du Vengeur; bien qu'il constitue le second membre d'une comparaison; il semble déjà dominer cette strophe, ornée aussi d'une belle épanaphore (« . . . *il est beau* de périr, / *Il est beau* . . .», IX, 2—3, cf. str. IV, v. 3):

> Vainqueur d'*Eole* et des *Pléiades*,[32]
> Je sens d'un souffle heureux mon navire emporté:
> Il échappe aux écueils des trompeuses Cyclades,
> Et *vogue à l'immortalité.*
>
> Mais des flots fût-il la victime,
> Ainsi que le VENGEUR, *il est beau* de périr,
> *Il est beau*, quand le sort vous plonge dans l'abîme,
> De paraître le conquérir.

L'«alliance de mots» *voguer* à *l'immortalité*[33] témoigne fort bien de l'ingéniosité phraséologique de Lebrun; si l'on y ajoute la musicalité du vers suivant («Il est *beau*, quand le *sort* vous *plonge* dans l'*abime*»: ō—ǭ—ǭ—ĭ), on a le droit de voir dans cette série d'images transformées en autant de symboles subjectifs — c'est-à-dire rapportés au poète lui-même — une préfiguration du vers final de *l'Infinito* léopardien: «E *naufragar* m'è *dolce* in questo mare».[34]

Les strophes suivantes (IX—XVII) servent à évoquer l'acte même de l'héroïque sacrifice; presque chacune d'elles surprend le lecteur moderne par ses images inédites. Après la lutte acharnée du «lion» contre les «léopards»[35] (str. X) et l'agitation révélée au moyen de trois sujets juxtaposés (*Le fer, l'onde, la flamme* entourent ses héros,» str. X, v. 2), la strophe XI met en scène, un peu à la manière de Victor Hugo, le moment des dernières réflexions:

> Captifs ! . . . La vie est un outrage:
> Ils préfèrent le *gouffre*[36] à ce bienfait honteux.
> L'Anglais, en frémissant, admire leur courage,
> Albion pâlit devant eux.

[31] L'épithète se rencontre déjà chez Racine *(Esther)* : «La *mer* la plus *terrible* et la plus orageuse» (L., s. v.).

[32] Le nom antique de ces constellations a ici un sens collectif pour désigner en général les astres défavorables. En ce qui concerne les perspectives astronomiques v. aussi la strophe VII sur *Argo*, nom de navire et d'étoile.

[33] Au point de vue de l'usage poétique, *voguer* est loin d'être un terme classique. Les premières attestations littéraires, au sens propre du mot, remontent à Voltaire (*Irène*, cf. L.).

[34] Ce n'est pas l'unique écho d'origine française dans le texte léopardien; on y retrouve aussi une célèbre pensée de Pascal («Le silence des espaces infinis m'effraie»): « . . . interminati /Spazi di là da quella, e sovrumani/ silenzi, e profondissima quiete /Io nel pensier mi fingo; ove per poco/ Il cor non si spaura».

[35] Selon L. ce terme de blason est un renvoi direct à l'Angleterre. On retrouve des exemples poétiques, dans un sens général, chez La Fontaine et Racine.

[36] Ce terme peu classique se rencontre aussi chez Delille dans une acception analogue: «Tu péris, et si jeune, ah ! nos sables peut-être, / Ou les *gouffres* des mers t'auront vu disparaître» (L.).

La paradoxe atteint son comble: c'est le *gouffre* qui, à ce moment fatal, semble préférable à une vie couverte de honte. Le sacrifice héroïque ne peut engendrer que le sentiment de gloire qui prend aussitôt le dessus: à la strophe XV reparaît aussi le mot d'ordre *Liberté*, associé cette fois au drapeau tricolore de la Révolution:

> Voyez ce *drapeau tricolore*[37]
> Qu'élève en périssant leur courage indompté.
> Sous le flot qui les couvre, entendez-vous encore
> *Ce cri:* «Vive la *Liberté*»?

C'est le motif de «ce cri» qui est repris, en guise d'anaphore, au début de la strophe suivante (XVI):

> *Ce cri!* . . . c'est en vain qu'il expire,
> Étouffé par la mort et par les flots jaloux.
> Sans cesse il revivra répété par ma lyre.
> *Siècles! il planera*[38] *sur vous!*

Les deux dernières strophes se composent presque uniquement d'exclamations; ce style «exclamatif» — beaucoup moins fréquent par exemple dans le domaine de l'élégie (5.) — est un héritage classique ce qui n'exclut pas le retour à une perspective hugolienne («*Siècles!* il planera sur vous!»). En ce qui concerne les tropes, c'est l'hyperbole qui s'allie le plus souvent à ce style «exclamatif»; on la retrouve aussi dans la strophe finale où le poète reprend, en guise de «coda», une allusion antique. Même par là il reste fidèle à l'esprit républicain de la Révolution qui, à bien des égards, impliquait un retour à l'atmosphère plutôt romaine qu'attique du pouvoir d'Etat (sous ce rapport il suffit de penser aux discours d'inspiration cicéronienne d'un Robespierre). Voici donc la strophe finale, conçue manifestement dans le but de faire admettre un bel oxymoron où l'idée de «naufrage» s'associe à celle de «victoire»:

> Et vous! héros de Salamine,
> Dont Thétis vante encor les exploits glorieux,
> Non! vous n'égalez point cette auguste ruine,
> Ce *naufrage victorieux!*

On ne saurait terminer l'analyse de ce célèbre spécimen de l'ode sans jeter un coup d'œil sur la structure syntaxique du même texte. Il est facile à établir que la phrase de Lebrun peut revêtir deux aspects.[39] Dans 11 cas la

---

[37] Le drapeau *tricolore*, introduit en 1789, est mentionné aussi par Delille: «Ce signe *tricolor* à peine est arboré» (L.). Il faut attendre Lamartine pour trouver, au moins en prose, des phrases comme celle de Lebrun: «Le *drapeau tricolore* a fait le tour du monde» (R.). Cf. *fior tricolore* dans un célèbre épigramme de G. Carducci (*Congedo*).

[38] La phrase est à rapprocher d'un vers allégorique de Delille: «Le Temps, un cercle en main, *plane* sur l'univers» (L.). Il serait facile de trouver aussi des exemples en prose comme la phrase suivante de J. J. Rousseau: «Mon âme erre et *plane* dans l'univers sur les ailes de l'imagination.» (ibid.)

[39] Sans tenir compte de la structure exceptionnelle de la strophe XVI (v. plus haut): 2, 1, 1. Inutile d'ajouter que cette segmentation est parfaitement motivée par le contenu.

strophe est constituée par une seule phrase — qu'on pourrait appeler «phrase strophique»[40] — et dans 5 cas il y a une forte césure après le 2e vers ce qui donne naissance à deux «phrases demi-strophiques» selon le schéma: 8—12/ 12—8.

Pour illustrer le premier procédé, il suffit de rappeler la strophe initiale:

Au sommet glacé du Rhodope, compl. nom.

Qu'il soumit tant de fois à ses accords touchants, {phrase verbale attributive

Par de timides sons le fils de Calliope compl. nom.; sujet

Ne préludait point à ses chants. {préd. verbal, compl. ind.

L'ampleur de la période est parfaitement motivée: par l'évocation d'un vaste cadre mythologique Lebrun recourt à ce que la poétique classique appelle «retardatio»: au bout du 4e vers on n'apprend pas encore quels «chants» se feront entendre (cf. «ses chants»). Cette figure détermine la structure entière de la strophe: après un vers nominal et une proposition attributive qui sert à qualifier le Rhodope, c'est-à-dire un complément de lieu, la première moitié du vers 3 ne contient qu'un complément de manière («par de timides sons») qui, faute de sujet et de prédicat, semble flotter dans le vide. Le sujet, indiqué au moyen d'une périphrase, est placé dans le second hémistiche du même vers, mais cette fois c'est le verbe qui reste en suspens. Le prédicat négatif du vers 4 («ne préludait point...») complète enfin la phrase, mais, au lieu d'apaiser, il ne fait qu'attiser la curiosité du lecteur.

Les strophes suivantes montrent, au point de vue syntaxique, une ampleur analogue; seule la strophe IV (v. plus haut) présente comme nouvelle variante la division en distiques; dans ce cas la division 8—12/12—8 créerait une symétrie trop rigoureuse, si le traitement des deux distiques ne trahissait pas quand même une différence notable. Après le 1er vers («A peine sa fureur commence»), il y a une pause métrique marquée aussi par la virgule; rien de pareil après le vers 3, puisque dans ce cas le sujet est de nouveau séparé de son prédicat; on doit donc y admettre un enjambement impliquant aussi une sorte de gradation et d'intonation ascendante (« ... lorsque sa bouche immense / Vomit leurs flots étincelants»). Tout compte fait, la structure des phrases contribue également à l'effet de cette pièce originale et vigoureuse.

5. En ce qui concerne l'élégie, il nous paraît nécessaire d'examiner au moins quatre exemples pour évoquer non seulement les particularités, mais aussi l'évolution du style élégiaque.

Le premier texte est Circé, une célèbre cantate polymétrique de Jean-Baptiste Rousseau (1671—1741). Comme on le sait, c'est la Cantate VII de l'auteur; il s'agit d'une adaptation poétique de la cantate — genre musical d'origine italienne — à un sujet antique. Comme précisément au XVIIIe siècle la cantate musicale tendait à devenir — grâce au talent de Bach — un genre plutôt sacré, on pourrait parler d'une sorte de l a ï c i s a t i o n

[40] La terminologie de la syntaxe stylistique est loin d'être élaborée; pour le moment nous parlons de phrases formées d'un seul vers, d'un distique, d'un tercet, etc. L'unité fondamentale devrait être ce que les Allemands appellent «Satzvers» et qui prédomine par exemple dans le folklore poétique.

d'inspiration humaniste de ce genre — au moins dans le domaine de la poésie.[41] D'autre part, si dans le cas précédent, nous venons d'assister à la *mythisation* d'un sujet contemporain, *Circé* témoigne du processus opposé, à savoir de la *démythisation* d'un sujet antique pour suggérer ce qu'il y a d'éternellement humain dans le sort d'une femme abandonnée. Dans la figure de Circé il n'est pas difficile de découvrir presque le noyau d'une tragédie racinienne, réduite à la scène finale, c'est-à-dire à son point culminant.

Dans ce qui suit, notre analyse se bornera à cet élément principal de l'action, constituée par trois motifs: l'évocation de la nature,[42] la complainte de Circé, un rondeau divisé en trois complets[43] et la scène finale, à savoir le suicide au bûcher de la malheureuse héroïne. Au point de vue stylistique chacune de ces trois parties pose des problèmes foncièrement différents:

I

Sur un rocher *désert*,[44] l'*effroi*[45] de la nature,
Dont l'*aride*[46] sommet semble toucher les cieux,
Circé, pâle, *interdite*, et la *mort* dans les yeux,
Pleurait sa *funeste* aventure.[47]
Là, ses yeux errant sur les flots,
D'Ulysse *fugitif*[48] semblaient suivre la trace,
Elle croit voir encor son *volage*[49] héros;
Et, cette *illusion* soulageant sa disgrâce,
Elle le rappelle en ces mots,
Ou'interrompent cent fois ses pleurs et ses sanglots:

[41] Ni la cantate musicale, ni la cantate poétique n'a encore été traitée d'une manière monographique. En tout cas la forme polymétrique, représentée par les cantates de J.-B. Rousseau, correspond exactement à une variété antérieure de la cantate musicale italienne, notamment à celle qui impliquait la combinaison de strophes conçues en différentes métres.

[42] On retrouve un tableau similaire par exemple dans la Cantate V qui évoque le souvenir d'Amymone, une des Danaïdes.

[43] Parfois on trouve une abondance presque inutile de ces rondeaux: dans la Cantate V (v. la note précédente) il y en a trois; il est question d'une alternance régulière des passages descriptifs ou narratifs et de ces couplets lyriques.

[44] *Désert* comme adjectif est fort rare au XVIIe siècle (La Fontaine, Racine, etc. L.); chez Voltaire on lit le vers: «Dans des sables brûlants, sur des *rochers déserts*» (L.), Lamartine chantera des «bords *déserts* des lacs mélancoliques» (ibid.).

[45] Dans l'expression *effroi de la nature* la notion d'*effroi* est presque personnifiée; cf. Voltaire: «Ô Dieu persécuteur, *effroi* du genre humain» (L.).

[46] L'épithète a un caractère racinien, cf. «D'un *aride* rocher fit sortir des ruisseaux» (*Athalie*, L.). Le mot est fréquent dans le langage poétique du XVIIIe siècle, cf. Voltaire: «Pour languir au désert de l'*aride* Arabie» (*Zaïre*, L.); Lefranc de Pompignan: «Ecoutez, ossements *arides*» (*La Résurrection des Morts*). Voir aussi la *Cantate V* de J.-B. Rousseau. «Sur les rives d'Argos, près des bords *arides* . . .».

[47] Les analogies de l'expression *funeste aventure* sont assez rares, cf. *péril funeste* (Corneille), *jour funeste* (Racine), *coup funeste* (id.) et surtout *hymen funeste* (Racine). Voir L. au mot *funeste*.

[48] Pendant bien longtemps *fugitif* (adj.) était rare dans le langage poétique. Bossuet parle d'*esclaves fugitifs*, Racine de *femmes fugitives* (*Bajazet*, L.).

[49] Qui ne se rappellerait, à propos de *volage*, les célèbres paroles de Phèdre sur Thésée: «*Volage* adorateur de mille objets divers» (acte II, scène 5).

Comme plus haut le quatrain de Lebrun, le dizain de J.-B. Rousseau *(abba/cd/cdcc)* est fondé sur une alternance régulière des alexandrins (v. 1—3, 6—8, 10) et des octosyllabes (v. 4—5, 9). La division du texte en phrases et en périodes engendre une série de stylèmes d'ordre syntaxique: il est évident que la strophe initiale est construite selon le schéma 4, 2,4 et que, entre les deux quatrains (v. 1—4; 6—10) le poète fait bien ressortir le distique placé au milieu de la strophe: «Là, les yeux errants sur les flots, / D'Ulysse fugitif semblent suivre la trace.» Le premier quatrain sert à évoquer le paysage auquel renvoie l'adverbe *là* au début du vers 5; au vers 6 le lecteur découvre non seulement l'ombre d'«Ulysse fugitif», c'est-à-dire de l'amant infidèle, mais aussi un douloureux soupir marqué de la répétition allitérante des *s* (...«*s*emble *s*uivre la trace»). Le second quatrain s'appuie également sur le distique central: l'idée représentée par l'épithète *fugitif* est reprise au moyen du qualificatif *volage* antéposé, aux vers 8 et 10 les syntagmes «*s*oulageant *s*a di*s*grâce» et «...cent fois *s*es pleurs et *s*es sanglots» continuent la série des allitérations sifflantes. Signalons enfin la gradation qui mène d'une simple *illusion* visuelle aux *pleurs* et aux *sanglots*.

Au point de vue lexical, ce dizain paraît beaucoup plus fidèle à l'usage du XVIIe siècle que l'ode de Lebrun; à peu d'exceptions près, les stylèmes lexicaux les plus frappants sont des épithètes adjectives (souvent antéposées). Les modèles et les sources d'inspiration rattachent assez solidement ce texte à la grande tragédie et surtout au style du Racine; il ne serait pas exagéré de dire qu'on se trouve en présence d'une transposition élégiaque des meilleures traditions du style de la tragédie racinienne.

II

La deuxième partie du poème, le rondeau susmentionné trahit nettement son inspiration de caractère plutôt musical que littéraire. Les trois quintils reposent sur le schéma A—B—A; autrement dit, c'est une anépiphore ou — comme disent les théoriciens russes — un «кольцо»:

(A) *C*ruel au*t*eur / des *t*roubles de mon âme,	*a*
Que la *p*itié / re*t*ar*d*e un *p*eu *t*es *p*as;	*b*
*T*ourne un moment / *t*es yeux sur ces *c*limats,	*b*
Et si ce n'est / *p*our partager ma *f*lamme,	*a*
Reviens *d*u moins / pour hâter mon *t*répas.	*b*
(B) Ce *t*riste *c*œur / *d*evenu *t*a victime	*a*
Chérit encor l'amour / qui l'a surpris;	*b*
Amour fatal! / ta haine en est le prix;	*b*
*T*ant de *t*endresse, / ô *d*ieux! / est-elle un crime,	*a*
Pour mériter / un si cruel mépris?	*b*
(A) Cruel auteur etc.	*b*

Avant de mourir, c'est à l'infidèle Ulysse que Circé adresse sa dernière complainte; dans ce contexte l'épithète *cruel*,[50] employée en guise d'anépi-

---

[50] Pour cet emploi de l'adjectif *cruel* cf. Racine: «Hélas! fus-je jamais si *cruel* que vous l'êtes?», mais l'analogie sémantique est loin d'être parfaite. Cf. encore: «Avec quels yeux *cruels* sa rigueur obstinée / Vous laissait à ses pieds peu s'en faut prosterner!» *(Phèdre*, acte III, scène 1.)

phore, prend une nuance *assez* insolite. Dans le langage galant on parlait souvent d'une *cruelle*, mais beaucoup moins de la *cruauté* d'un amant volage. Signalons dès maintenant une autre particularité du texte: à l'encontre de la 1ère strophe où abondent les *s* allitérants, dans la 2e c'est la répétition des occlusives qui prend le dessus. Entre deux séries d'occlusives dentales, J.-B. Rousseau intercale très adroitement une allitération labiale (v. 3: «*pour partager ma flamme*») qui s'appuie aussi sur la rime *pas / trépas* (v. 1, 5). Celle-ci n'est pas d'ailleurs un phénomène isolé: d'une manière fort singulière, toutes les rimes de la 1ère strophe du rondeau ont pour base une variété plutôt vélaire de la voyelle *a (âme / flamme; pas / climats / trépas)*. La monotonie voulue de ces rimes va de pair avec l'uniformité rythmique des décasyllabes groupés dans ce quintil; presque chaque vers est un «Satzvers» et la césure, transformée presque toujours en une coupe très brève, se trouve régulièrement après la 4e syllabe.

La 2e strophe est construite d'une manière non moins rigoureuse; toutefois, malgré les similitudes, on peut y relever aussi des traits nouveaux. Dans les rimes c'est la voyelle *i* qui domine; aux rimes «consonantiques» *victime / crime* (cf. plus haut *âme / flamme*) le poète oppose trois rimes «vocaliques»: *surpris / prix / mépris* (cf. plus haut *pas / climats / trépas*). Malgré cette monotonie bien calculée, le rythme des décasyllabes devient un peu plus varié: aux v. 7 et 9 la segmentation 4, 6 tend à se transformer en 6, 4 pour donner naissance à des décasyllabes «a maiore» (selon la terminologie italienne). Les allitérations fondées sur les occlusives s'estompent (cf. pourtant le v. 6); en revanche c'est la liquide *r* qui prédomine au v. 7 («*Chérit encor l'amour qui l'a surpris*»). Comme plus haut, les rimes en *-pri* ne font que souligner l'expressivité de ces soupirs étouffés, entremêlés de sanglots un peu rauques.[51]

Par rapport à la richesse des éléments d'expressivité phonique, le lexique offre moins de surprises. C'est le langage galant conventionnel qui prévaut (cf. *partager ma flamme*, etc.): il y a peut-être plus d'originalité dans la tournure *chérir l'amour* pour laquelle la lexicographie ne nous fournit aucune analogie précise.[52]

Retenons aussi le v. 9 qui énonce une maxime encore non formulée de cette manière («*Tant de tendresse, ô dieux, est-elle un crime?*»). Ce vers contient d'ailleurs deux césures (4, 2, 4) pour mettre en relief l'exclamation *ô dieux* et une très belle allitération fondée sur les occlusives dentales *t* et *d* (cf. la 1ère strophe).

Le chant de Circé s'évanouit dans l'air; la description du paysage se mêle aussitôt à une brève scène dramatique qui rappelle involontairement au lecteur moderne les sacrifices analogues de nos jours:

> C'est ainsi qu'en regrets sa douleur se déclare.   *a*
> Mais bientôt, de son art employant le secours,   *b*
> Pour rappeler l'objet de ses tristes amours   *b*
> Elle invoque à grands cris tous les dieux du Ténare,   *a*

---

[51] L'unique clausule suivie d'une pause métrique se trouve à la fin du vers 2, ce qui correspond au schéma 2—3 des phrases.

[52] Cf. pourtant l'expression cornélienne *chérir son erreur* (*Polyeucte*, R., s. v.).

Les Parques, Némésis, Cerbère, Phlégéton,   *c*

Et l'inflexible Hécate, et l'horrible Alecton.   *c*

Sur un autel sanglant l'affreux bûcher s'allume;   *d*

La foudre dévorante aussitôt le consume;   *d*

Mille noires vapeurs obscurcissent le jour;   *e*

Les astres de la nuit interrompent leur course,   *f*

Les fleuves étonnés remontent vers leur source   *f*

Et Pluton même tremble en son obscur séjour.   *e*

La troisième partie de la cantate se compose de 12 alexandrins. Presque chacun de ceux-ci est un «Satzvers»; le 1er vers résume l'idée maîtresse des trois couplets précédents; on y voit reparaître même l'allitération dentale que nous venons de décrire («... sa *douleur* se *déclare*»). Après tant de rimes «monocordes» cette strophe se distingue aussi par la variété phonique de ses clausules: le verbe *déclare*, avec son *a* ouvert, permet au poète de placer à la fin du vers 4 le nom de *Ténare* qui n'est rien d'autre que la bouche de l'Enfer sur un cap de la Péloponèse antique. Entre ces rimes presque «criardes» on entend résonner une rime très sombre à savoir *secours / amours*; après l'õ d'une rime formée par des noms mythologiques (*Phlégéton / Alecton*[53]) des rimes analogues se retrouveront à la fin de la strophe: d'une part *jour / séjour*, d'autre part *course / source*. La série de ces rimes sombres n'est interrompue que par les deux *u* de la rime *s'allume / consume* qui marque le moment de l'horrible sacrifice de soi-même. Abstraction faite de l'harmonie des clausules, la strophe entière abonde en vers expressifs qui, sans se borner aux lois de l'euphonie traditionnelle, produisent plutôt des effets dantesques; rappelons à ce sujet au moins deux vers qui contiennent déjà quelque chose de l'art hugolien: «Elle invoque à grands cris | tous les dieux du Ténare» «Et Pluton même tremble | en son obscur séjour.» Le rythme du dernier vers est également digne d'intérêt: ∪∪‿́‿‿́∪‿́ | ∪∪∪‿́∪‿́∪‿; c'est surtout la collision de deux ictus au premier hémistiche qui doit intéresser le métricien.

Chose bizarre, tous ces effets se manifestent au moyen d'un vocabulaire relativement simple qui dépasse à peine les traditions classiques. Pour *(se) déclarer* il serait facile de se référer à des analogies raciniennes;[54] on pourrait faire des réflexions analogues sur la plupart des unités lexicales et phraséologiques. Les mots un peu plus rares sont surtout des latinismes comme *invoquer* et *inflexible*;[55] une nuance de nouveauté se cache dans les syntagmes *la foudre dévorante* (comp. *le feu dévorant*, L.) et les *fleuves étonnés*; il est presque superflu d'ajouter que dans le second cas on est en présence d'une personnification non attestées par d'autres sources.[56]

6. L'élégie était pourtant un des genres les plus susceptibles d'évoluer selon les exigences de l'époque; tendant à une révélation plus ou moins directe

[53] Toutefois les deux noms servent à évoquer des réminiscences classiques fort différentes: *Phlégéton* est le nom d'un fleuve de feu dans le Tartare, tandis qu'*Alecton* est une furie comme Mégère et Tisiphone.

[54] «Seigneur, ma folle ardeur malgré moi *se déclare*» (Racine, *Phèdre*, acte II, sc. 5.).

[55] Pour *invoquer* cf. Corneille: «A l'envi l'un et l'autre [les deux chrétiens] étalaient sa manie... / Et traitaient de mépris les dieux qu'on *invoquait*» (*Polyeucte*, acte III, scène 2). Pour *inflexible* v. également Corneille (en parlant d'une femme): «A mes saints désirs la trouvant *inflexible*» (*Cinna*, acte V, scène 2, L.).

[56] Pour le syntagme attributif *les fleuves étonnés* la lexicographie ne nous fournit aucun point de repère.

des sentiments, elle ne pouvait rester trop longtemps dans la sphère du style post-classique. Outre les traditions gréco-latines, une de ses sources d'inspiration pouvait être aussi la *Bible* et avant tout le *Psautier* qui, dès les adaptations de Clément Marot et Théodore de Bèze, avait constitué un filon souvent peu apprécié dans l'évolution de la poésie française.

En lisant quelques strophes de l'*Ode imitée de plusieurs psaumes* de N.-J.-F. Gilbert (1751—1780) on se trouve en présence d'un texte qui témoigne non seulement de l'inspiration biblique, mais aussi des incertitudes régnant dans la division de la poésie en genres lyriques. Le caractère d'ode de ce poème s'efface pour céder la place au ton élégiaque; c'est pourquoi, paraît-il, ce texte figure dans certaines éditions sous le titre d'*Adieu à la vie*.[57]

Certes, le poème, conçu quelques jours avant la mort de ce «poète maudit»,[58] présente de nombreuses inégalités; il contient toutefois d'importantes innovations lexicales et phraséologiques dont les échos survivront même à la poésie romantique.

(I) J'ai révélé mon cœur au Dieu de l'innocence
    Il a vu mes pleurs pénitents;
    Il guérit mes remords, *il m'arme* de constance:
    Les malheureux sont ses enfants.

Cette strophe, faisant allusion à la confession du poète pendant sa maladie, est marquée d'un groupement ternaire et d'une anaphore: aux vers 2—3 les trois *il* font allusion «au Dieu de l'innocence.» Le poète n'espère de récupérer sa santé; c'est pourquoi il se borne à dire (au moyen d'une alliance inédite des mots); «Il *guérit* mes *remords*.» Au second hémistiche du v. 3 on trouve une métaphore plus conventionnelle: «il m'*arme* de *constance*.» Dans ce cas c'est plutôt la forme transitive du verbe qui constitue une nouveauté; dans les exemples antérieurs les poètes ont plutôt recouru à la forme réfléchie.[59] Il y a une différence bien évidente entre la fonction des deux formes: tandis que la forme réfléchie met en relief l'h o m m e comme l'unique source de redressement, la forme active souligne l'intervention d'une force surnaturelle.

Une autre innovation sémantique est liée à l'emploi de l'adjectif *incorruptible*, épithète antéposée du mot avenir: Dans son exaltation mystique, le poète mortellement blessé croit entendre, par autosuggestion, ces paroles consolatrices:

---

[57] Voir L. au mot *exil* où il y a une citation de Gilbert (les v. 33—34 de notre texte).

[58] La misère de Gilbert deviendra presque proverbiale, cf. une belle élégie d'Hégésippe Moreau qui sera traduite en hongrois par Petőfi pour illustrer le sort typique du poète incompris. A la légende de cette misère qui, d'après certaines sources, n'était pas aussi noire qu'on la suppose (v. l'*Anthologie poétique française* — *XVIIIᵉ siècle* — de M. Allem, Paris s. d. [1966], p. 397.) contribuèrent aussi les tristes événements de ses derniers jours: «Gilbert succomba aux suites d'une chute de cheval; transporté chez lui, et de là à l'hôpital, où il dut subir l'opération du trépan, il fut pris d'une sorte de fièvre cérébrale qui lui brouilla l'esprit; c'est alors, dans un moment de lucidité, quelques jours seulement avant de mourir, qu'il composa cette Ode imitée de plusieurs psaumes» (M. Allem, loc. cit.).

[59] Cf. Racine: «*Armez-vous* de courage et d'une foi nouvelle» (*Athalie*, L.); Fénelon: «*Arme-toi* de courage contre ton ennemi» (L.).

(V) J'éveillerai pour toi la pitié, la justice

De l'*incorruptible* avenir,
Eux-mêmes[60] épureront, par leur long artifice,
Ton honneur qu'ils pensent tenir.[61]

Depuis assez longtemps *incorruptible* avait un sens métaphysique: bien que Corneille ait parlé, dans un sens très concret, d'un *juge incorruptible*, l'adjectif est devenu un synonyme d' 'éternel' dans plusieurs syntagmes comme *Dieu incorruptible, pensées incorruptibles, beauté céleste incorruptible*, etc.[62] L'originalité de Gilbert consiste en ce qu'il a appliqué cet adjectif puisé dans le style sublime à sa propre gloire posthume. Il paraît pourtant signifi catif que nous n'ayons re**trouvé** l'expression *incorruptible avenir* chez aucun auteur postérieur.

La strophe suivante, malgré ses antécédents religieux, comporte des nuances presque baudelairiennes et verlainiennes:

(VI) *Soyez béni*, mon Dieu ! vous qui daignez me rendre

L'innocence et son noble orgueil;
Vous qui, pour protéger le repos de ma cendre,
Veillerez près de mon cercueil !

Le reste du texte — constitué par les trois dernières strophes — mérite d'être intégralement cité:

(VII) Au *banquet de la vie*, infortuné convive

J'apparus un jour, et *je meurs*:
Je meurs, et sur ma tombe, où lentement j'arrive,
Nul ne viendra verser des pleurs.

(VIII) *Salut*, champs que j'aimais, et vous, douce verdure,

Et vous, riant *exil* des bois !
Ciel, *pavillon* de l'homme, admirable nature,
Salut pour la dernière fois !

(IX) Ah ! puissent voir longtemps votre beauté sacrée

Tant d'amis sourds à mes adieux !
Qu'ils meurent pleins de jours, que leur mort soit pleurée,
Qu'un ami leur ferme les yeux !

Essayons de nous borner à quelques motifs. En ce qui concerne la métaphore «le *banquet* de la vie,» Gilbert l'a en commun — sans aucun exemple

[60] C'est-à-dire tes ennemis, cf. plus haut: «Mes ennemis, riant, ont dit dans leur colère: «Qu'il meure et sa gloire avec lui».
[61] La construction n'est pas très heureuse, le syntagme «par leur long artifice» se rapporte au dernier vers et non pas au verbe *épureront*.
[62] Cf. L. avec des citations de Corneille, Bossuet, Bourdaloue, etc.

antérieur — avec André Chénier.[63] L'exclamation *salut* (vers 1 et 4 de la strophe VIII) contient un appel anaphorique; ce procédé sera repris aussi par Lamartine.[64] Tout à fait original est le sens amélioratif du mot *exil* dans l'expression *riant exil des bois*. A première vue, c'est un oxymoron, mais il révèle aussi un sentiment essentiellement «préromantique»: le goût de la solitude. Les expressions de ce genre inspireront plus tard à Pouchkine, la première partie de sa méditation sur l'état de la campagne russe.[65] Au point de vue biographique, il faut encore ajouter que ce sens du mot *exil* est né sous la plume d'un provincial qui, dans ses derniers moments, devait rêver des bois de la Lorraine, son pays natal.

Pour terminer, voici une remarque sur l'emploi du terme *pavillon* au vers: «Ciel, *pavillon* de l'homme, admirable nature . . .» (strophe VIII, v. 3). Ce curieux exemple poétique a été signalé aussi par Littré, mais sans commentaire; on ne connaît aucun cas d'emploi analogue. Il n'en reste pas moins que cette expression doit être également ramenée à l'inspiration biblique de Gilbert, notamment à la tentative de représenter la voûte céleste non pas comme quelque chose de solide (cf. lat. *firmamentum* et ses correspondances en grec, en hébreu, etc.), mais comme une immense tente, comparable au *Sternenzelt* de Schiller *(Ode an die Freude)*. Néanmoins ces perspectives cosmiques sont à rapprocher aussi de l'exclamation *admirable nature*,[66] si apte à synthétiser toutes les nostalgies d'un mourant aspirant au moins à la gloire posthume.

7. En 1780 Gilbert avait déjà parlé de l'«admirable nature» ce qui n'est point étonnant au siècle de Rousseau; deux ans plus tard, en 1782, l'abbé Jacques Delille (1738—1813), ce fervent disciple et traducteur de Virgile,[67] publia ses *Jardins* dont un beau fragment figure souvent dans les anthologies.[68] La postérité n'était pas toujours compréhensive à l'égard de ce remarquable artiste du genre descriptif,[69] mort aveugle par une cruelle ironie du sort; c'est pourquoi il nous paraît particulièrement utile de soumettre ce texte — comme une nouvelle variété du style élégiaque — à une sorte de «close reading»:[70]

[63] Cf. «Au *banquet de la vie* à peine commencée, / Un instant seulement mes lèvres ont pressé / La coupe . . .» (L.).

[64] *«Salut* ! bois couronnés d'un reste de verdure» (L.).

[65] Cf. son poème Деревня (Le village).

[66] Cf. La Bruyère: «Tout est grand et *admirable* dans *la nature»* (L., au mot *admirable*). Comme il s'agit d'un exemple appartenant à un genre très différent, rien n'empêche d'attribuer à Gilbert cette trouvaille aussi.

[67] Sa traduction en vers des Géorgiques parut en 1770; il écrivait aussi d'importants essais sur l'utilité des traductions pour l'enrichissement de la langue et de la phraséologie littéraires. Dans ses dernières années il donna une traduction du *Paradis perdu* de Milton.

[68] Inutile de dire que le titre *L'Automne* (cf. M. Allem, *op. cit.*, p. 357.) est loin d'être authentique; néanmoins il renvoie bien aux motifs que la sensibilité des romantiques trouvera plus tard dans ces vers.

[69] Cf. les remarques si peu justifiables de M. Allem: «On l'a représenté, costumé en abbé, tournant le dos à la nature et se dirigeant vers le temple du mauvais goût. On sait qu'il abonde en périphrases qui font le tour du mot propre avec une ingéniosité incontestable, quoique souvent ridicule.» (*op. cit.*, p. 336.)

[70] Sur l'importance du «close reading» comme prémisse indispensable de toute analyse textuelle, v. M. Riffaterre, *Criteria for Style Analysis*, Word 1959, p. 155 et suiv.

L'AUTOMNE

Remarquez-les surtout lorsque la *pâle* automne
Près de la voir flétrir, embellit sa couronne;
Que de *variété*, que de pompe et d'*éclat*
Le pourpre, l'*orangé*, l'*opale*, l'*incarnat*,
5 De leurs riches couleurs étalent l'abondance.
Hélas ! tout cet *éclat* marque leur *décadence*.
Tel est le sort commun. Bientôt les *aquilons*
Des *dépouilles* des bois vont *joncher* les *vallons*;
De *moment* en *moment* la feuille sur la terre
10 En *tombant* interrompt le *rêveur solitaire*.
Mais ces *ruines* même ont pour moi des attraits.
Là, si mon cœur nourrit quelques profonds regrets,
Si quelque souvenir vient *rouvrir* ma *blessure*,
J'aime à mêler mon deuil au deuil de la nature;
15 De ces bois desséchés, de ces rameaux flétris,
Seul, errant, je me plais à *fouler* les *débris*.
Ils sont passés, les jours d'ivresse et de *folie*;
Viens, je me livre à toi, *tendre mélancolie*;
Viens, non le front chargé des nuages affreux
20 Dont marche enveloppé le chagrin ténébreux,
Mais l'œil *demi-voilé*, mais telle qu'en automne,
A travers des vapeurs un *jour plus doux* rayonne !
Viens, le regard *pensif*, le front calme, les yeux
24 Tout prêts à s'humecter de *pleurs délicieux*.

Évidemment, les mots et les expressions en italique sont tous des stylèmes; sans vouloir donner une analyse exhaustive du texte, bornons-nous de nouveau aux motifs qui, dans leur ensemble, témoignent d'une conception nullement commune à cette époque. Peu nombreux sont les textes qui montrent aussi nettement l'apparition du «promeneur solitaire» de J.-J. Rousseau dans le domaine de la poésie lyrique. Cette attitude manifestement rousseauiste se révèle au moyen d'un style très souple dont la simplicité touchante peut déjà se passer aussi bien de l'emphase post-classique que des images d'inspiration biblique d'un Gilbert. C'est déjà l'homme moderne qui goûte un admirable automne et qui, pour le décrire, — doit recourir aussi à plus d'un néologisme d'ordre phraséologique.[71]

Le premier stylème que nous avons à examiner est l'épithète «antropomorphe» de l'automne. Jusqu'au XVIIIe siècle *pâle* ne servait point à caractériser une saison ou une partie du jour; les lexicographes citent de Delille les constructions *automne orageux, automne nébuleux*, mais ils n'essaient même pas de commenter, au moyen de rapprochements et d'autres exemples, la *pâle automne* qui paraît dans ce texte. Tout porte à croire que ce syntagme est à rapprocher de l'expression *pâles journées* chez Chénier.[72] Entre les deux textes il y a cependant d'importantes différences: tandis que chez Chénier *pâle* a, au figuré, le sens de 'terne, incolore'; chez Delille l'épithète évoque

[71] La syntaxe du texte est beaucoup plus conventionnelle; nous allons pourtant renvoyer à quelques tropes comme la répétition anaphorique de *viens* aux vers 18—24.
[72] «Ma vie est *sans couleur*, et mes *pâles journées* / M'offrent de longs ennuis» (L.).

incomparablement mieux la p â l e u r d'un visage humain. En même temps l'expression *pâle automne* est à rapprocher aussi des vers 21—22 où l'auteur — sans découvrir la rime automne/monotone[73] — opère quand même avec une rime sombre fondée sur la clausule -one (prononcée éventuellement: -õn(ə): «Mais l'œil *demi-voilé*, mais telle qu'en *automne*, / A travers des vapeurs un jour plus doux[74] *rayonne*.» Dans ce cas c'est *demi-voilé* qui, sous l'angle de l'usage classique, est aussi inattendu que l'épithète *pâle* de l'automne.[75]

L'antithèse brièvement esquissée au vers 2 («Près de la voir *flétrir, embellit sa couronne*») est largement développée aux vers 3—6 qui, quoique commencés par l'exclamation «que de variété!» se termine par un mot aussi «négatif» que *décadence*. Examinons rapidement les stylèmes de ce passage. Le mot *variété* fut pendant longtemps réservé aux prosateurs,[76] mais Delille parle aussi ailleurs d'une variété rapportée aux impressions visuelles.[77]

Le vers commencé par l'exclamation «Que de *variété* . . .» se termine par *éclat*, c'est-à-dire par un terme qui sera repris aussi au vers 6. C'est au moyen de ce terme rarement mis en relation avec les feuilles d'automne que Delille introduit une énumération de couleurs et de nuances où deux nouvelles dénominations — l'*orangé* et l'*opale* — sont rangées entre des indications plus conventionnelles (la *pourpre*, l'*incarnat*[78]). Pour *orangé* et *opale* comme noms de couleur nous n'avons relevé aucun exemple poétique antérieur.[79] Le vers est fort caractéristique: il nous montre parfaitement, comment Delille sait mêler les motifs nouveaux aux éléments conventionnels du style poétique.

Le dernier accord de cette période, l'emploi poétique du mot *décadence* a une importance indéniable: sa présence atteste que dans certains cas existe une sorte de continuité entre les poètes lyriques du XVIIᵉ siècle et ceux du XVIIIᵉ.[80]

A partir du vers 7 («Tel est le sort commun . . .») l'horizon s'élargit; jusqu'au vers 17 le poète expose, avec un grand luxe de détails, les analogies et les

---

[73] *Monotone* n'est guère employé dans le langage poétique du XVIIIᵉ siècle, mais cf. Lamartine: «Comme un enfant bercé par un chant *monotone*, / Mon âme s'assoupit aux murmures des eaux» (L.).

[74] Il est évident que le syntagme *un jour plus doux* (ö — ū — ü — ū) contribue également à l'effet des voyelles sombres de la rime.

[75] Delille est mort presque entièrement aveugle, mais nous ne saurions dire, si vers 1782 sa vue était déjà atteinte. En tout cas, une explication purement physiologique de l'épithète *demi-voilé* de l'*œil* ne peut être écartée d'emblée.

[76] Outre un exemple tiré de Pascal, cf. La Rochefoucauld «Il faut de la *variété* dans l'esprit» (L.). Au XVIIIᵉ siècle La Motte emploie ce terme dans un contexte très caractéristique: «De la *variété* les grâces sont compagnes, / J'en veux dans mon ouvrage égayer la raison.»

[77] Cf. le vers: «Riche *variété*, délices de la vue» (L.).

[78] Pour *incarnat* — autre épithète «anthropomorphe» — cf. surtout La Fontaine: «Psyché leur fit [à des jeunes filles] un petit compliment, à quoi elles répondirent par l'*incarnat* qui leur monta aux joues» (L.).

[79] A l'origine l'*orangé* était un terme d'histoire naturelle, pour *opale* cf. Buffon: «De toutes les pierres chatoyantes l'opale est la plus belle» (L.).

[80] Cf. les vers suivants de Saint-Amant: «Que j'aime à voir la *décadence* / De ces vieux palais ruinés» (L.). Le terme est usité aussi dans le style satirique du XVIIIᵉ siècle: «Dès lors la poésie a vu sa *décadence*; / Infidèle à la rime, au sens, à la *cadence*, / Le compas à la main, elle va dissertant» (Gilbert, *Le dix-huitième siècle*, cf. par M. Allem, *op. cit.*, p. 402).

affinités qu'il essaie de découvrir entre la nature d'automne et la vie humaine. Dans cette atmosphère mystique presque tous les motifs tendent à transformer en symboles. Pour La Fontaine l'*aquilon* était encore un vent réel;[81] chez Delille la valeur symbolique du mot est déjà plus évidente.[82] Au vers suivant *dépouilles des bois* est un néologisme lexical et phraséologique qui ne tardera pas à être adopté par maints poètes mineurs comme par exemple Millevoye.[83] Au vers 9 l'expression adverbiale *de moment en moment* serait presque prosaïque,[84] si le doux murmure des *m* et les voyelles nasales ne lui prêtaient pas une expressivité qui contrebalancent même l'effet douteux, au point de vue stylistique, du verbe *interrompt*.

Quant à la mention du *rêveur solitaire*, il est facile d'y reconnaître l'élément le plus rousseauiste du texte entier; les analogies abondent,[85] mais c'est en vain qu'on chercherait des exemples poétiques antérieurs.

Le reste de nos remarques peut être beaucoup plus brièvement résumé. Il est curieux de signaler au vers 11 un sens assez vague du mot *ruines*;[86] la construction *rouvrir les blessures* s'appuie sur l'usage classique et postclassique;[87] enfin, en ce qui concerne l'expression «anthropomorphe» *le deuil de la nature*, nous devons la faire remonter plutôt à l'éloquence sacrée qu'au langage poétique traditionnel.[88]

Le vers 17 («*Ils* sont passés, *les jours* d'ivresse et de folie») n'est point étranger au style de la poésie galante non plus; néanmoins on y découvre, sous l'influence de la langue parlée, une curieuse anticipation du sujet au moyen d'un sujet pronominal et même une sorte d'antithèse à cette *tendre mélancolie* qui sert à introduire la période finale de ce passage («*Viens*, je me livre à toi, *tendre mélancolie*»). Le mot a été depuis longtemps introduit dans le langage poétique,[89] mais il faudra attendre «*la mélancolie tendre et la mélancolie enchanteresse*» de J. J. Rousseau[90] pour que d'autres poètes recourent également à ce bel oxymoron.[91] Comme si tous ces poètes de la fin du XVIIIᵉ siècle s'étaient inspirés d'un brillant mot de Voltaire: «La *mélancolie*, c'est le *bonheur* d'être *triste*.»[92]

L'oxymoron est d'ailleurs une figure aussi chère à ces premiers souffles de l'inspiration romantique que l'hyperbole à la poésie post-classique. C'est

---

[81] Cf. «Tout vous est *aquilon*, / Tout me semble Zéphyr» (L.).

[82] La rime *aquilon* / *vallon* sera reprise par Lamartine dans la dernière strophe de *L'Isolement*.

[83] «De la *dépouille* de ces bois / L'automne *avait jonché* la terre» (R.).

[84] On ne saurait citer aucun exemple poétique antérieur. Dans ce contexte l'hémistiche en question forme une sorte de rime intérieure avec l'expression *en tombant*.

[85] Nous nous bornons à citer les deux exemples suivants: «Ce *rêveur* poursuit toujours sa chimère» (*Emile*, L.); «Je suis devenu *solitaire* ou, comme ils le disent, insociable et misanthrope» (L.). Delille mettait souvent *solitaire* à la fin d'un vers («Quelque chose manquait à ce cœur *solitaire*» L.).

[86] Pour ce procédé sémantique nous n'avons pu trouver aucune analogie sure.

[87] Cf. surtout Racine («Vos regards vont *rouvrir mes blessures* . . .» *Andromaque*) et Voltaire («Il va périr mon cœur et *rouvrir ma blessure* . . .»). (L., au mot *blessure*).

[88] Cf. Massenet: «La terre . . . s'ébranle et se couvre de *deuil*» (L., au mot *deuil*). L'image métaphorique sera reprise par Lamartine: «Salut! derniers beaux jours; *le deuil de la nature* / Convient à ma douleur et plaît à mes regards» (*L'Automne*).

[89] Cf. Corneille dans *Cinna*: «Et laisse-moi de grâce, attendant Emilie, / Donner un libre cours à ma *mélancolie*» (L.).

[90] Cf. également L., au mot *mélancolie*.

[91] Cf. le vers «*Douce mélancolie*, aimable *messagère*» de A. Chénier (R.).

[92] Cité par R., au mot *mélancolie*.

par un second oxymoron que se termine la longue période caractérisée par un groupement ternaire déjà mentionné, à savoir la reprise anaphorique de *viens*. Le poète écarte «les nuages affreux» pour pouvoir terminer sa méditation élégiaque par un accord plus calme et plus harmonieux: «Viens, [a] le regard pensif, [b] le front calme, [c] les yeux / Tous prêts à s'humecter[93] de *pleurs délicieux*.»[94]

8. Il faut encore renvoyer à un texte illustrant aussi la simplification stylistique d'un autre genre: l'ode funèbre.[95] A ce propos il n'est pas superflu de rappeler le fait bien connu qu'au début du XVII[e] siècle précisément l'ode funèbre était un des genres les plus rhétoriques de la poésie; pour s'en convaincre il suffit de citer une seule strophe des célèbres *Consolations* de Malherbe à M. du Périer (VIII) La Mort a des rigueurs à mille autres pareilles;

> On a beau la prier,
> La cruelle qu'elle est se bouche les oreilles,
> Et nous laisse crier . . .

Comparons à ces alexandrins et à ces hexasyllabes, terminés souvent par des rimes grammaticales *(crier / prier)* les doux octosyllabes de Parny[96] (1733—1814) dans son poème *Sur la mort d'une jeune fille*:

Son âge échappait à l'enfance;	-ãs	a	
Riante comme l'innocence,	-ãs	a	
Elle avait les traits de l'Amour.	-ūr	b	∧
Quelques mois, quelques jours encore,	-ǫr	c	
5 Dans ce cœur pur et sans détour	-ūr	b	
Le sentiment allait éclore.	-ǫr	c	∧
Mais le Ciel avait au trépas	-pα	d	
Condamné ses jeunes appas.	-pα	d	∧
Au ciel elle a rendu sa vie,	-vĩ	e	
10 Et doucement *s*'est endormie	-mĩ	e	
*S*ans murmurer contre ses lois.	-u̯α	f	∧
Ainsi le *s*ourire *s*'efface;	-as	g	
Ainsi meurt *s*ans lai*ss*er de tra*c*e,	-as	g	
14 Le chant de l'oiseau dans les bois.	-u̯α	f	∧

Ces 14 vers représentent un aspect bien différent du langage poétique du XVIIIe siècle. Le vocabulaire a beaucoup moins d'importance que dans les autres poèmes; ce sont plutôt la segmentation syntaxique et l'instrumentation phonétique qui prédominent.

[93] Avant Delille ce synonyme plus élégant de *se mouiller* n'appartenait guère au style poétique. Cf. pourtant Diderot: «Je l'avais lu trois fois à la suite, et à la quatrième lecture j'en *humectais* encore les feuillets de quelques larmes» (L.). Plus tard Lamartine n'hésitera pas à écrire: «Et mon regard long, triste, errant involontaire, / Les suivait et de *pleurs* son chagrin s'*humectait*» (L.).
[94] Pour le syntagme *pleurs délicieux*, cf. nos remarques sur l'oxymoron: Gáldi, *op. cit.*, pp. 122—123.
[95] A propos des affinités qui rattachent certaines variétés de l'ode à l'élégie voir nos observations sur le titre du poème susmentionné de Gilbert (p. 231).
[96] Evariste-Désiré de Forges de Parny.

Considérons d'abord les fins de phrases déjà indiquées plus haut. Elles coïncident toujours avec la fin d'un vers; d'une manière générale, il y a aussi peu d'enjambements dans ce texte (v. 5, 7, 10) que dans un morceau de folklore poétique. Les pauses métriques plus importantes, marquées aussi de points, se trouvent à la fin des vers 3, 6, 8, 11 et 14. Il est impossible de ne pas y apercevoir certaines symétries: selon la terminologie de la « canzone » pétrarquesque, les vers 1—6 (plus exactement: 1—3, 4—6) correspondent à la « fronte » divisée en deux « pieds », et les vers 7—14 à la « sirima ». La seconde unité embrasse un distique central (v. 7—8) qui correspond éventuellement la « chiaxe » ou « diesi ») de la canzone — et deux « volte » (9—11, 12—14).

Au schéma très net de la structure syntaxique et, bien entendu, aussi à la répartition parallèle des divers motifs[97] s'oppose cependant — à la manière plutôt italienne que française — une autre structure: celle de la disposition des rimes. A la fin du premier « pied » (dans le sens italien du terme) le mot *Amour* reste sans rime: l'attention du lecteur se glisse rapidement vers le tercet suivant pour retrouver la seconde partie de la rime à un endroit un peu insolite.[98] Une vraie pause aussi bien sémantique que rythmique ne se trouve donc qu'à la fin du vers 6: toutes les rimes sont « terminées », c'est-à-dire que le « mot d'appel » est toujours complété par son « écho ».

Après les rimes incontestablement sombres ($\tilde{a}$—u—ϱ) on voit paraître la rime vocalique en *-pα* des vers 7—8.[99] L'expressivité de la voyelle α ne peut être contestée: elle est mise en relief, d'une part, par le mot *trépas* placé sous le coup de la rime, d'autre part par l'antithèse qui existe entre le mot *trépas* et l'expression *jeunes appas*. On doit voir précisément dans ce couple de mots le noyau même du poème; c'est après ces deux *-pα* évoquant des associations si différentes qu'est placée l'unique rime c l a i r e du texte; néanmoins la rime *vie / endormie* a la fonction d'unir deux périphrases euphémiques: [a] « Au Ciel elle a rendu sa *vie*, [b] Et *d*oucement s'es*t* endormie. » Au vers 8 la rime s'appuie aussi sur plusieurs allitérations intérieures qu'il est utile de transcrire de la manière suivante:

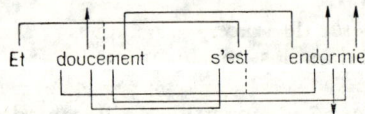

[97] Vers 1—3: Portrait d'ailleurs très vague de la jeune fille. Mots « plastiques »: *enfance, innocence, les traits de l'Amour*. — Vers 4—6: Adolescence; image impliquant une comparaison avec les fleurs. — Vers 7—8: Décision du Ciel; mythisation d'une mort *prématurée*. — Vers 9—12: Suite de la mythisation; euphémismes. Mot-clé: *sans murmurer*, pour traduire le sentiment de la résignation. — Vers 13—14: Le sens du verbe *meurt* est aussitôt atténué par la comparaison: « Ainsi *meurt* le chant de l'oiseau ... »

[98] Autrement dit: le premier « pied » n'a pas le même schéma des rimes que le second: *aab — cbc*.

[99] Faute de termes plus appropriés, nous appelons « rime vocalique » celle qui se termine en voyelle (CV); en revanche, les rimes — *our, -ore* sont pour nous des « rimes consonantiques » (du type VC). Evidemment, dans un texte chanté l'*e* instable peut sensiblement modifier ces effets de contraste.

Le schéma que nous venons d'esquisser est d'autant plus important qu'il contient aussi les germes des effets d'«harmonie impressive» — selon la terminologie de Grammont — qui veut caractériser les vers suivants. Au vers 11 la consonne initiale *sans* continue l'allitération des sifflantes (doucement — *s'est* . . .) et *murmurer* s'associe à l'allitération des consonnes nasales (doucement — endormie). Dans le syntagme *contre ses lois* la voyelle nasale ǫ̃ reprend les mêmes effets qui se rattachent aux mots doucement et endormie. Dans le dernier quatrain (v. 11—14, *fggf*) les diphtongues -*uα* et les *a* [α] de *s'efface* et *trace* créent une certaine monotonie des clausules; néanmoins les derniers vers sont dominés plutôt par la répétition insistante de la sifflante *s*; cet effet repris plus tard par Lamartine[100] et tant d'autres poètes, semble évoquer, sur le plan des correspondances, des sons et des parfums en allés. Il est d'ailleurs curieux de noter que les timbres bien sombres du dernier vers («Ainsi meurt . . . / Le *chant* d'un *oiseau dans* les *bois*») ne sont plus compatibles avec les échos phoniques de ce soupir prolongé.[101]

9. Les catégories de la poétique du XVIIIe siècle ne suffisent pas toujours à décrire et à classer la réalité des faits. Néanmoins, en ayant en vue aussi l'évolution ultérieure, il est utile d'intercaler entre l'élégie (*6—8.*) et l'idylle (*10.*) au moins un paragraphe sommaire consacré à un genre naissant: la m é d i t a t i o n.[102] Evidemment, on pourrait rattacher à l'idylle la plupart des textes de ce genre; d'autre part, cependant, le langage fort stylisé de la n o c t u r n e[103] que nous nous proposons d'examiner s'oppose également à la simplicité et à la spontanéité primesautière de l'idylle proprement dite.

Voici donc, pour illustrer la méditation, un passage d'André Chénier qu'une anthologie moderne publie sous le titre *Abîmes de clarté*.[104] L'oxymoron absolument inédit qui figure dans ce titre posthume (cf. plus bas, le vers 35) donne déjà une idée de la hardiesse de certains aspects peu appréciés du style poétique de Chénier.[105]

> Muse, *Muse nocturne*, apporte-moi ma *lyre*.
> Comme un fier *météore*, en ton brûlant *délire*,
> Lance-toi dans l'espace; et pour franchir les airs,
> Prends les *ailes* des vents, les *ailes* des éclairs,
> 5 Les bonds de la *comète* aux longs cheveux de flamme.
>
> *Mes vers impatients* élancés de mon âme
> *Veulent* parler aux Dieux, et *volent* où reluit
> *L'enthousiasme errant*, fils de la belle nuit.
> *Accours*, grande nature, *ô mère du génie.*
> 10 *Accours, reine du monde*, éternelle Uranie,

[100] Cf. par exemple: «*Soleil* mystérieux, flambeau d'une autre *sphère*» (*La foi*).

[101] Notre analyse doit être complétée par ce que H. Morier a dit de ce poème et de quelques autres textes poétiques du XVIIIe siècle: *op. cit.*, p. 129 («Le style mièvre»).

[102] Depuis Descartes, méditation était le nom traditionnel d'une sorte d'écrit composé sur un sujet de dévotion, ou de philosophie (L.). Pour la dénomination d'un genre poétique semblable, on ne connaît aucun exemple antérieur à Lamartine.

[103] Lagarde-Michard, *op. cit.*, p. 378.

[104] Pour caractériser son ingéniosité, il ne suffit point de se borner aux pièces d'anthologie généralement connues.

[105] Lagarde-Michard, *op. cit.*, p. 378.

Soit que tes pas divins sur l'astre du Lion
Ou sur les triples feux du superbe Orion
Marchent, ou soit qu'au loin, *fugitive* emportée,
Tu suives les détours de la voie argentée,
15 Soleils amoncelés dans le céleste azur
Où le peuple a cru voir les traces d'un lait pur;
Descends, non, porte-moi sur la *route brûlante*,
Que je m'élève au ciel, comme une *flamme ardente*.
Déjà ce corps pesant se détache de moi.
20 Adieu, *tombeau de chair*, je ne suis plus à toi.
Terre, fuis sous mes pas. L'éther où le ciel nage
M'aspire. Je parcours l'océan sans rivage.
Plus de nuit. Je n'ai plus d'un globe opaque et dur
Entre le jour et moi l'impénétrable mur.
25 *Plus de nuit*, et mon œil et se perd et se mêle
Dans les *torrents profonds de lumière éternelle*.
Me voici sur les feux que le langage humain
Nomme Cassiopée et l'Ours et le Dauphin.
Maintenant la Couronne autour de moi s'embrase.
30 Ici l'Aigle et le Cygne et la Lyre et Pégase.
Et voici que plus loin le Serpent tortueux
Noue autour de mes pas ses anneaux lumineux.
Féconde immensité, les esprits magnanimes
Aiment à se plonger dans tes vivants *abîmes*;
35 *Abîmes de clarté*, où, libre de ses fers,
L'homme siège au conseil qui créa l'univers;
Où l'âme remontant à sa grande origine
Sent qu'elle est une part de l'essence divine.

Ce fragment tiré du poème *Amérique* ne présente pas une structure aussi rigoureusement déterminée qu'un morceau lyrique plus bref. Son vocabulaire, à peu d'exceptions près, se compose d'unités lexicales et phraséologiques assez conventionnelles; c'est uniquement le contexte ou, si l'on veut, l'«enthousiasme errant» qui les transforme en stylèmes propres à Chénier. En tout cas, cette espèce d'enthousiasme est quelque chose d'exceptionnel dans le domaine de la poésie lyrique: on y a souvent reconnu l'admiration de l'astronomie moderne, mais on a beaucoup moins apprécié un autre aspect de l'enthousiasme de Chénier: son admiration à l'égard des progrès de l'aéronautique: n'oublions pas que ces vers datent des années des expériences des frères Montgolfier (1783) et que l'imagination d'un poète pouvait dès cette époque entrevoir la conquête de l'espace par l'homme. Voilà pourquoi cet «hymne à la nuit» se transforme si facilement en un «hymne à la lumière»,[106] mais aussi en un éloge du progrès de la science.

Pour révéler ces sentiments complexes et pour éviter la sécheresse de la poésie didactique, Chénier a dû recourir à des moyens stylistiques empruntés à d'autres genres, notamment à l'ode. Toutefois ces éléments traditionnels entrent dans une nouvelle synthèse où ils ne tardent pas à revêtir des

[106] *Ibid.*

fonctions bien différentes. Pour les saisir, nous allons recourir à la méthode d'une analyse complexe.[107]

Le texte de Chénier se compose d'une curieuse alternance de vers *isolés* et de périodes poétiques s'étendant à un certain nombre de vers. Les vers isolés sont presque toujours marqués de stylèmes particulièrement expressifs qui, à leur tour, servent à communiquer les points les plus saillants des idées et des sentiments. Dès le début on rencontre un vers isolé, dominé par une double invocation et par le syntagme *Muse nocturne* pour lequel nous n'avons aucune attestations antérieure. On croit avoir à faire à une attitude «pré-mussetiste», mais dans ce cas la mention de *la lyre* (préfiguration du *luth* mentionné par Musset) s'associe à une rime tout à fait insolite, à savoir au mot *délire* qui, évidemment, renvoie à une sorte de «fureur poétique».[108] Le dynamisme des premiers vers est d'ailleurs augmenté aussi par une comparaison bien hardie: l'envol de cette «Muse nocturne» est comparé à un *fier météore*[109] et ce rapprochement entraîne aussitôt une autre image «astrale», placée à la fin d'un groupement ternaire: (v. 4—5):

Prends { *les ailes* des vents,
{ *les ailes*[110] des éclairs,
{ Les bonds de la *comète*[111] aux longs cheveux de flamme.

Après cette invocation mêlée d'exhortations répétées (v. 1—5), la phrase suivante a un caractère plus subjectif: *les vers impatients*[112] qui jaillissent de l'âme du poète servent de support grammatical à deux verbes parallèles, réunis aussi par une allitération labiale:

[ils]
veulent porter aux Dieux,
et *volent* où *reluit*
L'enthousiasme errant, fils de la belle nuit.

Il est curieux de remarquer que dans ce contexte extatique, plein d'effets manifestement «pindariques»,[113] l'enthousiasme devient non seulement un esprit «errant», mais aussi un phénomène lumineux: il reluit comme un véritable génie («fils») de la nuit.

Le vers 9 est de nouveau un «Satzvers», une unité rythmique: c'est ici que l'«enthousiasme errant» revêt l'aspect d'une exaltation cosmique. La

[107] Autrement dit, on ne fait aucune distinction rigoureuse entre les divers domaines de la stylistique; on cède plutôt au charme du texte pour y découvrir au fur et à mesure les stylèmes les plus significatifs.

[108] Pour cette acception du terme *délire* v. Lemercier: «De tes esprits émus le *délire* s'empare» (L.).

[109] Pour *météore* comme image du langage poétique, L. ne cite que Béranger: «Hélas ! rapide *météore*, / Trop vite elle [la sylphide] a fui loin de nous».

[110] La répétition de la métaphore *les ailes* donne naissance à un parallélisme anaphorique des deux premiers membres du groupement ternaire.

[111] Pour l'emploi poétique du mot *comète*, les dictionnaires ne fournissent aucune attestation; il est vrai que le poème de Chénier n'a jamais été dépouillé par les lexicographes.

[112] Epithète insolite; cf. Corneille: «*Impatient désir* d'une illustre vengeance» (*Cinna*, L.); Racine: «Ton *cœur impatient* de revoir ta Troyenne» (*Andromaque*, L.).

[113] V. plus haut nos refléxions sur le caractère «pindarique» ou «antipindarique» de la poésie du XVIIIe siècle.

nature est personnifiée («*Accours*, grande nature ...») et même accompagnée d'un qualificatif fort surprenant: «ô mère de gloire». Malgré son caractère inédit, la dernière expression ne laisse subsister aucun doute: la Nature peut être présentée comme «mère de gloire», car elle offre toutes les possibilités au déploiement libre des facultés humaines. Un seul vers suffit à Chénier pour formuler l'optimisme de l'homme du XVIIIe siècle et sa foi dans le progrès de la science.

Au début du vers 10 le poète reprend l'impératif *accours* pour former une anaphore et pour introduire par cette seconde double invocation son hymne à Uranie, «reine du monde».[114] La phrase se distingue par son ampleur car cette période ne compte pas non moins de 9 vers. Après le 7e vers de ce passage (v. 16) il y a pourtant une césure syntaxique; le reste du texte dépend entièrement de deux impératifs aux sens opposés: «*Descends*, non, *porte*-moi sur la route brûlante.» Il est fort dommage que le vers 18, un des points culminants de l'acheminement des idées ne soit, au point de vue stylistique, qu'un écho assez pâle de l'expression *route brûlante*:[115] «Que je m'élève au ciel comme une *flamme ardente*». Cette conclusion n'est sauvée que par le sens métaphorique de *flamme*:[116] l'innovation sémantique est non seulement un fait lexical, mais une conséquence naturelle du contexte, animé d'un bout à l'autre par l'«enthousiasme errant» des espaces infinis. L'attitude de Chénier est diamétralement opposée à celle de Pascal et même de Léopardi (*L'Infinito*): l'homme moderne, assoiffé d'élargir le champ de ses investigations, ne s'humilie plus devant l'univers, mais s'arme pour en découvrir les secrets.

Les vers 19—20 sont également des unités syntaxiques indépendantes: le poète, ravi de ses nostalgies astrales,[117] dit adieu à son corps, «*tombeau de chair*»,[118] et à la terre qui doit «*fuir* sous ses pas». Il se sent soumis à la force d'attraction de l'espace: «l'éther m'*aspire*»[119] — entendons-nous au vers 22. A partir de ce passage, il n'y a pas que les pauses métriques qui deviennent plus fréquentes, mais aussi les unités syntaxiques, voire les phrases bornées à une partie relativement restreinte du vers. Ainsi s'explique la répétition anaphorique *plus de nuit* dans les vers 23 et 25; immédiatement après (v. 26) l'expression *torrents profonds de lumière éternelle* est destinée à faire sentir quelque chose de l'activité ininterrompue des forces cosmiques. Dans les évocations de ce genre où il est facile de reconnaître l'application des idées des encyclopédistes à la pensée poétique, quelques vers (27 et suiv.) retombent dans la mythisation conventionnelle; il est pourtant à noter que les astres et les constellations sont classées dans une catégorie très générale

[114] Tournure inattestée; seul Lamartine parlera de la Lune comme *reine des ombres* (*L'Isolement*, L.).

[115] L'expression *route brûlante* paraît être originale; la rime *brûlante / ardente* unit le verbe *brûler* à *ardre*, son synonyme archaïque.

[116] Pas d'antécédents dans le langage poétique; néanmoins *flamme* se rapporte souvent à l'ardeur des passions (Bossuet, Molière, Régnier, etc. L.).

[117] Cette attitude sera maintes fois reprise par les poètes romantiques et post-romantiques: même vers 1880 le plus grand poète roumain Mihail Eminescu cherchera à se présenter comme un démon volant, un Lucifer (pris au sens étymologique) qui s'identifie à l'étoile du berger (v. le poème *Luceafărul*).

[118] Image tout à fait originale; elle provient peut-être de l'éloquence sacrée.

[119] Emploi très hardi du verbe *aspirer* dont le sujet est l'*éther*. Pas d'exemples similaires dans le langage poétique antérieur.

(«les feux», v. 27) qui ramène de nouveau l'attention du lecteur sur l'astronomie scientifique. Même la naissance incessante de mondes nouveaux est ingénieusement évoquée par le syntagme *féconde immensité*; au point de vue sémantique, les trouvailles de ce genre élargissent d'une façon très heureuse la sphère d'emploi de certains mots et surtout des épithètes adjectives. L'univers n'est plus un amas inerte d'astres et de galactiques; comme auparavant dans la conception de Diderot, la matière même s'anime pour peupler ces *vivants abîmes* (v. 34). Jusqu'ici le mot *abîme* était toujours un synonyme de *gouffre*;[120] il fallait le génie d'André Chénier pour enrichir le langage poétique français non seulement d'une belle épanaphore («vivants *abîmes*; *Abîmes* . . .» v. 35—36), mais aussi de l'oxymoron inédit *abîmes de clarté*. En même temps, cette inoubliable image s'associe indissolublement à l'idée de liberté intellectuelle, puisque l'homme, «libéré de ses fers» et ayant déjà une idée de la nature de ces *abîmes*, «siège au conseil qui créa l'univers». Chénier admet donc avec les philosophes du XVIIIe siècle la perfectibilité de l'intelligence humaine et c'est précisément dans ces facultés intellectuelles qu'il croit entrevoir une étincelle de l'«essence divine». Inutile d'ajouter que dans ce contexte même la formule déiste pâlit devant la foi illimitée du poète dans le progrès.

10. Il est presque superflu de rappeler que les rêveries philosophiques d'André Chénier constituent une rare exception dans la poésie de l'époque et, en un sens plus précis, dans le domaine de la méditation. Passons à une autre variété du même genre qui, à bien des égards, s'appuie aussi sur un genre plus traditionnel, à savoir sur l'*idylle*. Il serait utile de jeter un coup d'œil sur les idylles de Jean-François Ducis et d'autres poètes; on y découvre également un enrichissement peu apprécié du vocabulaire poétique.[121] Néanmoins cette fois, pour plus de brièveté, nous nous bornons à analyser rapidement une des idylles moins connues de Parny, intitulée *Projet de solitude*. Cette touchante «invitation au voyage» ne pouvait être conçue que par un poète originaire des îles lointaines[122] admirées aussi par Bernardin de Saint-Pierre; chez Parny, auteur si lu pendant une bonne cinquantaine d'années, le goût de l'exotisme poétique s'allie non seulement au désir d'évasion, mais aussi à un sentiment d'i n s u l a r i t é qui aboutira plus tard au mythe moderne de l'Ile des Bienheureux. Dans cette atmosphère fort complexe, le vocabulaire conventionnel de la poésie galante s'enrichit d'éléments exotiques très précis, prêts à se transformer en symboles — un siècle avant le symbolisme proprement dit. Voici donc le texte choisi:[123]

> Fuyons ces *tristes lieux*, ô *maîtresse adorée*:   I   a
> Nous perdons en espoir la moitié de nos jours,   b
> Et la *crainte importune* y trouble nos amours.   b ∧
> Non loin de ce rivage est une île ignorée,   a
> 5 Interdite aux vaisseaux, et d'écueils entourée.   a ∧

[120] V. plus haut nos réflexions sur l'ode de J.-B. Rousseau, p. 226.
[121] Rappelons le cas d'un vieux poète qui n'hésite pas à se comparer à une *chouette*. Cf. à ce sujet aussi un texte de Clément Marot: «Quel qu'il soit, il n'est point poëte, / Mais fils aismé d'une *chouette* . . .» (L.).
[122] Parny est né à l'île Bourbon.
[123] Cf. F. Duviard, *Anthologie des poètes français (XVIIIe siècle)*, Paris s. d. [1948], pp. 179—180.

Un *zéphyr éternel* y rafraîchit les airs.   II   *a* ∧

Libre et nouvelle encor, la *prodigue nature*   *b*

Embellit de ses dons ce point de l'univers: *a* ∧

Des ruisseaux argentés roulent sur la *verdure,*   *b*

10 Et vont en serpentant se perdre au sein des mers;   *a* ∧

Une main favorable y reproduit sans cesse   III   *a* ∧

L'*ananas* parfumé des plus douces odeurs;   *b* ∧

Et l'*oranger touffu,* courbé sous sa richesse,   *a*

Se couvre en même temps et de fruits et de fleurs.   *b* ∧

15 Que nous faut-il de plus ? Cette *île fortunée*   *c*

Semble par la nature aux amants destinée.   *c* ∧

L'*Océan* la resserre, et deux fois en un jour   IV   *a* ∧

De cet *asile* étroit on achève le tour.   *a* ∧

Là, je ne craindrai plus un père inexorable.   *b* ∧

C'est là, qu'en *liberté* tu pourrais être *aimable,*   *b*

Et *couronner* l'amant qui t'a donné son cœur.   *c* ∧

Vous coulerez alors, mes paisibles journées,   *d*

Par les nœuds du plaisir l'un à l'autre enchaînées: *d* ∧

Laissez-moi peu de gloire et beaucoup de bonheur.   *c* ∧

25 *Viens; la nuit est obscure et le ciel sans nuage;*   V   *a* ∧

D'un éternel adieu saluons ce rivage,   *a* ∧

Où par toi seule encor mes pas sont retenus.   *b* ∧

Je vois à l'horizon *l'étoile de Vénus:*   *b*

Vénus dirigera notre course incertaine.   *c* ∧

30 *Éole* exprès pour nous vient d'enchaîner les vents;   *d* ∧

Sur les flots aplanis *Zéphire* souffle à peine;   *c* ∧

Viens; l'Amour jusqu'au bord conduira deux amants.   *d* ∧

Le poème s'ouvre par un vers isolé dont les deux hémistiches représente[nt] une sorte d'antithèse rythmique: tandis que le premier hémistiche («Fuyo*ns* ces *tristes lieux* . . .») se compose de trois ïambes (◡–́ ◡–́ ◡–́), le second hémistiche est fondé sur le rythme franchement ascendant de deux anapestes («ô maî*tresse* adorée»: ◌̀◡ –́ ◡◡–́). Le vers 2 motive le projet de fuite, mais il est curieux d'observer que les ictus font presque toujours résonner des voyelles sombres:

$$\tilde{\varrho} \qquad \psi\alpha \qquad\qquad \bar{u}$$

Nous per*don*s en *espoir* ¦ la moit*ié* de nos *jours*

Au vers 3 le premier hémistiche et même le début du second communiquent un sentiment de gêne qui s'accompagne d'un frémissement intérieur (d'où la consonne *r*, précédée ou suivie d'une occlusive sourde):

Et la *crainte* import*une*[124] ¦ y *trouble* . . .

La clausule pourrait bien marquer un moment de calme et de bonheur, mais il est évident que le syntagme *nos amours* a également une consonance

---

[124] Epithète assez fréquente de certains sentiments (L.), cf. *fierté importune* (Racine), *vœux importuns* (La Fontaine).

sombre, ce qui va de pair avec les autres motifs évoquant cette liaison hérissée de difficultés. C'est pourquoi l'idée de la fuite paraît parfaitement motivée. La fin du vers évoque déjà l'île féerique du bonheur et le vers suivant en fournit de nouveaux détails sans qu'il soit nécessaire de recourir à un effort de mythisation. Pour peindre cette solitude sauvage, opposée aux «tristes lieux» de la civilisation, le poète se borne à dire: «Interdite aux vaisseaux et d'écueils entourée.»

La «strophe» II présente un nouveau schéma des rimes (ababa); celui-ci sert à mettre en relief des mots aussi importants que la *prodigue nature* et *verdure*. Dans cette atmosphère d'enchantement exotique, rafraîchie par un *zéphyr éternel*[125] (v. 6), même les *ruisseaux argentés*[126] se transforment facilement en un symbole du délaissement et du calme délicieux (« . . . Et vont en serpentant[127] se perdre au sein des mers.»).

La «strophe» suivante (ababcc) est un sizain; malgré certains clichés usés comme une main *secourable*[128] on doit y apprécier aussi bien le nom exotique de l'*ananas*[129] comme stylème poétique, qu'un beau vers (13) servant à caractériser l'*oranger touffu*:[130] «se couvre en même temps *et de fruits et de fleurs*».[131] L'*île fortunée*[132] que le sort réserve aux amants est donc placée dans le cadre ensoleillé des ananas et des oranges comme autant de symboles d'une liesse exubérante. Le tableau est si serein que dans ce passage les vers de Parny n'admettent plus de rimes sombres. . .

La «strophe» IV est un huitain d'une structure assez insolite (aabbcddc). Là, entouré de l'immense océan, on n'a plus à craindre un *père inexorable*;[133] «c'est là qu'*en liberté* tu pourrais être *aimable*.» Au fond,[134] c'est dans ces vers qu'il faut chercher le noyau même de l'«invitation» de Parny, invitation qui, à proprement parler, équivaut à un cri de détresse: pourquoi les amoureux ont-ils à lutter contre la rigueur d'un *père inexorable* qui constitue le principal obstacle de leur bonheur? Le poète se range hardiment du côté de ceux qui veulent s'aimer *en liberté* et qui, même dans ces «tristes lieux» (v. 1), c'est-à-dire au sein d'une société pleine de préjugés essaient de se créer une «île fortunée». Le bonheur sentimental vaut davantage que toute espèce de gloire; c'est pourquoi cette «strophe» se termine par un vers diamétralement opposé à la philosophie de Gilbert, avide de gloire jusqu'à sa mort: «Laisse-moi peu de gloire et *beaucoup de bonheur*.»

[125] *Zéphyr* est un mot courant du langage poétique, mais on n'y ajoute presque jamais l'épithète *éternel*.

[126] Cf. Saint-Lambert: «L'émail des gazons frais, les *ruisseaux argentés*» (L.).

[127] *Serpenter* est rare chez les auteurs antérieurs; cf. pourtant Boileau: «Et des ruisseaux de lait *serpentaient* dans les plaines» (L.). Chez Voltaire on lit les vers suivants: «Près de ces bords fleuris, / Où la Seine *serpente* . . .» (ibid.).

[128] Mot venu du langage religieux, cf. Delavigne: «Notre-Dame d'Embrun, soyez moi *secourable*!» Boileau parle de la *bonté secourable* d'un roi (L.).

[129] Les grands dictionnaires (L., R., Quillet, Lar.) ne fournissent aucun exemple littéraire.

[130] Terme très rare du langage poétique; v. pourtant La Fontaine: «Le blé, riche présent de la blonde Cérès, / Trop *touffu* bien souvent épuise les guérets» (L.). V. aussi Delille: «Et des pampres *touffues* le luxe infructueux» (L.).

[131] A signaler la combinaison du polysyndète *et* . . . *et* . . . avec une allitération labiale fort expressive.

[132] Cf. «*Iles Fortunées*: ancien nom des îles Canaries» (L.).

[133] Cf. Corneille: «Mon père et mon devoir étaient *inexorables*» (*Polyeucte*, L.).

[134] Ce sens de l'adjectif est presque inexistant dans le langage poétique.

Enfin voici encore un huitain d'une structure semblable à la précédente (*aa bbcdcd*): il commence par un vers particulièrement souple (25) dont les tonalités parcourent toute une gamme de timbres clairs:

$$\underset{\text{Viens; / la nuit est obscure / et le ciel sans nuage . . .}^{135}}{\overset{i\tilde{e} \qquad \underset{}{u}i \qquad \bar{u} \qquad i\underset{}{e} \qquad \ddot{u}\bar{a}}{}}$$

Un peu plus bas (v. 28—29) le nom de Vénus forme une curieuse épanaphore: dans l'expression *étoile de Vénus*[136] il figure dans un synonyme légèrement stylisé de la dénomination courante (*étoile du soir* ou *du berger*), tandis qu'au début du vers suivant il flotte entre les deux acceptions du terme: est-il un nom d'étoile ou aussi un nom de déesse? Dans les vers suivants même la mention d'*Eole* et de *Zéphyr* ne sert qu'à évoquer le calme doux et profond de la nature: c'est de ce grand silence cosmique qu'émerge la belle figure étymologique du vers final: «Viens; l'*Amour* jusqu'au bord conduira deux *amants*».

Il est encore à noter que la strophique «latente» de ce poème (5—5—6—8—8) doit nous rappeler de loin la structure polymétrique de la cantate en tant que sous-genre de l'élégie (5.): la polymétrie a déjà disparu, mais ses traces se retrouvent dans la longueur inégale de ces «strophes» à peine déchiffrables au moyen de la disposition des rimes.

11. Après les genres que nous venons de passer en revue, il est indispensable d'examiner aussi un aspect beaucoup plus réaliste de la méditation, à savoir la s a t i r e. La veine satirique est un élément indissolublement lié à l'esprit du XVIIIe siècle; ses manifestations ont l'avantage de nous initier à des couches jusqu'ici négligées du langage poétique. Dans ce qui suit nous allons examiner intégralement une seule satire: le poème *Les vous et les tu* de Voltaire.[137] Cette pièce relativement peu connue va nous révéler encore une des possibilités du mélange des genres: si bizarre que cela puisse nous paraître, un certain ton élégiaque n'est point étranger à ce texte qui évoque avec une verve bien voltairienne les deux aspects de la carrière d'une cocotte ambitieuse.

> PHILIS, qu'*est devenu ce temps*
> Où, dans un *fiacre* promenée,
> Sans *laquais*, sans *ajustements*,
> De tes grâces seules ornée,
> 5 Contente d'un mauvais soupé
> Que tu changeais en *ambroisie*,
> Tu te livrais, dans ta *folie*,
> A l'amant *heureux et trompé*
> Qui t'avait consacré sa vie?
> 10 Le ciel ne te donnait alors,

Λ

---

[135] La douceur et la musicalité de ce vers sont dues aussi à l'absence presque totale de la liquide *r*; à la fin d'*obscur* elle se réduit à un souffle allongeant la voyelle précédente.

[136] Même Lamartine et Musset préfèrent parler de l'*étoile du soir* (R.).

[137] La plupart des satires sont un peu prolixes; ce texte relativement bref représente assez bien certains traits stylistiques de ce genre.

Pour tout rang et pour tous trésors,
Que les *agréments* de ton âge:
Un cœur tendre, un *esprit volage*,
Un *sein d'albâtre*, et de beaux yeux.   ∧
15 Avec tant d'attraits précieux,
Hélas! qui n'eût été *friponne*?   ∧
Tu le fus, objet gracieux;
Et (que l'Amour me le pardonne!)
Tu sais que je t'en aimais mieux.   ∧
20 *Ah! madame!* que votre vie,
D'honneurs aujourd'hui si remplie,
Diffère de ces doux instants!   ∧
Ce large suisse à cheveux blancs,
Qui ment sans cesse à votre porte,
25 Philis, est l'*image du Temps*:
Il semble qu'il chasse l'*escorte*
Des tendres Amours et des Ris;
Sous vos magnifiques *lambris*
Ces enfants tremblent de paraître.   ∧
30 Hélas! je les ai vus jadis
Entrer chez toi par la fenêtre
Et se huer dans ton *taudis*.   ∧
Non, madame, tous ces *tapis*
Qu'a tissus la *Savonnerie*,
35 Ceux que les Persans ont *ourdis*,
Et toute votre *orfèvrerie*,
Et ces *plats* si chers que Germain
A gravés de sa main divine,
Et ces *cabinets* où Martin
40 A surpassé l'art de la Chine;
Vos *vases japonais* et blancs,
Toutes ces *fragiles merveilles*;
Ces deux *lustres* de *diamants*
Qui pendent à vos deux oreilles,
45 Ces riches *carcans*, ces *colliers*,
Et cette *pompe enchanteresse*,
Ne valent pas un des baisers
Que tu donnais dans ta jeunesse.   ∧

Une dizaine de vers (1—9) constituent le portrait de l'ancienne Philis.[13]
L'héroïne moderne, malgré son nom, se promène ou, pour mieux dires
e s t   p r o m e n é e en *fiacre*;[139] après ce prélude ses grâces seules — sans
leaquais,[140] sans *ajustements*,[141] suffisent pour transformer même un *mauvai*

---

[138] Les pseudonymes grecs de ce genre étaient très fréquents dans la poésie galante
de l'époque. Outre la mode, déjà déclinante, des ornements mythologiques, il faut
tenir compte des traditions inaugurées, depuis la Renaissance, par l'idylle pastorale.
[139] Pour un exemple tiré des Mazarinades v. L. On retrouve chez L. aussi le texte
que nous analysons.
[140] Cf. Boileau: «Je l'ai connus *laquais*, avant qu'il fût commis» (L.).
[141] Cf. La Fontaine: «C'est un *ajustement* des mouches empruntés» (L.).

souper en *ambroisie*;[142] la petite, dans sa *folie*,[143] semble *se livrer* entièrement à un amant *heureux* et *trompé*.[144] Le cynisme fort réaliste de ce préambule — qui n'a encore rien à voir avec la satire proprement dite — n'est modéré que par la nostalgie d'un Voltaire vieillissant; n'appartenait-il pas, lui aussi, au cortège des amants «heureux et trompés»? En tout cas le vieux poète parle avec une réelle tendresse de celle dont les uniques trésors étaient, à cette époque-là, les *agréments*[145] de son âge. Malgré cela, le portrait n'est guère idéalisé: au *cœur tendre* et au *sein d'albâtre*[146] s'associe un *esprit volage*: ce curieux mélange de motif qui n'était d'ailleurs que trop naturel, ne pouvait avoir qu'une seule suite: «Avec tant d'attraits précieux, / Hélas! qui n'eût été friponne?»[147] (v. 15—16). «Tu le fus, *objet gracieux*» (v. 17) ajoute Voltaire, en avouant aussitôt — ce que le lecteur suppose déjà — qu'il l'en «aimait mieux» (v. 19). Après ces aveux où, comme nous venons de le voir, le cynisme se teint d'une bonne dose de mélancolie, la pause métrique devient une interruption particulièrement longue, un moment de recueillement qui incite à la réflexion. C'est de ce silence que jaillit l'exclamation *Ah, madame!* qui, suivie de trois vers rapides (20—22) marque la transition à la seconde partie — incontestablement satirique — du portrait. Au seuil de la porte de la courtisane en vogue paraît un «large suisse»[148] (vers 23) qui, contrairement au respect qu'inspire ses «cheveux blancs» (ibid.), «ment sans cesse» à la porte de sa patronne. Le même suisse semble chasser «l'escorte[149] des tendres Amours et des Ris» (v. 26—27); entre les «magnifiques *lambris*»[150] on ne retrouve plus la gaîté de la jeunesse de Philis, mais uniquement ce suisse, triste *image du temps*.[151] Le poète est assez cruel pour rappeler à l'orgueilleuse Philis d'où elle vient; chose singulière, ce passage se termine par un mot aussi brutal que *taudis*.[152] Après ce cri amer, le luxe de la courtisane enrichie est esquissé dans une période de 14 vers, au moyen de maints

[142] Cf. M. Régnier: «D'hommes vous faisant dieux vous paissait d'*ambroisie*» (L.). Un peu plus tard A. Chénier dira: «Que vos heureux destins, les délices du ciel, / coulent toujours trampés d'*ambroisie* et de miel» (ibid.).

[143] Ce sens de *folie* (qui s'est maintenue jusqu'à nos jours dans le nom des *Folies Bergères*) était très fréquent au XVIIIe siècle. Cf. aussi notre texte tiré des *Jardins* de Delille (p. 234).

[144] L'effet comique du texte résulte de l'opposition sémantique des deux épithètes. Cf. Montesquieu: «Nous étions tous deux *heureux*; tu me croyais *trompée*, et je te *trompais*» (*Lettres pers.*, L.).

[145] Cf. La Fontaine: «Son art de plaire, et de n'y *penser* pas, / *Ses agréments*, à qui tout rend hommage» (R.).

[146] Déjà Clément Marot parle d'une *gorge d'albâtre* (R.). Cf. Voltaire: «Il [Dieu] se plut à pétrir d'incarnat et d'*albâtre* / Les charmes arrondis du sein de Pompadour.»

[147] Auparavant le mot avait un sens nettement péjoratif. Cf. Molière: «Et je pense pas que Satan en personne / Puisse être si méchant qu'une telle *friponne*» (L.).

[148] Terme très rare dans le langage poétique (cf. *Les Plaideurs* de Racine, L.). L. renvoie aussi à ce texte de Voltaire.

[149] Cf. Racine: «Errant dans le palais sans suite et sans *escorte*, / La mère de César veille seule à sa porte» (L.).

[150] Cf. La Fontaine: «Le chaume devient or, tout brille en ce pourpris, / Tous ces événements sont peints sur le *lambris*» (L.).

[151] Autant que je sache, on a fort peu parlé du «symbolisme» des satires de Voltaire; il n'en reste pas moins que le poète en était parfaitement conscient.

[152] Cf. Voltaire: «De Philémon vous connaissez l'histoire, / Amants aimés dans le coin d'un *taudis*» (L.). Comme exemple poétique antérieur il suffit de renvoyer à un passage de Molière: «Et sortons de ce *taudis*, / Où l'on ne peut être assis» (*Le Bourgeois gentilhomme*, R.).

détails pittoresques. Le langage poétique — au moins en ce qui concerne la satire — s'enrichit sous nos yeux d'une série de motifs inédits.[153] Néanmoins l'ancien amant ne saurait être ébloui par cette *pompe enchanteresse*[154] et ses *fragiles merveilles*:[155] comme il ressort des derniers vers (47—48), toutes ces splendeurs fallacieuses «ne valent pas un des baisers / Que *tu* donnais dans ta jeunesse.» La conclusion reprend le ton élégiaque, mais n'est-elle pas en parfaite harmonie avec les principes même de cette pièce, digne de figurer parmi les meilleures pages du vieux Voltaire.

12. La satire n'est pas loin d'un genre non moins typique du XVIIIe siècle: l'*épigramme*. Dans le cadre de la présente ébauche stylistique nous ne pouvons essayer de proposer une sorte de typologie structuraliste de l'épigramme français; contentons-nous d'examiner la structure d'une maxime de J.-B. Rousseau sur le thème baroque du «theatrum mundi»:

Ce monde-ci n'est qu'une *œuvre comique*	*a*
Où chacun fait des rôles différents.	*b* ∧
Là, sur la scène, en *habit dramatique*,	*a*
Brillent prélats, ministres, conquérants.	*b* ∧
5 Par nous, *vil peuple*, assis aux derniers rangs,	*b*
Troupe futile et des grands *rebutée*,	*c*
Par nous, d'en bas, la pièce est écoutée,	*c* ∧
Mais nous payons, *utiles* spectateurs,	*d*
Et, quand la *farce* est mal représentée,	*c*
10 Pour notre argent nous sifflons les acteurs.	*d* ∧

Quel curieux dizain ! Bien que ce texte date de la première moitié du siècle (J.-B. Rousseau mourut en 1748), il est impossible de ne pas y reconnaître un esprit de révolte qui caractérisera encore mieux le demi-siècle suivant. Le grand drame de la vie n'est plus l'œuvre de la Providence; c'est une *œuvre comique*,[156] une *farce*[157] de valeur assez douteuse. Qui en est l'auteur? Le poète n'en souffle pas un mot, mais il n'oublie pas de signaler deux faits. D'une part, il insiste sur les différences sociales qui séparent le *vil peuple*, c'est-à-dire les *utiles spectateurs*, la «misera plebs contribuens» de ceux qui, en *habits dramatiques*,[158] c'est-à-dire dans des costumes dignes de leurs rangs, *brillent*[159] sur la scène comme «prélats, ministres, conquérants». Seuls les grands semblent diriger l'histoire et ils n'ont que du mépris pour la *troupe futile*[160] qui, malgré son état humiliant («des grands *rebutée*»[161]), se transforme

---

[153] Sur une description de la *Savonnerie* par Voltaire lui-même v. L. — Le mot *cabinet* est attesté aussi chez Corneille et Racine. — Pour les *vases japonais* les dictionnaires ne fournissent aucune documentation. — Le sens métaphorique de *lustre* (de diamants) manque également aux dictionnaires.

[154] Cf. aussi chez A. Chénier: «J'ai connu des grandeurs la *pompe enchanteresse*» (L.).

[155] Syntagme non attesté; cf. la construction *fragile innocence* chez La Fontaine (L.).

[156] Cf. Boileau: «Que la nature donc soit votre étude unique, / Auteur qui préludait aux honneurs du *comique*» (L.).

[157] Déjà J.-B. Rousseau a entrevu le sens qui sera donné plus tard à ce terme par Rimbaud: «La vie est la *farce* à mener par tous» (R.).

[158] Nous n'avons aucun exemple antérieur.

[159] Cf. Voltaire: «Tel *brille* au second rang qui s'éclipse au premier» (L.).

[160] Cf. Delille: «Ce papillon lui-même, à nos yeux si *futile* . . . » (L.).

[161] Pour un exemple chez Molière v. L.

involontairement en *utiles spectateurs* par rapport au drame, voire à la tragédie d'un pays.[162] Mais est-ce une masse inerte, réduite à une inaction totale? Le vers 7 qui rime à la clausule «des grands *rebutés*» pourrait le faire croire («Par nous d'*en bas* la pièce est écoutée»), mais le tercet final expose parfaitement le «ius murmurandi» d'un peuple fort peu content de la monarchie absolue; le dernier vers, insistant de nouveau sur les lourds fardeaux des masses, résonne presque comme une menace: «Pour notre argent *nous sifflons* les acteurs.»

Voilà ce qu'il est advenu du dizain classique de l'«ode pindarique» au XVIIIᵉ siècle: un moyen fort efficace de la satire sociale qui ne ménage aucune dignité, aucune institution. Seule la laïcisation définitive du motif «theatrum mundi» permettra un jour à Piron, cet autre poète avide de gloire, de formuler sa propre épitaphe comme une flèche dirigée contre l'Académie:

Ci-gît Piron, qui ne fut rien,
Pas même académicien.

13. Avant de terminer notre tour d'horizon, essayons de décrire au moins quelques particularités de la c h a n s o n du XVIIIᵉ siècle. Dans ce cas l'embarras de choix pose des problèmes assez délicats; pour compléter la galerie des auteurs examinés, choisissons *Le saule du malheureux*, un lied élégiaque de Jean-François Ducis, l'initiateur du culte de Shakespeare en France (1733—1816).

Les deux premières strophes évoquent d'une manière touchante le milieu champêtre où le poète cherche un refuge, un «riant exil»:[163]

Charmant vallon, le plus doux des déserts,
Où souvent *seul* j'ai *cherché* la nature,
J'entends déjà ton ruisseau qui *murmure*;
Je vois enfin tes saules toujours verts.
Chantez le saule et sa douce verdure.

Oui, les voilà ces *ramiers amoureux*,
Ces monts, ces bois, ces prés, cette *onde pure*.
Ah! devais-tu, *riche et simple nature*,
T'offrir si belle à l'oeil du malheureux?
Chantez le saule et sa douce verdure.

Au début du texte il convient de signaler la mise en relief du motif du *vallon*: le poète se plaît à souligner ce qui a un horizon restreint où l'homme ne se perd pas.[164]

---

[162] A remarquer la rime intérieure unissant *futiles* à *utiles*; c'est dans cette rime inédite que paraît culminer la verve satirique de l'auteur. La même rime est attestée aussi chez Delille: «Ce papillon lui-même, à nos yeux si *futiles* / Qui sait si de son vol l'erreur n'est pas *utile?*» (L.).

[163] Pour l'emploi amélioratif de ce mot v. notre commentaire sur l'*Ode* de Gilbert (p. 233).

[164] Sur ce trait du style lyrique de l'époque v. les judicieuses remarques de H. Morier, *op. cit.*, p. 129 et suiv. Auparavant le mot *vallon* était assez rare dans le langage poétique (cf. La Fontaine: «Et déjà les *vallons* / Voyaient l'ombre en croissant tomber du haut des monts» L.).

Au même vers, un autre mot «réhabilité» — au moins dans ce contexte — est le *désert*. Son emploi s'oppose très nettement à l'usage classique; la nouveauté de son contenu sémantique est encore soulignée par l'épithète: «*le plus doux des déserts.*»[165]

A partir du vers 2 commence la série des rimes en *-ure* qui s'associe, au moins dans la strophe initiale, à des allitérations sifflantes («*souvent seul*») et chuintantes («*charmant vallon . . . j'ai cherché . . .*»; «*J'entends déjà . . .*»); c'est la même impression musicale, composée de trois éléments phoniques (*s, ch, ü*) qui explique aussi le choix du refrain «*Chantez le saule et sa douce verdure.*» Ce refrain entraîne d'ailleurs des conséquences qui déterminent la prépondérance des rimes en *-ure* ou, si l'on veut, de la voyelle *u* qui caractérise le texte entier (str. I: *nature / murmure / verdure;* str. II: *pure / nature / verdure,* etc.).[166]

Au point de vue lexical, malgré les innovations sémantiques que nous venons de signaler, le texte paraît très conventionnel; les stylèmes sont à chercher plutôt dans le domaine de l'euphonie et de la syntaxe stylistique. Aux vers II, 1—2 on observe la répétition insistante d'une particule aussi simple que le pronom démonstratif; il n'en est pas moins vrai qu'après le préambule «Oui, les voilà . . .» la valeur déictique du pronom se transforme en un véritable geste oral: «. . . *ces* ramiers amoureux, / *Ces* monts, *ces* bois, *ces* prés, cette onde pure . . .» Au point de vue syntaxique c'est presque un polysyndète: le pronom sert à donner plus de relief aux membres d'une énumération formulée conformément aux exigences de ces décasyllabes groupés en quintils. La stylisation du vocabulaire est fort discrète: cf. *pigeon → ramier; vague → onde.*

Ce sont au fond les mêmes particularités qui caractérisent les deux dernières strophes:

> Me voilà donc, saule cher au malheur,
> Sous tes rameaux nourrissant ma *blessure.*
> Ah! *dis* au vent, *dis* à l'eau qui *murmure,*
> En s'enfuyant, d'emporter ma douleur.
> Chantez le saule et sa douce *verdure.*
>
> Puisse bientôt, ce sont mes derniers vœux,
> Quelque pasteur, voyant ma sépulture,
> Dire en passant: «On trompa sa *droiture.*
> Il fut sensible, et *mourut malheureux.*»
> Chantez le saule et sa douce verdure.

A propos de l'avant-dernière strophe, il faut attirer l'attention sur un motif pétrarquesque: le poète mourant confie sa douleur à la nature. Le vers 3 de cette strophe est d'ailleurs l'écho d'un vers antérieure (I,3); il est significatif que c'est précisément la rime verbale *murmure* qui marque de son empreinte cette espèce de «rondeau latent». En ce qui concerne la strophe

---

[165] A retenir aussi l'allitération *d — d* et les symétries du rythme anapestique: ◡◡⟋ ◡◡⟋.

[166] Evidemment, les rimes en *-ure* ne sont pas très nombreuses; c'est pourquoi un peu plus loin on trouve déjà des vers plus ou moins gauches comme par exemple III, 2: «Crédule espoir n'es-tu qu'une *imposture*?» Cf. aussi la note suivante.

finale, elle forme une curieuse antithèse avec la strophe précédente: aux vers élégiaques «Ah, *dis* au vent, *dis* à l'eau qui murmure, / En s'enfuyant, d'emporter ma douleur,» le poète oppose les paroles d'un pasteur qui dira un jour: «On trompa sa *droiture*. / Il fut *sensible*, et *mourut malheureux* . . .» Cette épitaphe laconique renferme le noyau d'une certaine critique sociale qu'on ne s'attendait guère à découvrir dans cette chanson sentimentale. D'une manière singulière, c'est l'idéal de *droiture*[167] qui constitue l'accord final de ces doux quintils.

14. Pour terminer nos analyses, voici quelques mots sur un texte généralement connu qui, à bien des égards, semble synthétiser toutes les variétés du style poétique du XVIIIe siècle. Il est question, comme nous l'avons déjà dit plus haut, du texte de la *Marseillaise* (1792) de Rouget de Lisle (1760—1836) qui, pour des raisons inconnues, ne figure presque jamais dans les anthologies poétiques de ce siècle. Passons donc en revue les 6 strophes authentiques de la *Marseillaise*,[168] en faisant quelques remarques sommaires sur le m é l a n g e   c o n s t a n t   des stylèmes les plus différents.

Strophe I — Aux vers 3—4 l'inversion, tout en étant une figure classique, est fonctionnellement bien motivée: elle sert à placer le mot *tyrannie* sous le coup de la rime: «Contre nous *de la tyrannie* / *L'étendard sanglant* est levé.» Au début du vers 6 le verbe *mugir* est rapporté aux soldats animés par une passion manifestement contre-révolutionnaire: «Entendez-vous dans les campagnes / *Mugir* ces féroces soldats?»[169] En ce qui concerne le refrain, on y remarque surtout, l'expression *sang impur* qui aura maints échos européens.[170]

Strophe II — Au premier vers le mot *horde* devient le pivot d'un groupement ternaire qui remplit presque deux octosyllabes

$$\text{Que veut cette } horde \left\{ \begin{array}{l} \text{d'esclaves} \\ \text{de traîtres} \\ \text{de rois couronnés?} \end{array} \right.$$

L'association *horde* — *roi* est des plus hardies; auparavant on entendait surtout par *hordes* certaines formations militaires plus ou moins barbares. Dans ce contexte tout ce qui dépend du terme de *horde* mérite notre attention: la «triade» *esclaves* — *traîtres* — *rois* n'est admissible que dans l'atmosphère créée par ce chant de guerre qui peut être considéré à juste titre comme un prélude aux poèmes politiques d'inspiration romantique d'Auguste Barbier. Néanmoins, le chantre le plus illustre de la Révolution ne reste point fidèle à ce style plein d'esprit novateur; un peu plus bas, les vers 3—4

[167] Pour l'emploi poétique de *droiture* v. aussi un autre texte de Ducis: «Un mortel généreux connaît mal l'imposture; / Aisément dans un autre il croit voir sa *droiture*» (traduction de *Macbeth*, L.).

[168] Dans certaines éditions (par exemple dans l'*Anthologie des Poètes lyriques français*, Paris s. d., préfacée par Charles Saratéa, pp. 198—200) on trouve encore une 7e strophe, intitulée *Couplet des Enfants*.

[169] A propos de cet emploi de *mugir* cf. un texte de Boileau: «Lorsqu'il entend de loin d'une gueule infernale / La chicane en fureur *mugir* dans la grand'salle» (L.).

[170] Nous pensons avant tout à l'expression lermontovienne черная кровь dans l'élégie Смерть поета (La mort du poète), écrite après le tragique duel de Pouchkine (1837).

témoigent encore de l'influence d'une sorte de «retenue classique»: «Pour qui ces ignobles *entraves*, / Ces *fers* dès longtemps préparés?» Non moins classique est la tournure qui termine ces octosyllabes: «C'est nous qu'on ose méditer / De rendre à l'antique esclavage!...». En tout cas, il est fort significatif que ce magnifique chant de la liberté contient une strophe encadrée, en guise d'antithèse, par les mots *esclaves* et *esclavage*.

Strophe III — Au début de la strophe il est curieux de voir que des «*cohortes*[171] *étrangères*» et des «*phalanges*[172] mercenaires» (vers 1, 3) étaient la *loi* même «dans nos foyers» français. La catachrèse, si vivement critiquée par certains auteurs,[173] caractérise aussi ce texte où la vivacité du chant de guerre se mêle souvent aux survivances du style de l'ode post-classique. C'est également de l'ode que vient la répétition emphatique de l'exclamation *quoi*!; grâce à ce procédé en un seul quatrain on observe une fusion indissoluble du «style exclamatif» et du «style interrogatif».[174] C'est le style, voire l'emphase traditionnelle de l'ode qui se manifestent aux vers 5—6 de cette strophe; au vers 6 c'est l'ordre des mots (S—C—V: «Nos fronts sous le joug se ploieraient») qui représente un trait plutôt archaïque de la syntaxe poétique.

Strophe IV — Conformément à la répétition de l'exclamation *quoi*! (str. III), c'est ici un verbe, l'impératif *tremblez*! (vers 1, 3) qui forme le noyau anaphorique d'un nouveau parallélisme. L'allitération «*T*remblez, *t*yrans!» est particulièrement réussie; après quelques vers un peu plus ternes l'inspiration du poète parvient à ranimer ce style pathétique dont même les rimes nouvelles sont parfois froides et peu expressives.[175] Dans la seconde moitié du huitain les occlusives expressives ne sont pas moins nombreuses (*«T*out est soldat...»; «S'ils *t*ombent...»; «La *t*erre...») et même les rimes comme par exemple *combattre* / *battre* ne font que renforcer ces accords fermement cadencés.

Strophe V — L'élan de l'inspiration lyrique n'exclut pas quelques sages conseils qui, au point de vue poétique, ont trouvé des formules assez heureuses («Guerriers magnanimes... / Épargnez ces tristes victimes / A regret s'armant contre vous»). Aux vers 5 et 6 l'anaphore se présente sous une forme peu commune: «*Mais* le despote sanguinaire, / *Mais* les complices de Bouillé...». La phrase reste en suspens: même aux vers suivants on ne trouve aucune phrase principale achevée: «Tous ces tigres qui sans pitié / Déchirent le sein de leur mère...» Malgré cette réticence (en tant que figure poétique), le sens de la phrase est parfaitement clair: pas de clémence pour ceux qui menacent de ruiner la patrie.

---

[171] L'emploi de ce terme antique est à ramener à une tendance générale du langage révolutionnaire: appliquer aux réformes et aux institutions modernes la terminologie de la république romaine. Cf. aussi chez Boileau: «Et bravant des sergents la timide *cohorte*...» (L.).

[172] Mot très peu employé dans le langage poétique; il est curieux de voir que le texte de la *Marseillaise* n'a jamais été dépouillé, paraît-il, par les lexicographes.

[173] Sur la fréquence de la catachrèse au XVIIIe siècle v. Le Hir, *op. cit.*, p. 142.

[174] Cf. les exemples cités plus haut, à propos de l'analyse d'une ode.

[175] Cf. *perfides* (projets) *parricides*. Il s'agit d'ailleurs de termes relativement rares dans le langage poétique antérieur. Cf. pourtant Corneille: «Ce *perfide* ennemi de la grandeur romaine» (L.). Pour *parricide* v. également quelques exemples cornéliens (ibid.).

Strophe VI. — Toute la strophe est dominée par une double invocation et par les impératifs symétriquement placés qui s'y rattachent:

Amour sacré de la Patrie,

                Conduis, soutiens nos bras vengeurs.

Liberté, liberté chérie,

            Combats avec tes défenseurs.

Le parallélisme implique d'importantes conséquences non seulement sur le plan de la syntaxe, mais aussi au point de vue sémantique: grâce à la personnification l'Amour de la patrie et la Liberté deviennent deux anges tutélaires de ces vengeurs qui, animés par les «mâles accents»[176] de ce chant, continuent à combattre aussi bien pour leur *gloire* que pour le *triomphe* de la liberté. Il est évident que toute la phraséologie de la strophe finale s'élève au niveau de la strophe initiale ce qui, malgré certaines inégalités que nous n'avons pas manqué de signaler, assure une haute valeur esthétique au texte de la *Marseillaise*, texte si étroitement lié à un moment décisif de l'histoire.

15. Peut-être n'est-il pas inutile de rappeler une remarque de Rivarol qui, à proprement parler, implique une défense catégorique du style conventionnel et d'un stock d'images formées par les grands auteurs. Selon Rivarol, «c'est le style métaphorique qui porte un germe de corruption; le style naturel ne peut être que vrai . . . les erreurs dans les figures ou dans les métaphores annoncent de la pauvreté dans l'esprit, et un amour de l'exagération, qui ne se corrige guère . . .»[177] Il serait curieux de dire si Rivarol ou d'autres autorités de la rhétorique et de la stylistique auraient approuvé les innovations lexicales et phraséologiques que nous venons de découvrir dans une bonne dizaine de texte.

En tout cas, un lecteur d'aujourd'hui ne saurait qu'approuver la plupart de ces innovations qui, malgré certaines inégalités indéniables, reflètent si bien l'ingéniosité stylistique de quelques poètes remarquables du siècle des Lumières. Malgré la critique conservatrice, ces auteurs étaient bien conscients des «glissements» dont nous avons parlé plus haut et qui préparaient la voie du romantisme triomphant au premier tiers du XIXe siècle.

[176] Pour cette expression L. ne nous fournit aucun autre exemple. R. cite de Ronsard: «Quel son *mâle* et hardi, quelle souche héroïque, / Et quel superbe vers entends-je ici sonner?»

[177] *Discours sur l'universalité de la langue française,* 1784, cité par Le Hir, *op. cit.,* p. 161.

JEAN-JACQUES ROUSSEAU EN ALLEMAGNE DANS LA DEUXIÈME MOITIÉ DU XVIIIᵉ SIÈCLE

par

JACQUES MOUNIER

Comment oser traiter un sujet aussi vaste et aussi diffus en quelques dizaines de pages? Ambition démesurée ou gageure, tous les soupçons portés à l'égard d'une telle entreprise sont justifiés et, d'avance, nous les acceptons. Deux voies se présentaient: affirmer notre point de vue en quelques formules lapidaires, de préférence paradoxales, ou bien exposer les multiples aspects de la question en les étayant par de copieuses références. Nous avons dû emprunter une troisième voie, périlleuse celle-là. Les écueils, en effet, sont légion. Signalons-les d'abord et ne les perdons pas de vue.

Rousseau, qui pourrait l'ignorer, n'a jamais foulé le sol allemand, n'a jamais connu le moindre vocable allemand, ne s'est jamais intéressé aux problèmes allemands. Les échanges épistolaires entre Rousseau et les Princes (ou les savants) allemands ou encore ses admirateurs bernois et zurichois se font en français et jamais il ne comblera le vœu d'Usteri et de ses vertueux amis qui l'avaient invité à Zurich.

Pourquoi citer des Suisses? Mais pourrions-nous négliger le pays natal de Rousseau et surtout cette Suisse alémannique, carrefour des lettres, pont entre les cultures française et allemande, lorsque nous étudions l'influence de Rousseau en Allemagne dans la deuxième moitié du XVIIIᵉ siècle? Cette Allemagne est une mosaïque d'Etats indépendants, certains minuscules, tous différents les uns des autres et l'accueil réservé aux écrits du Citoyen de Genève est lui aussi nécessairement différent suivant les structures politiques, sociales et économiques des Etats, suivant l'emprise de la religion, la sévérité de la censure ou le développement de l'esprit critique favorisé par l'obtention de libertés.

Accueil de Rousseau, influence de Rousseau. Mais accueil par qui? Influence sur qui? ou sur quoi? Que de nouveaux écueils!

Chacun entend encore les cris d'enthousiasme poussés par les jeunes Stürmer, adorateurs du «divin Jean-Jacques». Mais le compte rendu d'un journaliste anonyme, attentif et consciencieux, ou les réactions modérées d'un lecteur de bonne foi ne sont-ils pas plus significatifs que les exaltations de quelques zélateurs bruyants, à la gloire éphémère? Comment, cependant, apprécier la fraction du public allemand touchée par les écrits de Rousseau, lorsqu'on ignore le tirage des éditions et des traductions, le nombre des invendus et l'importance des prêts et que, pour l'époque, un périodique qui tire à 1000 exemplaires est estimé avoir du succès. Cette prétendue «fortune» de Rousseau risque bien de n'être en fait que celle que spécialistes des belles-lettres et écrivains en renom lui ont faite! Sont-ce des preuves suffisantes d'un quelconque «accueil» de Rousseau?

Quant à l'influence, sur qui s'exerce-t-elle? Assurément sur quelques esprits distingués, nous en avons des preuves irréfutables. Mais les idées, les sentiments, l'état d'esprit du public allemand, sont-ils modifiés — et comment, en quelle mesure — par la lecture et la pénétration des écrits de Rousseau? A qui accorder créance? Aux gazetiers, aux «grands» écrivains, aux francs-tireurs, à tous... ou alors à personne? Disons encore un mot de cette «influence» de Rousseau, car s'il y eut en son temps un «mythe Rousseau», il ne faudrait tout de même pas être aveugle au point de confondre obstinément Rousseau avec le «rousseauisme», cet agrégat informe et gigantesque de concepts et d'idées, d'émotions et de sentiments venus de tous bords et dont Rousseau, paraît-il, devrait reconnaître seul la paternité. A en croire certaines études, que leurs auteurs nomment sans rougir comparées, voire comparatistes, il semblerait que, sans Rousseau, l'humanité n'aurait jamais entendu ni les appels de la nature et de la sensibilité, ni la voix de la liberté et de la justice, ni l'amour de la vertu et du bien. Et d'autres, grâce au procédé facile de l'analogie, de retrouver Rousseau — ou ce qu'ils estiment être Rousseau! — partout où il leur plaît. Et similitudes d'abonder! Témoignage incontestable de respect et d'amour envers Jean-Jacques, mais dont la valeur scientifique est quasiment nulle. Ne soyons pas dupes, Rousseau n'a pas inventé tous les grands problèmes éternels de l'humanité! Mais son rôle ne serait-il pas suffisamment éminent, si nous pouvons dire de ses œuvres et de sa pensée qu'elles ont en quelque sorte servi de catalyseur, provoquant des réactions souvent déterminantes?

En 1750, Voltaire est à Berlin, admiré et fêté. Rousseau est encore inconnu. En 1751, le *Discours sur les sciences et sur les arts* paraît et, très rapidement, Rousseau connaît la gloire, surtout par les cris d'indignation qu'il provoque. Les milieux lettrés, la presse, le public, le Roi de Prusse et bien d'autres Princes croient au progrès de la raison, sur lequel ils fondent leur espoir d'une humanité meilleure et plus heureuse. Or, Rousseau ose s'insurger et sur quel ton! Lessing est le premier à réagir, en avril 1751.[1] Ravi par la rhétorique éloquente de Rousseau, il ne peut accepter les conclusions du premier *Discours*. La science et la moralité n'ont pas de rapports nécessaires et les arts sont en fait ce que les hommes veulent bien en faire. Quant au caractère efféminé des contemporains, n'est-ce pas un progrès sur la bestialité des temps passés? La critique, sans acrimonie, était pourtant radicale. Gottsched[2] sera moins indulgent: Rousseau parle et écrit en ignorant, car les sciences et les arts — l'histoire en est la preuve — n'ont jamais asservi l'homme; c'est au contraire grâce à leur progrès que nous ne vivons plus comme des bêtes stupides, mais avons gagné en politesse et en sociabilité. Gottsched traite de sophismes les affirmations erronées et injustifiées de Rousseau. Les autres comptes rendus et les autres jugements portés sur ce premier *Discours* sont eux aussi, dans l'ensemble, défavorables, qu'ils viennent de Leipzig, d'Erlangen ou de la plume de Haller dans les *Annonces de Göttingen*, même si ce dernier sait gré à Rousseau d'avoir au moins vitupéré contre l'incroyance que nombre de savants ont contribué à répandre. Haller est du reste le seul à tempérer ses critiques après la lecture du *Recueil de toutes les pièces qui ont été publiées à l'occasion du Discours de M. J. J. Rousseau* («esprit éclairé et fort savant, ami sérieux et diligent de la

[1] Compte rendu du *Premier Discours*, *Das Neueste aus dem Reiche des Witzes*, n⁰ 1, avril 1751.
[2] Gottsched, *Das Neueste aus der anmuthigen Gelehrsamkeit*, Band 1, pp. 469—486.

vertu, philanthrope» qui jamais n'a prêché le retour en arrière).[3] Les attaques de Gottsched redoubleront à la parution de chaque *Réponse* de Rousseau. La traduction du *Discours* par Tietz en 1752 passe inaperçue et ne modifie pas les positions.

Faut-il nous étonner de cet accueil? Certes pas. L'emprise de l'Aufklärung était forte et ses tenants ne pouvaient tolérer alors sa mise en cause. Tout reposant sur le progrès des sciences et sur la foi en la raison humaine, comment suivre les sophismes et les paradoxes néfastes de ce nouveau Diogène? Le public lui-même pouvait-il accepter celui qui semblait lui ôter tout espoir, ainsi que l'affirmaient, peut-être abusivement, journalistes et écrivains, défenseurs de l'Aufklärung en tête. Le ton de Gottsched et des partisans des Lumières triomphait.

L'accueil du *Discours sur l'inégalité* en 1755 sera sensiblement identique. Lessing, qui a seulement feuilleté cet ouvrage, écrit à Mendelssohn qu'il ne saisit pas la notion rousseauiste de «perfectibilité», mais son compte rendu en juillet 1755 loue le «hardi philosophe qui ne regarde aucun jugement tout fait et va droit vers la vérité». L'audace de Rousseau ne déplaît pas à Lessing, même si ses idées et ses assertions osées n'entraînent pas son adhésion. Il encourage son ami Mendelssohn à traduire ce second *Discours* (en 1756).[4] A Leipzig, à Erlangen, à Rostock et à Zurich, Rousseau reçoit le même accueil qu'à Berlin: on reconnaît ses talents littéraires, la force de son imagination et de son éloquence, mais on n'accepte pas ses idées, et sa conception de l'homme à l'état de nature, comprise à tort, on le devine, ne lui attire que mépris et ironie. Haller lui-même ne peut s'empêcher d'user envers Rousseau d'un langage voltairien. La fameuse lettre de Voltaire du 30 août 1755 donnait le ton: Rousseau, par esprit de contradiction, s'enfermait dans ses paradoxes, son état de nature était la négation du progrès de la raison, Rousseau devait être réfuté au nom de l'Humanité.

Rousseau avait conquis une gloire maudite. Personne n'avait été indifférent à ses deux *Discours*, mais qui l'avait vraiment bien lu et bien compris? Il aura de la peine à se défaire de l'étiquette d'homme de la nature qui «marche à quatre pattes» et pourtant, très curieusement, c'est à cette fausse image qu'il devra bientôt des élans d'enthousiasme!

Un revirement s'opère au profit de Rousseau lorsqu'il publie, en 1757, la *Lettre à d'Alembert*. Gottsched lui-même fait sa palinodie et accorde à l'auteur «la raison et l'amour de la vertu».[5] Haller applaudit aux attaques de Jean-Jacques contre les méfaits du théâtre et Bodmer s'enthousiasme pour les propos du vertueux censeur, défenseur de la morale et de la foi. Bodmer, séduit par Rousseau, moraliste et prédicateur, lui attirera de nombreux admirateurs parmi les jeunes écrivains, philosophes ou pasteurs suisses. Du côté de Lessing, les réticences sont plus grandes, les attaques de Rousseau contre le théâtre en général apparaissent comme exagérées et injustifiables. Les efforts de Lessing, sa réflexion sur le théâtre, ses buts son rôle, s'oppo-

---

[3] *Göttingische Anzeigen*, 26 février 1753, Band 1, p. 237 et 6 oct. 1753, Band 2, pp. 1090—96.
[4] Lettre de Lessing à Mendelssohn du 21 janvier 1756, *Briefe*, ed. P. Rilla, tome IX, p. 63. Compte rendu du 2ème *Discours* par Lessing, *Berlinische privilaegirte Zeitung*, 10 juillet 1755.
[5] *Das Neueste aus der anmuthigen Gelehrsamkeit*, janvier 1759, Band 9, p. 63—69.

sent manifestement à la position de Rousseau. C'était la réaction attendue d'un homme de théâtre, parmi d'autres, aux thèses d'un moraliste. La réfutation de l'esthéticien Sulzer ira dans le même sens.

1761: *La nouvelle Héloïse* paraît. Le sophiste et le censeur se transforment en romancier. Mais s'agit-il d'un roman d'amour? Le vertueux Rousseau se serait-il laissé séduire par les pièges de la passion ou du libertinage? Les réactions sont nombreuses et variées, mais il appert que le roman de Rousseau obtient en Allemagne, comme en France, un grand succès, ainsi que le notent Rousseau lui-même, Mendelssohn et d'autres. Un immense public, qui va des Grands à la petite bourgeoisie «éclairée» des villes et au milieu des pauvres pasteurs de province, dévore le long roman de Julie et de Saint-Preux. Les témoignages abondent, mais les avis et les positions sont loin d'être identiques, heureusement.

En schématisant quelque peu, disons que deux questions se posent aux lecteurs critiques: le talent de Rousseau et la valeur didactique de son roman. Ce second aspect attire du reste un intérêt quasi général, mais nous sommes déjà habitués à cette propension de la génération de Lessing et de Nicolai à tout juger au moyen de critères moraux rationnels, même le romanesque. Ajoutons pourtant que nombre de lecteurs, de lectrices surtout, ne jugent pas, mais sont enchantés et muets d'admiration, annonçant l'approche d'une nouvelle génération rousseauiste exaltée et peu critique, lasse du rationalisme.

Si l'on excepte l'hostilité, déjà déclarée de Gottsched, les qualités didactiques de *La nouvelle Héloïse* sont généralement reconnues et appréciées.[6] Gottsched approuve Bordes et sa *Prédiction*: Rousseau n'est ni un moraliste, ni même un philosophe, mais un hypocrite qui, sous le masque de la vertu, dissimule avec peine les passions et les vices. Son roman apparaît comme un ramassis d'obscénités honteuses et condamnables. Position extrême et unique, car les réactions de la presse allemande et suisse sont plutôt favorables: Rousseau a écrit un roman d'amour, il est vrai, mais «c'est ici l'amour comme il doit être» (Leipzig, 1761), l'amour de l'âme et non les passions ou les instincts terrestres. Et comment ne pas louer toutes ces lettres instructives et nombreuses sur les femmes, sur Paris, sur l'éducation des enfants, sur le suicide etc...? De Leipzig, de Zurich, de toutes parts, la critique fait l'éloge des longues dissertations morales et philosophiques. Haller, lui aussi, dans sa sévère *Revue*, salue la victoire de «la vertu sincère et fondée sur la religion» (1762), même si les premières parties du roman étaient scandaleuses.[7] L'enseignement religieux et moral plaît à Haller, quoique Rousseau soit inférieur à Richardson.[8] Sans doute le roman n'est-il pas parfait, mais les descriptions naturelles sont justes et vraies, Rousseau sait peindre et sentir la nature, malgré l'attrait qu'il éprouve pour le romanesque. Morale et nature, voilà ce qui entraîne l'adhésion générale et celle des Suisses allemands en particulier. Qu'il nous suffise de rappeler ici les deux lettres de 1761 de Julie Bondeli, défendant *La nouvelle Héloïse* avec perspicacité et justesse,

[6] *Das Neueste . . .*, nov. 1761, Band 11, pp. 860—69.
[7] Plusieurs comptes rendus élégieux de *La Nouvelle Héloïse* in *Neue Zeitungen von gelehrten Sachen*, 11 dec. 1760, 4 mai 1761, 3 mai 1762.
[8] Haller, *Göttingische Anzeigen*, 9 oct. 1762.

s'attirant les éloges de Rousseau, et les nombreuses marques d'admiration de Hess, de Bodmer, d'Usteri, de tant d'autres peu connus aujourd'hui, Bernois et Zurichois, fidèles lecteurs de Jean-Jacques.[9]

Mais *La nouvelle Héloïse* posait aussi des problèmes esthétiques et littéraires. L'accord, à ce propos, n'est pas général. Si Julie Bondeli devait soutenir le roman de Rousseau contre les clameurs «des fats et des petites maîtresses», selon ses propres termes, mais aussi contre les «esprits faux et les méchants» et même malheureusement contre certains hommes de mérite et d'esprit, il en était de même en Allemagne, où Hamann devait répondre vigoureusement aux critiques approfondies de Mendelssohn. L'analyse est impitoyable et aboutit à la condamnation du roman en tant que roman, car Mendelssohn aurait préféré que l'auteur «eût écrit des essais philosophiques». Il consacre plusieurs *Lettres* (en juin 1761), publiées dans une revue rationaliste berlinoise, à la critique de *La nouvelle Héloïse*. Indiquons les points principaux.

Comme Haller, Mendelssohn place Richardson avant Rousseau, en tant que romancier, bien sûr, car Rousseau est plus philosophe, mais «sa connaissance du cœur humain est plus spéculative que pragmatique, ses narrations inégales, son art du dialogue» insuffisant, ses situations mal choisies, son intrigue lâche, sans cesse entrecoupée «de longs sermons de morale». Les caractères des personnages, et même leur langage, ne sont pas mieux accueillis. Saint-Preux, un philosophe ? Bien plutôt un niais, un impuissant, un vélléitaire, qui parle de sa raison et agit comme un enfant et dont le prétendu langage de la passion n'est qu'outrance et «exclamations glacées». Julie ? Elle passe son temps à philosopher. Edouard ? Aucune originalité, un Anglais vertueux de convention. Wolmar seul est réussi. Ici seulement, Mendelssohn rejoint le jugement de Julie Bondeli.[10] Bref, le roman ne mérite pas le succès qu'il obtient, Rousseau a été incapable de réaliser un tout cohérent, ce n'est qu'une «chaîne d'anecdotes» sans lien interne. Toutefois la valeur philosophique de certaines lettres n'est pas mise en cause. Lessing approuvera Mendelssohn et, quelques années plus tard, dans sa *Dramaturgie de Hambourg*, il critiquera à son tour, citant bien souvent son ami, les caractères des héros de Rousseau, les faiblesses dramatiques, le manque de naturel et les outrances du langage.

Hamann devait réagir autrement. Il défend *La nouvelle Héloïse* qu'il place avant les romans de Richardson, grâce à une composition plus heureuse et une morale plus profonde. Sa correspondance révèle pourtant que le début du roman l'a agacé, mais il a fini par goûter l'ensemble.[11] Dans les *Idées chimériques* d'Abälardius Virbius, son porte-parole, il se moque ironiquement des prétentions de sagesse de Mendelssohn, défend contre lui Rousseau romancier, qui a su ne pas abuser du langage théâtral, mais a créé un dialogue vraiment romanesque qui est, pour Hamann, un pur chef-d'œuvre. Cette opinion lui attire une réponse très sèche de Nicolai: Saint-

---

[9] Julie Bondeli, lettres du 15 mars et du 30 avril 1761, in Sophie de La Roche, *Mein Schreibetisch*, Leipzig 1799, pp. 150—161.

[10] Voir les six *Lettres* de Mendelssohn du 4 au 25 juin 1761, in *Briefe, die neueste Literatur betreffend*, pp. 255—310.

[11] Hamann, *Chimärische Einfälle Abälarddi Virbii*, 1761, in *Kreuzzüge eines Philologen*.

Preux n'a pas le droit de siéger parmi les Sages, tout ce romanesque n'est qu'illusion et gallimatias. Nicolai était peu enclin à apprécier les éléments irrationnels, à l'inverse de Hamann, irréductible adversaire du rationalisme et de ses analyses desséchantes annonciateur du triomphe du sentiment sur la logique.

Mais Hamann n'est pas seul à accepter avec ferveur le roman dans son ensemble. Dans le pays de Gessner et de Haller, l'enthousiasme est débordant. Bodmer et ses amis goûtent les descriptions naturelles, l'amour simple et idyllique, les joies de la vie rustique loin de la corruption des villes, ils comprennent la voix du sentiment, ils se plongent avec délice, sans aucune réticence, dans ce mélange de sensibilité et de vertuomanie raisonneuse, de passion et de sagesse, de joies terrestres et de religiosité. Les critiques de Haller, limitées aux aspects souvent peu orthodoxes de la religion de Rousseau, ne nuisent pas à l'admiration enthousiaste des Suisses allemands. Quant à ceux pour qui l'orthodoxie ne pose pas ou peu de problèmes de conscience, comme Wieland et Sophie La Roche, sa cousine, ainsi que leurs amis, l'accueil de La *nouvelle Héloïse* est chez eux extrêmement favorable. Et il est indubitable que nombre de lecteurs et de lectrices ont dû dévorer avec passion ce roman qu'on s'arrachait, comme le note Mendelssohn dans son compte rendu. Nous ne connaissons pourtant qu'une traduction en allemand, celle de Gellius, du moins dans les années 60. Sans compter les *Extraits* de Formey, avide de profiter de la gloire de Rousseau pour vulgariser des leçons de sagesse et de morale et répandre les lumières. Mais quel fut son public ?

Des réactions peu nombreuses accueillent le *Contrat social*, lors de sa parution. On s'occupera de lui après 1789 ! En 1762, *La nouvelle Héloïse* et bientôt *Emile* attirent seuls l'attention, par leur nouveauté. Quelques comptes rendus de presse, entre autres celui de Haller, s'en prennent aux idées républicaines de Rousseau, mais surtout à la « religion civile ». A nouveau, on l'accuse d'être un sophiste, un homme à paradoxes. Son traducteur lui-même, Geiger, ne s'en prive pas dans une longue introduction. Et Formey ne manque pas d'abréger et d'expurger le *Contrat* de Rousseau afin de divulguer la pure doctrine politique de l'Aufklärung. Seuls les Suisses apprécient les conceptions républicaines de Rousseau, à moins que ce ne soit plutôt la rigueur du Citoyen de Genève. La courageuse campagne d'un Lavater contre les prévarications du bailli Grebel, la création de la revue politico-pédagogique *Der Erinnerer* et la teneur des articles qui y sont publiés, tout cela révèle l'influence de Rousseau. Mais il serait abusif de privilégier le *Contrat social*, car celui-ci ne peut être distingué, à l'époque, des autres œuvres de Rousseau.

Emile paraît. L'intérêt est vif dans un pays qui se passionne pour les problèmes d'éducation. Mais les réactions ne sont pas toujours favorables à cause des positions peu orthodoxes de Rousseau dans la *Profession de foi*. La religion fait passer la pédagogie au second plan. C'est ce qui transparaît dans la majorité des comptes rendus de la presse et en tête Haller dans ses *Göttingische Anzeigen* (juin 1763). Les conceptions pédagogiques de Rousseau sont traitées bien souvent, on s'en doute, de « chimériques » ou encore de « paradoxales », selon la terminologie bien connue ! Les adaptateurs, tels Feder ou Formey, fabricants d'Emiles nouveaux, chrétiens, utiles et autres reçoivent alors la palme refusée à Rousseau. Heureusement que d'autres lecteurs moins intolérants et plus perspicaces assurent à l'*Emile* la gloire et l'immortalité. N'en citons qu'un, mais de poids: Kant.[12] Ravi et éclairé par le génie de Rousseau, il en conservera quelques thèses essentielles comme le rôle du sentiment et l'impossibilité de faire dépendre la vertu et le bonheur des progrès de la raison. Rousseau lui permet d'échapper à l'optimisme facile de la tradition intellectualiste et rationaliste, de réintégrer la sensibilité dans la conception de l'homme. Premier pas qui compte dans la pensée kantienne. Les élèves du philosophe de Kœnigsberg, comme Herder ou Lenz, seront marqués par Rousseau, ce «Newton du monde moral», dès leur adolescence.

Faisant fi des réticences des gazetiers ou des rigoristes, le grand public, des «Grands» aux lecteurs plus modestes, apprécie l'*Emile*. Les exemples sont nombreux et connus, grâce aux correspondances de l'époque. Rousseau devient conseiller du Prince de Württemberg, la Princesse Galitzin élève ses enfants selon les principes de Rousseau, comme tant d'autres, les La Roche, les Tscharner, les Usteri et tous ceux qui n'ont pas laissé leur nom à la postérité, bons pères de famille, mères de famille attentives et enthousiastes. Les particuliers pratiqueront la doctrine de Rousseau avant même que ne soient créés des établissements spécialisés, favorables à la nouvelle pédagogie. Les conseils de Rousseau paraissaient utiles à tous les «amis des enfants» aux yeux desquels l'enseignement rationaliste devait être dépassé, si l'on voulait parvenir à l'épanouissement et à l'équilibre de l'enfant. Les critiques tatillonnes ne purent rien contre un élan de sympathie quasi général vers le sensible et compréhensif père d'Emile.

Cette sympathie s'exprime très clairement, et de toutes parts, lorsque Rousseau se voit condamné, chassé, poursuivi. Frédéric II lui-même ne propose-t-il pas à l'auteur du *Contrat social* un asile dans ses terres? Que de visites Jean-Jacques reçut-il alors! La rigueur des autorités françaises et suisses indigna. Et témoignages de sympathie d'affluer et admirateurs de solliciter du grand martyr une entrevue. Heureux les Usteri, les Tscharner, les Wegelin, les Lavater et jusqu'à cette étonnante Julie Bondeli qui purent voir et entendre l'extraordinaire Rousseau. Le malheur grandissait Jean-Jacques, mais la sympathie affectueuse ne risquait-elle pas d'aveugler tout sens critique? Pour certains de ses admirateurs, nous craignons bien que si.

Pourtant, dans l'ensemble, la génération de Lessing a su garder son sang-froid et juger Rousseau comme écrivain ou comme philosophe, avec des arguments. A l'exception peut-être de Gottsched, farouchement hostile, tous ont pesé le pour et le contre, même s'il allait de soi que l'accueil des thèses révolutionnaires de Rousseau devait être peu favorable parmi ceux qui mettaient leur confiance dans le savoir et la raison et refusaient de s'attaquer ouvertement à la foi traditionnelle. Les réactions des recenseurs étaient presque attendues. Celles du public sont différentes, dans la mesure où nous nous permettons de les apprécier! Elles sont certainement plus favorables, comme celles des milieux suisses allemands.

La nouvelle génération, celle de Goethe, ne discute plus; elle encense Rousseau, apôtre, selon les jeunes «génies», de la libération de l'homme (en tous domaines, bien sûr), héros incompris et persécuté, symbole du grand

---

[12] Voir les annotations de Kant sur les marges de son exemplaire des *Observations concernant le sentiment du Beau et du Sublime*, Werke, Berlin, tome XX.

homme brisé par une société mauvaise où règnent les préjugés et surtout l'intolérance.

N'ayons cependant crainte de poser quelques questions à ces zélateurs inconditionnels ! On se demande bien souvent, à les écouter, s'ils ont seulement lu les livres de Rousseau et s'ils les ont lus, est-ce entièrement et attentivement ? Sont-ils allés jusqu'au bout de *La nouvelle Héloïse* ? Connaissent-ils le rationaliste *Contrat social* ? Il semble que non. Leur enthousiasme va en général à certains grands thèmes qu'ils estiment provenir du seul Rousseau : retour à la nature, liberté du sentiment, révolte contre toute limitation. Thèmes rousseauistes, certes, mais que les Stürmer interprètent dans un sens souvent peu conforme à la pensée de Rousseau. Ainsi, pour lui, retour à la nature ne signifie pas déchaînement des instincts naturels, liberté du sentiment n'est pas synonyme d'exaltation ou de sensibilité débordante et la révolte contre les limitations ne conduit ni à l'anarchie, ni à la révolution. Les excentricités du jeune Goethe et de ses amis n'auraient certainement pas reçu l'assentiment de Rousseau, car les élèves appliquaient étrangement les prétendues leçons du Maître !

Ceci dit, il est indéniable que Rousseau a joué un rôle important dans la formation de cette nouvelle génération. Les exemples sont nombreux et bien connus. Nous serons brefs. Mais nous devons ajouter que, si ces bruyants Stürmer tiennent le devant de la scène, d'autres esprits plus pondérés et moins enthousiastes font contrepoids et se moquent ou s'indignent de cet accueil délirant, trop souvent injustifié, réservé à un Rousseau idéalisé et quasiment mythique.

Le ton des *Discours* plaît aux Stürmer, on s'en doute. Dégoût de la vie en société, retour à la nature, protestation contre la corruption, tout cela constitue leur «idéologie». Les drames du jeune Goethe et de Klinger développent inlassablement ces thèmes. Herder aussi voit dans le XVIIIᵉ siècle un siècle de déclin, malgré les progrès des sciences et des arts. Il croit toutefois au développement continu de l'histoire et ainsi ce siècle a-t-il sa place et son rôle. Si d'autres, comme Wieland, les Suisses allemands et même Haller, continuent à apprécier le goût de Rousseau pour la vie simple, vertueuse et tranquille, ils se refusent à suivre ceux qui condamnent l'ordre social, les valeurs consacrées et la culture comme les héros du jeune Klinger ou même le *Götz de Berlichingen*. Le *Diogène* de Wieland marque la limite qu'il ne faut pas dépasser et que les Stürmer transgressent. Même si le *Contrat social* ne semble pas être une lecture favorite de la jeune génération, certains leitmotive empruntés à Rousseau, mais amplifiés dans le sens de la révolte, réapparaissent dans les œuvres de l'époque, drames en particulier, à tel point que Wieland dans *Le miroir d'or* ou Haller dans *Fabius et Caton* estiment nécessaire de lutter contre la diffusion et l'éloge dangereux de ces idées subversives, républicaines, démocratiques, mais surtout anarchistes, prétendument inspirées par Rousseau. Comme si celui-ci était plus un anarchiste qu'un législateur.

Mais la faveur générale se porte avant tout sur *La nouvelle Héloïse*, ce «livre divin» (selon Jacobi), et sur l'*Emile*, le «meilleur livre écrit en français» (selon les termes de Lenz). Les œuvres, les correspondances, les témoignages divers, tout démontre incontestablement que ces deux chefs-d'œuvre de Rousseau ont conquis la nouvelle génération. Lecture de première main, lecture intégrale, lecture attentive, analyse sérieuse ? Non, sinon que très rarement ! L'enthousiasme naît de discussions passionnées dans des cercles d'amis, âmes sensibles, avides de justice, d'égalité, d'amour, mais générale- ment incapables de rigueur et d'esprit critique, cénacles de jeunes gens ardents comme Goethe, Lenz, Klinger, les frères Stolberg, les Jacobi, réunions de jeunes filles ou de jeunes femmes sentimentales comme Caroline Flachsland, fiancée de Herder, et ses amies, ou Sophie La Roche et sa fille, tant d'autres aujourd'hui oubliés, qu'il serait vain d'évoquer ici, car l'énumération serait trop longue. L'adoration de Rousseau est communicative, elle doit son origine et sa permanence à une parenté d'esprit indéniable, avivée et entre- tenue par un échauffement collectif des esprits. Nous retrouvons Héloïse dans les lettres de Goethe, de Wieland, de Jacobi, de Lenz et, jusque dans leurs œuvres, on a pu dégager des «influences» du roman de Rousseau, dans *Werther*, dans *Allwill*, dans *Woldemar*. Les allusions directes aux personnages sont même légion et certains ont affirmé que la paternité de tous les héros de ces drames et romans du Sturm-und-Drang revenait à Rousseau. N'allons pas si loin. Les analogies sont frappantes et multiples, sans aucun doute, mais aurait-on oublié le roman anglais ? Rousseau aurait-il donc inventé l'amour naturel et les délices de la passion, la vie simple et rustique, la douceur des épanchements, la sensibilité, la vertu ? Pourquoi pas le roma- nesque ! Et, de plus, *La nouvelle Héloïse* n'était-elle pas pour Rousseau l'illustration de ce que devait être une nouvelle société, fondée sur les liens sacrés du mariage, sur le respect de la famille et la croyance en Dieu ?

Les lecteurs de la génération de Goethe empruntaient ce qui leur était cher, quittes à altérer le sens de l'œuvre et de la pensée de Rousseau. L'ac- cueil qu'ils réservent à l'*Emile* révèle le même état d'esprit, mais le traité d'éducation entraîne des réalisations pratiques et collectives, preuves tan- gibles de l'influence de Rousseau et de l'intérêt qu'on porte à son plan péda- gogique. En général, cependant, c'est l'Evangile de la nature qui est le centre de cristallisation de tous les enthousiasmes. Mais, qu'est-ce que cet Evangile ? Malheureusement, c'est trop rarement celui que Rousseau conseillait de suivre, du moins ce ne sont bien souvent que des aspects secondaires ou défor- més de la pensée de Rousseau: bains froids, nudité, nourriture «naturelle», liberté laissée aux mouvements, aux inclinations, aux instincts, crainte et horreur de toute contrainte (physique, morale, intellectuelle), de toute discipline, bref plus d'abus et d'excentricités que de sages réformes ! Fallait-il pratiquer le naturisme, au sens le plus moderne du terme, pour se rapprocher de la nature ? Certains le pensèrent alors, le jeune Goethe lui-même ! Les voyages de Goethe, de Lavater, des frères Stolberg, de Jacobi et les excen- tricités qui les illustrèrent ne sont pas à rappeler ici. Ce n'est là qu'une cari- cature ridicule de Rousseau. Goethe ne manquera pas de le noter plus tard et de regretter ces comportements soi-disant dictés par l'admiration pour Rousseau. Tous ne sombraient pas dans l'outrance risible, heureusement Klinger, par exemple, que Goethe estime un «véritable enfant de la nature» se référera toute sa vie à l'*Emile* et à la pensée de Rousseau, même après avoir subi l'envoûtement de la philosophie kantienne. Son dernier roman, ou presque, *Histoire d'un Allemand des temps modernes* (1798), se termine sur l'invocation de Rousseau et ses *Considérations et pensées* (1801—1802) citent à tous propos l'auteur de l'*Emile*, du *Contrat social* et de *La nouvelle Héloïse*, unissant dans une semblable admiration les trois grands chefs- d'œuvre. Herder, pour sa part, saura toujours gré à Rousseau, malgré des erreurs et des exagérations, de lui avoir indiqué la voie qui doit conduire à une régénération de l'homme. Son enthousiasme pour l'*Emile* qu'il fait partager en 1771 à Caroline, sa fiancée, n'est pas un feu de paille. Et celui de Caroline, méritoire, car elle s'est efforcée de lire le texte en français, durera lui aussi.

Nous devrions citer encore Lenz et Sophie La Roche, et tant d'autres, mais la place nous manque. Rappelons au moins que l'*Emile* est certainement à l'origine de la création de plusieurs établissements d'enseignement, dont le but est d'appliquer concrètement les réformes préconisées par Rousseau, tel le célèbre Philanthropinum, réalisé grâce à l'appui du Prince de Dessau et que Basedow, puis Campe dirigeront. Salis, Bahrdt, Salzmann, Pfeffel, Pestalozzi, en Allemagne ou en Suisse, avec des fortunes diverses, créeront eux aussi des établissements similaires, d'inspiration rousseauiste. Et toute une abondante littérature pédagogique fleurira, soucieuse d'exposer, de commenter et d'illustrer — parfois aussi de discuter — les idées de l'auteur d'*Emile*.

Avec la génération du Sturm-und-Drang est né le «mythe Rousseau». Des lecteurs trop souvent dénués de sens critique ont dévoré les œuvres de Jean-Jacques, mais certaines œuvres seulement et, la plupart du temps, partiellement, sans aucun doute possible, car l'admiration qui est portée à Rousseau paraît contredire les conceptions des admirateurs eux-mêmes, preuve de leur ignorance, du moins de leur méconnaissance de Rousseau. Celui-ci, idéalisé, recréé au goût de la nouvelle génération, devient un porte-parole, voix sacrée de la Nature, héraut et prophète martyr. Les revendications qu'il est censé avoir exigées ne sont malheureusement pas toujours les siennes ! La «rousseaumanie» s'écarte de Rousseau et le déforme. Sa présence est toute-puissante, sa gloire immense, mais le connaît-on ? Les esprits pondérés, souvent réticents, de la génération précédente et, rapidement, des penseurs lucides comme Herder et Goethe, sauront indiquer la voie à suivre et éviter les outrances d'une admiration passionnée et aveugle.

1775: Goethe part pour Weimar. Le groupe des amis s'est déjà scindé. Le rousseauisme délirant des Lenz et autres a déjà agacé Herder et amusé Goethe. Quant à Rousseau, il ne produit plus, il se fait oublier, du moins il essaie, car les ragots colportés par les gazettes de France et d'Allemagne nuisent à la tranquillité du malheureux Jean-Jacques. Ne dit-on pas qu'il a lu ses Mémoires ? Et la curiosité de renaître et l'impatience d'augmenter, aiguisées par les journalistes de tous bords. Mais n'allons pas croire non plus que, d'un jour à l'autre, le culte rendu à l'idole a cessé. Il faudra attendre 1782, parution des six premiers livres des *Confessions*, pour assister à des retournements spectaculaires.

Après 1775 paraissent de nombreuses œuvres empreintes de thèmes rousseauistes, comme le *Waldbruder* de Lenz, récit autobiographique de ses malheurs à la cour de Weimar, dont le sous-titre révélateur précise: «un pendant aux souffrances du jeune Werther, où un jeune homme à l'amour malheureux se retire dans la solitude pour y vivre en disciple de Rousseau». Révélateur, en effet, car il indique clairement que Rousseau a été recréé au feu du génie de Goethe, mais est-ce encore Rousseau ? Jacobi traduit pour *Allwill* la préface rédigée par Rousseau pour *La nouvelle Héloïse*, ce «livre divin» avec lequel Dohm, par bonheur, a osé comparer *Woldemar*. Jacobi, l'égal du «plus grand génie qui ait jamais écrit en langue française» (selon ses termes), nous comprenons sa fierté! Romans rousseauistes, certes, comme *Stillings Jugend* de Jung-Stilling ou *Waldbruder* de Lenz, mais ces thèmes ont tant d'autres origines que Rousseau que parler de sa seule influence nous semble abusif et contestable. Nous formulerons les mêmes réserves à l'égard de la production dramatique de Klinger dont nous reconnaissons pourtant l'admiration qu'il porte à Rousseau. Le «divin Jean-Jacques» conserve donc les mêmes fidèles, les Klinger, Lenz, Jacobi, sans oublier les Suisses, Bodmer, Julie Bondeli et toujours Sophie La Roche dont les *Lettres de Rosalie* révèlent la force des préceptes de l'*Emile* et l'envoûtement d'*Héloïse*. Goethe, lors d'un voyage en Suisse en 1779, ne manquera pas d'aller verser des larmes à Meillerie, ému par le souvenir de Julie et de Saint-Preux, lui qui, peu de temps auparavant, dans le *Triomphe de la sensibilité* écrivait: «Et maintenant, voici la lie: 'La nouvelle Héloïse', 'Les souffrances de jeune Werther'...»

Avant la parution des *Confessions*, avant même la mort de Rousseau, la voix de la modération et l'esprit critique parviennent pourtant à se faire entendre. Rousseau est sans doute admirable, mais on peut discuter ses idées. C'est ce que fait Herder dans *Encore une philosophie de l'histoire* (1774) où il affirme sa foi dans le développement continu de l'humanité et dans l'action de la Providence. Les «maîtres» de la jeune génération rejoignent ainsi les esprits prudents comme Wieland ou comme Kant.

La mort de Rousseau, bientôt entourée de mystère, attire bien sûr l'attention générale. Moins d'un mois après, Johann Georg Jacobi, le frère de Fritz, fait paraître dans le *Mercure* de Wieland un éloge funèbre du bien-aimé philosophe, martyr de la vérité et apôtre de la vertu: «Je ne puis rien pour son ombre» — écrit Jacobi — «mais je peux avouer publiquement qu'il m'a, par ses écrits, rendu plus proche de la nature, qu'il a donné à mon cœur ses sentiments les plus purs, qu'il a élevé mon esprit et fait pressentir des cieux pleins d'amour.»[13] Hommage qui résume ce qu'avaient ressenti les admirateurs de Rousseau. Mais bientôt les anecdotes, parfois très fantaisistes, affluent dans la presse de langue allemande, qui traduit presque tout ce qui paraît dans la presse française: prétendues lettres de Rousseau, indignité de sa compagne, lectures en privé de ses Mémoires et aussi les doutes émis à l'égard de la mort naturelle du malheureux philosophe. Les témoignages précis des amis et des médecins, traduits et approuvés par Wieland dans son *Mercure*, auront beaucoup de peine à convaincre les esprits plus enclins à la fable et à la légende qu'à la stricte objectivité. Le suicide de Rousseau n'ajoutait-il pas encore à la figure du juste persécuté, acculé par les hommes méchants à la dernière extrémité? Les discussions, pour le moins oiseuses, devaient se poursuivre de longues années!

Cependant, ce qui aiguisait la plus grande curiosité, était la publication attendue des *Confessions* de Jean-Jacques. Les lecteurs allemands n'ignoraient pas leur existence et le climat très «rousseauiste» qui régnait encore en Allemagne vers les années 80 était propice à exacerber l'impatience de tous. On se rabattait en attendant sur les compilations, on lisait les *Souvenirs* de Sturz qui, grâce à des séjours en France et en Angleterre, avait pu rencontrer, affirmait-il, des amis et des relations de Rousseau; on pouvait chercher pâture dans les *Fragments* du jeune Girtanner qui apparaissent plus comme une apologie qu'une biographie de Rousseau, «l'un des plus grands hommes

---

[13] Jacobi, in *Der Teutsche Merkur*, septembre 1778, Band 23.

que notre siècle a produits», et certainement des plus malheureux![14] N'oublions pas non plus que les *Dialogues* paraissent dès 1780. Hamann les dévore et les préférera même — réaction unique — aux *Confessions*. Jacobi s'afflige et la presse, dans son ensemble, accueille froidement cette œuvre autobiographique de «Rousseau, juge de Jean-Jacques», qui révèle chez l'auteur un pitoyable état pathologique, mélange d'orgueil et de mythomanie. Que devaient nous apprendre les Mémoires?

La curiosité grandissante, toutefois, allait trouver un nouvel aliment: la brève anecdote du «ruban volé» qui devint rapidement une véritable affaire dans les gazettes allemandes. Becker publie ce récit en janvier 1780 dans les *Ephemeriden der Menschheit*, périodique dirigé par Iselin. Les réactions sont immédiates. Les plus significatives sont celles de Wieland qui s'efforce, dans son *Mercure*, de justifier la conduite apparemment injustifiable de Jean-Jacques en rappelant les traits essentiels de son caractère.[15] Il ne faut pas accuser cet «homme libre, bon et vrai», ce «cœur princier», ce «héros de notre siècle» en alléguant l'innocence et la pureté (prétendues!) de Marion. Rousseau était un martyr. Iselin lui aussi approuva Wieland qui s'empressa de renchérir de plus belle et sur le champ, lui qui, pourtant, souvenons-nous en, s'était gaussé en son temps de Jean-Jacques et de son retour à la nature. Quant à Becker, irrité des attaques portées contre lui et des doutes émis à l'égard de son honnêteté de traducteur, il ne manque pas de se justifier en dévoilant le sérieux de ses sources: la lecture des «*Confessions*», ô combien attendues, grâce à la bienveillance du Genevois Moultou. Heureux élu qu'on dut envier, mais qui annonçait au moins aux lecteurs allemands impatients qu'il ne fallait pas désespérer, car les Mémoires de Rousseau existaient, sans aucun doute possible. La voix discordante d'un Wekhrlin, réputé par son ton polémique, son admiration pour l'Aufklärung et l'Encyclopédie, son attitude moqueuse et critique à l'égard d'un Jean-Jacques idéalisé, ne troubla pas les admirateurs qui ne répondirent même pas à ses féroces accusations. Et qu'on n'aille pas insinuer que Rousseau aurait abandonné ses enfants! Campe, à l'instar d'autres collègues de la presse allemande, préfère conseiller un prudent silence; ou se laisser bercer par la douce musique de Rousseau, ses *Consolations des Misères de ma vie* qui enchantent un nombreux public, qui compte Goethe, Herder et les Cours de Gotha et de Saxe-Weimar.

Bref, à la veille de la parution des six premiers livres des *Confessions*, Rousseau est toujours admiré et il a déjà conquis un nouveau public, puisque des jeunes gens comme Schiller ou Jean-Paul Richter (dont le choix délibéré du double prénom à résonances rousseauistes est assez révélateur) se plongent dans les écrits de Rousseau ou s'intéressent à son destin. En quatorze strophes, Schiller compatit aux malheurs injustes que le philosophe, prophète et martyr, dut endurer et son poème se termine par ces mots remplis d'admiration et d'affectueuse sympathie:

«Tu n'étais pas fait pour ce monde —
Pour lui, tu étais trop brave, trop grand».[16]

[14] Christopher Girtanner, *Fragmente über J.J. Rousseaus Leben, Character und Schriften*, Göttingisches Magazin der Wissenschaften und Literatur, 1781, Band II, 1, pp. 89—146, Band II, 2, pp. 259—293.
[15] Pour les nombreuses réactions de Wieland, voir A. Fuchs, *Les apports français dans l'œuvre de Wieland, 1772—1789*, Paris 1934.
[16] Poème *Rousseau* de Schiller, *Anthologie pour l'année 1782*, 14 strophes.

Au printemps 1782: les six premiers livres des *Confessions* (suivies des «*Rêveries*») paraissent enfin, à Genève. Les traductions en allemand ne tardent pas. Quant aux réactions, elles sont nombreuses et variées, on le devine aisément. Disons que le ton est, dans l'ensemble, élogieux, surtout parmi les écrivains; les journalistes ayant professionnellement une attitude plus critique. Goethe est d'emblée ravi par les quelques pages qu'il vient de lire aussitôt, dès le 9 mai. «Ce sont comme des étoiles éclatantes . . . Quel cadeau pour l'humanité qu'un homme aussi noble».[17] Il ajoutera plus tard: «Qu'il est merveilleux d'avoir la révélation de l'âme d'un disparu et d'en connaître sincèrement les profondeurs intimes.» Jugement significatif et compréhensif: Goethe était conquis par la courageuse entreprise de Rousseau, par ce récit transparent, par cette sincérité totale; il acceptait les *Confessions* comme un tout, peu soucieux des quelques «historiettes grivoises» qui attireront les critiques des grincheux ou des vertuomanes. L'enthousiasme de Goethe était communicatif, car les éloges à l'égard des *Confessions* ne tarissent pas à Weimar, ni même à Gotha. Pourtant Wieland se tait, à notre étonnement. Aurait-il été déçu ou gêné, trompé peut-être dans son attente et sa sympathie? Il se peut. Herder, également, se tient sur la réserve, mal à l'aise devant les révélations exhibitionnistes de Rousseau. «Comme tu es tombé du ciel, Lucifer!» — écrit-il à Hamann et il suppose que le grand Kant aussi sera stupéfait. Hamann n'a pas les mêmes scrupules que Herder et il se délecte à la lecture des aveux de Jean-Jacques, toujours avide d'en apprendre davantage. Quant au philosophe de Kœnigsberg, Hamann nous dit avec humour «qu'il travaille sans doute à sa propre confession auriculaire ou à la confection de la Raison pure» et nous pouvons supposer que sa promenade régulière n'a pas été troublée par la lecture absorbante des Mémoires osés de Rousseau! Mais Hamann demeure bien l'un des plus fidèles admirateurs de Jean-Jacques, car il loue les *Dialogues* plus encore que les *Confessions* et il saisit, avec Herder, toute l'importance de l'*Essai sur l'origine des langues*, paru également en 1782.[18] Jacobi, enthousiaste lecteur de *La nouvelle Héloïse*, est littéralement abattu par les révélations des *Confessions*. «Ce livre m'a fait étonnamment souffrir et je donnerais beaucoup pour pouvoir l'oublier. Rousseau était certainement déjà à demi-fou lorsqu'il l'écrivit».[19] Cette explication plausible permettait d'excuser en partie Jean-Jacques qu'il avait tant aimé et tant vénéré. Comme Herder, n'aurait-il pas préféré conserver de Rousseau une image idéalisée, sinon mythique, celle que tous deux, avec tant d'autres, ils se faisaient du «divin Jean-Jacques» dans les années 60? Cuisante était la réalité, atroce la désillusion.

Les journalistes ne s'embarrassaient pas de tels scrupules, ni de tels remords. Une gazette de Halle, par exemple, estimait que cette «véritable histoire d'aventurier» guérirait au moins les admirateurs trop ardents de leur zèle et montrerait sous son vrai visage, méprisable certes, le célèbre Citoyen de Genève. Livre nuisible, aussi bien à la réputation de son auteur qu'à ses lecteurs. La déception n'était pourtant pas souvent aussi amère, mais les *Confessions* tant attendues n'apportaient pas ce qu'on avait espéré. Rousseau dépeignait sa jeunesse fougueuse et libertaire, s'arrêtant là où

---

[17] *Goethes Briefe*, Böhlau, Weimar, tome V, p. 323. et tome VI, p. 324.
[18] Voir *Hamanns Briefwechsel*, ed. A. Hankel, Wiesbaden, tome IV, pp. 404 et 413.
[19] *Jacobis auserlesener Briefwechsel*, Leipzig 1827, tome 1, p. 356.

il aurait été intéressant de le mieux connaître, comme écrivain et comme philosophe. Ceci dit, tous les recenseurs, ou presque, vantent la richesse des notations psychologiques et la justesse des remarques morales, l'intérêt passionnant des récits de rêves, l'approfondissement de la connaissance du moi secret, en un mot la sincérité. Cette courageuse et absolue franchise permet finalement à la critique de tenir pour secondaires les détails choquants des *Confessions* dont personne n'ose d'autre part contester les grandes qualités littéraires. Malheureusement, elles étaient encore incomplètes . . .

Mais, en 1782, paraît également l'*Essai sur les règnes de Claude et de Néron*, nouvelle mouture de Diderot où redoublent les attaques perfides contre le défunt Jean-Jacques. A la grande indignation des amis de celui-ci et à la joie des défenseurs de celui-là! On ne manque pas de rapprocher les *Confessions* de l'*Essai*. Un plumitif inconnu, Hanker (Epheu est son pseudonyme), traduit Diderot pour mieux le ravaler et défendre Rousseau, auquel il attribue toutes les qualités et toutes les vertus, un être irréprochable et à part. Nous ignorons quel fut le succès de ce livre; sans doute, très mince. Auguste de Gotha lui-même vient au secours de Rousseau, en termes moins haineux et plus modérés, il est vrai: Diderot a déformé la pensée de son ancien ami, les reproches qu'il formule sont injustifiés et l'auteur des *Bijoux indiscrets* n'a pas de leçons de morale et de vertu à donner au père de Julie et de Saint-Preux! Le prince espère que les lecteurs redresseront d'eux-mêmes le jugement partial de Diderot. Même si Rousseau n'est pas irréprochable, il a droit à notre admiration: «Destiné à un siècle meilleur, il portait en lui, en naissant, les vertus et les défauts des temps antiques.» Rousseau offrait ainsi les caractères éternels et respectables d'une belle âme antique. Mais notons que cette défense est publiée dans le *Journal de Tiefurt*,[20] périodique princier tiré à très peu d'exemplaires, pour distraire les Cours de Gotha et de Weimar. La portée est extrêmement limitée, ne soyons pas dupes.

Ainsi, malgré des réserves limitées, émanant d'une minorité, quelques réticences de la presse et la déception de Herder ou de Jacobi (et chez eux la consternation est empreinte de pitié et non de sarcasmes), malgré les regrets de certains qui attendaient plus de scandales, plus encore d'aveux et de révélations à sensation, Rousseau n'avait pas souffert de la publication des six premiers livres de ses *Confessions*. Son image n'en avait pas été ternie. Le culte avait à nouveau été rendu à l'idole et l'encens avait brûlé sur l'autel de Jean-Jacques. Les iconoclastes s'étaient tenus à distance et personne n'avait dangereusement attenté au «mythe». La victoire semblait toujours appartenir aux zélateurs de Rousseau.

Et pourtant, en 1784, Ludwig Wekhrlin repart en guerre contre la légende d'un «divin Jean-Jacques», «idole de son siècle» dont il faut reconnaître l'aveuglement. «Je sais qu'il est encore trop tôt pour renverser son piédestal», note le directeur du *Monstre gris*, mais «il est permis pour le moins de douter de la vertu de ce saint», car les témoignages d'une «foule d'hommes respectables et célèbres», et même des admirateurs de Rousseau, «avouent qu'il était plus fou que méchant».[21] Le culte aveugle et intolérant doit être remis en cause, et lui seul, car les qualités littéraires de Rousseau sont

[20] August von Gotha, in *Journal von Tiefurt* publié au tome VII des *Schriften der Goethe Gesellschaft*, Weimar 1893.
[21] *Das graue Ungeheuer*, 1784, Band III, n° 7, pp. 28—54.

incontestables. Ecrivain doué, éloquent, instructif même, Rousseau, pour Wekhrlin, était indigne du nom d'homme.

Cette note discordante semble ne pas avoir eu d'écho. Etait-ce mépris, sécurité d'une majorité solidement assise, ou prudence. Peut-être attendait-on aussi la publication de la «suite» des *Confessions*? L'affaire n'est donc pas réglée, les six premiers livres n'ont pas calmé l'appétit, on espère encore d'autres révélations. Aussi constatons-nous sans étonnement que tout ce qui touche à l'œuvre et surtout à la personne de Rousseau attire curiosité et intérêt. Le monde des lecteurs allemands demeure vigilant et ne néglige rien.

Laissons pour l'instant de côté les réactions suscitées par de nouvelles traductions ou de nouvelles éditions de *La nouvelle Héloïse* et de l'*Emile*, tâchons de nous en tenir au domaine biographique. L'accueil réservé aux *Mémoires de Madame de Warens*, aux *Mémoires* de Marmontel ou à *La vie de Jean-Jacques Rousseau* de Barruel-Beauvert est des plus froids ! Allégations fausses et présomptueuses, calomnies haineuses, mensonges et hypocrisies, voilà ce que sont ces *Mémoires* pour les journalistes indignés. Le livre de Barruel n'est qu'une compilation incohérente. Mieux vaut relire les premiers livres des *Confessions* ou aller en pèlerinage à Ermenonville. Ce que ne manquent pas de faire maints admirateurs comme Sophie La Roche, le jeune Humboldt et le pédagogue Joachim Campe. L'enthousiasme de celui-ci est proche du délire ! Une *Lettre de Paris* de 70 pages est consacrée à cette pieuse visite à Ermenonville. Campe est envoûté. Il a heureusement le bonheur de pouvoir rapporter dans sa bonne ville de Brunschwig une «relique de son saint» (selon ses propres termes !), une tabatière du «divin Jean-Jacques ».[22]

Le succès des six premiers livres des *Confessions* était assuré. Il était même confirmé par l'intérêt de nouveaux lecteurs comme Schiller qui cite souvent Rousseau dans sa correspondance et surtout le tout jeune Hoffmann, attiré par les souvenirs du petit musicien Rousseau. Mais le parti des adversaires ne se tient pas pour battu et les anecdotes relatées par la presse française servent souvent de matériaux aux accusateurs de Rousseau. A titre d'exemple, signalons l'article qui paraît dans le *Monstre gris*, déjà cité, sous la plume d'un rédacteur anonyme, en 1786. Après avoir ironisé sur les prétendues persécutions endurées par Rousseau, après avoir mis en lumière les contradictions qui caractérisent ses diverses attitudes, et son exhibitionnisme constant, le journaliste en vient aux *Confessions*, «monument de cynisme et d'immoralité», qui révèle combien basse et combien hypocrite fut la vengeance posthume de Rousseau.[23]

Les *Lettres sur les ouvrages et le caractère de J. J. Rousseau* de Madame de Staël ne passent pas inaperçues. Elles sont très rapidement traduites en Allemagne, ou imitées et font l'objet de nombreux commentaires dans la presse de langue allemande. Elles fournissent évidemment des arguments de poids aux admirateurs de Jean-Jacques qui s'efforcent de conserver l'image légendaire d'un Rousseau génial et éminemment vertueux. Des périodiques aussi différents que la *Neue Bibliothek der schönen Wissen-*

[22] Joachim Heinrich Campe, *Briefe aus Paris*, Braunschweigisches Journal, février 1790, pp. 143—211.
[23] *Das graue Ungeheuer*, 1786, Band VIII, n° 23, pp. 190—209.

schaften et le *Philosophisches Magazin* analysent avec compréhension et amour le caractère de Rousseau et tentent de justifier ses actions par l'extrême sensibilité, quasi maladive, du malheureux Jean-Jacques, être fragile, aisément blessé par la froide ironie, acculé au repli sur lui-même et accusé à tort d'orgueil, de méfiance et de misanthropie. Puisse la postérité reconnaître enfin le génie de Rousseau ! Restons-en là. Notons pourtant que le nombre et surtout la longueur des articles dithyrambiques prouvent que le culte du «divin Jean-Jacques» avait toujours des adeptes et que les lecteurs allemands ne semblaient pas se lasser de tels éloges. La «suite» des *Confessions* était attendue avec impatience.

Les livres VII à XII paraissent à la fin de 1789. «Nous n'en dirons pas plus» — estime une gazette de Gotha, en signalant à ses lecteurs cette publication[24] — «car la curiosité, qui trouvera là une abondante nourriture, jettera infailliblement ces Confessions entre les mains de tous les amis de la littérature.» Les réactions sont nombreuses. Certaines sont prévues, d'autres surprenantes, certaines lapidaires, d'autres riches; mais, dans l'ensemble, l'accueil est moins chaleureux que celui qui fut réservé aux premiers livres. Pourquoi cette évolution ? Avançons au moins cette hypothèse: rapidement, le nom de Rousseau est mêlé à celui des Révolutionnaires français, et les jugements «littéraires» — quelle que soit la prétention de leurs auteurs à l'impartialité — subissent le contrecoup des réactions politiques. Les positions nouvelles sont parfois reconnues, mais souvent, elles sont inconscientes.

On ne s'étonnera pas du dégoût de Fritz Jacobi, déjà très déçu par les six premiers livres. Cette fois, la mesure est pleine, Rousseau a définitivement perdu l'un de ses plus chauds admirateurs d'autrefois. Mais la fidélité de Klinger, toujours irréductible, se manifeste à nouveau; il est conquis par la sincérité de Jean-Jacques qui n'a pas reculé devant les plus pénibles aveux, descendant, avec l'audace insensée que l'on sait, jusque dans le tréfonds de son cœur. L'admiration de Fichte est elle aussi confirmée, les *Confessions* sont souvent citées et Rousseau fait partie de ses auteurs favoris. Même si les idées politiques et pédagogiques l'emportent sans aucun doute sur les écrits autobiographiques, Fichte admire l'homme et le plaint dans ses malheurs. Les persécutions rapprocheront bientôt les destins de ces deux philosophes malheureux. Herder, dans les *Lettres* fictives adressées à J. G. Müller, étudie les problèmes posés par le genre autobiographique et, à l'occasion, révise ses jugements sur Rousseau. Malade et insatisfait, il est en partie excusable, excepté de son égoïsme, et il fut certainement meilleur qu'il ne put se dépeindre lui-même. «Comme vainqueur de soi, nous devons lui décerner la palme», conclut Herder.[25] L'audace des *Confessions* s'estompe sans doute pour lui devant d'autres audaces qui, elles, remettent brutalement en cause l'Ordre et maintes valeurs consacrées. Ce qui explique peut-être aussi le silence de tant d'autres.

Le sort de Rousseau attire un sentiment de compassion à peu près général et si certains reprochent aux amis trop enthousiastes un aveuglement injustifiable et condamnable, on s'afflige des persécutions de Rousseau, même si celui-ci les a exagérées dans ses Mémoires. La sincérité rachète la honte des aveux. Mais surtout personne ne conteste l'immense intérêt des derniers

[24] *Gothaische gelehrte Zeitungen*, 28 novembre 1789.
[25] *Herders Sämtliche Werke*, Berlin, tome XVIII, pp. 359—376.

livres pour la connaissance de l'homme. Bref, il faut lire ces *Confessions*, à moins que l'on ne soit trop jeune ou que l'on fasse partie du «beau sexe», selon les conseils de plusieurs recenseurs !

L'accueil n'était donc pas défavorable. Mais la réputation de Rousseau allait bientôt subir de nouvelles attaques, particulièrement dans la très rationaliste *Berlinische Monatsschrift*, en été 1790, dans un très long article rédigé par un homme des Lumières, admirateur des Encyclopédistes, le Conseiller juridique von Ramdohr.[26] Un autre compte rendu, presque aussi long, paraîtra en 1792 dans la grande Revue d'Iéna, l'*Allgemeine Literatur-Zeitung*, d'un auteur anonyme, dont les prises de position à l'égard de Rousseau rejoignent celles de Ramdohr. Essayons de les résumer. Selon Ramdohr, on comprend plus facilement Rousseau si l'on sait distinguer son «moi réel» de son «moi idéalisé». Or, Rousseau, poussé par son imagination excessive, sacrifie constamment son moi réel au profit d'une image embellie et idéalisée. C'est ainsi qu'il se voudra martyr de la vertu et de la vérité et qu'il voudra vivre ce que les Encyclopédistes se bornaient à prêcher. Ambition démesurée, cause de toutes ses erreurs, mais aussi de tous ses malheurs. Le vrai Rousseau, celui que Ramdohr estime, n'apparaît que lorsqu'il ne se laisse pas prendre aux pièges de l'amour-propre, qu'il ne recherche plus l'admiration des autres, lorsqu'il écrit par exemple *La nouvelle Héloïse*. «Je distingue en Rousseau» — conclut très nettement Ramdohr — «l'homme qu'il fut réellement de celui que ses sectateurs veulent faire apparaître. Dans le premier cas, il a droit à ma pitié, à mon affection, à mon admiration», mais il refuse un Rousseau mythique, ce prétendu «exemple de vertu, de vérité et d'indépendance», qui s'arroge le titre usurpé de «meilleur des hommes» et qui pose au «héros moral». Mais Ramdohr avouait son admiration pour les talents de l'écrivain incomparable. Qu'aurait pensé Rousseau de cette dissociation ?

La longue dissertation de Ramdohr eut du succès. On la cite, on l'approuve, on s'en inspire, on durcit aussi ses affirmations. C'est ainsi que Rehberg, dans un ouvrage sur l'éducation dirigé contre l'auteur d'*Emile*, ou qu'un rédacteur anonyme de l'*Allgemeine Literatur-Zeitung* s'accordent pour déclarer que les *Confessions* sont un livre extrêmement dangereux, car il séduit et enchante, mais il faut se garder de cet envoûtement insidieux, il faut oser «se révolter contre la divinisation d'un être aussi mauvais», «arracher le voile de l'idole», bref, ne pas hésiter à condamner les *Confessions* qui représentent un véritable danger pour la moralité. Ces jugements datent de 1792; l'auteur des *Confessions* est surtout le «père de la Révolution», le chimérique Jean-Jacques apparaît comme un terroriste sanguinaire. L'accueil des derniers livres des *Confessions* reflète les positions politiques et les angoisses, le débat dépasse les préoccupations littéraires. Pendant plusieurs années, le nom de Rousseau évoque la Révolution. L'heure du *Contrat social* a sonné.

Mais revenons quelques années en arrière pour rappeler la curiosité toujours vive que provoquent de nouvelles traductions et de nouvelles éditions des grandes œuvres de Rousseau durant la période qui voit paraître les *Confessions*. D'une manière générale, la presse approuve Cramer et les «Réviseurs», car «les œuvres de Rousseau, plus que celles de tout autre écrivain, méritaient une nouvelle interprétation» (*Allgemeine Literatur-Zeitung*, 1er Octobre 1789), mais la réussite n'est pas toujours jugée complète

---

[26] *Berlinische Monatsschrift*, juillet-août 1790, pp. 50—85 et 148—183.

et les annotations ne reçoivent pas l'approbation de tous, surtout lorsqu'elles surchargent un «chef-d'œuvre de la représentation» tel que *La nouvelle Héloïse*.[27] Les remarques des «Réviseurs», spécialistes des questions pédagogiques comme Campe, Trapp, Stuve, Ehlers ou Reisewitz, offrent «un résumé de ce qu'on peut dire pour et contre Rousseau» (*Göttingische Anzeigen*, 31 décembre 1789), elles sont accueillies avec respect. Faut-il dire que ce sont plus de 2300 pages consacrées à la traduction commentée de l'*Emile*? Qu'ajouter après cela? Les chiffres parlent d'eux-mêmes et nous sommes obligés de reconnaître, avec ce journaliste anonyme de l'*Allgemeine Deutsche Bibliothek* que «le grand mérite de Rousseau est d'avoir appris aux penseurs à penser sur l'éducation»; pour le moins à polémiquer, car l'*Emile* sert toujours de référence à toute discussion pédagogique, Bible pour les uns, monument d'erreurs pour les autres. La place nous manque pour indiquer ici, même succinctement, les réactions diverses des «Réviseurs», de Rehberg, de Fichte et de tant d'autres à la lecture ou à la relecture de l'*Emile*. Nous pouvons affirmer que Rousseau alimente encore bon nombre de débats.

Les années 90 voient le succès du *Contrat social*, qui va servir la cause des défenseurs de la liberté et subir les attaques des partisans de l'ordre établi. Deux clans, deux idéologies, deux conceptions de la société et de l'homme s'affrontent. Pour les uns, comme Rehberg, Möser ou Eberhard, Rousseau est un homme dangereux qui n'aurait pas hésité à user de la violence pour contraindre les hommes à se conformer à ses principes abstraits. Et de citer à l'appui le comportement des Jacobins! Pour les autres, comme Fichte particulièrement, et plus tard Hölderlin, le «contrat» est un acte de la liberté de l'homme, l'affirmation de la loi morale de l'homme, il est donc conforme à «l'état naturel». Positions évidemment inconciliables. L'exil de Fichte et la «folie» de Hölderlin, courageux admirateurs du Citoyen de Genève, montrent sans doute que la violence, l'intolérance et le dogmatisme n'étaient pas imputables au seul Rousseau. Oser défendre les thèses du *Contrat social*, puis bientôt seulement prononcer le nom de Rousseau apparut comme une audace insensée, rarement tolérée par la censure, réprimée par la Justice établie, soucieuse d'étouffer les revendications égalitaristes ou libertaires. Rousseau, à la fin du XVIIIᵉ siècle, provoque en Allemagne un effroi quasi général, du moins chez ceux qui redoutent le pouvoir démocratique et qui, seuls, peuvent s'exprimer sans ennuis. Faudra-t-il s'étonner de l'hostilité de la nouvelle génération, celle des frères Schlegel? Après 1793, les admirateurs de Rousseau seront fort rares.

Mais il est temps de conclure. Une étude de l'influence des conceptions politiques, constitutionnelles et économiques de Rousseau en Allemagne à la fin du siècle ou celle de la fortune de Jean-Jacques dans la génération des Schlegel nous conduiraient trop loin, hors des limites que nous nous sommes fixées. La période survolée est assez vaste et assez riche! Nous avons pu constater une courbe ascendante de la fortune et de l'influence de Rousseau, suivie d'un brusque déclin ou plutôt d'un silence souvent prudent. L'attitude de l'*Aufklärung* est, à quelques exceptions près, essentiellement critique. Sa foi dans les progrès de la raison l'oppose à l'auteur des *Discours*, mais elle approuve le censeur et le moraliste, le philosophe et l'homme de

---

[27] *Allgemeine Literatur-Zeitung*, nᵒ 67, 10 mars 1792, pp. 529—536 et nᵒ 68, 12 mars 1792, pp. 537—544.

bien qui défend la vérité et la vertu. Le romancier est moins bien accueilli, le pédagogue déçoit, le «Vicaire» dérange. Rousseau obtient cependant un succès plus grand en Suisse alémannique. Avec l'explosion du Sturm-und-Drang, l'esprit critique est débordé, un véritable culte est instauré. Rousseau n'est plus discuté, son œuvre n'est plus analysé. On adore, on loue, on encense. Mais connaît-on bien l'homme? Lit-on attentivement et intégralement ses écrits? Dans l'ensemble, non! Rousseau est l'incarnation de quelques grandes revendications, le héraut de quelques thèmes prédominants. Les zélateurs se créent un Rousseau mythique et le «rousseauisme» défigure le vrai Jean-Jacques. Aussi l'influence affirmée bruyamment est-elle souvent discutable. Un climat prétendument «à la Rousseau» favorise les malentendus. Seul est incontestable l'enthousiasme souvent délirant des Stürmer, mais, dans la plupar⁴ des cas, il est de courte durée, du moins dans ses outrances. Car l'homme excite la plus vive curiosité et la publication de ses *Confessions* est attendue avec l'impatience générale. Les six premiers livres, bien accueillis, malgré certaines réticences, parfois sérieuses, déçoivent: on attendait mieux et plus! Le clan des admirateurs passionnés l'emporte toujours, mais des jugements défavorables osent s'exprimer et gagnent des sympathies. Quand paraît la fin des *Confessions*, les troubles politiques et l'agitation révolutionnaire fournissent aux adversaires de Rousseau de terribles arguments: on voit où conduisent les excès de l'imagination et la croyance intolérante en des principes généraux. On fait encore l'éloge de la sincérité, des notations psychologiques et des éminentes qualités littéraires des *Confessions*, mais on n'hésite pas à ajouter que «le meilleur des hommes» est le «Père de la Révolution». Gloire maudite entre toutes. Reconnaître son admiration pour Rousseau devient une position politique, même si des esprits raisonnables s'efforcent de dissocier l'artiste incomparable du dangereux sophiste ou du théoricien subversif. Quand sonne l'heure du *Contrat social*, les amis et les admirateurs allemands de Jean-Jacques Rousseau ont intérêt à garder un silence prudent.

MADAME DE GENLIS ET SES DEUX VOYAGES EN ANGLETERRE

par

JACQUES E. BERTAUD

Au cours d'une vie qui fut aussi longue que celle de Voltaire, Stéphanie-Félicité Brûlart, née Ducrest, comtesse de Genlis, puis marquise de Sillery (26 janvier 1746—31 décembre 1830), connut successivement une bonne partie du règne de Louis XV, celui de Louis XVI, la Révolution, le Premier Empire et la Restauration. Elle s'éteignit quelques mois après l'avènement de Louis-Philippe, dont elle avait été «le gouverneur» de 1782 à 1790. Sa production littéraire, commencée en 1779,[1] s'étend approximativement sur le dernier quart du XVIIIe siècle et le premier tiers du XIXe. En vérité, c'est une tâche ingrate que de parler d'une femme qui, pendant et après cette carrière si longue et si diverse, traversée par les orages de l'époque la plus dramatique de notre histoire, a fait l'objet de tant de critiques malveillantes; une femme qui, après son heure de gloire et lorsqu'elle n'est pas tout à fait oubliée, ne vit le plus souvent dans la mémoire des hommes que comme une figure assez comique ou, quand elle est prise au sérieux, comme un personnage odieux, noirci par des accusations vraies ou fausses, mais en tout cas presque toujours exagérées. Comme le dit un de ses biographes: «Nous n'en finirions pas si nous rappelions seulement les noms des écrivains qui l'ont accablée de leurs sarcasmes».[2]

---

[1] Par la publication chez Panckoucke, en juillet de cette année-là, du premier tome de son *Théâtre à l'usage des jeunes personnes*, qui s'appellera par la suite *Théâtre d'Education*. Précisons toutefois que Mme de Genlis se vit imprimée avant 1779; trois comédies, recueillies en 1781 dans le tome I de son *Théâtre de Société*, parurent d'abord anonymement dans le *Parnasse des dames*, probablement en 1776. Le détail de ces publications, l'accueil de la critique et d'autres faits qui ne peuvent être examinés ici seront exposés dans notre étude sur *Madame de Genlis et l'Angleterre*, encore en cours de rédaction. Elle constitue le sujet d'une thèse pour le Doctorat de l'Université de Paris, entreprise sous la direction de M. le Professeur Jacques Voisine, à qui nous sommes redevable, non seulement du sujet lui-même, mais aussi de précieux conseils, dispensés avec bienveillance depuis plusieurs années.

[2] Honoré Bonhomme, *Madame la Comtesse de Genlis* (. . .), Paris 1885, p. 66. Parmi les causes variées de cette hostilité persistante envers Mme de Genlis, il faut citer sa nomination comme «gouverneur» des princes d'Orléans (cf. *infra*, n. 15) et l'arrivée au Palais-Royal de deux petites Anglaises, Paméla et Hermine, qui furent élevées par la comtesse dans cette véritable petite école constituée par les enfants d'Orléans, les propres filles de Mme de Genlis, sa nièce Henriette de Sercey et son neveu César Ducrest, sans compter les élèves de passage. Jusqu'à une époque récente, Paméla a fait couler beaucoup d'encre et nous ne pouvons entrer dans le détail de cette polémique. Qu'il nous suffise de dire qu'en gros nous sommes en présence de deux thèses opposées; l'une qui accepte la propre version de Mme de Genlis, c'est-à-dire l'adoption, à des fins pédagogiques, de cette Anglaise, orpheline de père, et l'autre qui, faisant de celle-ci, la fille adultérine du futur Philippe-Egalité et de Félicité de Genlis, échafaude toute une démonstration pour le prouver. Le principal tenant de cette deuxième thèse est

18*

275

Certes, il existe une bonne biographie de Mme de Genlis, la seule qui puisse en fait prétendre à faire autorité, mais elle a l'inconvénient d'avoir été écrite il y a soixante ans, si bien qu'en dépit de ses indubitables qualités d'objectivité et d'originalité, cette consciencieuse étude comporte, par la force des choses, trop de lacunes et sans doute d'erreurs pour pouvoir être qualifiée de définitive. En outre, comme le titre l'indique et malgré une cinquantaine de pages qu'il consacre à la fin de son livre[3] à l'œuvre de la comtesse, Jean Harmand s'intéresse plutôt au personnage historique qu'à l'écrivain proprement dit. Ainsi, ce qui est vrai de la vie de Mme de Genlis l'est encore bien plus de son œuvre. Malgré la récente publication de deux livres sur le sujet,[4] tout, pratiquement, reste à faire dans ce domaine, à commencer par une bibliographie sérieuse. C'est là le premier travail qui s'imposerait au chercheur désireux d'appuyer toute étude valable de Mme de Genlis, non seulement sur les documents classiques: archives, correspondances, mémoires, journaux et périodiques contemporains de la vie de l'auteur, mais aussi sur l'analyse d'une œuvre dont on devine très tôt en la lisant qu'elle contient d'abondants éléments autobiographiques.

Une dernière remarque générale à faire sur les études qu'on a consacrées à Mme de Genlis, c'est qu'à côté des détails biographiques ou anecdotiques la concernant, d'ailleurs souvent stéréotypés et répétés à satiété d'un ouvrage à l'autre, l'aspect sur lequel la plupart des commentateurs se sont arrêtés touche à ses idées pédagogiques,[5] et cela au détriment du reste de son œuvre,

---

J. Turquan, co-auteur de *La Belle Paméla* (Paris 1923), jugé, avec raison à nos yeux, par Amédée Britsch, de l'école adverse, comme un «ouvrage qui ne manque ni de verve, ni d'information», mais «gâté par le parti-pris» (cf. *Lettres de L.-J.-P. d'Orléans duc de Chartres à Nathaniel Parker Forth (1778—1785)*, Paris 1926). Toutefois, la réalité de la liaison entre le duc et la gouvernante a été prouvée par G. Maugras dans *L'Idylle d'un gouverneur*, Paris 1904. Ce fut une autre cause de scandale.

[3] Jean Harmand, *Madame de Genlis. Sa vie intime et politique* (. . .), Préface d'Emile Faguet (. . .), Paris 1912, traduit en anglais l'année suivante, sous le titre *A Keeper of Royal Secrets. Being the Private and Political Life of Madame de Genlis*, New York 1913.

[4] Alice M. Laborde, *L'Œuvre de Madame de Genlis*, Paris 1966, et Anna Nikliborc, *L'Œuvre de Mme de Genlis*, *Romanica Wratislaviensia*, IV, Wrocław 1969. On trouve dans le second un plus grand effort de synthèse que dans le premier qui, tout compte fait, n'est guère plus qu'une bonne anthologie.

[5] C'est Sainte-Beuve qui a principalement contribué à fixer ce «portrait en costume de pédagogue», selon la formule d'E. Faguet. L'auteur des *Causeries du Lundi* (v. tome III, Garnier, 1852, pp. 16—30, chronique du 14. 10. 1850) est, tout compte fait, sévère pour cette femme-auteur, dont «l'originalité la plus réelle consistait en cette vocation et cette verve de pédagogie poussée jusqu'à la manie», seul côté par lequel, selon lui, elle «a chance de vivre». Dans son *Histoire critique des doctrines de l'éducation en France* (Hachette, 1881, II, pp. 120—8.), G. Compayré accepte les conclusions de Sainte-Beuve et range Mme de Genlis parmi les contradicteurs de Rousseau, tout en soulignant ce qu'elle lui doit. Il condamne plus qu'il n'approuve cette éducation où il ne trouve «rien de naturel», où «tout est tendu, affecté».

On pourra encore consulter sur cet aspect de l'œuvre de Mme de Genlis: J. Pons, *L'Education en Angleterre entre 1750 et 1800. Aperçu de l'influence pédagogique de J.-J. Rousseau*, Paris 1919, pp. 172—7. — W. M. Kerby, *The Educational Ideas and Activities of Mme la Comtesse de Genlis* (. . .), Paris 1926, ouvrage extrêmement décevant (cf. le jugement de M. Wahba dans l'article cité ci-dessous, p. 229, n. 19) — Phyllis J. Ward, *Madame de Genlis, educationist*, (Ph. D. Cantab. 1934), thèse non publiée, dont le principal mérite est de réfuter le trop sommaire classement de notre auteur parmi les épigones de Rousseau. L'article de la même dans la *R.L.C.*, tome 16, pp. 731—4,

qui est considérable — selon les critiques, le nombre de volumes qui la composent approche ou dépasse la centaine — et qui, nous l'avons dit, n'a pas encore bénéficié d'un examen approfondi. Cependant, c'est son œuvre d'éducatrice qui nous intéresse au premier chef ici, car c'est avant et pendant la Révolution, époque des deux séjours en Angleterre, qu'elle a été principalement écrite et diffusée des deux côtés de la Manche. Cette période est aussi celle où Félicité de Genlis se livre corps et âme à ses activités d'institutrice. L'œuvre qu'elle produit en conséquence a le mérite de comprendre à la fois une théorie de l'éducation et des applications pratiques, sous la forme de livres élémentaires destinés à la formation intellectuelle et morale de l'enfance. Toutefois, à cause de l'inévitable comparaison avec Rousseau, c'est avant tout le côté théorique de cette œuvre qui a retenu l'attention des critiques; une étude des livres que Mme de Genlis a écrits pour les enfants reste donc à faire.[6]

Sans prétendre avoir encore accompli tous ces défrichements préalables avant de rédiger le présent article, nous espérons du moins pouvoir montrer, dans ce qui pourrait être l'ébauche d'un ou deux chapitres détachés d'une éventuelle biographie de Mme de Genlis, comment il est possible, si l'on tient compte de textes et de documents négligés jusqu'ici, de jeter quelque lumière sur une période de sa vie qui intéresse plus spécialement le comparatiste et qui n'a peut-être pas reçu toute l'attention qu'elle mérite. Il semble en effet que les biographes de notre auteur soient passés assez vite sur les deux séjours qu'elle fit en Angleterre, le premier en juillet 1785 et le second en 1791—1792. H. Bonhomme mentionne seulement «le voyage en Angleterre», c'est-à-dire le second, bien qu'il donne le texte d'une lettre où il est clairement question du premier. J. Harmand, dans un chapitre qu'il intitule «Voyage (au singulier) en Angleterre», donnant au premier abord l'impression que Mme de Genlis n'y alla qu'une fois, consacre à peine sept ou huit pages sur vingt-quatre aux deux voyages proprement dits, le deuxième occupant presque toute la place et le premier n'ayant droit qu'à une quinzaine de lignes par parenthèse. Hâtons-nous d'ajouter qu'en cela J. Harmand ne fait que suivre Mme de Genlis, qui commence à raconter son premier

est un bref résumé du second séjour — Magdi Wahba, *Madame de Genlis in England*, in *Comparative Literature* (Univ. of Oregon, Vol. XIII, 1961, pp. 221—238). M. Wahba se propose essentiellement d'étudier l'accueil fait en Angleterre aux idées pédagogiques de Mme de Genlis entre 1781 et 1792, accueil qui, selon lui, contraste avec les controverses et l'indignation morale auxquelles donnèrent lieu l'*Emile* et l'*Héloïse* de Rousseau, à partir du moment où la Révolution «began to threaten the peace of mind of conservative opinion in England». Cet article contient d'utiles références à des ouvrages concernant la littérature pédagogique de cette époque, ainsi que des renseignements précis sur les traductions anglaises des premières œuvres de Mme de Genlis. Nous y renvoyons notre lecteur.

[6] Une telle étude comporterait l'examen d'ouvrages comme le *Théâtre à l'usage des jeunes personnes* (1779—1780), les *Annales de la vertu, ou Cours d'histoire à l'usage des jeunes personnes* (1781), les *Veillées du Château, ou Cours de morale à l'usage des enfans* (1784), la *Nouvelle Méthode d'enseignement pour la première enfance* (1801), les *Nouveaux Contes moraux* (1802), etc. Les plus connus de ces livres ont droit en général à un court commentaire dans les ouvrages consacrés à l'histoire de la littérature enfantine. Parmi les bibliographies les plus récentes, on pourra consulter *The World of Children's Literature*, par Anne Pellowski, New-York—London 1968, et *A Critical History of Children's Literature* (Revised Edition), Collier-Macmillan, 1970.

séjour à la fin du tome III de ses *Mémoires*,[7] mais en y mêlant tout de suite les souvenirs du second, dont le récit, plus long, remplit aussi environ vingt-cinq pages du tome IV (pp. 89—113). Dans une biographie anglaise plus récente, les deux voyages sont bien traités séparément et dans l'ordre chronologique, mais là encore on s'appuie principalement sur les *Mémoires*, sans mettre suffisamment leur exactitude en question.[8]

Il ne saurait s'agir ici de traiter les deux séjours en détail. Nous mettrons donc l'accent sur le premier, parce qu'il a été souvent négligé par les critiques et qu'en raison de sa brièveté et de sa richesse en contacts, il offre, dans les limites d'une courte étude, la possibilité d'un développement suivi et à peu près complet. Quant au second, dont la matière, à elle seule, aurait excédé la capacité du présent article, nous nous contenterons d'en donner une rapide vue d'ensemble.

LE PREMIER SÉJOUR (JUILLET 1785)

Mme de Genlis avait fait le projet d'un voyage outre-Manche bien avant 1785. Nous avons là-dessus non seulement son propre témoignage,[9] mais encore celui d'Edward Gibbon, qui, dans une lettre du 16 décembre 1777 à Dorothea Gibbon lui expliquant qu'il ne voulait pas trop s'éloigner de Londres à ce moment-là, donnait entre autres la raison suivante:

«I expect without knowing the day a French Lady of quality Madame de Genlis to whom I have very great obligations. Whenever she informs me of her arrival in London, I must instantly fly (on the wings of meer friendship) to receive and attend her . . .»[10]

---

[7] pp. 272—301. Nous citons cet ouvrage d'après la 2ᵉ édition en 8 vol. des *Mémoires inédits de Madame la Comtesse de Genlis, sur le dix-huitième siècle et la Révolution française, depuis 1756 jusqu'à nos jours*, Paris 1825. L'auteur entreprit de les rédiger en 1812, mais elle les avait commencés beaucoup plus tôt, le troisième volume datant presque tout entier de l'émigration. D'autre part, 3 des 7 volumes manuscrits d'un journal particulier qu'elle avait tenu pendant quinze ans, «passés de suite dans le plus grand monde», furent perdus après le départ de France en 1792. Parmi ceux-ci se trouvait le journal du second voyage en Angleterre (v. *Mémoires* I, pp. 29—33). Notons, à ce propos, que les deux séjours outre-Manche sont bien des voyages, l'émigration ne commençant officiellement pour Mme de Genlis qu'au moment où le départ pour Tournai en décembre 1792 inaugure un long exil de huit ans en Belgique, en Suisse, en Hollande et en Allemagne.

[8] Violet Wyndham, *Madame de Genlis*, Londres 1958. Comme le livre de J. Harmand, dont il s'inspire, cet ouvrage est dans son ensemble une réhabilitation. Ne visant pas à la découverte de faits nouveaux mais utilisant adroitement, à l'intention du grand public, les principales sources écrites, Mrs. Wyndham brosse un tableau clair et vivant, plein de notions justes quant à la psychologie de Mme de Genlis. Une brève et spirituelle (pour ne pas dire ironique) évocation de la vie de notre auteur avait été publiée par Austin Dobson, en 1866, dans l'*Englishwoman's Domestic Magazine*, recueillie ensuite dans *Four Frenchwomen* (Chatto & Windus, 1890, et World's Classics, O.U.P., 1923). Un peu auparavant, Julia Kavanagh, dans ses *French Women of Letters: Biographical Sketches*, London 1862, s'était plus particulièrement intéressée à l'œuvre de la romancière et avait très judicieusement analysé les causes et les conséquences de l'ambiguïté d'une réputation qui, au fond, méritait mieux (v. surtout II, pp. 30—33).

[9] «J'avois toujours eu un désir passionné de faire un petit voyage en Angleterre. Enfin j'y cédai un peu avant la révolution» (*Mémoires*, III, p. 272).

[10] *The Letters of Edward Gibbon*, Ed. J. E. Norton, London 1956, II, p. 170.

Nous n'avons pu trouver la nature exacte de la dette d'amitié à laquelle il est fait allusion ici, mais nous savons que l'historien anglais venait de séjourner six mois à Paris cette année-là (de mai à novembre) et qu'il avait été reçu et fêté un peu partout. Les lettres qu'il écrit alors témoignent du plaisir qu'il trouve à voir ses connaissances s'étendre «over the most valuable parts of Paris». Il ne fait donc guère de doute qu'il a été reçu au Palais-Royal et y a probablement rencontré Mme de Genlis, qui fut toujours très obligeante pour les visiteurs anglais, surtout de renom. Environ deux ans après, le 15 octobre 1779, elle lui écrivait une assez longue lettre pour accompagner l'envoi du premier volume de son *Théâtre à l'usage des jeunes personnes* et lui exprimait son regret de ne pouvoir y joindre les autres volumes, ceux-ci ne devant paraître que trois semaines plus tard. Elle en était d'autant plus fâchée, disait-elle, que Gibbon y aurait vu «un éloge de la bienfaisance et de la générosité des Anglois, qui naissoit naturellement du récit d'une histoire que j'ai vu arriver à Spa».[11] Le passage qui suit dans la même lettre intéresse encore plus notre propos:

«J'ai déjà eu l'honneur de vous écrire, Monsieur, il y a un an, et une très longue lettre, dans laquelle je vous remerciois de la bonté que vous aviez eue de vous charger de m'arrêter un logement à Londres, et je vous annonçois que le malheur des tems me privoit du plaisir de voir un païs que j'ai toujours si ardemment désiré connoître. Je m'en suis dédommagé *(sic)* en quelque sorte en faisant connoissance avec une partie des grands hommes qui ont illustré l'Angleterre. Je sais enfin parfaitement l'anglois, et pour vous en donner l'idée je lis Shakespear avec la plus grande facilité; mais mon poëte favori c'est Milton, et je l'aime au point que je sais une très considérable partie de son admirable Paradis Perdu, par cœur. Je sais aussi beaucoup de vers de Pope; je crois que je vous ferois rire si vous me les entendiez déclamer, cependant les Anglois m'entendent, et c'est tout ce que je veux. J'étois même bien tentée de vous écrire en anglois, mais j'ai pensé que vous me trouveriez trop de présomption, et c'est bien assez d'avoir celle d'envoyer à l'auteur d'un des plus beaux ouvrages d'histoire que nous ayons, un ouvrage fait pour des enfans.»[12]

Il est dommage que Mme de Genlis n'ait pas suivi sa première idée et écrit sa lettre en anglais; nous aurions pu vérifier si effectivement elle savait parfaitement cette langue, affirmation qui, à première vue, peut paraître exagérée; elle corrige cette impression, il est vrai, en faisant allusion à son

---

[11] Il s'agit de *L'Aveugle de Spa*, comédie en un acte (t. 2. du *Théâtre* en 4 vol. de 1780, ou t. 3. du même en 7 vol. de 1785). Voir en particulier la scène II, où Félicie (c'est-à-dire l'auteur) dit à «Miladi Semur»: «Vous êtes si sensible! . . . Et d'ailleurs, je crois qu'en général les Angloises sont plus compatissantes que nous; elles ont moins de fantaisies, moins de coquetterie; & la coquetterie étouffe & détruit presque toutes les vertus». Un peu plus loin, elle lui dit encore: « . . . vous y verrez que nous nous piquons de vous imiter sur tous les points, à l'exception d'un seul, la bienfaisance. Nous exagérons toutes vos modes, nous prenons vos usages, vos manières; mais nous n'avons pas encore adopté cette généreuse coutume établie universellement parmi vous, de faire des souscriptions pour encourager les talens, ou pour secourir les infortunés.»

[12] *The Miscellaneous Works of Edward Gibbon, Esq* (. . .) John Murray, 1814, II, p. 236—7. Mme de Genlis avait donc écrit à Gibbon en 1778 et sa lettre était restée sans réponse, mais l'historien était coutumier du fait. A notre connaissance, ces rapports épistolaires n'auront pas de suite. Mme de Genlis n'hésitera pas à porter plus tard un jugement sévère sur le grand ouvrage de l'historien anglais (v. *Mém.* II, pp. 377—8). L'éloge de 1779 allait, il est vrai, au 1er volume seulement, paru en 1776.

accent défectueux et nous apprend, en passant, qu'elle s'est exercée à la parler avant même de venir en Angleterre. Ce qu'elle veut dire en fait, c'est qu'elle est capable de lire les poètes anglais dans le texte; un passage des *Mémoires* relatif à une période un peu antérieure nous le confirme:

«J'avois pris aussi un maître de langue angloise; et, comme j'avois une très-grande mémoire, je lisois couramment les poëtes au bout de cinq mois.» (II, 275)

En réalité, loin de penser qu'elle avait atteint d'un coup la perfection, Félicité continuera de lire et d'étudier l'anglais pendant de longues années. En mai 1785 par exemple, nous la voyons assister régulièrement aux leçons que les princes d'Orléans, ses élèves, prennent avec un certain Mr. Powell; elle considère cela comme un grand privilège, qu'elle n'est pas du tout prête à céder au sous-gouverneur Lebrun. Aussi lui rappelle-t-elle assez vertement qu'il sait et parle l'anglais depuis plusieurs années et qu'il a déjà «*profité* pendant 3 ans 1/2 des Leçons données aux p(rin)ces».[13]

Ne quittons pas Gibbon sans citer un dernier passage de la lettre que la comtesse lui écrivait le 15 octobre. Après lui avoir dit qu'on joue ses pièces «ici de tous les côtés» et qu' «on les traduit même en italien à Gènes, et en allemand à Hambourg», elle ajoute:

«(...) mais j'avoue que je serois bien plus flattée qu'elles le fussent en anglois, car si je n'étois pas françoise, et si après la France on me donnoit le choix d'une patrie, bien certainement je voudrois être angloise. Je ne connois que deux nations sur la terre, la mienne et la vôtre, pourquoi faut-il ... je ne veux pas m'arrêter à de si tristes réflexions, j'aime mieux espérer qu'une heureuse paix comblera bientôt tous les désirs des bons citoyens des deux nations.»

Les sentiments exprimés ici sont peut-être en partie dictés par le désir de plaire et aussi de se ménager quelque appui en vue de la traduction de son *Théâtre* en anglais, mais nous les croyons d'autre part sincères. Ne s'expliquent-ils pas d'ailleurs par le cosmopolitisme et l'anglophilie généralisés de l'époque et plus particulièrement par l'influence du Palais-Royal, où le ton est donné par le duc de Chartres, anglomane réputé?[14] Nous ne serons donc pas surpris de constater qu'au moment où Mme de Genlis met pour la première fois le pied sur le sol de cette seconde patrie, ses impressions sont colorées à la fois par le sentiment qu'elle confiait à Gibbon en 1779 et par la fierté qu'elle ressent devant l'accueil flatteur qui lui est fait.

Cet accueil s'explique par la relative célébrité qui l'a précédée outre-Manche; elle la doit à sa double réputation de comtesse attachée depuis

---

[13] *Journal de l'éducation des princes.* Trois des cahiers de ce journal (pour les années 1785, 1787 et 1788), les seuls qui semblent avoir échappé à la tourmente révolutionnaire, se trouvent au Musée Condé à Chantilly. Ils sont de la main de Lebrun, avec annotations également manuscrites de Mme de Genlis (on en trouvera quelques extraits, pour l'année 1787, dans *Gouverneur de Princes*, 1900, pp. 166—175, par M. de Chabreul).

[14] Cf. Amédée Britsch, *La jeunesse de Philippe-Egalité (1747—1785)*, Paris 1926, *passim* et surtout Chap. XI. A vrai dire, parallèlement à son enthousiasme pour l'Angleterre, et comme nous l'avons déjà vu à propos de *L'Aveugle de Spa* (cf. *supra*, n. 10), on décèle aussi chez Mme de Genlis une irritation qui se manifeste devant les outrances d'une certaine anglomanie de surface (v. par exemple son *Anglomane ennemi des Anglois*, dans le tome 10 de la 1ère éd. des *Mémoires*, pp. 233—240, et le personnage du Baron dans *Les Vœux téméraires*, Hambourg 1798, I. *passim*).

prés de quinze ans à la Maison d'Orléans[15] et de femme-auteur dont trois importants ouvrages pédagogiques ont déjà été publiés et presque aussitôt traduits en anglais.[16] Nous pouvons aussi nous demander si, antérieurement à 1785, certaines relations anglaises nouées en France n'ont pas préparé le terrain. Nous avons émis, à propos de Gibbon, l'hypothèse d'un tel contact. Y en a-t-il eu d'autres? Il est plus que probable qu'au Palais-Royal comme à Villers-Cotterets, à Chantilly, chez le prince de Condé, comme à l'Isle-Adam ou au Temple, chez le prince de Conti, à Spa comme dans le salon de telle ou telle grande dame, Mme de Genlis a eu l'occasion d'entrer en rapport avec des Anglais. Malheureusement, en partie à cause du désordre et de l'imprécision des *Mémoires* de la comtesse à cet endroit comme en bien d'autres, il est difficile d'en faire la preuve. C'est à peine si elle cite deux ou trois noms comme ceux de «M. Conway (. . .), fils de mylord Erford (Hertford)», qu'elle connut à Sillery, où il passa six mois, et plus tard à Spa (II, 89 et 304—5), ou de lady Pembroke, qu'elle avait «beaucoup vue jadis à l'Ile-Adam» (III, 340), avant d'être présentée par elle à la reine Charlotte, lors de la visite de juillet 1785.

Il y a à la Bibliothèque Nationale un ouvrage qui représente peut-être la trace d'un autre contact anglais. C'est un exemplaire des *Seven Discourses Delivered in the Royal Academy by the President*, publiés à Londres en 1778, et qui porte, de la main de Joshua Reynolds, la dédicace «To Madame la Comtesse de Genlis from the Author». Toujours est-il que le célèbre peintre anglais sera un des premiers, sinon le premier, à faire les honneurs de son pays à la comtesse, peu après l'arrivée de celle-ci en Angleterre. Il fait ainsi part de la nouvelle le 5 juillet au duc de Rutland:

«Madame la Comtesse de Genlis is just arrived. I had the honour of her company yesterday to dinner. She speaks English tolerably well, and has very pleasing manners. To-day she is gone to Windsor, the Queen having sent to desire to see her (. . .)»[17]

Une lettre de Horace Walpole, datée du lundi soir, 4 juillet 1785, commente aussi l'arrivée de Félicité à Londres:

«I will read no more of Rousseau; his *Confessions* disgusted me beyond any book I ever opened. His hen, the schoolmistress, Madame de Genlis, the

[15] Mme de Genlis entra au Palais-Royal comme dame d'honneur de la duchesse de Chartres à la fin de 1770 ou au début de 1771. En juillet 1779, elle fut nommée gouvernante des deux petites princesses, nées le 23 août 1777. Un peu avant la mort de l'aînée des jumelles (le 6 février 1782), la comtesse devint «le gouverneur» des ducs de Valois (le futur Louis-Philippe) et de Montpensier. Sur la sensation causée à Paris par l'incroyable nouvelle, voir *Anecdotes secrètes du 18e siècle* (. . .). Par P. J. B. N(ougaret), Paris 1808, II, p. 103.

[16] A savoir le *Théâtre d'Education*, *Adèle et Théodore* et *Les Veillées du Château*. Pour ces traductions anglaises, on pourra se reporter à l'étude de M. Wahba (cf. *supra*, n. 5), à compléter toutefois, en ce qui concerne les traductions publiées en feuilleton dans divers périodiques anglais, par l'ouvrage de Robert D. Mayo, *The English Novel in the Magazines 1740—1815*, Evanston—London 1962 (v. Index à Genlis).

[17] *Letters of Sir Joshua Reynolds*, Collected and Edited by F. Whiley Milles, Cambridge 1929, Letter LXXXV, p. 126. Dans un manuscrit de Mme de Genlis déposé à la Bibliothèque Nationale (N. ac. fr. 4360), on peut lire la note suivante: «j'ai vu à Londres en 1785 chés le cher reynolds un portrait en miniature qu'il possédoit le seul original de Milton, quoique l'ouvrage ne fut pas beau il l'avoit acheté 100 louis . . .» Mme de Genlis arriva à Londres le mercredi 29 juin (v. *The Gazetteer and Daily Advertiser* du 2 juillet, British Museum, Burney Collection, 759b).

newspapers say, is arrived in London. I nauseate her too; the eggs of education that both he and she laid, could not be hatched till the chickens would be ready to die of old age. I revere genius; I have a dear friendship for common sense; ... but I abhor extravagance that is given for the quintessence of sense, and affectation that pretends to be philosophy.»[18]

Pareil anathème, qui se comprend si l'on voit bien qu'il englobe Rousseau et son présumé disciple en jupon et que l'hostilité de Walpole pour le premier déteint sur le second, étonne cependant lorsqu'on sait que, six ans auparavant, Mme du Deffand avait fait de grands éloges de Mme de Genlis dans plusieurs lettres adressées à son cher Horace, qui, de son côté, lui avait conseillé de «former une liaison» avec la comtesse. Il avait lu et grandement apprécié le *Théâtre d'Education*, du moins le premier volume que lui avait envoyé la vieille marquise, quelques mois avant de mourir.[19] Il est vrai que Walpole avait eu le temps d'oublier tout cela et que sa virulente attaque vise surtout *Adèle et Théodore*, que la critique anglaise n'avait pas accueilli sans réserves, à cause précisément du caractère quelque peu utopique du plan d'éducation de Mme de Genlis.[20]

Coloré par la magie du souvenir et par le désir de se faire valoir, le récit du premier séjour tel qu'il nous est fait dans les *Mémoires* est un tableau sans ombres, surtout dans ce résumé qui nous en donne une idée d'ensemble:

«Mon voyage en Angleterre fut excessivement brillant. Nulle femme ne pouvoit entrer dans la chambre des communes. Cette chambre, par un arrêté particulier, m'accorda la permission d'assister à une séance. Je n'eus pas la permission d'y mener avec moi une autre femme. Ce fut milord Inchiquin qui m'y conduisit. On ne jouoit point la tragédie l'été; on donna pour moi une représentation d'*Hamlet*. Le récit de toutes ces choses fut mis dans tous les papiers anglois, avec les réflexions les plus obligeantes pour moi. On inséra aussi dans ces papiers une infinité de vers faits pour moi, entre autres une belle ode par M. Hayley, et qui se trouve dans ses œuvres. Je reçus des marques d'intérêt et d'estime des personnages les plus distingués de l'Angleterre (. . .) Je ne fis point mettre toutes ces choses dans nos papiers françois; je ne les mandai même pas à mes amis: je me contentai de les écrire dans mon journal. Il est vrai que je fus, dans ce voyage, tellement livrée à la société, que j'écrivis bien peu de lettres: toutes mes heures étoient employées en courses, en visites et en fêtes.» (III, 336—7)

En nous aidant des précisions données par Mme de Genlis elle-même dans les cinq ou six pages des *Mémoires* qui suivent cet extrait,[21] mais en les

[18] *Horace Walpole's Correspondence*, ed. by W. S. Lewis, Yale et London vol. 33, pp. 475—6. V. aussi plus loin, *ibid.*, p. 479 (9. 7. 1785).
[19] Cf. *ibid.*, vol. 7, pp. 161, 163, 165, 203, 212, 219, 228. Voir aussi dans le même volume, pp. 445—460, *Madame Du Deffand's Journal*, où l'on peut suivre les relations entre les deux femmes en cette dernière année de la vie de la marquise.
[20] Voir en particulier l'opinion d'Enfield dans la *Monthly Review*, LXX, 338 (cf. M. Wahba, *op. cit.*, p. 231). Le critique du *Gentleman's Magazine* (LIII, pp. 2, 860 et 946, *passim*), dont M. Wahba résume aussi les objections, se trompe en pensant qu'*Adèle et Théodore* était destiné aux jeunes filles et par conséquent ne leur convenait guère; comme l'*Emile*, c'est un traité à l'intention des parents et des éducateurs.
[21] Voici un sommaire des pp. 337—343, dans l'ordre suivi par l'auteur: Elle est invitée chez lord Gordon par le prince de Galles; elle passe trois jours chez Burke, qui lui fait visiter Oxford; ils s'arrêtent en chemin chez la duchesse de Portland; chez Burke, elle voit William Windham et Joshua Reynolds; description des vitraux de ce

confrontant avec d'autres témoignages qui recoupent ou infirment le sien, essayons de rétablir l'ordre chronologique de faits présentés ici pêle-mêle et d'en ramener le récit quelque peu embelli à de plus justes proportions.

Nous savons déjà par J. Reynolds que la réception de Mme de Genlis par la reine Charlotte à Windsor eut lieu le 5 juillet, alors que les *Mémoires* la placent après les trois jours passés chez Burke, c'est-à-dire au plus tôt, comme nous le verrons, le 20 ou le 21. Le *Daily Universal Register* du jeudi 7 commente ainsi la nouvelle:

«Madame la Comtesse de Genlis, so well known throughout all Europe by her writings, as well as by her excellent qualifications of head and heart has been received by her Majesty at Windsor with very peculiar marks of favour and regard; and we make no doubt but every attention will be paid her during her stay in this country, by those who are in the possession of genius themselves, or who are sensible to the merit of talents in others.»

Une réputation européenne, sans aucun doute, de nombreux talents, certes, mais du génie, c'est une autre histoire. Un des premiers à répondre à la prière de la souveraine fut probablement lord Mansfield, âgé alors de quatre-vingts ans. Il s'empressa d'écrire à Mme de Genlis, c'est elle qui nous l'apprend, pour demander à la voir. Elle reçut «avec plaisir ce respectable vieillard, rempli d'esprit et d'instruction»; elle ajoute dans une note: «Il avoit eu des liaisons intimes avec Pope, et l'on voyoit chez lui plusieurs portraits de ce poëte célèbre» (III, 341). Faut-il voir là une preuve qu'elle se rendit à Kenwood, la résidence de lord Mansfield, située entre Hampstead Heath et Highgate, dans le nord de Londres? Quant à la visite du Lord Chief Justice, elle a dû avoir lieu entre le 7 et le 9 juillet, car le 6 il était en tournée à Chelmsford, le 8 il participait au débat des Communes et le 10, à l'occasion de la Sainte-Félicité, donc après avoir vu la comtesse, il lui envoyait une corbeille de «roses mousseuses».[22] Une lettre de Mrs. Boscawen à Mrs. Delany écrite le 14 juillet, d'où il ressort que le mardi précédent (le

---

dernier dans la chapelle du Christ, à Oxford; de retour à Londres, elle reçoit un message de la reine, par son lecteur, «M. du Luc» (Jean-André Deluc, 1727—1817), l'invitant à aller à Windsor; elle déjeune chez la sous-gouvernante des princesses, «madame de Lafitte» (Marie-Elisabeth Bouée, dame de la Fite, 1736—1794); elle est présentée à la reine par Lady Pembroke (épouse du 10e comte de Pembroke); l'audience dure deux heures; la reine lui envoie «une corbeille remplie de superbes ananas»; son jardinier de Kew, «M. Iton» (William Aiton, 1731—1794) a ordre de lui laisser prendre toutes les plantes et les graines qu'elle désire; charme du jardin de Kew; elle reçoit lord Mansfield, «grand-juge d'Angleterre» (William Murray, 1er comte de Mansfield, 1705—1793); il lui envoie «une corbeille remplie de roses mousseuses» pour sa fête; visite du château et du parc de Blenheim; un valet de chambre français de la duchesse de Marlborough lui apporte, de la part de celle-ci, «une immense corbeille pleine d'ananas». — Elle voit «avec grand détail tout ce qu'il y a de curieux à Londres et dans ses environs»; elle est reçue par Horace Walpole; on lui donne une fête dans les jardins du poète Waller; description de ces jardins; elle écrit à «M. Bridget» (Bridgen, de son vrai nom), gendre de Samuel Richardson; elle voit la maison, le portrait et la tombe du romancier, mais décline l'offre qui lui est faite de traduire *Paméla* «littéralement»; elle se lie avec Mlle Wilkes et dîne deux fois chez le père de celle-ci.

[22] Il lui donnera aussi un rosier entier qu'elle rapportera à Paris pour le remettre «au fameux fleuriste Descemet» (1732—1810). Elle pourra ainsi se vanter d'avoir fait «la conquête de la rose mousseuse» (en anglais «moss-rose» et «rose moussue», selon Littré).

12) on parla de Mme de Genlis à Kenwood en termes très élogieux,[23] nous confirme que c'est avant ce mardi-là que se place la rencontre avec lord Mansfield. D'autre part, il est peu probable que Mme de Genlis l'ait reçu le lundi, puisque ce jour-là Fanny Burney a passé toute la matinée avec elle et a trouvé qu'elle était «the sweetest as well as most accomplished French-woman» qu'elle eût jamais rencontrée.[24] Nous allons bientôt retrouver Fanny Burney, mais pour l'instant continuons de suivre notre voyageuse au jour le jour, dans la mesure où nous avons pu combler les lacunes de son emploi du temps.

«On ne jouait point la tragédie l'été; on donna pour moi une représentation d'*Hamlet*». C'est ainsi, nous nous le rappelons, que Félicité consigne dans ses *Mémoires* un autre honneur qui lui fut fait. Le *Daily Universal Register* du mercredi 13 juillet 1785 nous apprend précisément que la tragédie de *Hamlet* sera jouée au Theatre Royal, Hay-Market, «By Particular Desire, This Evening», et sera accompagnée d'un divertissement avec chants, danses, et dialogues, intitulé *Harlequin Teague; or The Giant's Cause Way* (pièce de l'Irlandais John O'Keefe, créée en 1782), avec Mrs. Goodwin dans le rôle de Colombine, plus une «Ranelagh Masquerade», le tout couronné par un grand spectacle de ballet. C'est bien à cette soirée particulièrement brillante du 13 juillet que Mme de Genlis a assisté, mais elle aura cependant eut l'illu-sion, ou l'aura plus tard cultivée, qu'une exception a été faite en sa faveur, alors que la réalité fut plus banale. En effet, si l'on consulte, jour par jour, le *Daily Universal Register* pour les mois de juin et juillet, on s'aperçoit que la mention «by desire» revient plus d'une fois et que c'était donc une pratique courante de réclamer la reprise de tel ou tel spectacle: d'autre part, le nu-méro du 23 juin du même journal annonce pour le lendemain «the Tragedy of *Hamlet*; Hamlet by Mr. Lacy ... with (by desire) *Peeping Tom*.» Par conséquent, la représentation du 13 juillet, avec le même Mr. Lacy dans le rôle de Hamlet (et le journal souligne qu'il le joue pour la seconde fois cette saison), n'a pas tout à fait le caractère exceptionnel que Félicité lui prête dans ses *Mémoires*. Il se peut toutefois qu'elle ait exprimé le désir de voir la pièce qui, depuis les *Lettres philosophiques* de Voltaire, était sans doute considérée en France comme la plus typiquement shakespearienne de toutes et qu'un des admirateurs anglais de la comtesse se soit empressé d'accéder à son désir.

Dans ses *Anecdotes* (1784—1796, *Correspondence*, vol. 12, 257), H. Wal-pole a recueilli pour la postérité une réflexion faite, paraît-il, par Mme de Genlis lors de la soirée au Haymarket:

«Madame de Genlis being in England in July 1785, went to see *Hamlet*. When she heard the passage 'from whose bourn no traveller returns', she said sensibly, 'Comment donc! Ne voilà-t-il pas le revenant?' This remark was quite new.»

La remarque de la comtesse n'a peut-être pas été aussi spontanée que Walpole semble le croire. Le passage qu'il cite vient du fameux monologue de Hamlet (III, 1, v. 77—8) et, bien que Voltaire l'omette dans son adapta-

<hr>

[23] *The Autobiography and Correspondence of Mary Granville, Mrs Delany* (...), 2nd series, London 1862, pp. 261—2. Lettre citée par M. Wahba (*op. cit.*, 227, n. 14), moins cependant une phrase qui nous intéresse ici.

[24] *Diary and Letters of Madame D'Arblay* (...) with Preface and Notes by Austin Dobson, London 1904, II, 288. Lettre à Mrs Phillips du 11 juillet 1785.

tion peu fidèle de la tirade, nous pouvons être certains que Mme de Genlis, qui, de son propre aveu, pratiquait Shakespeare dans le texte depuis des années, le connaissait de longue date.

Deux jours après cette représentation, le vendredi 15 juillet, Félicité écrivait à Fanny Burney, avec qui nous savons qu'elle avait passé toute la matinée du lundi précédent, pour s'excuser de n'avoir pu la recevoir dans l'intervalle et pour la remercier du présent que la romancière anglaise lui avait fait de l'ouvrage de son père, le Dr. Charles Burney (son *Histoire de la Musique* probablement). Elle terminait sa lettre ainsi:

«Je pars dans l'instant pour Oxford; adieu ma chère amie; n'oubliez pas que vous avez pris l'engagement de m'aimer. Pour moi, je vous aime depuis l'instant où j'ai lu *Evelina* et *Cecilia*, et le bonheur de vous entendre et de vous connaître personnellement, a rendu ce sentiment aussi tendre qu'il est bien fondé.»[25]

Alors que l'extraordinaire renommée des deux romans de Frances Burney, publiés respectivement en 1778 et 1782, était parvenue jusqu'à Mme de Genlis, l'Anglaise, de son côté, ava itdécouvert le *Théâtre d'Education*, grâce à Mme de la Fite qui, un jour, lut avec sa fille *La Rosière de Salency*, pour distraire «la pauvre Mademoiselle Beurney», restée sans nouvelles de sa sœur.[26] A la fin de 1785 et surtout au cours des années 1786 et 1787, Mme de Genlis va tenir une assez grande place dans le journal de Fanny Burney, pour qui les bruits scandaleux qui circulent sur le compte de Félicité et la réprobation violente et universelle qui en découle vont bientôt poser un cas de conscience délicat. La reine Charlotte consultée par sa dame d'atour tranchera la question en lui suggérant de ne pas répondre à la lettre du 15 juillet, celle que nous venons de citer, et de se refuser désormais à toute correspondance. En dépit du «zèle indiscret» et des instances réitérées de Mme de la Fite, qui semble bien avoir été poussée tout du long par Mme de Genlis après le retour de celle-ci en France, Fanny Burney tiendra bon, non sans grands débats intérieurs cependant, car elle veut croire malgré tout à l'innocence de celle qu'elle considère encore comme une femme d'un rare mérite et d'un charme captivant.[27]

Le lendemain de la lettre à Fanny Burney, le samedi 16, nous trouvons Félicité à Beaconsfield, chez Edmund Burke, où Reynolds et William Windham sont également présents. Dans son *Journal* pour juillet 1785, Windham note:

«16th. Went to Beaconsfield; conveyance, Sir Joshua's coach; object of visit, to meet Madame de Genlis. Her manners were what we should call French, but not remarkable either in that or any other respect.»[28]

---

[25] *ibid.*, II, 288—9.

[26] *ibid.*, II, 263, *Diary* au 9. 10. 1784. Sur Mme de la Fite, cf. *supra*, n. 21. *La Rosière de Salency* fait partie du tome IV du *Théâtre à l'usage des jeunes personnes*, «volume (. . .) uniquement destiné à l'éducation des enfans de Marchands, d'Artisans . . . (Préface)». F. Burney qualifie la pièce de «very interesting and touchingly simple little drama».

[27] V. *ibid.*, II, pp. 302, 341—342, 345—346, et III, pp. 11—15, 25, 117—118, 172—174, 248—250, 261—262, 308—309. Selon F. Burney (v. III, 15), la reine alla jusqu'à regretter, en 1786, l'audience particulière qu'elle avait accordée à Mme de Genlis, disant qu'elle y avait été contrainte «Against her own judgment, (. . .) from the impudent vehemence of one of Madame de Genlis's friends here».

[28] *The Diary of the Right Hon. William Windham* (. . .), Longmans 1866, p. 56. On consultera aussi: *Memoir of the Life and Character of the Right Hon. Edmund Burke*

De son côté, Félicité commente ainsi cette visite dans ses *Mémoires*:

«Le fameux M. Burke, que je ne connoissois que de réputation, quitta sa maison de campagne pour venir me prendre à Londres, en m'offrant de me mener voir l'université d'Oxford, en m'arrêtant trois jours à sa maison de campagne, qui étoit sur la route. J'y consentis. Dans cette course, nous nous arrêtâmes d'abord chez la duchesse de Portland, qui se trouvoit sur notre chemin. C'est elle qui jadis avoit donné asile à J.-J. Rousseau, qui ensuite se brouilla très-injustement avec elle.

Au moment où nous arrivâmes, on nous apprit que la duchesse étoit à la mort, elle mourut dans la nuit; mais on nous ouvrit son parc, où nous nous promenâmes trois heures: il étoit superbe (. . .) Je passai trois jours très-agréables chez M. Burke, je vis là M. Windham, qui a été si célèbre depuis; il étoit de la société la plus douce et la plus aimable; j'y vis aussi le chevalier Reinolds, le meilleur peintre de portraits de l'Angleterre. M. Burke me conduisit à Oxford, où nous passâmes deux jours. J'admirai dans la chapelle du Christ les beaux vitraux peints nouvellement alors par Reinolds; il y avoit représenté l'Espérance d'une manière ingénieuse; elle étoit vue par derrière, la tête élevée vers les cieux, et les bras tendus vers des nuages.»[29]

Nous devons, à propos de la visite d'Oxford, éclaircir une énigme. Sur la foi d'une lettre de H. Walpole, que nous citerons un peu plus loin, on a dit et répété que si Mme de Genlis était allée à Oxford c'était pour y recevoir son grade de docteur, sans se demander pourquoi notre comtesse, d'habitude si empressée à tenir le compte exact des honneurs qui lui furent rendus en Angleterre et même encline à en rajouter, a passé celui-là sous silence. M. Wahba est le seul qui, à notre connaissance, ait exprimé un doute à l'égard de cette nouvelle, mais sans se référer à la lettre de Walpole qui en est la source, ni donner les raisons précises de son scepticisme.[30] L'explication est pourtant bien simple; elle nous a été obligeamment fournie par Mr. I. G. Philip, archiviste à la Bodléienne, qui nous a fait remarquer qu'aucun grade universitaire, honorifique ou non, n'était, ni n'aurait pu être décerné à des personnes du sexe féminin au XVIIIe siècle et que, par conséquent, ce serait perdre son temps que de poursuivre des recherches dans cette direction. Quant à la phrase en question de la lettre de Walpole, elle ne constitue pas, toujours selon Mr. Philip, une affirmation catégorique et doit être considérée comme une plaisanterie. On imagine assez bien en effet l'épistolier anglais

---

(. . .), by James Prior Esq., 2nd ed., London 1826, I, 460—461 et II, 407, sur Butler's Court, la maison de Burke à Beaconsfield. On lira également les deux anecdotes concernant Mme de Genlis et racontées par Prior sur un ton peu flatteur (II, 176—7); elles sont reproduites en partie dans *The Correspondence of Edmund Burke*, ed. by T. W. Copeland, Cambridge & Chicago V, 1965, pp. 226—7, et résumées par D. C. Bryant (*E. Burke and His Literary Friends*, St Louis 1939, pp. 306—7), qui signale l'erreur commise par Prior en les plaçant en 1791.

[29] III, 338—9. On trouvera dans la correspondance de J. Reynolds (*op. cit.*, cf. *supra*, n. 17) deux lettres au Rev. John Oglander (du 27. 12. 1777 et du 9. 1. 1778, pp. 58—61) donnant une description par Reynolds des vitraux en question et la reproduction d'une gravure les représentant (The West Window of New College Chapel — From Earlom's engraving, 1787). On voit très bien, sous la partie centrale consacrée à la Nativité, dans le 5e compartiment en partant de la gauche, la figure de l'Espérance, telle que la décrit Mme de Genlis.

[30] M. Wahba, qui ne cite que des sources secondaires, dit ceci: «I have not been able to discover any evidence for this curious assertion, which betrays considerable ignorance of the English universities in the eighteenth century» (*op. cit.*, 227, n. 14).

dans le rôle du pince-sans-rire donnant ainsi une nouvelle dont la cocasserie devait être évidente à l'époque, mais n'est plus perçue aujourd'hui que par les initiés.[31]

Nous n'avons pas le moyen de savoir avec certitude si les deux jours consacrés à Oxford s'ajoutent aux trois jours passés dans la maison de campagne de Burke, ou si Mme de Genlis s'est absentée de Londres seulement trois jours en tout. Bien qu'il faille pencher, semble-t-il, pour la première hypothèse, l'extrait des *Mémoires* cité plus haut à ce sujet est loin d'être clair et cette relative obscurité s'accroît si, considérant l'arrêt chez la duchesse de Portland, l'on cherche à interpréter les expressions «dans cette course» et «sur notre chemin». En fait, Bulstrode, le domaine de la duchesse, se trouvant à quelque six kilomètres avant Beaconsfield quand on vient de Londres, la visite du parc a dû avoir lieu au moment où Burke est allé chercher son invitée, c'est-à-dire le vendredi 15 juillet, jour où Mme de Genlis écrivait à Fanny Burney: «Je pars dans l'instant pour Oxford». Cela prouve qu'une fois de plus notre auteur s'est trompée dans l'ordre des faits, car si la duchesse de Portland était probablement bien «à la mort» le 15 déjà, elle ne s'éteignit pas «dans la nuit», comme l'affirme Félicité, mais deux jours plus tard, le dimanche 17.[32]

Une autre visite notée par la comtesse dans ses *Mémoires* (III, 342), celle du château et du parc de Blenheim, est probablement à placer pendant les deux jours passés à Oxford, vu le peu de distance qui sépare cette ville de Blenheim. De même, la fête qu'on lui donna dans les jardins du poète Waller, qui se trouvent à Hall Barn, près de Beaconsfield, s'inscrit certainement dans le programme du séjour chez Burke. Tout cela tiendrait difficilement dans l'espace de trois jours.

Nous avons une autre raison de penser que Mme de Genlis s'absenta au moins cinq jours de Londres: de retour dans la capitale, elle envoie à Jane Burke une lettre datée du 22 juillet 1785; il est donc probable qu'arrivée le 15 à Beaconsfield, elle en est repartie le 20 ou le 21 et a écrit peu après sa lettre de remerciement. Comme à notre connaissance celle-ci est inédite, et à cause de l'intérêt qu'elle présente, nous la reproduisons ici intégralement:

«j'ai si mal exprimé dans mon mauvais anglois La tendre reconnoissance que m'ont inspiré *(sic)* Madame, Les preuves d'amitié et L'accueil si aimable que j'ai reçu de vous et de monsieur burke, que je ne puis me défendre de vous renouveller encore tous les remercimens que je vous dois à L'un et à L'autre. j'ai bien mal parlé à baconsfields, mais j'ai senti vivement tout ce que peut inspirer de doux et de tendre Le plaisir d'admirer de près un homme justement célèbre, par des talens supérieurs, et Les qualités Les plus atta-

---

[31] Malgré le doute qui a pu subsister à ce sujet, rien n'excuse l'accumulation d'erreurs qu'on trouve dans une seule phrase d'un ouvrage récent, à propos du doctorat d'Oxford: «Forte de son voyage en Angleterre de l'année 1778 (?), au cours duquel elle a été fêtée par le grand Burke qui lui a remis la médaille (??) de docteur de l'Université d'Oxford . . . etc.» (Marguerite Castillon du Perron, *Louis-Philippe et la Révolution française*, Perrin 1963, I, pp. 70—71). Même désinvolture envers l'histoire dans un article d'André Castelot intitulé «La pédagogue et le régicide» (*Historia*, No. 290, Janvier 1971, pp. 24—35).

[32] Cf. *Gentleman's Magazine*, vol. 55, II, 575, et *Jackson's Oxford Journal*, No. 1682, July 23, 1785.

chantes et j'ai joüi de La satisfaction de le voir dans son intérieur aussi heureux qu'il est digne de L'être. Le tableau que vous m'avés offert tous les deux ne s'effacera point de mon souvenir.

je me flatte madame que monsieur votre fils viendra en france (,il) m'est doux et même nécessaire d'espérer que je pourrai lui être de quelque utilité. et je compte que je serai La 1ère personne qu'il préviendra de son arrivée; c'est un droit que m'a donné L'amitié que vous avés bien voulu me témoigner, et je le réclame d'avance. je vous supplie madame d'exprimer à toutes Les personnes que j'ai eu L'avantage de voir chés vous combien j'ai été sensible à L'indulgence si aimable quelles m'ont montré *(sic)*. ainsi qu'à my lord inchiquin et aux dames qui étoient chés lui car je me rappelle qu'étant *au bout de mon anglois* je suis partie de Cliveden d'une manière beaucoup trop silencieuse. je dois désirer quon me juge non sur ce que j'ai pu paroître mais sur ce que j'ai du penser et sentir.

recevés madame L'assurance si vraie de ma reconnoissance et des tendres sentimens que je vous ay consacrés pour ma vie et avec Lesquels j'ai L'honneur d'être Madame, votre très humble et très obéissante servante ducrest genlis.»[33]

La façon dont Mme de Genlis insiste sur l'insuffisance de son anglais souligne implicitement l'importance qu'elle accorde à cette aptitude à bien s'exprimer. De fait, la pratique des langues vivantes est un des articles fondamentaux de son système d'éducation et celui par lequel elle fait vraiment figure de précurseur. Il y a aussi que le séjour à Beaconsfield fut peut-être le seul moment du premier voyage où elle ne put converser en français, Burke étant, de son propre aveu, peu expert à manier notre langue.[34] Quant à Richard, le fils de Jane et Edmund Burke, il fera effectivement un court séjour en France, au mois de novembre de la même année, et nous savons qu'il fut reçu par Mme de Genlis. Il alla à Paris, à Saint-Leu, où il fut présenté au marquis de Dampierre, protégé du duc de Chartres, qui s'occupa de lui, et à Fontainebleau, où il fut présenté à la reine et aux Polignac; le roi s'enquit de son père et de lui auprès de lady Clermont, qui lui rapporta les termes élogieux du souverain à l'égard du grand orateur. Dans la lettre à sa mère où il raconte toutes ces choses, le jeune Richard se réjouit des honneurs qu'on lui fit uniquement à cause de la renommée de son père, avantage qui vaut à ses yeux ceux de la richesse et du rang.[35]

La lettre de Mme de Genlis à Jane Burke nous fournit aussi la preuve qu'étant à Beaconsfield la comtesse a été reçue par lord et lady Inchiquin, voisins et amis des Burke, dans leur résidence de Cliveden; celle-ci, pittoresquement située sur une terrasse dominant la Tamise, entre Maidenhead et

[33] Northampton County Record Office, 517 N, 1381+, Wentworth Woodhouse Monuments in the Sheffield City Libraries. Lettre publiée ici avec la permission de: Earl Fitzwilliam and Earl Fitzwilliam's Wentworth Estates Company, and the City Librarian.

[34] Cf. *The Correspondence of E. Burke, op. cit.* (cf. *supra*, n. 28), VII, App. I, 584 et IX, 3. On trouvera en outre, dans ce dernier volume, des lettres en français de Burke qui montrent l'insuffisance qu'il reconnaît lui-même (pp. 14—16, 22—29, 35—37, 52—53).

[35] *Ibid.*, V, 231—5 (Richard Burke, Jr. to Jane Burke, 9 Nov. 1785). Dans le vol. II (pp. 411 sq.), une série de lettres de janvier 1773 nous renseignent sur le premier voyage de Richard en France, où son père le conduisit; il séjourna dans une famille d'Auxerre.

Beaconsfield, avait été construite sur le même plan que la propriété des Burke, mais en plus petit.[36] C'est donc sans doute après cette réception, dans la dernière semaine de son voyage, que Félicité fut conduite à la Chambre des Communes par «milord Inchiquin», qui avait dû lui promettre cette faveur à Cliveden. Si l'on en croit le passage des *Mémoires* déjà cité, elle put y assister à une séance grâce à la permission qui lui fut accordée «par un arrêté particulier». La bibliothèque de la Chambre des Communes ne conserve pas trace d'un tel arrêté, bien qu'il soit vrai, comme l'affirme notre visiteuse qu'aucune femme ne pouvait pénétrer dans la salle des séances. Cette interdiction dura de 1778 à 1834, date de l'incendie qui dévasta l'ancienne Chambre des Communes, située à cette époque à l'emplacement de ce qui est aujourd'hui St. Stephen's Hall. La salle avait alors un faux plafond qui faisait qu'elle était surmontée d'une sorte de vaste grenier au centre duquel une ouverture composée de huit lucarnes assurait la ventilation de la Chambre des Communes. Dans ce local sombre et déprimant, éclairé par une seule chandelle, certaines dames privilégiées et recommandées par quelque membre du Parlement, pouvaient venir s'asseoir sur le banc circulaire qui cernait l'ouverture et, la porte refermée à clé derrière elles, assister d'en haut, juste au-dessus du lustre de la salle des séances, à un débat des Communes. Les vingt-cinq billets d'entrée distribués quotidiennement étaient très recherchés et, à supposer que Mme de Genlis obtint un de ces billets, l'on peut penser que c'est ce qui lui fit croire qu'elle avait bénéficié d'un véritable passe-droit, surtout si l'on tient compte du fait qu'avec le passage du temps, les événements ont toujours tendance à grossir dans son souvenir.[37]

Le dernier jalon précis que nous ayons du séjour de juillet 1785 est constitué par la lettre que Walpole envoie le samedi 23 à la comtesse d'Upper Ossory pour lui raconter en détail la visite faite la veille à Strawberry Hill par Mme de Genlis, qui, de son côté, ne consacre qu'une petite phrase de ses *Mémoires* à l'événement («M. Horace Walpole, l'ami si intime de madame du Deffant, me donna à déjeuner dans son prieuré gothique», III, 343). Il va sans dire que nous préférons le bavardage à la fois étudié et narquois de l'homme de lettres anglais à la concision incolore de la comtesse française, qui ne s'oublie pas assez pour être un bon témoin de ce qui se passe autour d'elle. Ecoutons donc Horace Walpole:

«You surprise me, Madam, by saying the newspapers mention my disappointment of seeing Madame de Genlis — how can such arrant trifles spread? it is very true, that, as the Hill would not go to see Madame de Genlis, she has come to see the Hill. Ten days ago Mrs. Cosway sent me a note that *Madame* desired a ticket for Strawberry Hill. I thought I could not do less than offer her a breakfast, and named yesterday sennight. Then came a message that she must go to Oxford and take her Doctor's degree — and then another, that I should see her yesterday, when she did arrive with Miss

[36] Sur lord Inchiquin, 5th Earl of Inchiquin (Ireland), 1726—1808, cf. Sir Lewis Namier & John Brooke, *The History of Parliament*, III, 222.

[37] Cf. Harry Graham, *The Mother of Parliaments*, London 1910, pp. 270—2, et *The Houses of Parliament. An Illustrated Guide to the Palace of Westminster*, 11th ed., London 1967. Ajoutons toutefois que, malgré l'interdiction dont nous parlons, il n'était pas rare de voir des femmes assister aux séances (cf. P. D. G. Thomas, *The House of Commons in the Eighteenth Century*, Oxford 1971, p. 149).

Wilkes and Pamela, whom she did not even present to me, and whom she has educated to be very like her in the face. I told her I could not attribute the honour of her visit but to my late dear friend Madame du Deffand. It rained the whole time, and was dark at midnight, so that she could scarce distinguish a picture — but you will want an account of her, and not of what she saw or could not see. Her person is agreeable, and she seems to have been pretty. Her conversation is natural and reasonable, not *précieuse* and affected and searching to be eloquent, as I had expected. I asked her if she had been pleased with Oxford, meaning the buildings, not the wretched oafs that inhabit it. She said she had had little time; that she had wished to learn their plan of education, which, as she said sensibly, she supposed was adapted to our Constitution — I could have told her that it is directly repugnant to our Constitution, and that nothing is taught there but drunkenness and prerogative, or, in their language, Church and King. I asked if it is true that the new edition of Voltaire's works is prohibited; she replied, severely, — and then condemned those who write against religion and government, which was a little unlucky before her friend *Miss Wilkes*. She stayed two hours, and returns to France to-day *to her duty*. I really do not know whether the Duc de Chartres is in England or not — She did lodge in his house in Portland Place — but at Paris, I think, has an hotel where she educates his daughters.»[38]

Cette lettre contient plusieurs affirmations à retenir, dont une, rappelons-le, concernant le doctorat d'Oxford, a déjà pu être classée comme une bonne plaisanterie de la part de Walpole. Nous y apprenons en outre que Mrs. Cosway, l'épouse du peintre Richard Cosway et miniaturiste réputée elle-même, servit d'intermédiaire entre Walpole et Mme de Genlis; c'est la preuve que les deux femmes se connaissaient et étaient probablement entrées en relations auparavant, soit à Londres, soit à Paris. Le second nom qui retient notre attention ici est celui de Miss Wilkes, «Polly», la fille chérie du célèbre «ami de la liberté». En 1785, ce dernier n'est plus, selon ses propres termes, qu'«un volcan éteint» et nous ne pensons pas qu'il faille donner à cette fréquentation de Félicité la moindre signification politique ou «philosophique». Certes, Polly, qui avait fait, l'année précédente, un séjour en France de mai à août, chez la duchesse de la Vallière, était ainsi que son père dans les meilleurs termes avec les d'Holbach, Mme Helvétius et J.-B. Suard, toutes personnes qu'elle vit alors régulièrement à Paris; mais le nom de Mme de Genlis n'apparaît pas dans les lettres envoyées par Wilkes à sa fille en 1784 et il semble bien que ce soit cette dernière qui fit les premières avances, après l'arrivée de la comtesse à Londres. Les *Mémoires* sont plus explicites à cet endroit qu'à l'accoutumée:

«Mademoiselle Wilkes, fille du célèbre Wilkes, du parti de l'opposition, vint me voir; c'étoit une personne de trente-cinq ans, fort laide, mais très spirituelle, sachant beaucoup de langues, et d'une instruction fort remarquable; elle fut si aimable pour moi que je me liai intimement avec elle. Son père étoit très-fameux par ses querelles avec le gouvernement, la hardiesse de ses opinions, et la violence avec laquelle son parti l'avoit fait nommer lord-maire. Je dînai deux fois chez lui; sa conversation étoit amusante; il

---

[38] *H. Walpole's Correspondence*, vol. 33, pp. 482—3. On trouvera d'utiles éclaircissements dans les notes qui accompagnent le texte de cette lettre.

avoit beaucoup vu Voltaire pendant son séjour à Londres; il me dit que Voltaire savoit très-mal l'anglois, qu'il n'étoit pas en état de sentir la beauté des poëtes. Il me conta beaucoup de traits de sa jalousie et de son animosité contre Pope; tout le monde sait qu'il eut la bassesse de le dénoncer comme *papiste*. Je vis chez M. Wilkes une chose qui me surprit étrangement: lorsque M. Wilkes quitta la place de lord-maire, la ville de Londres, selon l'usage, lui fit un présent: elle lui donna un superbe morceau d'argenterie, représentant en plein relief l'assassinat de César au sénat. Ce présent fut fait avant la révolution, dont il sembloit être un prélude; il étoit placé pompeusement sur la cheminée du salon.» (III, 362—3)

C'est probablement Mme de Genlis qui, ne manquant jamais une occasion de nourrir son hostilité envers Voltaire, mit chez Wilkes la conversation sur le philosophe. Quant à Walpole, on peut se demander pourquoi il fit de même avec Mme de Genlis en lui posant une question sur la récente édition des œuvres de Voltaire. Sachant d'avance la réponse qu'il allait s'attirer, peut-être voulait-il simplement taquiner sa visiteuse, dont la sévère opinion sur le philosophe de Ferney était bien connue. Il est certain cependant que, malgré son ton moqueur et l'évidente insinuation au sujet de la naissance illégitime de Paméla, dont la présence aux côtés de Mme de Genlis au cours de ce séjour ne semble être attestée que par lui, il a l'air d'avoir été agréablement surpris par la simplicité et le bon sens de celle qu'il avait traitée de «maîtresse d'école» et de «poule» de Rousseau, moins de vingt jours auparavant.

Les derniers mots de la lettre de Walpole nous montrent qu'il n'a gardé qu'un vague souvenir des renseignements fournis autrefois par Mme du Deffand. Depuis 1782, le duc de Chartres n'a plus qu'une fille, la future Madame Adélaïde. S'il est effectivement locataire d'une maison au no. 35 Portland Place, il est à peu près certain que, quoiqu'il fût en Angleterre en même temps que la gouvernante, il ne vint pas à Londres cette année-là.[39] Enfin, c'est par Walpole que nous apprenons aussi que Félicité rentra en France le 23 juillet; elle note dans ses *Mémoires*:

«(...) mon passage fut très orageux: j'éprouvai une des plus terribles tempêtes que l'on ait vues dans ce détroit. J'arrivai à Saint-Leu au bout de six semaines d'absence: la joie de mes élèves fut extrême, ainsi que la mienne.» (III, 372)

Le *Journal* du Musée Condé enregistre cette joie. Le 27 juillet, jour de son retour à Saint-Leu, où le petit pensionnat passait sept ou huit mois de l'année, un cortège où figurait une charrette garnie de feuillage et de fleurs préparée la veille alla à sa rencontre, mais la manqua, «et c'est la voyageuse qui reçut son monde sur l'escalier parmi l'attendrissement général».[40]

Ce voyage de trois semaines à Londres et dans ses environs, on le voit, fut bien rempli, surtout si l'on ajoute au compte rendu précédant celui des

[39] Cf. Amédée Britsch, *op. cit.* (v. *supra*, n. 2), pp. 8—15 et 34—38.

[40] A. Britsch, *op. cit.* (v. *supra*, n. 14), pp. 379—380. Selon cet auteur, Mme de Genlis avait quitté Saint-Leu le 25 juin, ce qui fait une absence de 31 jours pleins exactement, et non de six semaines comme elle le dit dans ses *Mémoires*. Voir aussi H. Bonhomme, *op. cit.* (cf. *supra*, n. 2), p. 50: «Quand je suis venue seule en Angleterre avec M. Myris, j'y passai cinq semaines et trois jours. Je n'avois qu'une femme de chambre et deux domestiques, etc ...» (Lettre de Mme de Genlis au duc d'Orléans, envoyée de Londres, le 17. 1. 1792).

faits et gestes de Mme de Genlis que nous n'avons pu encore dater, même approximativement, à savoir la réception, chez lord Gordon, par le prince de Galles qui n'avait pas pu l'inviter à Carlton House, toute sa maison étant partie pour Brighton, et la visite de la maison de Richardson, qui donne lieu dans les *Mémoires* au commentaire suivant:

«Richardson n'est pas enterré à Westminster, les Anglois ne font pas de cet auteur autant de cas que nous, parce qu'il n'est pas compté au rang des bons écrivains, et qu'il a mal peint le grand monde qu'il ne connoissoit pas; mais il a si bien peint le cœur humain, les passions et la vertu, il a si bien connu le cœur d'une femme honnête, ingénue et sensible, qu'il méritera toujours d'être placé au premier rang des moralistes.»[41]

Elle put, lors de cette visite, s'asseoir sur le banc de Richardson («le bras droit de ce banc s'ouvroit et renfermoit une écritoire»), dans le jardin de Parson's Green, et contempler son «portrait de grandeur naturelle et à l'huile», dont Mr. Bridgen, le gendre du romancier fit faire pour elle une copie en miniature qu'il lui envoya un mois après son retour en France.

Ce serait mal connaître Félicité que de croire que c'est là tout. Elle avait ce qu'on pourrait appeler la mystique de l'emploi du temps, pour elle-même aussi bien que pour les autres, à tel point qu'elle consacra à cette implacable divinité un ouvrage de plus de 250 pages, qui porte précisément ce titre, *De l'emploi du temps*, et qu'elle publia en 1823.

«Toutes mes occupations et mes courses, dit-elle fièrement, ne m'empêchèrent pas à mon premier voyage, de prendre, pendant mon séjour à Londres, deux maîtres: l'un de déclamation angloise; l'autre étoit un bijoutier qui m'apprit à faire de jolis ouvrages en semences de perles collées.» (III, 363)

Une chose frappe le lecteur qui parcourt d'un trait le récit du séjour de 1785 dans les *Mémoires*: il n'y trouve aucune description de monuments ou de rues, aucun portrait individuel ou collectif. Londres et Oxford, en tant que villes, brillent par leur absence. Remarquons en passant que même la question que Walpole voulut poser sur l'architecture d'Oxford fut mal interprétée et qu'on lui répondit sur le plan d'éducation de l'université. Les châteaux visités n'existent que par leurs parcs et les souvenirs qui s'attachent aux personnages rencontrés et tournent autour de corbeilles de fleurs ou de fruits (des ananas à profusion!). A part les brèves descriptions du vitrail de Reynolds à Oxford, du «morceau d'argenterie» de Wilkes et du portrait de Richardson, les seules autres qui se détachent, accentuant ainsi la prédominance des souvenirs «botaniques», sont celles de Kew et des jardins du poète Waller.

Il reste enfin un souvenir auquel Mme de Genlis fait un sort particulier en écrivant ses *Mémoires* bien des années après son voyage. C'est celui de l'hommage que lui rendit le poète Hayley sous la forme d'«une belle ode . . . qui se trouve dans ses œuvres» et qui, nous l'avons vu, ne serait qu'un exemple de l'«infinité de vers» faits pour elle et insérés dans les journaux au moment de son séjour. Force nous est de constater qu'en nous confiant cela, Félicité a, volontairement ou non, incliné une fois encore les faits dans le sens d'un honneur exceptionnel, qui aurait coïncidé avec sa présence en

---

[41] III, 361. Richardson est, avec Addison, un des écrivains anglais dont l'éloge revient le plus souvent sous la plume de Mme de Genlis. Voir en particulier: *Adèle et Théodore*, 1822, I, 423, *Les Veillées du Château*, Préface, et *Bélisaire*, 1808, Préface.

Angleterre. Or, si l'on consulte la première édition des *Poems and Plays* de William Hayley, publiée à Londres en 1785, on trouve bien une *Ode to the Countess de Genlis*, mais elle est datée 1784 et surtout l'auteur précise dans sa préface que l'«Ode to that elegant and instructive female author» est inédite. Le doute que nous éprouvons sur la véracité des dires de la comtesse à ce sujet est renforcé par le fait que nous n'avons jusqu'ici pas retrouvé le moindre distique qui ferait partie de cette «infinité de vers» écrits pour elle en Angleterre. Sa mémoire a-t-elle magnifié les quatre vers imprimés à sa louange dans le *Mercure de France* du 25 juin 1785, en les ajoutant au souvenir un peu confus des quinze strophes dithyrambiques de William Hayley? Toutefois, le fait que ce poème fut écrit avant la visite de Mme de Genlis et ne parut probablement pas dans les journaux, comme elle le suggère, ne lui enlève rien de sa signification à nos yeux.

Hayley, dont Southey disait: «Everything about that man is good except his poetry», a beau être un poète médiocre, les vers qu'il dédie à Mme de Genlis expriment assez bien les raisons de l'accueil favorable fait aux premiers ouvrages de la comtesse par un public conscient de la nécessité de donner à la jeunesse des livres adaptés à son intelligence et destinés à former son cœur et son esprit. Hayley salue en Mme de Genlis l'apôtre de la morale et l'amie des enfants et des mères. Il commence par stigmatiser l'inanité et la frivolité qui caractérisèrent les œuvres romanesques françaises jusqu'au moment où «le génie de cette terre généreuse» suscita une main féminine pour redresser les torts causés «à la vertu, à la vérité et au goût» par une fausse philosophie, génératrice de livres immoraux et licencieux. Mme de Genlis vint enfin et, mêlant l'inspiration religieuse à la sagesse et à la fantaisie, elle sut inventer des fictions dramatiques et romanesques capables de protéger la jeunesse du mal et de lui enseigner la vertu, en exerçant sur elle, par leur beauté et leur pathétique, un charme tout-puissant.

Les deux dernières strophes du poème peignent le tableau édifiant de la mère et de l'enfant penchés sur les «chastes» pages de Mme de Genlis; la première pour y apprendre dans la joie l'art de l'éducatrice, le second pour y chercher un «plaisir instructif», que traduiront ses larmes et ses paroles de gratitude:

> Whenever youth, with curious view,
> Instructive pleasure shall pursue,
> The little lively student there,
> With rapt attention's keenest air,
>   Shall o'er thy volumes bend:
> And while his tears their charm confess,
> His grateful voice shall in their author bless
> The spirit-kindling guide, the heart-enchanting friend.[42]

Nous pouvons imaginer le plaisir qu'a pu prendre Félicité à lire ces vers qui célébraient en elle le personnage qu'elle ambitionnait d'être avant tout et qui est celui dans lequel la postérité l'a fixée. Quel épilogue plus digne pouvait-on trouver au premier séjour anglais que ce temoignage d'admiration sincère?

[42] *Poems and Plays*, By William Hayley, Esq. (. . .), London 1785, I, pp. 149—156. Voir aussi la préface en tête des six volumes et l'*Impromptu to Mr. Meyer* (pp. 183—4), également de 1784, tout à l'éloge de Voltaire et de Rousseau.

Dans l'intervalle de plus de six ans qui sépare les deux voyages, Mme de Genlis continue de se consacrer presque exclusivement à sa tâche d'éducatrice et sa production littéraire diminue considérablement. Pourtant un livre important sort de sa plume pendant cette période; c'est *La Religion considérée comme l'unique base du bonheur et de la véritable philosophie.* Publié en 1787 et traduit en anglais la même année, il consacre son auteur dans son double rôle de championne de la religion et d'ennemie des philosophes.[43] C'est assez pour que les sarcasmes se déchaînent de nouveau. La *Correspondance littéraire* de Grimm, qui avait accueilli favorablement, et même chaleureusement, le premier volume du *Théâtre* de Mme de Genlis en 1779, ne manqua pas de faire un long compte rendu du nouvel ouvrage pour en souligner tous les défauts et dénoncer la présomption de celle qu'un quatrain satirique qualifia de «mère de l'église», à la suite de cette publication.[44] En 1787 également, on voit paraître en Ecosse une anthologie composée des plus beaux contes et autres extraits remarquables d'*Adèle et Théodore* et des *Veillées du Château*; elle est intitulée *The Beauties of Genlis* et témoigne de la permanence du renom de notre auteur outre-Manche.[45]

C'est cependant dans des circonstances bien différentes de celles du premier voyage que Félicité se rend en Angleterre pour la deuxième fois. Alors qu'en 1785 elle était seulement accompagnée de Paméla, du peintre Myris et de sa femme de chambre, une véritable petite troupe traverse cette fois la Manche. Il y a, en plus de la gouvernante, sa petite-fille, Eglantine de Lawœstine, âgée de cinq ans, sa nièce Henriette de Sercey, Paméla, la princesse Adelaïde d'Orléans, le botaniste et pharmacien Pierre-Philippe Alyon, le domestique Horain et sans doute quelques autres personnes, comme l'artiste Charles Lepeintre, dont la présence fut intermittente. Le premier séjour ne dura que trois semaines; elle restera plus d'un an la seconde fois et séjournera principalement dans trois villes, à savoir Bath, Londres et Bury St. Edmunds, dans le Suffolk; elle fera en outre plusieurs expéditions dans d'autres provinces.[46] Dans l'ensemble, elle mènera une vie beaucoup plus retirée, aura à se débattre parmi des difficultés financières et, en contraste avec les hommages du premier séjour, se heurtera à des réactions hostiles qui iront croissant avec l'aggravation des événements en France.

[43] D. Mornet dans *Les Origines intellectuelles de la Révolution Française (1715—1787)*, Paris 1967, au chapitre intitulé *Les résistances de la tradition religieuse et politique*, cite l'ouvrage de Mme de Genlis comme une étape importante de ce mouvement, aussitôt après Palissot et ses *Philosophes*. Certains écrits antérieurs de la comtesse lui auraient permis de faire commencer plus tôt le rôle qu'elle ne jouera pleinement qu'après le retour d'exil.

[44] Cf. *Correspondance secrète* (. . .) publiée (. . .) par M. de Lescure, Paris 1866, II, 210—1.

[45] Pour d'autres preuves, ainsi que sur les raisons et les limites de cette popularité, voir M. Wahba, *op. cit.*, pp. 232—236.

[46] Par un dépouillement de la presse provinciale, nous avons pu établir quelques dates, dont voici deux des plus importantes: arrivée à Bath, entre le 29 octobre et le 2 novembre 1791 (*Bath Chronicle* du 3); arrivée à Bury St. Edmunds, le dimanche 12 février (792 (*Bury & Norwich Post* du 15). Pour le voyage dans les provinces (Newmarket, Cambridge, Derbyshire, pays de Galles, Portsmouth, île de Wight), voir *Mémoires* IV, 115—7.

La principale raison de ce revirement vient de ce que, dès 1789, Mme de Genlis prend fait et cause pour la Révolution et qu'à tort ou à raison on l'englobe bientôt parmi les fauteurs d'intrigue du Palais-Royal, quand on ne fait pas d'elle l'âme d'un complot orléaniste. La maîtresse du duc de Chartres s'est muée en égérie du duc d'Orléans, le futur Philippe-Egalité. Cela lui suscite une nouvelle catégorie d'ennemis, plus acharnés encore que les premiers.[47] Ce courant d'hostilité traverse la Manche avec la gouvernante et, unissant contre elle les adversaires anglais de la Révolution et les émigrés royalistes, qui voient des Jacobins partout, la poursuit jusqu'à son départ en novembre 1792, qui se fera presque sous la menace.

Les anciens amis de 1785 se lamentent ou invectivent. Fanny Burney a peine à croire à pareille métamorphose:

«What a woeful change from that elegant, amiable, high-bred Madame de Genlis I knew six years ago! the apparent pattern of female perfection in manners, conversation, and delicacy.»[48]

Elle se réjouit que «Madame Brulard» n'ait pas cherché à renouer avec elle, mais, au nom de la haute qualité morale de ses œuvres, se déclare disposée à croire, plutôt que mille ennemis déclarés, une seule personne qui serait prête à la justifier. Walpole, un instant réconcilié avec «la maîtresse d'école» en juillet 1785, condamne sans appel «That scribbling trollop Madame de Sillery» (Lettre à la comtesse d'Upper Ossory du 4-2-1792).

On constate un même retournement chez Burke, l'hôte si obligeant de Beaconsfield lors du premier séjour. Il est vrai qu'il n'était à ce moment-là qu'un homme politique aux idées libérales, réputé pour son éloquence. Il faut attendre 1790 pour que ses *Réflexions sur la Révolution de France*, dont le succès est foudroyant, fassent de lui l'inspirateur passionné et prestigieux de la Contre-Révolution. Ses traces ne seront que tardivement suivies par une Mme de Genlis transformée en restauratrice du catholicisme et de la monarchie, rôle qu'elle assumera, comme beaucoup d'autres, autant sans doute par intérêt et opportunisme politique que par une conviction antérieure, retrouvée à la suite d'un drame personnellement vécu et à la lumière d'une foi religieuse qu'elle ne perdit jamais. Mais cette Mme de Genlis-là, Burke ne la connaîtra pas. En 1795, deux ans avant de mourir, il enverra à Mrs. Crewe cette prière, qui fait un curieux pendant antithétique aux vers que Hayley avaient dédiés à la «charmante magicienne» de 1784:

«I hope and supplicate, that all providant and virtuous Wives and Mothers of families, will employ all the just influence they possess over their Husbands and Children, to save themselves and their families from the ruin that the Mesdames de Staals and the Mesdames Rolands, and the Mesdames de Sillery, and Mrs. Helena Maria Williams, and the Mrs. Woolstencrofts &c &c &c &c &c and all that Clan of desperate, Wicked, and mischievously ingenious Women who have brought, or are likely to bring Ruin and shame upon all those that listen to them.»[49]

---

[47] La question des positions politiques de Mme de Genlis et de son véritable rôle auprès de Philippe-Egalité ne peut être abordée ici. Les textes qui en traitent surabondent, y compris ceux où Félicité présente sa propre justification. C'est peut-être J. Harmand qui tire la meilleure conclusion des pièces du procès (voir surtout *op. cit.*, 3e Partie, pp. 193—6 et chap. I à III; 4e Partie, pp. 349—355).

[48] *Diary and Letters of Madame D'Arblay*, V, 78.

[49] *The Correspondence of E. Burke*, VIII (1968), 304 (11 August 1795).

Au moment où Burke écrivait ces lignes, «Mrs. Genlis, *alias* Sillery, *alias* Brulart, as she would be styled at the Old Bailey», pour parler comme Walpole, se trouvait en Allemagne, où, plus que jamais considérée comme une Jacobine, elle était en butte à bien des affronts. L'année suivante, elle entreprit des démarches pour qu'on la rayât de la liste des émigrés et envoya, entre autres, au ministre de la Justice du Directoire, un document intitulé *Mémoire et Réclamations de la Citoyenne Genlis*; on trouve le passage suivant concernant le second séjour en Angleterre:

«(. . .) Je suis partie de France la première fois en 1791 pour aller prendre les eaux de Bath et pour conclure en Angleterre un arrangement pour la vente des vins de Sillery, et pour faire un voyage instructif pour deux de mes élèves que j'y menois (Mlle d'Orléans et ma nièce); voyage que mon goût pour les lettres me rendoit doublement intéressant. Je partis avec des passeports en bonne forme; Pethion alors au comble de sa popularité vint avec moi, ainsi que Mr. Voidel présentement en France: ainsi ce départ ne fut certainement pas une *émigration* et mes passeports ne limitoient point le tems de mon absence. Je passai à Londres où je laissai Pethion, je ne m'arrêtai dans cette ville que pour changer de chevaux. Mr. Voidel vint avec nous à Bath, il n'y resta que 6 jours et repartit pour la France avec Pethion qu'il reprit à Londres. Je restai à Bath deux mois de suite, vivant dans la plus profonde solitude; ensuite je voyageai trois mois dans toutes les provinces d'angleterre. Après ces voyages je fus dans une maison de campagne chez Mr. Sheridan près de Londres, où j'ai resté cinq semaines. (. . .) j'avois voyagé, pour des raisons de négoce, de santé, et comme institutrice, et comme littérateur. (. . .) Je revins dans les premiers jours de novembre 1792 (. . .)»[50]

Ce n'est pas ici la place de comparer ce récit avec les versions des mêmes événements que Félicité a données dans les *Mémoires* et ailleurs. Si nous l'avons préféré aux autres, c'est qu'autant que nous le sachions, il est inédit et qu'en dépit de ses graves inexactitudes et omissions volontaires — pas un mot de Paméla, ni de Bury St. Edmunds, où elle passa pourtant plus de huit mois! —, il est le plus précis de tous sur certains détails comme ceux qui concernent Pétion et Voidel. Surtout, il énumère clairement les raisons qu'eut Mme de Genlis de faire ce voyage; il n'y a pas lieu de douter qu'aucune de celles-ci ait été inventée pour les besoins de la cause, bien que cet écrit cherche à prouver que son auteur ne tombe pas sous le coup des décrets sur l'émigration. A ces raisons, il faut ajouter le souvenir attendri qu'elle gardait de son premier séjour. Projetant dès avril 1791 de passer l'hiver suivant en Angleterre, elle consigna ce sentiment dans ses *Leçons d'une gouvernante*, publiées cette année-là. La phrase, reprise textuellement dans les *Mémoires*, décrit l'Angleterre comme

«(le) pays que mon goût particulier, la reconnoissance et l'amitié me rendoient également cher, et où j'espérois être plus heureuse qu'en France,

[50] Archives Nationales, F7 6521, No. 1291. Dans ses *Mémoires*, Mme de Genlis se contredit sur l'arrêt à Londres, à quelques pages d'intervalle (voir IV, pp. 100 et 112). La version du présent document est corroborée par d'autres textes. A propos des vins de Sillery, voir les *Travels in France* d'Arthur Young, à la date du 8 juillet 1789. Il considère M. de Genlis comme «the greatest wine-farmer in all Champagne» et dit ceci de sa femme: «I did not like to pass the door of Madame de Genlis without seeing her: her writings are too celebrated»; mais les Genlis n'étaient pas à Sillery ce jour-là.

si je pouvois trouver le bonheur loin de ma famille, de mes élèves et de ma patrie.» (IV, 75)

D'autres traits communs rapprochent les deux séjours. Outre les relations amicales qu'elle entretient avec quelques personnes,[51] moins en vue sans doute, mais tout aussi hospitalières que celles du premier voyage, Félicité poursuit la seconde fois ses efforts systématiques pour se perfectionner dans la langue anglaise et enrichir sa connaissance de la littérature, un des motifs de son déplacement, comme nous venons de le voir. Dès le début de son séjour, elle met à profit, pour elle et pour ses élèves, les ressources culturelles de Bath, sa première étape, qui, à cette époque, se trouve à l'un des sommets de sa prospérité et de son rayonnement mondain. En particulier, son théâtre, tout en restant le banc d'essai des salles londoniennes, devient progressivement l'égal de celles-ci et les vedettes de la capitale n'estiment déroger en venant jouer dans la célèbre ville d'eau. C'est ce que suggèrent les *Mémoires*:

«Il y avoit une excellente troupe de comédiens qui jouoient la tragédie et la comédie. Je louai une loge, et, pour nous bien familiariser avec la *langue parlée*, nous allions presque tous les jours au spectacle; nous entendîmes parfaitement presque tout de suite la tragédie; il n'en fut pas de même de la comédie: la vitesse du débit, les façons de parler familières et proverbiales, et les fréquentes abréviations nous déroutoient continuellement. Mais nous portions toujours avec nous les pièces imprimées, où nous lisions ce que notre oreille ne nous faisoit pas comprendre; et, de cette manière, au bout de six semaines, nous entendions l'anglois comme les Anglois mêmes.» (IV, 112)

Ainsi, tout en apprenant et en enseignant à la fois l'anglais parlé de façon vivante, Félicité satisfaisait sa passion pour le théâtre. Le seul regret qu'elle aura de quitter Londres, où elle restera environ six semaines en se rendant de Bath à Bury St. Edmunds, sera d'avoir à se priver des représentations théâtrales, la petite ville du Suffolk n'ayant pas de salle, d'où son empressement à aller voir «toutes les belles pièces de théâtre» durant ce deuxième séjour londonien.[52]

[51] Citons entre autres: Sir Richard Colt Hoare (1758—1838) qui la reçut dans son château de Stourhead, dans le Wiltshire, après le départ de Bath; Thomas Charles Bunbury (1740—1821), qui envoyait tous les samedis à Mme de Genlis, alors à Bury, «un âne chargé de fruits superbes et de fleurs» (*Mém.*, IV, 114); Mr. Hervey, futur lord Bristol (1769—1859), qui forma, à l'époque du séjour de Bury, une solide et durable amitié avec Mme de Genlis, et plus encore avec la princesse d'Orléans; les fameuses «Ladies of Llangollen» (Lady Eleanor Butler et Sarah Ponsonby), qui reçurent Mme de Genlis dans leur cottage de Plasnewydd, ce qui donna lieu à un morceau de bravoure dans les *Souvenirs de Félicie* (1804), repris dans les *Mémoires* (III, 343—356) et loin d'être sans intérêt; Sheridan, enfin, qui tomba amoureux de Paméla, et fut l'hôte de Mme de Genlis et ses compagnes dans sa maison d'Isleworth (sur les péripéties de cette fin de séjour, voir *Mémoires*, IV, 127—139).

[52] Cf. lettre citée par H. Bonhomme (voir *supra*, n. 40), du 17 janvier 1792. C'est précisément l'époque où George Romney accompagne Mme de Genlis et ses élèves au théâtre et qu'il peint les portraits de la gouvernante et de Paméla. Dans sa *Life of George Romney* (Chichester, 1809, pp. 144—153 et pp. 166—171), William Hayley, l'encenseur de 1784, raconte comment, au cours d'un séjour qu'il fit à Paris en août 1790 en compagnie du peintre et d'un ami commun, les trois voyageurs furent chaleureusement reçus par Mme de Genlis, qu'ils ne connaissaient pas. C'est donc Hayley qui servit d'intermédiaire entre Romney et la comtesse, dont le portrait par le peintre anglais, bien qu'il ne soit qu'une esquisse, est un des plus vivants qu'on ait faits d'elle.

Avec cette question du théâtre, nous sommes amenés naturellement à considérer la conclusion que Mme de Genlis donne à ses deux voyages, dès la fin du tome III de ses *Mémoires*, où plus de six pages sur huit sont consacrées aux auteurs dramatiques anglais, et cela pourra servir de point de départ au bref bilan provisoire de son expérience anglaise, par lequel nous nous proposons de clore notre examen des séjours en Angleterre.

BILAN DE L'EXPÉRIENCE ANGLAISE DE MME DE GENLIS

Aux impressions plus ou moins estompées que lui ont laissées les pièces vues ou lues pendant les deux voyages, se mêle, à l'époque de la rédaction des *Mémoires*, le souvenir de lectures faites avant 1785 ou après 1792 et sans doute aussi celui des critiques traditionnellement dirigées contre le théâtre anglais, depuis qu'on écrivait en France des *Observations* ou des *Remarques* sur l'Angleterre, avec leurs inévitables parallèles entre les deux conceptions dramatiques. Le verdict de la comtesse est sévère:

«Je lus beaucoup d'ouvrages anglois et je fus frappée du mépris ridicule que les écrivains de ce pays affectent pour les autres nations. Ce manque de dignité et de bienséance en est un aussi de grandeur et de goût. Avec quelle injustice ils ont jugé notre littérature en pillant et en copiant nos écrivains !» (III, 363)

Citant à l'appui un texte de Dryden, qui, «dans sa tragédie de la Mort d'Antoine et de Cléopâtre, déchire tous nos poëtes» (il s'agit en fait de la préface de *All for Love; or, The World Well Lost*), elle continue:

«Tous les auteurs anglois, et même le sage Addisson, n'ont pas été plus équitables pour nous. Comment sommes-nous représentés dans les comédies angloises? Les François y sont constamment traités comme des fats imbéciles, et, ce qui peut paroître singulier, comme des poltrons. Enfin on ne met les François sur le théâtre anglois que pour les représenter sous les traits les plus odieux et les plus ridicules. Dans les ouvrages les plus nouveaux on retrouve la même injustice et la même haine. Que l'on compare tout ceci avec la généreuse bonhomie de nos auteurs, qui ont tant loué les écrivains anglois et leur nation ! Que l'on compare l'équité angloise et l'équité françoise, le goût anglois et le goût françois ! C'est, je crois, sans vanité nationale, tout ce que nous pouvons désirer de plus avantageux pour nous.» (*ibid.*, 364—5)

Elle passe ensuite un certain nombre de pièces en revue et en conclut que leurs sujets et leurs situations ne sont le plus souvent qu'«un inconcevable tissu d'horreurs». S'il faut peut-être voir là un écho de la campagne de moralisation qui, dans l'Angleterre de la deuxième moitié du XVIIIe siècle, aboutit à l'expurgation de nombre de pièces de la période antérieure, il y a surtout l'expression d'une indignation personnelle. Celle d'une moraliste, qui, précisément, ne voit dans la littérature qu'un prétexte à faire de la morale, et, qui plus est, de ne la faire qu'avec de bons sentiments; celle aussi d'une championne de la foi catholique, car ce qui scandalise le plus Mme de Genlis dans le théâtre anglais, ce sont les «moqueries indécentes sur la religion catholique et les calomnies les plus atroces contre les ministres de notre culte . . .» (III, 369) qui s'y trouvent.

Ce qu'on peut observer dans la vie réelle ne lui donne guère meilleure opinion des Anglais, qu'elle chicane sur des bagatelles (n'oublions pas toutefois que ceci fut écrit au moins dix ans après le second séjour): la mode extravagante et dangereuse des «*Wiskys*» par exemple, ces «voitures démesurément élevées», «les détails frivoles des modes nouvelles et des habits de femmes» étalés dans les journaux, «le goût des romans et des contes de revenans», leur luxe, qui «surpasse de beaucoup le nôtre». Si les Français, à cause de leur gaîté, «passent facilement pour des étourdis», les Anglais, taciturnes, «se font, à peu de frais, une réputation de sagesse». Enfin, ces derniers «exaltent sans cesse le mérite de leur nation», et c'est un point sur lequel nous devrions les imiter, en acquérant cette «vanité respectable que nous n'avons pas assez».

Nous sommes loin, semble-t-il, des protestations d'amitié pour la seconde patrie qui remplissaient la lettre à Gibbon du 15 octobre 1779. Des deux attitudes, laquelle est la plus vraie et la plus fondamentale? Ni l'une, ni l'autre, vraisemblablement. Mme de Genlis, selon la règle du contraste et de l'ambiguïté qui semble dominer son caractère aussi bien que sa vie et son œuvre, n'en est pas à une contradiction près. Mais surtout, plus qu'elle ne le croit, elle a subi l'influence des courants politiques et philosophiques de l'époque mouvementée qu'elle a traversée; en particulier, elle s'est laissé entraîner d'abord par l'anglophilie et le cosmopolitisme du siècle des Lumières, puis, partiellement, par l'anglophobie et le nationalisme de l'aube du XIXe siècle.[53]

Afin de conclure avec plus de certitude sur un tel sujet, il faudrait aussi pouvoir rendre compte de la place de l'Angleterre dans l'œuvre de Mme de Genlis en procédant au dépouillement dont la nécessité a été soulignée au début de cette étude. Tout compte fait, par ses résultats, l'expérience anglaise de la comtesse est assez mince. Nous l'avons déjà dit, rien ne bouge, rien ne vit; les rues, le peuple, ses mœurs et ses coutumes, le climat même, tout semble absent. On a souvent l'impression qu'elle n'a pas *vu* l'Angleterre, ou qu'elle l'a vue essentiellement à travers une fraction de sa littérature, de telle sorte qu'il est difficile de distinguer entre ce qui vient de l'expérience directe et ce qui a une origine livresque. Ne dit-elle pas elle-même que, pendant le second séjour, elle ne lut que des livres anglais, à raison de six heures par jour et en faisant des extraits de toutes ses lectures (*Mém.*, IV, 118—9)? Le petit nombre d'objets, de scènes ou de personnages qui ont été observés sur place se rattachent, soit aux honneurs qui lui furent rendus et qui flattèrent sa vanité de femme et d'écrivain, soit au penchant qu'elle a à faire des contes moraux de tout ce que la vie lui présente. Nous n'en voulons pour preuve que cette méditation sur le *Cimetière de Bury*, le seul écrit qu'elle dit avoir composé au cours de son deuxième voyage:

«Le cimetière de cette ville est surtout remarquable par la beauté des monumens antiques dont il est entouré; on me conta que ce cimetière est le lieu de rendez-vous des amans, pendant le printemps et l'été; ils s'y réunissent le soir au clair de la lune. Il me semble qu'il n'y a qu'un amour légitime,

---

[53] Précisons ici que les *Mémoires* ne font que reproduire en le condensant un texte qui parut dès 1803 dans le *Mercure* (v. *Suite des Souvenirs de Félicie*, Paris, 1807, pp. 12—63) et que *Les Mères rivales*, roman épistolaire de notre auteur, contient une importante lettre sur l'Angleterre (v. éd. de Berlin en 4 vol., An X, III, lettre XXXIII). Celle-ci constitue un portrait du peuple anglais plein d'aperçus très justes sur cette nation, pour laquelle finalement Mme de Genlis éprouve une grande admirtion.

profond et pur, qui puisse s'exprimer dans un tel lieu. Le vice, ou un sentiment léger, formé par le caprice, ne se plairoient parmi ces tombeaux, ces ruines et sous l'ombrage des cyprès. Là, on ne sauroit prononcer avec légèreté et sans y penser, le serment d'aimer jusqu'à la mort ! Je me représente avec intérêt deux jeunes amans, gênés par un tuteur avare (car je veux qu'ils ne soient point sous l'autorité des auteurs de leurs jours, puisqu'ils se donnent un rendez-vous secret), je les vois arriver et se trouver seuls ensemble pour la première fois de leur vie. Je les vois s'approcher avec le saisissement et l'innocence d'une première passion, s'asseoir sur une tombe en face d'un de ces tombeaux gothiques dont ce lieu est entouré. Je vois couler leurs larmes ! . . . L'agitation violente qu'ils éprouvent forme un contraste frappant avec la tranquillité même de cet asile de la mort ! C'est ici que toutes les passions humaines viennent s'anéantir pour l'éternité, et c'est ici, jeunes amans, que vous osez vous livrer au sentiment le plus tumultueux qui puisse troubler l'âme; c'est ici que vous jurez d'aimer éternellement ! . . . Ils parlent ! . . . Avec quelle attention je les écoute ! . . . Le calme de la nuit, la douce clarté de la lune, les reflets harmonieux qu'elle produit sur ces vénérables monumens; ces sapins et ces cyprès qui s'élèvent avec majesté parmi ces tombeaux, et dont les belles formes pyramidales se dessinent en noir foncé sur ces tours antiques; cette réunion d'objets imposans, funèbres, religieux, en inspirant une profonde mélancolie, exalte tous les sentimens. Que l'entretien de ces amans sera touchant et pur ! . . . C'est dans des fêtes, c'est au bal que les amans emploient le langage fantastique des poëtes; c'est là que l'on parle à sa maîtresse de ses grâces, de sa beauté, et qu'on la compare à Vénus; mais ici l'amour s'exprime comme la sainte amitié; son langage est celui de l'âme, de la vertu, et c'est l'Eternel qu'on prend à témoin du serment que l'on croit irrévocable. Hélas ! ce serment, peut-être, est prononcé sur la tombe d'une victime de l'amour ! . . . Ah ! s'il en est ainsi, ce fut une femme, sans doute . . . La séduction ou l'inconstance d'un ingrat a creusé son tombeau ! . . . Peut-être fut-elle l'amie de celle qui foule aux pieds sa cendre, et qui s'expose aux mêmes dangers ! . . . Imprudente et jeune amante ! rappelle-toi ce souvenir. Oh ! tu viens rêver au bonheur sur les bords d'un abîme; tu paieras cher un moment d'illusion; tu as perdu pour long-temps la paix et la tranquillité ! . . . Cependant tu sortiras pure de ce premier entretien; mais n'en accorde pas un second, tu y perdrais l'innocence: va, tu as connu de l'amour tout ce qu'il a de doux et d'enchanteur; il n'est pas en son pouvoir de te rendre jamais le charme de ce premier rendez-vous.» (*Mém.*, III, 356—9)

Point n'était besoin d'aller en Angleterre pour écrire cela. Il suffisait d'avoir lu Young, Hervey ou Gray, ou encore quelqu'un de leurs innombrables imitateurs français.[54] Il suffisait tout simplement d'avoir respiré l'air du temps.

[54] Cf. A. Monglond, *Le Préromantisme français*, Paris 1965, I, pp. 145—161, et Ph. Van Thieghem, *Les Influences étrangères sur la littérature française*, P.U.F., Paris, 2e éd., pp. 103—113.

IRREGULAR GENIUS: SOME ASPECTS OF MILTON AND SHAKESPEARE ON THE CONTINENT AT THE END OF THE EIGHTEENTH CENTURY

by

J. H. TISCH

I. INTRODUCTION

One of the truly judicious comparatists of our time has singled out the gradual shift in the intellectual leadership of Europe "from classical France to preromantic England" as the most characteristic development of the eighteenth century.[1] For centuries, France and England *"s'étaient façonnées l'une sur l'autre, selon la dialectique des longs antagonismes"*.[2] The great triple war of the middle of the century was not the only decisive duel between the two nations for possession of new spheres; it has its peaceful but dramatic counterpart in the energetic cultural and literary expansion of England that, having dealt with Absolutism and its taut social structure, rose to be a cherished European ideal, the promised land of liberty. *"Montesquieu a fixé pour toujours ce moment de l'histoire des idées."*[3]

It forms part of the notorious complexity of the 18th century that the continent discovered two vastly different and seemingly incompatible identities of "the happy island": England, the fountainhead from which basic intellectual inspirations of the Enlightenment had flowed, and England the cradle of emotive anti-rationalism and literary sentimentalism — up to 1750 *"une Angleterre philosophique et politique"*, after 1760 *"une seconde Angleterre: celle du mystère, des brumes, des tempêtes de l'âme."*[4]

"Pre-Romantic" (in English literature loosely interchangeable with "Post-Augustan"[5] is a widely accepted but awkward blanket term whose validity has been seriously questioned. The notion of "Pre-Romanticism" is useful as a common denominator for nascent forces which collectively (though with varying degrees of radicalism) through their potent cumulative effect challenged the primacy of classicist dogmatism and, against deeply entrenched prejudices, brought about a revulsion from the rationalist outlook on poetry. This elaboration of new modes of feeling and of a transformed view of literature foreshadowed the salient ideological and technical innovations, the "tremendous creative renewal"[6] of Romanticism.

---

[1] W. P. Friederich, *Outline of Comparative Literature*, Chapel Hill, 1954, p. 202. — Only works actually referred to in the text of this essay are listed in the footnotes; for further information see the sections dealing with literary relations with the continent in volumes II (1971) and III (1969) of the *New Cambridge Bibliography of English Literature and* of course the current general and specialized bibliographies in *Yearbook of Comparative Literature, Annual Bibliography of English Language and Literature, Philological Quarterly, Journal of English and Germanic Philology* etc.

[2] R. Pomeau, *L'Europe des Lumières*, Paris, 1966, p. 71.

[3] P. Hazard, *La Pensée Européenne au XVIII*ème *Siècle*, Paris, 1946, I, p. 247.

[4] P. Guth, *Histoire de la littérature française*, Paris, 1967, I, p. 522f.

[5] B. H. Bronson, *Facets of the Enlightenment*, Berkeley and Los Angeles, 1968, p. 160.

[6] L. R. Furst, *Romanticism in Perspective*, London, 1969, p. 279.

The term "Pre-Romantic" however, tends to obscure divergencies apparent on closer scrutiny between the so-called "Pre-Romantics" and the Romantics themselves, especially in countries where the latter espoused purely aesthetic subjective ideals that had little in common with the social concern of their 18th-century predecessors. While English Romanticism was, down to details of thought and diction, firmly rooted in the early 18th century,[7] this evolutionary pattern of organic growth did not recur exactly on the continent. Caution is also indicated lest the 'reactive' concept of Pre-Romanticism should evoke a simplistic antithetical view of the 18th century, suppressing or blurring the plurality of perspectives. At least in "its positive beginnings Pre-Romanticism is complementary to the Enlightenment," and a network of intersecting and intertwining strands extends beyond[8] the turn of the century. "Classical" and "Pre-Romantic" impulses may emanate from one and the same author, often, but not invariably, at different times and in different environments. Not only did for instance in Germany a rationalistic undercurrent keep the interest in Pope alive,[9] but the melancholy medievalism of his *Eloisa to Abelard* appealed to Pre-Romantic sensibilities to which the bulk of Pope's poetry might have been alien.

It should be emphasized that English literature did not create continental Pre-Romanticism; the stimulation of Pre-Romantic idols whose works attained European diffusion — Shakespeare, Young, Ossian, Sterne, Richardson, even Milton — in many countries released, enhanced and consolidated the emotional ferment, the partly submerged "Romanticism of the Enlightenment,"[10] i.e. latent indigenous energies of a poetic revival that were biding their time to burst out triumphantly.

Pre-Romantic Sentimentalism has been investigated and documented by Van Tieghem[11] and others in valuable studies that sometimes appear overeager to synthesize broad similarities at the expense of equally significant national and individual differences (and the full story of e.g. German Pre-Romanticism has still to be written).

A distinctive feature of European Pre-Romanticism resides in the magnetism of minor poets, their prominent function as models capable of enriching some of the greatest talents of the age, in the tremendous and, in relation to their artistic magnitude and attainment, disproportionate[12] international impact made by figures such as Young, Macpherson or Gessner whose popularity not infrequently eclipsed the admiration for Shakespeare.

It is a truism to state that England in the 18th century produced a literature of startling originality. Its achievements culminated in the prose genres, especially in the meteoric brilliance of the novel, but in the spheres of drama or epic did not include anything remotely comparable to Shakespeare or

---

[7] H. Oppel, Englische und deutsche Romantik. Gemeinsamkeiten und Unterschiede, *Die Neueren Sprachen*. N.F. 5, 1956, p. 465.

[8] L.R. Furst, *Romanticism, The Critical Idiom* 2, London, 1969, p. 24.

[9] J. H. Heinzelmann, Pope in Germany in the Eighteenth Century, *Modern Philology*, *10*, 1913, p. 24.

[10] To borrow the title of M. Lamm's study of the mystical-sentimental strain in 18th-century Sweden, *Upplysningstidens romantik*, 1918 and 1920.

[11] E. g. P. Van Tieghem, *Ossian et l'Ossianisme dans la littérature européenne au XVIII*ème *siècle*, Groningen, 1920, and P. Van Tieghem: *Le Préromantisme, Études d'histoire littéraire européenne*, Paris, 1930.

[12] K. Krejči, *Geschichte der polnischen Literatur*, Halle/Saale, 1958, p. 170.

Milton who, in their native country, together with Spenser, were reaching the status of classics, exerted a wide-spread direct influence (Milton's at least equalled Pope's) and enjoyed high esteem. The century saw over a hundred editions of *Paradise Lost* (or more than twice as many as of Shakespeare's plays). Milton "was talked about (and even read) by all classes of people . . . It would be difficult to imagine a more exalted poetic reputation."[13]

The two sections of this essay that follow, devoted to Milton and Shakespeare respectively, attempt to throw some light on selected aspects of these authors on the continent where their momentum was of more lasting significance than e.g. the feverish craze unleashed by Ossian's intoxicatingly cadenced "Northern" prose poetry which for Mme de Staël was practically synonymous with the "Romantic" but whose magic faded and in several countries gave way to sceptic disenchantment well before 1800.

Both Milton and Shakespeare were disparaged for their "perverse barbarities" and acclaimed as embodiments of inspiration and imaginative freedom, as oracles of creative genius by 18th-century critics. Both were received perhaps less as historical realities of intrinsic value than as stirring myths, as catalysts and rousing symbols of rejuvenation, protest and change, and their innovatory impetus coalesced to an amazing degree with that of the 18th-century Pre-Romantics. The formative influences Goethe jotted down for *Poetry and Truth* — "The effect of the English models, at first Milton, Young. Later especially novels. At last Shakespeare" — are symptomatic of at least some major predilections of the age. Particularly on German soil "the divine poet" (Klopstock), Young (like Thomson) profited from the general enthusiasm for Milton;[14] their (at bottom heterogeneous) influences merged inextricably in Bodmer's *Noah*[15] and above all in the "German Milton," Klopstock, among German poets of note "the most sympathetically allied to Young in spirit and purpose."[16]

Like the champion of Ossian in Germany, Michael Denis, Klopstock learnt English in order to read Milton in the original language,[17] and, in the words of Robson-Scott, he "united in his single person almost all the varied ingredients of pre-Romanticism and owing to the prestige of his poetry, gave them a general currency which they would otherwise have lacked."[18] It was not unusual for both Klopstock and Young to be rated above Milton by their contemporaries.

Shakespeare's discovery on the continent in the 18th century, which has been described as "*un des aspects les plus significatifs du pré-romantisme*

---

[13] J. Thorpe, ed., *Milton Criticism. Selection from Four Centuries*, London, 1956, p. 8.

[14] Cf. L. M. Price, *Die Aufnahme englischer Literatur in Deutschland 1500—1960*, Berne and Munich, 1961, p. 120f.

[15] See J. H. Tisch, *Between the Idyllic and the Sublime — Some Aspects of the Reception of Milton in Switzerland* in R. W. Last, ed., *Affinities. Essays in German and English Literature. Dedicated to the Memory of Oswald Wolff (1897—1968)*, London, 1971, p. 9.

[16] J. L. Kind, *Edward Young in Germany*, New York, 1906, p. 90.

[17] Cf. H. C. Sasse, Michael Denis as a Translator of Ossian, *Modern Language Review*, 60, 1965, p. 548.

[18] W. D. Robson-Scott, *The Literary Background of the Gothic Revival in Germany*, Oxford, 1965, p. 38.

européen",[19] was closely associated with the vogue of Ossian (translated like Shakespeare by the prolific Le Tourneur) that engulfed Europe, as well as with electrifying ideas (the poet "a second Maker; a just Prometheus under Jove") culled from the writings of Shaftesbury ("whose name streaks through most of the literature of the eighteenth century,"[20] and who impressed Neoclassicists and Pre-Romantics alike) and with the new doctrine of original genius that was so effectively funnelled into European minds by Edward Young's *Conjectures on Original Composition* of 1759.

If Germany looms large in this essay, this is of course a concomitant of her prominence in 18th-century English-Continental literary relations, and of the singularly dynamic reorientation of aesthetics, taste and thought (not inappropriately styled the "English revolution" in German letters [Borinski]) in which the Swiss intelligentsia, keenly alive to English literature, was deeply involved.[21] As early as 1739 Gottsched admits in a letter to Bodmer *"Es scheint, als wenn die Engländer die Franzosen bald aus Deutschland verjagen wollten,"* and it cannot be gainsaid that "all the main literary or intellectual movements of eighteenth-century Germany owe their primary inspiration to England."[22] Within less than 100 years Germany against heavy odds had made up enormous cultural leeway, advancing from the humble station of poor relation to a vanguard position; towards the end of the 18th century "creatively and critically alike, learned Europe spoke German."[23] By that time, German poets, after an immensely fruitful period of discipleship, and still respecting Milton, still vitally affected by Shakespeare, assumed a self-confident posture of disinterest towards literary developments — including a milestone such as the publication of Wordsworth's and Coleridge's *Lyrical Ballads* 1798 — in contemporary England.[24]

English literature encouraged the European emancipation from Neoclassical precepts of which France was the stronghold. Yet the notion of *"L'Europe Anglaise"* supplanting suddenly as if by magic the primacy of Paris as Europe's cultural capital stands — like so many commonplaces of history — in need of differentiation. Not only did the French cultural hegemony persist throughout the era in substantial regions of Europe (none other than Edmund Burke shortly before his death 1797, the year of Campo Formio, referred to England as "the moon shone upon by France"[25]) but the scin-

[19] P. Van Tieghem, Shakespeare devant la critique continentale au XVIIIᵉ siècle, *Essais et Etudes Littéraires* 1 1945/46, p. 151.

[20] D. B. Schlegel, *Shaftesbury and the French Deists*, Chapel Hill, 1956, p. 10; Cf. H. Wolffheim, *Die Entdeckung Shakespeares — Deutsche Zeugnisse des 18. Jahrhunderts*, Hamburg, 1959, p. 41: *"Dadurch ... dass Young in der Nacheiferung gerade Shakespeares die Bedingungen für neue Genies proklamierte, wurde er zum europäischen Stifter der neuen deutschen Genielehre."*

[21] See J. H. Tisch, *Milton and the German Mind in the Eighteenth Century* in F. R. Brissenden, ed., *Studies in the Eighteenth Century*, Canberra, 1968, p. 205f.

[22] W. D. Robson-Scott, *op. cit.*, p. 57. Cf. J. Voisine who, in his review of L. M. Price (see footnote 14 above), *Etudes Germaniques*, *18*, 1963, p. 220, views English-German literary relations in the 18th and early 19th centuries as *"plus importantes alors qu'à aucune autre époque."*

[23] L. Magnus, *English Literature in its Foreign Relations 1300 to 1800*, London, 1927, p. 237.

[24] Cf. E. C. Mason, *Deutsche und englische Romantik*, Göttingen, 1959, p. 12 f.

[25] Cf. S. Skalweit, *Edmund Burke und Frankreich*, Cologne and Opladen, 1956, p. 75.

tillating counterpoint of Gallomania and Anglomania, the dialectical inter-play of antagonism, rivalry, affinity and cross-fertilization between the two leading (and then uncommonly similar) nations illustrates the point that "*L'Europe anglaise, superposée à la française, confirme celle-ci, ou la complète autant qu'elle s'y oppose.*"[26] What has been stressed with regard to the Polish Enlightenment ("In most cases, the translations instead of coming directly from the Thames to the Vistula, pursued the customary route of travellers — the high road from Paris")[27] highlights the role played by France as an authoritative intermediary throughout much of Europe. As a main recipient of, and port of transshipment for, linguistic Anglicisms[28] and works of English literature (e.g. over 150 English novelists were introduced to con-tinental readers through French translations), France herself, also inter-nally experiencing a signal dissemination of foreign literatures,[29] "*aidait l'Europe à se libérer de la suprématie intellectuelle de la France.*"[30]

II. MILTON

The "English revolution" in German letters referred to above deeply affected the intellectual life of the German-speaking regions, and in this context Milton rose to the position of an exemplary aesthetic program, an almost religious creed. It has been claimed that Milton's significance for German 18th-century literature was hardly inferior to Shakespeare's, that Milton was the first English poet "to inspire respect and win fame for our literature on the Continent of Europe,"[31] and that the rise of both Shake-speare and Milton from obscurity to acceptance on the continent followed largely parallel lines. The names of Shakespeare and Milton became indeed shibboleths, battle cries, dividing clashing factions; they mark at various times progressive, even revolutionary positions; they grow near-synonymous with the liberation from classicist domination, with the dawn of a new era of dramatic and poetic taste. *Paradise Lost* and the "Miltonic" emerge as an artistic and spiritual force in 18th-century Germany. But whereas Shakespeare, still often called the third German classic, was welcomed by the Germans like a fellow-countryman born in exile, Milton did not become an integral part of the German literary heritage. No translator of genius took up his cause. One can only surmise as to the reasons why the German-speaking cultural area did not match its profound appreciation of Milton's art by a Milton translation comparable to the outstanding German render-

[26] R. Pomeau, *op. cit.*, p. 72.
[27] Sister M. F. Tumasz, Eighteenth century English Literature and the Polish Enlight-enment (1764—1822), *Dissertations Abstracts*, 24 (1964) p. 4179 (Fordham).
[28] See St. de Ullmann, Anglicism and Anglophobia in Continental Literature, *Modern Languages*, 27, 1946, p. 12 f. *Cf.* R. A. Charles, French Mediation and Inter-mediaries, 1750—1815, in P. A. Shelley, ed. *Anglo-German . . . Crosscurrents*, Chapel-Hill, 1957, pp. 1—38 on an aspect of France's contribution to the literary traffic in the opposite direction; in this case from Germany to England.
[29] Cf. P. Van Tieghem, *L'Année littéraire (1754—1790) comme intermédiaire en France des littératures étrangères*, reprint, Geneva, n. d. p. 20.
[30] P. Hazard, *op. cit.* II, p. 243.
[31] J. G. Robertson, Milton's Fame on the Continent, *Proceedings of the British Academy*, 1908, p. 1.

ings of Shakespeare. But all the same, Milton exercised a profound influence on the "emergence of German as a literary language", to use Blackall's phrase, and on the rise of rhymeless verse. The new poetic ideals that had been distilled from his work cried out for more adequate forms and media. The sonorousness and dignity, the "sublime" quality of Milton's style, constitute one of the roots of the new German poetic diction that was born during this period. The reception of Milton was also closely linked with the revival of interest in the epic; 18th-century Germany was swept by enthusiasm for this genre that the Germans had so sadly neglected, but of which *Paradise Lost* embodied the very idea. The work of the "Christian Homer" was admired as the realisation of the epic's most rigorous formal and thematic requirements. In short, the progress of Milton's art and thought in Germany was accompanied by heated exchanges of opinion on several then vital problems of aesthetics and poetics, and coincided with an important chapter in the history of literature and ideas.

In the enthusiasm for Milton, two decisive factors in the development of 18th-century German literature are said to have coalesced — the impact of English letters and the religious, irrational revival. This religious undercurrent is hardly more audible anywhere than in Switzerland, especially in the polyglot circle around J. J. Bodmer (1698—1783), a vicar's son, "*ein Geist von höchster europäischer Ausstrahlung*",[32] and an able champion of English literature, who virtually re-discovered *Paradise Lost* decades after it had first been rendered into German by Milton's contemporary E. Th. Haak (1605—90) (to whose fragmentary translation E. G. v. Berge is heavily indebted for the first printed German version of *Paradise Lost*, 1682), and untiringly disseminated a knowledge of and a respect for Milton in the German-speaking countries. The grandeur of Milton instilled in Bodmer, despite his rationalist background, a deep awareness of the function and scope of the imagination. Through him and his collaborator J. J. Breitinger, *das Wunderbare* (the miraculous) came to be representative of crucial aesthetic issues, as a peculiar synthesis of a new flair for the enigmatic, irrational side of poetic imagery, and protestant dogma of an English-Swiss mould. There is evidence that the impressive rise of the literary Zurich in the 18th century should be understood as a direct continuation of the traditions of the "theological" Zurich. In the activities of Bodmer and his circle, theology and aesthetic theory sustain each other. It is certainly not fortuitous that Milton's fame in Germany owed so much to theological and pietist circles. (Incidentally, the author of the first German translations of *Paradise Regained* and *Samson Agonistes*, 1752, was a clergyman, Simon Grynäus of Basle). Bodmer's prose translation of *Paradise Lost* (1732 etc.) provided the decisive impulse for the young Saxon poet and student of theology Fr. G. Klopstock (1724—1803) to emulate Milton, whom he admired as the founder of sacred Christian heroic poetry and the fellow seer-poet, in his monumental hexameter epic *Der Messias* that earned his author

[32] M. Bircher, Die früheste deutsche Coriolan-Übersetzung, *Shakespeare-Jahrbuch* 104, 1968, p. 122; Bircher rightly emphasizes Bodmer's significance for the reception — not only of Milton, but also — of Shakespeare: "*Wenn auch Bodmer kein Werk Shakespeares übersetzt, ja, ihm nicht einmal einen Aufsatz gewidmet hat, so sind doch seine Verdienste um die Aufnahme des 'Engelländischen Sophocles' im deutschen Sprachgebiet nicht abzuschätzen*" (ibid.).

the rather misleading title "The German Milton"-"a very *German* Milton indeed!" as Coleridge mockingly commented.

There is something paradoxical about the way in which Klopstock — "more than Milton", as Schönaich maliciously describes him —, the most gifted German follower of Milton to respond imaginatively to his model on a large scale, gradually replaces that model as an example for German (and even foreign) writers who (the young Hölderlin among them) find access to Milton once removed, as it were. *Der Messias* is in the last analysis in tone, and particularly in spirit, worlds apart from Milton's epic. Nothing could more vividly illuminate the misunderstanding — fundamental yet creative — upon which a great deal of the cult of the German as well as the English Milton was founded than the fact that Klopstock's basically un-Miltonic work with its seraphic emotionalism and not *Paradise Lost* itself led the Miltonic, anti-Gottschedian school to victory. As Klopstock's "Pre-Romantic" response to *Paradise Lost* and Milton's significance for Bodmer and Breitinger's postulate of the *"hertzrührende Schreibart,"* of emotive aesthetics indicate, the appeal to the heart was an important avenue for Milton's reception by German-speaking readers in the century of the Enlightenment.

While the main wave of Milton's impetus that had taken a strong hold on the later 18th-century Germany lost its vitalizing momentum long before 1800, a number of further translations (including Bürde's genteel blank verse version of *Paradise Lost*, 1793) notwithstanding, it betrays the diversified significance of English models in the 18th century, that both Goethe and Schiller in their youth as well as in their classical periods were stimulated by the author of *Paradise Lost*. For Goethe, Milton belonged to his early formative influences, and his admiration for the "true poet," the master of style never completely faltered despite some later scepticism towards the content of Milton's major epic. Without *Paradise Lost*, the poetic cosmos of Goethe (who as late as 1829 read and praised *Samson Agonistes*) would have been the poorer. The world of *Faust*, with its heavenly exposition, its visionary longings, its cosmic splendour, its stark manifestation of evil bears the stamp of Miltonic inspiration which, as plans indicate, was also to have been manifest in the projected continuation of the *"Walpurgisnacht"*. From 10th August to 16th October 1799, Goethe had Zachariä's hexameter translation on loan from the Weimar library, and it is fascinating to watch how, in some *Faust* scenes written at the very end of the century, Goethe's superb imagination and diction play productively and sometimes rhapsodically (e.g. in the hymnal words of the Archangels in the "Prolog im Himmel") on the allegedly uncongenial subject matter of *Paradise Lost*.

In Schiller we have perhaps the German poet who is most akin to Milton in regard to his ardent ethical seriousness, the often misunderstood uncompromising rigour of his message, the fusion of the didactic with the sublime. For the Storm and Stress Schiller and some of his contemporaries, who sense a kindred revolutionary spirit in Satan, *Paradise Lost* held a curious fascination, foreshadowing Byronism that was to absorb such sympathies and energies. The affinity of Schiller's imagination with the polarities of the poetic and theological structure of Milton's epic permeates his early plays which are impregnated with Miltonic touches and may also extend to the cosmic-rhetorical *Jugendlyrik*. Karl, the noble brother in Schiller's volcanic *Robbers*, a kind of modern Cain and Abel drama, is sympathetic with Satan, the extraordinary *Genie* "who could not suffer anybody to be above him," and Schiller to a certain degree presents him as a fallen angel in almost romantic terms, as one would imagine a humanized interpretation of Satan by Goethe (or in pictorial art, by Henry Fuseli). In my opinion, the inward similarity with the texture of Milton's thought never completely disappears in Schiller's dramatic and philosophical œuvre. In his essay *Vom Erhabenen* (1793) he cites Satan as an aesthetic example of sublimity and admirable strength of character, and in his analysis of basic poetic types, *Über naive und sentimentalische Dichtung* (1795), he celebrates Milton's "magnificent" depiction of Adam and Eve and the state of innocence in Paradise as *"die schönste mir bekannte Idylle in der sentimentalischen Gattung."*[33]

Besides the aura of defiantly Luciferian revolt surrounding *Paradise Lost*, a totally different facet, the patriarchal, nostalgically pastoral elements of the poem (cf. e.g. France Anne-Marie du Bocage's *Le Paradis Terrestre*, 1748) acquired crucial importance in Germany in the 18th century, especially in its latter part during which, in conjunction with nature sentimentalism and a craving for a spiritual Arcadia, the more lyrical side of Milton inspired numerous, on the whole undistinguished, idyllic biblical epics and *Patriarchaden*. More than once Schiller's references to Milton point to the realm of that concept that as a near synonym for "Miltonic", throws light on what Milton meant for the 18th-century German mind, and co-ordinates various aspects of the reception of Milton: the sublime. The history of Milton enthusiasm in 18th-century Germany overlaps to a large degree the rise of the sublime as an artistic and emotional category, an aesthetic—philosophical notion, from Wernicke, Bodmer, Haller, Pyra and Klopstock to Herder, Schiller and Kant. Milton generally evoked the impression of almost unprecedented greatness and moral integrity, and *Paradise Lost* was viewed as the realization of poetry in its loftiest form. Bodmer's assertion that there is hardly a higher peak to which the human mind can elevate itself than Milton reflects an overwhelming and transforming experience that almost equals the impact of Shakespeare on his German followers and is summed up on the threshold of the new century by Mme de Staël in *De la Littérature* (1800): *"Peut-on élever l'âme et l'imagination à une plus grande hauteur que dans le Paradis Perdu?"*[34]

Holland, instrumental as she was in the dissemination of English letters in the 18th century — her function as an important mediator is personified

[33] *Sämtliche Werke*, ed. G. Fricke and H. G. Göpfert, Munich, 1958—59, V. p. 749.
[34] For details concerning this section, see J. H. Tisch, Milton and the German Mind in the Eighteenth Century, in *Studies in the Eighteenth Century*, ed. F. R. Brissenden, Canberra, 1968, p. 205—229; J. H. Tisch, Von Satan bis Mephistopheles: Milton und die deutsche Klassik, *Proceedings of the Australian Goethe Society*, 1966/67, Nedlands, 1969, pp. 90—118; J. H. Tisch, Between the Idyllic and the Sublime — Some Aspects of the Reception of Milton in Switzerland, in *Affinities. Essays in German and English Literature*, ed. R. W. Last, London, 1971, pp. 3—18. — While Pizzo's statement: *"Weder den Romantikern noch den Klassikern sagte das* V. P. [*Verlorene Paradies*] *etwas"* (E. Pizzo, *Milton's Verlornes Paradies im deutsche Urteile des 18. Jahrhunderts*, Berlin, 1914, p. 142) is sweeping to the point of distortion, the predominantly unsympathetic attitude of the German Romantics is indeed a peculiar phenomenon warranting closer investigation.

in the distinguished pioneering figure of Justus van Effen[35] — seemed predestined to become a fertile soil for Miltonic influences. Volume IX of the *Journal Littéraire* (1717) contained the memorable *Dissertation sur la poésie anglaise* by Justus van Effen, in which in the context of the discussion of epic poetry Milton is dealt with in detail, not without criticism. A Dutch blank verse translation of *Paradise Lost* appeared as early as 1728; later versions favoured, not incongruously, the familiar constraint of the Alexandrine, the sonorous metre of Vondel's *Lucifer* and *Adam in ballingschap*.[36] Milton, "far from being welcomed in Holland with enthusiasm, as might have been expected from an apparent sympathy in religion and politics," was for complex reasons on the whole coolly received. Holland where, it should be added, the anti-rationalist poetic revival was rather timid, compared with England or Germany,[37] remained "either actively hostile . . . or else passively indifferent," an attitude towards Milton that did not materially change throughout our period.[38]

As in the case of Holland, Milton's influence in Scandinavia was limited, and largely filtered through the medium of Klopstock's poetry. During the 18th century, only Danish translations of *Paradise Lost* (1790) and *Paradise Regained* (1792) were published. But lofty Miltonic strains in the work of J. H. Kellgren (1751—1795), B. Lidner (1757—93), J. O. Wallin (1779—1839) and Thomas Thorild (1759—1808), the vocal prophet of the new era of Swedish literature that broke away from the fetters of "Gustavianism," reveal how Milton's spaciously imaginative poetry stimulated and enriched "Pre-Romanticism" in Northern Europe.

The Italians were undoubtedly among the pioneers of an unbiased appreciation of Milton. While various earlier attempts to render *Paradise Lost* into Italian remained unpublished (including the version Antonio Conti wrote while in England, 1715/16), the complete Italian blank verse translation by Paolo Rolli (1687—1765), an exponent of Italian Anglomania who spent almost 30 years in London and became Italian master to the Royal family and Handel's favourite librettist, appeared in 1735. Rolli's *Del Paradiso Perduto* was reprinted repeatedly (still as late as 1794, i.e. the year in which the first book of Mariotti's translation appeared; new renderings in fact continued into the Romantic age).

Rolli who — successfully — aims at a translation that is both literal and poetic ("*io pretendo d'aver non solo litteralmente tradotto i sensi del Milton, ma pur anche la Poesia*")[39] already had joined issue with a mighty opponent in his spirited *Remarks upon M. Voltaire's Essay on the Epick Poetry of the European Nations* (1728), "the first piece of writing in English published by an Italian author."[40] But after these auspicious beginnings critical inter-

---

[35] See W. J. B. Pienaar, *English Influences in Dutch Literature and Justus van Effen as Intermediary*, Cambridge, 1929.

[36] Cf. H. H. Meier, "*Nachwort*" to his translation of *Paradise Lost*, Reclam, Stuttgart 1969, p. 402.

[37] Cf. Th. Weevers, *Poetry of the Netherlands in its European Context 1170—1930*, London, 1960, pp. 147—148.

[38] Cf. H. Scherpbier, *Milton in Holland*, Amsterdam, 1933, pp. 204—206.

[39] Cited in G. E. Dorris, Paolo Rolli and the first Italian translation of Paradise Lost, *Italica*, 62, 1965, p. 215.

[40] E. H. Wilkins, *A History of Italian Literature*, Cambridge, Mass. 1954, p. 327.

est on the whole seems to have ossified into aloofness, and Voltairian intransigence.

Spain certainly recognized Milton's poetic stature; translations were attempted — two were published in the early 19th century, when the War of Independence brought Spain and England closer together (the first Portuguese version did not appear until 1823). But Spanish literature does not bear the imprint of any noteworthy influence, and critical opinions, limited in range, tended to lean on Italian authorities. The Miltonic traits of Felix José Reinoso's epic *La inocencia perdida* (1799), and the protracted controversy over the poetic utilization of Christian marvels do not go far towards refuting the assumption, facile though it may appear, that Milton was never likely to make an impact on "a country which has so little sympathy with the England of the Commonwealth."[41]

Considering the general time-lag affecting western culture in Russia, it is remarkable that Milton received considerable attention among Russian writers at a fairly early stage. It is illuminating that A. Kantemir's first ode, ostensibly inspired by Horace, is tangibly indebted to *Paradise Lost*, which the poet — for six years (from 1732 onwards) Russia's diplomatic representative in London — paraphrased from the Italian translation of Paolo Rolli, presumably not long after the publication of the *Paradiso* in 1735.[42]

In Russia, A. G. Stroganov's manuscript translation (circulating since 1745) of Milton's major epic, and N. J. Novikov's printed version of 1780 were followed by various others, also of shorter works (e.g. *Il Penseroso* 1799/1800; *Lycidas* 1801), and found their theoretical counterpart in some discerning criticism, of which the comprehensive study of Milton in a St. Petersburg literary journal in 1802 deserves special mention (*Korifei, ili kliuch literatury*, III). "Indeed, few Western classics were better known in Russia during this period than *Paradise Lost*."[43]

The history of Milton in Hungary opens in 1788 on a polemical note with the *paradicsomi harcz*, the discussion triggered off by the publication of extracts from D. Szabó's hexameter translation of *Paradise Lost* in the journal *Magyar Museum*. The prose version of the epic (from the French) by the officer-poet A. Bessenyei, published in 1796, is undistinguished, but the preface appears to disclose an awareness of the limitations of normal expression which Bessenyei shares with many 18th century translators touched by the galvanic force of Milton's expansive diction.[44]

Milton was first mentioned in Polish writings in 1770, the earliest translation of *Paradise Lost* (made from the English and not without a touch of grandeur) by Father Hyacinth Przybylski appeared in 1791, followed by a translation of *Paradise Regained* in 1792. Przybylski's work provides another illustration of the strain imposed by the pressure of Milton's style

[41] E. A. Peers, Milton in Spain, *Studies in Philology*, 23, 1926, p. 183.
[42] Cf. V. J. Boss, Kantemir and Rolli, Milton's Il Paradiso Perduto, *Slavic Review*, 21, 1961, p. 441 f.
[43] E. J. Simmons, *English Literature and Culture in Russia (1553—1840)*, reprint. New York, 1964, p. 115.
[44] Cf. H. V. Wlislocki, Miltons erste ungarische Übersetzer, *ZfVergl. Lit. Gs.* 4, 1891, p. 116 f.

on the linguistic resources of his translators (in Przybylski's version it manifests itself in a riot of neologisms and other innovations). An antagonist of Przybylski, F. D. Dmochowski published selections from the longer of Milton's epics (1801—1803), but his endeavours were gravely hampered by the limitations of his model, the wooden French prose translation by Louis Racine (1755). "The task of initiating the Polish reader with Milton's work proved thus a failure."[45]

The accomplished version of *Paradise Lost* which the versatile J. Jungmann (1773—1847), a classicist by training and close to the Englightenment but a leader of the Czech literary Renaissance, published in 1811, throws light on yet another facet of Milton's significance around the turn of the century: here as a programmatically elevated source of linguistic inspiration (together with the *Bible Králická*) for the patriotic task of strengthening and perfecting a national literary idiom. "Service to Czech literature through service to the Czech language: this is Jungmann's real contribution."[46]

The 18th century in France presents the curious picture of Milton as a poet of repute, early translated (1729 etc.), not infrequently discussed and perhaps better known than all other foreign literary figures but without any significant following; as distinct from Germany, his real impact was not to come until after the turn of the century, with the advent of Romanticism in which Milton ranked among the major trail-blazing forces — an indication of the often unpredictably staggered chronology not only of "national" patterns of literary reception but also of the relevance of individual English authors on the continent.

Voltaire in his *Essay upon Epick Poetry* (1727) with the voice of dignified admiration drew European attention to Milton's greatness (as he was to do a little later with regard to Shakespeare, although his persevering claims of pioneering discovery are exaggerated at least in the case of Milton). Soon however Voltaire's sympathies cooled off, and his less laudatory and progressively harsher verdicts shaped French critical attitudes towards Milton in the 18th century to a large extent. Whether it can be maintained "that the French literature of the first twenty or thirty years of the nineteenth century represents the most intense period of Miltonic influence on any alien literature"[47] is a matter for discussion. But there can be no doubt that the Renaissance of Milton in France, significantly riding on the tide of a religious revival, and his full recognition are associated with the name of Chateaubriand. His devoted and perceptive involvement with the true Milton, whom he triumphantly confronts with the distorting rationalist strictures of the preceding century, culminated fittingly in his *Génie du Christianisme* (1802) (where he even rehabilitates Milton's much maligned religious background: *"Pour tout homme impartial, une religion qui a fourni un tel merveilleux et qui de plus a donné l'amour d'Adam et d'Eve n'est pas une religion anti-poétique"*)[48] and much later (1836— by that time at least a dozen French versions and some 40 imitations had appeared) in his faithful and congenial translation of *Paradise Lost, "l'ouvrage de ma vie."*

---

[45] St. Helsztynski, Milton in Poland, *Studies in Philology*, 26, 1929, p. 148.
[46] M. Souckova, *The Czech Romantics*, S'Gravenhage, 1958. p. 20.
[47] As Robertson suggests, *loc. cit.* p. 20.
[48] Cited in J. M. Telleen, *Milton dans la littérature française*, Paris, 1904, p. 119.

Besides this significant early 19th-century approbation of Milton by the restorer of faith in France, one should not overlook another remarkable phenomenon. In a world-historical phase of the old century, arguments from major prose tracts by Milton (who after all had first become known on the continent as a controversial political figure and a brilliant, hard-hitting prose writer) became a formidable weapon in the struggle for liberty in the hands of Mirabeau,[49] the passionate leader of the Revolution who selected Milton "above all other political writers to guide the French at a time of national crisis towards a fuller realization of their inherent rights."

III. SHAKESPEARE

The impact of Shakespeare on German writers in the eighteenth century "came with the force of a quasi-divine revelation"[50] and while this encomiastic, emotional and nostalgic reception has to be viewed as forming part of a European historical process and being, at least up to Herder's enthusiastic Shakespeare essay of 1773, strongly influenced by foreign criticism,[51] its intensity and depth have no parallels anywhere on the continent. "*Shakespeare hat in Deutschland so tief gewirkt wie nirgends und die deutsche Literatur befruchtet wie kein anderer Dichter.*"[52] It was a discovery leading to a profound and, as English observers had to admit, almost unique appreciation of Shakespeare that notwithstanding its philosophical bias helped (like the involvement with Milton) to build German literature. It coloured the image of the English dramatist in several other countries in Northern and Eastern Europe and created the basis for Shakespeare's international fame, despite the fact that in a sense it was founded on a myth and that it involved a far-reaching transformation and even distortion of the "real" Shakespeare.[53]
The familiar theme "Shakespeare in Germany" has been treated thoroughly though not exhaustively by numerous studies which tend to operate[54] with too schematic and linear a sequence of literary period concepts. We shall merely focus our attention on the years immediately before and after the turn of the century, a time when Germany compensated for her political impotence by a splendid flowering of literature and thought. Here, in examining Shakespeare's significance, we once again, as so often in our observations on the complex *siècle des lumières*, discern side by side contrasting, seemingly contradictory but ultimately complementary trends.

---

[49] As D. M. Wolfe, Milton and Mirabeau, *PMLA*, 49, 1934, p. 1116f. has shown with reference to Mirabeau's *De la liberté de la Presse*, 1788 and *Théorie de la Royauté après la Doctrine de Milton*, 1789; quotation from p. 1127.
[50] W. Witte, Deus absconditus. Shakespeare in Eighteenth-Century Germany in *Papers. Mainly Shakespearian*, ed. G. I. Duthie, Edinburgh, 1964, p. 76.
[51] Cf. H. Wolffheim, *Die Entdeckung Shakespeares Deutsche Zeugnisse des 18. Jahrhunderts*, Hamburg, 1959, p. 78: "*Der weitere Prozeß der Aufnahme und Aneignung ist seit Herder ein innerdeutscher Vorgang.*"
[52] W. Muschg, Deutschland ist Hamlet, in W. M., *Studien zur tragischen Literaturgeschichte*, Berne and Munich, 1965. p. 227.
[53] Cf. K. Ziegler, Shakespeare und das deutsche Drama, in *Shakespeare, Seine Welt — Unsere Welt*, ed. G. Müller-Schwefe, Tübingen, 1964, p. 84, cf. p. 90.
[54] As K. S. Guthke reminds us: Richtungskonstanten in der deutschen Shakespeare-Deutung des 18. Jahrhunderts, *Shakespeare-Jahrbuch*, 98, 1962, p. 64 f.

If we try to accentuate them by dissecting them, we hope that the incisions are not made too arbitrarily. Having left the boisterously idolatrous, subjective, blatantly self-centred and imitative phase of his Shakespeare experience behind and having integrated Shakespearian elements and impulses permanently into his own art, Goethe approaches the towering phenomenon, Shakespeare, in a frame of mind that is still admiring but more critical and objective; this mature wisdom is in tune with his classical outlook and with his stance as a theatrical producer. In his capacity as the director of the Weimar theatre (since 1791) Goethe carefully stylizes several of Shakespeare's plays along the consistent lines of a heightened, anti-naturalist, dignifiedly declamatory presentation.

Schiller, since his debut hailed as the "German Shakespeare", like Goethe, had offered fervent homage to Shakespeare's superhuman talent and eagerly followed the celebrated model, a discipleship that although progressively more emancipated, intensified his own drama throughout his life; as Pascal points out, Schiller's whole conception of "high tragedy" is indebted to Shakespeare.[55] But his illuminating experiment in re-creating, during this momentous and seminal era of German theatrical history, Shakespeare's *Macbeth* (a play that already had experienced strange vicissitudes of interpretation in Germany) for the Weimar stage resulted in a "*Neudichtung aus dem Geiste der klassischen Weltanschauung.*"[56] Schiller's *Macbeth*, performed on 14th May 1800, constitutes a precious document revealing how he asserted his own artistic identity in relation to Shakespeare (who emerged from Schiller's *On Naive and Reflective Poetry* 1795 as a kind of corrective opposite to his own "sentimental" type). *Macbeth*, for Schiller of crucial importance, as was *Hamlet* for Goethe, is rewritten in rhetorical euphonious diction as a (highly stageworthy) classical character and Nemesis tragedy, expounding Schiller's sublimated image of man and the near-allegorical trial, vindication and restoration of moral order. The demonic, imaginative, elemental is lifted from Shakespeare's bewildering *chiaroscuro* into the lucidity of articulate reflection. It is perhaps indicative of the complex role played by Shakespeare in Germany that Schiller's monumental *Wallenstein* trilogy, "nearest among all his works to the amplitude and mystery of Shakespeare"[57] whose affinities with *Macbeth* are tangible and which Schiller completed shortly before he produced his translation, is more Shakespearian than Schiller's intellectualizing and moralizing reading of Shakespeare's sombre tragedy that transformed the witches into antique deities of fate, and from A. W. Schlegel elicited the irritated cry "Macbeth is out of joint!" And yet, Schiller's venture stands in immediate proximity (and not only chronologically speaking) to Schlegel's great translation that — an illustration of the fruitful dialectics of the period — provides a common basis for Romantic *and* classical endeavours striving towards the true, authentic, original Shakespeare. Both the

[55] R. Pascal, *Shakespeare in Germany. 1740—1815*, Cambridge, 1937, p. 23; cf. p. 22: "Of all great German playwrights, Schiller owes the heaviest debt to Shakespeare." See also P. Steck, Der Einfluß Shakespeares auf die Technik der Meisterdramen Schillers, *Shakespeare-Jahrbuch, 96*, 1960, p. 106f.

[56] H. H. Borcherdt, Schillers Bühnenbearbeitungen Shakespearescher Werke, *Shakespeare-Jahrbuch, 91*, 1955, p. 54.

[57] W. F. Mainland, Schiller and Shakespeare — Some Points of Contact, in *Affinities. Essays in German and English Literature*, ed. R. W. Last, London, 1971, p. 27.

formalized, realism-shunning Weimar style of Shakespeare productions and A. W. Schlegel's reverently faithful and yet daringly creative German rendering of 16 plays (1797—1801; another translation followed in 1810 and the enterprise was later continued by less inspired collaborators) marked the end of an era, the victory over the domination of the 'adapted', mutilated, coarsened or sentimentalized, of the naturalistically and melodramatically presented Shakespeare.[58]

Goethe had broken new ground with a production of *King John* in 1791 that (still based on Eschenburg's translation) by and large followed Shakespeare's text, and three years after the first performance of one of Schlegel's versions (Iffland's *Hamlet* in Berlin) he guided Shakespeare worship on the Weimar stage to a climax with Schlegel's *Julius Caesar* in 1803. Schlegel's translation, metrically influential and linguistically of sparkling boldness, represents the epoch-making final stage in an amazing process of productive acclimatization and established Shakespeare as a naturalized German classic. *"Eine Epoche in der Geschichte Shakespeares als deutscher Geist wird durch sie beendet. Was ihr folgt ist die Geschichte Shakespeares als deutsches Theater."*[59]

The famous Shakespeare chapters in *Wilhelm Meisters Lehrjahre* (1795/96), "Goethe's most important contribution to the criticism of English literature,"[60] which treat *Hamlet* like an absolute, self-contained reality, came as the first penetrating interpretation of a Shakespearian play in German. The Romantics' eager acceptance of the novel's plausible if historically unjustified passive, philosophical and sentimental portrait of the hero (that launched the Prince of Denmark as a mythical figure and as a symbol of Romantic *Weltgefühl*) as well as of the organic-morphological approach Goethe (developing Shaftesbury's notion of "inward form") brought to bear on Shakespeare's work, once again expose the traditional classical-Romantic dualism as a simplistic construction.[61]

Some of the features that characterize the Romantic attitude to Shakespeare undeniably belong to Storm and Stress heritage, and yet one cannot help noticing a marked transformation and even reversal of Storm and Stress values and positions in Romanticism. In the anglophile — and anti-feudal — "Pre-Romantic" atmosphere of *Sturm und Drang*, German enthusiasm for Shakespeare burnt with frenzied heat, fanned by the hymnic force of Young's *Conjectures on Original Composition*, one of the movement's central documents (publ. 1759, the year of Lessing's startling homage to

[58] Cf. K. S. Guthke, Shakespeare im Urteil der deutschen Theaterkritik des 18. Jahrhunderts, in K. S. G., *Wege zur Literatur*, Berne and Munich, 1967, p. 246. — With the publication of Schlegel's translation, the important role Switzerland played in the early history of German Shakespeare editions comes almost abruptly to an end, and there is little critical discussion after 1800, for a time; cf. *Shakespeare und die Schweiz*, ed. E. Stadler, Berne, 1964, p. 19. and E. Graf, *Die Aufnahme der englischen und amerikanischen Literatur in der deutschen Schweiz von 1800—1830*, Zurich, 1951, p. 91.

[59] F. Gundolf, *Shakespeare und der deutsche Geist*, Berlin 1922[6], p. 356.

[60] J. Boyd, *Goethe's Knowledge of English Literature*, Oxford, 1932, p. 29.

[61] Cf. M. Joachimi-Dege, *Deutsche Shakespeare-Probleme im XVIII. Jahrhundert und im Zeitalter der Romantik*, Leipzig, 1907, p. 183: "*Die romantische Shakespeare-forschung und — Interpretation beginnt Hand in Hand mit der klassischen . . .Erst mit der Zeit treten die Romantiker in der Shakespeareliteratur in Gegensatz zu den Klassikern.*"

Shakespeare in the 17th *Literaturbrief*, and available in two German translations in 1760). Shakespeare was revered with intuitive vagueness as the manifestation of nature, of the "Original," as the heroic liberating, irrational genius independent of all rules. The uninhibited emulation of Shakespeare's supposed formlessness served as a rebellious, militantly anti-Neoclassicist gesture. In German Romanticism, the pervasive Shakespearomania, the emotive exaltation, continue, albeit at a higher level of sophistication. But in the sympathetic and often brilliant utterances of Tieck, F. and A. W. Schlegel and others in the 1790's and early in the 19th century, the object of these eulogies appears in a radically changed light. The captivating sensuous, rapturous image of the wild untutored 'Genie', Shakespeare, has been ousted by the concept of Shakespeare as the supreme fulfilment of Romantic poetry, ("*Shakespeares Universalität ist wie der Mittelpunkt der romantischen Kunst*")[62] the "*tiefsinnige Künstler,*" the deliberate, form-conscious, technically perfect artist, the disciplined creative genius. Neglected aspects of Shakespeare's œuvre at last come into their own, e.g. the poetic dimensions of his dramas, the evocative power of their language, the blending of comic and tragic moods, and, of course, the elusive world of his comedies, in particular the magic unreality of *A Midsummer Night's Dream* and the *Tempest* (which are now even treasured as the keys to the very essence of Shakespeare's art). The Romantic writers' later drift towards symbolic metaphysical drama, from Shakespeare towards Calderón lies outside the scope of this essay which is primarily concerned with the transformative processes at the turn of the century.[63]

If after Germany, where, in the 18th century, Shakespeare was received with almost unique spiritual intensity and ecstatically hailed as a liberator, we turn briefly to France (and Italy) as well as to Russia, this selective but not altogether arbitrary arrangement does not suggest a lack of interest in, and contact with, Shakespeare's work in all the countries to which no reference is made.[64] It does, however, take into account the tardiness and lack of originality of the response to Shakespeare predominant in what have been called, in this respect, the derivative regions of Europe.

In France, the turn of the century hardly represents a highwatermark in the reaction to Shakespeare; on the contrary his fortunes seem to be temporarily at a low ebb, and notable transformations in critical postures on the whole do not become discernible until later.

Towards the end of the 18th century, melodrama, pantomime and opera took possession of Shakespeare, exploiting the horrors, the marvels, the sombreness — sensational, extrovert elements which form an integral part of the Elizabethan world and of Shakespeare's dramatic cosmos but wrenched from their vibrantly poetic context produced little more than caricatures of the original (such as *Les Visions de Macbeth ou les Sorcières d'Ecosse*,

---

[62].*Athenäum-Fragment* 247, cited in Joachimi-Dege, *op. cit.* p. 179; cf. pp. 144, 159 and 164.

[63] On the new attitude to Shakespeare in the critical work of Schelling and the later F. Schlegel see Pascal, *op. cit.* p. 33. f.

[64] Cf. e. g. R. Pennink, *Nederland en Shakespeare, Achttiende Eeuw en Vroege Romantiek*, 's-Gravenhage, 1936, p. 270. with regard to Holland: "*Als Shakespeare — ik reken nu tot circa 1840 — geen grote factor is geworden in het Nederlandse geestesleven, ligt het niet daaraan, dat de klank van zijn naam en faam niet was doorgedrongen.*"

mélodrame à grand spectacle, Paris 1817, but composed earlier), introducing a vestigial Shakespeare to social classes without literary training. This drastic coarsening emphasis on the outward trappings recalls the bold popularizing experiments of Jean-François Ducis whose vogue in fact lasted well into Romanticism. His successful adaptations that brought almost half a dozen of Shakespeare's tragedies — with their plots and moods reworked nearly beyond recognition — onto the — eminently capable — French stage (from *Hamlet*, 1769 to *Othello*, 1792), throw light on the ambivalence surrounding the genius of Shakespeare in Neoclassical Europe, and on the established taste whose dictates, as Voltaire fully realized, ruled out the presentation of an unadulterated text. The real, "total" Shakespeare remained largely unknown. As Jusserand points out,[65] "Had he [Ducis] altered Shakespeare less, he could not have had him played at all." Paradoxically, Ducis' sweeping changes, designed to render Shakespeare palatable to the French in terms of classical regularity and decorum (which has aptly been called "the orthodoxy of the Eighteenth century,"[66]) also enhanced the pathetic and terrible aspects[67] and turned Shakespeare virtually into a forerunner of French melodrama.

In view of the absence of a genuine historical sense, and of the conservative rigidity of the time-honoured proprieties governing dramatic art,[68] it would be futile to look for a revolution of French 18th-century taste. Symptoms of a Shakespeare cult that allegedly advanced in the wake of, say, Sebastien Mercier's progressive essays and of Le Tourneur's influential translation should be seen in proper perspective — as resulting in a widening of the conventions in the favourable if to some extent freakish atmosphere of Anglomania, but not in a profound metamorphosis and definitive emancipation under Shakespeare's influence, the numerous manifestations of passionate admiration and articulate propagandist acclaim notwithstanding.

Many 18th-century critics regarded Milton's *Paradise Lost* as "the most lofty, but most irregular Poem, that has been produc'd by the Mind of Man," as J. Dennis in 1704 admiringly described it.[69] To this antithesis of sublimity and regularity, the polarity of the *génie inculte* Shakespeare and the *axiomes du bon goût*, and the stock responses this confrontation produced,

---

[65] J. J. Jusserand, *Shakespeare in France under the Ancien Régime*, London, 1899 p. 439.

[66] J. W. Draper, The Theory of Translation in the Eighteenth Century, *Neophilologus*, 6, 1921, p. 241.

[67] Cf. H. E. Brooks, Eighteenth Century French Translations and Adaptations of Shakespeare, *Dissertation Abstracts*, 21, 1960—61, pp. 2701—2702, Northwestern Univ. It should be noted that Pierre Antoine la Place's pioneering Shakespeare translation (in his *Théâtre Anglois* 1745/46) reveals massive alterations at variance with the liberal stance of his *Discours sur le Théâtre Anglois*. Even a "revolutionary theorist" (Jusserand) such as Mercier bows to the ruling taste when adapting Shakespeare for the stage.

[68] Shakespeare's *"pièces étaient en contradiction sur tous les points avec une doctrine dramatique qui s'était établie et précisée peu à peu en France au siècle précédent, et qui, à l'époque qui nous occupe, régnait à peu près exclusivement sur tous les théâtres de l'Europe, même en Espagne et en Angleterre."* P. Van Tieghem, Shakespeare devant la critique continentale au XVIIIᵉ siècle, *Essais et Etudes Littéraires*, I, 1945/46, p. 154.

[69] J. Thorpe, ed., *Milton Criticism. Selections from Four Centuries*, London, 1956, p. 344.

provide an illuminating parallel. *Défauts et beauté*, the recognition (though often grudging or condescending) of Shakespeare's merit and the horrified, indignant indictment of his apparent defiance of unities and rules; Shakespeare as a morbidly fascinating monstrosity of incorrectness, a showpiece of barbaric genius, a colossal unbridled talent but hardly as a model to be emulated (except for some isolated inorganic borrowings) — these juxtapositions and contrasts mould the sharply polarized history of Shakespeare reception in 18th-century France and to a large degree elsewhere.

In this connection, the significance of Voltaire, the first French Shakespearean of stature and unquestionably the exponent of the taste of his age, can hardly be overrated. If it was Voltaire's historical mission to ensure international circulation for certain philosophical ideas, he also attained European influence in his dual role as Shakespeare's seminal advocate and abusive antagonist (who in his old age regretfully admitted *"c'est moi qui le premier montrai au Français quelques perles que j'avrais trouvées dans son énorme fumier"*). As a dramatist, Voltaire was instinctively attracted by Shakespeare's sheer dramaturgical brilliance,[70] but in imitating, rather faint-heartedly and without deeper sympathy, a limited range of external devices, he manifestly attempted to draw on the wealth of Shakespeare's imaginative stagecraft without making any concessions of form. His opinions, especially their reactionary bias "gained steadily increasing potency" and "came finally to be accepted as incontrovertible gospel,"[71] and their retarding effect on the critical assessment of Shakespeare reached well into the 19th century. Voltaire's utterances — from the 1730's, in particular from the XVIIIth of his *Lettres Philosophiques*, 1734 (perhaps the most important European document of its kind from the first half of the century) in which he discovers and welcomes Shakespeare, the Corneille of the English, as an uncontrolled genius full of fecundity, great despite his faults, but *"sans la moindre étincelle de bon goût et sans la moindre connaissance des règles,"* to the notorious letter to the Academy of 1776, provoked by the indefatigable labours of Shakespeare's 'shield-bearer', the translator Le Tourneur, and the climax of Voltaire's militant disparagement of the barbarian Shakespeare — prove in the last analysis fairly consistent. His "fluctuating pronouncements may almost all be described as variations on a single paradoxical formula of which now one and now the other element was emphasized."[72]

And yet, against Voltaire's formidable strictures and the inertia of well-settled Neoclassical taste, Shakespeare gradually gained ground, a trend to which Diderot and others contributed through their intuitive awareness of Shakespeare's greatness, along with Garrick's renowned Shakespeare recitations in the *salons* of Paris and with the endeavours of enlightened if somewhat cavalier translators. Pride of place belongs to La Place who in 1745/46 erected a landmark of European relevance with his first French version of ten Shakespearean plays, and who in his eulogizing and remark-

[70] As G. Larroumet pointed out many years ago, Voltaire. L'influence de Shakespeare sur son théâtre, *Revue des cours et conférences*, Paris, 8, 1900, p. 262.
[71] Th. R. Lounsbury, *Shakespeare and Voltaire*, New York, 1902, p. 443.
[72] C. H. Herford, A sketch of the History of Shakespeare's influence on the continent, *Bulletin of the John Rylands Library*, 9, 1925, p. 23.

ably liberal *Discours sur le Théâtre Anglois* with which he prefaces his translation, vigorously challenged the right of his fellow-countrymen to "impose on the rest of the world a narrow French standard of taste."[73] It was through the monumental translation of all 36 plays by Pierre Le Tourneur (1776—82), a creditable but still pale, "bowdlerized and sentimentalized" rendering dedicated to Louis XVI (which, unlike the quaint products of *"le bon Ducis"*, did not conquer the French stage) that *"le dieu du Théâtre,"* as Le Tourneur reverently styles him in his Johnsonian *Discours*, in an era delighting in graveyard poetry and Youngian and Ossianic gloom became *"le poète du sombre."* Le Tourneur, together with the fervent Shakespeare enthusiast Mercier and Ducis (who ironically enough succeeded to Voltaire's seat in the French Academy) form a Pre-Romantic literary faction, centred in Rousseau, an anti-Voltairian circle where Shakespeare was *"un mot de passe, un signe de ralliement dans l'amitié, — et un ferment de renouveau."*[74]

But Shakespeare's hour in France, as it turned out, a veritable apotheosis, did not arrive until the early 19th century when, under German influence, appreciation and emulation of his work reached its peak; it even had become feasible to place the English dramatist above Racine. It is a respectable and by no means untrue cliché that French Romanticism won its battle under the banner of Shakespeare, which the leader of the movement, Shakespeare's devoted disciple Victor Hugo so provocatively brandished. But this triumphant breakthrough (of Shakespeare's reputation rather than of a total understanding of his art) should not obscure the lingering survival of classicist reservations. None other than Chateaubriand, a warm admirer of both Milton, as we have seen, and of Shakespeare's innate genius, seems to revert to the dramatic propriety of the *ancien régime* when, while recognizing Shakespeare's penetrating vision of human nature, he depreciates his artistic example by implication as Gothic, barbarous, and dangerous to imitate.

It is hardly surprising that homage to Shakespeare in Italy for a long time proved rather distant, since it was restrained by the secure grip conformity in the shape of canonical Neoclassicist tenets had on followers and critics, from the *"Settecentisti puri"*, such as Conti, Rolli, Maffei, Quadrio and Pignotti,[75] to Vittorio Alfieri who, "a genuine son of the didactic eighteenth century" (Collison-Morley), in his own words was "well aware" of Shakespeare's "faults" and turned away from the English poet's seductive example to preserve his own originality and individuality. The intriguing aura of controversy around Shakespeare may have somewhat dimmed Alfieri's lustre in Pre-Romantic days; conversely it has been held that "the appearance of a great tragic poet . . . to reinforce classical tradition" was "an important factor in counteracting the growth of Shakespeare's influence" towards the end of the 18th century.[76]

Shakespeare entered Italy under the auspices of Voltaire, and his unspectacular progress to the threshold of Romanticism was in keeping with

[73] A. Ralli, *A History of Shakespearian Criticism*, I, New York, 1959, p. 56.
[74] C. Pichois, Préromantisme, Rousseauistes et Shakespeariens (1770—1778), *Revue Litt. Comparée 33*, 1959, p. 355.
[75] Cf. A. Nulli, *Shakespeare in Italia*, Milan, 1918, p. 153.
[76] L. Collison-Morley, *Shakespeare in Italy*, Stratford-on-Avon, 1916, p. 62. cf. p. 65.

these premises and the respect accorded to Classicist ideals. A glance at Spain reveals a similar pattern: there is evidence of gleams of insight, of independent judgments and serious translation (Leandro Fernandéz de Moratín: *Hamlet*, 1795), but Shakespeare criticism, even the opinions of Moratín who had visited England and whom some would regard as the highest embodiment of Spanish dramatic endeavours in the 18th century, remains permeated with the tenacious *"preocupaciones galoclásicas."*[77]

Antonio Conti "has the honour of being the first to mention Shakespeare's name — if only in mutilated form — in Italian literature,"[78] in a remarkable letter prefixed to his own tragedy *Il Cesare* published at Faenza in 1726 (*Julius Caesar* incidentally was the first of Shakespeare's plays to be wholly translated into Italian — 1756): *"Sasper è il Cornelio degl' Inglesi, ma molto piu irregolare del Cornelio, sebbene al pari di lui pregno di grandi idee, e di nobili sentimenti"* — a passage which might account for Bodmer's puzzling spelling of Shakespeare's name and may be echoed in Voltaire's phrase of 1734 ("amended" in later editions of his *Lettres Philosophiques*), *"Shakespeare qui passoit pour le Corneille des Anglois."*

As we observed earlier, the Milton translator Paolo Rolli was, like Conti (who spent several years in London) a living link between Italy and England (*"Essere o no, la gran question è questa,"* his blank verse version of Hamlet's soliloquy represents the first Italian translation of any Shakespearean text). And yet, the formula he coined, in his life of Milton, with regard to Shakespeare, *"Bellezze ed irregolarità,"* evidences the prevailing Neoclassicist sensibility.

While the admiration for Shakespeare in 18th-century Italy, where Pope enjoyed a popularity unsurpassed by any other English author, was not totally barren, it did not act as a great shaping force, and even the modest contribution it made to the dramaturgical range of the later Enlightenment had first been filtered through Voltaire's eclectic Shakespeare imitations. No play of Shakespeare was staged before the end of the century, and even beyond 1800 Le Tourneur's ubiquitous French translation on which Giustina Renier-Michiel's undistinguished *Opere Drammatiche di Shakespeare* (1798/1800 — like Le Tourneur's, in prose) were based, as was the rhapsodic praise Manzoni (who did not know English) lavished upon the *"sommo poeta,"* largely determined the Italian image of "that bright luminary of the English stage" as Lamberti termed him in 1796.

Some signs of opposition against the sway of formalistic Classicist rectitude became manifest, heralding long-term changes, even though the claims of creative imagination were only tardily vindicated: Shakespeare served as a rallying cry for those venturing to challenge and reject the unities; the rise of the *comédie larmoyante* — perhaps a marginal but an interesting factor — resulted in an extension of the sociological basis for Shakespeare's

---

[77] Cf. A. Par, *Shakespeare en la Literatura Española*, I Madrid/Barcelona, 1935, p. 112.

[78] J. G. Robertson, *Studies in the Genesis of Romantic Theory in the Eighteenth Century*, Cambridge, 1923, p. 103, ; *Cf.* the same author's The Knowledge of Shakespeare on the Continent at the Beginning of the Eighteenth Century, *Modern Language Review*, 1, 1906 pp. 319—320. On Conti's *"posizione ammirative"* between Shakespeare and " '*il più purgato e il più florido' teatro francese"* see F. Ulivi, Antonio Conti e il classicismo del Settecento, *Lettere Italiane*, 7, 1955, p. 166f.

acceptance; and needless to say, the infectious Youngian—Ossianic fashion that pervaded Europe provided an attractive if mild antidote to Voltairian aspersions. However, the Italian *"Pre-Romantici,"* some of whom, in the dramatic sphere, were united in their predilection for Voltaire's tragedies, appear uncertain to the point of ambiguity in their attitudes, as exemplified by Vinzenzo Monti who revered Shakespeare but as a dramatist adhered to classical form, "Romantic by temperament and anti-Romantic by conviction,"[79] like so many "transitional" figures in the later 18th century. There was no real continuity between these earlier advocates of a new view of literature and the actual Romantics. In the light of modern research a figure who spent three of the seven decades of his life in England where he belonged to the most intimate circle of Samuel Johnson, *"mio venerato maestro,"* and who "was to some degree, unknowingly, responsible for the 'Romantic' trend in Italy,"[80] should be looked upon not only as a significant Anglo-Italian mediator but in particular as an eloquent apologist of Shakespeare: the talented Anglomaniac Giuseppe Baretti. With his gallant defence of Shakespeare against Voltaire's vitriolic diatribe, the *Lettre à l'Académie Française* 1776 (his *Discours sur Shakespeare et sur M. de Voltaire* of the following year) and his anachronistic perception of poetic greatness, Baretti occupies a historical position, not unlike that of Bodmer, the undaunted champion of Milton whose vision of, and sustaining belief in, the creative aspect of poetry gave him such a powerful edge of superiority over his Voltaire-oriented opponent Gottsched.

In Russia, too, Shakespeare's œuvre may not have asserted itself as a vitalizing force until after the turn of the century. But ever since Catherine the Great, a German, had, in the 1780s, broken the ice with her clumsily amateurish imitations, Shakespeare "was abundantly translated, paraphrased and discussed."[81] The qualities that imbue Nikolay Karamzin's alert version of *Julius Caesar* (1787) and its bold and perspicacious preface mirror a comprehension of "the magnificent interpreter of human nature" much in advance of the well-worn Voltairian notion of Shakespeare as an inspired barbarian — a stance that befitted the Pre-Romantic author of the Sternian *Letters of a Russian Traveller* (1791f.), even though the 18th century lineaments of Karamzin's views are clearly visible under the tinge of sentimentalism. But his impetus, by and large, fell flat. "Almost alone of major English authors, Shakespeare failed to find competent translators until well into the 19th century";[82] no play of Shakespeare was staged until 1806, and even then the preponderance of Neoclassical theatrical practice was inimical to productions freed from the usual distortions. Shakespeare's works were, it is true, known and appreciated — journals continued to be instrumental in the dissemination of English letters — without having been acclimatized, let alone naturalized.

In Russia, as in most parts of Europe, the caesura and turning point in the complex processes originating from the discovery and discussion of

---

[79] J. M. Cohen, *A History of Western Literature*, Harmondsworth, 1956, p. 221.
[80] G. A. Tucci, Baretti and the Shakespearean Influence in Italy: A Study in Eighteenth Century Polemics in Italy, *Dissertations Abstracts, 20*, 1960, p. 4664, New York.
[81] C. H. Herford, *loc. cit.* p. 25.
[82] M. S. Anderson, Some British Influences on Russian Intellectual Life and Society in the 18th Century, *Slavonic and East European Review, 39*, 1960, p. 158.

Shakespeare seem to lie outside the lines of demarcation of the 18th century. But the startling reversal of criteria applied in the evaluation of Shakespeare in early 19th-century Russia was, as were analogous phenomena for instance in France (and Italy) linked, albeit indirectly, through the medium of German Romanticism with the past. The Russians were now able to draw on vital energies first released in 18th-century Germany (where the Neo-classical system had not taken root) by an interlocking trend of Enlightenment and Storm and Stress, i.e. their positive attitude towards the seeming indiscipline of Shakespeare's genius. "Russia's Shakespearean devotion in the first quarter of the nineteenth century was of the German variety."[83] After a relatively undramatic passage through the receptively cosmopolitan, still strongly Frenchified atmosphere of the 18th century, Shakespeare now, around 1820, came to the fore (together with Byron and Scott) as an inspiring emblem of Romanticism.[84] The veneration of Shakespeare aroused by a sense of affinity with a poet who appeared to adumbrate traits of Romantic art was buttressed by a more intellectual appreciation modelled on German writings. The Russian Romantic movement handsomely made amends for the omissions, both emotional and critical, of the preceding century.

Romanticism coincided with the heyday of English culture in Russia, yet it constituted the last era in which a foreign literature left a momentous and lasting mark on Russian literature. Shakespeare, on the continent frequently the symbolic spearhead of the rebellion against Neoclassical abstractions, strengthened Russia's quest for emancipation from French, and despite the nexus with Shakespeare idolatry in Germany, also German authority.

Even when the Shakespearian wave was at its height, only one solitary attempt at creative emulation was made. Few would deny that Alexander Pushkin, in following Shakespeare in his historical drama *Boris Godunov* (staged 1831), soared to an exalted artistic level. However, it lends a revealing if sobering twist to the eventful and distinguished history of English literature on the continent to realize that Shakespearian tragedy in Russia, not unlike the Miltonic epic in Klopstock's Germany, turned out to be a noble but still-born genre.[85]

---

[83] E. J. Simmons, English Literature in Russia, *Harvard Studies and Notes in Philology and Literature, 13*, 1931, p. 302.

[84] Romanticism, as distinct from the "Golden Age" of Russian poetry which, though coeval with the flowering of Romanticism in Western Europe, has been characterized as "a posthumous child of the eighteenth century," D. S. Mirsky, *A History of Russian Literature* ed. F. J. Whitfield, London, 1949, p. 71.

[85] The statements contained in the preceding paragraphs should be corrected and supplemented by the findings of recent Soviet scholarship, e. g. I. Levidova's *Bibliography of Russian Translations and Literature on Shakespeare in Russian 1748—1962*, Moscow, 1964, the first entry in which is A. Sumarokov's adaptation of *Hamlet*, publ, in 1748. Special importance attaches to the magisterial work *Shakespeare and Russian Culture*, publ. by the Soviet Academy in 1965, with M. P. Alekseev as part author and chief editor. Both these works are in Russian. — Shakespeare's profound impact on the literature of Hungary and other countries of East Central Europe remains to be discussed in another article. — Editors' note. — For Shakespeare's reception on the continent see now the excellent section 'Die Wirkungsgeschichte' in I. Schabert(ed.), *Shakespeare-Handbuch pp.* 662ff. (Stuttgart, 1972). This book was published after the manuscript of this chapter had been forwarded to the Editors.

IV. CONCLUSION

Even within the restricted compass of these pages the multifacetted, fluctuating and often puzzling nature of the reception of English literature on the continent in the 18th century may have conveyed something of the complexity of the age as a whole. One cannot cross even a corner of the huge field of these literary relations without noticing recurrent factors: the staggered chronological pattern, the unequal rate of progression, geographically speaking; the bewildering ramifications of literary transmission and the transcontinental cosmopolitan mobility of crucial works (Ossian makes his first appearance in Russia through the passages contained in Goethe's *Werther* translated in 1781), the diversity of national curves of development within the overall unity, the vast gamut of possibilities,[86] the wide spectrum of refractory metamorphic distortions and creative misunderstandings, the coalescence of seemingly jarring and sometimes far from synchronous elements, the difficulty involved in distinguishing between an author's influence and his *fortuna* abroad, and the often glaring discrepancies between quantitative "popularity" and actual impact, between fascination and emulative realisation.

Let us now turn to the more positive constants that can be detected. The discovery of the wealth and brilliance of England's literary heritage came as a revelation to the continent, and the European ascendancy of her authors from Milton and Shakespeare to Richardson, Fielding, and Byron rested by and large on constituent qualities critics grew accustomed to finding in English works of literature: originality, assurance and naturalness combined with sophistication, and unspoilt by convention, rule or dogma; immediacy and untrammelled imaginative freedom, an invigorating infusion of creativeness. These qualities, as we have seen, fostered the decisive transformations of the era and engendered a new image of literature (typefied for many in the irregular genius of Milton and Shakespeare) and an awareness of its historical dimension.

The 18th century became the age of bi- and multilateral relations, of a marked reciprocal interaction of literatures. The highly varied responses to works of English literature on the continent throw into relief the unmistakable national contours of the countries concerned, the individuality of their respective mentalities and sensibilities. But the "era of unified West European literature had by 1800 arrived,"[87] and the influence of England, commensurate with the expansive spatial spread of the Enlightenment "at work from the Netherlands and the Scandinavian countries upon the north to Italy on the south, from Spain and Portugal upon the west to Russia in the east,"[88] helped to make European letters truly European, to

---

[86] Cf. e. g. P. Van Tieghem, *Ossian en France*, Paris, 1917, II p. 472 on the multiple role of Ossianic poetry: "*Les poèmes attribués au Barde de Morven ont offert successivement ou à la fois un document littéraire, un monument historique, un idéal moral des tableaux qui séduisent l'imagination ou qui émeuvent la sensibilité.*"

[87] M. B. and L. M. Price, *The Publication of English Humaniora in Germany in the Eighteenth Century*, Berkeley and Los Angeles, 1955, p. ix.

[88] C. Vaughan, The influence of English poetry upon the Romantic revival on the continent, *Proceedings of the British Academy*, 1913/14, p. 261.

nurture a cosmopolitan tolerant spirit of give and take that provided a counterweight to cultural isolationism. As Goethe remarked to Eckermann in 1827 with regard to this polyphony of stimulation and constructive criticism: *"Es ist aber sehr artig, daß wir jetzt bei dem engen Verkehr zwischen Franzosen, Engländern und Deutschen, in den Fall kommen, uns einander zu kritisieren. Das ist der große Nutzen, der bei einer Weltliteratur herauskommt und der sich immer mehr zeigen wird."*[89]

It is hoped that the foregoing pages may also have drawn attention to the alliance of forces connecting the cult of Shakespeare and Milton with the dethronement of Neoclassicism. These and other facets of the memorable advance of English literature on the continent might induce the observer to couch his conclusions in sharp-edged dichotomies and neat polarities, thus aggravating the dangers inherent in the abstractions, not to say the verbal phantoms of literary history. It may be tempting to depict the 18th century in terms of a linear sequence of currents, a geometric progression of movements following on each other's heels and pointing with teleological unequivocalness to Romanticism as their ultimate goal. However, this trust in the schematic confrontation of periods[90] has long been shaken. It has been recognized that "such antitheses are inherently unreal; the evolution of thought shows no such sharp contrasts, no such hard and fast lines."[91] We tend to see Pre-Romanticism not as an intermediate stage between hermetically sealed periods but as a continuous line of 18th-century development running parallel to, and only eventually phasing out, Classicism[92] — even in Voltaire, the eponym of the Neoclassical age, rationalism and *"sensibilité"* exist side by side — and the Romantic movement itself as "the product of a protracted process of evolution."[93]

Conversely, the Enlightenment has emerged as a comprehensive phenomenon whose internal tensions and contradictions are embedded in a framework of relative unity and cohesion. Comprising both a reassertion of "immutable" classical principles and a critical reappraisal of such beliefs, thus ushering in a notion of poetry that transcended pure reason, the Enlightenment bears witness to the intricate dialectics of continuity and discontinuity, traditionalism and change in a century that was so lavishly energized and made richer by the inspiration of English literature.

[89] See G. M. Vajda, Goethes Anregung zur vergleichenden Literaturbetrachtung, *Acta Litteraria Academiae Scientiarium Hungaricae*, 10, 3—4, 1968, p. 226f.

[90] Cf. also J. H. Tisch, Baroque, in J. M. Ritchie, ed.: *Periods in German Literature*, London, 1966, p. 21f. on these problems.

[91] J. G. Robertson, *Studies in the Genesis of Romantic Theory in the Eighteenth Century*, Cambridge, 1923, p. 190.

[92] Cf. K. Krejči, Les tendances Préromantiques dans les littératures des renaissances nationales du XVIIIᵉ et XIXᵉ siècles, in N. Banašević, ed., *Actes du Vᵉ Congrès de l'Association Internationale de Littérature Comparée*, Belgrade/Amsterdam, 1969, p. 165. Krejči asserts: *"qu'il s'agit ici d'un courant parallèle, qui accompagne le classicisme européen presque dès ses débuts, prend successivement le dessus sur lui et prépare ainsi la révolution romantique."*

[93] L. R. Furst, *Romanticism*, London, 1969, p. 14. The same author repeatedly underlines the evolutionary character of the development of English literature, see e. g. her *Romanticism in Perspective*, London, 1969, p. 251.

GERMAN *ILLUMINATI* IN HUNGARY

by

MÁRIA KAJTÁR

The Order of the *Illuminati* was founded by Professor Adam Weishaupt of Ingolstadt in May, 1776. Although related to the freemason movement, it was different in some essential features.

Essays dealing with the ideology of the Bavarian order of the *Illuminati*, studies and bibliographies, or at least some of them,[1] consider this order an offshoot of the freemason movement, others[2] treat it as an independent intellectual and political trend. There seems to be some truth in each of these theories; the order was more or less independent of the freemason movement in different countries and showed different types of organization. Nevertheless, in its essential aspects, that is, not in external organization but in its links with the Enlightenment, in its attitude to historical reality, the movement of the *Illuminati* differs essentially from the freemason trend.

Conditions for the emergence of the order in Bavaria can be explained by referring to the Central and East European type of development. In the late eighteenth century the arrested development of Central and East European countries provided a suitable atmosphere for any organization or movement which advocated the ideological-political aims of the Enlightenment but, owing to the specific nature of social development, these conditions did not lead to open revolutionary activity.

From the middle of the eighteenth century, in Bavaria, too, conditions were favourable for the emergence of an organization which, though connected with the Enlightenment, differed from it in its ideological makeup. In the semi-feudal circumstances of Bavaria, in accordance with general German conditions, the bourgeoisie wanted to make itself heard. During the reign of Joseph Maximilian III, under the impact of the Enlightenment, there were signs of a flowering in intellectual life (for example, the foundation of the Bavarian Academy, educational reforms, introduction of compulsory schooling, measures to raise the general cultural level of the people.) The seeming expulsion of Jesuits from ideological-political leadership — as in other European countries — resulted also in Bavaria in a more tolerant treatment of questions of religion, and in a more worldly spirit in the principles and methods of education. However, Catholic Bavaria, unlike the Protestant German states, had common frontiers with Austria and was more intimately tied to Rome, so that the Jesuits had deep roots in

---

[1] Lajos Abafy, *Geschichte der Freymaurerei in Ungarn*, Budapet, 1900. — Kálmán Benda, *A magyar Jakobinusok* (The Hungarian Jacobins), Budapest, 1957. — S. Pietack *Goethe als Freimaurer*, Leipzig, 1880.
[2] H. Hettner, *Geschichte der deutschen Literatur im 18. Jahrhundert*, Berlin, 1961. — — W. Krauss, *Studien zur deutschen und französischen Aufklärung*, Berlin, 1963. — G. Schuster, *Die geheimen Gesellschaften, Verbindungen und Orden*, Leipzig, 1880.

the political-cultural life of the country, which could not be annulled, either by legislation or by special measures. In the background of political and cultural life they continued to exercise an influence, often openly advocating their positions.

THE HISTORY AND SOCIAL BASE OF THE *ILLUMINATI* IN BAVARIA

From the point of view of the history of Bavarian *Illuminati*, the Jesuits played a particularly important role, if for no other reason, then because their founder, Weishaupt, was himself educated by Jesuits. The man who would later become a philosopher and hold a high office in his order, becoming a kind of "dictator", had learned from his masters the art of ruling over his fellow men in a strict hierarchic structure, and he also learned the way of making use of the activities of his subordinates within that hierarchy for his own ends. Thus his life and work was characterized by the dilemma of how to adhere to and how to break away from Jesuitism at the same time. Weishaupt was a characteristic figure of the second trend of the German Enlightenment. He was also representative of a certain type of eighteenth-century German intellectual, and thus subject to the influences which had a strong impact on the German intelligentsia in the second third of the century. Among these influences were the ancient philosophy and the French Enlightenment and philosophy. This part of the German intelligentsia was capable of adopting rationalism to the extent of being able to turn its back on mysticism. This rationalism made Weishaupt reject the mystical and irrational elements of 18th-century German freemasonry. However, his break was not complete, since his work retained a good deal from the ceremonies of the freemasons. For example, he continued to use geographic terms in a classicistic form (Österreich-Aegypten, Bayern-Achaia, etc.) and the *Illuminati* names of persons (Zwack-Cato, Weishaupt-Spartacus).[3]

[3] The structure of the order of the *Illuminati* according to the original documents as given by Weishaupt in his *Originalschriften*:
I. *Classe* 1. *Vorbereitung*
        2. *Noviziat*
        3. *Minervalis*
        4. *Illuminatus minor*
(Members of the first class were not initiated in the mysteries and admisson depended on intention of subjection. Degrees of requirement in Class I were elaborated by Weishaupt in detail in his *"Das Verbesserte System"*.)
II. *Classe* 1. *Symbolische* (a) *illuminatus minor*
                   (b) *illuminati dirigentes*
                       (Schottische Richter)
(The formalities of the symbolic and Scottish grade and the ceremonies had been elaborated by Knigge who tried to introduce the freemason rituals into the *Illuminatus* Order.)
III. *Classe* 1. *Kleinere Mysterien*
         2. *Grössere Mysterien* (a) *Magnus*
                        (b) *Rex*
(The requirements of the grades of *Magnus* and *Rex* were not elaborated.)
The members above the Scottish grade had been called *Aeropagites* and only they had been initiated into the mysteries, the "more dangerous doctrines" of philosophy. Weishaupt lectured to them on the subjects of *Materialismus* und *Idealismus* — these appeared in 1786 and only they could know about organizations of a political nature.

The chronological events of the history of the Bavarian order hasve been well investigated and exact philological data and information on all issues are available.[4] This movement of short though stormy duration can be reconstructed from original documents, the works of Weishaupt and the pamphlets of contemporary *Illuminati*.[5]

The external chronological history of the order can be divided into three phases. The first of these is a period lasting from its foundation in 1776 to 1780. The characteristics of this period hardly indicate the beginnings of a later movement of great significance. Its members were mostly students, Weishaupt's disciples, university students, teachers and intellectuals. Though Weishaupt had worked out his basic ideas in the first versions of his shorter writings, they reflect neither a comprehensive world image nor extensive culture. In addition, the bibliographical data of his works and the dates of publication prove that his ideas matured only later.[6] Most of these publications appeared between 1785—1786. Neither its social basis, nor the number of its members justifies the wide and rapid circulation of the ideas of the *Illuminati* at a later period.

However, the situation changed in 1780 when Adolf Freiherr von Knigge entered the order. Critics consider the peak of the movement to last until 1784 when persecutions began. The place of Knigge, an extremely interesting and contradictory man, in the history of the *Illuminati* is just as contradictory as his career as a writer and journalist. While devoting his excellent organizational sense and his contacts with higher circles to the interests of the movement, his individualism, which disregarded any obligation to the rules and statutes of the order, constantly violated its principles. His attitude caused disputes within the order itself, leading to the break-up of the membership into factions. The differences in the personalities of the leaders concealed deeper ideological controversies which kept rising to the surface in their direction of the movement.

Knigge strove to produce a closed system. He finished by leaving the order in 1784. It would be hard to decide today whether he was led to this action by personal reasons, or else by an acute sense of political instinct, sensing approaching danger, and wanting to leave the sinking boat in time.

From about 1784, the third and declining period in the history of Bavarian *Illuminati* began. In 1784 the ruler of Bavaria prohibited any kind of secret organization. Secret informers infiltrated the order in 1785 in the persons of Privy Councillor Utschneider, the Reverend Cosandry and others, including the professors of the Marianische Akademie, who provided exact information to the Prince and the police on the organization of *Illuminati* and on their aims. Many of the members, beginning with some who had played socially

---

[4] E. Engel, *Geschichte des Illuminatenordens. Ein Beitrag zur Geschichte Bayerns*, 1906. — Schuster, *op. cit.*
[5] A. Weishaupt, *Schilderung der Illuminaten*, Nürnberg, 1786. — *Vollstaendige Geschichte der Verfolgungen der Illuminaten in Bayern*, 1786.
[6] *Vollstaendige Geschichte der Verfolgungen der Illuminaten in Bayern*, 1786. — *Apologie der Illuminaten*, Leipzig, 1786. — *Einige Originalschriften des Illuminatenordens . . .* München, 1787. — *System und Folgen des Illuminatenordens in Briefen*, München, 1787. — *Kurze Rechtfertigung meiner Absichten*, 1787. — *Das verbesserte System der Illuminaten mit allen seinen Einrichtungen und Graden*, Frankfurt — Leipzig, 1787. — *Schilderung der Illuminaten*, Nürnberg, 1786. etc.

an insignificant role to important political personalities (as the Marquis Constanzo, Counciller Zwack, Court Counciller Zinzendorf), were obliged to flee. Weishaupt resigned his professorship and emigrated first to Regensburg and subsequently to the court of the Prince of Gotha.

The life and fate of Weishaupt cannot be separated from his order. After the order was dissolved, he himself became frustrated as was typical of German intellectuals who miscarried the fate of revolutions; he was unable to transform the results of thought into action, and his futile argumentative life ended in failure. In a letter addressed to Cosandry in 1786 he estimated his life and activity to be a breath of air. The letter is argumentative, passionate and not very polite in expressing Weishaupt's resignation, nostalgia and the sincere pain felt over an unfought battle: "*Man wollte meinen Einfluss auf die Jugend, die mir sehr anhing, schwaechen. Man wollte mich ausser alle Wirksamkeit setzen, mich noch vorher laecherlich machen, um zu diesem Ende eine Comödie spielen*" ... "*Ich glaube mich zu etwass bessern aufbehalten, als das Gelaechter meiner Feinde zu werden . . . . . . ich sah also, dass von den Bedrückungen, die ich schon seit 13 Jahren erfahre, kein Ende abzusehen sei. Ich hielt es also für Pflicht, für meine Ruhe zu sorgen.*"[7]

THE IDEOLOGY OF THE BAVARIAN ILLUMINATI

The majority of Weishaupt's works are devoted to an exposition of the ideology and programme of the *Illuminati*. In analysing *Illuminati* ideology, it must be taken into consideration that Weishaupt did not aim at establishing a philosophical system but rather intended to justify his practical activity on an ideological plane both before his friends and enemies. It was mainly by means of a concrete programme that he intended to expound the main theses of his ideology.

All his ideas focused on two kinds of questions: what is the world we inhabit like and what should it be made into? Two philosophical disciplines emerged in the centre of his activity: ontology and ethics, the latter inseparable from politics. However, the fact that we try to organize his philosophy around these two points does not necessarily mean that Weishaupt developed a uniform system. The chief characteristic of Weishauptian "philosophy" was eclecticism, which was not uncommon with the thinkers of the last two phases of the period, and in this respect, too, Weishaupt was a typical representative of the period.

As far as the basic conflict between idealism and materialism is concerned, Weishaupt did not give an unambiguous answer; not unlike those of other philosophers of the period, his works exemplified an objective idealism coupled with materialistic elements. As a disciple of Wolff and Feder, he was a Leibnizian and as such a pronounced adherent and supporter of theology. He recognized the existence of a superior power independent of human consciousness, calling it God. However, his concept of God differed from the anthropomorphic Christian God and rather resembled the pantheistic concept of Leibniz. His ideal is a godlike purposefulness which is given in nature but which, nevertheless, cannot manifest itself unfailingly since

[7] *Apologie der Illuminaten*, Beylage A. An den Herren Abbé Cosandry, p. 190.

the secular powers, in alliance with the Churches, falsify it. Weishaupt thus arrives at the central question which is constantly present in his philosophy, viz. *religion*. His religion-centredness can be traced back to both subjective and objective factors. He could never become entirely independent of the Jesuits: although throughout his life he waged war against their principles, he adopted their methods. He also had to cope with the problem of religion, constantly present in the intellectual and cultural thought of the Enlightenment. In connection with diverse subjects in both his educational and strictly philosophical works, he always returned to religion. As a result of his idealism Weishaupt was never adverse to religion but only to the Churches.

Weishaupt did not simply state "what the world was like" but linked up his analysis with the politico-ethical issue of "what the world ought to become."

Against the real given world reflecting the theses of its present socio-ethical state, he always poses an antithesis: against the inevitable acceptance of existing reality he raises the utopistically conceived social arrangements of the future. He deals with this question in his *Originalschriften*.[8]

Weishaupt conceives of the emergence of class societies in a Wolffian and Rousseauistic manner, as based on the principle of natural rights. Weishaupt considered the state strictly necessary from an ethical-philosophical standpoint. The existence of a supreme power *("Oberster Gewalt")* was just and justified in the present, as long as state and individual interests pointed to different directions. The state is meant to assume a regulating function. It becomes an ethical institution when the rulers and the state apparatus form an alliance with secret societies, since the direct aim of the latter is to improve morals and, by increasing the number of individuals of good morals, society as a whole is bound to become moral. Only then can a social contract be realized between the moral individuals of society and the moral interests of society.

Moreover, the final aim of Weishaupt's utopistic ideas is a community existing in the spirit of liberty, standing above individual nations and uniting mankind, through basic principles and rights to be laid down in the Codex of Nations. This would be at the same time a codex of family and individual human rights corresponding to the national interest. Since, he reasons, there will no longer be independent peoples and nations, egoism, intolerance, patriotism (the latter always used as a negative attribute) will duly disappear.

In direct contradiction to himself, Weishaupt conceived his utopistic state as the earthly realization of the teachings of Christ. His arguments against the existing social order were built on certain tenets of Christian doctrine. In the course of history Christ was the only being capable of showing the path leading directly to liberty and equality. In approaching the theory of the state from this angle, Weishaupt came practically to the same conclusion as the materialistic conception of society: a state above nations: *"Es wird eine Zeit kommen, wo ein Hirt und ein Schafstall sein wird,"* he writes, thus everybody becoming equal, without belonging to nation and classes.

---

[8] *Originalschriften der Illuminatenordens, welche bey dem gewesenen Regierungsrath Zwack durch vorgenommenen Hausvisitation zu Landhut den 11. und 12. Oktober 1786 vorgedrungen worden*, München 1887, J. Stobl.

If people understand the inner core of the teachings of Christ, and if by means of secret societies they realize its essence, then the alliance between states and Churches which aimed at oppressing people will cease. This, however, will not be possible unless people cultivate their minds. To this end Christianity and Enlightenment will serve the same purpose.

Concerning the methods and tactics to promote the realization of the final aim, Weishaupt expounded the theory of general morality. In a state where a general morality rules, there must be general freedom too. A society based on general morality and rights can only be realized if the state can make use of the order and purposefulness prevailing in nature. These lines reveal the historical view of French Enlightenment and the main ideas of Wolff's "flat teology" (v. Engels). His vocabulary, images, the structure and strict discipline of his sentences *follow the images of an indivisible mechanism* and linguistic rigour. In this mechanism everything happens according to a predestined aim. In imitation of the changes of nature, historical changes do not occur abruptly but slowly, without force and revolution, in an evolutionary manner due to the gradual enlightenment of the human spirit and the concomitant changes in morality. In these changes man does not figure in any way except as "the promoter of birth." Finally it is not man himself who, according to his own will and laws, contributes to changes in society, but the change must occur according to a self-propelled mechanism of nature. In this process man can only function as an instrument.

However, man as such, is of tremendous importance in Weishaupt's hierarchy of ideas. Weishaupt views man in two dimensions: first as a tiny component responsible for the regular function of nature as a whole, secondly as the final aim and as such, of incomparable significance. In this respect Weishaupt's humanism, man-centredness, is undeniable: *"Oh, gewiss mit und aus Menschen ist alles zu machen"* — he says. Although apt to adopt the good and the moral, man as given must be changed and moulded. How and into what — answers to these questions are to be found in the most clearly elaborated discipline of philosophy: ethics.

The basic categories of his ethics (his key-words, if we may analyse his text from a semantic viewpoint) are as follows: precision, order, discipline and a sense of subjection; aloofness from passions; compassion; self-knowledge, submissiveness, faithfulness: condemnation of self-satisfied action; consideration above all for the interests of the community; unconditional submission to superiors.

His ethical principles suffer greatly owing to the fact that he aims at the complete annihilation of the individual personality which would in turn entail the loss of man's creative ability, his personal sense of responsibility and his sense of duty. In Weishaupt's ideology the individual hardly exists, not even as conceived in the narrowest sense.

One of the central categories of his anti-individualism is the *community (die Gesellschaft)*, society. (By community he understands the community of the organization of *Illuminati*; the union of the members without discrimination as to wealth, social, occupational and denominational differences.) For him a community is a defensive formation against any enemy.

However, paradoxically, this behaviour pattern also justifies the expression of Weishaupt's most humanistic ethical principles: man is not a unit who stands alone but is part of a community, and as such he is obliged to share the sufferings of his fellow men, to stand by them in persecution.

Weishaupt considers education as the chief instrument for the formation and shaping of man. Education plays a key role in his theory. He believes that every man can be educated. He considers the most important methods of education to be reading (the letters of Seneca, Epictetus, Abbt, Cicero, Feder, Montaigne are "recommended readings for *Pflanzschule*"), discussion on a strictly hierarchical basis of philosophical subjects and the affairs of the order, and the influence of the personality of the teacher himself. In this case teacher and superior in the order are generally one and the same person. The superior is expected to exercise his power over his alumnus unnoticed. In Weishaupt's ethics the influence of Platonic ideas is evident.

Reflecting on the ethical consequences of the political institutions of his age, Weishaupt tried to provide an ideal for state and morality in his ideology. Its essence was, as is true of most ethics-centred philosophies, to show man how to understand himself and find happiness within the social context of his age, or, should this not be possible in the given historical circumstances, within a future society which is inevitable and which in his view will be an optimal one.

THE PLACE OF THE MOVEMENT OF BAVARIAN *ILLUMINATI* IN THE GERMAN ENLIGHTENMENT

Weishaupt and other members demanded freedom and equal rights for every individual in the name of the Enlightenment. At the same time, the organization was built on an extremely narrow social basis, yet it comprised men of diverse ideological persuasions. Weishaupt himself aimed at relying on the bourgeois intelligentsia. Knigge, on the other hand, brought in the aristocracy in no small number. For a short time even Karl August, Prince of Weimar, Ernst, Prince of Gotha and Ferdinand, Elector of Braunschweig counted among the *Illuminati*. We also find members of the German nobility, intellectuals, artists, writers, even Goethe himself,[9] among the *Illuminati*.

Among the members the names of Herder, Lessing, Nicolai, Jacobi and Schlosser can be found, names which witness the desire of German intellectuals to find a new path and new directions. However, there are indications that they did not take their membership in this "secret society" seriously. We may also add that among the *Illuminati* there were hardly any plebeian members, and even if there were, they played no role.

Indeed, at this time a process which became highly characteristic of the bourgeois revolutions of Eastern and Central Europe started in Germany: in want of a bourgeoisie, here the nobility partly took over their role. The evolutionary contradictions arising from this peculiarity are well known. A bourgeoisie mingling with the aristocracy and the nobility could not seriously mean, nor was it in its interest (especially late in the eighteenth

---

[9] On Goethe's interest in the *Illuminati* see R. Friedenthal, *Goethe élete és kora* Budapest 1971, p. 28. Original: *Goethe — sein Leben und seine Zeit*, München 1963.

century), to produce real economic and political equality for the plebeian and the peasant. This was historically absurd, even though Weishaupt as an *Illuminatus* assumed the name of Spartacus, a constant reminder of the paragon of popular revolutions.

AUSTRIAN AND HUNGARIAN VARIANTS OF THE *ILLUMINATI* MOVEMENT

CONDITIONS FOR THE EMERGENCE OF THE MOVEMENT IN AUSTRIA AND HUNGARY

After its dissolution in Bavaria and the escape of its members, the ideology of the Bavarian *Illuminati* movement was modified and, by accommodating itself to changing economic, social and cultural conditions, it found fertile soil in the eastern countries of Europe.

The Enlightenment movement within the Catholic church had already begun to develop during the reign of Maria Theresa in Austria. The central figure of this movement was Gerhard van Swieten who obtained permission from the monarch for the introduction of the first ecclesiastical reforms. However, the process fully matured during the reign of Joseph II, in the ecclesiastical and social reforms of the monarch. Although this paper is only concerned with the Austrian connections of the *Illuminati* of Bavaria from 1790 to 1794, that is, in the period following the death of Joseph II, it is nevertheless, essential to refer to certain basic features of Josephinism, since this trend launched the fermentation, in Austria and particularly in Hungary, that culminated in the Jacobinist movement, with which also the history of Austrian and Hungarian *Illuminati* had links. Kálmán Benda in his study, "Josephinism and Jacobinism in the Habsburg Monarchy"[10] offers an excellent summary of the historical research on the first years of these movements. According to him, Josephinism, that is to say, the Austrian version of enlightened absolutism, did not essentially differ from other varieties. All endeavoured to preserve feudalism, although by different means. The early philosophers of the Enlightenment influenced through German media the political principles of Joseph II, "however, in the Eastern part of Europe where the bourgeoisie remained backward, the Enlightenment provided new arguments to absolute governments and their allies, the aristocracy, in order to consolidate their own power . . . Joseph II had no intention of overthrowing feudalism, but with the modernization of the state apparatus, the extension of its sphere of interest, the slight restriction of ecclesiastical and gentry power with moderate bourgeois support and state control over the peasantry, wanted to preserve the essentials of feudalism."[11] Joseph's mistake was that he alienated the only class on which he could have relied, the Hungarian nobility, since there was as yet no Hungarian bourgeoisie. In conjunction with his peasant policy his alienation of the nobility doomed his system to failure.

[10] Kálmán Benda, *A magyar jakobinusok iratai* (Papers of the Hungarian Jacobins), Budapest 1952, Introductory essay.
[11] K. Benda, *op. cit.*, p. 14.

Still at the end of the reign of Joseph II, under the impact of the 1789 French events, a change occurred in the attitude of this enlightened monarch of Eastern Europe, and he endeavoured to form a closer alliance with the nobility. It was in this political atmosphere that Leopold II ascended to the throne. The two years of his rule were not as unambiguously reactionary as had been formerly asserted by historians. Benda confirmed in his above-mentioned study that "the reform efforts of Leopold did not lag behind those of Joseph either from a political or from a social point of view. However, his method was more flexible, especially as far as the hereditary provinces were concerned. Leopold's policy in Hungary naturally received other acoustics. In order not to lose the country, he was compelled to let reaction take the upper hand despite his personal intentions. The adherents of Joseph II, the Josephinist intelligentsia, sided in 1790 with the anti-Habsburg patriotic nobility movement, and Leopold was compelled to turn against tlhem and was forced to lean on the clergy, reactionary but unques tionably oyal to the dynasty, which had been pushed into the background by his brother.

"However, by the end of 1791 the situation changed in many ways. Anti-Habsburg efforts had lost their support from abroad, and under the impact of the French Revolution, the majority of the nobility sided with the king, thus enabling Leopold to make a renewed attempt to launch his social reforms."[12]

He was prevented, however, from carrying out these endeavours by his death, and his successor, Francis I, (lacking initiative and diplomatic tact) embarked on a policy of repressive measures, claiming that the only possibility of defending the old system against the revolution was through rigid adherence to it.

THE HISTORY OF THE *ILLUMINATI* MOVEMENT IN AUSTRIA
AND HUNGARY

The history of the Austrian and Hungarian *Illuminati* between 1790—1791 faithfully reflected the fluctuation of political and diplomatic events. Confronted with the complexity of social and political circumstances, the *Illuminati* had broken away from Weishauptian ideas, although they were well acquainted with his writings and were familiar with the history of his organization.

However, in its general framework and outward appearance the Austro-Hungarian variety of illuminism differed from the Bavarian one. While Weishaupt and his movement had had nothing to do with the freemasons, the two *Illuminati* centres of the Monarchy, in Vienna and Pest and Buda, had close ties with the freemasons, particularly between 1790—1791. The *Illuminati* movement within the Monarchy was in point of fact the highest degree of freemasonry. According to data provided by Walter Markow, until the death of Joseph II, each of the well-known 42—47 lodges in the Monarchy represented the Josephinist trend. The members of the lodges were 11 per cent landowners and noblemen, 58 per cent officials, 5 per cent

[12] *Ibid.*, p. 26.

churchmen, 15 per cent free professionals, 10 per cent merchants, 1 per cent sundry). At that time there were some 2000—3000 freemasons in the Monarchy.

It is noteworthy that the Austrian and Hungarian *Illuminati* were so intimately connected that they cannot be treated separately from each other. The link between the two movements needs no explanation, being part and parcel of a geographical, historical, economic, political and cultural relationship characteristic of the countries in the Habsburg Monarchy from the seventeenth century and until the First World War.

The members of the Hungarian *Illuminati* circles were at home in the Viennese lodges and could obtain information and ideas from them, particularly before 1790. The interaction was, of course, reciprocal with the Hungarian freemason and *Illuminati* movements, also influencing the Viennese.

The reconstruction of the Hungarian-Austrian variant of the *Illuminati* movement and its more objective evaluation is rendered extremely difficult owing to the scarcity of available material. This is mainly due to the fact — as also pointed out by Martinovics in a report written for the court — that neither the Austrian nor the Hungarian *Illuminati* prepared written documents of their activities, profiting from the Bavarian example. They kept up contact by means of verbal messages and meetings. An exception is the diary of Alajos Lipót Hoffmann, an *Illuminatus* and court agent who lectured at the German department of the University of Pest until 1790 (*Aktenmaessige Darstellung der Deutschen Union und Ihrer Verbindung mit den Illuminaten — Freymaurer — und Rosenkreuzorden*, Wien, 1796), who described himself and the dual character and contradictions of the movement. More data on the history and ideology of the movement could be found if we had access to the private writings of Emperor Francis and the freemason documents to which Kálmán Benda refers in the introduction of his book *Papers of the Hungarian Jacobins*, but to which he himself had no access.[13] Thus in reconstructing the movement only the reports of agents, particularly those of Martinovics, can serve as direct sources. They, however, must be used with caution because for personal reasons or lack of information they often distort or falsify data and names. This is why, when dealing with the history of the *Illuminati* movement in the Monarchy, I have tried to rely on data which can be corroborated from different sources or can be checked by the footnotes that Benda added to the papers.

ILLUMINATI IN VIENNA

In Vienna the movement became a real threat to the state around 1790 when it developed into a considerable organization. Historians regard 1790 as a landmark when the failure of the system of Joseph II, the seeming mystery of Leopold's policy and the repressive measures of Francis forced the democratic intelligentsia and those inclined to their views to come out, however cautiously, in the open.

In Vienna, as early as the 1780s, a so-called Union Lodge (French-English-American Union, elsewhere: German-French-English-American Union) emerged which also included the majority of *Illuminati* in Vienna. Its name

[13] *Ibid.*, p. 39.

already pointed to an international orientation. The ruling circles of the Monarchy sensed danger and became polarized themselves on the question of the *Illuminati*. After the death of Joseph II, Martinovics and Hoffmann in their secret reports insisted repeatedly that the *Illuminati* movement of Vienna was becoming more and more radical. However, this turn to the left must be interpreted with caution, since "there was more talk about it than existed in actual fact." This moderate radicalism aimed at preventing revolution by reforms consisted in the ideal of a "well-groomed Monarchy", to be explained by the class status of the majority of the membership, and particularly by their professions. The majority of the membership were court officials of bourgeois origin (such as Widmann, an administrative official, Schlossing, a secretary of state and historian of law, the tutor of Emperor Francis, Joachim Braun, court clerk and Becken, councillor), ecclesiastical personalities (Poschinger, a Dominican monk, Gruber, professor of diplomacy at the University of Vienna, Jacob Meissner, the director of the Piarist school at Nikolsburg), also aristocrats and poets, like Blumauer and Alxinger and such men of high position as Sonnenfels, Martini and Van Swieten.

The subjects that were discussed at lodge meetings and reading circles — as L. A. Hoffmann mentions in his memoirs — included particularly the theory of the state, ethics, religion and educational policy. Martini, Van Swieten, and Sonnenfels even succeeded in accomplishing practical reforms. In their basic principles they did not entirely break away from Weishaupt. Hoffman writes of their aims in these words: "We have united in order to realize the aims of the founder of Christianity, dethroning superstition and fanaticism by means of a quiet alliance functioning to further God's achievement."[14] Their reformism was far removed from a revolutionary nature and their caution was understandable. For the members who were court officials a revolution similar to the 1789 events would have meant an end to their existence; for members of the churches, on the other hand, a radical institution according to the religious-philosophical orientation of the Enlightenment would have meant an unacceptable step towards atheism.

In reports written by Martinovics on the *Illuminati* of Vienna, despite many intentional errors and distortions (he tries, for example, to present every revolutionary action as stemming from the activity of secret societies), he correctly interprets the Enlightenment as the source of *Illuminati* ideas.

It is characteristic of the activity of the Viennese *Illuminati* movement — despite some of its radical members and features — that their only objective was the continuation of the trend begun by Joseph II and nothing more radical than that.

THE *ILLUMINATI* OF HUNGARY

The Hungarian organization was similar to the one in Austria. In the beginning men who were familiar with *Illuminati* ideas, particularly freemasons and the democratic intelligentsia, did not form a close-knit organization. They met at loosely arranged, casual meetings and at lectures and conferences — which did not make use of the mystical ceremonies charac-

---

[14] *Ibid.*, p. 85.

teristic of secret societies — where they discussed current problems. After 1790, probably in the wake of the Austrian-Bavarian model, it became necessary to adopt the secret organization form, owing to the radicalization of philosophical thought. It was late in 1790 and early in 1791 that the Reading Circle of Buda at Pest-Buda *(Societas Eruditorum)* was established, with members professing radical ideas, including Hajnóczy, Szentmarjay, Berzeviczy and Verseghy. Side by side with the *Societas Eruditorum*, several similar "reading and self-training" circles emerged at Pest-Buda, which were organized in imitation of the German *"Lesekabinett"*. Besides these groups other circles consisting of aristocrats and noblemen played a considerable role in propagating the ideas of the Enlightenment in Hungary. It was in February, 1792 that a certain Ferenc Zugrovics, Orczy's clerk, reported to the court the existence of a circle around László Orczy[15] and accused his master of holding "atheistic, revolutionary and republican" meetings "in condemnation of the government." In the reports other groups are mentioned, for example those of Counts Haller and Török, Baron Podmaniczky and others. How much truth there was in these rumours can hardly be checked today, nor can we prove what connections these groups had with the *Illuminati*. It can well be assumed that these gatherings included the same free-thinking, enlightened individuals as the reading circles.

The social basis and centre of the *Illuminati* of Pest was the University with its professors and students. Károly Koppi, Antal Kreil (of Bavarian origin), Schraud and Hoffmann had all been *Illuminati*, men familiar with the Enlightenment, who were at the same time informers of the court. Kreil even belonged to the secret organization of the Jesuits and reported on their affairs to the court. According to the reports of Martinovics and those of other sources, the following men also belonged to the university group of the *Illuminati* in Hungary: András Szathmáry, clerk of the University of Pest; Ferenc Gyurkovics, professor of political sciences; Professor Albert Barics, all names which occur most frequently in the reports. Beside the above-mentioned founders the following members are referred to in the Reading Circle of Buda: János Nagyváthy, Szabó Szentjóbi, Sándor Lányi, Szolártsik, Pál Őz and Baron József Podmaniczky. These different groups, however, maintained intimate contacts with each other, meeting jointly, for example, in the house of Ferenc Abaffy, one of the leading personalities of Hungarian freemasonry. It was especially Szolártsik who reported on these meetings to the court.

Nor were the lodges, reading circles and clubs of Pest isolated from other lodges and groups functioning in the country. In the provincial residences of aristocratic patrons of the sciences and of the Enlightenment these intellectual communities had naturally developed in every part of the country.

There were significant lodges in Transylvania, the Upper Region, near Tokaj and Sárospatak. Nevertheless, the centre was still in Pest-Buda, a further indication that the city was beginning to develop into the capital of the country: administration, cultural life and other activities had begun to concentrate there.[16]

---

[15] *Ibid.*, p. 42.
[16] See Elemér Jancsó, *A magyar szabadkőművesség irodalmi és művelődéstörténeti szerepe a 18. században* (The historical and cultural role of Hungarian freemasonry in the 18th century), Cluj 1936.

As far as the ideological platform of various groups and clubs was concerned, until 1790, the death of Joseph II, members had been kept together by their enthusiasm for Josephinism. After 1790, among the groups and even within them, a polarization began. A portion of their members had been expelled from public life during the reign of Leopold, as, for example, the Hungarian middle nobility and non-noble intelligentsia. Another portion, particularly those of German and Austrian origin, recognizing the dynastic political objectives of Leopold and the continuation of the Josephinist line in his principles of government, became loyal to the emperor and accepted commissions in public and secret life. This process of differentiation culminated during the reign of Francis, in reaction to his policy. Some of the lodge members renounced their former principles, while a smaller portion became ever more radical, turning against the emperor; some of them even joined the Jacobins.

The general picture concerning the lodges turned out somewhat differently in the case of the *Illuminati*. After 1790, the first Hungarian organizations of the *Illuminati* consisted mainly of foreign intellectuals. In the spirit of the Enlightenment, they demanded full bourgeois transformation but strictly under the supervision of the Austrian dynasty, never denying their loyalty either to king or court. However, the paths of the two factions of Hungarian *Illuminati* separated; after 1790 they even turned against each other. During the reign of Francis I, as a reaction against burgeoning Habsburg absolutism, the second group comprising the nobility with their allies, the democratic intelligentsia, more sharply emphasized the unity of the Enlightenment, national independence and the necessity of national transformation. Thirdly, it would be impossible to overlook those factions of the patriotic aristocratic opposition who revolted against foreign rule but wished neither bourgeois transformation nor the elimination of feudalism.

However, this polarization did not mean that the groups of different persuasions segregated in practice. If we can believe the lists included in the reports, then even after 1790, Károly Koppi, Antal Kreil, Haller, Podmaniczky and Török met where they had before.

The names of the radical intelligentsia occurred, however, less frequently, or not at all, in these reports which may be due to two reasons. The paths of men like Hajnóczy, Nagyváthy, Berzeviczy either diverged from the ideas of the lodges or else they really succeeded in ensuring the secrecy of their meetings and conversations. It was this group which in 1794 combined the ideas of the Enlightenment with that of national independence, and changed these ideas into the activism of the Jacobinist movement.

In its wide political and cultural ramifications, the movement of the Hungarian *Illuminati* can be considered as an intermediate step between the revolutionary nature of the reformism of freemasonry and the Jacobinist movement. In its objectives, hopes and ideals the democratic nobility and the intelligentsia surpassed the reformism of freemasonry in the ideal of a bourgeois republic, the realization of which may have been effected by the Jacobinist movement if, owing to the internal mistakes of the organization and the backwardness of conditions in Hungary, it had not been foredestined to failure.

From the late 1780s more and more is heard of the left-wing faction of the freemasons, the *Illuminati*, and from 1790 it is possible to trace this process of radicalization in the light of surviving pamphlets and reports.

A leaflet written by Károly Koppi, a leading personality in the Hungarian *Illuminati* movement, in 1790 (*"A Warning by a Loyal Citizen of our Free Country to the Authorities and Rulers of Hungary"*), voices the hopes which the Hungarian nobility attached to the reign of Leopold. It considers the circumstances of the 1790s suitable for the reorganization of the affairs of the country and for the consolidation of the relationship between the ruler and the people. The leaflet is a Hungarian variant of Montesquieu and the French law of nature, stating that laws are bound to protect the happiness of the people by guaranteeing human and civil rights. In Koppi's 1790 work there was no allusion yet to a republic, or equality — not even in general terms. His principles only went beyond Josephinism in the matter of religion where instead of tolerance he demanded full religious liberty.

Special light is thrown on the general mood of 1791 in Hungary by the meetings of the *Illuminati* which were becoming ever more radical as revealed in a report written by the Pest bookseller and court agent, Ignác Strohmayer. Strohmayer's report is less suspect than those of other agents, because unlike the others, he writes succinctly, dwelling only on essential points, and his statements can be corroborated with general historical events. In 1791 the progressive factions joined the patriotic organization of the nobility in opposition to the Habsburgs, and Leopold was compelled to lean on reactionary clerical elements. The report of Strohmayer describes this situation in an account of a conversation between the Deputy-Constable of County Zala and János Spissich: "It is entirely wrong to believe that the country as a whole is dissatisfied, though in every county there is secret dissension."[17] The counties were merely waiting for parliament to meet to give expression to their dissatisfaction. This mood was aggravated by the agitation of *Illuminati* and freemason club members who discussed at their meetings daily politics, the events and achievements of the 1790 parliament, and did not dwell on abstract topics.

It was in 1791 that Martinovics began to send his reports to the Chief of Police, Gotthardi. Although his reports are far from reliable, being verbose and seldom to the point, behind the flood of words we can nevertheless detect that those sitting in the lodges became more and more radical, or else had turned away from politics. Late in 1791, he spoke of the dissolution of the *Illuminati* "church" in Hungary. This was only partially true, since the lodges dissolved only formally and the membership remained in contact with each other. But it is also true that the activity of the lodges went hand in glove with the dominant political trends. Late in 1791, overtures on the part of the nobility towards the Habsburgs enabled Leopold to make allowances to the Hungarians and attempt to introduce a moderate social reform plan.

However, with the death of Leopold, all the reform attempts that Joseph II and Leopold had wished to introduce were interrupted by the overt reactionary political measures of Francis I. Between 1792—1794, the *Illuminati* lodges in Hungary reacted to the politics of Francis, activized themselves again, and formed an organization. The informers reported in March, 1792 that the *Illuminati*, shocked by the warfare planned against the French

---

[17] Benda, *op. cit.*, p. 100.

and the French Constitution, were planning to attempt a rescue of the French Republic. Reports came in of increasing support for France and of expressions of sympathy. It was reported that both in Vienna and Pest the *Illuminati* planned to disseminate their ideas to the lower classes, to the peasants and plebeians and that they continued to call themselves democrats. Martinovics summed up the aims of the *Illuminati* in the following words: to end the oppressive power of the Monarchies, to prevent wars contradictory to the interests of the people, to end the prerogatives of birth, and the profanation of religion. They agreed that the French Revolution was the real school of democracy for every nation; Martinovics also reminded the court that by insisting on democratic principles the *Illuminati* went beyond Josephinism, that instead of reforms there was a danger of revolution, and he energetically warned the court that unrest created by the *Illuminati* might spread throughout the Empire.

Reports dating from the end of 1793 already speak less of the organization of *Illuminati* but more of the circulation of Jacobinic ideas.

THE REFLECTION OF THE *ILLUMINATI* IDEA IN HUNGARIAN
LITERATURE

Illuminati ideas and questions posed by them undoubtedly became part and parcel of the cultural life of the period. Their influence as an integral, even though not the most important, element of the Hungarian and Austrian Enlightenment is incontestable.

Thus we must put the question to what extent can we find in our restricted field, in one of the most important sections of the cultural life, in literature this influence and whether it can be directly traced.

To start with, we shall have to clarify what we understand by literature in late 18th-century Hungary. If we think in terms of contemporary concepts, it is indeed difficult to measure the effect of this influence in literature. In the literary activity of our really great classical writers, it is not easy, sometimes even impossible, to detect this influence. In the midst of the turbulent ideas of the period and the manifold foreign and local influences affecting writers, it seems impossible to disentangle what was exactly due to the *Illuminati*. The thoughts and ideas they discussed during their meetings and conversations occur in a far too complex manner, encompassed in the general ideology of the Enlightenment, so that it would be impossible to trace them one by one. It is evident, however, that writers and intellectuals professing similar ideas and agreeing in their political views had known of this movement.

Ferencz Kazinczy writing to György Aranka said, for example, "Did you ever hear about the *Illuminati*? These men are active in Vienna too. Their aim is, as far as I can make it out (I have never belonged to them, I swear to you before the Everlasting Lord and Master!) *avertere superstitionem, opprimere Tyrannismus, benefacere*. Isn't this the greatest bliss of life?" In his *Pályám emlékezete* (Memories from my career) he writes that when visiting Vienna he took part in a freemason lodge meeting where he met Blumauer and Alxinger. So it is quite evident that Kazinczy was familiar with this movement; and Batsányi too was in touch with the *Illuminati* of

Pest as he speaks of them in his poem entitled *Levél Szentjóbi Szabó László-hoz* (Letter addressed to László Szentjóbi Szabó): *"S hát mint vagytok ti más buda-pesti barátaink? Mit mível a bölcs Koppi? Miképp nevelkednek alatta a haza jobb csemetéi?"* (How are you all, my friends in Buda-Pest? How is the wise Koppi? How do the promising youths of this country progress under him?) However, from Batsányi we hear not only words of agreement but also the warning of a realistic politician who was in disagreement with Martinovics and could see the true nature of the Hungarian-Austrian relationship, as is clear from his defence *Hazámnak akartam szolgálni. A felségsértéssel és hazaárulással vádolt költő a maga ügyében.* (I meant to serve my country. The poet in his own defence when charged with treason to his sovereign and his country).

A number of other similar examples could be cited but they are hardly sufficient to claim that any work written by a writer of the Enlightenment was inspired by the *Illuminati*. An attempt to prove the literary influence of the Hungarian *Illuminati* (not less than that of the Bavarians or Austrians) would be far-fetched in this respect and would entail the danger of overestimating the literary side of the movement. (Not to mention the fact that as far as the great figures of the literature of the period are concerned, we have no idea whether or not they belonged to the *Illuminati*. If we know that they were freemasons or Jacobins, it is not the same as the more restricted movement of the *Illuminati*.)

However, if we extend the concept of literature, if we include, for example, the pamphlets of the late 18th century among the literary genres — strictly in keeping with the concepts of the age — there is copious material to deal with. True, the majority of these writers wished to serve with their works political aims and not aesthetic and artistic ones. The authors wrote about social and religious questions, scientific problems. Moreover, the fact that a prose work bears the marks of a pamphlet does not exclude its literary merits and the value of pamphlets produced in the late eighteenth century is enhanced by the fact that they adequately reflect the spirit of the age sometimes in prose, in writings which could serve as a model for the Hungarian essay.[18]

The subjects of these pamphlets form the following groups:

I. Problems of bourgeois transformation and national independence. Alajos Batthyany's *Ad amicam aurem*, a pamphlet written in 1790 gives an "official" treatment of the whole complex of questions — although the author, to the best of my knowledge, did not belong to the *Illuminati* movement. His ideal state is a constitutional monarchy, with restricted rights for the ruler and special emphasis on individual liberty. Disgusted with the events of the French Revolution, he offers advice to rulers and to governmental representatives, to the clergy and the people, on how to behave in order to achieve slow evolution and to avoid revolution by means of reforms. In his pamphlet utopistic ideas are mixed with practical suggestions for urgent reforms.

[18] Cf. Géza Ballagi, *A politikai irodalom Magyarországon 1825-ig* (Political literature in Hungary until 1825), Budapest, 1888. — Denis Silagi, *Jakobiner in der Habsburger Monarchie*, Wien, 1962. — György Kókay, *A magyar hírlap- és folyóiratirodalom kezdetei (1780—1795)* (Beginnings of newspaper and periodical literature in Hungary), Budapest, 1970.

The legal treatises of Hajnóczy (*De comitiis regni Hungariae*, 1790; *De diversis subsidiis publicis dissertatio*, 1792; *Gedanken eines ungarischen Patrioten über einige zum Landtag gehörige Gegenstände*, 1790; *Ratio proponendarum in comitiis Hungariae legum*, 1790; *Dissertatio politico-publicae de regiae potestatis in Hungaria limitibus*, 1790; *Reflexiones in premissas leges*, 1792; etc.) can hardly be classed as pamphlets, owing to their style and tone yet as far as their substance, their deep sense of realistic political insight, is concerned, they can truly compete with the most outstanding pamphlets. Hajnóczy believed to be able to achieve bourgeois development by practical and directly applied internal reforms. His interest ranges from constitutional rights to ecclesiastical and civil law. The freedom of the press and religion, urban development and trade, legislation on real property and taxation all get an important place in his writings.

The pamphlets of Martinovics on these questions all date from 1793, when he saw that he had lost the favour of Francis, recognized the impact of the despotic and regressive methods of the emperor. He sensed that in Hungary the atmosphere was turning more antagonistic to the court. In order to win over the nobility, in August 1793 he dictated to Laczkovics his proposal for a constitution; in other pamphlets he meant to prepare the ground emotionally for the same. However, he did all this by offering to the nobility what was due to the people. The plan of the constitution was not too interesting, yet the pamphlets were, for they exemplify perfectly Martinovics's change of mood and the difference between his papers written between 1790—1792 and the latter ones. In his pamphlets entitled *Punctae quae comitatuum . . .* (1793), *Ad deputatos Hungariae Legistratores* (1793), and *Monitum ad Hungaros*, (1793) he demanded constitutionalism, tax exemption for the nobility and the safeguarding of the happiness of the people in a constitution based on civil rights. The Hungarian constitution, in allotting all power to the aristocracy, excluded the nobility — he writes — from the idea of the nation. He also stated that in Hungary there was no "national public fund"; trade, commerce and science were backward and the Enlightenment did not develop in a satisfactory manner. He also demanded the restriction of royal power. Both his pamphlets and his constitutional proposals rested particularly on the idea of a social contract fostered by the Enlightenment as well as the peculiarities of the Hungarian situation.

These pamphlets mark a definite advance as compared to his work *Status regni Hungariae*, where he only gave generalities, considering theocracy (particularly of the Jesuits), and the rule of the aristocracy as the chief evils of Hungary. At that time he himself abhorred revolution and thought that the people ought to be given their rights before they would awake to consciousness and extort them by force.

His letters and pamphlets addressed to the Habsburg rulers, Leopold II and Francis I — perhaps better termed his monologues — became progressively more revolutionary in tone. His first letter addressed to Leopold (*Lettre adressée à Sa Majesté l'Empereur, le 15 Novembre 17*90) mainly criticised the foreign policy of the ruler, expounding the idea, prevalent in the Enlightenment and popular among the *Illuminati*, that it was not the king but his advisers who were wicked.

His anonymous pamphlet *Oratio pro Leopoldo rege II* (1792) already shows in a more complex manner the duplicity of the political efforts of Martinovics. Previous to the pamphlet Martinovics in a letter offered his services to Leopold to protect him from the nobility, which had been incited against him by *Illuminati* and Jesuits. "He wanted to prove via historical and philosophical arguments that the king did not forswear his path and was ruling better and more mercifully than could be wished."

However, in the pamphlet he failed to prove his point, or at least the court reaction gives this impression — Martinovics in his pamphlet enumerated indirectly all the injustices, lawless actions, bad methods of rulership which had characterized Leopold's rule and with an unexpected sally he advised the Protestants to run to the rescue of the king.

While in the *Oratio* he shyly and in a debatable manner criticized the policy of the House of Habsburg, he omitted to mention the independence efforts of Hungary. But in his letter addressed in October, 1792 to Emperor Francis — an inspired anonymous pamphlet which, from a literary point of view, is most successful — putting all caution aside, he turns in a Jacobinist-revolutionary manner against the King. During the lawsuit against him he confessed to being the author of *Moniteur* and to having written his letters in imitation of Count Gorani, letters which had been attributed to the count by the secret police. After criticizing the foreign policy of Leopold, he returned to the period of Francis, stating that by following the trend represented by Leopold instead of carrying on the line of Joseph II, he poisoned even further the political atmosphere at home and abroad. Discussing policy in Hungary, he drew the conclusion that Hungary wanted independence because "The people do not love you, everything goes to show that you are not fit to rule and you are surrounded by depraved, wicked and silly persons."

Among the pamphlets written in favour of Hungarian independence of special note are Gergely Berzeviczy's "*Austria's Rule in Hungary*" which in its argumentation demonstrates tact and sobriety, and an essay, "*The Confrontation of English and Hungarian Administration*" by György Aranka, published in *Magyar Kurir* in 1791. We have already referred to Károly Koppi's *Ad inclitos et amplissimos . . .*, a pamphlet insisting particularly on bourgeois transformation and the restriction of Papal and nobility power, from a freemason and Josephinist angle, in the name of human and civil rights.

A fine piece preparatory to the 1790 parliamentary campaign is Ferenc Verseghy's *A Magyar Hazánk anyai szózattya az ország napjára készülő magyarokhoz* ("A motherly appeal by Hungary to the Hungarians preparing for the great day of the country"), a poem giving voice to the current views of freemason lodges and other reading circles of the Josephinist intelligentsia.

Finally there is a verse pamphlet written in German by an unknown writer, entitled "*O Pannonen, o Ihr Hunen*" which incites to a struggle for freedom, independence and revolution.

Naturally, "counter-pamphlets" also appeared in this period, directed against those who gave voice to the aspirations of Hungarians and the nobility. These were written by adherents of the Court and Habsburg interests, as for example L. A. Hoffmann's *Babel* and *Ninivé* (and Elek Horányi's immediate reply *Anti-Ninivé*, in 1790) or János Molnár's *Politisch-kirchliches Manch-Hermaeon*.

II. Another group of pamphlets treats the problems of *religion and education*. The writings and ideas of the Hungarian *Illuminati* and Jacobins coincide closely with those of the Bavarians. The reader is especially captivated by the pamphlets of János Laczkovics attacking the Church, religion and the clergy. As compared to the others they are particularly distinguished by their racy, elegant Hungarian style which does not lack a touch of humour and a bit of sarcasm either. Laczkovics translated his *"Expulsion of Jesuit monks from China"* in 1791 from the German original by the Austrian pamphleteer, J. Rautenstrauch, and also his *"Traveller Hoping to be Instructed in the Christian Faith."* Both writings satirize the inconsistencies of Christian religion and after having rationally refuted all theological doctrines — the author draws the conclusion that it is no longer possible to exercise power over enlightened mankind with lies of this kind.

In contrast to Laczkovics's pamphlet written with literary ambition and witty skill, the treatise of Ferenc Verseghy, entitled *"Of the Origin and Progress of Religion,"* written in 1790, represents the opposite tendency within the genre, following mainly the scientific principle. Its ideological content is also different from Laczkovics's work, for Verseghy defends the Christian religion and attacks the clergy.

Hajnóczy, Martinovics, János Nagyváthy and other, anonymous authors deal also with religion and the question of church authority — coming particularly to the conclusion that in Hungary church property ought to be confiscated, since the church has no right whatsoever to enjoy privileges without work.

Another favourite subject of the Enlightenment, *education* is often approached in these writings. However, only in connection with the above-mentioned subjects, as a secondary point. In one of Martinovics's essays, *Monitum ad Hungaros*, the education of the nation is placed in importance above that of the individual because, according to him, only a cultured and polished nation can withstand both anarchy and tyranny.

In Hajnóczy's projects and essays the question of education is always included. His pamphlet *Glosses on an Educational Project* (1792) is devoted entirely to this problem. His educational principles can be summed up briefly as follows: an ethico-philosophical education is important, yet the essence of education is love on a mutual basis; the talented children of the poor must be given the same education as anybody else.

III. Finally, practically every pamphlet after 1790 is concerned with the most exciting question of interest to the Hungarian intelligentsia and the politically minded nobility, namely *the events of the French Revolution*. Martinovics wrote his *Einwendungen wider die französische Konstitution* in 1791 more or less at the commission of the court. He maintained that the spirit of the constitution could in reality not be realized, although he thought it should safeguard the freedom and security of men. Martinovics considered the monarchical system as the most desirable and wanted the king to maintain the essentials of the constitution without listening to evil advisers. It is interesting to note that behind the lines of the pamphlet which condemns the French constitution — perhaps contrary to the author's intention — the outlines of an exemplary bourgeois constitution emerge.

János Szlávy's fragment of a pamphlet, *Notes written by a Hungarian Soldier, a Prisoner of War in France* is of an entirely different nature. He talks away in a pleasant narrative manner about that revolutionary country and describes its citizens and constitution as an example to be followed. Intermittently he tries to clarify concepts such as liberty and equality.

We must make mention of a philosophical treatise by Martinovics, entitled *Mémoires philosophiques ou la nature dévoilé* which in one of its chapters deals in detail with the problems of freemasonry and the *Illuminati* movement. In this fine analytical essay Martinovics came nearest to the Weishauptian *Illuminati* trend.

UTOPIA AND *ILLUMINATUS* IDEOLOGY

However, there is a genre in the achievements of which the influence of the *Illuminati* can be more effectively demonstrated. This genre is the utopistic novel of the 18th century.

From the middle of the 18th century onwards, the utopistic novel flourished throughout Europe. Its ideological roots can be traced back to the ideology of the Enlightenment itself. In France, for example, a yearly average of several hundred utopistic novels appeared from 1739 onwards. They satisfied a commercial literary demand and in the course of time most of them, with a few exceptions, have been forgotten.

The utopistic novel was influenced by writers like Defoe, Swift, Rousseau, and Montesquieu. The settings of the utopistic novel were unknown islands, faraway lands, the Moon, or the future, and its characters were more like abstract principles walking on legs than human beings.

In the history of the German novel utopistic fiction plays a sorry part, as an appendix to the aesthetic principles of Winckelmann and Gottsched who did not include the utopistic novel, nor the novel proper in the category "of higher artistic forms". For about a hundred years between Grimmelshausen's Baroque *Simplicissimus* (1670) and Wieland's Classic *Agathon* (1766—67) no important work appeared in this genre. After the appearance of *Agathon*, the novel was beginning to be noticed. Friedrich von Blanckenburg's *Versuch über den Roman* which appeared in 1774 is also characterized by the fact that it transposed the essence of the Classicist theory of the epic, based on Aristotelian principles, to the novel, and thus all the essential difference between the two genres practically disappeared. Von Blanckenburg only took notice of two novels, *Agathon* and *Tom Jones*, and to the analysis of these he later added an exhaustive critique of *Werther*.

However, the novel was not truly recognized as a separate genre before Schlegel produced his aesthetics *Von der Entheilung der schönen Künste*. Academic aesthetics, nevertheless, did not recognize, neither then not later, the Robinsonades or the utopistic novels which in Germany appeared in large numbers. The first German Robinsonade, *Der teutsche Robinson*, published in 1722, rivalled the popularity of *Werther*. Side by side with these commercial products, Schnabel's *Insel Felsenburg* and Gellert's *Geschichte der schwaebische Graefin* are of real literary merit.[19]

[19] A. Nivelle, *Kunst und Dictungstheorien zwischen Aufklärung und Romantik* Berlin, 1963.

In my opinion Freiherr von Knigge's utopias[20] should not be forgotten. In their time they were popular and widely read. Recently a number of articles have appeared on Knigge,[21] rediscovering his realistic art. His satiric tendency, sarcasm and bitter humour are once again appreciated. I can only agree with Hedvig Voegt who considers Knigge as one of the first propagators of Jacobinism in Germany.

His novel *Geschichte Peter Clausens* (The history of Peter Claus, 1785) was the continuation of the German *Schelmroman* of the 17th century, an antecedent to *Wilhelm Meister*, although lacking the drive of Grimmelshausen or the depth of the Goethean œuvre.

Utopia proper, bearing the title *Der Traum des Herrn Bricks* (The dream of Mr. Brick), appears in an episode in the history of Peter Claus. It constitutes and independent part both in plot and structure within the novel. It consists of four parts. In the first part Mr. Brick travels to the Island of Tahiti on the ship of Captain Cook. The action takes place in a definite time and locality. In the idyllic conditions prevailing on the island the reader is estranged from 18th-century German reality. In the second part the reader is led into a utopistic world. Mr. Brick falls asleep in a boat and on awaking finds himself on an unknown Island where Rousseauistic conditions prevail. However, Mr. Brick who came here from 18th-century Germany cannot adjust, insisting that "I could not stay on that lovely spot. I felt too weak to raise myself to the level where these noble creatures existed. Ever since childhood, I was raised in wickedness, driven by restless passions. How could I have found myself happy in heavenly bliss where the perfect harmony of body, spirit and reason ruled?" In the third chapter he wanders on to a neighbouring country where dreadful social conditions prevail, which resemble exactly those which existed in Germany. It is particularly in this chapter that Knigge's powerful descriptive realism becomes evident. Indirectly, by means of an anti-utopia he characterizes the monarch who oppresses the people and is, besides, a silly ass, because instead of making his peasants cultivate the land, he is waging useless wars, making the caste of the "crooked nose bearers," the "Schiefnasigen" partake in power, who enjoy it on account of their birth, not their talent. It is in this chapter that Mr. Brick encounters a man of a philosophical turn of mind, and the subject of their long talks turns inadvertently to secret societes and the ideas of the *Illuminati*. By 1785, Knigge no longer had any illusions concerning this movement. In these talks he points to the contradictions and naiveté of the movement, the passive behaviour of the Bavarian *Illuminati*, the lack of aims and objectives and the difference between *"handeln"* and *"lehren"*. As a final argument he speaks as follows to the unknown Mr. Brick (who incidentally enumerates the arguments of Weishaupt in defence of the order):

---

[20] *Peter Clausens Geschichte in drei Teilen*, Riga, 1783—1785., *Benjamin Noldmanns Geschichte der Auyklaerung in Abyssinien* . . . Riga, 1792.

[21] Hedwig Voegt *Die deutsche jakobinische Literatur und Publicistik*, Berlin, 1972. A. v. Knigge, *Der Traum des Herren Brick, Essays, Satyren, Utopien*. Hrsg: H. Voegt, Introduction dealing with Knigge.

Jürgen Walter, *Adolph Freiherrn Knigges Roman*, "*Benjamin Noldmanns Geschichte der Aufklaerung in Abyssinien.*" *Kritischer Rationalismus als Satire und Utopie im Zeitalter der deutschen Klassik*. Germanisch-Romanisch Monatschrift. N° 2., 1971.

"Don't say a word! All this is merely youthful ardour and fancy which captivated me too, in the beginning. In this project there are as many contradictions as words to describe it. I am not ashamed to confess that in the beginning I also supported it heart and soul, but now I see that I was wrong... Let me point out briefly what these projects are bound to become according to the lessons of history. General enlightenment in the whole world? — What a contradiction! Can you imagine that, given the immense differences between fates, passions and situations, every man should want to sacrifice his life for one clever aim? All this could only happen where no state has ever existed, as in that happy country I described above, but not in my country where so-called culture has such deep roots."

The nostalgic tone of this work reaches its culmination in the fourth chapter when Mr. Brick, during his wanderings, arrives in a country with a communistic system of society. Unfortunately, this chapter remained unfinished.

In contrast to the German tradition, Hungarian literature can produce fewer examples of the utopistic novel. I have been able to find only a single "novel" conceived in the spirit of *Illuminatism*. It was written by János Nagyváthy, and is entitled *A tizenkilencedik században élt igaz magyar hazafi örömórái* (The Happy Hours of a True Hungarian Patriot of the Nineteenth Century). Nagyváthy himself was a member of a lodge "called" Generosity *("Nagyszívűség")* in Pest, and his work was published in 1792 by the lodge. Of Nagyváthy, Kazinczy wrote to Aranka one year before the work was published, i.e. in 1791: "At Pest "Generosity" published the three following pieces. 1. Reminiscences of the Red Friar on contemplating the Ruins of the Church. Translated by De la Plume (Nagyváthy), 2. Change of Religion (by the same author), 3. L'horoscope de la Pologne, All this by Nagyváthy. This man is about 35 years of age. S. Pataki Calvinist Scribe and Losontzi was *concreator* . . . A very talented man. Stone mason."

Nagyváthy's *A True Hungarian Patriot in the Nineteenth Century* can be called a novel only with the best of intentions, since the modest story frames merely hold philosophico-political theses together.

The true Hungarian patriot belonged to the middle nobility, he fell asleep and had a reassuring dream. The nobility and the serfs had formed an alliance and patriotic harmony reigned between them. The nobleman called the liberated serf his companion in work. The nobility had resigned its material privileges and equality based on natural laws ruled everywhere, following the example of the great English and French nations. Nor did religious differences disturb this harmony, as different denominations lived peacefully side by side.

In Nagyváthy's utopia the ideology of the *Illuminati* has no theoretical basis as in Knigge's. However, this is of no importance, since it is evident that this piece of writing reflects the democratic-radical branch of freemasonry and the *Illuminati* movement. Nagyváthy foreshadows the programme of the 1848 bourgeois democratic revolution.

ÉLÉMENTS ROMANTIQUES DANS LE POÈME
«DEI SEPOLCRI» DE FOSCOLO

par

TIBOR KARDOS

I

De Sanctis, à qui la postérité s'adresse de plus en plus souvent en cher-
chant des explications authentiques aux phénomènes de l'histoire littéraire
italienne, était pénétré des espoirs de son siècle en plein essor, tout en voyant
aussi ses ombres; il écrivit à propos de *Dei Sepolcri* de Foscolo, reconnaissant
les valeurs de ce grand poème où le poète malheureux, arrivé au zénit poétique de sa vie, concentre tous les rêves, les enthousiasmes et les amertumes
de ses premières années d'adulte: «Ce chant est la première voix lyrique de
la nouvelle littérature, la mise en valeur de la nouvelle conscience, de l'homme
nouveau . . . Foscolo frappait à la porte du XIXe siècle.» Et c'est au même
De Sanctis que l'on doit une conception de *Dei Sepolcri*, réapparue depuis,
sous centaines de formes diverses, déformée et affaiblie: ce poème présente
à l'humanité les illusions perdues de la vie et de l'immortalité.[1] Mais les
meilleurs connaisseurs du XXe siècle de Foscolo (M. Fubini, W. Binni) ont
sauvegardé l'explication positive de De Sanctis sur les illusions de *Dei
Sepolcri*. Il est vrai que Fubini, dans son œuvre classique où il donne une
analyse extrêmement subtile, complexe et humaniste de *Dei Sepolcri*, refuse
de mettre un accent absolu sur cet aspect du poème.[2] Mais, dans la même
œuvre, en examinant la correspondance de Foscolo, il rapproche l'illusion
de cette grande âme inquiète de celle de Leopardi, et arrive à la conclusion
que cette illusion est une chose réelle: «Ce n'est pas la nostalgie du cœur,
mais l'essentiel même de l'histoire de l'humanité.»[3] Dans l'édition de l'épi-
thaphe d'Ippolito Pindemonte, qui porte le même titre, il retourne à la vieille
thèse selon laquelle c'est le motif de l'illusion «perdue» qui est au centre du
poème de Foscolo.[4] Binni trouve — et c'est une trouvaille heureuse — que
les illusions sont en même temps des valeurs morales absolues: «illusioni-
valori».[5]

[1] Pour la citation, v. F. De Sanctis, *Storia della letteratura italiana*, Milano 1935,
C. E. Bietti, vol. III, pp. 207—210, sur les illusions; *op. cit.*, pp. 208—209; *Ugo Foscolo*, Saggi critici, Bari 1952, pp. 97, 102—103. — L'évolution du problème peut être
suivie dans: M. Fubini, *Ugo Foscolo*, Firenze 1963, pp. 42—43. — W. Binni, *Foscolo e
la critica*, Firenze 1962. — La critique hongroise n'a pas analysé la question. La thèse
ancienne mais remarquable, faite à la Faculté de Pécs sous la direction de Jenő Koltay-Kastner de Gy. Lukic: *Ugo Foscolo et le romantisme*, Pécs 1928, a surtout traité
Jacopo Ortis et l'œuvre critique de Foscolo; *Dei Sepolcri* y est cité une seule fois
(p. 29). Jenő Koltay-Kastner, dans son excellent exposé, *Ugo Foscolo*, Irodalomtörténeti
dolgozatok, Szeged 1960, pp. 1—74, fait plutôt allusion aux rapports avec l'étranger
et au but social et éducatif du poème (pp. 74—75). On voudrait continuer leur travail
à partir de ce point.
[2] Cf. M. Fubini, *op. cit.*, pp. 167—200, 179—180.
[3] *Op. cit.*, 43.
[4] V. I. Pindemonte, *I sepolcri, A Ugo Foscolo*. A cura di Mario Fubini. *Lirici del
Trecento*, A cura di B. Meier. Milano—Napoli s. a. Ricciardi vv. 65—70, p. 1029.
[5] Cf. W. Binni, *op. cit.*, p. 39.

347

Sur un point important de cette parabole critique, B. Croce dit aussi quelque chose d'invariablement valable. Tout d'abord, il précisa que Foscolo, bien qu'il nommât illusions la beauté, la vertu, l'amitié, la patrie, l'humanisme, reconnaissait leur nécessité et les acceptait pratiquement toutes. C'est ainsi que le poète donnait l'exemple, et c'est pourquoi la jeunesse du Risorgimento italien s'enthousiasmait pour lui. L'affirmation de Croce est donc liée à tout cela: Foscolo avait réussi à franchir les limites du pessimisme de la vision du monde mécanique du XVIIIᵉ siècle par sa force d'action «concrète», par sa sensibilité extrêmement forte pour l'histoire et pour la liberté.[6]

Il est évident que les sources primordiales du pessimisme de Foscolo étaient ses propres expériences amères, et aussi l'exemple de Vico. Dans la philosophie du «ricorso», malgré l'élaboration brillante de l'évolution historique, il y a quelque chose de fondamentalement tragique. Ce trait tragique se manifeste moins dans le caractère déterminé du développement de l'action humaine que dans la répétition des périodes, indépendamment de ce qu'on y distingue les traits d'une évolution en spirale ou qu'on nie cette évolution complètement. Que la nature humaine soit fondamentalement la même, c'est également étayé par la conviction humaniste de Foscolo. Il a un autre trait commun avec Vico, et c'est la manière dont il aime l'homme avec toutes ses faiblesses, et dont il a pitié de lui dans ses misères. Mais chez lui, ce trait est une chose vécue et primordiale. Quand le sort de Venise fut scellé par la paix de Campoformio, en 1797, il écrivit *(La giustizia e la pietà)*:

> «. . . . . l'infinite angosce
> Dell'infelice umanità !»[7]

Il esquisse sans aucun doute la préface à Plutarque en 1801 en se nourrissant d'éléments empruntés à Vico, et cela pouvait bien précéder son amitié avec Lomonaco: l'allusion à la «scienze dell'umana natura» vise selon toute probabilité cette exigence qui devrait être indispensable à l'égard des législateurs, des hommes d'État et des philosophes. Dans cette Préface il parle des «erreurs et crimes» de son siècle et ajoute qu'à son avis: il n'y a pas de différence entre passé et présent, seule l'apparence change.[8]

Dans la rédaction définitive, ou au moins fondamentale, des *Ultime lettere di Jacopo Ortis*, parue un an plus tard (1802), il évoque avec Plutarque «les crimes et les misères de l'humanité» en ces termes: «Col divino Plutarco potrò consolarmi de'delitti e delle sciagure dell'umanità, volgendo gli occhi ai pochi illustri, che, quasi primati dell'uman genere, sovrastano a tanti secoli e a tante genti.»[9]

L'exemple éclatant des exploits des héros est donc bien supérieur à l'«éternelle» tragédie historique, et nous voici dans le cercle sans issue mais à la fois magnifique, des illusions et des valeurs — des héros, des actes, des

---

[6] Cf. B. Croce, *Foscolo. Poesia e non poesia*, Vol. VIII, Bari 1955, p. 74.

[7] U. Foscolo, *Liriche ed epigrammi*, Bologna 1961, Zanichelli, a cura di E. Chiòrboli. *La giustizia e la pietà*, Canto II, vv. 3—4, p. 107.

[8] Foscolo, *Proemio ai Discorsi sopra gli uomini illustri di Plutarcho, Prose*, vol. I, Bari 1912, a cura di V. Cian, p. 213.

[9] Foscolo, *Ultime lettere di Jacopo Ortis*. 18 octobre, *op. cit.*, vol. I, p. 257.

modèles d'outre-tombe. C'est dans *Dei Sepolcri* que cet ordre de valeurs, unique selon lui, se manifeste avec les plus brillantes couleurs.

Il vaut la peine d'esquisser brièvement les motifs dont surgit le débat séculaire sur les illusions « perdues ». Il est vrai que Foscolo, dans la préface à longue haleine de son poème, peint une image tragique de la course incessante des choses du monde vers le destin fatal de la Terre:

> «............. l'uomo e le sue tombe
> E l'estreme sembianze e le reliquie
> Della terra e del ciel traveste il tempo. »

(vers 20—22)

C'est une image matérialiste et sensualiste. Les *Frammenti su Lucrezio*, conçus à la même époque, expriment la même pensée, mais sous une forme plus souple, et avec plus de force:

« Dico a me stesso: perché vivi? tu e tutta l'umana razza, qual mai fine dovete adempiere nel mondo? Chi mi ha preceduto nacque, visse, morì, e lasciò dopo di sè una mano di posteri, che non fanno che riprodursi per nascere, vivere, morire. Le nazioni si struggono vicendevolmente e, divenute senza rivali, se stesse; e il romano combattea col romano. O umana razza, quale è la meta di tante fatiche? Niuno lo sa, e ognuno nondimeno si affanna per vivere. »

Foscolo reconnaît la lutte continue dans l'histoire, même s'il ne reconnaît pas ses motifs, son ordre, ses forces motrices. Et c'est alors, juste à ce moment, qu'il lie l'explication de l'action humaine, en tant qu'action instinctive, à la lutte et à l'instinct vital, à l'inquiétude et à la volonté d'agir: « Ma né l'uomo è contento della semplice vita. Loda la tranquillità appunto perché non l'acquista mai; e, se mai l'avesse, la fuggirebbe come si odia la sazietà. Il supremo motore di tutti i suoi pensieri, di tutte le sue membra è la noia ... Ora il primo motore di tutte le azioni è la noia, la quale ci fa cercare occupazioni e desideri nuovi, quando sono soddisfatti quelli che ci rodevano. »[10]

La « noia » est plutôt un état de tension inactive qu'un simple ennui. Déjà Croce s'en était aperçu et il l'exprimait lorsqu'il dit: « l'ennui force Foscolo à agir ». Le poète, à la fin de ce manuscrit, écrit: « Però, veggendo Epicuro che questa noia ci faceva scorrere di desiderio in desiderio, e di pianto in pianto e di fatica in fatica avvicinarsi al sepolcro, riponea tutta la sua felicità nella indolenza ... »[11]

C'est probablement pour cette raison qu'il dit, dans la rédaction de 1802 de *Jacopo Ortis*, que l'homme semble être lui-même l'ouvrier de ses malheurs, mais que les malheurs sont les conséquences de l'ordre universel, et que l'espèce humaine avance orgueilleusement et aveuglement vers son destin.[12]

Et, dans les *Frammenti su Lucrezio*, l'idée de *Dei Sepolcri* sur les « illusions » réapparaît avec toute sa force douloureuse. Car s'il s'était occupé de l'agri-

---

[10] Foscolo, *Frammenti su Lucrezio, Prose*, vol. II, Bari 1913, p. 201.
[11] Foscolo, *op. cit.*, II, p. 200, voir note 2.
[12] Cf. la note 42, dans la lettre des 19—20 febbraio 1798. Mais il écrit de la même façon dans la première rédaction. Voir Foscolo, *Ultime lettere di Jacopo Ortis*, 8 gennaio 1798, *Prose*, vol. I, p. 106; 19 gennaio 1798, ibid. p. 108.

culture, de l'artisanat, de la science présomptueuse («boriose scienze»), des mathématiques ou de l'astronomie et non pas de l'étude de l'homme, il n'aurait pas tant de fois éprouvé de la compassion («compassione») et du mépris («disprezzo») envers lui-même: «non mi si farebbero svanire le illusioni, che, come mere apparenze, velano il vuoto della vita; non avrei perduta la speranza del cielo, e la superbia di non morire affatto, e di lasciare dopo il mio corpo il mio spirito».[13] On a besoin des illusions.

Il est donc logique que c'est au moment de la complète résignation qu'apparaît dans *Dei Sepolcri* le motif de «l'illusion», en guise de protestation et de consolation, apparemment contre les dispositions «rationnelles» du gouvernement napoléonien:

«Ma perché pria del tempo a sè il mortale
Invidierà l'illusion che spento
Pur lo sofferma al limitar di Dite?»

(vers 22—25)

Nous savons que le gouvernement milanais ne faisait que renouveler de vieilles dispositions prises par les Autrichiens pour rendre les sépultures plus démocratiques; mais le vrai sujet du poème est, avec ce point de départ, le destin de l'homme sur terre. Foscolo, le penseur sensualiste-matérialiste découvre que l'immortalité des héros de l'humanité est strictement liée à ce monde, mais elle cesse d'exister avec l'expiration du temps accordé à cette planète et à ses êtres vivants; l'immortalité existe donc jusqu'au moment où l'action humaine elle-même existe, et elle y trouve sa raison, son but. Il prononce une vérité insolite en Italie au seuil du XIXᵉ siècle. Et pourtant, cette ode, cette hymne, cette élégie — on peut l'appeler comme on veut — déclare en conclusion finale que, dans le cadre de l'histoire l'homme est un géant:

«E tu onore di pianti, Ettore, avrai
Ove fia santo e lagrimato il sangue
Per la patria versato, e finchè il sole
Risplenderà su le sciagure umane.»

(vers 292—295)

Ce n'est pas de l'indifférence, mais de la majesté, de la solidarité, de l'enthousiasme. Cette idée a pour base une découverte, c'est qu'en dehors de l'histoire il n'y a rien. Et il s'agit justement de cela: chez Foscolo, c'est la grandeur de «l'operosa umana prole»[14] qui est accentuée, et par conséquent «l'illusion» foscolienne est profondément humaniste et diffère à maints égards de la conception de Pindemonte sur l'illusion, et même de celle de Leopardi. Chez Pindemonte, une fois les rêves et les espoirs perdus — écrit Fubini —, c'est la philosophie qui prend leur place et apporte à l'homme un

---

[13] *Frammento su Lucrezio, op. cit.* vol. II, p. 202.
[14] «l'operosa umana prole» v. id. *Sermone Primo,* vv. 52—53, *Poesie,* 1926, a cura di Enrico Bianchi, p. 87.

bonheur froid et une paix non moins froide. Chez Léopardi, au contraire, le grand sentiment et les brasiers de l'imagination ne sont point suivis du calme, mais de l'infélicité.[15]

II

Il n'est pas inutile d'examiner textuellement comment se dessine le problème de l'illusion et, corrélativement, de l'action vertueuse dans *Dei Sepolcri*, la plus belle œuvre de Foscolo, en accordant une attention particulière à ce que souligne Foscolo dans les notes écrites sur le poème, ensuite dans son autodéfense adressée à Monsignor Guillon, et même dans le fragment en prose concernant les *Grazie*: il «voulait exprimer des sentiments ardents et innocents», «le vrai et la beauté morale» qui «inspirent l'imagination». Après les désillusions personnelles, après avoir perdu son frère, puis sa douce patrie, après tant d'injustices, Foscolo, le poète, veut créer son univers non pas d'après les conclusions sans espoir de la froide raison, mais restant obstinément auprès des critères de «l'époque des illusions». Tout cela est sans doute une attitude esthétique inspirée (sentimentalement) de Marmontel et (historiquement) de Vico. En effet, si Foscolo s'obstinait à créer — car la création est l'unique forme de vie possible pour un poète —, il devait se tenir à une poétique correspondant aux époques «poétiques» de l'enfance et de l'adolescence de l'humanité, comme l'avait pensé Vico.[16] C'est ainsi que Foscolo, bien qu'il eût perdu tout espoir, bien qu'il fût absolument persuadé de la fin tragique de l'histoire humaine, ne se plongeait pas dans l'indifférence ou dans un bas cynisme, mais au contraire, il célébrait, avec plus de passion que jamais, la vertu des héros, la liberté et le pouvoir créateur de l'homme. Cette attitude est profondément stoïque et elle n'est pas loin du sérieux solennel de l'«épicurien» Lucrèce, dont la lecture se reflète clairement dans de nombreuses expressions de ce chant, et dont Foscolo écrit ses notes émouvantes justement à cette époque. L'enfant du médecin italien de Zante exprime le désespoir des précurseurs de la nouvelle bourgeoisie italienne, cette couche sociale très valeureuse: ce désespoir est une conséquence grave de la mystification napoléonienne. Et bien sûr, il découle aussi de ce fait historique et social, vu clairement par Gramsci en premier, que les intellectuels italiens se sont isolés du peuple.[17] La force d'un Antée manque à la vie de cette bourgeoisie, à cette vie historique de tant de siècles, car, en dernière analyse, c'est uniquement ce rapport qui pourrait lui prêter de la force.

III

On dirait donc que cette attitude en apparence contradictoire de Foscolo, même si elle n'est pas pourvue de sincérité, est incertaine, et on peut l'expliquer uniquement par le développement social italien. Elle est sans doute

---

[15] Cf. note 4.

[16] Les notes de Foscolo v. Foscolo, *Poesie*, ibid. pp. 97, 120; G. B. Vico, *La Scienza Nuova*, a cura di Fausto Nicolini, Bari 1928, vol. I, Libro I, Sezione I, Cap. XXII—XXIII; Sez. II, Cap. XXI—XXIX, XXXVII, XLIII—XLV, L—LIII, LIV—LVI; Libro II, Sez. VI—XI; Libro III—V.

[17] Cf. A. Gramsci, *Gli intellettuali e l'organizzazione della cultura*, 1952, Einaudi. pp. 3—19, 40—42.

aussi présente dans les épopées dramatiques modernes de diverses nations bourgeoises européennes, qui ont pour sujet les problèmes capitaux de l'humanité. Ce jeune homme italo-grec pressentait une attitude que même un Goethe, au cours des luttes de toute une vie humaine, ne pouvait refuser, malgré toutes les protestations démiurgiques et malgré tous les efforts de *Faust*. C'est le même individualisme d'un développement bourgeois européen qui, là aussi, fraie le chemin et sera vaincu. Et cette pensée se dégage avec encore plus de lucidité du drame de crise d'Ibsen: il est naturel que la désillusion de *Peer Gynt* et la conclusion très peu conciliante du drame nous suggèrent de sérieux doutes en ce qui concerne le jugement définitif d'Ibsen sur l'état et l'avenir de sa patrie. Mais parce que la perspective de *Peer Gynt* s'ouvre sur l'humanité entière, il est clair qu'Ibsen ne pouvait entrevoir une perspective plus optimiste de la situation d'alors, même dans un sens plus large et plus intégral. Quant à Foscolo, il porte toujours en lui une sorte d'espoir désespéré, faute de quoi il ne tenterait pas d'encourager ses compatriotes par l'héroïsme de *Dei Sepolcri*. En effet, Foscolo est possédé d'une puissante force d'agir qui ne cesse d'exploser jusqu'au dernier moment de sa vie:

«Quello spirto guerrier ch'entro mi ruggie»

dit-il dans sa fameuse épigraphe sur lui-même[18] et il mentionne dans d'autres œuvres aussi *(Frammenti su Lucrezio)* «ce feu qui faisait rage» en lui. Même si ce trait n'est pas une réaction au monde extérieur, mais il est ancien et hérité, il est ramené de toute façon à la surface à la suite d'événements comme, dans le cas de Foscolo: la compassion envers les opprimés et les pauvres, la tragédie de Venise, la patrie perdue, sa dégradation militaire, etc. L'explosion s'accomplit soit dans des actes de dévouement militaires, soit dans le journalisme, soit dans la création littéraire, et prouve encore une fois le sens étrange de cette «noia» qui est en même temps un «fuoco» chez Foscolo. Et c'est surtout le fait d'écrire qui est essentiel et qui joue le rôle de l'action, comme c'est le cas pour son prédécesseur et idéal, Alfieri, et son successeur, Leopardi:

«Aggiungi ch'io ho sempre scritto, perché non ho potuto fare, e cercava così di mandar fuori del mio petto un certo fuoco che ruggiva dentro di me, e che cresce con gli anni; onde il cuore mandò sempre i sensi miei all'ingegno, e l'ingegno alla penna . . .»[19]

IV

Les facteurs culturels ont évidemment un rôle important dans la prise de conscience de la personnalité morale de Foscolo, et ces facteurs ne peuvent être négligés. Sa «noia» — bien que le rapport entre la réflexion et l'action soit exactement le contraire chez lui — nous suggère l'«acidia» de Pétrarque et particulièrement l'ambiance qui domine *I Trionfi* et qui se dégage du

[18] «Quello spirto guerrier ch'entro mi ruggie» v. Foscolo, *Alla Sera* V. 14. *Liriche ed epigramme*, ed. Chiòrboli, p. 114.
[19] Sur la tentative de libération de Foscolo (l'histoire des hébreux du ghetto de Zante), sur son logement misérable de Venise, sur ses idées de réforme agraire cf. J. Koltay-Kastner, *op. cit.*, pp. 8, 19. — Pour la citation, v. Foscolo, *Frammenti su Lucrezio*, ibid. vol. II, p. 195.

premier sonnet de *Canzoniere*: la nostalgie des innombrables beautés de la vie, la plongée dans l'eau de la vie, puis la découverte de ce «che quanto piace al mondo è breve sogno».

Les commentaires sur *Dei Sepolcri* font volontiers allusion à ce que l'anéantissement absolu du monde, concentré dans ces deux vers de Foscolo:

> «E l'estreme sembianze e le reliquie
> Della terra e del ciel traveste il tempo»
>
> (vers 21—22)

correspondrait à un vers du célèbre chant de Pétrarque, *Spirto gentil* . . . qui dit:

> «E tutto quel ch'una ruina involve»   (LIII.35.).

Cela est vrai, mais chez Pétrarque la pensée que tout ce qui vit est sujet à l'anéantissement, est exprimée — au point de vue du contenu — plus largement et plus profondément, et c'est justement dans *I Trionfi* qu'il parle du triomphe du Temps. Le Temps triomphe sur la Gloire, d'après le contenu général de cette partie; la même idée se reflète dans quelques brèves et vigoureuses expressions, comme «fuggir del Sole» et «la ruina del mondo manifesta» (*Trionfo del Tempo*, 69.). La conclusion très claire de l'atmosphère de cette partie annonce déjà Foscolo:

> «Tutto vince e ritoglie il Tempo avaro;
> Chiamasi Fama ed è morir secondo
> né più che contro 'l primo è alcun riparo;
> così 'l Tempo trionfaì nomi e 'l mondo.»[20]

La correspondance fondamentale entre *I Trionfi* de Pétrarque et *Dei Sepolcri* de Foscolo ressort dans l'une des pensées directrices et introductrices du *Trionfo della Fama*, où Pétrarque déclare:

> «vidi da l'altra parte giugner quella
> che trae l'uom dal sepocro e 'n vita il serba».[21]

La Gloire sauve donc l'homme de la Tombe, mais cette vie d'outre-tombe, promise par Pétrarque, est déjà exclue du monde de la foi. C'est une immortalité humaniste, une vie terrestre et non plus celle d'outre-tombe, une vie vécue parmi des hommes et non pas parmi des spectres: c'est cette même vie qu'imaginera Foscolo.

Le premier pas que fit Foscolo pour prendre conscience de l'action humaine triomphante de la tombe, nous porte vers son adolescence effervescente et vers ses premiers souvenirs littéraires, quand il lisait Pétrarque (dès les années 1794—95) et l'admirait — c'est en 1795 qu'il le nomma «tenero cantatore di Laura»[22] — et quand il écrivit une ode à Dante qu'il avait reconnu

[20] F. Petrarca, *Triumphus Temporis*, vv. 142—145. *Rime, Trionfi e Poesie latine*, Milano-Napoli, a cura di Ferdinando Neri, p. 531.
[21] Petrarca, *Triumphus Fame*, vv. 8—9. p. 553.
[22] V. Foscolo, *Poesie*, v.Bianchi p. 18. «me ne venni con gli idilli del nostro Gesnero e col tenero cantatore di Laura» ad Aurelio de'Giorgio Bertola.

comme un «esprit d'éternelle gloire». Un connaisseur hongrois de Foscolo écrit que le poète subit l'influence de «la nouvelle branche de tendance socialiste» de la poésie d'épitaphe «qui naquit avec le poème de Legouvé, récité pour la première fois à l'Académie de Paris le 6 octobre 1797 et édité en 1801». Ce poète «proteste contre la pauvreté de la cérémonie des funérailles et souligne l'efficacité des sépultures dans l'éducation d'une nation».[23]

Il est très probable qu'il y ait eu des rapports entre les divers motifs. Il y a toutefois beaucoup d'obstacles s'opposant à ce que Legouvé ait eu une influence sur Foscolo en ce qui concerne les bases idéologiques. L'auteur français avait fait la lecture de son poème dans le lointain Paris le 6 octobre 1797, et dès le 17 octobre commençait pour Foscolo une période si mouvementée — fuite, changements incessant de lieu et de profession — qu'il serait hardi de penser qu'il eût si vite reçu le poème de Legouvé. Il est plus vraisemblable de supposer que Foscolo rencontra ce poème quatre ans plus tard. Mais à cette époque la pensée de la mémoire et de la tombe des grands héros, auteurs de grands exploits — pensée apte à éveiller des nations — était depuis longtemps mûrie en lui: elle s'épanouit et même apparaît dans toute sa grandeur dans ses poèmes de jeunesse, dans la première esquisse de *Jacopo Ortis*, créée entre 1796 et 1798. Dans le *Bonaparte liberatore* de style pétrarquien *(Italia mia, Spirto gentil)*, conçu avant la paix de Campoformio, en 1797, il évoque «les ombres des Brutus qui montrent fièrement aux siècles l'épée baignée de sang du père et du fils». Il est clair que derrière cette phrase se cache la connaissance et le culte précoce d'Alfieri. Le texte d'une ode contemporaine et du même style pétrarquien, *Ai novelli repubblicani*, ainsi que la note y jointe, évoquent de nouveau «la larva notturna» de Tiberius Gracchus qui donne des conseils héroïques. Ce motif d'origine pétrarquienne apparaît dans toute sa beauté — tout comme dans *Dei Sepolcri* — dans le premier *Jacopo Ortis*, celui de 1798. Dans celui-ci entrent en scène, au lieu du spectre des Brutus et des Gracchus, le culte sentimental et héroïque des tombes, les illusions et la fatalité de l'espèce humaine. On y entrevoit même certaines idées et tournures qui font penser à Vico (la corrélation entre l'ancienne religion héroïque et les héros antiques), et tout cela plusieurs années avant son amitié avec Lomonaco.[24]

Il faut toutefois noter que l'autre grande ode de Pétrarque, le *Spirto gentil*, célèbre les tombes des héros d'éternelle mémoire en général et mentionne l'esprit vivant, en particulier, dans les tombeaux de marbre des «grandi Scipioni» et du «fedel Bruto» dont la gloire durera jusqu'à la fin des temps et qui en même temps est en relation réciproque avec les vivants, en tant que conscience vivante et critique; l'esprit des héros de jadis survivra donc avec la patrie romaine et la postérité.[25]

[23] Foscolo, *A Dante*, ibid. pp. 21—23; sur l'influence de Legouvé et de Delille cf., en conformité avec Belvederi et Cian, J. Koltay-Kastner, *op. cit.*, 34—35, v. encore la note 68.

[24] V. Foscolo, *Bonaparte liberatore*, vv. 8—10, *Liriche*, ed. Chiòrboli, p. 113; *Ai novelli repubblicani*, vv. 53—63, ed. Bianchi, la note de l'auteur au poème p. 60; *Ultime lettere di Jacopo Ortis*, rédaction bolognaise, 1798, *Al lettore, Prose*, vol. I, p. 77; *op. cit.*, 8 settembre 1797, vol. I, p. 81; *op. cit.*, 21 settembre 1797, vol. I, p. 84; *op. cit.*, 23 ottobre 1797, vol. I, p. 94; *op. cit.*, 8 gennaio 1798, p. 106; *op. cit.*, 19 gennaio 1798, p. 108; *op. cit.*, 14 maggio 1798, p. 129.

[25] F. Petrarca, *Spirto gentil . . .* vv. 32—42.

De plus, l'esprit d'outre-tombe des héros de la liberté romaine suscitait l'intérêt grâce à une œuvre moderne de grande influence. Il s'agit de *Le notti romane* de A. Verri. La pièce fut présentée aux spectateurs italiens pour la première fois en 1792, puis répétée en 1796.

La dédicace *Al lettore* de *Jacopo Ortis*, invariée dans toutes les rédactions, présente l'œuvre comme un texte écrit pour remplacer les «larmes» qu'il ne peut verser sur la «tombe» de cet ami qui, par son «héroïsme», pourrait être un «modèle et consolation». Dans *Jacopo Ortis* même apparaît toute la courbe du romanesque des tombes: depuis la mort presque inaperçue de l'homme simple qui laisse en ses proches un bon souvenir, de la reconnaissance et de l'amour, jusqu'à Pétrarque dont le souvenir appartient à tout le peuple italien: la petite compagnie de Jacopo Ortis s'approche de la maisonnette d'Arqua de ce grand poète «simili a' discendenti degli antichi repubblicani, quando libavano sopra i mausolei de' loro maggiori morti per la patria, o a' que' sacerdoti che, taciti e riverenti, s'aggiravano per li boschi abitati da qualche divinità» (Lettera X.). Et la seconde rédaction milanaise de 1802 ne pouvait qu'accentuer cette pensée. Mais dans cette seconde rédaction, Foscolo ne cite plus le sonnet qu'Alfieri avait écrit à Arqua même, et qui figure encore dans l'édition de Bologne. Les pierres précieuses, l'or seraient dignes d'orner le tombeau de Pétrarque — juge Alfieri — mais non; ce sont les tombeaux des monarques qui doivent être décorés de pierres précieuses, il faut en orner les monuments où l'on ne peut pas poser de lauriers: ici, suffit le nom de cet esprit divin.[26] Voici donc les liens étroits chez Foscolo, du culte des tombes, de l'action héroïque et du romanesque des mérites du créateur avec Pétrarque et Alfieri.

Dans les lettres de Jacopo Ortis, datées du printemps, de l'été, de l'automne de 1797 et de l'année 1798 — il paraît que, pour l'essentiel, cette datation est très juste — surgissent l'une après l'autre les tournures et les idées caractéristiques à *Sepolcri*: que l'homme «vit dans l'illusion de pouvoir prolonger son existence», que l'humanité est assujettie à un «destin implacable», que nous sommes entourés de «la creuse apparence des choses». Et pourtant, il lui semble déjà à cette époque qu'«Omero, Ossian e Dante, i tre maestri di tutti gli ingegni sovrumani hanno investito la mia fantasia ed infiammato il mio cuore», ou, si ce ne sont pas eux-mêmes, ce sont au moins «le loro ombre divine ... assise su le vòlte eccelse che sovrastano l'universo, a dominare l'eternità».[27] Voici les thèses et les antithèses, les contradictions aiguës de *Dei Sepolcri*!

Il est cependant indiscutable que l'inspiration pétrarquienne lui parvient en partie à travers une appréciation de Pétrarque par Alfieri. *Filippo*, *Timoleone*, les deux tragédies de *Brutus* et leurs dédicaces, ainsi que deux autres écrits d'esprit révolutionnaire d'Alfieri: *Del principe e delle lettere* et *La virtù sconosciuta* contiennent certaines idées proches de celles qui travaillent en Foscolo, comme la force impulsive des exploits et du nom même des héros (surtout par le théâtre: sur l'exemple d'Alfieri, Foscolo fit aussi cette expérience); à une époque de rien, où l'homme n'a pas la possibilité d'accom-

---

[26] Foscolo, *op. cit.*, *Prose*, vol. I, p. 94. — Le sonnet d'Alfieri v. *Son. XXVIII*. *Opere di Vittorio Alfieri*, introduzione e scelta a cura di Vittore Branca, p. 1139.
[27] Foscolo, *Ultime lettere di Jacopo Ortis* rédaction bolognaise, 14 maggio 1797, *Prose*, vol. I, p. 129.

plir des actions héroïques, il faut écrire, enthousiasmer, il faut ainsi créer une opinion publique: et c'est le devoir des «scrittori-tribuni». L'impulsion spontanée des esprits ardents, ainsi que le désir d'agir des «abbondi caldi e ferocissimi spiriti» et «la superba e divina febbre dell'ingegno» d'Alfieri sont très proches de la «noia» de Foscolo, «il primo motore di tutte le azioni» et de ce «certo fuoco che ruggiva» en lui.[28] Les expériences directe et indirecte sont difficilement séparables dans l'inspiration d'un écrivain: dans ce casci non plus, on ne les distingue pas.

V

Si l'on veut pénétrer plus profondément le poème *Dei Sepolcri*, il deviendra clair que même dans sa structure il y a un trait qui nous fait penser à *I Trionfi*. Pétrarque, dans l'une des esquisses de son œuvre, nous explique comment il part vers des rivages toujours nouveaux pour retrouver ses héros:

> «uomini e fatti gloriosi e magni
> per le parti di mezzo e per le streme,
> ové sera e mattina il sol si bagni».[29]

L'un des critiques contemporains de Foscolo, l'abbé Guillon, lui reproche justement cette façon fiévreuse de rechercher ses héros, cette errance perpétuelle dans des pays lointains: «Young, Hervey, Gray ne voyageaient pas tant, il leur suffisait de méditer sur les tombes qu'ils avaient devant eux et sur leurs compatriotes.» En effet, Foscolo parle d'abord des tombeaux d'Italie, il glorifie les lieux commémorant la Santa Croce de Florence. Ensuite, en allant vers l'Occident, où le soleil «se plonge dans les profondeurs du soir», il mêle à ses louanges la mémoire de Nelson. Enfin, il s'en vole vers l'Orient, où «se lève le soleil», pour chanter l'éloge des héros de Marathon et de Troie.

Le poète de *Dei Sepolcri* fut fortement inspiré par la typologie pétrarquienne des héros, c'est-à-dire par cette démarche poétique qui personnifie les choses — pour mettre en mouvement l'imagination — par périphrases,

[28] Ecrire à une époque où l'action héroïque est impossible, v. la préface de *Timoleone* d'Alfieri adressée à Pasquale de'Paoli: «Io perciò dedico questa mia tragedia a voi, come a uno di quei pochissimi che avendo idea bene diritta d'altri tempi, d'altri popoli e d'altro pensare, sareste quindi stato degno di nascere ed operare in un secolo men molle alquanto del nostro.» v. *Tragedie e vita di Vittorio Alfieri*, Firenze 1842. S. Centofanti. Volume unico p. 179. — V. encore la préface à *Washington*, devant le *Bruto*, I. *op. cit.*, p. 357. — Préface au «peuple italien futur» devant le *Bruto* II, v. Vittorio Alfieri, *Opere*, ed. Branca, p. 859; *Del principe e delle lettere*, Libro III, cap. IV, *op. cit.*, p. 992; cap. XI, p. 1017; *La virtù sconosciuta*, *op. cit.*, p. 1024—25. — L'«impulso» chez Alfieri: «il naturale suo impulso». «sublime impulso», v. *Del principe e delle lettere*, Libro III, cap. VI, Alfieri, *Opere*, ed. Branca, p. 999: le désir d'agir: «abbondi caldi e ferocissimi spiriti, a cui nulla manca per fare alte cose, che il campo ed i mezzi.»; *op. cit.*, cap. XI, p. 1017: la fièvre de l'esprit: «la superba e divina febbre dell'ingegno e del cuore» *op. cit.*, Libro III, cap. VI, p. 999: sur les écrivains-tribuns: «tribuni-scrittori», «sublimi tribuni dei non liberi popoli»; *op. cit.*, Libro III, cap. X, p. 1014. — Pour la conception foscolienne de l'ennui: «ora il primo motore di tutte le azioni è la noia», Foscolo, *Frammento su Lucrezio*, *Prose*, vol. II, pp. 200, 201, 202.; pour «un certo fuoco che ruggiva dentro di me» Foscolo, *Frammenti su Lucrezio*. *Prose*, vol. II, p. 195., cf. encore la note 18.

[29] Appendice ai *Trionfi* 2. *Triumphus Fame* I. Redazione anteriore vv. 16—18; Petrarca, *Rime, Trionfi e Poesie latine*, p. 564.

et caractérise les héros par leurs exploits et leurs mérites, souvent sans même les nommer. De même, l'alignement des héros nous apparaît dans *Il Trionfo della Fama* de Pétrarque comme nous le reverrons chez Foscolo, avec certaines modifications caractéristiques. Pétrarque distingue d'une part les héros de l'épée et de la lutte, d'autre part les philosophes, les rhétoriciens et les écrivains. Par ce système, il suit certains schémas antiques où le héros de la vie théorique est opposé au héros de la vie active dans la littérature biographique. Foscolo garde la méthode pétrarquienne, mais il en crée une variante romantique. D'un côté, ce sont Dante, Pétrarque, Machiavel — les écrivains. Il y range Michel-Ange le sculpteur et Galilée l'astronome. De l'autre côté nous avons devant nous les héros de la liberté et de la patrie qui luttaient l'épée à la main, Nelson, les combattants grecs et les héros de Troie. Mais ils sont tous unis par l'idée qu'ils représentent *la nation* par leur esprit créateur, et que dans le destin de la plupart d'entre eux se manifeste *le moment historique de la lutte pour l'indépendance*. On découvre aussi tout le temps des parentés dans la rédaction. Si Pétrarque, dans la forme provisoire de *I Trionfi*, décrit ainsi les philosophes en pleine méditation sur les choses célestes:

> «e vidi a quella man gente salvestra
> tacita e grave, che pensando avea
> fatta al ciel con l'ingegno alta fenestra»,[30]

il nous est facile d'évoquer les fameux vers de Foscolo où il fait l'éloge de Michel-Ange, créateur d'un nouveau ciel humain, et de Galilée qui pénètre les secrets de la nature céleste:

> «E l'arce di colui che nuovo Olimpo
> Alzò in Roma a' Celesti; e di chi vide
> Sotto l'etereo padiglion rotarsi
> Più mondi, e il sole irradiarli immoto . . .»

(vers 159—162).

Et ajoutons qu'on peut découvrir, outre les faits du texte, une autre allusion à la connaissance précoce de *I Trionfi* dans la partie II de l'édition de 1798 de Bologne, dite «corrigée» de *Jacopo Ortis* où l'auteur cite avec Ossian *Il Trionfo della Morte* (Lettre LXIV). Cette circonstance est intéressante même si l'on considère ladite édition comme apocryphe.

VI

De ce qui a été dit jusqu'ici, il est clair que les graines du jardin de Pétrarque fleurissent d'une autre fleur chez Foscolo, car le «terrain» historique et les conditions «atmosphériques» ont complètement changé au cours de cinq siècles. Les différences sont d'abord nuancées, puis caractéristiques et même capitales.

La notion de la «gloire» du poète de Laura, le précurseur de l'humanisme est devenue, sous l'influence du sentimentalisme, beaucoup plus humaine.

[30] Appendice ai *Trionfi* 3. *Triumphus Fame* III. Altra redazione vv. 4—6, *op. cit.*, p. 571.

Chez Foscolo la «gloire» n'est pas une simple évocation de grands exploits qui n'ont au fond aucune relation directe avec la postérité. Au contraire, chez Foscolo la «fama» basée sur l'action morale, est imprégnée de sentiments ardents. La gloire deviendra une forme romantique de réciprocité presque familiale de la coexistence humaine, de celle des vivants et des morts, et c'est par ces nouveaux attributs qu'il multiplie la force pédagogique de la gloire de la Renaissance:

> «. . . . . Celesta è questa
> Corrispondenza d'amorosi sensi,
> Celeste dote è negli umani; e spesso
> Per lei si vive con l'amico estinto . . .»

(vers 29—32).

Bien sûr, c'est uniquement dans *I Trionfi* que la gloire pétrarquienne est si clairement différenciée et qu'elle devient si abstraite. Les Scipio et le Brutus du *Spirto gentil* sont pleins de sentiments ardents pour l'avenir lointain de la patrie et, par conséquent, leur gloire aussi est marquée de ce ton chaleureux. De plus, Pétrarque même devient un poète sentimental aux yeux de Foscolo. C'est ce que prouve l'apparition de la figure du poète soit dans la préface d'un poème envoyé à l'adresse d'un disciple de Gessner (Bertola), soit dans l'une des scènes les plus sentimentales de *Jacopo Ortis*. Le personnage principal du roman de sa première époque sur Laura, l'épigraphe du cycle écrit à l'occasion de la mort de son père, en témoignent tous également. Et Pétrarque, auteur d'odes héroïques, ne s'oppose point à la figure du poète sentimental.

Si, à la fin de l'édition de 1798, dite apocryphe de *Jacopo Ortis*, en faisant l'inventaire de la bibliothèque, on n'y trouve, parmi les «libri di sentimento e poesia», que Pétrarque et Werther, après Hervey, Arnaud, Voltaire et Plutarque, alors cette allusion sera sans doute authentique par son esprit. Si, chez Pétrarque, l'alignement des héros immortels a élargi l'horizon vers les quatre points cardinaux, chez Foscolo le changement incessant des divers pays deviendra un moyen artistique pour accentuer le caractère universel et en même temps fortement humain de ses thèses. C'est pourquoi il semble préférable de souligner plutôt les éléments familièrement vifs, sentimentaux et actuels de Foscolo, et moins l'universelle souffrance humaine, le constant, l'«éternel» humain.[31] *Dei Sepolcri* n'est pas un poème de n'importe quelle époque, il généralise un moment historique précis. Car, comme nous l'avons déjà mentionné, les personnages de Foscolo représentent les héros actifs ou créateurs de la pensée laïque et du sentiment national des temps modernes, et en plus, les Italiens luttent tous pour la liberté: les sculpteurs comme les savants! Ou encore, voyons un peu leur style caractéristique à périphrases. Chez Pétrarque, ce sont les traces de la poétique du Moyen-Age finissant, méthode poétique bien connue de Dante. C'est la croyance esthétique d'une époque où l'on cherchait volontiers le sens allégorique sous l'enveloppe de la réalité: la périphrase permettait une parallélisation beaucoup plus large et en même temps fascinait l'imagination. Foscolo accepte cet héritage pé-

---

[31] Cf. M. Fubini, *op. cit.*, p. 181.

trarquien, malgré les reproches de ses critiques. C'est pourquoi sa poésie est «obscure» — comme le lui reproche même son ami Pindemonte. Et pourtant, les périphrases de Foscolo prêtent à sa poésie et surtout au poème écrit sur les *Sepolcri*, non seulement un ton énigmatique et solennel, mais aussi très tendu. Foscolo, comme conséquence naturelle de sa tension sentimentale, ne se contente pas de nommer les choses par leur nom, ou d'employer une épithète incolore, bien que juste; dans son poème il refuse cette méthode en tant que ressource poétique.

Un autre fait révélateur, c'est qu'en parlant de l'amour de Pétrarque (*Saggio sopra l'amore del Petrarca*), il découvre dans le poète d'Arrezzo «la plus brûlante passion du cœur humain», c'est-à-dire la faculté psychique qu'il admirait le plus chez les hommes. Ce qui plus est, il aime en Pétrarque le chantre du principe fondamental de l'univers, l'amour: «Tutto è amore — diss'io . . . l'universo non è che amore! E chi lo ha mai più sentito e meglio dipinto del Petrarca? Adoro come divinità que' pochi geni che si sono innalzati sopra gli altri mortali; ma il Petrarca io . . . l'amo; e mentre il mio intelletto gli sacrifica come a nume, il mio cuore lo invoca padre e amico consolatore.»[32] Et nous sommes de nouveau entourés de cette atmosphère chaleureusement panthéiste, familiale et sentimentale dans laquelle Foscolo se plonge toujours. Le feu poétique, qui se manifeste en même temps que le sentiment douloureux de la solitude, est déjà une couleur caractéristique de la poésie de Pétrarque, et crée l'ambiance d'une fraternité intime entre le modèle et le disciple tardif. Mais tout cela était inévitable et peut être considéré comme un élément caractéristique de la naissance du sentimentalisme européen.

Ce n'est pas sans raison que les commentateurs de *Dei Sepolcri* ont souligné la nostalgie douloureuse que reflète le poème vis-à-vis de la nature:

> «. . . . . Ove più il Sole
> Per me alla terra non fecondi questa
> Bella d'erbe famiglia e d'animali . . .»

> (vers 3—5),

et qu'au fond, il y a une grande affinité entre cette nostalgie et le fameux sonnet de *Canzoniere* qui commence par *Zeffiro torna* (CCCX). En effet, l'idée que le monde des plantes constitue une unique et grande famille, doit être considérée comme une invention pétrarquienne. Pétrarque parlait des «fleurs et herbes» comme de la «douce famille» du «printemps». Il est intéressant que Foscolo, dans un calque, avait saisi la nature de la même manière quand il fut touché pour la première fois par la douceur de l'expression pétrarquienne (dans le *Jacopo Ortis* milanais). Dans la lettre du 20 novembre des *Ultime lettere di Jacopo Ortis* il décrit sa visite dans la maison et le jardin d'Arqua de Pétrarque. Il y prononça les paroles suivantes évoquant avec fidélité le jardin et son habitant de jadis:

«Io salutava a ogni passo la famiglia de' fiori e dell'erbe, che a poco a poco alzavano il capo chinato dalla brina.» Cette phrase est encore influencée par la mémoire de la petite fleur gelée de Dante et elle nous invite à voir l'image

---

[32] Foscolo, *Ultime lettere di Jacopo Ortis*, rédaction bolognaise, 14 maggio 1798, *Prose*, vol. I, p. 132.

pétrarquienne. Mais le poète parle déjà dans *Dei Sepolcri* de «la belle famille des animaux et des plantes». Ce n'est plus un élément archéologique des sentiments humains, recueilli pour nous enrichir quelque peu, comme le croit Fubini.[33] L'image s'est élargie, une nouvelle tension s'est emparée d'elle: parce qu'elle contient tout ce qui vit, et la beauté de la nature vivante, palpitante et la réjouissance fraternelle de l'homme. Pétrarque avait lancé une suite de pensées et une évolution sentimentale qui, au cours des siècles, ont reçu un nouvel accent: c'est déjà l'univers de Rousseau. De Sanctis le pressentait lui-même un peu, en écrivant: «Cet écrivain avait quelque chose de dantesque, mais c'était un Dante aux nerfs à fleur de peau, qui était devenu élégiaque, pétrarquien, proche de Rousseau.»[34] Il nous fait vraiment penser à Dante par sa volonté d'agir, par le rôle décisif de la sphère politique et morale, par la concision de l'expression. Par ailleurs, il se rattachait à Pétrarque — comme nous l'avons vu — dès l'époque de *Bonaparte liberatore*, jusqu'à *Dei Sepolcri* et même plus tard. Et chez lui Pétrarque tourna en Rousseau pour qui la nature et les sentiments naturels étaient devenus brusquement des mots d'ordre guerriers.

VII

C'est en cette période ardente que les deux génies et les deux époques se trouvent le plus près les uns des autres. Les lecteurs sentimentaux et d'instinct romanesque du XVIIIᵉ siècle jouissaient d'un Pétrarque de la solitude provinciale et de la nostalgie du bonheur. C'est en lisant Pétrarque qu'ils reconnurent, comme Pindemonte (et Foscolo) «les délices de la souffrance», cet état d'âme si caractéristique du sentimentalisme. Car Ossian ne fit que renforcer cette vieille idée pétrarquienne, l'idée du «nouvel Ulysse» comme il se plaisait à se nommer. Ici, ne manquons pas de noter que Jacopo Ortis est également présenté par Foscolo comme le «nouvel Ulysse», pseudonyme symbolique de Pétrarque.

Du reste, quelques années plus tard il écrit — en France, au bord de l'Atlantique, en mûrissant *Dei Sepolcri* — une *Epistola* d'esprit et de style horatiens, en réponse à Monti, et dans laquelle on trouve un vers très intéressant à nos yeux, le souvenir ressuscité d'angoissants cauchemars pétrarquiens:

«Passa la vita sua, colma d'oblio».[35]

Le navire («la nave mia») est remplacé dans le vers par la «vie» («la vita sua»), mais en dehors de la troisième personne plus indifférente, il ne change rien au texte original, il ne fait qu'interpréter, résout l'expression allégorique. Il veut évoquer le désespoir, le désir de mort de Pétrarque, en se rappelant le premier vers du sonnet, mais il sait peut-être, lui aussi, que le sens du vers est complètement changé. Pétrarque voulait dire: les passions peuvent être mortelles, et pour lui elles le devinrent vraiment au moment où il les écrivit. Foscolo dit: voici son destin, celui d'un exilé — une vie errante et l'oubli. La vie errante et inquiète de Pétrarque-Ulysse trouve un sens nouveau dans le destin amer du compatriote exilé et s'enrichit de couleurs romantiques

---

[33] Cf. M. Fubini, *op. cit.*, p. 195.

[34] F. De Sanctis, *Ugo Foscolo*, p. 80.

[35] «Passa la vita sua colma d'oblio», Foscolo, *A Vincenzo Monti*, 1805, *Liriche*, ed. Chiòrboli, p. 283.

dans l'action active et «passive»: c'est lui qui introduit l'exil, en tant qu'institution nouvelle, dans l'histoire italienne.[36]

Les images sur la nature de *Jacopo Ortis*, et particulièrement l'idylle d'Arqua, la visite de la maison, du jardin, de la tombe de Pétrarque, correspondent si profondément à la façon de vivre pétrarquienne qu'elles ont attiré l'attention des commentateurs. Ainsi, Troccoli pense que dans cette scène l'expression et l'atmosphère du ton initial de *Dei Sepolcri* sont vraiment présentes surtout par le motif déjà mentionné de la nature, de «la famille des fleurs et herbes».[37] Cela est vrai, mais — nous l'avons vu — le processus même, l'influence multiple et inquiétante de Pétrarque est beaucoup plus compliquée, complexe et pénétrante.

Les faits prouvent que la lecture de Pétrarque peut être ramenée à une époque très précoce de la vie de Foscolo, probablement à son séjour à Venise, c'est-à-dire aux années 1794—1795. En examinant les débuts littéraires vénétiens de Foscolo, Carlo Dionisotti s'intéresse à l'influence du traducteur d'Ossian, Cesarotti, et de son milieu. Il constate que, sous l'influence de cette école, il se produit un changement dans la création poétique de Foscolo: il s'éloigne des odes, et, au sens plus étroit du mot, de la lyre et se tourne vers une lyre plus lâche, plus vaste, et aussi vers la prose. Dans le plan d'étude de Foscolo, préparé vers 1796, figure une œuvre en prose alors intitulée «Lettres à Laura» — à quoi ferait-elle allusion, sinon à un roman lyrique et sentimental? Il semble que les critiques, après tant d'analyses toujours reprises au cours de six décennies, éclaircissent le sort des premiers romans d'Ugo Foscolo.[38] Tout porte à croire que l'épisode de Lauretta de la rédaction bolognaise de 1798 — qui se réalisera entièrement dans le *Jacopo Ortis* milanais de 1802 — dérive de ce roman. En ce qui concerne cet épisode de Lauretta — qui devient folle d'amour — tout en étant une variante de texte assez fidèle du *Voyage sentimental* de Sterne («Pauvre Marie») et de la pièce écrite en 1786 par Marsolier des Vivetières, *Nina ou La folle d'amour*, on ne saurait nier son caractère de vécu; le nom même de Laura en témoigne. Plusieurs connaisseurs de la question, ainsi le dernier qui identifie à juste titre Laurette «à la Laura du roman épistolaire perdu», pensent que ce nom serait le pseudonyme d'une amoureuse vénétienne de Foscolo. Les opinions sont partagées sur l'objet de cet amour: peut-être est-ce le souvenir d'un amour malheureux pour une fille inconnue, ou peut-être le nom de Laura cache-t-il celui d'Isabella Teotochi-Albrizzi.[39] De toute façon, le pseudonyme de Laura suggère l'influence dominante de Pétrarque chez le jeune Foscolo. Comme Alfieri, qui fut le premier idéal en poésie moderne du jeune Foscolo, admirait Pétrarque, de même l'adolescent Foscolo l'admirait aussi. Pétrarque est déjà présent dans les premiers vers. Mais l'école Cesarotti «déchaîne» en lui Pétrarque, et Pétrarque «déchaîne» ses passions et ses états d'âme lyriques.

[36] B. Croce, *op. cit.*, p. 75.

[37] Foscolo, *Dei Sepolcri*, commentaire de Giuseppe Troccoli au vers 5; Foscolo, *Liriche e prose*, Firenze 1958.

[38] Pour l'influence de Cesarotti et de son milieu sur Foscolo cf. C. Dionisotti, *Venezia e il noviziato poetico del Foscolo*, Lettere Italiane, Anno XVIII, 1966, gennaio-marzo, pp. 18—27. — Sur le roman *Laura* cf. P. Fasano, *Laura e Lauretta. Il primo romanzo di Ugo Foscolo*, La Rassegna della Letteratura Italiana, 1966, gennaio-aprile, pp. 65—86.

[39] Fasano, *op. cit.*, p. 77.

Si les *Jacopo Ortis* bolognais et milanais doivent beaucoup à l'esprit de Pétrarque, il faut reconnaître que la mort héroïque, cette idée romantique et éducatrice du grand modèle, continue encore plus à déferler dans l'œuvre. Nous pensons ici, entre autres, aux moments émouvants et concrets, comme par exemple l'histoire de la lettre — celle qui précède l'excursion à Arqua — du 12 novembre de l'édition milanaise, où il décrit ses méditations sur les cyprès plantés récemment: «E quando l'ossa mie fredde dormiranno sotto quel boschetto, omai ricco ed ombroso, forse nelle sere d'estate al patetico susurrar delle fronde si uniranno i sospiri degli antichi padri della villa, i quali, al suono della campana de' morti, pregheranno pace allo spirito dell'uomo dabbene e raccomanderanno la sua memoria ai lor figli.»[40]

Cette image sentimentale annonce de toute évidence une nouvelle formulation plus humaniste de la gloire, le monde sentimental nouveau, mais d'une sensibilité humaine, des «cyprès». Dans le jardin et auprès du tombeau de Pétrarque, Foscolo a l'impression d'être venu auprès du tombeau de son père; et même, nous sommes témoins bien avant *Dei Sepolcri* — dans toutes les deux rédactions de *Jacopo Ortis* — de la naissance d'une nouvelle religion humaine: «La casa di quel sacro italiano sta crollando per la irreligione di chi possiede un tanto tesoro ... O Italia, placa l'ombra de' tuoi grandi!»[41] Et déjà en 1797, dans le second chant de *La giustizia e la pietà*, ensuite dans *Jacopo Ortis*, il ne limite pas le culte des tombes à sa propre personne, il ne l'étend pas uniquement à l'Italie et à la nation italienne. Ses méditations concernent toute l'espèce humaine et toute l'histoire de l'humanité, quand il parle de «l'infinite angoscie dell'infelice umanità», de «le sciagure dell'umanità», c'est-à-dire quand il nous fait percevoir l'universalité de la clausule du grand poème.[42]

On peut se demander si le culte de Pétrarque, remontant à la première adolescence de Foscolo, gagna quelque chose par Pindemonte, le grand ami, avec qui il discuta le problème de *Dei Sepolcri* dans le salon d'Isabella Teotochi-Albrizzi, à Venise — bien qu'assez tard, en 1806 —, car Foscolo lui-même appelait son ami «un disciple italien de Pétrarque».[43] La poésie lyrique de Pindemonte est vraiment riche en souvenirs pétrarquiens, mais en plus, lui-même fait allusion à certains vers de *I Trionfi* (*Triumphus fame*, II. 145—147) dans sa lettre poétique écrite sur *Dei Sepolcri* et adressée à Foscolo; il se souvient des «héros bienfaisants» qui s'illustrèrent «soit dans la guerre, soit dans la paix».[44]

[40] Foscolo, *Ultime lettere di Jacopo Ortis*, rédaction milanaise, 12 nov. 1797, *Prose*, vol. I, p. 262.

[41] Foscolo, *op. cit.*, p. 267.

[42] « . . . l'infinite angoscie dell'infelice umanità», Foscolo, *La giustizia e la pietà*, *Liriche ed epigramme* (ed. Chiòrboli), p. 107; *Ultime lettere di Jacopo Ortis*, rédaction bolognaise: «la sua vita del pianto segreto sparso su le disgrazie dell'uomo onesto», 3 septembre 1797, *Prose*, vol. I, p. 79; *op. cit.*, rédaction milanaise: «piangevo le nostre sciagure . . . il mio sciagurato paese», 2 octobre 1797, *Prose*, vol. I, p. 255; *op. cit.*: «col divino Plutarcho potrò consolarmi de'delitti e delle sciagure dell'umanità». 18 octobre 1797, p. 257; *op. cit.*, «gli uomini cercano per una certa fatalità le sciagure con la lanterna», 20 novembre 1797, p. 266; *op. cit.*, «fatale infelicità de'mortali», 29 avril 1797, p. 297; *op. cit.*, «pare che gli uomini sieno i gabbri delle proprie sciagure, ma le sciagure derivano dall'ordine universale e il genere umano serve orgogliosamente e ciecamente a'destini», 19—20 février 1798, vol. II, p. 33; *op. cit.*, «ho pianto sempre sulle miserie dell'umanità». vol. II, p. 55.

[43] *Lirici del Settecento*, p, 992.

[44] *Ibid.* p. 1044.

VIII

On voit que, grâce à un goût commun, les contemporains feuilletaient Pétrarque avec émotion et d'une manière de voir nouvelle. On peut dire la même chose d'une autre source connue de Foscolo, que le poète même avouait comme telle devant tous: ce sont les Grecs et surtout Homère. Beaucoup ont relevé que c'est à cette époque qu'il traduisit l'*Iliade* et se mit à interpréter l'*Odyssée*, et que ces œuvres l'inspirèrent profondément dans la création du poème *Dei Sepolcri*.[45] Mais il vaut la peine d'observer comment Foscolo invoque les idéaux grecs en définissant le genre de *Dei Sepolcri*: «Ho desunto questo modo di poesia da' Greci, i quali dalle antiche tradizioni traevano sentenze morali e politiche, presentandole non al sillogismo de' lettori, ma alla fantasia ed al cuore.»[46]

Dans d'autres écrits théoriques, dans les fragments qui accompagnent les *Grazie*, Foscolo se réfère aux hymnes homériques ainsi qu'à Callimaque et Pindare. Il développe ici ses intentions de plusieurs points de vue. Il faut souligner que ces fragments furent écrits au cours de la création laborieuse des *Grazie*, et que cette œuvre fut conçue à partir des mêmes mobiles que *Dei Sepolcri*. C'est pourquoi l'ambiance mêlée de *Dei Sepolcri* est caractérisée de près par cette prise de position théorique: «A taluni dispiacerà forse questa novità di mescolare il didattico, l'epico e il lirico in un solo genere, nè io credo che l'autore brami ch'io ne faccia le sue discolte: ma dirò solo che non è novità, perché gli inni attribuiti ad Omero, quei di Callimaco su le nozze di Teti e Peleo sono per l'appunto misture de' tre generi e tale fu forse la prima poesia . . .»[47]

Il était persuadé que dans la poésie grecque il existait encore un Gesamtkunstwerk primitif, du moins dans l'univers de la poésie, et qu'il existait aussi une influence élémentaire au point de vue moral et politique, exercée sur la société entière. Cette pensée n'est point privée d'éléments romantiques.

La renaissance de ce monde grec, en tant que sujet poétique, est actuelle et romantique. Le fait que *Dei Sepolcri* est presque complètement privé d'allusions directes aux Romains, comme s'ils n'avaient jamais existé, est particulièrement digne d'attention. Pourtant, Foscolo aimait l'époque républicaine de l'histoire romaine, tout comme la littérature romaine. Cette lacune a un sens profond, la démarche poétique est parfaitement intentionnelle, puisque dans l'édition milanaise des *Ultime lettere di Jacopo Ortis* (28 octobre), il glorifie les peuples qui, «per non obbedire a' romani, ladroni del mondo, diedero alle fiamme le loro case, le loro mogli, i loro figli e se medesimi . . .»[48] Ugo Foscolo, héros romantique de la liberté nationale, retourne aux Grecs combattant les Perses, et ce retour ne s'ajoute plus à cette tendance de la culture européenne qui exploitait le monde hellénique en tant que foyer et norme historiques de la beauté classique, mais à une

---

[45] Cf. F. De Sanctis, *Ugo Foscolo*, pp. 103—104. — G. Barbarisi, *Introduzione alle versioni omeriche del Foscolo*, GSLI, Anno CXXXII, 1935, pp. 568—609. — M. Fubini, *op. cit.*, pp. 168—170, 198—200.

[46] Dans les premiers vers de *Dei Sepolcri*, ed. Troccoli.

[47] Foscolo, *Frammenti della ragione poetica . . . del carme. Sistema degli inni*, ed. Chiòrboli, p. 199.

[48] Foscolo, *Ultime lettere di Jacopo Ortis*, 28 ottobre 1797, *Prose*, vol. I, p. 256.

manière de voir qui préparait une conception nouvelle, romantique sur les Grecs: celle de Vico, et plus tard, à leur suite à tous deux, celle de Leopardi. Son enthousiasme pour les héros grecs de la liberté et son respect pour Florence, cette nouvelle Athène, sont strictement liés, et feront écho dans le romantisme européen. Byron lisait volontiers la littérature italienne. Il goûtait les confessions du poète italo-grec, les *Lettere di Jacopo Ortis*, et même s'il regrette qu'une œuvre semblable ne soit plus jamais née de la plume de Foscolo,[49] on croit — avec des preuves à l'appui — que l'auteur de *Childe Harold* fit connaissance de *Dei Sepolcri* au cours de son séjour en Italie. Ce poème, avec *Jacopo Ortis*, était très proche de sa décision héroïque d'aller lutter, et s'il le fallait, de mourir, pour la liberté grecque.

IX

Il est certain que l'hellénisme de Foscolo tire sa force de la conception historique de Vico dès ses années de jeunesse vénétiennes. Les relations profondes entre le philosophe et le poète ont éveillé l'attention sensible de De Sanctis, et depuis, elles constituent une question toujours actuelle. Foscolo avait accepté intégralement les préceptes de Vico sur le progrès de la civilisation humaine, à notre avis sous l'influence précoce de Cesarotti, propagateur zélé de Vico, influence qui fut renforcée plus tard par celle de Lomonaco. Ses idéaux historiques et héroïques, sa poétique, ses principes se rencontrent à une époque historique et humaine très proche de celle de Vico, c'est-à-dire au temps d'Homère, où les cités grecques luttaient pour leur liberté contre les Perses. Il faut ajouter que cette inspiration grecque de nature sentimentale et d'origine vicoïenne qui eut un si grand effet sur l'imagination de Foscolo, est d'autant plus vicoïenne qu'elle veut reconnaître l'importance de la science et de l'art modernes à cette nouvelle époque «humaine».[50]

C'est pourquoi il accentue la grandeur de Machiavel, de Michel-Ange, de Galilée. Michel-Ange apparaît très tôt, dans le premier *Jacopo Ortis* — à côté d'Homère, Ossian, Dante et Pétrarque —, et l'édition définitive de *Jacopo Ortis*, celle de Milan, les évoque en compagnie de tous les grands hommes italiens du poème, dans l'interprétation qui sera développée dans

---

[49] La renaissance des Muses de la barbarie est liée à Florence, aux yeux de Foscolo. *Op. cit.*, rédaction milanaise, 25 settembre 1798, *Prose*, vol. II, p. 9. — Les réalisations littéraires et artistiques de Florence et de l'Italie, ainsi que son propre rôle sont considérés dans les *Grazie* comme une renaissance de la Hellade. Cf. Foscolo, *Le Grazie*, Inno secondo, Vesta vv. 665—672, ed. Bianchi, p. 172 et *passim* presque chaque page. — Byron sur *Jacopo Ortis* cf. Fr. Veglione, *Ugo Foscolo in Inghilterra*, Catania 1910, pp. 15—17; J. Koltay-Kastner, *op. cit.*, p. 17. La remarque de De Sanctis est digne d'attention: «Byron e Leopardi discendevano da Foscolo». Cf. F. De Sanctis, *Ugo Foscolo*, p. 110.
[50] De Sanctis, *Storia della letteratura italiana*, vol. III, p. 208.; De Sanctis, *Ugo Foscolo*, p. 108. — W. Binni, *op. cit.*, pp. 22—23, 53, 58. — B. Croce, *Foscolo*, pp. 75, 81. — M. Fubini, *op. cit.*, pp. 257—258, 260, 262. — Le fait qu'il s'agit surtout de Cesarotti, qui avait eu une si grande influence sur Foscolo dans sa jeunesse, et non pas du rôle de Francesco Lomonaco, est attesté d'une part par l'influence de Cesarotti sur toute la poésie de jeunesse de Vico et sur *Jacopo Ortis*, d'autre part par le rôle énorme de Cesarotti dans celle de Vico. Pour ce dernier cf. B. Croce, *Bibliografia Vichiana*. Accresciuta e rielaborata da Fausto Nicolini, Napoli 1947, vol. I, pp. 390—393. — Le rôle de Lomonaco est mis en relief chez M. Fubini, *L'amicizia di Ugo Foscolo e di Francesco Lomonaco*, GSLI, Anno CX, 1937, pp. 1—87.

Dei Sepolcri: «Dianzi io adorava le sepolture del Galileo, del Machiavelli e di Michelangelo; contemplandole io tremava, preso da un brivido sacro. Coloro che hanno eretti que' mausolei sperano forse di scolparsi della povertà e delle carceri con le quali i loro avi punivano la grandezza di que' divini intelletti?» Ensuite il fait mention d'Alfieri, «l'unico mortale, ch'io desiderava conoscere», et bientôt c'est la fameuse scène de Parini. En un mot, tous les héros italiens de *Dei Sepolcri* apparaissent bien plus tôt.[51]

De plus, dans «l'édition corrigée» bolognaise de *Jacopo Ortis*, l'Arioste est mentionné comme l'«italico Omero», et ce n'est qu'une variante du «toscano Omero», surnom donné par Vico à Dante.[52] Même si l'on admet que ce n'est pas le texte de Foscolo, mais celui d'Angelo Sassoli, «le jeune lettré», ce fait est toujours digne de réflexion et il s'accorde bien avec les éléments vicoïens du *Jacopo Ortis* bolognais, considéré comme authentique.

C'est justement le motif vicoïen qui témoigne incontestablement de l'esprit très humain de *Dei Sepolcri*. L'apparition du concept de «l'homme-sauvage» et cette pensée vicoïenne que cet «homme-sauvage» accède de la condition d'animal à celle d'homme, grâce aux institutions sociales, n'avaient point obtenu l'approbation de l'abbé Guillon:

> «Dal dì che nozze e tribunali ed are
> Diero alle umane belve esser pietose
> Di se stesse e d'altrui, toglieano i vivi
> All'etere maligno ed alle fere
> I miserandi avanzi che Natura
> Con veci eterne a sensi altri destina.»

(vers 91—96)

Ce créateur solennellement sévère juge les choses sans se nourrir d'«illusions» et reconnaît la loi inexorable de la nature. La pensée de la consolation d'outre-tombe manque totalement à son poème. Mais le poète trouve des paroles humaines fondées sur la solidarité humaine: les hommes vénèrent les cendres de leurs chers défunts. Les larmes versées à cause des «sciagure dell'umanità» représentent un geste caractéristique de cette attitude humaine. Et ces larmes ne sont pas d'un sentimentalisme gratuit, mais le signe d'un nouvel humanisme, un humanisme héroïque et fervent qui aspire à la liberté et au bonheur. Fubini, dans son analyse subtile, sourit en parlant de la vision de Foscolo sur le destin «baigné de larmes» de l'humanité: «in quella grande onda di pianto».[53] Mais les exemples du poète: les pleurs des orphelins, des mourants, des opprimés, les larmes de Jupiter qui est incapable de détourner la fatalité, les pleurs du grand Hector, sont tous de tels tournants du sort, de tels exemples de colère et d'héroïsme, qu'on n'a pas envie de sourire de cet humanisme en larmes.

---

[51] Foscolo, *Ultime lettere di Jacopo Ortis*, rédaction milanaise, 27 agosto 1798, *Prose*, vol. II, p. 5.
[52] Foscolo, *Vera storia di due amanti infelici*, 10 giugno 1798, *Prose*, vol. I, p. 167. — G. B. Vico. *op. cit.*, Libro III, Sez. I, cap. I.
[53] M. Fubini, *op. cit.*, p. 197.

X

L'humanisme de Foscolo se réalise dans une solitude désespérée. Le poète ne cherche pas la consolation, parce qu'il est certain de ne pas la trouver. La critique contemporaine n'a rien compris au poème de Foscolo. Le jugement de Monsignor Guillon était injuste, et même celui de Pindemonte ne peut être considéré comme trop indulgent. Le grand ami trouve *Dei Sepolcri* décousu, obscur; il reproche au poète l'admiration des Grecs et qu'il soit tourmenté par des problèmes «antiques» qui en réalité n'existent pas. Ce n'est pas surprenant si l'on considère que même le sensible Fubini trouve que, dans *Dei Sepolcri*, il s'agit uniquement des problèmes éternels et presque pas du présent actuel et vivant, tout au plus y voit-il un chagrin personnel et résigné. Pindemonte ne dit vrai que dans des choses insignifiantes, tandis que Monsignor Guillon, bien que son jugement fût injuste et tendancieux, soulève une question fondamentale. En écrivant des louanges sur les épitaphes de Young, Hervey et Gray, il fait l'observation suivante: «Tous leurs poèmes sont exaltés par l'espoir de la future résurrection. De cela, Monsieur Foscolo ne dit pas un mot.» Il n'est pas étonnant que Foscolo ait compris et l'allusion de l'abbé Guillon, et le danger qui y était caché, dans la situation donnée. En réponse à la critique de Guillon, il expose son opinion en détail, «Young et Hervey méditaient sur les tombes en fidèles chrétiens ..., Gray écrivait comme le fait un philosophe ..., mais l'auteur considère les tombes dans un but politique, et il a l'intention de réveiller chez les Italiens l'esprit d'une compétition politique, par les exemples d'autres nations qui respectent la mémoire et les tombes de leurs grands hommes. C'est pourquoi il doit parcourir un chemin plus long que Young, Hervey et Gray, et c'est pourquoi il est devenu le propagateur de la résurrection des vertus et non pas du corps.»[54]

La riposte est merveilleuse: Monsignor Guillon accuse Foscolo d'impiété devant l'opinion publique, le poète matérialiste rejette l'argumentation sur l'abbé, en démontrant ironiquement qu'il s'occupe uniquement de la résurrection du corps, tandis que sa propre conception aspire aux valeurs morales, à la résurrection des vertus héroïques.

Et de plus, Foscolo dépasse cette conception et témoigne d'une façon de penser encore plus élevée, d'où l'on voit à quel point il est éclairé, et à quel point sa pensée est nuancée. Il parle de ce type d'homme sans valeur qui ne laisse derrière lui aucune hérédité sentimentale qui, pour survivre la mort d'une manière ou d'une autre:

«O ricovrarsi sotto le grandi ale
Del perdono d'Iddio; ma la sua polve
Lascia alle ortiche di deserta gleba
Ove nè donna innamorata preghi,
Nè passeggier solingo oda il sospiro
Che dal tumulo a noi manda Natura.»

(vers 45—50)

[54] Le passage de N. Guillon v. Foscolo, *Dei Sepolcri*, au vers 200, ed. Troccoli. Traduit d'après la traduction en hongrois de l'auteur.

L'expression «le grandi ale del perdono d'Iddio» est empruntée aux *Psaumes* et elle permet de dessiner plus exactement le schéma de la conception religieuse de Foscolo.[55] Le poète, pieux dans son enfance et son adolescence, était devenu un adepte des Lumières et du matérialisme sensualiste, et le devenait de plus en plus.

La conclusion de la rédaction milanaise de *Jacopo Ortis* (1802) met un signe d'égalité entre «le néant» («dal nulla») et «l'incompréhensible éternité» («o dalla incomprensibile eternità»). Jacopo Ortis prie Dieu avant son suicide: s'il ne peut s'unir à sa Thérèse, que Dieu le laisse dans «le néant» («nel nulla»). Ses dernières paroles pour décrire son suicide sont: «gettandomi nella notte della morte».[56] Chronologiquement, les œuvres *Frammenti su Lucrezio* (vers 1803) et *Commento alla «Chioma di Berenice»* (1803) sont encore plus proches de *Dei Sepolcri*. Dans la seconde on enrégistre sans contradiction le thèse d'Epicure et de Lucrèce: l'homme qui doit se libérer de la peur de la mort après une vie consacrée aux plaisirs sereins de l'esprit, s'unira à la matière. Et «non esservi altro mondo dopo questo, toglie ogni principio di religione, alla quale sogliono rifuggire i mortali nelle loro disavventure.»[57] Il n'est pas loin non plus de cette conception dans *Commento*: il parle des religions comme des produits nécessaires et parfaitement humains, et de leur mythologie comme des appuis possibles de la poésie.[58]

En fin de compte, Foscolo hésite entre le matérialisme pur, la religion naturelle de Rousseau et la religion historico-philosophique de Vico. Son vague déisme a vraiment plus de rapports avec les sentiments qu'avec les considérations de la raison. Mais ce qu'en dit De Sanctis n'est pas du tout acceptable, à savoir qu'on pressent en lui un avant-coureur de la restauration religieuse et un porte-parole précoce de Chateaubriand.[59] Il regarde en avant du haut de sommets plus élevés: ce sont les faîtes de Vico, et il est très loin de la piété vulgaire de son milieu bourgeois.

Sa conception de l'héroïsme est au fond stoïque (il lit Sénèque: c'est à lui qu'il emprunte le pseudonyme de Didimo-Didymus), et c'est pourquoi son intérêt se tourne vers la destinée terrestre de l'homme et vers les devoirs sociaux du poète.[60] On fait à juste titre une comparaison entre les vers de *Dei Sepolcri* évoquant les grands qui reposent dans la Santa-Croce et cette partie de l'*Orazione inaugurale* de Pavie: «Né le barbarie de' Goti, né le animosità provinciali, né le devastazioni di tanti eserciti, spensero in quest'aure quel fuoco immortale, che animò gli Etruschi e i Latini, che animò Dante nelle calamità dell'esilio, e il Machiavelli nelle angosce della tortura, e Galileo nel terrore della Inquisizione, e Torquato nella vita raminga, nella persecuzione de' retori, nel lungo amore infelice; nella ingratitudine delle corti, né tutti questi, né tant'altri grandissimi ingegni, nella domestica povertà. Prostratevi su' loro sepolcri, interrogateli come furono grandi e infelici, o come l'amor della patria, della gloria e del vero accrebbe la constanza del

---

[55] *Psaumes*, XVII, 8.
[56] Foscolo, *Ultime lettere di Jacopo Ortis*, 23 marzo 1798, ore 1, *Prose*, vol. II, p. 59.
[57] *Frammenti su Lucrezio*, *Prose*, vol. II, p. 199.
[58] *Commento alla «Chioma di Berenice»*. *Discorso quarto*, *Prose*, vol. II, pp. 262—266.
[59] Cf. F. De Sanctis, *Storia della letterature italiana*, vol. III, p. 208.
[60] Devant le *Commento alle «Chioma di Berenice»*, dans une citation de Sénèque, figure «Didymus grammaticus», v. Foscolo, *op. cit.*, *Prose*, vol. II, 228.

loro cuore, la forza del loro ingegno e i loro beneficii verso di noi.»[61] Et cette conception est identique à la scène florentine déjà citée du *Jacopo Ortis* milanais.

XI

Dans cette introduction aux discours prononcés à Pavie, les héros malheureux guidés par l'amour de la patrie, de la gloire et de la vérité, et qui doivent, en plus, supporter la misère quotidienne, ne diffèrent point du poète de *Dei Sepolcri*. Bien sûr, il fallait d'abord transformer leur caractère à sa propre image, pour pouvoir ensuite en dessiner ses propres traits imaginaires. Il acceptait donc le portrait peu réaliste de Trajano Boccalini et de Rousseau sur Machiavel: d'après eux cet homme d'État florentin voulait démasquer les tyrans pour montrer «combien de larmes et de sang surgissent» de leur règne. Ce portrait change sensiblement chez Foscolo la vérité historique. Mais il encourage la lutte du peuple italien pour l'indépendance et la liberté dans l'esprit de ce genre de malentendus féconds. Il est beaucoup plus proche de la vérité dans son jugement sur Michel-Ange et Galilée. Il présente Michel-Ange comme un démiurge qui éleva un «nouvel Olympe», c'est-à-dire créa une mythologie héroïque, mais tout humaine, du christianisme. Il en est de même pour Galilée qu'il perçoit le premier en poésie comme l'explorateur de mondes nouveaux.

L'image complète du panthéon foscolien est composée des héros de la politique, de l'art et de la science, auxquels se joint la poésie, représentée par Dante et Pétrarque, Alfieri et Parini, ainsi que l'héroïsme actif de Nelson et des combattants grecs. Du point de vue de la solennité et de l'universalité, il est l'opposé vivant de la médiocrité des héros d'Ippolito Pindemonte. Or, Pindemonte présente, lui aussi, une espèce de panthéon dans son poème, le «panthéon» de la monarchie constitutionnelle et des bons bourgeois. Voici par exemple le tombeau du seigneur «humanitaire», c'est-à-dire du «bon roi». Tout près, c'est le tombeau du bon ministre qui accomplit un devoir vraiment difficile, parce qu'il était, d'après Pindemonte, «ministre et citoyen» en une personne! Vient ensuite le «bon capitaine» qui «sut aimer l'homme» («risum teneatis amici?»). Et finalement, c'est le tombeau du philosophe, qui, selon Pindemonte, devait être un penseur pratique, sinon il ne dirait pas de lui qu'il imaginait des «vérités utiles».[62]

Certes, l'ami de Foscolo, dans sa lettre poétique écrite sur *Dei Sepolcri*, paraît être un poète médiocre, et il n'est pas digne de l'appréciation exagérée de Foscolo qui lui écrit ces vers tendres et reconnaissants:

«Nè da te, dolce amico, udrò più il verso
E la mesta armonia che lo governa . . .»

(vers 8—9)

---

[61] V. Foscolo, *Origine e ufficio della letteratura*, *Opere*, Edizione Nazionale, vol. VII, Firenze 1933. Le Monnier cap. XV, p. 37.
[62] I. Pindemonte, *I Sepolcri*, vv. 280—292. *Lirici del Settecento* p. 1043.

Excepté quelques belles strophes, quelques vers attendrissants, nés aux moments heureux de l'inspiration, la poésie de Pindemonte est pâle, même s'il écrit de temps en temps des confidences sincères, avec cet accord comme note fondamentale:

> «Malinconia
> ninfa gentile
> la vita mia
> consegno a te.»[63]

Il est impossible de mettre en doute la bonne foi de Pindemonte, quand il fait certaines observations critiques à son ami, dans son épître poétique, et qu'il lui reproche l'obscurité de ses expressions poétiques. Il se peut que dans ces reproches d'un goût préromantique sur le rôle exagéré que jouent la mythologie grecque et l'histoire mythique révolue dans la poésie de son ami, il se cache quelque vérité:

> «Perché tra l'ombre della vecchia etade
> stendi lungi da noi voli si lunghi?»[64]

Mais quand il veut lui donner l'exemple de sa propre poésie, pour pleurer sa propre douleur, la «douce Elise», au lieu des héros farouches de Marathon, au lieu d'Ajax, d'Ulysse, d'Hector que pleure Foscolo, le résultat reste bien en arrière de celui de son ami. Car le poète italo-grec est accablé des souvenirs et des chagrins de sa patrie d'origine et de sa patrie élue, mais derrière «le voile d'étranges poèmes» il met en vers les idéaux vivants et les douleurs du présent.

Le poète né en Grèce, et parlant d'abord le grec comme langue maternelle, ressentait profondément les souffrances du peuple de sa mère, cette tension toujours croissante du pays où, près de deux décennies après la création de *Dei Sepolcri*, éclata l'insurrection générale contre le régime turc. Foscolo éprouve alors toutes les inquiétudes et tous les tourments de cette lutte. Les douze dernières années de sa vie se déroulent dans l'angoisse et l'action pour le sort de sa petite patrie, les îles Ioniennes. Il veut y retourner, pour vivre et renaître au sein du peuple.[65]

Au moment de la création de *Dei Sepolcri* (seconde moitié de 1806) nous sommes au début de cette évolution. Cette lutte pour la liberté eut son Marathon, mais elle eut surtout ses Thermopyles. En plus, c'est juste à cette époque — vers 1805—1806 — que Foscolo se plonge dans l'univers homérique: c'est alors qu'il traduit l'*Iliade* et l'*Odyssée*. Quand il parle de la côte de Hellespont, de la haute marée qui apporte en hurlant

> «Alle prode retèe l'armi d'Achille
> Sovra l'ossa d'Aiace»
>
> > (vers 219—220),

---

[63] Pindemonte, *op. cit., La Malinconia*, p. 930.
[64] Pindemonte, *I Sepolcri*, vv. 344—345. p. 1046.
[65] Cf. J. Koltay-Kastner, *op. cit.*, 64—70. Pour les articles publicistes relatifs à son pays natal grec v. Foscolo, *Opere*, Ed. Nazionale, vol. XIII, Parte 1 (Scritti Sulle Isole Jonie e su Parga), pp. 1—593.

quand il raconte la mort de la nymphe Electre et les derniers jours de Troie, en vérité, il ne s'en remet pas à l'imagination, il ne se détache point de la réalité: c'est l'ambiance de ses jours et de ses nuits. S'il voit à présent les flots sauvages de la Manche, c'est de sa première jeunesse que reviennent vers lui «le vaste pays des vents», la mer ionienne et son mugissement «hurlant». Les héros homériques ressuscités dans l'âme sensible du traducteur exprimaient les sentiments qui agitaient aussi bien l'époque de Foscolo que l'époque lointaine de l'Antiquité — mutatis mutandis — qui, dans le domaine de certains problèmes moraux et même politiques, avaient trouvé ses homologues dans l'imagination de Foscolo. Les héros antiques de Marathon ne connaissaient évidemment pas l'idée de la nation de la société bourgeoise moderne en formation au temps de Foscolo, ou plus tard encore, mais la solidarité entre les hommes libres des cités grecques, le panhellénisme au riche contenu culturel, qui les opposa hardiment aux rois perses pour la défense de leur indépendance, vivaient fortement en eux. Foscolo, en tant que soldat aux sentiments révolutionnaires de l'armée napoléonienne, avait dû subir des injustices auxquelles il répondit en renonçant à son rang militaire. Dans *Dei Sepolcri*, l'injustice sera récompensée dans la mort, sinon avant, d'après l'exemple éternel d'Ajax, héros sévère et magnanime:

«. . . . . a' generosi
Giusta di glorie dispensiera è Morte»

(vers 220—221)

Et le jugement divin les atteint tous, même Ulysse:

«Nè senno astuto, nè favor di regi
All'Itaco le spoglie ardue serbava,
Chè alla poppa raminga le ritolse
L'onda incitata dagl'inferni Dei.»

(vers 222—225)

La tragédie d'Ajax et d'Ulysse est suivie du drame personnel et de la vengeance d'un Foscolo enfui de Venise:

«E me che i tempi ed il desio d'onore
Fan per diversa gente ir fuggitivo,
Me ad evocar gli eroi chiamin le Muse
Del mortale pensiero animatrici.»

(vers 226—229)

On s'est déjà aperçu que Foscolo aimait particulièrement la figure d'Hector. «L'ornement des chants funèbres», comme il le nommait, lui paraissait être le plus grand parmi les héros homériques, à cause de sa haute moralité et de sa fin tragique. Mais il se pleurait lui-même en la personne d'Hector. Or, se pleurer sous le masque d'antiques héros épiques: cela peut être une forme voilée et décente de l'individualisme «sensible», c'est-à-dire sentimental. Il faut néanmoins accentuer le caractère «politique» et historique — comme le dit Foscolo — des héros grecs; et ce sont toujours les traits du poète qui s'y reflètent.

Les combattants de Marathon et de Troie sont tous les personnages de gigantesques scènes historiques, où se décide le destin de peuples entiers, ou encore dans lesquelles le progrès historique arrive à un tournant décisif. Ainsi la douce figure effacée d'Elise de Pindemonte reste, malgré toutes les douleurs de son poète, une affaire personnelle, quelle actuelle que soit la figure d'Elise, tandis que les gestes émouvants et plaintifs, le chant plein de dignité de la Cassandre foscolienne intéressent toute l'humanité. Et dans ce chant, il s'agit justement de la récompense que recevront les héros comme Hector, grâce à la gloire et à la poésie. Car Foscolo croit en un monde éthique présent et futur qui durera jusqu'à la fin de l'histoire de l'humanité:

> «Ove fia santo e lagrimato il sangue
> Per la patria versato ...»
>
> (vers 293—294)

XII

Les éléments de la poésie des épitaphes du sentimentalisme et du préromantisme changèrent totalement dans l'univers poétique de Foscolo, réellement inspiré d'Homère, de Pétrarque et des génies du peuple italien. Dans la lettre poétique de Pindemonte, on retrouve les types et les situations poignants de Hervey: le jeune homme aux beaux espoirs, saisi par la mort à la fleur de l'âge, la jeune fille qui s'effondre au moment de ses noces et sa tombe où poussent de mauvaises herbes, tandis que le hibou ulule au clair de la lune. Ces poèmes écrits dans le mauvais goût commun, manquent complètement chez Foscolo.

Il y a quand même, chez lui aussi, de scènes nocturnes et funèbres au cimetière — des scènes peut-être volontairement exagérées[66] —, mais ce ne sont pas les tombes des jeunes qui l'étonnent: c'est la misérable sépulture du prêtre des Muses. Il s'agit de la tombe de Parini, qui n'eut droit qu'à une dalle anonyme, prescrite pour tous selon l'ancien arrêté repris par le gouvernement napoléonien:

> «.............. E senza tombe giace il tuo
> Sacerdote, o Talia, che a te cantando
> Nel suo povero tetto educò un lauro
> Con lungo amore, e t'appendea corone.»
>
> (vers 53—56)

Les voix et les lumières fantomatiques de la nuit sont destinées à accompagner l'ordre de Napoléon, le nouveau Prométhée, et de ses compagnons:

> «.............. A lui non ombre pose
> Tra le sue mura la città, lasciva
> D'evirati cantori allettatrice;

[66] Cf. M. Fubini, *op. cit.* p. 196.

Non pietra, non parola; e forse l'ossa
Col mozzo capo gl'insanguina il ladro
Che lasciò sul patibolo i delitti.
Senti raspar fra le macerie e i bronchi
La derelitta cagna ramingando
Sulle fosse, e famelica ululando;
E uscir del teschio, ove fuggia la Luna,
L'ùpupa, e svolazzar su per le croci
Sparse per la funerea campagna,
E l'immonda accusar col luttuoso
Singulto i rai di che son pie le stelle
Alle obbliate sepolture. Indarno
Sul tuo poeta, o Dea, preghi rugiade
Dalla squallida notte. Ahi! sugli estinti
Non sorge fiore, ove non sia d'umane
Lodi onorato e d'amoroso pianto.»

(vers 72—90)

C'est une autre atmosphère, c'est un autre univers: le monde de l'humanisme
où l'on revendique les droits à la grandeur humaine, où le bon vieux assis
sous ses chers tilleuls et la douce lumière de la poésie récompensent le désert
du cimetière nocturne. Dans cette description la colère morale, la critique
sociale contre le «Sardanapal lombard» l'emportent sur le frisson larmoyant
et sentimental:

«Cui solo è dolce il muggito de'buoi
Che dagli antri abduàni e dal Ticino
Lo fan d'ozi beato e di vivande.»

(vers 59—61)

Foscolo regarde donc vers le passé, mais tout en se tournant vers l'avenir.
Le goût présent le pousse à s'en faire l'écho, mais il le dépasse.

A la suite des poèmes d'Ossian, la littérature préromantique européenne
allait être inondée des scènes de bataille farouches de l'histoire, mais ces
scènes ne furent nulle part plus justifiées que dans *Dei Sepolcri*. Marathon,
le champ de bataille de ceux qui tombèrent pour la liberté grecque, garde
toujours vivants les événements de ce jour d'éternelle mémoire: car les
Grecs reconnaissants perpétuaient leurs souvenirs par les sépultures. Voici
la scène nocturne des ombres des combattants que le marin errant sur la
mer — peut-être Pindemonte, peut-être lui-même — voit se dessiner dans
la nuit et qui finit par une résignation émue:

«. . . . . Il navigante
Che veleggiò quel mar sotto l'Eubea,
Vedea per l'ampia oscurità scintille
Balenar d'elmi e di cozzanti brandi
Fumar le pire igneo vapor, corrusche
D'armi ferree vedea larve guerrierè
Cercar la pugna; e all'orror de'notturni
Silenzi si spandea lungo ne'campi

Di falangi un tumulto, e un suon di tube,
E un incalzar di cavalli accorrenti
Scalpitanti su gli elmi a'moribondi,
E pianto, ed inni, e delle Parche il canto.»

(vers 201—212)

Ce ne sont pas des scènes inventées, mais les flammes de l'imagination décrites d'après une mémoire vivante. Il nous faut accepter que chez lui, les lieux communs de la poésie d'épitaphe et héroïco-sentimentale contemporaine ont perdu leurs traits caractéristiques et s'enrichissent d'une nouvelle signification dans un nouvel ordre de valeurs, c'est-à-dire dans les limites de la mythologie foscolienne. Le poète de *Dei Sepolcri* se sentait sans doute plus proche d'Homère, de Tyrtaïos, de Dante, du Pétrarque de l'*Italia mia*, du *Spirto gentil*, de *I Trionfi*, du Shakespeare magicien de tragédies historiques; il se considérait plutôt comme un rénovateur de la «poesia storica» inexistante,[67] que comme un poète d'épitaphes. Cela ne veut pas dire qu'on ait des doutes quant à la réalité de ses expériences anglaises et françaises du genre, de la lecture sensible d'auteurs tels que Young, Hervey, Gray, Legouvé et Delille.[68]

Mais l'esprit animateur de *Dei Sepolcri* — comme nous l'avons déjà prouvé — est tout autre chose, une chose beaucoup plus complexe, beaucoup plus grandiose. Ses proportions gigantesques: le monde entier, son mouvement incessant: c'est-à-dire toute l'histoire, la force humaine créatrice et active en pleine fonction; bref, le génie humain, l'héroïsme final: donc la force morale et l'amour de la liberté, forment en tant que valeurs suprêmes de l'être humain, une image magnifique du monde romantique. Foscolo créa ce monde d'une manière vraiment poétique, en élevant son poème au-dessus de toute espèce de poésie d'épitaphe, italienne ou étrangère.[69]

XIII

Une dernière question, d'ailleurs capitale: où placer *Dei Sepolcri* dans l'œuvre foscolienne? Sa place peut être indiquée dans le domaine d'exploits héroïques, dans les limites de la conception de gloire d'une grande tension sentimentale. Ce poème serait-il un sommet sans précédents et solitaire que le poète n'aurait jamais plus atteint? Ou suit-il la ligne toujours ascendante de sa permanente évolution poétique? Ces questions ne sont point superflues, puisque certains critiques italiens de marque, tels que Croce et surtout Flora, ont pris parti pour les *Grazie* comme sommet de la production poétique foscolienne, bien que ce poème soit resté inachevé. En effet, les *Grazie* constituent

[67] Foscolo, *Commento alla «Chioma di Berenice»*, *Discorso quarto*, *Prose*, vol. II, pp. 262—270.
[68] Les modèles étrangers d'Ugo Foscolo sont démontrés entre autres par V. Cian, *Per la storia del sentimento e della poesia sepolcrale in Italia*, GSLI, Anno XX, 1892, pp. 205—235. — R. Belvederi, *Ugo Foscolo*, Rovigno 1915. — Pour d'autres bibliographies v. Binni, *op. cit.*, pp. 44—46. — Au même endroit, il critique sévèrement l'accusation de plagiat de Foscolo: W. Binni, *op. cit.*, p. 46. — Sur les précédents italiens directs du poème de Foscolo: modérément G. Manacorda, *Studi Foscoliani*, Bari 1921, excessivement N. L. Rizzo, *La poesia sepolcrale in Italia*, Napoli 1927.
[69] Cette opinion est partagée par l'excellent connaisseur moderne de Foscolo, M. Fubini, *op. cit.*, pp. 176—177.

une suite à l'ambiance solennelle de *Dei Sepolcri* — comme le croyait De Sanctis — mais elles ne l'atteignent ni dans son entité harmonique, ni dans la force concentrée de l'inspiration, ni dans le pouvoir de l'expression.[70] Et ce n'est ni la solennité pindaresque, ni l'austérité d'un Parini qui nous fait admirer le poète de *Dei Sepolcri*, mais le haute degré de l'ardeur sentimentale, la libre volée de l'imagination, qui s'y manifeste malgré le ton étouffé caractéristique des hymnes: ce ne sont pas des traits classiques, mais des traits romantiques.

Il serait erroné de chercher une différence fondamentale entre *Dei Sepolcri* et l'œuvre précédente de Foscolo. L'atmosphère enchantée des poèmes comme *Alla Sera*, *A Zacinto*, *In morte del fratello Giovanni*, et même certains passages réussis de la prose un peu emphatique des *Ultime lettere di Jacopo Ortis* ne sont point inférieurs à quelques traits stylistiques de *Dei Sepolcri*. *Dei Sepolcri*, comme ces poèmes, sont caractérisés par la même force passionnée, la même douleur — ce sont les séquelles de son propre destin et en même temps l'état d'âme de la classe la plus sensible et de certaines couches de la société italienne, après l'assujettissement consécutif au traité de Campoformio. La première phrase de la préface dramatique des *Ultime lettere di Jacopo Ortis* (édition milanaise) sera sans doute le leitmotiv de Foscolo: «Il sacrificio della nostra patria è consumato: tutto è perduto; e la vita, seppure ne verrà concessa, non ci resterà che per piangere le nostre sciagure e le nostre infamie.»[71] Ce drame historique italien est visiblement l'une des «misères humaines» au-dessus desquelles volera le chant désespéré de la Cassandre de *Dei Sepolcri*. Mais ce sentiment tragique n'est pas récent chez Foscolo. Il est lié de prime abord à l'événement qui provoqua la catastrophe matérielle de sa famille: la mort de son père[72]; et il apparaîtra bientôt, ça et là, comme facteur fondamental de ses états d'âme. Ce ton tragique résonne dans le poème à la mode du genre épigramme, intitulé *Il proprio ritratto*:

«. . . . . ma il core,
Ricco di vizi e di virtù, delira:
Forse da morte avrò fama e riposo.»

L'idée grecque de la fatalité qui résonne dans le chant des Parques de *Dei Sepolcri*, le poursuit depuis des années, pour entrer finalement dans le grand poème. Foscolo sentait dès le début l'attraction d'une force gigantesque, le pressentiment de l'anéantissement. C'est pourquoi il écrit ces mots révélateurs sur l'avenir, en se tournant vers la *Serag*:

«Vagar mi fai co'miei pensier sull'orme
Che vanno al nulla eterno . . .»

Dans son poème lyrique où il se souvient de son lieu de naissance, l'île Zante il lutte avec le pressentiment que le destin lui accordera, au lieu de la gloire

---

[70] Cf. B. Croce, *Ugo Foscolo*, pp. 80—86. — Fr. Flora, *Storia della letteratura italiana*, Milano 1940, Vol. III, pp. 67—69, 72, 79—81.

[71] Foscolo, *Ultime lettere di Jacopo Ortis*, **2** ottobre 1797, *Prose*, vol. I, p. 255.

[72] Toute l'atmosphère du cycle engendré en 1794—95 a le même aspect et dépasse absolument le souvenir de l'événement qui eut lieu six ans plus tôt (en 1788). Voir Foscolo, *In morte del padre*, *Liriche ed epigrammi* (ed. Chiòrboli), VI, pp. 63—74.

tant désirée et embellie de sentiments, l'antithèse: «l'enterrement sans larmes». Cette voix se répète plus fort à l'heure lugubre de la mort de son frère Giovanni:

> «Sento gli avversi numi e le secrete
> Cure che al viver tuo furon tempesta,
> E prego anch'io nel tuo porto quiete.
> Questo di tanta speme oggi mi resta!
> Straniere genti, almen l'ossa rendete
> Allora al petto della madre mesta.»

On a souligné à juste raison dans une étude statistique qui énumère les événements de sa vie, qu'en 1827 il fut accompagné de très peu de gens à son dernier voyage et enterré dans un petit cimetière anglais à Chiswick, tout comme il l'avait prévu dans la scène douleureusement idyllique de *Dei Sepolcri*:[73]

> «Pietosa insania, che fa cari gli orti
> De'suburbani avelli alle britanne
> Vergini, dove le conduce amore
> Della perduta madre; ove clementi
> Pregaro i Geni del ritorno al prode
> Che tronca fe' la trionfata nave
> Del maggior pino, e si scavò la bara.»

(vers 130—136)

Quand il associe l'héroïsme magnanime de Nelson aux pleurs des mères, «la gloire» devient familière, proche de l'homme: nulle pensée poétique n'est capable d'en exprimer plus. Mais il est naturel que celui qui meurt pour son peuple, pour sa patrie — ceux, au moins, que nous connaissons pour tels —, celui-là meurt pour «sa mère». Sur les tombes du Foscolo révolutionnaire fleurissent les fleurs tendrement soignées de l'action héroïque, de l'amour de la liberté et de la gloire romantique. Le poète, plongé dans ses méditations, s'encourage par des images pétrarquiennes, vicoïennes et homériques, pour créer ses images à lui gigantesques sur les peuples, les héros et l'histoire.

Ce poème révèle spontanément certains traits testamentaires, tout comme quelques grands vers visionnaires de Petőfi.

Chez Foscolo, les images qui tourbillonnent autour de la vie et du repos éternel, de la mort, de l'exploit héroïque et de la gloire, ne sont pas simplement des motifs toujours repris, mais le processus de sa tragédie perpétuelle qui se manifeste sans cesse, et qui vient d'une part de ses propres défauts et ainsi de facteurs personnels négatifs de son destin, d'autre part de la situation catastrophique de Venise, de toute l'Italie. Une telle affluence de sentiments et d'images — due à la réalité amère et au désir ardent de créer et d'agir — semble être quelque chose de réel, même si les mobiles en sont

---

[73] C'est Giuseppe Troccoli qui fait allusion à cette coïncidence douloureuse, *Dalle Ultime lettere alla poesia Dei Sepolcri, e a quella delle Grazie*. En tête de l'introduction du même titre d'Ugo Foscolo, *Liriche e prose*, pp. 9—48.

romantiques. Et il n'y a qu'une seule chose qui console le poète, parce qu'il n'y a qu'une seule chose qui est au-dessus de lui; c'est la poésie, les Muses:

«Siedon custodi de'sepolcri; e quando
Il tempo con sue fredde ale vi spazza
Fin le rovine, le Pimplee fan lieti
Di lor canto i deserti, e l'armonia
Vince di mille secoli il silenzio.»

(vers 230—234)

C'est ainsi que le poème de Foscolo, *Dei Sepolcri*, devient un véritable document de la grandeur humaine. C'est avec une force poétique et avec une imagination rares dans la littérature mondiale, avec une grande chaleur humaine et d'immenses perspectives historiques, qu'il préconise la valeur absolue du dévouement et de la création. Et c'est pourquoi *Dei Sepolcri* représentait une force d'action concrète de la société contemporaine; c'est ainsi que ce poème devint l'ouverture du Risorgimento italien, et c'est ainsi que son auteur put être, non seulement aux yeux de Giuseppe Mazzini, mais aussi aux yeux de deux générations vibrantes, le modèle par excellence «des idées et de l'action».

INDEX

Müller, J. G. 270
Myris 294

Nagyváthy, János 336—337, 343, 346
Namier, Sir Lewis 289
Napione, Gianfranco Galeani 195, 211—212
Napoléon I, 192, 196, 206, 371
Nerval, Gérard de 136—137, 146
Newton, Isaac 58, 63, 65, 144, 163, 166
Nicolai, Friedrich 23, 258—260, 331
Nicoll, A. 83—84, 103—104, 107—108
Nicolson, M. H. 163
Nievo, I. 206
Nisard, Paul 72
Nivelle, A. 344
Novalis (Friedrich Hardenberg) 136, 141, 146
Novikov, N. J. 310
Nulli, A. 318

Ogiorboli, E. 348
Oglander, John 286
Oldmixon, John 101
Oldys, William 180
Omodeo, Adolfo 189
Oppel, H. 302
Orczy, László 336
Ordonnec, Karl von 123
Ormond, Earl of 124
Orsi, G. G. 193
Ortis, Jacopo 355, 360, 367
Ossory, Upper, comtesse 289, 295
Otway, Thomas 84, 93
Oxford, Robert Harley, Earl of 124

Pagano, M. 199, 216
Paine, Thomas 129, 136
Palissot, Ch. 294
Panard, Charles-François 122, 161
Panckoucke, Charles-Joseph 275
Paoli, Pasquale 356
Par, A. 319
Parini, Giuseppe 199, 201—203, 205, 208, 216—217, 365, 368, 371, 374
Parnell, Thomas 169, 181
Parny, Evariste-Désiré de Forges 237, 243, 245
Pascal, Blaise 62, 64, 66—67, 224, 235, 242
Pasolini, P. P. 206
Peacock, Thomas Love 51—52
Peers, E. A. 310
Pellowski, Anne 277
Pembroka, Lady 283
Pennink, R. 315
Pepi, A. 198
Percy, Thomas 39, 117, 129—130, 144, 160, 165, 167—168
Pergoli, B. 199
Perkins, Merle L. 71, 76
Perron du (Castillon) 287
Pestalozzi, J. H. 264

Peter, the Great, of Russia 59, 69, 78
Petersen 215
Petőfi, Sándor 150, 223, 231, 375
Petrarch (Petrarque) F. 72, 130, 192—193, 197—198, 223, 353—364, 368, 371, 373
Petronio, G. 190—191, 195
Petty, William 60
Pfeffel, Konrad 264
Pheidias 14—15
Philanthropos (pseudonym) 91—92
Philip I. G. 286
Philippe-Égalité 275, 295
Philippe V, of Spain 56
Philips 284
Philips, Ambrose 101, 162
Philips, John 172
Philips, Mrs Kath. 91, 95, 170
Piccolomini 198
Pichois, C. 318
Pienaar, W. J. B. 309
Pietack, S. 325
Pignotti 318
Pindar (Pindare) 163, 197, 208, 222, 363
Pindemonte, I. 217, 347, 350, 359—360, 362, 366, 368—369, 371—372
Piranesi, Giovanni Battista 123, 189, 217
Piromalli, A. 190
Piron, Alexis 161, 250
Pizzo, E. 308
Place (la) Pierre Antoine 316
Plato (Platon) 9—11, 13—16, 19, 23, 29, 34, 43—44, 53—54, 78
Plautus 105—106
Plebe, A. 190
Plotinus 15—16, 48
Plutarch (Plutarque) 22, 348, 358
Podmaniczky, József 336—337
Poe, Edgar Allan 141
Polybius (Polybe) 68
Pomeau, René 63, 68, 70, 73, 301, 305
Pomfret, John 131, 142, 155
Pons, J. 276
Ponsonby, Sarah 297
Pope, Alexander 19, 29, 42, 69, 85, 95, 118—119, 121, 124—126, 129—130, 136, 141—143, 145, 148—149, 154, 156, 159, 162—164, 167, 172, 174—176, 182—184, 186, 279, 302—303, 319
Poschinger 335
Poussin, Gaspard 36
Pound, Ezra 130
Powel 280
Praxiteles 15
Praz, Mario 200
Prévost, abbé 63, 216
Price, L. M. 303—304
Price, M. B. 322
Prior, James 286
Prior, Matthew 118, 124, 127, 131, 143, 161, 164, 169, 181
Przybylski, Father Hyacinth 310—311

384

Prod'homme, J. G. 75
Prud'hon, Pierre-Paul 123
Puppo, Mario 191, 194—195, 200, 202, 205, 210—211, 213
Pushkin (Pouchkine) A. 233, 252, 321
Pyra, J. J. 308

Quillet, L. R. 245
Quinault, Phillipe 67
Quintilian 14

Racine, Jean de 22, 24, 56—58, 61, 64—65, 71—75, 223—224, 227—228, 230—231, 236, 241, 244, 248—249, 318
Racine, Louis 311
Radcliffe, Mrs. 120
Ralli, A. 318
Ramdohr F. W. B. von 271
Randolph, Thomas 163
Ransom, John Crowe 52—54
Rautenstrauch, J. 343
Ravenscroft, Edward 99
Reeve, Cleman 120
Régnier, M. 248
Rehberg 271—272
Reiner-Michiel, Giustina 319
Reinoso, Felix, José 310
Reisewitz 272
Retz, Cardinal 55, 65
Reynolds, Sir Joshua 35—37, 45, 281—283, 285—286, 292
Rezzonico, C. C. 217
Rhode 215
Rich, John 96
Richards, I. A. 52
Richardson, Samuel 120, 122, 138, 153, 186, 258—259, 283, 292, 302, 322
Richelieu, cardinal 64
Richter, Jean-Paul 141, 266
Ridgway, Ronald S. 62
Riffaterre, M. 233
Rimbaud, Arthur 249
Rivarol, Antoine 126, 254
Rizzo, N. L. 373
Robert Paul 219—220
Robertson, J. G. 305, 311, 319, 323
Robespierre, Maximilien 62, 225
Robson-Scott, W. D. 303—304
Rochester, John Wilmat Earl of 118
Roger, Jacques 62
Rogers, A. K. 47
Rolli, Paolo 216, 309—319
Romney, George 297
Ronsard, Pierre de 254
Rosa, A. 190
Rosario, R. 189
Roscommon W. Dillon, Earl of 91
Rosiello, L. 194, 199
Roquier 199
Roucher, Jean-Antoine 122
Roudaut, Jean 60
Rouget de Lisle 252
Rougement, Denis de 69

Rousseau, Jean-Baptiste 142, 161, 222, 226—229, 233, 243, 249
Rousseau, Jean-Jacques 22, 39, 43, 47, 63, 122, 138—139, 144—145, 155, 196, 217, 221, 225, 233—234, 236, 255—273, 276—277, 281—282, 291, 293, 318
Rulhière, Claude-Carloman de 161
Russell, Thomas 130, 181, 186
Ruttkay, K. G. 99
Rymer, Thomas 25, 86

Sackville, C. 206
Sade, Marquis de 140
Saint-Amant, Marc-Antoine Girard de 235
Sainte-Beuve, Charles—Augustin de 65, 67, 276
Saint-Évremond, Charles de 55—56, 64
Saint-Lambert, Jean François de 122, 245
Saint-Simon, Louis de Rouvroy 55, 57—58, 61, 64
Salinari, C. 190
Salis 264
Sallay, Géza 204
Saluzzo, D. 217
Salom 216
Salvatorelli, Luigi 189
Salviati, Leonardo 193
Salvini, I. 193
Salza, A. 196
Salzmann, Christian Gotthilf 264
Sappho 217
Saratéa, Charles 252
Sasse, H. C. 303
Sassoli, Angelo 365
Savage, Richard 173, 176
Savioli, F. C. 201
Scarron, Paul 69
Schelling, F. W. J. 17, 48, 133, 315
Scherpbier, H. 309
Schiaffini, A. 194
Schiller, Friedrich 39—40, 233, 266, 269, 307—308, 313
Schlegel, August Wilhelm 48, 133, 136, 313—315
Schlegel, D. B. 304
Schlegel, Friedrich 133, 201, 315
Schlegel, Johann Elias 22, 344
Schlegel (brothers) 17, 39, 272
Schlosser, Johann Georg 331
Schlossing, Friedrich Wilhelm 335
Schnabel, Johann Gottfried 344
Schopenhauer, Arthur 12, 141, 202
Schönaich 307
Schraud 336
Schuster, G. 325, 327
Schwarz, Gyula 78
Scott, John of Amwell 128, 162—163, 321
Sée, Henri 59, 78
Sénancour, Étienne Privert 136